studies in jazz

Institute of Jazz Studies
Rutgers—The State University of New Jersey
General Editors: *Dan Morgenstern & Edward Berger*

Studies in Jazz No. 2

Metuchen, N.J., London, 1982

The Scarecrow Press and the Institute

Art Tatum

A Guide to His Recorded Music

ARNOLD LAUBICH

RAY SPENCER

of Jazz Studies, Rutgers University

Library of Congress Cataloging in Publication Data

Laubich, Arnold, 1929-
    Art Tatum, a guide to his recorded music.

    (Studies in jazz ; no. 2)
    Discography.
    "Published music": p.
    Includes indexes.
    1. Tatum, Art, 1910-1956--Discography. 2. Jazz
music--Discography. I. Spencer, Ray, 1917-
II. Title. III. Series.
ML156.7.T37L4 1982   016.7899'12542'0924 82-10752
ISBN 0-8108-1582-6

PREFACE

Arnold Laubich and Ray Spencer have produced a labor of love and innovation. Only a passion for the music of Art Tatum could demand the burden of time needed to pursue the details that form this meticulously constructed discography.

Tatum was a genius. He changed the jazz piano. Not everyone plays like Tatum; few have the technique or courage to imitate him or to hazard a Tatum sound. Mary Lou Williams noted that Tatum "does all the things others try to do and can't." A. B. Spellman observed that Tatum's "keyboard mastery was complete;" he had absolute control. Most are influenced by him; all have to contend with his style and talent. If Tatum is not accepted fully he has to be rejected consciously. He cannot be ignored.

This discography is the state of the art. Its coverage is complete. The organization of materials leaves little to chance. If a fact exists on Tatum's recorded contributions, it is in this volume. Edward Berger, Curator of the Rutgers Institute of Jazz Studies, identifies this discography as "the most visually comprehensive." The use of a data processor in the grasp of the devoted intelligence possessed by Arnold Laubich and Ray Spencer provides all the detail of Walter Allen's monumental Hendersonia but through the use of a computer rather than a pen and pad. This is the discography process of the future: the prototype.

That it is a complete discography is obvious, but it does not stop there. Scholars will relish the sparkling gems in the rest of the book, especially the ten pages of research tools at the back of the book. A Matrix Cross Reference List enables one to locate an index for any performance through a matrix number. The Quick Dating Guide is another useful feature.

All who must deal with timing, especially those presenting recorded material for radio, will be most pleased with another innovation. Others have presented the time of alternate takes, but here all timing is presented. Phil Schaap found this seemingly simple task to be an incredible aid to his broadcast planning.

The elusive foreign issues, the bane of all discographers, have been ferreted out.

The section on "Imitatums," those who directly and deliberately followed the master, is a unique addition. Not really necessary, but certainly it will be the part read first by pianists.

The first volume in the Rutgers Institute of Jazz Studies Series was the towering, many-faceted study of Benny Carter by Morroe and Edward Berger and James Patrick. This second study is a most worthy companion. It should serve as a model for any complete discography. We are all indebted to the authors for their sustained effort and for the brilliance of their design. This discography is an appropriate memorial for a genius.

William M. Weinberg

CONTENTS

ART TATUM
October 13, 1909 - November 5, 1956
Courtesy of Frank Driggs

FOREWORD

Art Tatum's position and status in the history of the development of jazz piano improvisation has remained steady in the years since his death in November 1956. He is at the pinnacle of a comprehensive, orchestral, solo piano approach as an exciting performer, a smooth technician, and most of all, an intensely creative musician. Tatum is the most articulate representative of the tradition formed from the merging of ragtime, Dixieland and blues piano into stride and from there into and through the piano developments of the swing era. During the emergence of the bebop style in the 1940's, when scores of musicians shifted their focus to pursue the new directions, Tatum remained firmly committed to his own broad course. From his well-defined position he released a stream of new harmonic combinations and rhythmic experiments that ultimately influenced not only his peers but younger generations of musicians as well.

Born on October 13, 1909, Tatum reached adolescence in an age when having a piano in one's living room was common, when ragtime and novelty piano interpretations were as popular as hymns and light classics. Blind in one eye, and with very limited vision in the other under the best of circumstances, Tatum nevertheless learned to read music both from printed scores and by the Braille method. As Tatum developed, he took as his heroes the giants of the Harlem stride tradition, those men who had combined a history of ragtime and popular piano with knowledge of the Dixieland tradition, of the musical developments in New York City with study of classics. These musicians, who were attentive to technique and touch and style as well as sensitive to the sounds and sights of the streets, provided a natural direction for Tatum who seemed to have an unlimited capacity for taking in the sounds around him. He met many musicians who passed through Toledo on road tours, and he and his friends got early experience playing for tips and for their own amusement in various Toledo night spots. He combined this with some basic classical training and anything he could hear on radio, piano rolls, and recordings.

Tatum invigorated the more formal patterns of ragtime and stride and parlor piano with a flexibility that made original designs out of cliches, jokes out of patter matter and genius strokes out of crusty formulas. He invented decorative devices only to outwit them before they ran their course in an ascending or descending or spinning pattern. As he developed, his hands bespoke individual intelligences, so independent were they when enunciating separate rhythms or contrapuntal melodies and so powerful when metamorphosing into a single-minded, unified, keyboard-breadth idea. Most of the time the hands cooperated, conventional mates, each fulfilling its designated function. The left hand set down Tatum's rich harmonic progressions while providing an unshakeably secure rhythmic foundation. The right hand sang, reshaped, and commented upon the melodies.

Knowing that there is a a predetermined harmonic structure and melodic line is essential to hearing a Tatum interpretation. The harmonic lines may be altered, reworked or rhythmically rephrased for moments at a time, but they are still the base underneath Tatum's superstructures. The melodic lines may be transformed into fresh shapes with only a note or a beat or a phrase particle retained to associate the new with the original, yet the melody remains, if only in the listener's imagination.

Tatum's obvious technical abilities, his sometime penchant to adorn his improvisations with frills and trills and his keyboard largesse may obscure for a new listener the total musician behind the rococo facade. The astonishing harmonic asides are explicit moments of full sail for a musician whose creative genius was present at all times in all phrases - in the silences, in the figures and melodic variations. in the conscientiously thoughtful bass lines, and in his rhythmic precision and clarity of beat.

The genius inside is what prevents Tatum's recordings from sounding dated. No matter what style he plays in, or the simplicity or density or character of a performance, there is an essential creativity which defies standardization, categorization and the aging process itself. Younger musicians who grew up respecting Tatum's position as an elder in the musical styles they associate with him, continue to listen to his performances for the invigorating effect these will have on their own work. What they hear, and what will keep the interpretations fresh long after the performance styles have disappeared from our conventional expectations is a master musical thinker - a creator and composer as well as an interpreter. Tatum provides fresh insights to those who think they already understand the paths on which they are travelling and reveals new avenues to those who believe the area has already been thoroughly charted. No one has ever successfully challenged Tatum in the comprehensive harmonic/melodic solo domain that belongs to him.

This volume is a handbook of information about Art Tatum recordings and selected related materials. It is the first book-length authoritative discography of the recorded performances of Art Tatum and is up to-date as of June 1982. It is an invaluable instrument for anyone interested in information about the professional recordings of Tatum or in his transcriptions originally made for radio broadcasts, personal appearances on radio and television which have been preserved, concert appearances, and some rare performances originally taped in night clubs, private homes and after-hours spots. A substantial amount of new information appears in these pages A great deal of material has been re-released in the last decade which has not appeared until this time in any published catalogue. More material has become accessible for the first time on records. Wonderful surprises have been uncovered. Some of these have been released on record; others will, we hope, become publicly available in the near future.

The amount of new information which has emerged in the last few years attests to a renewed interest in the recorded music of Tatum, and has provided impetus to the efforts of the authors of this text and others who have been able to collect information from hitherto undisclosed sources.

Apart from the wealth of specific reference material that is made available by the publication of this book, the text yields a rich portrait of Tatum as a recording artist and working musician. While he is remembered most often for his contribution to the art of solo piano performances, these pages illustrate how frequently he recorded with others. In his first official recording performance, August 5, 1932, Tatum appeared within a small ensemble accompanying the singer Adelaide Hall. His final professional recording date was a quartet engagement with Ben Webster on tenor sax, Red Callender on bass, and Bill Douglass on drums. Recorded on September 11, 1956, just two months before Tatum's death, the album was praised by critics and Webster himself considered "Night and Day" to be his finest recorded performance. The last available issues are from radio broadcasts of club dates from October, 1956 by the Art Tatum Trio which at that time included Everett Barksdale on guitar and Bill Pemberton on bass; most frequently during the 1950's the trio was composed of Tatum, Barksdale and Slam Stewart.

Considering the impact it made, the life of the original Art Tatum Trio, with Tiny Grimes on guitar and Slam Stewart on bass, was surprisingly short. The three men decided to collaborate while in Hollywood early in 1943 and the trio dissolved shortly after a June 1944 recording date with Asch in

New York. This trio recorded only enough music for two albums for consumer purchase; all of their other perfomances included in these lists have been transferred to recordings from radio transcriptions, V-Discs, or tapes of radio broadcasts and club appearances. Among the most exciting recently issued performances by the trio is the bebop Tatum twirl through "Exactly Like You," originally taped in 1944 during an engagement at "Frenchie's Pink Pig" in Milwaukee.

A brief survey of other Tatum ensemble recordings includes some 1937 Deccas featuring "Art Tatum And His Swingsters," a small ensemble with Lloyd Reese on trumpet and Marshall Royal on clarinet. In 1941 Tatum heads a small group for a magnificent series of recordings accompanying the well known blues singer Big Joe Turner. Some wonderful material from 1941 was released for the first time by Onyx records in 1973. From the private collection of Jerry Newman, these performances provided our only glimpse to date of the much discussed "after-hours" part of Tatum's musical personality, revealing him in various situations uptown, in Harlem spots, thoroughly at ease, and making music strictly for fun.

A little later in the 1940's recordings preserve Tatum's appearance at the Metropolitan Opera House in New York, a session with the Barney Bigard Sextet, various engagements for the Armed Forces Radio Service including one with the Les Paul Trio, in a musical segment from the film, "The Fabulous Dorseys," and among a field of superb musicians assembled for a special radio broadcast in 1945.

Between 1954 and 1956 Norman Granz arranged a series of small group recording dates for Tatum, and there are treasures among these fortunate collaborations: Tatum with Benny Carter and Louis Bellson in June, 1954; with Roy Eldridge, Alvin Stoller and John Simmons on March 23d and 29th, 1955; with Lionel Hampton and Buddy Rich in August, 1955, and that group with additional musicians in September, 1955; with Red Callender and Jo Jones in January 1956; with Buddy DeFranco, Red Callender and Bill Douglass in February, 1956 and finally with Ben Webster in the above mentioned September 1956 quartet date.

The recorded ensemble material reveals Tatum in a variety of performance circumstances on occasions when he is more or less interested in adapting himself to the conditions and the musicians. Sometimes, he seems to be attempting, uncomfortably, to cooperate within an ensemble where he is not at all at ease. Elsewhere, Tatum's dynamic energies dominate a group to the extent that the performances sound as if he were physically dragging the other musicians, sometimes even the members of his own trio, through the beats. Balancing these are the moments of graceful simplicity with Big Joe Turner, of elegance, musicianship and obvious mutual respect with Benny Carter, of exciting competition and shared exhilaration in some of the Tatum-Hampton extended up-tempo sails, of Tatum's generous informal accompaniments for singers, and of his hard-driving collaboration as part of the rhythm section with the Esquire All-Stars.

For the most part, the recorded solo piano material more directly reflects Tatum's tendency to select from the classics of the popular song literature, yet boogie-woogie and blues are represented, as are some spoofs on the semi-classics and a few original compositions. Anecdotes by those who heard him play in informal circumstances indicate that his personal repertoire was much broader than is revealed by a collection of titles representing professional performances.

A chronological listening to selected performances will illustrate Tatum's gradual changes in his approach to the piano keyboard, to the elements which are emphasized and to the way in which his hands work in relation to one another during a

XII

performance. One will note changes in choice of style, the movement away from early decorations of melodic lines to longer, more integrated phrases, the gradual pattern of left hand accompaniment changing from early harmonic substitutions to an intensification of the harmonic rhythms and to a variety of left hand choices and techniques, and an overall move towards a contrapuntal as well as a harmonic balance between the upper and lower registers of the keyboard.

There are fascinating moments in store for those who are interested in following the various interpretations of performances that have been recorded more than once. Some turn out to be more or less fixed interpretations which simply gain more luster and speed in subsequent performances; others evolve gradually, retaining some elements of previous performances, transforming others, and adding new materials within the structures; others reflect rather dramatic changes of approach and leave to the imagination the process of development that took place in the unrecorded practice and performance of these tunes.

Among the most enlightening and revealing of the solo performances released in the past decade is Tatum's 1941 piano-vocal after-hours "Toledo Blues" interpretation. So out-of-character in terms of Tatum's professional performance posture, it is an intimate and fond caress of the blues tradition...a simple celebration among friends. The release of the 1932 test pressing of "Tiger Rag" offers a rare opportunity to visit a Tatum interpretation that was to become infinitely more secure and polished before its first issued performance recorded in the spring of 1933. The recently released complete performances, on the Smithsonian label, from the private party collection of 1955, restore comprehensibility to performances that were rendered rhythmically awkward and musically unbalanced by their ill-advised editorial cuts. Tatum's as yet

XIII

unreleased elegant spoof and transformation of Chopin's "Waltz in C♯ Minor" would surely have caused Chopin to tap his toes and pick up his ears and would tickle the fancy of anyone who remembers the piece from his early days of piano practice.₆

Appropriately, this first published volume devoted to Art Tatum is a catalogue and a source book to his recorded material. It presents a solid foundation from which to proceed with future research. To the best of their abilities, the authors have untangled the confusions and corrected omissions in the limited previously published discographical data relating to Tatum. They have traced the recorded sources, identified reissues and have comprehensibly organized the mass of issued and unissued materials. They have thoughtfully included related materials that pertain to Tatum's recorded works and they have given us an instrument which will prove to provide valuable information at any point in one's introduction to, or study of, the music of Art Tatum. Most of all, this volume is a fundamental step toward the preservation of Tatum's contributions to the development of jazz piano improvisation and thus to the history of American popular music.

Felicity A. Howlett

INTRODUCTION

So much praise has been heaped upon Art Tatum over the years, and he is held in such high esteem by both musicians and cognoscenti, that it is surprising to discover that no book has ever been written about him or his work. There has, however, been a welcome resurgence of interest in recent years, perhaps spurred by the twenty-fifth anniversary of his death in 1956. Contemporary Keyboard Magazine devoted most of its October 1981 issue to him, and the 1981 Kool (formerly Newport) Jazz Festival featured an evening of eight pianists plus Slam Stewart, Tiny Grimes, and Eddie Daniels in a "Tribute to Art Tatum." The Smithsonian Institution has released a Tatum record of rare performances, and both the Book-Of-The-Month Club and Time-Life Records have issued boxed sets of his work. Norman Granz, a long time Tatum booster, continues to reissue on the Pablo label and has also released a complete LP of formerly unissued takes. Other releases have emerged, bringing forth both new and reissued material.

The need for a comprehensive discography of Art Tatum performances has long been evident and this volume is intended to fill that void.

For the Art Tatum devotee, the discography provides a means of untangling the confusion engendered by the many reissues in the years since Tatum's death, and distinguishes these from performances previously unreleased. Many of these recordings have liner notes which offer little, erroneous, or no information about the origins of the material or, indeed, whether the performances are reissues at all. We have tried to provide a roadmap of Tatum performances which may have already been encountered in one's own collection, and to point the way to sources of old material previously thought to be unavailable, as well as new material previously undreamt of. It also serves to aid in the identification of future releases which are bound to

XV

appear, many of them of pieces listed in the Unissued Sessions section.

For the neophyte, this book acts as a springboard and serves as a guide in the assembly of a representative collection.

For the researcher, this volume offers the first published information about many previously unlisted recordings, as well as dates and places of available recordings where such data was not previously known. For example, there are listings taken from the original Decca Master Books which have long resisted the clutches of discographers. The Matrix Cross Reference List should be especially valuable to the researcher.

For the record collector or dealer, the Compilation of Issued Discs offers an easy way to identify the contents of records identified on auction or sale lists solely by label name and catalogue number. An arrow in the Chronological Discography identifies orginal issues for those who treasure them.

For the musician who is interested in playing as well as listening to Tatum's music, the list of Published Music, keyed to the records, provides a closer, invaluable look at the innards of Tatum's output, work which continues to influence countless pianists and other instrumentalists. Musicians will enjoy the Imitatums section, which offers a look at efforts by others to emulate specific Tatum recordings or to intentionally play in the style of Art Tatum.

For those with access to a player piano, the list of Piano Rolls will undoubtedly be of interest because all of them are currently available.

For all of us, the Title List gives an overview of the kinds of tunes preferred by Tatum, most often the American popular song. Composers and lyricists are identified so that one may investigate how Tatum treats one's own favorites. The list of Films, although unfortunately so very short, contains details of the two known film clips in which Tatum appeared.

Simply stated, the purpose of this book is to act as a catalyst for further research, and to aid in the acquisition of materials to best and most fully enjoy the piano playing of the man we believe to be the most influential jazz pianist of our time.

We have not included biographical information, anecdotes, lists of appearances, influences which Tatum had upon others or they upon him, a bibliography, nor any detailed musical analysis. These are all the subject of another volume on Art Tatum in preparation by the authors in collaboration with Felicity A. Howlett.

We have adhered to what might be called a "session emphasis," in that we have tried to cluster information about all selections which were performed at the same place on the same date and time. The sessions are separated from each other by dashed lines to make them more readily distinguishable. Even though "discography" implies a transfer to disc, we have kept sessions intact. Those pieces which remain unissued from sessions where some material has become available on disc appear in the Chronological Discography. Where no part of a session has ever been issued on disc, details cannot truly belong in the discography and therefore we have provided a separate section entitled "Unissued Sessions." Once again dashed lines separate one session from another for clarity.

In order to furnish a practical and convenient method of cross referencing from one list to another, we have implemented a system of index numbers. These numbers make their first appearance prominently in the upper left hand corner preceding each performance in the Chronological Discography. They identify that performance in each succeeding list. Apart from their function for the purpose of ready identification, the numbers themselves have no significance and none should be attributed to them.

In the interest of readability we have not used the ditto marks, dashes, and "all titles also on ..." comments often found in other discographies to conserve space. Each listing in the Chronological Discography is self-contained, and record sizes and speeds are noted in order to add meaning to the catalogue numbers. Similarly, the country of origin has not been merged into the manufacturer's name (as in "BrE", for example) nor have abbreviations been used for the manufacturer's name.

It is our hope that the listings will produce many revelations for the reader. We trust that the Tatum collector who believes he "has everything Tatum ever recorded" will not be chastened by the presence of new listings, but rather that he will be encouraged and stimulated to acquire what he lacks and to contact us with information about what we missed. It is apparent that a work of this scope must inevitably contain errors of commission and omission, and for these we apologize. We welcome corrections and additions as supportive of the ultimate goal, which is to disseminate as much complete and accurate information as is possible. We might add that some entries which appear to be prima facie in error are not. For example, it may seem strange that Jazztone would issue both J-SPEC-100 and J-SPEC-101 with almost identical contents, and that the United States Veterans Administration would issue its "Here's to Vets" series first on 16 inch transcriptions and then on 12 inch transcriptions, and that Pablo, in issuing thirteen individual LP's in its "Art Tatum Solo Masterpieces" series all over the world, would have the first eight volumes numbered alike everywhere, only to have the remaining volumes numbered one way in the United States and Canada and differently in all other countries. These anomalies do exist. (Incidentally, when we went to the printer Volume 13 had not yet been issued separately in the United States or Canada.) The authors would appreciate any and all additional information, corrections, or comments, and may be contacted c/o Arnold Laubich, 469 Fifth Avenue, New York, NY 10017, USA.

It should be apparent that a book of this nature would not be possible without the kind and gracious cooperation of many people. A special note of thanks is due to Felicity Howlett, for her significant assistance to this project. Also especially noteworthy was the time, effort, and substantial contribution of Mike Doyle, Jim Feely, Mike Lang, Bill Miner, Bob Porter and Jerry Valburn, and to them we express our gratitude. We would also like to acknowledge the valuable assistance of, and thank the following, for their help: Clive Acker, Bob Altschuler, Eric Anderson, Ray Avery, Ed Berger, Raffaele Borretti, Joe Boughton, Jack Bradley, Aaron Bridgers, Dominic Brigaud, Michael Brooks, Dave Carey, Dave Chertok, John Clement, Vince Cosgrave, Ken Crawford, Les Crystal, Michael Cudahy, John R. T. Davies, Charles Delaunay, Frank Driggs, Steve Ettinger, Harry Fein, Harold Flakser, Livingston Freeman, Milt Gabler, Norman Granz, Ben Hafey, Steve Hartig, Bill Haseltine, Jim Hedrick, Wally Heider, Haywood Horne, John Hozack, Larry Imber, Walter Keepers, John Kelly, Wayne Knight, Rüdiger Litza, Karsten Lohmann, Rainer Lotz, Bob McCunney, Jack McKinney, Dan Morgenstern, Jaime Müller, Ken Noble, Dennis Oppenheim, Les Paul, Chris Pirie, Lothar Polomski, Brian Priestley, Henry Quarles, Jerry Raskin, Ed Roeloffs, Mort Savada, Phil Schaap, Don Schlitten, Dick Schmelzle, Wolfgang Schmidt, Kenn Scott, Dick Sears, Yasuo Segami, Manfred Selchow, Heinz Sprenger, Joe Springer, Mike Sutcliffe, J. R. Taylor, Warren Taylor, Charlie Teagarden, Fred Turco, Jim Turner, Louis Ventrella, Pierre Voran, Bob Wessels, Lars Westin, Bozy White, Martin Williams, Art Zimmerman and George Ziskind.

June, 1982

Arnold Laubich
Ray Spencer

THE CHRONOLOGICAL DISCOGRAPHY

The Chronological Discography covers all disc recordings known to the authors on which Art Tatum appears. Records issued by government agencies, such as the Armed Forces Radio Service, are included. In a few cases where the manufacturer assigned a catalogue number to a proposed Tatum issue which was never released, such number is shown with an appropriate explanatory note.

Please refer to the corresponding number in Figure 1 for each of the explanations below.

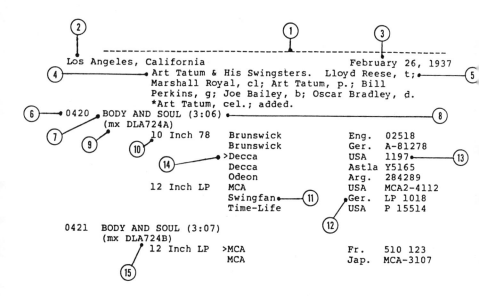

① A dashed line signals the end of the previous session. Each session represents a group of performances made on the same date at the same location, and a dashed line is used above and below to distinguish the performances from that particular session.

(2) The city and state where the session took place.

(3) The date of the session.

(4) The nature of the performances; whether they were piano solos, or if by a group, its name.

(5) If applicable, the names and instruments of other performers. Abbreviations used to describe the instruments appear in the Appendix.

(6) The index number. This is a number assigned to each specific performance so that it may be readily identified when referred to in succeeding lists. The index numbers are purely arbitary and have no significance other than as a device for identifying a particular performance.

(7) The published title of the selection played. If a significant difference exists in the way the title is listed on a particular record label or jacket, details are provided in the "Compilation of Issued Discs."

(8) The playing time of the performance. All times are necessarily approximate due to the great variation in equipment speeds and power supplies. Often a reissue by the original manufacturer is significantly longer or shorter in playing time than the original. Where possible, the time given is that which appears in the manufacturer's master book. One should be cautious about relying on times for performance identification.

9 The master, or matrix ("mx") number:

In the case of 78 rpm records or other "direct-to-disc" recordings, this is a sequential number (within a series) assigned at the time of performance, and is usually found pressed in the record surface between the last grooves and the label. The prefixes and suffixes provide useful information about additional performances of the same tune ("alternate takes") made at the same recording session, as well as other information. For example, the Decca matrix number "DLA724B" indicates the second ("B") take of the title recorded at the Decca Los Angeles studio on the same date. The matrix number identifies the performance. (The same cannot be said for the catalogue number, as is described further below.)

In the case of LP's, EP's and other issues which contain more than one track per side, the matrix number applies to all tracks on a side and is not uniquely associated with the performance. Such a matrix number simply identifies the pressing.

V-Discs were special 78 rpm records issued by military units of the United States government for distribution to the troops and were not intended for commercial use. They bore matrix numbers which were determined by the government, as well as serial numbers which were assigned by the record manufacturers. Both of these numbers are found embossed consecutively in the record surface between the last grooves and the label; sometimes the matrix number is given first and sometimes the serial number. The "Chronological Discography" always lists the matrix number first, followed by the serial number.

(10) The diameter of the record, in inches, followed by additional details about the characteristics of the disc.   See the Appendix for details.

Transcriptions were special recordings made for radio broadcast use.   Those made for commercial use were generally distributed to radio stations on a subscription basis, and were not made for general circulation.   Transcriptions made for one of the many United States government agencies typically were for broadcast by the Armed Forces Radio Service, or on the Voice of America. These, too, were not intended to be sold to the public.   Both types of transcriptions have found their way into the hands of collectors and various record companies and are often reissued.

(11) The manufacturer's trade name which appears on the record label.   If the trade name on the record jacket differs significantly from that on the label, details are provided in the "Compilation of Issued Discs," and the latter also cross references labels which are sometimes known by more than one name. V-Discs (see above, 9) bearing the legend, "War Department-Music Section-Athletic & Recreation Branch-Special Services Division, A.S.F.," or "War Department-Music Section-Entertainment & Recreation Branch-Special Services Division, A.S.F.," are commonly called "Army" and are so referred to here.   So too are those labelled "Army-Navy-Marine Corps.-Coast Guard."   Those labelled "Navy Department, Bureau of Naval Personnel" are called "Navy."   Labels are listed alphabetically within size and speed categories.

(12) The country in which the record was pressed and issued.   Within label name, USA issues are listed first because they tend to be most available and best known.   Other issuing countries are listed

XXIII

alphabetically. Within country, issues are
listed numerically. See the Appendix for a list
of abbreviations.

(13) The manufacturer's catalogue number of the
record, as it appears on the record itself. If
the record jacket is numbered in a significantly
different way, such variation is noted where the
record is listed in the "Compilation of Issued
Discs." If the record is part of a set, the set
number is cross referenced in the "Compilation of
Issued Discs." If a separate number is not shown
for the set, it is the same as the number listed
for the individual disc.

(14) The arrow points to the original issue.

(15) An illustration of an alternate take, (a second
performance) of the same tune. The master number
suffix was incremented by the manufacturer to
distinguish between the performances.

Every effort has been made to list performances
in strict chronological order. However, because of
the peculiar circumstances of the performances made
for Decca in August and October of 1934 (Index
numbers 0140 through 0262) it was deemed advisable to
group these by title to avoid confusion. Normally,
record companies assign matrix numbers sequentially
according to the performance date. Decca did this on
August 22, 1934, and August 24, 1934, when Tatum
recorded at their New York studios. Decca assigned
suffix "A" to the first take, and used "B" if there
was a second take. Subsequently, Tatum returned to
the studio on October 9th and re-recorded several of
the same titles, as well as some new ones. Instead
of assigning new matrix numbers when a title was
repeated on another date, Decca used the suffix "C"
(and "D" when there was yet another take), thus
implying that these were all recorded at the first

session. Things became even more complicated later on. Apparently these early records were still selling and Decca may have lost damaged, or worn out the masters. Accordingly, they brought Tatum back into the studios, this time in Los Angeles on February 22, 1940, (six years later!) to play four of the same titles (as well as others). "Emaline," (0910), "Moonglow," (0920), "Love Me," (0930), and "Cockails For Two," (0940), which were then reissued by Decca. but they used the old catalogue numbers, 155 and 156! Thus it is possible to buy these records, with the same catalogue number, listing the same titles, but actually containing different performances made six years apart.

UNISSUED SESSIONS

The format of this section is similar to that of the main chronological discography except that information associated with record issues is inapplicable and does not appear. Included are details of all known performances which were reproduced on disc, wire, tape, transcription or other similar audio recording media. Most have survived in some form in private collections.

If a session was recorded for the Armed Forces Radio Service or a similar governmental group, and has not been issued commercially, it nevertheless appears in the main Chronological Discography rather than in this list. Such discs are offered for sale in auction lists and by dealers, even though they may be difficult to obtain

In order to provide continuity where part of a session has been issued on disc, the unissued performances have also been listed in the main Chronological Discography rather than in this list.

This section therefore contains those known sessions no part of which has been made available on disc. They exist today mostly on tape or cassette. Of course these listings can only represent our "best efforts," since the extent of the existence of private recordings made by individuals from their radios, etc., can never be fully known. The purpose of the inclusion of such listings is:

> To make the collector aware that these did or do exist and perhaps can be obtained by trade for personal use or research.

> To provide a possible means of identification of future disc releases which may come from these sources.

> To document other performers with whom Art Tatum played and to list other titles, or types of music, or vocals, some of which may differ in character from those which were commercially released.

> To help in establishing other dates and places where Tatum performed.

Index numbers in this section bear the prefix "T," and are numbered higher than index numbers in the Chronological Discography. They are cross referenced by the Title List, the Musician Index, and the Quick Dating Guide.

COMPILATION OF ISSUED DISCS

This is a listing of known issued discs which contain one or more tracks on which Art Tatum performs. Discs are listed alphabetically by manufacturer's label name; within label they are in alphanumeric sequence by catalogue number as it appears on the disc, and within catalogue numbers they are listed alphabetically by country of manufacture.

The titles on each disc are listed alphabetically for convenience, and the index number appears to the left of each title. Only titles on which Tatum appears are listed. Record sizes and speeds are also shown, and if they are preceded by an "s," the record has been electronically rechannelled for stereo. If the record is part of a set and the set itself bears a different catalogue number, that number is given below the label name. If the set number is not noted in the listing for an individual disc, it is the same as the number of that disc. Sets are also listed by the set number, and there is a cross reference to the discs within the set which contain titles on which Tatum appears.

TITLE LIST

Titles are in alphabetical order. Each is preceded by the index number which locates it within the Chronological Discography or, if the index number has a "T" prefix, within the Unissued Session list. The title is followed by the approximate time of the performance, if known, and the first appearance of a title is followed by the name of the composer. Where the composer did not write the words, the names of lyricists are given after the "/" mark. Multiple composers or lyricists are linked with hyphens.

MUSICIAN INDEX

This list is used to locate performances in which Art Tatum appeared with a particular musician or orchestra. Musicians are listed alphabetically. The musician's name is followed by the instrument which he played, and beneath that is a list of each index number of the performances on which he played with Tatum. The list includes performances from both the Chronological Discography and the Unissued

Session list; the latter numbers are preceded by the letter "T."

THE IMITATUMS FILMS, PUBLISHED MUSIC, PIANO ROLLS

Each of these sections provides an explanation within itself, or is reasonably self-explanatory.

APPENDICES

The appendices include a guide to abbreviations, a matrix cross-reference list which makes it possible to easily locate an index number for any performance to get further information if the matrix number is known, a list of other discographies which were reviewed in the course of this work, and a Quick Dating Guide. The latter readily identifies the year performed for any index number in the Chronological Discography or the Unissued Session list, and has been placed at the back of the book for convenience.

New York, New York   August 5, 1932
        Unissued test pressing incorrectly attributed
        in the Brunswick files to Jimmy Lord, a
        horn player.
        Piano solo.
0001 TIGER RAG (1:58)
      (mx TO 1192)
                   Brunswick   USA   Unissued
        12 Inch LP >Aircheck   USA   21
                   Time-Life   USA   P 15514

New York, New York   August 5, 1932
        Issued under the name of Adelaide Hall.
        Personnel unconfirmed except for the pianists
        and trumpeter, but probably included the
        following: Charlie Teagarden, t; Jimmy Dorsey(?),
        cl; Francis Carter and Art Tatum, p; Dick
        McDonough(?), g; Adelaide Hall, v.
0010 STRANGE AS IT SEEMS (3:06)
      (mx B12148A)
        10 Inch 78 >Brunswick   USA   6376
                   Brunswick   Eng. 1348

0011 STRANGE AS IT SEEMS (3:08)
      (mx B12148B)
                   Brunswick   USA   Unissued

0020 I'LL NEVER BE THE SAME (3:09)
      (mx B12149A)
        10 Inch 78 >Brunswick   USA   6362
                   Brunswick   Eng. 1348

0021 I'LL NEVER BE THE SAME (3:17)
      (mx B12149B)
                   Brunswick   USA   Unissued

New York, New York   August 10, 1932
        Issued under the name of Adelaide Hall.
        Francis Carter and Art Tatum, p; Adelaide
        Hall, v.
0030 YOU GAVE ME EVERYTHING BUT LOVE (3:12)
      (mx B12166A)
        10 Inch 78 >Brunswick   USA   6376
                   Brunswick   Eng. 01442
                   Parlophone   Eng. F1425

0031 YOU GAVE ME EVERYTHING BUT LOVE
      (mx B12166B)
                   Brunswick   USA   Unissued

0040 THIS TIME IT'S LOVE (3:09)
      (mx B12167A)
        10 Inch 78 >Brunswick   USA   6362
                   Brunswick   Eng. 01442
                   Parlophone   Eng. F1425

New York, New York   March 21, 1933
        Piano solos.
0050 TEA FOR TWO (3:11)
      (mx B13162A)
        10 Inch 78 >Brunswick   USA   6553
                   Brunswick   Eng. 01554
                   Brunswick   Fr.   A-500337
                   Brunswick   Ger. A-9905
                   Special Editions   USA   5015-S
        7 Inch 45EP Columbia   Eng. SEG7540
                    Columbia   Jap. EM-72
                    Fontana   Eng. TFE.17235
        12 Inch LP CBS   Holl. 62615

1

		CBS Realm Jazz	Eng.	RM52601
		Columbia	USA	CS9655
		Columbia	Eng.	33SX1506
		Columbia Spec.Prod.	USA	JLN 24028
		Epic	USA	LN 24028
		Epic	USA	LN3295
		Time-Life	USA	P 15514

0051   TEA FOR TWO*
       (mx B13162B)

| | | Brunswick | USA | 6553 |

*Note: Existence of this alternate take is unconfirmed.
It is listed by inference, because there is a written
transcription of this tune done by J. Lawrence Cook
and marked, "Brunswick 6553," which is significantly
different than the "A" take, listed at 0050. Cook
was a well known transcriber for piano rolls and it
is possible that he worked with this alternate take.

0060   ST. LOUIS BLUES (2:30)
       (mx B13163A)

10 Inch 78	>Brunswick		USA	6543
	Brunswick		Eng.	01506
	Brunswick		Fr.	A-500265
	Brunswick		Fr.	A-9433
	Columbia		Astla	DO-1227
7 Inch 45EP	Columbia		Eng.	SEG7540
	Columbia		Jap.	EM-72
12 Inch LP	CBS Realm Jazz		Eng.	RM52601
	Columbia		USA	CS9655
12 Inch TX	AFRS Amer.Pop.Mus.		USA	149
	AFRS Amer.Pop.Mus.		USA	194

0061   ST. LOUIS BLUES*
       (mx B13163B)

| 10 Inch 78 | >Brunswick | USA | 6543 |

*Existence of this alternate take is unconfirmed.

0070   TIGER RAG (2:17)
       (mx B13164A)

10 Inch 78	>Brunswick	USA	6543
	Brunswick	Eng.	01506
	Brunswick	Fr.	A-500265
	Brunswick	Fr.	A-9433
	Columbia	Astla	DO-1227
7 Inch 45EP	Columbia	Eng.	SEG7540
	Columbia	Jap.	EM-72
	Fontana	Eng.	TFE.17235
12 Inch LP	CBS	Eng.	M 80244
	CBS	Holl.	62615
	CBS	Fr.	64946
	CBS Realm Jazz	Eng.	RM52601
	Columbia	USA	CS9655
	Columbia	USA	KG32355
	Columbia House	USA	P3S5932
	Epic	USA	LN3295
	Time-Life	USA	P 15514

0080   SOPHISTICATED LADY (3:14)
       (mx B13165A)

10 Inch 78	>Brunswick	USA	6553
	Brunswick	Eng.	01554
	Brunswick	Fr.	A-500337
	Brunswick	Ger.	A-9905
	Special Editions	USA	5015-S
7 Inch 45EP	Columbia	Eng.	SEG7540
	Columbia	Jap.	EM-72
	Fontana	Eng.	TFE.17235
12 Inch LP	CBS	Holl.	62615
	CBS Realm Jazz	Eng.	RM52601
	Columbia	USA	CS9655
	Columbia	Eng.	33SX1506
	Columbia Spec.Prod.	USA	JLN 24028
	Epic	USA	LN3295
	Epic	USA	LN 24028

```
                            Epic              USA  LA-16000
                            Philips           Eng. BBL7511
---------------------------------------------------------------
Cleveland, Ohio                               February 27, 1934
          Radio Broadcast. Piano solos, with announcer.
0090  YOUNG AND HEALTHY (1:30)

            12 Inch LP    Aircheck          USA   21
                          Epitaph           USA   E-4006
                         >RI Disc           Swiss RI-DISC 7

0100  MORNING, NOON, AND NIGHT (3:19)

            12 Inch LP    Aircheck          USA   21
                          Epitaph           USA   E-4006
                         >RI Disc           Swiss RI-DISC 7

0110  WHEN DAY IS DONE (2:51)

            12 Inch LP    Aircheck          USA   21
                          Epitaph           USA   E-4006
                         >RI Disc           Swiss RI-DISC 7

0120  STAR DUST (2:57)

            12 Inch LP    Aircheck          USA   21
                          Epitaph           USA   E-4006
                         >RI Disc           Swiss RI-DISC 7

0130  CHINATOWN, MY CHINATOWN (1:34)

            12 Inch LP    Aircheck          USA   21
                          Epitaph           USA   E-4006
                         >RI Disc           Swiss RI-DISC 7

---------------------------------------------------------------
     Note: For index numbers between 0140 and 0262,
     chronological order has been sacrificed in order
     to preserve the sequence of matrix numbers for each
     set of takes. Please see "How To Use This Book,"
     page XVIII, for further details about this group.

New York, New York                            August 22, 1934
          Piano solos.
0140  MOONGLOW (2:35)
      (mx 38387A)
            10 Inch 78    Brunswick         Eng.  01877
                         >Decca             USA   155
            12 Inch LP    MCA               Fr.   510.081
                          MCA               Jap.  MCA-3073

0141  MOONGLOW
      (mx 38387B)
                          Decca             USA   Unissued

0150  I WOULD DO ANYTHING FOR YOU (2:36)
      (mx 38388A)
            10 Inch 78   >Brunswick         Eng.  02015
                          Brunswick         Ger.  A-9790

0151  I WOULD DO ANYTHING FOR YOU
      (mx 38388B)
                          Decca             USA   Unissued

---------------------------------------------------------------
New York, New York                            October 9, 1934
          Piano solos.
          (See note preceding [0140].)
0152  I WOULD DO ANYTHING FOR YOU (2:36)
      (mx 38388C)
            10 Inch 78   >Decca             USA   1373
                          Decca             Can.  1373
            12 Inch LP    MCA               Fr.   510.081
                          MCA               Jap.  MCA-3073

                              3
```

```
                     Odeon              Arg.    284465
0153  I WOULD DO ANYTHING FOR YOU
      (mx 38388D)
                     Decca              USA     Unissued

-----------------------------------------------------------
New York, New York                      August 22, 1934
      Piano solos.
      (See note preceding [0140].)
0160  WHEN A WOMAN LOVES A MAN (3:04)
      (mx 38389A)
            10 Inch 78  >Decca          USA     741
                         Decca          Can.    741
            12 Inch LP   MCA            USA     MCA2-4112

-----------------------------------------------------------
New York, New York                      October 9, 1934
      Piano solos.
      (See note preceding [0140].)
0161  WHEN A WOMAN LOVES A MAN
      (mx 38389C)
                         Decca          USA     Unissued

0162  WHEN A WOMAN LOVES A MAN (2:38)
      (mx 38389D)
            10 Inch 78   Brunswick      Eng.    01978
                        >Decca          USA     741
                         Odeon          Arg.    284030
            12 Inch LP   MCA            Fr.     510.081

-----------------------------------------------------------
New York, New York                      August 22, 1934
      Piano solos.
      (See note preceding [0140].)
0170  EMALINE (2:34)
      (mx 38390A)
            10 Inch 78   Brunswick      Eng.    01862
                        >Decca          USA     155
                         Decca          Eng.    BM 01204
                         Decca          Eng.    M.30777
            12 Inch LP   MCA            Fr.     510.081
                         MCA            Jap.    MCA-3073

0180  LOVE ME (2:53)
      (mx 38391, 38391A)
            10 Inch 78   Brunswick      Eng.    02015
                         Brunswick      Ger.    A-9790
                        >Decca          USA     156
            12 Inch LP   MCA            Jap.    MCA-3073

0190  COCKTAILS FOR TWO (2:46)
      (mx 38392, 38392A)
            10 Inch 78  >Decca          USA     156
                         Decca          Eng.    M.30777
            12 Inch LP   MCA            Jap.    MCA-3073

-----------------------------------------------------------
New York, New York                      August 24, 1934
      Piano solo.
      (See note preceding [0140].)
0200  AFTER YOU'VE GONE (3:06)
      (mx 38426A)
            10 Inch 78  >Brunswick      Eng.    01862
                         Brunswick      Fr.     A-505015
                         Decca          Eng.    BM 01204

-----------------------------------------------------------
New York, New York                      October 9, 1934
      Piano solos.
      (See note preceding [0140].)
0201  AFTER YOU'VE GONE (2:28)
      (mx 38426C)
            10 Inch 78  >Decca          USA     468
            12 Inch LP   MCA            Fr.     510.081
```

4

```
                           MCA                Jap.  MCA-3073

0202  AFTER YOU'VE GONE
      (mx 38426D)
                           Decca             USA   Unissued
------------------------------------------------,--------------
New York, New York                            August 24, 1934
      Piano solo.
      (See note preceding [0140].)
0210  STAR DUST
      (mx 38427A)
                           Decca             USA   Unissued
-------------------------------------------------------------
New York, New York                            October 9, 1934
      Piano solos.
      (See note preceding [0140].)
0211  STAR DUST (3:17)
      (mx 38427C)
           10 Inch 78    Brunswick           Eng.  02051
                        >Decca               USA   306
                         Decca               Eng.  BM 01203
           12 Inch LP    MCA                 USA   MCA2-4112
                         MCA                 Fr.   510.081
                         MCA                 Jap.  MCA-3073

0212  STAR DUST
      (mx 38427D)
                           Decca             USA   Unissued
-------------------------------------------------------------
New York, New York                            August 24, 1934
      Piano solos.
      (See note preceding [0140].)
0220  I AIN'T GOT NOBODY
      (mx 38428A)
                           Decca             USA   Unissued
-------------------------------------------------------------
New York, New York                            October 9, 1934
      Piano solos.
      (See note preceding [0140].)
0221  I AIN'T GOT NOBODY (3:21)
      (mx 38428C)
           10 Inch 78    Brunswick           Eng.  01978
                        >Decca               USA   741
                         Decca               Can.  741
                         Odeon               Arg.  284030
                         Odeon               Arg.  286310
           12 Inch LP    MCA                 USA   MCA2-4112
                         MCA                 Fr.   510.081
                         MCA                 Jap.  MCA-3073

0222  I AIN'T GOT NOBODY
      (mx 38428D)
                           Decca             USA   Unissued
-------------------------------------------------------------
New York, New York                            August 24, 1934
      Piano solos.
      (See note preceding [0140].)
0230  ILL WIND (2:55)
      (mx 38429A)
           10 Inch 78   >Brunswick           Eng.  02051
                         Decca               Eng.  BM 01203
           12 Inch LP    MCA                 USA   MCA2-4112
                         MCA                 Fr.   510.081

0240  THE SHOUT (2:42)
      (mx 38430A)
           10 Inch 78    Brunswick           Eng.  01877
                         Brunswick           Fr.   A-505015
                        >Decca               USA   468
           12 Inch LP    MCA                 USA   MCA2-4112

                              5
```

```
                            MCA                    Fr.    510.081
                            MCA                    Jap.   MCA-3073

0241  THE SHOUT
      (mx 38430B)
                            Decca                  USA    Unissued

0250  BEAUTIFUL LOVE
      (mx 38431A)
                            Decca                  USA    Unissued

-----------------------------------------------------------
New York, New York                                 October 9, 1934
          Piano solos.
          (See note preceding [0140].)
0251  BEAUTIFUL LOVE (2:51)
      (mx 38431C)
          10 Inch 78   Brunswick                   Eng.   02489
                       Brunswick                   Ger.   A-81298
                       >Decca                      USA    306
          12 Inch LP   MCA                         USA    MCA2-4112
                       MCA                          Fr.    510.081
                       MCA                          Jap.   MCA-3073

0252  BEAUTIFUL LOVE (3:18)
      (mx 38431D)
          10 Inch 78   >Decca                      USA    306

-----------------------------------------------------------
New York,New York                                  August 24, 1934
          Piano solo.
          (See note preceding [0140].)
0260  LIZA (2:41)
      (mx 38432A)
          10 Inch 78   >Decca                      USA    1373
          12 Inch LP   MCA                         USA    MCA2-4112
                       MCA                          Fr.    510.081
                       MCA                          Jap.   MCA-3073

-----------------------------------------------------------
New York, New York                                 October 9, 1934
          Piano solos.
          (See note preceding [0140].)
0261  LIZA
      (mx 38432C)
                            Decca                  USA    Unissued

0262  LIZA (3:03)
      (mx 38432D)
          10 Inch 78   Brunswick                   Eng.   02489
                       Brunswick                   Ger.   A-81298
                       >Decca                      USA    1373
                       Decca                       Can.   1373
          12 Inch LP   MCA                         Fr.    510.081

-----------------------------------------------------------
Cleveland, Ohio                                    September 26, 1935
          Radio broadcast, "The Fleischmann Hour,"
          on NBC radio, New York City.
          Piano solo.
0270  LULU´S BACK IN TOWN (2:44)*
      (mx RG 200)
          12 Inch LP   Aircheck                    USA    21
          16 Inch TX   >Recollections at 30 USA    22
      *Time includes 26 second introduction by Rudy Vallee.
      Music time is 2:18.

-----------------------------------------------------------
New York, New York                                 December, 1935
          Piano solos.
0280  BOOTS AND SADDLE (2:15)
      (mx MS-96544-1)
          12 Inch LP   Ariston                     It.    AR/LP/12023
                       Jazz Panorama               Swed.  JPLP15
                       Jazz Panorama               Swed.  LP15
```

```
                    Oscar Disco      It.   OS 050
                    Saga             Eng.  6915
        16 Inch TX >Standard         USA   A675
                    Standard         USA   Q104

0290 AFTER YOU'VE GONE (2:25)
     (mx MS-96544-1)
        12 Inch LP  Ariston          It.   AR/LP/12023
                    Jazz Panorama    Swed. JPLP15
                    Jazz Panorama    Swed. LP15
                    Oscar Disco      It.   OS 050
                    Saga             Eng.  6915
        16 Inch TX >Standard         USA   A675
                    Standard         USA   Q104

0300 DIXIELAND BAND (2:30)
     (mx MS-96544-1)
        12 Inch LP  Ariston          It.   AR/LP/12023
                    Jazz Panorama    Swed. JPLP15
                    Jazz Panorama    Swed. LP15
                    Oscar Disco      It.   OS 050
                    Saga             Eng.  6915
        16 Inch TX >Standard         USA   A675
                    Standard         USA   Q104

0310 THE SHOUT (1:35)
     (mx MS-96544-1)
        12 Inch LP  Jazz Panorama    Swed. JPLP15
                    Jazz Panorama    Swed. LP15
        16 Inch TX >Standard         USA   A675
                    Standard         USA   Q104

0320 TIGER RAG (2:10)
     (mx MS-96545-1)
        12 Inch LP  Jazz Panorama    Swed. JPLP15
                    Jazz Panorama    Swed. LP15
        16 Inch TX >Standard         USA   A675
                    Standard         USA   Q104

0330 STAY AS SWEET AS YOU ARE (2:30)
     (mx MS-96545-1)
        12 Inch LP  Ariston          It.   AR/LP/12023
                    Jazz Panorama    Swed. JPLP15
                    Jazz Panorama    Swed. LP15
                    Oscar Disco      It.   OS 050
                    Saga             Eng.  6915
        16 Inch TX >Standard         USA   A675
                    Standard         USA   Q104

0340 MONDAY IN MANHATTAN (2:15)
     (mx MS-96545-1)
        12 Inch LP  Ariston          It.   AR/LP/12023
                    Jazz Panorama    Swed. JPLP15
                    Jazz Panorama    Swed. LP15
                    Oscar Disco      It.   OS 050
                    Saga             Eng.  6915
        16 Inch TX >Standard         USA   A675
                    Standard         USA   Q104

0350 I WOULD DO ANYTHING FOR YOU (2:10)
     (mx MS-96545-1)
        12 Inch LP  Ariston          It.   AR/LP/12023
                    Jazz Panorama    Swed. JPLP15
                    Jazz Panorama    Swed. LP15
                    Oscar Disco      It.   OS 050
                    Saga             Eng.  6915
        16 Inch TX >Standard         USA   A675
                    Standard         USA   Q104

0360 THEME FOR PIANO (1:00)
     (mx MS-96545-1)
        12 Inch LP  Ariston          It.   AR/LP/12023
                    Jazz Panorama    Swed. JPLP15
                    Jazz Panorama    Swed. LP15
                    Oscar Disco      It.   OS 050
```

```
                          Saga               Eng.   6915
            16 Inch TX  >Standard            USA    A675
                          Standard           USA    Q104

0370   IN THE MIDDLE OF A KISS (2:35)
       (mx MS-96546-1)
            12 Inch LP    Ariston            It.    AR/LP/12023
                          Jazz Panorama      Swed.  JPLP15
                          Jazz Panorama      Swed.  LP15
                          Oscar Disco        It.    OS 050
                          Saga               Eng.   6915
            16 Inch TX  >Standard            USA    A684
                          Standard           USA    Q105

0380   ROSETTA (2:15)
       (mx MS-96546-1)
            12 Inch LP    Ariston            It.    AR/LP/12023
                          Jazz Panorama      Swed.  JPLP15
                          Jazz Panorama      Swed.  LP15
                          Oscar Disco        It.    OS 050
                          Saga               Eng.   6915
            16 Inch TX  >Standard            USA    A684
                          Standard           USA    Q105

0390   I WISH I WERE TWINS (2:15)
       (mx MS-96546-1)
            12 Inch LP    Ariston            It.    AR/LP/12023
                          Jazz Panorama      Swed.  JPLP15
                          Jazz Panorama      Swed.  LP15
                          Oscar Disco        It.    OS 050
                          Saga               Eng.   6915
            16 Inch TX  >Standard            USA    A684
                          Standard           USA    Q105

0400   DEVIL IN THE MOON (3:15)
       (mx MS-96546-1)
            12 Inch LP    Ariston            It.    AR/LP/12023
                          Jazz Panorama      Swed.  JPLP15
                          Jazz Panorama      Swed.  LP15
                          Oscar Disco        It.    OS 050
                          Saga               Eng.   6915
            16 Inch TX  >Standard            USA    A684
                          Standard           USA    Q105
```

```
Chicago, Illinois                     December 21, 1935
       Recorded for Decca, but never issued by them in the
       USA.  Although listed in the Decca Master Book and
       on the label as a piano solo, this performance is
       actually by a small group with a vocalist.  The
       trumpeter is believed to be Guy Kelly, but the
       other personnel are unknown (other than Art Tatum, p).
       The other instruments are believed to include:
       two cl, d, b, v.
0410   BOOTS AND SADDLE (3:07)
       (mx C-90541 in the Decca Master Book; 90541-A on Odeon disc)
            10 Inch 78  >Odeon              Arg.   284465
            12 Inch LP   Jazz Archives      USA    JA-40
```

```
Los Angeles, California               February 26, 1937
       Art Tatum And His Swingsters.  Lloyd Reese,
       t; Marshall Royal, cl; Art Tatum, p; Bill
       Perkins, g; Joe Bailey, b; Oscar Bradley, d.
0420   BODY AND SOUL (3:06)
       (mx DLA724A)
            10 Inch 78    Brunswick         Eng.   02518
                          Brunswick         Ger.   A-81278
                         >Decca             USA    1197
                          Decca             Astla  Y5165
                          Odeon             Arg.   284289
            12 Inch LP    MCA               USA    MCA2-4112
                          Swingfan          Ger.   LP 1018
                          Time-Life         USA    P 15514
```

8

```
0421  BODY AND SOUL (3:07)
      (mx DLA724B)
              12 Inch LP   >MCA                  Fr.   510 123
                            MCA                  Jap.  MCA-3107

0430  WITH PLENTY OF MONEY AND YOU (2:40)
      (mx DLA725A)
              10 Inch 78    Brunswick            Eng.  02417
                           >Decca                USA   1198
                            Decca                Astla Y5168
                            Decca                Eng.  BM 02518
                            Decca                Eng.  M.39029
                            Odeon                Arg.  284255
              12 Inch LP    Swingfan             Ger.  LP 1018

0431  WITH PLENTY OF MONEY AND YOU (2:41)
      (mx DLA725B)
              12 Inch LP    MCA                  USA   MCA2-4112
                           >MCA                  Fr.   510 123
                            MCA                  Jap.  MCA-3107

0440  WHAT WILL I TELL MY HEART* (3:06)
      (mx DLA726A)
              10 Inch 78    Brunswick            Eng.  02417
                           >Decca                USA   1197
                            Decca                Eng.  M.39029
                            Decca                Astla Y5165
                            Odeon                Arg.  284289
              12 Inch LP    MCA                  USA   MCA2-4112
                            MCA                  Fr.   510 123
                            MCA                  Jap.  MCA-3107
                            Swingfan             Ger.  LP 1018
      *Art Tatum, p and cel.

0441  WHAT WILL I TELL MY HEART*
      (mx DLA726B)
                            Decca                USA   Unissued
      *Art Tatum, p and cel.

0450  I´VE GOT MY LOVE TO KEEP ME WARM (3:02)
      (mx DLA727A)
              10 Inch 78    Brunswick            Eng.  02518
                            Brunswick            Ger.  A-81278
                           >Decca                USA   1198
                            Decca                Astla Y5168
                            Decca                Eng.  BM 02518
                            Odeon                Arg.  284255
              12 Inch LP    MCA                  USA   MCA2-4112
                            MCA                  Fr.   510 123
                            MCA                  Jap.  MCA-3107
                            Swingfan             Ger.  LP 1018

0451  I´VE GOT MY LOVE TO KEEP ME WARM
      (mx DLA727B)
                            Decca                USA   Unissued

------------------------------------------------------------
New York, New York                       November 29, 1937
          Piano solos.
0460  GONE WITH THE WIND (2:48)
      (mx 62822A,2-62822A)
              10 Inch 78    Brunswick            USA   80159
                            Brunswick            Eng.  02564
                            Brunswick            Ger.  A-81407
                            Brunswick            Ger.  82455
                            Brunswick            Nor.  82455
                           >Decca                USA   1603
                            Decca                Astla Y5206
                            Decca                Eng.  BM 01232
                            Decca                Eng.  F 8069
              7 Inch 45     Brunswick            USA   9-80159
              7 Inch 45EP   Coral                Ger.  EPC 94 122
              10 Inch LP    Brunswick            USA   BL58023
                            Coral                Fr.   CVM.40006
                            Festival             Astla CFR10 648
```

9

	12 Inch LP	Ace of Hearts	Eng.	AH.109
		Brunswick	USA	BL54004
		Cathala	Fr.	BLP 100.005
		Coral	Ger.	COPS 3443
		Coral	Jap.	LPCM-2009
		MCA	USA	MCA2-4019
		MCA	Fr.	510.081
		MCA	It.	MAPD 7028
		MCA	Jap.	MCA-3074
		Swaggie	Astla	S1223
		Time-Life	USA	P 15514
		Vogue Coral	Eng.	LVA.9047
	12 Inch TX	AFRS Amer.Pop.Mus.	USA	434
	16 Inch TX	AFRS Basic Mus.Lib.	USA	P-2035

0461 GONE WITH THE WIND
(mx 62822B)

| | | Decca | USA | Unissued |

0470 STORMY WEATHER (3:07)
(mx 62823A,2-62823A)

	10 Inch 78	Brunswick	USA	80159
		Brunswick	Eng.	02564
		Brunswick	Ger.	A-81407
		Brunswick	Ger.	82455
		Brunswick	Nor.	82455
		>Decca	USA	1603
		Decca	Astla	Y5206
		Decca	Eng.	BM 01232
		Decca	Eng.	F 8069
		Odeon	Braz.	288.099
	7 Inch 45	Brunswick	USA	9-80159
	7 Inch 45EP	Coral	Ger.	EPC 94 122
		Festival	Astla	XP 45 658
	10 Inch LP	Brunswick	USA	BL58023
		Coral	Fr.	CVM.40006
	12 Inch LP	Ace of Hearts	Eng.	AH.109
		Brunswick	USA	BL54004
		Cathala	Fr.	BLP 100.005
		Coral	Ger.	COPS 3443
		Coral	Jap.	LPCM-2009
		MCA	USA	MCA2-4019
		MCA	Fr.	510.081
		MCA	It.	MAPD 7028
		MCA	Jap.	MCA-3074
		Swaggie	Astla	S1223
		Time-Life	USA	P 15514
		Vogue Coral	Eng.	LVA.9047
	12 Inch TX	AFRS Amer.Pop.Mus.	USA	149
		AFRS Amer.Pop.Mus.	USA	194
	16 Inch TX	AFRS Basic Mus.Lib.	USA	P-2035

0471 STORMY WEATHER
(mx 62823B)

| | | Decca | USA | Unissued |

0480 CHLOE (3:21)
(mx 62824A)

	10 Inch 78	Brunswick	USA	80160
		Brunswick	Eng.	02591
		Brunswick	Ger.	A-81552
		>Decca	USA	2052
		Decca	Eng.	BM 02591
		Decca	Fr.	MU-60517
	7 Inch 45	Brunswick	USA	9-80160
	10 Inch LP	Brunswick	USA	BL58023
		Coral	Fr.	CVM.40006
	12 Inch LP	MCA	USA	MCA2-4112
		MCA	Fr.	510.081
		MCA	Jap.	MCA-3074
	16 Inch TX	AFRS Basic Mus.Lib.	USA	P-2035

```
0481   CHLOE (3:02)
       (mx 62824B)
                  10 Inch 78   >Decca                 Can.   2052
                  12 Inch LP    Meritt                USA    4

0490   THE SHEIK OF ARABY (2:40)
       (mx 62825A)
                  10 Inch 78    Brunswick             USA    80160
                                Brunswick             Eng.   02591
                                Brunswick             Ger.   A-81552
                               >Decca                 USA    2052
                                Decca                 Can.   2052
                                Decca                 Eng.   BM 02591
                                Decca                 Fr.    MU-60517
                   7 Inch 45    Brunswick             USA    9-80160
                  10 Inch LP    Brunswick             USA    BL58023
                                Coral                 Fr.    CVM.40006
                  12 Inch LP    MCA                   USA    MCA2-4112
                                MCA                   Fr.    510.081
                                MCA                   Jap.   MCA-3074
                  16 Inch TX    AFRS Basic Mus.Lib.   USA    P-2035

----------------------------------------------------------------
                                              August, 1938
                  Piano solos.
0500   THE MAN I LOVE (2:45)
       (mx 025348-1)
                  12 Inch LP    Black Lion            Eng.   BLP30194
                                Caracol               Fr.    CAR.428
                                Varese Internat'l     USA    VS 81021
                  16 Inch TX    Keystone              USA    KBS402
                               >Standard              USA    Q126

0510   RUNNIN' WILD (2:25)
       (mx 025348-1)
                  12 Inch LP    Black Lion            Eng.   BLP30194
                                Caracol               Fr.    CAR.428
                                Varese Internat'l     USA    VS 81021
                  16 Inch TX    Keystone              USA    KBS402
                               >Standard              USA    Q126

0520   I CAN'T GET STARTED (3:00)
       (mx 025348-1)
                  12 Inch LP    Black Lion            Eng.   BLP30194
                                Caracol               Fr.    CAR.428
                                Varese Internat'l     USA    VS 81021
                  16 Inch TX    Keystone              USA    KBS402
                               >Standard              USA    Q126

0530   HAPPY FEET (1:45)
       (mx 025348-1)
                  12 Inch LP    Black Lion            Eng.   BLP30194
                                Caracol               Fr.    CAR.428
                                Varese Internat'l     USA    VS 81021
                  16 Inch TX    Keystone              USA    KBS402
                               >Standard              USA    Q126

0540   ROYAL GARDEN BLUES (2:25)
       (mx 025349-1)
                  12 Inch LP    Black Lion            Eng.   BLP30194
                                Caracol               Fr.    CAR.428
                                Varese Internat'l     USA    VS 81021
                  16 Inch TX    Keystone              USA    KBS452
                               >Standard              USA    Q126

0550   AIN'T MISBEHAVIN' (2:35)
       (mx 025349-1)
                  12 Inch LP    Black Lion            Eng.   BLP30194
                                Caracol               Fr.    CAR.428
                                Varese Internat'l     USA    VS 81021
                  16 Inch TX    Keystone              USA    KBS452
                               >Standard              USA    Q126
```

11

```
0560   STAR DUST (2:30)
       (mx 025349-1)
               12 Inch LP    Black Lion          Eng.   BLP30194
                             Caracol             Fr.    CAR.428
                             Varese Internat'l   USA    VS 81021
               16 Inch TX    Keystone            USA    KBS452
                            >Standard            USA    Q126

0570   IN A SENTIMENTAL MOOD (2:22)
       (mx 025349-1)
               12 Inch LP    Black Lion          Eng.   BLP30194
                             Caracol             Fr.    CAR.428
                             Varese Internat'l   USA    VS 81021
               16 Inch TX    Keystone            USA    KBS452
                            >Standard            USA    Q126

-----------------------------------------------------------
                                          August, 1938
            Piano solos.
0580   SWEET LORRAINE (2:35)
       (mx 025350-1)
               12 Inch LP    Jazz Anthology      Fr.    JA5177
                             Jazz Piano          Dan.   JP5005
                             Varese Internat'l   USA    VS 81021
               16 Inch TX    Keystone            USA    KBS472
                            >Standard            USA    Q129

0590   I'LL GET BY (2:25)
       (mx 025350-1)
               12 Inch LP    Jazz Anthology      Fr.    JA5177
                             Jazz Piano          Dan.   JP5005
                             Varese Internat'l   USA    VS 81021
               16 Inch TX    Keystone            USA    KBS472
                            >Standard            USA    Q129

0600   I'LL NEVER BE THE SAME (2:35)
       (mx 025350-1)
               12 Inch LP    Jazz Anthology      Fr.    JA5177
                             Jazz Piano          Dan.   JP5005
                             Varese Internat'l   USA    VS 81021
               16 Inch TX    Keystone            USA    KBS472
                            >Standard            USA    Q129

0610   JUDY (2:20)
       (mx 025350-1)
               12 Inch LP    Jazz Anthology      Fr.    JA5177
                             Jazz Piano          Dan.   JP5005
                             Varese Internat'l   USA    VS 81021
               16 Inch TX    Keystone            USA    KBS472
                            >Standard            USA    Q129

0620   ELEGIE (2:25)
       (mx 025351-2)
               12 Inch LP    Jazz Anthology      Fr.    JA5177
                             Jazz Piano          Dan.   JP5005
                             Varese Internat'l   USA    VS 81021
               16 Inch TX    Keystone            USA    KBS414
                            >Standard            USA    Q129

0630   BODY AND SOUL (2:30)
       (mx 025351-2)
               12 Inch LP    Jazz Anthology      Fr.    JA5177
                             Jazz Piano          Dan.   JP5005
                             Varese Internat'l   USA    VS 81021
               16 Inch TX    Keystone            USA    KBS414
                            >Standard            USA    Q129

0640   CAN'T WE BE FRIENDS (2:20)
       (mx 025351-2)
               12 Inch LP    Jazz Anthology      Fr.    JA5177
                             Jazz Piano          Dan.   JP5005
                             Varese Internat'l   USA    VS 81021
               16 Inch TX    Keystone            USA    KBS414
                            >Standard            USA    Q129
```

```
0650   MAKE BELIEVE (2:10)
       (mx 025351-2)
              12 Inch LP    Jazz Anthology       Fr.    JA5177
                            Jazz Piano           Dan.   JP5005
                            Varese Internat´l    USA    VS 81021
              16 Inch TX    Keystone             USA    KBS414
                            >Standard            USA    Q129

       ------------------------------------------------------------
                                                 August 1939
              Piano solos.
0660   GET HAPPY (1:55)
       (mx 042276-1)
              12 Inch LP    Black Lion           Eng.   BLP30194
                            Caracol              Fr.    CAR.428
              16 Inch TX    >Standard            USA    Q135

0670   BEGIN THE BEGUINE (2:45)
       (mx 042276-1)
              12 Inch LP    Black Lion           Eng.   BLP30194
                            Caracol              Fr.    CAR.428
              16 Inch TX    >Standard            USA    Q135

0680   IT HAD TO BE YOU (2:30)
       (mx 042276-1)
              12 Inch LP    Black Lion           Eng.   BLP30194
                            Caracol              Fr.    CAR.428
                            Smithsonian          USA    R 029
              16 Inch TX    >Standard            USA    Q135

0690   HUMORESQUE (2:20)
       (mx 042276-1)
              12 Inch LP    Black Lion           Eng.   BLP30194
                            Caracol              Fr.    CAR.428
              16 Inch TX    >Standard            USA    Q135

0700   HALLELUJAH (2:05)
       (mx 042277-1)
              12 Inch LP    Black Lion           Eng.   BLP30194
                            Caracol              Fr.    CAR.428
              16 Inch TX    >Standard            USA    Q135

0710   LULLABY IN RHYTHM (2:00)
       (mx 042277-1)
              12 Inch LP    Black Lion           Eng.   BLP30194
                            Caracol              Fr.    CAR.428
              16 Inch TX    >Standard            USA    Q135

0720   OH, YOU CRAZY MOON (2:25)
       (mx 042277-1)
              12 Inch LP    Black Lion           Eng.   BLP30194
                            Caracol              Fr.    CAR.428
                            Smithsonian          USA    R 029
              16 Inch TX    >Standard            USA    Q135

0730   OVER THE RAINBOW (3:50)
       (mx 042277-1)
              12 Inch LP    Black Lion           Eng.   BLP30194
                            Caracol              Fr.    CAR.428
                            Smithsonian          USA    R 029
              16 Inch TX    >Standard            USA    Q135

       ------------------------------------------------------------
Los Angeles, California                          April 12, 1939
              Piano solos.
0740   TEA FOR TWO (2:32)
       (mx DLA1759A)
              10 Inch 78    Brunswick            USA    80162
                            Brunswick            Eng.   02772
                            Brunswick            Ger.   A-82196
                            >Decca               USA    2456
                            Decca                Belg.  60.516
                            Decca                Can.   2456
                            Decca                Fr.    MU-60516
                            Odeon                Arg.   286291
```

	Odeon	Braz.	288.050
7 Inch 45	Brunswick	USA	9-80162
7 Inch 45EP	Coral	Ger.	EPC 94 122
10 Inch LP	Brunswick	USA	BL58023
	Coral	Fr.	CVM.40006
	Festival	Astla	CFR10 648
12 Inch LP	Ace of Hearts	Eng.	AH.109
	Brunswick	USA	BL54004
	Brunswick	Ger.	LPBM87507
	Cathala	Fr..	BLP 100.005
	Coral	Ger.	COPS 3443
	Coral	Jap.	LPCM-2009
	MCA	USA	MCA2-4019
	MCA	Fr.	510082
	MCA	It.	MAPD 7028
	MCA	Jap.	MCA-3074
	Swaggie	Astla	S1223
	Vogue Coral	Eng.	LVA.9047

0741 TEA FOR TWO
(mx DLA1759B)

	Decca	USA	Unissued

0750 DEEP PURPLE (3:12)
(mx DLA1760A)

10 Inch 78	>Decca	USA	2456
	Decca	Can.	2456
	Decca	Fr.	MU-60516
	Odeon	Braz.	288.050

0751 DEEP PURPLE (3:15)
(mx DLA1760B)

10 Inch 78	Brunswick	Eng.	02772
	Brunswick	Ger.	A-82196
	>Decca	USA	2456
	Decca	Belg.	60.516
	Decca	Fr.	MU-60516
	Odeon	Arg.	286310
12 Inch LP	MCA	Fr.	510082

August, 1939

Piano solos.
0760 ALL GOD´S CHILLUN GOT RHYTHM (1:55)
(mx 042377-1)

12 Inch LP	Alamac	USA	QSR 2428
	Alamac	Fr.	180.050
	Ariston	It.	AR/LP/12023
	DJM	Eng.	DJD 28002
	DJM	Eng.	DJLMD.8002
	GNP Crescendo	USA	GNP9026
	GNP Crescendo	Jap.	LAX-3089
	Jazz Panorama	Swed.	JPLP15
	Jazz Panorama	Swed.	LP15
	Jazz Series 4000FC	It.	JAZ4006
	Koala	USA	K.O. 14278
	Mercury	Jap.	BT-5049
	Oscar Disco	It.	OS 050
	Saga	Eng.	6915
	Trip	USA	JT-IX-(2)
	Trip	USA	TLX-5813
	Vogue	Fr.	DP.31B
	Vogue	Eng.	VJD 511-2
16 Inch TX	>Standard	USA	Q140
	Standard	USA	Q183

0770 SWEET EMALINA, MY GAL (2:00)
(mx 042377-1)

12 Inch LP	Alamac	USA	QSR 2428
	Alamac	Fr.	180.050
	Ariston	It.	AR/LP/12023
	DJM	Eng.	DJD 28002
	DJM	Eng.	DJLMD.8002
	Ember	Eng.	CJS848
	Jazz Panorama	Swed.	JPLP15

```
                              Jazz Panorama      Swed. LP15
                              Koala              USA   K.O. 14278
                              Mercury            Jap.  BT-5049
                              Olympic            USA   OL-7120 (E)
                              Oscar Disco        It.   OS 050
                              Phoenix 10         USA   PHX313
                              Saga               Eng.  6915
                              Trip               USA   JT-IX-(2)
                              Trip               USA   TLX-5813
                              Up Front           USA   UPF 156
                 16 Inch TX  >Standard           USA   Q140
                              Standard           USA   Q183

0780  INDIANA (2:05)
      (mx 042377-1)
                 12 Inch LP   Alamac             USA   QSR 2428
                              Alamac             Fr.   180.050
                              Ariston            It.   AR/LP/12023
                              DJM                Eng.  DJD 28002
                              DJM                Eng.  DJLMD.8002
                              Ember              Eng.  CJS848
                              Jazz Panorama      Swed. JPLP15
                              Jazz Panorama      Swed. LP15
                              Koala              USA   K.O. 14278
                              Mercury            Jap.  BT-5049
                              Olympic            USA   OL-7120 (E)
                              Oscar Disco        It.   OS 050
                              Saga               Eng.  6915
                              Trip               USA   JT-IX-(2)
                              Trip               USA   TLX-5813
                 16 Inch TX  >Standard           USA   Q140
                              Standard           USA   Q183

0790  DAY IN - DAY OUT (3:30)
      (mx 042377-1)
                 12 Inch LP   Discophon          Span. (S) 4174
                              DJM                Eng.  DJD 28002
                              DJM                Eng.  DJLMD.8002
                              Ember              Eng.  CJS848
                              Jazz Anthology     Fr.   JA5177
                              Koala              USA   K.O. 14278
                              Mercury            Jap.  BT-5049
                              Olympic            USA   OL-7120 (E)
                              Polydor            Eng.  623274
                              Smithsonian        USA   R 029
                              Sonet              Dan.  SLPS1937
                              Storyville         Dan.  SLP 829
                              Storyville         Jap.  ULS-1550
                              Trip               USA   JT-IX-(2)
                              Trip               USA   TLX-5813
                 16 Inch TX  >Standard           USA   Q140
                              Standard           USA   Q183

0800  FINE AND DANDY (1:50)
      (mx 042378-1)
                 12 Inch LP   Alamac             USA   QSR 2428
                              Alamac             Fr.   180.050
                              Discophon          Span. (S) 4174
                              DJM                Eng.  DJD 28002
                              DJM                Eng.  DJLMD.8002
                              Ember              Eng.  CJS848
                              GNP Crescendo      USA   GNP9026
                              GNP Crescendo      Jap.  LAX-3089
                              Jazz Anthology     Fr.   JA5177
                              Jazz Series 4000FC It.   JAZ4006
                              Koala              USA   K.O. 14278
                              Mercury            Jap.  BT-5049
                              Olympic            USA   OL-7120 (E)
                              Phoenix 10         USA   PHX313
                              Pick               Braz. 308.0013
                              Polydor            Eng.  623274
                              Sonet              Dan.  SLPS1937
                              Storyville         Dan.  SLP 829
                              Storyville         Jap.  ULS-1550
                              Trip               USA   JT-IX-(2)

                              15
```

```
                    Trip                    USA     TLX-5813
                    Up Front                USA     UPF 156
                    Vogue                   Belg.   VK 30
                    Vogue                   Eng.    VJD 511-2
                    Vogue                   Fr.     DP.31B
        16 Inch TX  >Standard               USA     Q140
                    Standard                USA     Q183

0810  I´VE GOT THE WORLD ON A STRING (2:25)
      (mx 042378-1)
        12 Inch LP  Alamac                  USA     QSR 2428
                    Alamac                  Fr.     180.050
                    Discophon               Span.   (S) 4174
                    DJM                     Eng.    DJD 28002
                    DJM                     Eng.    DJLMD.8002
                    GNP Crescendo           USA     GNP9026
                    GNP Crescendo           Jap.    LAX-3089
                    Jazz Anthology          Fr.     JA5177
                    Jazz Series 4000FC      It.     JAZ4006
                    Mercury                 Jap.    BT-5049
                    Polydor                 Eng.    623274
                    Sonet                   Dan.    SLPS1937
                    Storyville              Dan.    SLP 829
                    Storyville              Jap.    ULS-1550
                    Trip                    USA     JT-IX-(2)
                    Trip                    USA     TLX-5813
                    Vogue                   Belg.   VK 30
                    Vogue                   Eng.    VJD 511-2
                    Vogue                   Fr.     DP.31B
        16 Inch TX  >Standard               USA     Q140
                    Standard                USA     Q183

0820  I GOTTA RIGHT TO SING THE BLUES (2:10)
      (mx 042378-1)
        12 Inch LP  Alamac                  USA     QSR 2428
                    Alamac                  Fr.     180.050
                    Discophon               Span.   (S) 4174
                    DJM                     Eng.    DJD 28002
                    DJM                     Eng.    DJLMD.8002
                    GNP Crescendo           USA     GNP9026
                    GNP Crescendo           Jap.    LAX-3089
                    Jazz Anthology          Fr.     JA5177
                    Jazz Series 4000FC      It.     JAZ4006
                    Mercury                 Jap.    BT-5049
                    Phoenix 10              USA     PHX313
                    Polydor                 Eng.    623274
                    Sonet                   Dan.    SLPS1937
                    Storyville              Dan.    SLP 829
                    Storyville              Jap.    ULS-1550
                    Trip                    USA     JT-IX-(2)
                    Trip                    USA     TLX-5813
                    Vogue                   Eng.    VJD 511-2
                    Vogue                   Fr.     DP.31B
        16 Inch TX  >Standard               USA     Q140
                    Standard                USA     Q183

0830  I´M COMING VIRGINIA (2:35)
      (mx 042378-1)
        12 Inch LP  Alamac                  USA     QSR 2428
                    Alamac                  Fr.     180.050
                    Discophon               Span.   (S) 4174
                    DJM                     Eng.    DJD 28002
                    DJM                     Eng.    DJLMD.8002
                    GNP Crescendo           USA     GNP9026
                    GNP Crescendo           Jap.    LAX-3089
                    Jazz Anthology          Fr.     JA5177
                    Jazz Series 4000FC      It.     JAZ4006
                    Mercury                 Jap.    BT-5049
                    Polydor                 Eng.    623274
                    Sonet                   Dan.    SLPS1937
                    Storyville              Dan.    SLP 829
                    Storyville              Jap.    ULS-1550
                    Trip                    USA     JT-IX-(2)
                    Trip                    USA     TLX-5813
                    Vogue                   Eng.    VJD 511-2
```

```
                         Vogue                    Fr.   DP.31B
         16 Inch TX   >Standard                   USA   Q140
                         Standard                 USA   Q183

--------------------------------------------------------------
Los Angeles, California                     February 22, 1940
       Piano solos.
 0840  ELEGIE (3:10)
       (mx DLA1936A,DLA1936-AT1)
         10 Inch 78   Brunswick              Eng.   03162
                        Brunswick            India  0.3162
                      >Decca                 USA    18049
                        Decca                USA    25199
          7 Inch 45   Decca                  USA    9-25199
          7 Inch 45EP Decca                  USA    91573
         10 Inch LP   Decca                  USA    DL5086
                        Festival             Astla  CFR10 506
         12 Inch LP   Ace of Hearts          Eng.   AH133
                        Brunswick            Eng.   LAT.8358
                        Brunswick            Ger.   LPBM87507
                        Coral                Eng.   CP62
                        Coral                Ger.   COP 2686
                        Decca                USA    DL8715
                        Longines             USA    LWS262
                        MCA                  USA    MCA2-4019
                        MCA                  Fr.    510082
                        MCA                  Fr.    MAP 2686
                        MCA                  It.    MAPD 7028
                        MCA                  Jap.   MCA-3074
                        Swaggie              Astla  S1223
                        Time-Life            USA    P 15514

 0841  ELEGIE
       (mx DLA1936B)
                        Decca                USA    Unissued

 0850  HUMORESQUE (3:00)
       (mx DLA1937A,DLA1937-AT1)
         10 Inch 78   Brunswick              Eng.   03162
                        Brunswick            Ger.   A-82493
                        Brunswick            India  0.3162
                      >Decca                 USA    18049
                        Decca                USA    25199
          7 Inch 45   Decca                  USA    9-25199
          7 Inch 45EP Decca                  USA    91573
         10 Inch LP   Decca                  USA    DL5086
                        Festival             Astla  CFR10 506
         12 Inch LP   Ace of Hearts          Eng.   AH133
                        Brunswick            Eng.   LAT.8358
                        Brunswick            Ger.   LPBM87507
                        Coral                Eng.   CP62
                        Coral                Ger.   COP 2686
                        Decca                USA    DL8715
                        MCA                  USA    MCA2-4019
                        MCA                  Fr.    510082
                        MCA                  Fr.    MAP 2686
                        MCA                  It.    MAPD 7028
                        MCA                  Jap.   MCA-3074
                        Swaggie              Astla  S1223

 0860  SWEET LORRAINE (2:57)
       (mx DLA1938A)
         10 Inch 78   Brunswick              Eng.   04318
                      >Decca                 USA    18050
                        Decca                USA    25200
                        Decca                Astla  Y6088
                        Decca                Belg.  60.060
          7 Inch 45   Decca                  USA    9-25200
          7 Inch 45EP Brunswick              Ger.   10116EPB
                        Decca                USA    91573
         10 Inch LP   Decca                  USA    DL5086
                        Festival             Astla  CFR10 506
         12 Inch LP   Ace of Hearts          Eng.   AH133
                        Brunswick            Eng.   LAT.8358
                        Brunswick            Ger.   LPBM87507
```

```
                      Coral                 Eng.   CP62
                      Coral                 Ger.   COP 2686
                      Decca                 USA    DL8715
                      MCA                   USA    MCA2-4019
                      MCA                   Fr.    510082
                      MCA                   Fr.    MAP 2686
                      MCA                   It.    MAPD 7028
                      MCA                   Jap.   MCA-3074
                      Swaggie               Astla  S1223
                      Time-Life             USA    P 15514
          16 Inch TX  AFRS Downbeat         USA    434

0870  GET HAPPY (2:40)
      (mx DLA1939A)
          10 Inch 78  >Decca                USA    18050
                      Decca                 USA    25200
                      Decca                 Astla  Y6088
                      Decca                 Belg.  60.060
           7 Inch 45  Decca                 USA    9-25200
           7 Inch 45EP Brunswick            Ger.   10116EPB
                      Decca                 USA    91573
          10 Inch LP  Decca                 USA    DL5086
                      Festival              Astla  CFR10 506
          12 Inch LP  Ace of Hearts         Eng.   AH133
                      Brunswick             Eng.   LAT.8358
                      Brunswick             Ger.   LPBM87507
                      Coral                 Eng.   CP62
                      Coral                 Ger.   COP 2686
                      Decca                 USA    DL8715
                      MCA                   USA    MCA2-4019
                      MCA                   Fr.    510082
                      MCA                   Fr.    MAP 2686
                      MCA                   It.    MAPD 7028
                      MCA                   Jap.   MCA-3074
                      Swaggie               Astla  S1223
                      Time-Life             USA    P 15514
          16 Inch TX  AFRS Downbeat         USA    322
                      AFRS Downbeat         USA    415
                      AFRS Swing Years      USA    135

0880  LULLABY OF THE LEAVES (3:01)
      (mx DLA1940A)
          10 Inch 78  Brunswick             Eng.   04318
                      >Decca                USA    18051
                      Decca                 USA    25201
                      Decca                 Astla  Y5562
                      Decca                 Can.   18051
           7 Inch 45  Decca                 USA    9-25201
           7 Inch 45EP Brunswick            Ger.   10116EPB
                      Decca                 USA    91574
          10 Inch LP  Decca                 USA    DL5086
                      Festival              Astla  CFR10 506
          12 Inch LP  Ace of Hearts         Eng.   AH133
                      Brunswick             Eng.   LAT.8358
                      Brunswick             Ger.   LPBM87507
                      Cathala               Fr.    BLP 100.005
                      Coral                 Eng.   CP62
                      Coral                 Ger.   COP 2686
                      Decca                 USA    DL8715
                      MCA                   USA    MCA2-4019
                      MCA                   Fr.    510082
                      MCA                   Fr.    MAP 2686
                      MCA                   It.    MAPD 7028
                      MCA                   Jap.   MCA-3074
                      Swaggie               Astla  S1223
          16 Inch TX  AFRS Today's the Day  USA    36

0890  TIGER RAG (2:09)
      (mx DLA1941A)
          10 Inch 78  Brunswick             Eng.   04319
                      Brunswick             Ger.   A-82493
                      >Decca                USA    18051
                      Decca                 USA    25201
                      Decca                 Astla  Y5562
                      Decca                 Can.   18051
```

```
                          Swaggie              Astla S1223

0940  COCKTAILS FOR TWO (2:48)
      (mx DLA1946A)
            10 Inch 78     Brunswick          Nor.  233649
                          >Decca              USA   156
                           Decca              USA   25202
             7 Inch 45     Decca              USA   9-25202
             7 Inch 45EP   Decca              USA   91574
            10 Inch LP     Decca              USA   DL5086
                           Festival           Astla CFR10 506
            12 Inch LP     Ace of Hearts      Eng.  AH133
                           Brunswick          Eng.  LAT.8358
                           Brunswick          Ger.  LPBM87507
                           Cathala            Fr.   BLP 100.005
                           Coral              Eng.  CP62
                           Coral              Ger.  COP 2686
                           Coral              Ger.  COPS 3443
                           Decca              USA   DL8715
                           MCA                Fr.   510082
                           MCA                Fr.   MAP 2686
                           MCA                Jap.  MCA-3074
                           Swaggie            Astla S1223

---------------------------------------------------------------
Los Angeles, California                      July 26, 1940
          Piano solos.
0950  ST. LOUIS BLUES (2:26)
      (mx DLA2068A)
             8 Inch 78     Esquire Jazz Book, USA   Unnumbered
                           1944(cardboard demo
                           with brief excerpt)
            10 Inch 78     Brunswick          USA   80161
                           Brunswick          Eng.  03121
                          >Decca              USA   8550
                           Decca              Eng.  BM 03121
                           Odeon              Arg.  286291
                           Odeon              Braz. 288.099
             7 Inch 45     Brunswick          USA   9-80161
             7 Inch 45EP   Coral              Ger.  EPC 94 020
            10 Inch LP     Brunswick          USA   BL58023
                           Coral              Fr.   CVM.40006
                           Festival           Astla CFR10 648
            12 Inch LP     Ace of Hearts      Eng.  AH.109
                           Brunswick          USA   BL54004
                           Brunswick          Ger.  LPBM87507
                           Cathala            Fr.   BLP 100.005
                           Coral              Eng.  CRL57223
                           Coral              Ger.  COPS 3443
                           Coral              Jap.  LPCM-2009
                           MCA                USA   MCA2-4019
                           MCA                Fr.   510082
                           MCA                It.   MAPD 7028
                           MCA                Jap.  MCA-3075
                           Swaggie            Astla S1223
                           Vogue Coral        Eng.  LVA.9047
            16 Inch TX     AFRS Basic Mus.Lib. USA  P-2035

0951  ST. LOUIS BLUES
      (mx DLA2068B)
                           Decca              USA   Unissued

0960  BEGIN THE BEGUINE (2:37)
      (mx DLA2069A)
            10 Inch 78     Brunswick          USA   80161
                           Brunswick          Eng.  03121
                          >Decca              USA   8502
                           Decca              Eng.  BM 03121
             7 Inch 45     Brunswick          USA   9-80161
             7 Inch 45EP   Coral              Ger.  EPC 94 020
            10 Inch LP     Brunswick          USA   BL58023
                           Coral              Fr.   CVM.40006
                           Festival           Astla CFR10 648
            12 Inch LP     Ace of Hearts      Eng.  AH.109
                           Brunswick          USA   BL54004
```

```
                      Brunswick              Ger.  LPBM87507
                      Coral                  Ger.  COPS 3443
                      MCA                    USA   MCA2-4019
                      MCA                    Fr.   510082
                      MCA                    It.   MAPD 7028
                      MCA                    Jap.  MCA-3075
                      Swaggie                Astla S1223
                      Vogue Coral            Eng.  LVA.9047
          16 Inch TX  AFRS Basic Mus.Lib.    USA   P-2035
                      AFRS Purple Heart      USA   205

0961  BEGIN THE BEGUINE
      (mx DLA2069B)
                      Decca                  USA   Unissued

0970  ROSETTA (2:45)
      (mx DLA2070A)
          10 Inch 78  Brunswick              USA   80162
                      Brunswick              Eng.  04319
                     >Decca                  USA   8502
                      Decca                  Fr.   MU-60515
                      Odeon                  Arg.  286320
           7 Inch 45  Brunswick              USA   9-80162
           7 Inch 45EP Coral                 Ger.  EPC 94 122
                      Festival               Astla XP 45 658
          10 Inch LP  Brunswick              USA   BL58023
                      Coral                  Fr.   CVM.40006
          12 Inch LP  Ace of Hearts          Eng.  AH.109
                      Brunswick              USA   BL54004
                      Brunswick              Ger.  LPBM87507
                      Coral                  Ger.  COPS 3443
                      Coral                  Jap.  LPCM-2009
                      MCA                    USA   MCA2-4019
                      MCA                    Fr.   510082
                      MCA                    It.   MAPD 7028
                      MCA                    Jap.  MCA-3075
                      Time-Life              USA   P 15514
                      Swaggie                Astla S1223
                      Vogue Coral            Eng.  LVA.9047

0971  ROSETTA
      (mx DLA2070B)
                      Decca                  USA   Unissued

0980  INDIANA (2:45)
      (mx DLA2071A)
          10 Inch 78 >Decca                  USA   8550
                      Decca                  Fr.   MU-60524
                      Odeon                  Arg.  286341
          12 Inch LP  Ace of Hearts          Eng.  AH133
                      Brunswick              Eng.  LAT.8358
                      Brunswick              Ger.  LPBM87507
                      Cathala                Fr.   BLP 100.005
                      Coral                  Eng.  CP62
                      Coral                  Ger.  COP 2686
                      Decca                  USA   DL8715
                      MCA                    USA   MCA2-4019
                      MCA                    Fr.   510082
                      MCA                    Fr.   MAP 2686
                      MCA                    It.   MAPD 7028
                      MCA                    Jap.  MCA-3075
                      Swaggie                Astla S1223

0981  INDIANA
      (mx DLA2071B)
                      Decca                  USA   Unissued

------------------------------------------------------------
New York, New York                        November 11, 1940
          Recorded by Jerry Newman in his apartment.
          Murray McEachern, tb; Art Tatum, p.
1000  BEAUTIFUL LOVE[1] (3:41)
```

```
          12 Inch LP    Carrere           Fr.   67.406
                        Jazz Anthology    Fr.   JA5111
                        Jazz Society      Fr.   67.406
                       >Onyx              USA   ORI 205
                        Onyx              Jap.  MP2349
                        Polydor           Eng.  2344 043
                        Polydor           Ger.  2310 325
          [1]This title was released with only the piano solo excerpt.
          All issues listed play (1:43).

1010  LAUGHING AT LIFE[2] (3:03)

          12 Inch LP    Carrere           Fr.   67.406
                        Jazz Anthology    Fr.   JA5111
                        Jazz Society      Fr.   67.406
                       >Onyx              USA   ORI 205
                        Onyx              Jap.  MP2349
                        Polydor           Eng.  2344 043
                        Polydor           Ger.  2310 325
          [2]Murray McEachern, tb and as.  This title was
          released with only the piano solo excerpt.
          All issues listed play (1:00).

1020  ALL THE THINGS YOU ARE[3] (3:40)

          12 Inch LP    Intercord Xanadu  Ger.  INT.197.105
                       >Xanadu            USA   112
                        Xanadu            Fr.   VG405-JX.6610
          [3]Murray McEachern, as, instead of tb.

1030  OH! LADY BE GOOD[4] (3:47)

                                                      Unissued
          [4]Also includes Unknown, t; Herbie Fields, ts; Unknown, b.

1040  BODY AND SOUL[5] (7:49+)

                                                      Unissued
          [5]Also includes Herbie Fields, as; Unknown, b.
          This recording was interrupted to change acetates.

-----------------------------------------------------------
New York, New York                             January 21, 1941
          Art Tatum and His Band. Joe Thomas, t;
          Edmond Hall, cl; Art Tatum, p; John Collins,
          g; Billy Taylor, b; Eddie Dougherty, d.
1050  WEE BABY BLUES* (2:50)
      (mx 68605A, 68605AA, 68605-D)
          10 Inch 78   >Decca             USA   8526
                        Decca             USA   48062
                        Decca             Astla Y5892
                        Decca             Eng.  F 8059
                        Decca             Jap.  JDL 6025
                        Odeon             Arg.  284832
           7 Inch 45EP  Vogue Coral       Fr.   ECV18032
          10 Inch LP    Brunswick         USA   BL58038
          12 Inch LP    Brunswick         Eng.  LAT.8168
                        Brunswick         Ger.  LPBM87015
                        Decca             USA   DL8385
                        Decca             USA   DL8400
                        Decca             USA   DL78385
                        Decca             USA   DXF140
                        MCA               USA   MCA2-4019
                        MCA               USA   MCA2-4062
                        MCA               Fr.   510 105
                        MCA               It.   MAPD 7028
                        MCA               Jap.  JDL-6025
                        MCA               Jap.  MCA-3107
                        MCA               Jap.  MCA-3524
                        ORL               It.   8166
                        Time-Life         USA   P 15514
          12 Inch TX    AFRS Amer.Pop.Mus. USA  887
          *Also includes Joe Turner, v.
```

22

1060 STOMPIN´ AT THE SAVOY (3:12)
      (mx 68606A, 68606AA)
                10 Inch 78   >Decca   USA   8536
                 7 Inch 45EP Vogue Coral   Fr.   ECV18032
                10 Inch LP   Brunswick   USA   BL58038
                12 Inch LP   Brunswick   Ger.   LPBM87527
                             MCA   USA   MCA2-4019
                             MCA   Fr.   510 105
                             MCA   It.   MAPD 7028
                             MCA   Jap.   MCA-3107
                             Time-Life   USA   P 15514

1070 LAST GOODBYE BLUES* (3:10)
      (mx 68607A, 68607AA)
                10 Inch 78   >Decca   USA   8536
                             Odeon   Arg.   284832
                 7 Inch 45EP Vogue Coral   Fr.   ECV18032
                10 Inch LP   Brunswick   USA   BL58038
                12 Inch LP   Albatros   It.   VPA8474
                             Brunswick   Ger.   LPBM87019
                             MCA   USA   MCA2-4019
                             MCA   USA   MCA-1325
                             MCA   Fr.   510.080
                             MCA   Fr.   510 105
                             MCA   It.   MAPD 7028
                             MCA   Jap.   MCA-3107
                             MCA   Jap.   MCA-3519
                             Swingfan   Ger.   LP 1018
                             Time-Life   USA   P 15514
      *Also includes Joe Turner, v.

1080 BATTERY BOUNCE (2:28)
      (mx 68608A, 68608AA, 68608-D, XYZ68608-Tl)
                10 Inch 78   Brunswick   Eng.   03430
                             Brunswick   India 0.3430
                            >Decca   USA   8526
                             Decca   Astla Y5892
                             Decca   Eng.   F 8059
                 7 Inch 45EP Vogue Coral   Fr.   ECV18032
                10 Inch LP   Brunswick   USA   BL58038
                12 Inch LP   Brunswick   Ger.   LPBM87527
                             MCA   USA   MCA2-4019
                             MCA   Fr.   510 105
                             MCA   It.   MAPD 7028
                             MCA   Jap.   MCA-3107
                             MCA   Jap.   MCA-3004
                             Time-Life   USA   P 15514

New York, New York   April 6, 1941
          Radio broadcast, "What´s New, with
          Benny Goodman," a P. Lorillard
          program on NBC radio. Piano solo.
1090 GEORGIA ON MY MIND* (2:15)

                12 Inch LP   Carrere   Fr.   67.406
                             Jazz Anthology   Fr.   JA5111
                             Jazz Society   Fr.   67.406
                            >Onyx   USA   ORI 205
                             Onyx   Jap.   MP2349
                             Polydor   Eng.   2344 043
                             Polydor   Ger.   2310 325
      *All issues show incorrect date and source for this performance.

New York, New York   May 7, 1941
          Private live recording by Jerry Newman at
          Reuben´s, 242 West 130th St., NYC. Art
          Tatum, p.
1100 SWEET LORRAINE (3:01)

                12 Inch LP   Carrere   Fr.   67.406
                             Jazz Anthology   Fr.   JA5111
                             Jazz Society   Fr.   67.406
                            >Onyx   USA   ORI 205

23

```
                              Onyx          Jap.  MP2349
                              Polydor       Eng.  2344 043
                              Polydor       Ger.  2310 325

1110   FINE AND DANDY*  (4:03)

       12 Inch LP   Carrere          Fr.   67.406
                    Jazz Anthology   Fr.   JA5111
                    Jazz Society     Fr.   67.406
                   >Onyx             USA   ORI 205
                    Onyx             Jap.  MP2349
                    Polydor          Eng.  2344 043
                    Polydor          Ger.  2310 325
         *Also includes Reuben Harris, wh.

1120   BEGIN THE BEGUINE (3:52)

       12 Inch LP   Carrere          Fr.   67.406
                    Jazz Anthology   Fr.   JA5111
                    Jazz Society     Fr.   67.406
                   >Onyx             USA   ORI 205
                    Onyx             Jap.  MP2349
                    Polydor          Eng.  2344 043
                    Polydor          Ger.  2310 325
```

```
New York, New York                        June 13, 1941
        Art Tatum And His Band.  Joe Thomas, t;
        Art Tatum, p; Oscar Moore, g; Billy Taylor,
        b; Yank Porter, d; Joe Turner, v.
1130  LUCILLE (3:03)
      (mx 69356A, 69356AA)
            10 Inch 78  >Decca              USA   8577

1131  LUCILLE (3:25)
      (mx 69356B, 69356BB, XYZ69356, XYZ69356-Tl)
            10 Inch 78   Brunswick         Eng.   03430
                         Brunswick         India  0.3430
                         Brunswick         Swiss  88066
                        >Decca             USA    8577
            12 Inch LP   MCA               USA    MCA2-4019
                         MCA               Fr.    510 105
                         MCA               It.    MAPD 7028
                         MCA               Jap.   MCA-3107

1140  ROCK ME MAMA (2:57)
      (mx 69357A, 69357AA)
            10 Inch 78  >Decca             USA    8577
            12 Inch LP   MCA               USA    MCA2-4019
                         MCA               USA    MCA-1325
                         MCA               Fr.    510.080
                         MCA               Fr.    510 105
                         MCA               It.    MAPD 7028
                         MCA               Jap.   MCA-3107
                         MCA               Jap.   MCA-3524

1150  CORRINE, CORRINA (2:28)
      (mx 69358A, 69358AA)
            10 Inch 78  >Decca             USA    8563
                         Decca             USA    29924
                         Decca             USA    48062
            12 Inch LP   MCA               USA    MCA2-4019
                         MCA               Fr.    510 105
                         MCA               It.    MAPD 7028
                         MCA               Jap.   MCA-3107
                         MCA               Jap.   MCA-3524
                         MCA Coral         Ger.   82040-4
                         Time-Life         USA    P 15514

1160  LONESOME GRAVEYARD BLUES (3:05)
      (mx 69359A, 69359AA, XYZ69359-Tl)
            10 Inch 78   Brunswick         Eng.   03462
                         Brunswick         India  0.3642
                         Brunswick         Swiss  88066
                        >Decca             USA    8563
```

24

```
                          Decca               Eng.   BM 03462
            12 Inch LP    MCA                 USA    MCA2-4019
                          MCA                 Fr.    510 105
                          MCA                 It.    MAPD 7028
                          MCA                 Jap.   MCA-3107

1161  LONESOME GRAVEYARD BLUES (3:09)
      (mx 69359B)
            10 Inch 78   >Decca              USA    8563
```

```
New York, New York                          July 26, 1941
            Private live recording by Jerry Newman at
            Gee-Haw Stables, W. 132d St., NYC.  Art Tatum, p.
1170  MIGHTY LAK A ROSE (3:36)

            12 Inch LP    Carrere             Fr.    67.406
                          Jazz Anthology      Fr.    JA5111
                          Jazz Society        Fr.    67.406
                         >Onyx                USA    ORI 205
                          Onyx                Jap.   MP2349
                          Polydor             Eng.   2344 043
                          Polydor             Ger.   2310 325

1180  KNOCKIN´ MYSELF OUT* (4:03)

            12 Inch LP    Carrere             Fr.    67.406
                          Jazz Society        Fr.    67.406
                         >Onyx                USA    ORI 205
                          Onyx                Jap.   MP2349
                          Polydor             Eng.   2344 043
                          Polydor             Ger.   2310 325
        *Art Tatum, p and v; Chocolate Williams, b and v.
```

```
New York, New York                          July 26 or 27, 1941
            Private live recording by Jerry Newman at
            Gee-Haw Stables, W. 132d St., NYC.  Art Tatum, p.
1190  TOLEDO BLUES[1]  (4:08)

            12 Inch LP    Carrere             Fr.    67.406
                          Jazz Society        Fr.    67.406
                         >Onyx                USA    ORI 205
                          Onyx                Jap.   MP2349
                          Polydor             Eng.   2344 043
                          Polydor             Ger.   2310 325
                          Time-Life           USA    P 15514
        [1]Art Tatum, p and v; Chocolate Williams, b.  All issues
        listed are abridged versions, playing (3:30).

1200  BODY AND SOUL (3:32)

            12 Inch LP    Carrere             Fr.    67.406
                          Jazz Anthology      Fr.    JA5111
                          Jazz Society        Fr.    67.406
                         >Onyx                USA    ORI 205
                          Onyx                Jap.   MP2349
                          Polydor             Eng.   2344 043
                          Polydor             Ger.   2310 325

1210  STAR DUST[2]  (3:46)

                                                     Unissued
        [2]Also includes Chocolate Williams, b; Ann Robinson, v.

1220  EMBRACEABLE YOU[3]  (3:51)

                                                     Unissued
        [3]Also includes Chocolate Williams, b; Ethel White, v.

1230  I SURRENDER DEAR[4]  (4:27)

                                                     Unissued
        [4]Also includes Chocolate Williams, b; Charlie Shavers, v.
```

1240 THERE'LL BE SOME CHANGES MADE[5] (3:29)

	12 Inch LP	Carrere	Fr.	67.406
		Jazz Anthology	Fr.	JA5111
		Jazz Society	Fr.	67.406
		>Onyx	USA	ORI 205
		Onyx	Jap.	MP2349
		Polydor	Eng.	2344 043
		Polydor	Ger.	2310 325

[5]Also includes Chocolate Williams, b; Ollie Potter, v.

New York, New York   September 16, 1941
        Private live recording by Jerry Newman at
        Clark Monroe's Uptown House, 198 W. 134th St,
        NYC. Frank Newton, t; Art Tatum, p; Ebenezer
        Paul, b.
1250 OH! LADY BE GOOD (4:30)

	12 Inch LP	Carrere	Fr.	67.406
		Jazz Anthology	Fr.	JA5111
		Jazz Society	Fr.	67.406
		>Onyx	USA	ORI 205
		Onyx	Jap.	MP2349
		Polydor	Eng.	2344 043
		Polydor	Ger.	2310 325
		Time-Life	USA	P 15515

1260 SWEET GEORGIA BROWN (7:19)

	12 Inch LP	Carrere	Fr.	67.406
		Jazz Anthology	Fr.	JA5111
		Jazz Society	Fr.	67.406
		>Onyx	USA	ORI 205
		Onyx	Jap.	MP2349
		Polydor	Eng.	2344 043
		Polydor	Ger.	2310 325
		Time-Life	USA	P 15515

Los Angeles, California   c. 1943
        The Art Tatum Trio. Art Tatum, p; Tiny
        Grimes, g; Slam Stewart, b.
1270 MELODY IN F (5:08)

	16 Inch TX	>AFRS Jubilee	USA	11

1280 (Title unknown)

	16 Inch TX	>AFRS Jubilee	USA	17

1290 (Title Unknown)

	16 Inch TX	>AFRS Jubilee	USA	31

1300 AFTER YOU'VE GONE

	16 Inch TX	>AFRS Jubilee	USA	32

1310 SWEET LORRAINE

	16 Inch TX	>AFRS Jubilee	USA	32

New York, New York   December 4, 1943
        Leonard Feather's All Stars. Cootie Williams, t;
        Coleman Hawkins, ts; Edmond Hall, cl; Art Tatum, p;
        Al Casey, g; Oscar Pettiford, b; Sid Catlett, d.
        Note: According to Milt Gabler, who produced
              them, the original 78 rpm issues for masters
              A-4692 and A-4694 did not show "-1" suffixes
              because they were the original choices. At
              that time the other takes were not produced
              and were considered immaterial.
1320 ESQUIRE BOUNCE (3:12)

```
            (mx A4691-1)
                10 Inch 78   >Commodore          USA   547
                              Commodore          USA   7540
                 7 Inch 45    Commodore          USA   45-7540
                 7 Inch 45EP  Sonet              Dan.  SXP 2005
                10 Inch LP    Commodore          USA   FL20 025
                12 Inch LP    Atlantic           USA   SD2-306
                              Commodore          USA   XFL14936
                              Commodore          Jap.  GXC-3146
                              Fontana            Eng.  TL5273
                              Jazztone           USA   J-1221
                              London             Eng.  HMC5006
                              London             Fr.   180006
                              London             Ger.  6.24056
                              London             Jap.  SLC 450
                              Mainstream         USA   56017
                              Mainstream         USA   S/6017
                              Mainstream         USA   56037
                              Mainstream         USA   S/6037
                              Mainstream         Jap.  SL 1210
                              Sonet              Dan.  SLP1001
                              Time-Life          USA   P 15515
                              Tulip              Can.  105
                              Vogue              Fr.   INT40020
                              Vogue              Fr.   INT40025

1321  ESQUIRE BOUNCE (3:10)
      (mx A4691-2)
                12 Inch LP   >Atlantic           USA   SD2-306
                              Commodore          USA   XFL14936
                              London             Ger.  6.24056

1330  MOP-MOP (Boff-Boff) (3:00)
      (mx A4692-1)
                12 Inch LP   >Commodore          USA   XFL14936
                              London             Ger.  6.24056

1331  MOP-MOP (Boff-Boff) (3:08)
      (mx A4692-2)
                10 Inch 78   >Commodore          USA   548
                              Commodore          USA   7541
                 7 Inch 45    Commodore          USA   45-7541
                 7 Inch 45EP  Sonet              Dan.  SXP 2005
                10 Inch LP    Commodore          USA   FL20 025
                12 Inch LP    Atlantic           USA   SD2-306
                              Commodore          USA   XFL14936
                              Commodore          Jap.  GXC-3146
                              Fontana            Eng.  TL5273
                              Jazztone           USA   J-1221
                              London             Eng.  HMC5006
                              London             Fr.   180006
                              London             Ger.  6.24056
                              London             Jap.  SLC 450
                              Mainstream         USA   56008
                              Mainstream         USA   S/6008
                              Mainstream         USA   56037
                              Mainstream         USA   S/6037
                              Mainstream         Jap.  PS-1240
                              Mainstream         Jap.  SL 1210
                              Sonet              Dan.  SLP1001
                              Vogue              Fr.   INT40015
                              Vogue              Fr.   INT40020

1340  MY IDEAL* (3:07)
      (mx A4693-1)
                10 Inch 78   >Commodore          USA   548
                              Commodore          USA   7541
                 7 Inch 45    Commodore          USA   45-7541
                 7 Inch 45EP  Sonet              Dan.  SXP 2005
                10 Inch LP    Commodore          USA   FL20 025
                12 Inch LP    Atlantic           USA   SD2-306
                              Commodore          USA   XFL14936
                              Commodore          Jap.  GXC-3146
                              Fontana            Eng.  TL5273
                              London             Eng.  HMC5006
```

```
                     London              Fr.    180006
                     London              Ger.   6.24056
                     London              Jap.   SLC 450
                     Mainstream          USA    56037
                     Mainstream          USA    S/6037
                     Mainstream          USA    56002
                     Mainstream          USA    S/6002
                     Mainstream          Jap.   PS-1291
                     Mainstream          Jap.   SL 1210
                     Sonet               Dan.   SLP1001
                     Time-Life           USA    P 15515
                     Vogue               Fr.    INT40014
                     Vogue               Fr.    INT40020
        *The original issue was labelled, "Coleman Hawkins with
        Leonard Feather's All Stars."

1341  MY IDEAL* (3:07)
      (mx A4693-2)
             12 Inch LP  >Atlantic       USA    SD2-306
                          Commodore      USA    XFL14936
                          Commodore      Jap.   GXC-3147
                          London         Ger.   6.24056
                          London         Jap.   SLC 512
        *The original issue was labelled, "Coleman Hawkins and
        Leonard Feather's All Stars."

1350  ESQUIRE BLUES (3:15)
      (mx A4694-1)
             12 Inch LP  >Commodore      USA    XFL14936
                          London         Ger.   6.24056
                          London         Jap.   SLC 512

1351  ESQUIRE BLUES (3:16)
      (mx A4694-2)
             10 Inch 78   >Commodore     USA    547
                           Commodore     USA    7540
              7 Inch 45    Commodore     USA    45-7540
              7 Inch 45EP  Sonet         Dan.   SXP 2005
             10 Inch LP    Commodore     USA    FL20 025
             12 Inch LP    Atlantic      USA    SD2-306
                           Commodore     USA    XFL14936
                           Commodore     Jap.   GXC-3146
                           Fontana       Eng.   TL5273
                           Fontana       Eng.   TL.5294
                           Jazztone      USA    J-1221
                           London        Eng.   HMC5006
                           London        Fr.    180006
                           London        Ger.   6.24056
                           London        Jap.   SLC 450
                           Mainstream    USA.   56009
                           Mainstream    USA    S/6009
                           Mainstream    USA    56037
                           Mainstream    USA    S/6037
                           Mainstream    Jap.   SL 1210
                           Sonet         Dan.   SLP1001
                           Time-Life     USA    P 15515
                           Vogue         Fr.    INT40008
                           Vogue         Fr.    INT40020

---------------------------------------------------------------
New York, New York                        December 5, 1943
        Radio broadcast, "Chamber Music Society of
        Lower Basin Street," on NBC radio.  Art Tatum, p,
        with orchestra.
1360  SUGAR FOOT STOMP (2:07)

             10 Inch LP   Mecolico       Eng.   1/8
             12 Inch LP   Joker          It.    SM 3117
             16 Inch TX   >AFRS Yank Swing  USA  82
                           Session

        Same broadcast, the Art Tatum Trio.  Art
        Tatum, p; Tiny Grimes, g; Slam Stewart, b.
1370  SWEET GEORGIA BROWN (3:10)
```

28

```
                10 Inch LP    Mecolico            Eng.  1/8
                12 Inch LP    Joker               It.   SM 3117
                16 Inch TX    >AFRS Yank Swing    USA   81
                               Session
```

```
Los Angeles, California                          c. 1943/1944 (Mfg.
                                                    date March 11, 1944)
                The Art Tatum Trio.  Art Tatum, p; Tiny
                Grimes, g; Slam Stewart, b.
1380  EXACTLY LIKE YOU (3:22)

                12 Inch LP    Shoestring          USA   SS-105
                16 Inch TX    AFRS Basic Mus.Lib. USA   P-68
                              >AFRS Jubilee       USA   69

1390  SWEET LORRAINE (3:17)

                16 Inch TX    >AFRS Jubilee       USA   69
```

```
                                                 c. 1944
                The Art Tatum Trio.  Art Tatum, p; Tiny
                Grimes, g; Slam Stewart, b.
1395  I KNOW THAT YOU KNOW (2:37)

                16 Inch TX    >AFRS Remember      USA   H54-586
```

```
New York, New York                               January 5, 1944
                The Art Tatum Trio.  Art Tatum, p; Tiny
                Grimes, g; Slam Stewart, b.
                Note:  There are various suffixes to the
                matrix numbers which appear on the labels
                of the issues shown in each group below,
                all of which play the same.
1400  I GOT RHYTHM (2:15)
      (mx WN1360)
                10 Inch 78    Brunswick           USA   80102
                7 Inch 45EP   Brunswick           USA   EB 71020
                              Coral               Ger.  EPC 94 020
                10 Inch LP    Brunswick           USA   BL58013
                              Coral               Fr.   CVM.40007
                              Festival            Astla CFR10 648
                              Vogue Coral         Eng.  LRA.10011
                12 Inch LP    Ace of Hearts       Eng.  AH.109
                              Brunswick           USA   BL54004
                              Coral               Ger.  COPS 3443
                              Coral               Jap.  LPCM-2009
                              MCA                 USA   MCA2-4019
                              MCA                 Fr.   510 105
                              MCA                 It.   MAPD 7028
                              MCA                 Jap.  MCA-3075
                              Time-Life           USA   P 15515
                              Vogue Coral         Eng.  LVA.9047
                12 Inch TX    AFRS Amer.Pop.Mus.  USA   149
                              AFRS Amer.Pop.Mus.  USA   434
                16 Inch TX    >World Jam Session  USA   JS32
                              World Program Svce  USA   367

1410  COCKTAILS FOR TWO (2:37)
      (mx WN1361; USA V-Discs have mx VP1234, serial B42325)
                10 Inch 78    Brunswick           USA   80131
                12 Inch 78    V-Disc (Army)       USA   456
                              V-Disc (Navy)       USA   236
                7 Inch 45     Brunswick           USA   9-80131
                7 Inch 45EP   Brunswick           USA   EB 71021
                10 Inch LP    Brunswick           USA   BL58013
                              Coral               Fr.   CVM.40007
                              Festival            Astla CFR10 648
                              Vogue Coral         Eng.  LRA.10011
                12 Inch LP    Ace of Hearts       Eng.  AH.109
                              Brunswick           USA   BL54004
                              Caracol             Fr.   CAR 426
                              Coral               Jap.  LPCM-2009
```

```
                      Joker                    It.     SM 3119
                      MCA                      USA     MCA2-4019
                      MCA                      Fr.     510 105
                      MCA                      It.     MAPD 7028
                      MCA                      Jap.    MCA-3075
                      V-Disc                   It.     VDL 1006
                      Vogue Coral              Eng.    LVA.9047
        16 Inch TX    World Program Svce       USA     WM1276/1280
                     >World Jam Session        USA     JS32
                      World Program Svce       USA     393

1420   I AIN´T GOT NOBODY (2:33)
       (mx WN1362)
        10 Inch 78    Brunswick                USA     80131
         7 Inch 45    Brunswick                USA     9-80131
         7 Inch 45EP  Brunswick                USA     EB 71021
        10 Inch LP    Brunswick                USA     BL58013
                      Coral                    Fr.     CVM.40007
                      Vogue Coral              Eng.    LRA.10011
        12 Inch LP    MCA                      Fr.     510 105
                      MCA                      Jap.    MCA-3075
                      Time-Life                USA     P 15515
        16 Inch TX    World Program Svce       USA     WM1276/1280
                     >World Jam Session        USA     JS32
                      World Program Svce       USA     393

1430   AFTER YOU´VE GONE (2:25)
       (mx WN1363)
        10 Inch 78    Brunswick                USA     80141
         7 Inch 45EP  Brunswick                USA     EB 71021
                      Festival                 Astla   XP 45 658
        10 Inch LP    Brunswick                USA     BL58013
                      Coral                    Fr.     CVM.40007
                      Vogue Coral              Eng.    LRA.10011
        12 Inch LP    Ace of Hearts            Eng.    AH.109
                      Brunswick                USA     BL54004
                      Coral                    Ger.    COPS 3443
                      Coral                    Jap.    LPCM-2009
                      MCA                      USA     MCA2-4019
                      MCA                      Fr.     510 105
                      MCA                      It.     MAPD 7028
                      MCA                      Jap.    MCA-3075
                      Vogue Coral              Eng.    LVA.9047
        12 Inch TX    AFRS Amer.Pop.Mus.       USA     149
                      AFRS Amer.Pop.Mus.       USA     194
                      AFRS Amer.Pop.Mus.       USA     345
        16 Inch TX   >World Jam Session        USA     JS32
                      World Program Svce       USA     345

1440   MOONGLOW (2:33)
       (mx WN1364)
        10 Inch 78    Brunswick                USA     80114
         7 Inch 45EP  Brunswick                USA     EB 71020
                      Coral                    Ger.    EPC 94 020
        10 Inch LP    Brunswick                USA     BL58013
                      Coral                    Fr.     CVM.40007
                      Festival                 Astla   CFR10 648
                      Vogue Coral              Eng.    LRA.10011
        12 Inch LP    Ace of Hearts            Eng.    AH.109
                      Ace of Hearts            Eng.    AH133
                      Brunswick                USA     BL54004
                      Brunswick                Eng.    LAT.8358
                      Coral                    Eng.    CP62
                      Coral                    Ger.    COP 2686
                      Coral                    Ger.    COPS 3443
                      Coral                    Jap.    LPCM-2009
                      Decca                    USA     DL8715
                      MCA                      USA     MCA2-4019
                      MCA                      Fr.     510 105
                      MCA                      Fr.     MAP 2686
                      MCA                      It.     MAPD 7028
                      MCA                      Jap.    MCA-3075
                      Vogue Coral              Eng.    LVA.9047
        16 Inch TX    World Program Svce       USA     WM1276/1280
                     >World Jam Session        USA     JS32
```

```
1450   DEEP PURPLE (3:03)
       (mx WN1365)
              10 Inch 78    Brunswick            USA    80141
               7 Inch 45EP  Brunswick            USA    EB 71021
                            Festival             Astla  XP 45 658
              10 Inch LP    Brunswick            USA    BL58013
                            Coral                Fr.    CVM.40007
                            Vogue Coral          Eng.   LRA.10011
              12 Inch LP    Ace of Hearts        Eng.   AH.109
                            Brunswick            USA    BL54004
                            Coral                Ger.   COPS 3443
                            Coral                Jap.   LPCM-2009
                            MCA                  USA    MCA2-4019
                            MCA                  Fr.    510 105
                            MCA                  It.    MAPD 7028
                            MCA                  Jap.   MCA-3075
                            Vogue Coral          Eng.   LVA.9047
              16 Inch TX   >World Jam Session    USA    JS31

1460   I WOULD DO ANYTHING FOR YOU (2:29)
       (mx WN1366)
              10 Inch 78    Brunswick            USA    80102
               7 Inch 45EP  Brunswick            USA    EB 71020
              10 Inch LP    Brunswick            USA    BL58013
                            Coral                Fr.    CVM.40007
                            Vogue Coral          Eng.   LRA.10011
              12 Inch LP    Ace of Hearts        Eng.   AH133
                            Brunswick            Eng.   LAT.8358
                            Coral                Eng.   CP62
                            Coral                Ger.   COP 2686
                            Decca                USA    DL8715
                            MCA                  USA    MCA2-4019
                            MCA                  Fr.    510 105
                            MCA                  Fr.    MAP 2636
                            MCA                  It.    MAPD 7028
                            MCA                  Jap.   MCA-3075
              16 Inch TX    AFRS Today´s the Day USA    77
                           >World Jam Session    USA    JS31
                            World Program Svce   USA    393

1470   LIZA (1:54)
       (mx WN1367; USA V-Discs have mx VP1234, serial B42325)
              12 Inch 78    V-Disc (Army)        USA    456
                            V-Disc (Navy)        USA    236
              12 Inch LP    Black Lion           Eng.   BLP30203
                            Caracol              Fr.    CAR 426
                            Freedom              Fr.    FR.11007
                            Joker                It.    SM 3119
                            V-Disc               It.    VDL 1006
              16 Inch TX   >World Jam Session    USA    JS31
                            World Program Svce   USA    367

1475   TEA FOR TWO (0:03)
       (No mx assigned; cut one, aborted)

1480   TEA FOR TWO (2:05)
       (mx WN1368; cut two)
              12 Inch LP    Black Lion           Eng.   BLP30166
                            Freedom              Fr.    BLP30166
                            Intercord Black Lion Ger.   147.000
              16 Inch TX   >World Jam Session    USA    JS31
                            World Program Svce   USA    367

1488   HONEYSUCKLE ROSE (0:20)
       (No mx assigned; cut three, aborted)

1489   HONEYSUCKLE ROSE (2:24)
       (No mx assigned; cut four)
                            World Jam Session    USA    Unissued
```

```
1490  HONEYSUCKLE ROSE (2:19)
      (mx WN1369 [cut five])
                10 Inch 78    Brunswick          USA    80114
                 7 Inch 45EP  Brunswick          USA    EB 71020
                10 Inch LP    Brunswick          USA    BL58013
                              Coral              Fr.    CVM.40007
                              Festival           Astla  CFR10 648
                              Vogue Coral        Eng.   LRA.10011
                12 Inch LP    Ace of Hearts      Eng.   AH.109
                              Brunswick          USA    BL54004
                              Cathala            Fr.    BLP 100.005
                              Coral              Ger.   COPS 3443
                              Coral              Jap.   LPCM-2009
                              MCA                USA    MCA2-4019
                              MCA                Fr.    510 105
                              MCA                It.    MAPD 7028
                              MCA                Jap.   MCA-3075
                              Vogue Coral        Eng.   LVA.9047
                12 Inch TX    AFRS Amer.Pop.Mus. USA    149
                16 Inch TX    World Program Svce USA    WM1276/1280
                             >World Jam Session  USA    JS31
                              World Program Svce USA    345
```

```
New York, New York                            January 16, 1944
          Radio broadcast, "Chamber Music Society of
          Lower Basin Street," on WJZ radio.  Louis
          Armstrong, t; Jack Teagarden, tb; Coleman
          Hawkins, ts; Art Tatum, p; Al Casey, g;
          Oscar Pettiford, b; Sid Catlett, d.
1500  BASIN STREET BLUES* (3:37)

                12 Inch LP   >Aircheck           USA    27
      *Louis Armstrong, t and v; Jack Teagarden, tb and v.

1510  ESQUIRE BLUES (2:17)

                12 Inch LP   >Aircheck           USA    27

1520  HONEYSUCKLE ROSE (1:59)

                12 Inch LP   >Aircheck           USA    27
```

```
New York, New York                            January 18, 1944
          Esquire All-Star Concert from the Metropolitan
          Opera House.  The basic band seemed to consist
          of Roy Eldridge, t; Jack Teagarden, tb; Barney
          Bigard, cl; Coleman Hawkins, ts; Art Tatum, p;
          Al Casey, g; Oscar Pettiford, b; Sid Catlett, d.
          Unless otherwise indicated the four-man rhythm
          section (Tatum, Casey, Pettiford and Catlett)
          backed on all the numbers.  The personnel listings
          below each title group are of identifiable soloists.
          Selections from this concert on which Tatum did
          not perform are not included in the following list.
1530  ESQUIRE BLUES/INTRODUCTIONS[1] (5:10)

                10 Inch LP    Palm Club          Fr.    #2
                12 Inch LP    Dan                Jap.   VC-5029
                              Elec               Jap.   KV-401
                              FDC                It.    FDC1007
                              Festival           Fr.    100.350
                              Jazz Anthology     Fr.    JA5146
                              Jazz Society       Swed.  AA522
                              Palm 30            Eng.   P.30:07
                              Radiola            USA    Release #50
                              S R International  Ger.   30 182 0
                              Saga               Eng.   6922
                              Up Front           USA    5028/2
                16 Inch TX   >AFRS Jubilee       USA    67
      [1]Features Roy Eldridge, t; Jack Teagarden, tb;
         Barney Bigard, cl; Coleman Hawkins, ts; Art
         Tatum, p; Al Casey, g; also introductions of all.
```

```
1540    MOP-MOP (4:38)[2]
        (mx VP-467, serial D4-TC-30)
                12 Inch 78  >V-Disc (Army)        USA    152
                             V-Disc (Navy)        USA    135
                10 Inch LP   Palm Club            Fr.    PALM 01
                12 Inch LP   Ariston              It.    AR/LP/12059
                             Dan                  Jap.   VC-5011
                             Dan                  Jap.   VC-5029
                             Decca                Ger.   PD 12005
                             Discomania           Jap.   101
                             Elec                 Jap.   KV-401
                             FDC                  It.    FDC1001
                             Festival             Fr.    100.350
                             Jazz Anthology       Fr.    JA5102
                             Jazz Society         Swed.  AA522
                             Joker                It.    SM 3132
                             Palm 30              Eng.   P.30:07
                             Radiola              USA    Release #50
                             Redwood              Can.   R.W.J.1001
                             S R International     Ger.   30 182 0
                             Saga                 Eng.   6922
                             Up Front             USA    5028/2
                             Windmill             Eng.   WMD 248
                16 Inch TX   AFRS One Night StandUSA     187
        [2]Features Roy Eldridge, t; Jack Teagarden, tb;
           Barney Bigard, cl; Art Tatum, p; Al Casey, g;
           Sid Catlett, d.

1550    DO NOTHIN´ TILL YOU HEAR FROM ME[3] (3:28)
        (mx JDB100, serial B45590)
                12 Inch 78  >V-Disc (Army)        USA    672
                 7 Inch 45EP Bravo                Eng.   BR374
                10 Inch LP   Palm Club            Fr.    #2
                12 Inch LP   Astor                Astla  GGS-1389
                             Bulldog              Eng.   BDL 1007
                             DJM                  Eng.   DJM 22047
                             Dan                  Jap.   VC-5014
                             Dan                  Jap.   VC-5029
                             Decca                Ger.   PD 12006
                             Elec                 Jap.   KV-401
                             Everest              USA    FS-265
                             FDC                  It.    FDC1007
                             Festival             Fr.    100.100
                             Festival             Fr.    100.350
                             Jazz Anthology       Fr.    JA5146
                             Jazz Society         Swed.  AA522
                             Joker                It.    SM 3131
                             Kings of Jazz        It.    KLJ20.002
                             Omniamusic Napoleon It.     OLP-19002
                             Ozone                USA    3
                             Palm 30              Eng.   P.30:07
                             Phoenix 10           USA    PHX-312
                             Pickwick             USA    SPC 3335
                             Radiola              USA    Release #50
                             S R International     Ger.   30 182 0
                             Saga                 Eng.   6918
                             Saga                 Eng.   6922
                             Saga                 Eng.   ERO-8014
                             Swing House          Eng.   SWH 27
                             Trip                 USA    TLP-5024
                             Up Front             USA    5028/2
                             Vogue                Fr.    LDM.30206
                16 Inch TX   AFRS Yank Swing      USA    91
                             Session
        [3]Features Billie Holiday, v.

1560    I LOVE MY MAN (Billie´s Blues)[4] (4:04)
        (mx VP-670, serial D4-TC-170)
                12 Inch 78  >V-Disc (Army)        USA    248
                             V-Disc (Navy)        USA    28
                 7 Inch 45EP Bravo                Eng.   BR374
                10 Inch LP   Palm Club            Fr.    #2
                12 Inch LP   Ariston              It.    AR/LP/12059
                             Dan                  Jap.   VC-5014
                             Dan                  Jap.   VC-5029
```

33

		Decca	Ger.	PD 12006
		Elec	Jap.	KV-401
		FDC	It.	FDC1001
		Festival	Fr.	100.101
		Festival	Fr.	100.350
		Jazz Society	Swed.	AA522
		Joker	It.	SM 3131
		Joker	It.	SM 3428
		Kings of Jazz	It.	KLJ20.002
		Omniamusic Napoleon	It.	OLP-19002
		Ozone	USA	3
		Palm 30	Eng.	P.30:07
		Radiola	USA	Release #50
		S R International	Ger.	30 182 0
		Saga	Eng.	6918
		Saga	Eng.	6922
		Saga	Eng.	ERO-8014
		Swing House	Eng.	SWH 27
		Up Front	USA	5028/2
	16 Inch TX	AFRS One Night Stand	USA	187
		AFRS Yank Swing Session	USA	121

[4]Features Billie Holiday, v.

1570   I CAN'T GIVE YOU ANYTHING BUT LOVE[5] (3:15)

		Palm Club	Fr.	014
10 Inch LP				
12 Inch LP		Dan	Jap.	VC-5029
		Elec	Jap.	KV-401
		FDC	It.	FDC1007
		Festival	Fr.	100.350
		Jazz Anthology	Fr.	JA5146
		Palm 30	Eng.	P.30:07
		Radiola	USA	Release #50
		S R International	Ger.	30 182 0
		Saga	Eng.	6922
		Up Front	USA	5028/2
	16 Inch TX	>AFRS One Night Stand	USA	186

[5]Features Louis Armstrong, t and v; Jack Teagarden,
   tb; Barney Bigard, cl; Coleman Hawkins, ts.

1580   I GOTTA RIGHT TO SING THE BLUES[6] (3:39)

10 Inch LP		>Palm Club	Fr.	PALM 14
12 Inch LP		Dan	Jap.	VC-5029
		Decca	Ger.	PD-12008
		Elec	Jap.	KV-401
		FDC	It.	FDC1007
		Festival	Fr.	100.350
		Jazz Society	Swed.	AA522
		Joker	It.	SM 3133
		Palm 30	Eng.	P.30:07
		Radiola	USA	Release #50
		S R International	Ger.	30 182 0
		Saga	Eng.	6922
		Up Front	USA	5028/2
	16 Inch TX	AFRS One Night Stand	USA	187

[6]Features Louis Armstrong, t; Jack Teagarden, tb and v.

1590   SWEET LORRAINE[7] (3:20)
       (mx VP-468, serial D4-TC-31)

		V-Disc (Army)	USA	Unissued Test Pressing
12 Inch LP		Black Lion	Eng.	BLP30203
		Dan	Jap.	VC-5029
		Elec	Jap.	KV-401
		Europa Jazz	It.	EJ-1011
		FDC	It.	FDC1010
		Festival	Fr.	100.350
		Freedom	Fr.	FR.11007
		Jazz Anthology	Fr.	JA5146
		Jazz Society	Swed.	AA522
		Palm 30	Eng.	P.30:07
		Radiola	USA	Release #50

```
                    S R International    Ger.  30 182 0
                    Up Front             USA   5028/2
        16 Inch TX  AFRS One Night StandUSA    187
                   >AFRS Yank Swing      USA   90
                    Session
   [7]Features Art Tatum, p; with Oscar Pettiford, b; and
      Sid Catlett, d; only.

1600  I GOT RHYTHM[8]  (8:15)

        10 Inch LP   Palm Club           Fr.   PALM 14
        12 Inch LP   Dan                 Jap.  VC-5029
                     Elec                Jap.  KV-401
                     FDC                 It.   FDC1007
                     Festival            Fr.   100.350
                     Jazz Anthology      Fr.   JA5146
                     Jazz Society        Swed. AA522
                     Palm 30             Eng.  P.30:07
                     Radiola             USA   Release #50
                     S R International    Ger.  30 183 8
                     Saga                Eng.  6922
                     Up Front            USA   5028/2
        16 Inch TX  >AFRS One Night StandUSA    186*
        *Has some voice-over and is abbreviated.
   [8]Features Louis Armstrong and Roy Eldridge, t; Jack
      Teagarden, tb; Barney Bigard, cl; Coleman Hawkins,
      ts; Red Norvo, x; Art Tatum, p.

1610  BLUES[9]  (2:47)
      (mx VP-469, serial D4-TC-34)
        12 Inch 78  >V-Disc (Army)       USA   163
        10 Inch LP   Palm Club           Fr.   #2
        12 Inch LP   Ariston             It.   AR/LP/12059
                     Dan                 Jap.  VC-5029
                     Decca               Ger.  PD 12005
                     Elec                Jap.  KV-401
                     FDC                 It.   FDC1001
                     Festival            Fr.   100.350
                     Jazz Society        Swed. AA522
                     Joker               It.   SM 3132
                     Joker               It.   SM 3428
                     Palm 30             Eng.  P.30:13
                     Radiola             USA   Release #50
                     S R International    Ger.  30 183 8
                     Saga                Eng.  6922
                     Up Front            USA   5028/2
                     Windmill            Eng.  WMD 248
        16 Inch TX   AFRS One Night StandUSA    186
   [9]Features Roy Eldridge, t; Jack Teagarden, tb;
      Barney Bigard, cl; Al Casey, g.

1620  THEME FOR COCA-COLA/INTRODUCTIONS*[10]  (1:31)

        12 Inch LP   Aircheck            USA   27
                     Dan                 Jap.  VC-5029
                     Elec                Jap.  KV-401
                     FDC                 It.   FDC1007
                     Jazz Anthology      Fr.   JA5146
                    >Radiola             USA   Release 50
        16 Inch TX   AFRS One Night StandUSA    186**
        *The introductions were made a second time, because a
         segment of the program was broadcast for the "Victory
         Parade of Spotlight Bands", sponsored by Coca-Cola.
        **Lacks theme but has introductions.
   [10]Features Louis Armstrong and Roy Eldridge, t;
      Jack Teagarden, tb; Barney Bigard, cl; Coleman
      Hawkins, ts; Lionel Hampton and Red Norvo, vib.

1630  ESQUIRE BOUNCE[11]  (1:50)
      (mx VP-469, serial D4-TC-34)
        12 Inch 78   V-Disc (Army)       USA   163
        10 Inch LP   Palm Club           Fr.   #2
        12 Inch LP   Aircheck            USA   27
                     Ariston             It.   AR/LP/12059
                     Dan                 Jap.  VC-5011
```

```
                         Dan                    Jap.  VC-5029
                         Elec                   Jap.  KV-401
                         FDC                    It.   FDC1001
                         Palm 30                Eng.  P.30:13
                         Radiola                USA   Release #50
                         S R International      Ger.  30 181 2
                         Saga                   Eng.  6923
                         Up Front               USA   5028/2
            16 Inch TX   AFRS One Night StandUSA      186*
                         AFRS One Night StandUSA      187**
                         AFRS One Night StandUSA      188**
                        >AFRS Spotlight BandsUSA      261
                         US Dept. of State      USA   AJ32
                           VOA Amer.Jazz Series
          *Has some voice over, and is abbreviated.
          **Contains only a small portion, used as a theme.
     [11]Features Coleman Hawkins, ts; Art Tatum, p;
          Al Casey, g.

1640   BASIN STREET BLUES[12] (3:57)
       (mx VP-665, serial D4-TC-165)
            12 Inch 78  >V-Disc (Army)          USA   234
                         V-Disc (Navy)          USA   14
            10 Inch LP   Palm Club              Fr.   PALM 01
            12 Inch LP   Aircheck               USA   27
                         Ariston                It.   AR/LP/12059
                         Dan                    Jap.  VC-5006
                         Dan                    Jap.  VC-5029
                         Decca                  Ger.  PD-12008
                         Discomania             Jap.  101
                         Elec                   Jap.  KV-401
                         FDC                    It.   FDC1001
                         Festival               Fr.   100.350
                         Jazz Anthology         Fr.   JA5102
                         Jazz Society           Swed. AA522
                         Joker                  It.   SM 3133
                         Joker                  It.   SM 3428
                         Palm 30                Eng.  P.30:13
                         Radiola                USA   Release #50
                         S R International      Ger.  30 181 2
                         Saga                   Eng.  6923
                         Up Front               USA   5028/2
            16 Inch TX   *AFRS Spotlight BandsUSA     261
          *Incomplete start.
     [12]Features Louis Armstrong, t and v; Jack Teagarden,
          tb and v; Coleman Hawkins, ts.

1650   I'LL GET BY[13] (1:25)
       (mx JDB100, serial B45590)
            12 Inch 78  >V-Disc (Army)          USA   672
            10 Inch LP   Palm Club              Fr.   PALM 01
            12 Inch LP   Aircheck               USA   27
                         Dan                    Jap.  VC-5014
                         Dan                    Jap.  VC-5029
                         Decca                  Ger.  PD 12006
                         Elec                   Jap.  KV-401
                         FDC                    It.   FDC1007
                         Festival               Fr.   100.101
                         Festival               Fr.   100.350
                         Jazz Anthology         Fr.   JA5146
                         Jazz Society           Swed. AA522
                         Joker                  It.   SM 3131
                         Kings of Jazz          It.   KLJ20.002
                         Omniamusic Napoleon    It.   OLP-19002
                         Ozone                  USA   3
                         Palm 30                Eng.  P.30:13
                         Radiola                USA   Release #50
                         S R International      Ger.  30 181 2
                         Saga                   Eng.  6923
                         Up Front               USA   5028/2
            16 Inch TX   AFRS One Night StandUSA      188
                        >US Dept. of State      USA   AJ32
                           VOA Amer.Jazz Series
     [13]Features Billie Holiday, v.
```

1660   TEA FOR TWO[14] (3:28)
        (mx VP-472, serial D4-TC-35)
            12 Inch 78   >V-Disc (Army)   USA   163
            10 Inch LP   Palm Club   Fr.   #2
            12 Inch LP   Aircheck   USA   27
                          Ariston   It.   AR/LP/12059
                          Dan   Jap.   VC-5030
                          Elec   Jap.   KV-401
                          FDC   It.   FDC1001
                          Festival   Fr.   100.351
                          Jazz Society   Swed.   AA522
                          Palm 30   Eng.   P.30:13
                          Radiola   USA   Release #51
                          S R International   Ger.   30 181 2
                          Saga   Eng.   6923
                          Up Front   USA   5028/2
            16 Inch TX   AFRS One Night Stand USA   188
                          AFRS Yank Swing   USA   86
                          Session
        [14]Features Roy Eldridge, t; Barney Bigard, cl;
            Art Tatum, p; Lionel Hampton, vib.

1665   THEME FOR COCA-COLA/CONCLUSION*[15] (0:37)

            12 Inch LP   Aircheck   USA   27
                          Dan   Jap.   VC-5030
                          Elec   Jap.   KV-401
                         >Radiola   USA   Release 51
            *This ended the broadcast which began at [1620].
        [15]Features the basic band, no soloists.

1670   BACK O´ TOWN BLUES[16] (3:27)
        (mx VP-1025, serial D4-TC-511)
            12 Inch 78   >V-Disc (Army)   USA   366
                          V-Disc (Navy)   USA   148
            10 Inch LP   Palm Club   Fr.   #2
            12 Inch LP   Ariston   It.   AR/LP/12059
                          Dan   Jap.   VC-5006
                          Dan   Jap.   VC-5030
                          Decca   Ger.   PD-12008
                          Elec   Jap.   KV-401
                          FDC   It.   FDC1001
                          Festival   Fr.   100.351
                          Jazz Anthology   Fr.   JA5102
                          Jazz Society   Swed.   AA523
                          Joker   It.   SM 3133
                          Palm 30   Eng.   P.30:13
                          Radiola   USA   Release #51
                          S R International   Ger.   30 181 2
                          Saga   Eng.   6923
                          Up Front   USA   5028/2
        [16]Features Louis Armstrong, t and v; Art Tatum, p.

1680   MUSKRAT RAMBLE[17] (2:09)

            10 Inch LP   >Palm Club   Fr.   PALM 14
            12 Inch LP   Dan   Jap.   VC-5030
                          Elec   Jap.   KV-401
                          FDC   It.   FDC1010
                          Festival   Fr.   100.351
                          Jazz Anthology   Fr.   JA5146
                          Palm 30   Eng.   P.30:13
                          Radiola   USA   Release #51
                          S R International   Ger.   30 181 2
                          Up Front   USA   5028/2
        [17]Features Louis Armstrong, t; Barney Bigard, cl;
            Coleman Hawkins, ts.

1690   BUCK JUMPIN´[18] (2:42)

            10 Inch LP   Palm Club   Fr.   PALM 01
            12 Inch LP   Dan   Jap.   VC-5030
                          Elec   Jap.   KV-401

		FDC	It.	FDC1007
		Festival	Fr.	100.351
		Jazz Society	Swed.	AA523
		Palm 30	Eng.	P.30:13
		Radiola	USA	Release #51
		S R International	Ger.	30 181 2
		Saga	Eng.	6923
		Up Front	USA	5028/2
16 Inch TX		AFRS One Night Stand	USA	186
		>US Dept. of State	USA	AJ32
		VOA Amer.Jazz Series		

[18]Features Al Casey, g.

1700 STOMPIN´ AT THE SAVOY[19] (3:09)

10 Inch LP	>Palm Club	Fr.	PALM 14
12 Inch LP	Dan	Jap.	VC-5030
	Elec	Jap.	KV-401
	FDC	It.	FDC1010
	Festival	Fr.	100.351
	Jazz Anthology	Fr.	JA5146
	Jazz Society	Swed.	AA523
	Palm 30	Eng.	P.30:13
	Radiola	USA	Release #51
	S R International	Ger.	30 181 2
	Up Front	USA	5028/2
16 Inch TX	AFRS One Night Stand	USA	186

[19]Features Roy Eldridge, t; Jack Teagarden, tb;
Barney Bigard, cl; Coleman Hawkins, ts; Art Tatum, p.

1710 FOR BASS FACES ONLY[20] (4:59)

10 Inch LP	>Palm Club	Fr.	PALM 14
12 Inch LP	Dan	Jap.	VC-5030
	Elec	Jap.	KV-401
	FDC	It.	FDC1010
	Festival	Fr.	100.351
	Jazz Anthology	Fr.	JA5146
	Jazz Society	Swed.	AA523
	Palm 30	Eng.	P.30:13
	Radiola	USA	Release #51
	S R International	Ger.	30 181 2
	Up Front	USA	5028/2
16 Inch TX	AFRS One Night Stand	USA	188

[20]Features Roy Eldridge, t; Coleman Hawkins, ts;
Oscar Pettiford, b.

1720 MY IDEAL[21] (3:06)
(mx JDB91, serial B45464)

12 Inch 78	>V-Disc (Army)	USA	665
10 Inch LP	Palm Club	Fr.	PALM 01
12 Inch LP	Ariston	It.	AR/LP/12059
	Dan	Jap.	VC-5011
	Dan	Jap.	VC-5030
	Decca	Ger.	PD 12005
	Elec	Jap.	KV-401
	FDC	It.	FDC1001
	Festival	Fr.	100.351
	Jazz Society	Swed.	AA523
	Joker	It.	SM 3132
	Palm 30	Eng.	P.30:14
	Radiola	USA	Release #51
	S R International	Ger.	30 183 8
	Saga	Eng.	6923
	Up Front	USA	5028/2
	Windmill	Eng.	WMD 248
16 Inch TX	AFRS One Night Stand	USA	186

[21]Features Coleman Hawkins, ts; Art Tatum, p.

1730 ROSE ROOM[22] (5:33)
(mx VP-470, serial D4-TC-33)

12 Inch 78	V-Disc (Army)	USA	152
10 Inch LP	Palm Club	Fr.	PALM 01
12 Inch LP	Ariston	It.	AR/LP/12059
	Dan	Jap.	VC-5030

		Elec	Jap.	KV-401
		FDC	It.	FDC1001
		Festival	Fr.	100.351
		Jazz Anthology	Fr.	JA5102
		Palm 30	Eng.	P.30:14
		Radiola	USA	Release #51
		S R International	Ger.	30 183 8
		Saga	Eng.	6923
		Up Front	USA	5028/2
	16 Inch TX	AFRS One Night Stand	USA	187
		>US Dept. of State	USA	AJ32
		VOA Amer.Jazz Series		

[22]Features Barney Bigard, cl; Sid Catlett, d.

1740 FLYING HOME[23] (8:27+2:40 reprise called "Drum Duet")
      (1st half: mx JDB102, serial B45592; 2d half: mx JDB103, serial
      B45593)

	12 Inch 78	>V-Disc (Army)*	USA	674
	10 Inch LP	Palm Club	Fr.	PALM 01
	12 Inch LP	Ariston	It.	AR/LP/12059
		Dan	Jap.	VC-5011
		Dan	Jap.	VC-5030
		Decca	Ger.	PD 12005
		Discomania	Jap.	101
		Elec	Jap.	KV-401
		FDC	It.	FDC1001
		Festival	Fr.	100.351
		Jazz Anthology	Fr.	JA5102
		Jazz Society	Swed.	AA523
		Joker	It.	SM 3132
		Joker	It.	SM 3428
		Palm 30	Eng.	P.30:14
		Radiola	USA	Release #51
		S R International	Ger.	30 183 8
		Saga	Eng.	6923
		Up Front	USA	5028/2
		Windmill	Eng.	WMD 248

      *The V-Disc is titled "Flying On a V-Disc", Parts 1 & 2
[23]Features Roy Eldridge, t; Barney Bigard, cl;
    Coleman Hawkins, ts; Sid Catlett, d; Lionel
    Hampton, d and vib.

1750 VIBE BLUES (Jammin´ the Blues)[24] (4:13)

	10 Inch LP	>Palm Club	Fr.	PALM 14
	12 Inch LP	Dan	Jap.	VC-5030
		Elec	Jap.	KV-401
		FDC	It.	FDC1010
		Jazz Anthology	Fr.	JA5146
		Jazz Society	Swed.	AA523
		Palm 30	Eng.	P.30:14
		Radiola	USA	Release #51
		S R International	Ger.	30 183 8
		Up Front	USA	5028/2
	16 Inch TX	AFRS One Night Stand	USA	188

[24]Features Roy Eldridge, t; Jack Teagarden, tb;
    Lionel Hampton and Red Norvo, vib.

Los Angeles, California   c. 1944
        Art Tatum with the Les Paul Trio. Art
        Tatum, p; Calvin Goodin, g; Les Paul, g;
        Clinton Nordquist, b.
1760 JA-DA (3:28)
      (mx SSL-286)

	12 Inch LP	Shoestring	USA	SS-105
	16 Inch TX	>AFRS Basic Mus.Lib.	USA	P-172

1770 HUMORESQUE* (4:13)
      (mx SSL-286)

	12 Inch LP	Shoestring	USA	SS-105
	16 Inch TX	>AFRS Basic Mus.Lib.	USA	P-172

      *Piano solo by Art Tatum.

```
1780   IT HAD TO BE YOU* (3:53)
       (mx SSL-286)
              12 Inch LP   Shoestring              USA   SS-105
              16 Inch TX  >AFRS Basic Mus.Lib. USA   P-172
       *Piano solo by Art Tatum.

1790   I'VE FOUND A NEW BABY (3:36)
       (mx SSL-373)
              12 Inch LP   Shoestring              USA   SS-105
              16 Inch TX  >AFRS Basic Mus.Lib. USA   P-205

1800   OH! LADY BE GOOD (3:26)
       (mx SSL-373)
              12 Inch LP   Shoestring              USA   SS-105
              16 Inch TX  >AFRS Basic Mus.Lib. USA   P-205

1810   SOMEBODY LOVES ME (4:40)
       (mx SSL-373)
              12 Inch LP   Shoestring              USA   SS-105
              16 Inch TX  >AFRS Basic Mus.Lib. USA   P-205
                           AFRS Mail Call          USA   132

       ------------------------------------------------------------
Milwaukee, Wisconsin                            April, 1944
              Private live recording from Frenchie's
              Pink Pig by Michael J. Cudahy.  The Art
              Tatum Trio.  Art Tatum, p; Tiny Grimes,
              g; Slam Stewart, b.
1815   EXACTLY LIKE YOU (4:56)

              12 Inch LP  >Smithsonian            USA   R 029

1816   STORMY WEATHER (4:48)

                                                  Unissued

1817   SWEET LORRAINE (4:12)

                                                  Unissued

       ------------------------------------------------------------
New York, New York                              May 1, 1944
              The Art Tatum Trio.  Art Tatum, p; Tiny
              Grimes, g; Slam Stewart, b.
1820   THE MAN I LOVE (4:10)
       (mx T-1-A-1, T-1-A-3, T-1-A-3 #2,  T-1-A-3 #3)
              10 Inch 78LP Blue Star              Fr.    179
                           Dial                   USA    1036
                           Esquire                Eng.   10-156
                           Metronome              Swed.  B515
              12 Inch 78   Celson                 It.    RA8004
                          >Comet                  USA    T-1
               7 Inch 33EP Guilde du Jazz         Fr.    J701
              10 Inch LP   Blue Star              Fr.    6810
                           Dial                   USA    LP206
              12 Inch LP   Blue Star              Fr.    BLP6810
                           Crystal                Fr.    12.501
                           Explosive              Fr.    528012
                           Fontana                It.    LPU8001
                           Hall of Fame           USA    JG-607
                           Jazz Anthology         Fr.    JA5208
                           Jazztone               USA    J-1203
                           Jazztone               USA    J1280
                           Music Parade           It.    LEL 14
                           Tulip                  Can.   TLP 104

1830   DARK EYES (4:40)
       (mx T-1-B-1, T-1B-1, T-1-B-3, T-1-B-3 #3)
              12 Inch 78   Celson                 It.    RA8008
                          >Comet                  USA    T-1
              10 Inch LP   Blue Star              Fr.    6810
                           Dial                   USA    LP206
                           Jazztone               USA    J-SPEC-100
                           Jazztone               USA    J-SPEC-101
              12 Inch LP   Artia-Parliament       USA    WGM-2AB
```

			Artia-Parliament	USA	WGM(s)-2AB
			Artia-Parliament	USA	WGM-2A
			Bellaphon	Ger.	BLST 6557
			Blue Star	Fr.	BLP6810
			CID	Fr.	CVM42.004
			Columbia	Eng.	33SX1557
			Core	USA	100C
			Crystal	Fr.	12.501
			Explosive	Fr.	528012
			Fonit	It.	8001
			Fontana	It.	LPU8001
			Guest Star	USA	G1403
			Guest Star	USA	GS1403
			Hall of Fame	USA	JG-607
			Jazz Anthology	Fr.	JA5208
			Jazztone	USA	J-1203
			Jazztone	USA	J1280
			Mode	Fr.	MDINT.9168
			Mode	Fr.	MDINT9201
			Music Parade	It.	LEL 14
			Pop Jazz	USA	WGM 2A
			Royal Roost	USA	RLP 2213
			Royal Roost	USA	LP-2256
			Royal Roost	Jap.	YW-7803-RO
			Royal Roost	Jap.	YY-7002-RO
			Roulette	USA	RE-110
			Roulette	Jap.	YW-7503-RO
			Tulip	Can.	TLP 104
			Vogue	Eng.	LAE.12209
	12 Inch TX		AFRS Amer.Pop.Mus.	USA	149
			AFRS Amer.Pop.Mus.	USA	194

1840 BODY AND SOUL (4:30)
(mx T-2-A-4, T2A4-RE)

	10 Inch 78LP	Dial		USA	1046
	12 Inch 78	Celson		It.	RA8008
		>Comet		USA	T-2
	7 Inch 33	Storia della Musica Jazz		It.	046
	10 Inch LP	Blue Star		Fr.	6810
		Dial		USA	LP206
	12 Inch LP	Bellaphon		Ger.	BLST 6557
		Blue Star		Fr.	BLP6810
		CID		Fr.	CVM42.004
		Columbia		Eng.	33SX1557
		Crystal		Fr.	12.501
		Fonit		It.	8001
		Jazz Anthology		Fr.	JA5208
		Mode		Fr.	MDINT.9168
		Royal Roost		USA	RLP 2213
		Royal Roost		USA	LP-2256
		Royal Roost		Jap.	YW-7803-RO
		Royal Roost		Jap.	YY-7002-RO
		Roulette		USA	RE-110
		Roulette		Jap.	YW-7503-RO
		Time-Life		USA	P 15515
		Tulip		Can.	TLP 104
		Vogue		Eng.	LAE.12209

1850 I KNOW THAT YOU KNOW (4:15)
(mx T-2-B-3, T2B3-RE)

	10 Inch 78LP	Blue Star		Fr.	179
		Dial		USA	1036
		Esquire		Eng.	10-156
		Metronome		Swed.	B515
	12 Inch 78	Celson		It.	RA8004
		>Comet		USA	T-2
	7 Inch 33	Storia della Musica Jazz		It.	046
	7 Inch 33EP	Guilde du Jazz		Fr.	J701
	10 Inch LP	Blue Star		Fr.	6810
		Dial		USA	LP206
	12 Inch LP	Bellaphon		Ger.	BLST 6557
		Blue Star		Fr.	BLP6810
		CID		Fr.	CVM42.004

		Columbia	Eng.	33SX1557
		Crystal	Fr.	12.501
		Explosive	Fr.	528012
		Fonit	It.	8001
		Fontana	It.	LPU8001
		Hall of Fame	USA	JG-607
		Jazz Anthology	Fr.	JA5208
		Jazztone	USA	J-1203
		Jazztone	USA	J1280
		Mode	Fr.	CLVLXR401
		Mode	Fr.	MDINT.9168
		Music Parade	It.	LEL 14
		Musidisc	Fr.	30 CV 1522
		Royal Roost	USA	RLP 2213
		Royal Roost	USA	LP 2256
		Royal Roost	Jap.	YW-7803-RO
		Royal Roost	Jap.	YY-7002-RO
		Roulette	USA	RE-110
		Roulette	Jap.	YW-7503-RO
		Tulip	Can.	TLP 104
		Vogue	Eng.	LAE.12209
		Vogue	Fr.	DP.64B
	12 Inch TX	AFRS Amer.Pop.Mus.	USA	149
		AFRS Amer.Pop.Mus.	USA	194
	16 Inch TX	AFRS Downbeat	USA	330

1860 ON THE SUNNY SIDE OF THE STREET (4:26)
(mx T-3-A-3, T3A3-RE)

	10 Inch 78LP	Blue Star	Fr.	191
	12 Inch 78	Celson	It.	RA8006
		>Comet	USA	T-3
	7 Inch 33EP	Guilde du Jazz	Fr.	J701
	10 Inch LP	Blue Star	Fr.	6810
		Dial	USA	LP206
	12 Inch LP	Bellaphon	Ger.	BLST 6557
		Blue Star	Fr.	BLP6810
		CID	Fr.	CVM42.004
		Columbia	Eng.	33SX1557
		Crystal	Fr.	12.501
		Explosive	Fr.	528012
		Fonit	It.	8001
		Guest Star	USA	G1403
		Guest Star	USA	GS1403
		Hall of Fame	USA	JG-607
		Jazz Anthology	Fr.	JA5208
		Jazztone	USA	J-1203
		Jazztone	USA	J1280
		Mode	Fr.	MDINT.9168
		Music Parade	It.	LEL 14
		Royal Roost	USA	RLP 2213
		Royal Roost	Jap.	YW-7803-RO
		Royal Roost	Jap.	YY-7002-RO
		Roulette	USA	RE-110
		Roulette	Jap.	YW-7503-RO
		Tulip	Can.	TLP 104
		Vogue	Eng.	LAE.12209
	12 Inch TX	AFRS Amer.Pop.Mus.	USA	149
		AFRS Amer.Pop.Mus.	USA	194
	16 Inch TX	Office of War Info, Music of Jazz Bands	USA	51

1870 FLYING HOME (4:20)
(mx T-3-B-3, T3B3-RE)

	10 Inch 78LP	Blue Star	Fr.	191
		Dial	USA	1046
	12 Inch 78	Celson	It.	RA8006
		>Comet	USA	T-3
	7 Inch 33EP	Guilde du Jazz	Fr.	J701
	10 Inch LP	Blue Star	Fr.	6810
		Dial	USA	LP206
	12 Inch LP	Bellaphon	Ger.	BLST 6557
		Blue Star	Fr.	BLP6810
		CID	Fr.	CVM42.004
		Columbia	Eng.	33SX1557
		Crystal	Fr.	12.501

```
                        Explosive         Fr.   528012
                        Fonit             It.   8001
                        Fontana           It.   LPU8001
                        Forum             USA   F-9056
                        Hall of Fame      USA   JG-607
                        Jazz Anthology    Fr.   JA5208
                        Jazztone          USA   J-1203
                        Jazztone          USA   J1280
                        Mode              Fr.   MDR9161
                        Mode              Fr.   MDINT.9168
                        Music Parade      It.   LEL 14
                        Royal Roost       USA   OJ-1
                        Royal Roost       USA   RLP 2213
                        Royal Roost       Jap.  YW-7803-RO
                        Royal Roost       Jap.  YY-7002-RO
                        Roulette          USA   RE-110
                        Roulette          Fr.   CLVLXR.600A
                        Roulette          Jap.  YW-7503-RO
                        Time-Life         USA   P 15515
                        Tulip             Can.  TLP 104
                        Vogue             Eng.  LAE.12209
```

```
New York, New York                           May 21, 1944
         Radio broadcast, "Philco Hall of Fame," on
         NBC radio.  The Art Tatum Trio.  Art Tatum, p;
         Tiny Grimes, g; Slam Stewart, b.
1880  HUMORESQUE* (1:54)

         12 Inch LP  >Aircheck            USA   21
      *Piano solo by Art Tatum.

1890  I KNOW THAT YOU KNOW (3:28)

         12 Inch LP  >Aircheck            USA   21
```

```
New York, New York                           June 21, 1944
         Art Tatum Trio.  Art Tatum, p; Tiny
         Grimes, g; Slam Stewart, b.
         Note: It is not known whether each piece was rehearsed
         just prior to recording, or if all rehearsal took
         place at the beginning.
         The final issued performances begin at 1950.
1900  BOOGIE (3:38) (Rehearsal excerpts featuring quote from, and
               titled as, "Long, Long Ago")

         10 Inch LP  >Folkways            USA   FP 33
                      Folkways            USA   FJ2293
         12 Inch LP   Folkways            USA   FJ12293
                      Folkways            USA   FJ2893

1910  BOOGIE (1:51) (Rehearsal excerpts with riff based on "Tutt´Amor"
               and titled, "Variations On a Theme By Flotow")

         10 Inch LP  >Folkways            USA   FP 33
                      Folkways            USA   FJ2293
         12 Inch LP   Folkways            USA   FJ12293
                      Folkways            USA   FJ2893

1920  IF I HAD YOU (3:25)  (Rehearsal excerpts)

         10 Inch LP  >Folkways            USA   FP 33
                      Folkways            USA   FJ2293
         12 Inch LP   Folkways            USA   FJ12293
                      Folkways            USA   FJ2893

1921  IF I HAD YOU (1:48)  (Rehearsal excerpts)

         10 Inch LP  >Folkways            USA   FP 33
                      Folkways            USA   FJ2293
         12 Inch LP   Folkways            USA   FJ12293
                      Folkways            USA   FJ2893
```

1930 THE JAPANESE SANDMAN (1:35) (Rehearsal excerpt titled,
                                   "Warm Up With Sandman")

                 10 Inch LP >Folkways   USA   FP 33
                             Folkways   USA   FJ2293
                 12 Inch LP Folkways   USA   FJ12293
                             Folkways   USA   FJ2893

1940 SOFT WINDS (4:08) (Rehearsal excerpt titled, "Thou Swell")

                 10 Inch LP >Folkways   USA   FP 33
                             Folkways   USA   FJ2293
                 12 Inch LP Folkways   USA   FJ12293
                             Folkways   USA   FJ2893

1941 SOFT WINDS (4:16) (Rehearsal excerpt titled, "Thou Swell")

                 10 Inch LP >Folkways   USA   FP 33
                             Folkways   USA   FJ2293
                 12 Inch LP Folkways   USA   FJ12293
                             Folkways   USA   FJ2893

1942 SOFT WINDS (4:00) (Rehearsal excerpt titled, "Thou Swell")

                 10 Inch LP >Folkways   USA   FP 33
                             Folkways   USA   FJ2293
                 12 Inch LP Folkways   USA   FJ12293
                             Folkways   USA   FJ2893

1950 BOOGIE (3:45)
      (mx MA1251, 1251-1)
                 12 Inch 78 >Asch   USA   452-1
                             Melojazz   Fr.   7003
                             Stinson   USA   452-1
                 10 Inch LP Stinson   USA   SLP-40
                 12 Inch LP Jazz Anthology   Fr.   JA5208
                             Stinson   USA   SLP 40
                             Time-Life   USA   P 15515
                             Tulip   Can. TLP 104

1960 TOPSY (4:07)
      (mx 12551)
                 12 Inch 78 >Asch   USA   452-2
                             Melojazz   Fr.   7004
                             Stinson   USA   452-2
                 10 Inch LP Stinson   USA   SLP-40
                 12 Inch LP Asch   USA   AA2
                             Jazz Anthology   Fr.   JA5208
                             Stinson   USA   SLP 40
                             Tulip   Can. TLP 104
                             Xtra   Eng. XTRA 1007

1961 TOPSY (4:14)

                 12 Inch LP >Xtra   Eng. XTRA 1007

1970 IF I HAD YOU (3:24)
      (mx 1256-1, MA1256)
                 12 Inch 78 >Asch   USA   452-1
                             Melojazz   Fr.   7003
                             Stinson   USA   452-1
                 7 Inch 45EP Melodisc   Eng. EPM7-108
                 10 Inch LP Stinson   USA   SLP-40
                 12 Inch LP Jazz Anthology   Fr.   JA5208
                             Stinson   USA   SLP 40
                             Tulip   Can. TLP 104
                             Xtra   Eng. XTRA 1007

1980 SOFT WINDS (3:51)
      (mx 12571)
                 12 Inch 78 >Asch   USA   452-2
                             Melojazz   Fr.   7004
                             Stinson   USA   452-2
                 7 Inch 45EP Melodisc   Eng. EPM7-108
                 10 Inch LP Stinson   USA   SLP-40

```
            12 Inch LP    Jazz Anthology    Fr.    JA5208
                          Stinson           USA    SLP 40
                          Tulip             Can.   TLP 104
                          Xtra              Eng.   XTRA 1007

----------------------------------------------------------
New York, New York                            June 25, 1944
            Radio broadcast, "New World A Coming," Program
            #17, on WMCA radio.  Roy Eldridge and Charlie
            Shavers, t; Vic Dickenson and Benny Morton,
            tb; Edmond Hall, cl; Ben Webster, ts; Art
            Tatum, p; Al Casey, g; Slam Stewart, b;
            Arthur Trappier, d.
1983  FINE AND MELLOW* (3:38)

            12 Inch LP   >Totem            USA    1037
      *Also includes Billie Holiday, v.

1984  ROYAL GARDEN BLUES (2:46)
      (mx PS502)
            10 Inch 78   >Gazell           Swed.  2033
            12 Inch LP    Black Lion       Eng.   BLP30166
                          Freedom          Fr.    BLP30166
                          Intercord Black LionGer. 147.000
                          Queen Disc       It.    Q-020
                          Totem            USA    1037

1985  ALL OF ME* (1:43)

            12 Inch LP   >Totem            USA    1037
      *Also includes Billie Holiday, v.

1986  I GOT RHYTHM (2:30 + 0:30 reprise* behind narrator)
      (mx PS503)
            10 Inch 78   >Gazell           Swed.  2033
            12 Inch LP    Black Lion       Eng.   BLP30166
                          Freedom          Fr.    BLP30166
                          Intercord Black LionGer. 147.000
                          Queen Disc       It.    Q-020
                          Totem            USA    1037*

----------------------------------------------------------
New York, New York                             July 5, 1944
            Radio broadcast.  "Mildred Bailey Show," on
            WABC radio.  Piano solo.
1990  HUMORESQUE (3:33)

            16 Inch TX   >AFRS Yank Swing  USA    116,Part 2,
                          Session                 Series H-2
            Note: Announcer is Georgia Gibbs.

----------------------------------------------------------
                                             Fall, 1944
            Live performance.  Piano solo.
2000  AIN'T MISBEHAVIN' (4:28)

            12 Inch LP    Aircheck         USA    21
                          Black Lion       Eng.   BLP30166
                          Freedom          Fr.    BLP30166
                          Intercord Black LionGer. 147.000
            16 Inch TX   >AFRS Command     USA    141*
                          Performance
            *Announcer is Dinah Shore.

----------------------------------------------------------
                                  *September 18, 1944
            Piano solo.
2010  SMOKE GETS IN YOUR EYES (3:08)
      (mx HD5-MM-6636-1)
            12 Inch LP    Aircheck         USA    21
                          Joyce            USA    LP-5005
            16 Inch TX   >AFRS Jubilee     USA    97
                          AFRS Jubilee     USA    123
         *Original manufacturing date. Recording date unknown.
```

```
        ------------------------------------------------------------
New York, New York                          December 20, 1944
         Art Tatum, p; Remo Palmieri, g;
         Specs Powell, d.
2020   I CAN'T GIVE YOU ANYTHING BUT LOVE (3:06)

              16 Inch TX  >AFRS Mildred Bailey USA    13
                           Series

        ------------------------------------------------------------
New York, New York                          December 21, 1944
         Piano solos.
2030   FINE AND DANDY (2:45)
       (mx 1-1)
              10 Inch 78  >Asch               USA    356-1
                           Melodisc           Eng.   1157
                           Melojazz           Fr.    7012
               7 Inch 45EP Melodisc           Eng.   EPM7-108
              10 Inch LP   Stinson            USA    SLP-40
              12 Inch LP   Stinson            USA    SLP 40

2031   FINE AND DANDY (2:42)
       (mx 1-2)
              12 Inch LP   Folkways           USA    FJ2852
                          >Xtra               Eng.   XTRA 1007

2040   IT HAD TO BE YOU (2:33)
       (mx 2-1)
              10 Inch 78  >Asch               USA    356-1
                           Melojazz           Fr.    7011
                           Polydor            Fr.    580.019
              10 Inch LP   Stinson            USA    SLP-40
              12 Inch LP   Folkways           USA    FJ2852
                           Stinson            USA    SLP 40
                           Xtra               Eng.   XTRA 1007

2050   JA-DA (2:27)
       (mx 3-1)
              10 Inch 78  >Asch               USA    356-2
                           Melodisc           Eng.   1157
                           Melojazz           Fr.    7012
              10 Inch LP   Stinson            USA    SLP-40
              12 Inch LP   Folkways           USA    FJ2852
                           Stinson            USA    SLP 40
                           Xtra               Eng.   XTRA 1007

2060   WHERE OR WHEN (2:40)
       (mx 4-1)
              10 Inch 78  >Asch               USA    356-2
                           Melojazz           Fr.    7011
                           Polydor            Fr.    580.019
              10 Inch LP   Stinson            USA    SLP-40
              12 Inch LP   Folkways           USA    FJ2852
                           Stinson            USA    SLP 40
                           Xtra               Eng.   XTRA 1007

2070   SWEET AND LOVELY (2:51)
       (mx 5-1)
              10 Inch 78  >Asch               USA    356-3
                           Melojazz           Fr.    7013
                           Stinson            USA    356-3
               7 Inch 45EP Melodisc           Eng.   EPM7-108
              10 Inch LP   Stinson            USA    SLP-40
              12 Inch LP   Stinson            USA    SLP 40
                           Xtra               Eng.   XTRA 1007

2080   DANNY BOY (2:45)
       (mx 6-1)
              10 Inch 78  >Asch               USA    356-3
                           Melojazz           Fr.    7013
                           Stinson            USA    356-3
              10 Inch LP   Stinson            USA    SLP-40
              12 Inch LP   Folkways           USA    FJ2852
                           Stinson            USA    SLP 40
                           Xtra               Eng.   XTRA 1007

                              46
```

            Barney Bigard Sextet. Joe Thomas, t;
            Barney Bigard, cl; Joe Thomas, ts;
            Art Tatum, p; Billy Taylor, b; Stan
            Levey, d.
2090 CAN'T HELP LOVIN' DAT MAN OF MINE (3:08)
     (mx BW63)
            10 Inch 78 >Black & White   USA   14
            12 Inch LP   Golden Tone   USA   C-4068
                         Overseas   Jap. ULS-1559R
                         Storyville   Dan. SLP 807
                         Tops   USA   L1508

2100 PLEASE DON'T TALK ABOUT ME WHEN I'M GONE (2:51)
     (mx BW64)
            10 Inch 78 >Black & White   USA   14
            12 Inch LP   Harlem Hit Parade   USA   HHP5011
                         Overseas   Jap. ULS-1559R
                         Prestige   USA   P-24052
                         Storyville   Dan. SLP 807
                         Tops   USA   L1508

2110 SWEET MARIJUANA BROWN* (2:51)
     (mx BW65)
            10 Inch 78 >Black & White   USA   13
            12 Inch LP   Konsa   USA   8400
                         Overseas   Jap. ULS-1559R
                         Stash   USA   ST-100
                         Stash   USA   ST120
                         Storyville   Dan. SLP 807
        *Joe Thomas, ts and v.

2120 BLUES FOR ART'S SAKE (2:47)
     (mx BW66)
            10 Inch 78 >Black & White   USA   13
            12 Inch LP   Overseas   Jap. ULS-1559R
                         Storyville   Dan. SLP 807
                         Time-Life   USA   P 15515
                         Tops   USA   L1508

----
                                               c. 1945
        Live performance. Art Tatum, p.
2150 DANNY BOY (2:32)

            12 Inch LP   Kaydee   USA   KD-2
            16 Inch TX >AFRS Jubilee   USA   142

2160 HOW HIGH THE MOON* (1:59)

            12 Inch LP   Kaydee   USA   KD-2
            16 Inch TX >AFRS Jubilee   USA   142
        *Also includes unknown bassist.

Los Angeles, California   January 17, 1945
        Second Esquire Jazz Concert at the
        Philharmonic Auditorium. Art Tatum, p.
2170 THE MAN I LOVE (2:27)

            12 Inch LP   DJM   Eng. DJD 28002
                         DJM   Eng. DJLMD.8002
                         FDC   It.   FDC1009
                         Mercury   Jap. BT-5050
                         Palm 30   Eng. P.30:16
                         Phoenix 10   USA   PHX313
                         Saga   Eng. 6925
                         Sunbeam   USA   SB-219
                         Trip   USA   JT-IX-(2)
                         Trip   USA   TLX-5813
                         Up Front   USA   UPF 156
            16 Inch TX >AFRS Basic Mus.Lib. USA P-232

2180   I CAN´T GIVE YOU ANYTHING BUT LOVE* (2:20)

```
            12 Inch LP    Decca              Ger.   PD 12005
                          DJM                Eng.   DJD 28002
                          DJM                Eng.   DJLMD.8002
                          Ember              Eng.   CJS848
                          FDC                It.    FDC1009
                          Joker              It.    SM 3132
                          Mercury            Jap.   BT-5050
                          Olympic            USA    OL-7120 (E)
                          Palm 30            Eng.   P.30:16
                          Saga               Eng.   6925
                          Sunbeam            USA    SB-219
                          Trip               USA    JT-IX-(2)
                          Trip               USA    TLX-5813
            16 Inch TX  >AFRS Mail Call      USA    132
                         AFRS Basic Mus.Lib  USA    P-233
        *Also includes Junior Raglin, b.
```

California   c. May, 1945
            Piano solos.
2190   HALLELUJAH (3:07)
       (mx ARA-1040-1-A,ARA-1040-1-B,ARA-1040-1C)

```
            10 Inch 78  >ARA                 USA    4501
            12 Inch LP   Black Lion          Eng.   BLP30166
                         Freedom             Fr.    BLP30166
                         Intercord Black LionGer.   147.000
                         Smithsonian         USA    R 029
```

2191   HALLELUJAH (2:40)
       (mx METRO-1040)

```
            10 Inch 78  >Metro Hollywood     USA    23004
                         Rex Hollywood       USA    23004
            10 Inch LP   Rem Hollywood       USA    LP-3
            12 Inch LP   Black Lion          USA    BL-158
                         Black Lion          Eng.   2460-158
                         Black Lion          Eng.   BLP30166
                         Black Lion          Fr.    180.059
                         Black Lion          It.    BLP30124
                         Freedom             Fr.    BLP30.124
                         Freedom             Fr.    BLP30166
                         Intercord Black LionGer.   28 440-6 U
                         Intercord Black LionGer.   147.000
                         Jazz Man            USA    JAZ-5024
                         Smithsonian         USA    R 029
```

2200   POOR BUTTERFLY (3:10)
       (mx ARA-1041-1-A, ARA-1041-1-B)

```
            10 Inch 78  >ARA                 USA    4502
                         Metro Hollywood     USA    23004
                         Rex Hollywood       USA    23004
            10 Inch LP   Rem Hollywood       USA    LP-3
            12 Inch LP   Black Lion          USA    BL-158
                         Black Lion          Eng.   2460-158
                         Black Lion          Eng.   BLP30166
                         Black Lion          Fr.    180.059
                         Black Lion          It.    BLP30124
                         Freedom             Fr.    BLP30.124
                         Freedom             Fr.    BLP30166
                         Intercord Black LionGer.   28 440-6 U
                         Intercord Black LionGer.   147.000
                         Jazz Man            USA    JAZ-5024
            16 Inch TX   AFRS Remember       USA    782
```

2210   SONG OF THE VAGABONDS (3:00)
       (mx ARA-1042-1, ARA-1042-1-A, ARA-1042-1-B)

```
            10 Inch 78  >ARA                 USA    4504
                         Metro Hollywood     USA    23003
                         Rex Hollywood       USA    23003
            10 Inch LP   Rem Hollywood       USA    LP-3
            12 Inch LP   Black Lion          USA    BL-158
                         Black Lion          Eng.   2460-158
                         Black Lion          Eng.   BLP30166
                         Black Lion          Fr.    180.059
```

```
                        Black Lion            It.   BLP30124
                        Freedom               Fr.   BLP30.124
                        Freedom               Fr.   BLP30166
                        Intercord Black LionGer.    28 440-6 U
                        Intercord Black LionGer.    147.000
                        Jazz Man              USA   JAZ-5024
            16 Inch TX  AFRS Basic Mus.Lib. USA     P-774

2220  LOVER (2:58)
      (mx ARA-1043-1-A, ARA-1043-1-B)
            10 Inch 78  >ARA                  USA   4502
                        Metro Hollywood       USA   23003
                        Rex Hollywood         USA   23003
            10 Inch LP  Rem Hollywood         USA   LP-3
            12 Inch LP  Black Lion            Eng.  BLP30166
                        Freedom               Fr.   BLP30166
                        Intercord Black LionGer.    147.000
            16 Inch TX  AFRS Basic Mus.Lib. USA     P-774

2230  MEMORIES OF YOU (3:08)
      (mx ARA-1044A, ARA-1044-A, ARA-1044-B)
            10 Inch 78  >ARA                  USA   4501
                        Metro Hollywood       USA   23002
                        Rex Hollywood         USA   23002
            10 Inch LP  Rem Hollywood         USA   LP-3
            12 Inch LP  Black Lion            USA   BL-158
                        Black Lion            Eng.  2460-158
                        Black Lion            Eng.  BLP30166
                        Black Lion            Fr.   180.059
                        Black Lion            It.   BLP30124
                        Freedom               Fr.   BLP30.124
                        Freedom               Fr.   BLP30166
                        Intercord Black LionGer.    28 440-6 U
                        Intercord Black LionGer.    147.000
                        Jazz Man              USA   JAZ-5024
                        Smithsonian           USA   R 029

2240  RUNNIN' WILD (2:55)
      (mx ARA-1045-1-A, ARA-1045-1-B)
            10 Inch 78  >ARA                  USA   4503
                        Metro Hollywood       USA   23002
                        Rex Hollywood         USA   23002
            10 Inch LP  Rem Hollywood         USA   LP-3
            12 Inch LP  Black Lion            USA   BL-158
                        Black Lion            Eng.  2460-158
                        Black Lion            Eng.  BLP30166
                        Black Lion            Fr.   180.059
                        Black Lion            It.   BLP30124
                        Freedom               Fr.   BLP30.124
                        Freedom               Fr.   BLP30166
                        Intercord Black LionGer.    28 440-6 U
                        Intercord Black LionGer.    147.000
                        Jazz Man              USA   JAZ-5024
            16 Inch TX  AFRS Basic Mus.Lib. USA     P-774

2250  YESTERDAYS (3:07)
      (mx ARA-1046-1, ARA-1046-1-A, ARA-1046-1B, ARA-1046-1-B)
            10 Inch 78  >ARA                  USA   4503
                        Metro Hollywood       USA   23001
                        Rex Hollywood         USA   23001
            10 Inch LP  Rem Hollywood         USA   LP-3
            12 Inch LP  Black Lion            Eng.  BLP30166
                        Freedom               Fr.   BLP30166
                        Intercord Black LionGer.    147.000
                        Smithsonian           USA   R 029
            16 Inch TX  AFRS Jubilee 1947     USA   Unnumbered
                        Christmas Show

2260  THE KERRY DANCE (2:32)
      (mx ARA-1047-1A, ARA-1047-1-A, ARA-1047-1-B)
            10 Inch 78  >ARA                  USA   4504
                        Metro Hollywood       USA   23001
                        Rex Hollywood         USA   23001
            10 Inch LP  Rem Hollywood         USA   LP-3
            12 Inch LP  Black Lion            USA   BL-158
```

```
                        Black Lion               Eng.    2460-158
                        Black Lion               Eng.    BLP30166
                        Black Lion               Fr.     180.059
                        Black Lion               It.     BLP30124
                        Freedom                  Fr.     BLP30.124
                        Freedom                  Fr.     BLP30166
                        Intercord Black LionGer.  28 440-6 U
                        Intercord Black LionGer.  147.000
                        Jazz Man                 USA     JAZ-5024
          16 Inch TX    AFRS Basic Mus.Lib. USA   P-774
```

Hollywood, California   c. 1945
        Live performance at MacGregor Studios
        for AFRS. Murray McEachern and his
        AFRS Orchestra. Gene LaFrenier, t; Bob
        Goodrich, t; Phil Candreva, t; Les Jenkins,
        tb; Bob McReynolds, tb; Ray Coniff, tb;
        Murray McEachern, cl; Skeets Herfurt, as;
        Payton Laguere, as; Babe Russin, ts;
        Art Tatum, p.; Les Paul, g; Jud Denaut, b;
        Unknown, d.

2270 BEGIN THE BEGUINE[1] (3:14)
      (mx JDB20, serial B44988 & mx JDB20, serial D6-TC-5058)
```
          12 Inch 78    V-Disc (Army)[2]     USA    634
          10 Inch LP    Palm Club            Fr.    PALM 18
          12 Inch LP    Black Lion           Eng.   BLP30203
                        Freedom              Fr.    FR.11007
                        Giants of Jazz       USA    GOJ-1018
                        Shoestring           USA    SS-105
          16 Inch TX    AFRS Basic Mus.Lib.  USA    P-545
                        >AFRS Swingtime      USA    H52-37
```
      [1]Piano solo by Art Tatum.
      [2]The V-Disc issue of this performance had "Indiana"
         on the same side. The latter was performed later and
         appears at [2720].

2280 CHEROKEE (5:37)
```
          12 Inch LP    Giants of Jazz       USA    GOJ-1018
          16 Inch TX    >AFRS Swingtime      USA    H52-37
```

2290 DOWN BY THE OLD MILL STREAM[3] (3:39)
```
          16 Inch TX    >AFRS Swingtime      USA    H52-37
```
      [3]Also includes Jack Martin and Martha Stewart, v;
         Mel Torme and the Mel-Tones, vg.

                                              October 23, 1945
        Radio broadcast, "Chesterfield Supper
        Club,". Art Tatum, p; unknown, b.
2300 SWEET LORRAINE (2:06)
```
          12 Inch LP    >Aircheck            USA    21
```

2310 HOW HIGH THE MOON* (2:12)
```
          12 Inch LP    >Aircheck            USA    21
```
      *The last chord is played by the studio orchestra.

New York, New York   October 26, 1945
        Piano solos.
2320 GERSHWIN MEDLEY (4:16)
      (mx VP1692, serial B44382)
```
          12 Inch 78    >V-Disc (Army)       USA    604
          10 Inch LP    Palm Club            Fr.    PALM 18
          12 Inch LP    Black Lion           Eng.   BLP30203
                        Freedom              Fr.    FR.11007
```

```
2330  SHE´S FUNNY THAT WAY (3:35 + 0:30 spoken intro. by Tatum)
      (mx VP1709, serial B44530)
            12 Inch 78  >V-Disc (Army)      USA   604
            10 Inch LP   Palm Club          Fr.   PALM 18
            12 Inch LP   Black Lion         Eng.  BLP30203
                         Dan                Jap.  VC-5010
                         Freedom            Fr.   FR.11007

2340  LOVER (3:50)
      (mx VP1710, serial B44441)
            12 Inch 78  >V-Disc (Army)      USA   620
            10 Inch LP   Palm Club          Fr.   PALM 18
            12 Inch LP   Black Lion         Eng.  BLP30203
                         Freedom            Fr.   FR.11007

2350  BODY AND SOUL (3:07 + 0:16 spoken intro. by Tatum)
      (mx VP1711, serial B44523)
            12 Inch 78  >V-Disc (Army)      USA   620
            10 Inch LP   Palm Club          Fr.   PALM 20
            12 Inch LP   Black Lion         Eng.  BLP30203
                         Freedom            Fr.   FR.11007

2354  I´M BEGINNING TO SEE THE LIGHT (3:06)
      (mx JDB72, serial B45222)
            12 Inch 78  >V-Disc (Army)      USA   663
            10 Inch LP   Palm Club          Fr.   PALM 20
            12 Inch LP   Black Lion         Eng.  BLP30203
                         Europa Jazz        It.   EJ-1011
                         Freedom            Fr.   FR.11007

2355  NINE TWENTY SPECIAL (2:26)
      (mx JDB72, serial B45222)
            12 Inch 78  >V-Disc (Army)      USA   663
            10 Inch LP   Palm Club          Fr.   PALM 20
            12 Inch LP   Black Lion         Eng.  BLP30203
                         Freedom            Fr.   FR.11007

---------------------------------------------------------
                                          c. 1945
          Piano solos.
      Note: These are generally believed to have been recorded
      c. 1945.  However, the authors have a copy of Standard 191
      which bears the following legend, in ink: "Production Test
      1/22/44."  Therefore, if this notation is accurate, these
      performances took place on or before January 22, 1944.
2360  YOU TOOK ADVANTAGE OF ME (2:10)
      (mx ND3-MM-7196-1)
            10 Inch LP   Mecolico           Eng.  1/8
            12 Inch LP   Alamac             USA   QSR 2428
                         Alamac             Fr.   180.050
                         DJM                Eng.  DJD 28002
                         DJM                Eng.  DJLMD.8002
                         GNP Crescendo      USA   GNP9025
                         GNP Crescendo      Jap.  LAX-3088
                         Jazz Piano         Dan.  JP5005
                         Jazz Series 4000FC It.   JAZ4005
                         Joker              It.   SM 3117
                         Koala              USA   K.O. 14278
                         Mercury            Jap.  BT-5049
                         Pick               Braz. 308.0013
                         Trip               USA   JT-IX-(2)
                         Trip               USA   TLX-5813
                         Vogue              Eng.  VJD 511-1
                         Vogue              Fr.   DP.31A
            16 Inch TX  >Standard           USA   Q190

2370  BODY AND SOUL (2:50)
      (mx ND3-MM-7196-1)
            10 Inch LP   Mecolico           Eng.  1/8
            12 Inch LP   GNP Crescendo      USA   GNP9025
                         GNP Crescendo      Jap.  LAX-3088
                         Jazz Series 4000FC It.   JAZ4005
                         Joker              It.   SM 3117
                         Pick               Braz. 308.0013
                         Vogue              Belg. VK 30

                         51
```

		Vogue	Eng.	VJD 511-1
		Vogue	Fr.	DP.31A
	16 Inch TX	>Standard	USA	Q190

2380 I GUESS I´LL HAVE TO CHANGE MY PLANS (2:20)
   (mx ND3-MM-7196-1)

	10 Inch LP	Mecolico	Eng.	1/8
	12 Inch LP	Alamac	USA	QSR 2428
		Alamac	Fr.	180.050
		DJM	Eng.	DJD 28002
		DJM	Eng.	DJLMD.8002
		GNP Crescendo	USA	GNP9025
		GNP Crescendo	Jap.	LAX-3088
		Jazz Piano	Dan.	JP5005
		Jazz Series 4000FC	It.	JAZ4005
		Joker	It.	SM 3117
		Koala	USA	K.O. 14278
		Mercury	Jap.	BT-5049
		Pick	Braz.	308.0013
		Trip	USA	JT-IX-(2)
		Trip	USA	TLX-5813
		Vogue	Eng.	VJD 511-1
		Vogue	Fr.	DP.31A
	16 Inch TX	>Standard	USA	Q190

2390 WHAT IS THIS THING CALLED LOVE (2:35)
   (mx ND3-MM-7196-1)

	10 Inch LP	Mecolico	Eng.	1/8
	12 Inch LP	Alamac	USA	QSR 2428
		Alamac	Fr.	180.050
		DJM	Eng.	DJD 28002
		DJM	Eng.	DJLMD.8002
		GNP Crescendo	USA	GNP9026
		GNP Crescendo	Jap.	LAX-3089
		Jazz Piano	Dan.	JP5005
		Jazz Series 4000FC	It.	JAZ4006
		Joker	It.	SM 3117
		Koala	USA	K.O. 14278
		Mercury	Jap.	BT-5049
		Trip	USA	JT-IX-(2)
		Trip	USA	TLX-5813
		Vogue	Belg.	VK 30
		Vogue	Eng.	VJD 511-2
		Vogue	Fr.	DP.31B
	16 Inch TX	>Standard	USA	Q190

2400 CRAZY RHYTHM (2:15)
   (mx ND3-MM-7196-1)

	10 Inch LP	Mecolico	Eng.	1/8
	12 Inch LP	DJM	Eng.	DJD 28002
		DJM	Eng.	DJLMD.8002
		GNP Crescendo	USA	GNP9026
		GNP Crescendo	Jap.	LAX-3089
		Jazz Series 4000FC	It.	JAZ4006
		Jazz Piano	Dan.	JP5005
		Joker	It.	SM 3117
		Koala	USA	K.O. 14278
		Mercury	Jap.	BT-5049
		Pick	Braz.	308.0013
		Trip	USA	JT-IX-(2)
		Trip	USA	TLX-5813
		Vogue	Belg.	VK 30
		Vogue	Eng.	VJD 511-2
		Vogue	Fr.	DP.31B
	16 Inch TX	>Standard	USA	Q190

2410 CAN´T WE BE FRIENDS (2:30)
   (mx ND3-MM-7197-1)

	10 Inch LP	Mecolico	Eng.	1/8
	12 Inch LP	Alamac	USA	QSR 2428
		Alamac	Fr.	180.050
		DJM	Eng.	DJD 28002
		DJM	Eng.	DJLMD.8002
		Ember	Eng.	CJS848
		GNP Crescendo	USA	GNP9026

```
                       GNP Crescendo       Jap.   LAX-3089
                       Jazz Series 4000FC  It.    JAZ4006
                       Joker               It.    SM 3117
                       Mercury             Jap.   BT-5049
                       Olympic             USA    OL-7120 (E)
                       Pick                Braz.  308.0013
                       Trip                USA    JT-IX-(2)
                       Trip                USA    TLX-5813
                       Vogue               Belg.  VK 30
                       Vogue               Eng.   VJD 511-2
                       Vogue               Fr.    DP.31B
          16 Inch TX  >Standard            USA    Q190

2420  LIMEHOUSE BLUES (2:15)
      (mx ND3-MM-7197-1)
          10 Inch LP   Mecolico            Eng.   1/8
          12 Inch LP   Alamac              USA    QSR 2428
                       Alamac              Fr.    180.050
                       DJM                 Eng.   DJD 28002
                       DJM                 Eng.   DJLMD.8002
                       Ember               Eng.   CJS848
                       GNP Crescendo       USA    GNP9026
                       GNP Crescendo       Jap.   LAX-3089
                       Jazz Piano          Dan.   JP5005
                       Jazz Series 4000FC  It.    JAZ4006
                       Joker               It.    SM 3117
                       Mercury             Jap.   BT-5049
                       Olympic             USA    OL-7120 (E)
                       Phoenix 10          USA    PHX313
                       Pick                Braz.  308.0013
                       Trip                USA    JT-IX-(2)
                       Trip                USA    TLX-5813
                       Up Front            USA    UPF 156
                       Vogue               Eng.   VJD 511-2
                       Vogue               Fr.    DP.31B
          16 Inch TX  >Standard            USA    Q190

2430  AMONG MY SOUVENIRS (2:45)
      (mx ND3-MM-7197-1)
          10 Inch LP   Mecolico            Eng.   1/8
          12 Inch LP   DJM                 Eng.   DJD 28002
                       DJM                 Eng.   DJLMD.8002
                       Ember               Eng.   CJS848
                       GNP Crescendo       USA    GNP9026
                       GNP Crescendo       Jap.   LAX-3089
                       Jazz Piano          Dan.   JP5005
                       Jazz Series 4000FC  It.    JAZ4006
                       Joker               It.    SM 3117
                       Mercury             Jap.   BT-5050
                       Olympic             USA    OL-7120 (E)
                       Phoenix 10          USA    PHX313
                       Pick                Braz.  308.0013
                       Trip                USA    JT-IX-(2)
                       Trip                USA    TLX-5813
                       Up Front            USA    UPF 156
                       Vogue               Belg.  VK 30
                       Vogue               Eng.   VJD 511-2
                       Vogue               Fr.    DP.31B
          16 Inch TX  >Standard            USA    Q190

2440  I'M GONNA SIT RIGHT DOWN AND WRITE MYSELF A LETTER (2:40)
      (mx ND3-MM-7197-1)
          10 Inch LP   Mecolico            Eng.   1/8
          12 Inch LP   DJM                 Eng.   DJD 28002
                       DJM                 Eng.   DJLMD.8002
                       GNP Crescendo       USA    GNP9026
                       GNP Crescendo       Jap.   LAX-3089
                       Jazz Series 4000FC  It.    JAZ4006
                       Joker               It.    SM 3117
                       Mercury             Jap.   BT-5050
                       Trip                USA    JT-IX-(2)
                       Trip                USA    TLX-5813
                       Vogue               Belg.  VK 30
                       Vogue               Eng.   VJD 511-2
                       Vogue               Fr.    DP.31B
```

```
                16 Inch TX   >Standard              USA   Q190

2450  STAY AS SWEET AS YOU ARE (2:40)
      (mx ND3-MM-7197-1)
                10 Inch LP   Mecolico              Eng.  1/8
                12 Inch LP   DJM                   Eng.  DJD 28002
                             DJM                   Eng.  DJLMD.8002
                             GNP Crescendo         USA   GNP9026
                             GNP Crescendo         Jap.  LAX-3089
                             Jazz Series 4000FC    It.   JAZ4006
                             Joker                 It.   SM 3117
                             Mercury               Jap.  BT-5050
                             Phoenix 10            USA   PHX313
                             Pick                  Braz. 308.0013
                             Trip                  USA   JT-IX-(2)
                             Trip                  USA   TLX-5813
                             Up Front              USA   UPF 156
                             Vogue                 Eng.  VJD 511-2
                             Vogue                 Fr.   DP.31B
                16 Inch TX   >Standard              USA   Q190

2460  SOMEBODY LOVES ME (2:17)
      (mx ND3-MM-7197-1)
                12 Inch LP   DJM                   Eng.  DJD 28002
                             DJM                   Eng.  DJLMD.8002
                             Epitaph               USA   E-4006
                             GNP Crescendo         USA   GNP9025
                             GNP Crescendo         Jap.  LAX-3088
                             Jazz Series 4000FC    It.   JAZ4005
                             Mercury               Jap.  BT-5050
                             RI Disc               Swiss RI-DISC 7
                             Trip                  USA   JT-IX-(2)
                             Trip                  USA   TLX-5813
                             Vogue                 Belg. VK 30
                             Vogue                 Eng.  VJD 511-1
                             Vogue                 Fr.   DP.31A
                16 Inch TX   >Standard              USA   Q191

2470  WHY WAS I BORN (2:36)
      (mx ND3-MM-7198-1)
                12 Inch LP   DJM                   Eng.  DJD 28002
                             DJM                   Eng.  DJLMD.8002
                             Epitaph               USA   E-4006
                             GNP Crescendo         USA   GNP9025
                             GNP Crescendo         Jap.  LAX-3088
                             Jazz Series 4000FC    It.   JAZ4005
                             Mercury               Jap.  BT-5050
                             Phoenix 10            USA   PHX313
                             RI Disc               Swiss RI-DISC 7
                             Trip                  USA   JT-IX-(2)
                             Trip                  USA   TLX-5813
                             Up Front              USA   UPF 156
                             Vogue                 Eng.  VJD 511-1
                             Vogue                 Fr.   DP.31A
                16 Inch TX   >Standard              USA   Q191
2480  IF I COULD BE WITH YOU (2:41)
      (mx ND3-MM-7198-1)
                12 Inch LP   DJM                   Eng.  DJD 28002
                             DJM                   Eng.  DJLMD.8002
                             Epitaph               USA   E-4006
                             GNP Crescendo         USA   GNP9025
                             GNP Crescendo         Jap.  LAX-3088
                             Jazz Series 4000FC    It.   JAZ4005
                             Mercury               Jap.  BT-5050
                             Pick                  Braz. 308.0013
                             RI Disc               Swiss RI-DISC 7
                             Trip                  USA   JT-IX-(2)
                             Trip                  USA   TLX-5813
                             Vogue                 Eng.  VJD 511-1
                             Vogue                 Fr.   DP.31A
                16 Inch TX   >Standard              USA   Q191
```

54

```
2490   TEA FOR TWO (2:29)
       (mx ND3-MM-7198-1)
              12 Inch LP    DJM               Eng.  DJD 28002
                            DJM               Eng.  DJLMD.8002
                            Ember             Eng.  CJS848
                            Epitaph           USA   E-4006
                            Mercury           Jap.  BT-5050
                            Olympic           USA   OL-7120 (E)
                            RI Disc           Swiss RI-DISC 7
                            Trip              USA   JT-IX-(2)
                            Trip              USA   TLX-5813
              16 Inch TX   >Standard          USA   Q191

2500   MEAN TO ME (2:32)
       (mx ND3-MM-7198-1)
              12 Inch LP    DJM               Eng.  DJD 28002
                            DJM               Eng.  DJLMD.8002
                            Epitaph           USA   E-4006
                            GNP Crescendo     USA   GNP9025
                            GNP Crescendo     Jap.  LAX-3088
                            Jazz Series 4000FC It.   JAZ4005
                            Mercury           Jap.  BT-5050
                            Phoenix 10        USA   PHX313
                            Pick              Braz. 308.0013
                            RI Disc           Swiss RI-DISC 7
                            Trip              USA   JT-IX-(2)
                            Trip              USA   TLX-5813
                            Up Front          USA   UPF 156
                            Vogue             Belg. VK 30
                            Vogue             Eng.  VJD 511-1
                            Vogue             Fr.   DP.31A
              16 Inch TX   >Standard          USA   Q191

2510   IT'S ONLY A PAPER MOON (2:41)
       (mx ND3-MM-7199-1)
              12 Inch LP    Epitaph           USA   E-4006
                            GNP Crescendo     USA   GNP9025
                            GNP Crescendo     Jap.  LAX-3088
                            Jazz Series 4000FC It.   JAZ4005
                            Pick              Braz. 308.0013
                            RI Disc           Swiss RI-DISC 7
                            Vogue             Belg. VK 30
                            Vogue             Eng.  VJD 511-1
                            Vogue             Fr.   DP.31A
              16 Inch TX   >Standard          USA   Q191

2520   JUST A GIGOLO (2:19)
       (mx ND3-MM-7199-1)
              12 Inch LP    Epitaph           USA   E-4006
                            GNP Crescendo     USA   GNP9025
                            GNP Crescendo     Jap.  LAX-3088
                            Jazz Series 4000FC It.   JAZ4005
                            RI Disc           Swiss RI-DISC 7
                            Vogue             Eng.  VJD 511-1
                            Vogue             Fr.   416039
                            Vogue             Fr.   DP.31A
              16 Inch TX   >Standard          USA   Q191

2530   THREE LITTLE WORDS (2:16)
       (mx ND3-MM-7199-1)
              12 Inch LP    DJM               Eng.  DJD 28002
                            DJM               Eng.  DJLMD.8002
                            Epitaph           USA   E-4006
                            GNP Crescendo     USA   GNP9025
                            GNP Crescendo     Jap.  LAX-3088
                            Jazz Series 4000FC It.   JAZ4005
                            Mercury           Jap.  BT-5050
                            RI Disc           Swiss RI-DISC 7
                            Trip              USA   JT-IX-(2)
                            Trip              USA   TLX-5813
                            Vogue             Eng.  VJD 511-1
                            Vogue             Fr.   DP.31A
              16 Inch TX   >Standard          USA   Q191
```

```
2540   I GOTTA RIGHT TO SING THE BLUES (2:32)
       (mx ND3-MM-7199-1)
                  12 Inch LP     DJM                 Eng.   DJD 28002
                                 DJM                 Eng.   DJLMD.8002
                                 Ember               Eng.   CJS848
                                 Epitaph             USA    E-4006
                                 GNP Crescendo       USA    GNP9025
                                 GNP Crescendo       Jap.   LAX-3088
                                 Jazz Series 4000FC  It.    JAZ4005
                                 Mercury             Jap.   BT-5050
                                 Olympic             USA    OL-7120  (E)
                                 RI Disc             Swiss  RI-DISC 7
                                 Trip                USA    JT-IX-(2)
                                 Trip                USA    TLX-5813
                                 Up Front            USA    UPF 156
                                 Vogue               Eng.   VJD 511-1
                                 Vogue               Fr.    DP.31A
                  16 Inch TX    >Standard            USA    Q191

2550   ON THE SUNNY SIDE OF THE STREET (2:25)
       (mx ND3-MM-7199-1)
                  12 Inch LP     DJM                 Eng.   DJD 28002
                                 DJM                 Eng.   DJLMD.8002
                                 Ember               Eng.   CJS848
                                 GNP Crescendo       USA    GNP9025
                                 GNP Crescendo       Jap.   LAX-3088
                                 Jazz Series 4000FC  It.    JAZ4005
                                 Mercury             Jap.   BT-5050
                                 Olympic             USA    OL-7120  (E)
                                 RI Disc             Swiss  RI-DISC 7
                                 Trip                USA    JT-IX-(2)
                                 Trip                USA    TLX-5813
                                 Vogue               Belg.  VK 30
                                 Vogue               Eng.   VJD 511-1
                                 Vogue               Fr.    DP.31A
                  16 Inch TX    >Standard            USA    Q191

----------------------------------------------------------
New York, New York                          c. 1946
       Piano solos.
       *Note: Titles from this group which are marked
       with an asterisk are listed here because they
       have been commercially issued and attributed
       to Art Tatum.  They are not believed to have
       been played by Tatum; they were probably played
       by Frank Paparelli.
2570   GANG O´ NOTES (2:42)

                  12 Inch LP     Black Lion          USA    BL-158
                                 Black Lion          Eng.   2460-158
                                 Black Lion          Fr.    180.059
                                 Black Lion          It.    BLP30124
                                >Fontana             Eng.   FJL.904
                                 Fontana             Holl.  883 904JCY
                                 Freedom             Fr.    BLP30.124
                                 Intercord Black LionGer.   28 440-6 U
                                 Jazz Man            USA    JAZ-5024
                                 Savoy               USA    MG12162,
                                                            (Unissued)

2580  *FIFTY SECOND STREET BLUES (3:44)

                  12 Inch LP     Black Lion          USA    BL-158
                                 Black Lion          Eng.   2460-158
                                 Black Lion          Fr.    180.059
                                 Black Lion          It.    BLP30124
                                >Fontana             Eng.   FJL.904
                                 Fontana             Holl.  883 904JCY
                                 Freedom             Fr.    BLP30.124
                                 Intercord Black LionGer.   28 440-6 U
                                 Jazz Man            USA    JAZ-5024
                                 Savoy               USA    MG12162,
                                                            (Unissued)
```

2590 *JUST BEFORE DAWN (3:27)

```
         12 Inch LP    Black Lion            USA    BL-158
                       Black Lion            Eng.   2460-158
                       Black Lion            Fr.    180.059
                       Black Lion            It.    BLP30124
                      >Fontana               Eng.   FJL.904
                       Fontana               Holl.  883 904JCY
                       Freedom               Fr.    BLP30.124
                       Intercord Black LionGer.     28 440-6 U
                       Jazz Man              USA    JAZ-5024
                       Savoy                 USA    MG12162,
                                                    (Unissued)
```

2600 CRYSTAL CLEAR (2:57)

```
         12 Inch LP   >Fontana               Eng.   FJL.904
                       Fontana               Holl.  883 904JCY
                       Savoy                 USA    MG12162,
                                                    (Unissued)
```

2610 *A MIDNIGHT MELODY (4:02)

```
         12 Inch LP    Black Lion            USA    BL-158
                       Black Lion            Eng.   2460-158
                       Black Lion            Fr.    180.059
                       Black Lion            It.    BLP30124
                      >Fontana               Eng.   FJL.904
                       Fontana               Holl.  883 904JCY
                       Freedom               Fr.    BLP30.124
                       Intercord Black LionGer.     28 440-6 U
                       Jazz Man              USA    JAZ-5024
                       Savoy                 USA    MG12162,
                                                    (Unissued)
```

2620 APOLLO BOOGIE (2:25)

```
         12 Inch LP    Black Lion            USA    BL-158
                       Black Lion            Eng.   2460-158
                       Black Lion            Fr.    180.059
                       Black Lion            It.    BLP30124
                      >Fontana               Eng.   FJL.904
                       Fontana               Holl.  883 904JCY
                       Freedom               Fr.    BLP30.124
                       Intercord Black LionGer.     28 440-6 U
                       Jazz Man              USA    JAZ-5024
                       Savoy                 USA    MG12162,
                                                    (Unissued)
```

2630 *TOO SHARP FOR THIS FLAT (3:36)

```
         12 Inch LP   >Fontana               Eng.   FJL.904
                       Fontana               Holl.  883 904JCY
                       Savoy                 USA    MG12162,
                                                    (Unissued)
```

2640 *THIS AND THAT (3:32)

```
         12 Inch LP   >Fontana               Eng.   FJL.904
                       Fontana               Holl.  883 904JCY
                       Savoy                 USA    MG12162,
                                                    (Unissued)
```

2650 BETWEEN MIDNIGHT AND DAWN (2:47)

```
         12 Inch LP    Black Lion            USA    BL-158
                       Black Lion            Eng.   2460-158
                       Black Lion            Fr.    180.059
                       Black Lion            It.    BLP30124
                      >Fontana               Eng.   FJL.904
                       Fontana               Holl.  883 904JCY
                       Freedom               Fr.    BLP30.124
                       Intercord Black LionGer.     28 440-6 U
                       Jazz Man              USA    JAZ-5024
                       Savoy                 USA    MG12162,
```

2660 *PLAYING IN RIDDLES (4:02)
```
              12 Inch LP  >Fontana          Eng.  FJL.904
                           Fontana          Holl. 883 904JCY
                           Savoy            USA   MG12162,
                                                  (Unissued)
```

2670 BLUES ON THE ROCKS** (3:04)
```
                           Savoy            USA   MG12162,
                                                  (Unissued)
```
Note: Savoy Records had acetates of all of the above titles, which they never issued. The acetates bore titles corresponding to lead sheets which do exist, and credit Art Tatum as the composer. Since these original titles were purely arbitrary to begin with, the issued titles have been used in this discography to avoid confusion. The table below shows the correct original titles as listed on the Savoy acetates and the lead sheets:

Title As Listed Above:	Title on Savoy Acetate:
Gang O´ Notes	Playing In Riddles
Fifty Second Street Blues	Crystal Clear
Just Before Dawn	Blues On the Rocks
Crystal Clear	Just Before Dawn
A Midnight Melody	Fifty Second Street Blues
Apollo Boogie	This and That
Too Sharp For This Flat	A Midnight Melody
This and That	Apollo Boogie
Between Midnight and Dawn	Gang O´ Notes
Playing In Riddles	Between Midnight and Dawn

**The Savoy acetate marked "Too Sharp For This Flat" has not been issued, and is arbitrarily listed here as "Blues On the Rocks," which was the remaining title used on the Savoy acetates.

Hollywood, California   January 21, 1946
          Piano solos.
2680 WHERE OR WHEN (3:53)
      (mx JDB18B, serial D6-TC-5056*; mx JDB34B, serial D6-TC-5067)
```
          12 Inch 78  >V-Disc (Army)        USA   644
          10 Inch LP   Palm Club            Fr.   PALM 18
          12 Inch LP   Black Lion           Eng.  BLP30203
                       Freedom              Fr.   FR.11007
                       Shoestring           USA   SS-105
                       V-Disc               It.   VDL 1008
          16 Inch TX   AFRS Basic Mus.Lib.  USA   P-545
```
          *Note: This is an unissued test pressing which also contains a 0:03 spoken introduction by Tatum.

2685 LOUISE (3:02)
      (mx MM4607)
```
          16 Inch TX  >AFRS Jubilee         USA   167
```

2690 SONG OF THE VAGABONDS (2:14)
      (mx JDB34B, serial D6-TC-5067)
```
          12 Inch 78   V-Disc (Army)        USA   *644
          10 Inch LP   Palm Club            Fr.   *PALM 18
          12 Inch LP   Aircheck             USA   21
                       Black Lion           Eng.  *BLP30203
                       Freedom              Fr.   *FR.11007
                       V-Disc               It.   VDL 1008
          16 Inch TX  >AFRS Jubilee         USA   168
```
          *These versions lack the last three notes.

2700 NIGHT AND DAY (1:26)
      (mx SSL-1087)
```
          12 Inch LP   Shoestring           USA   SS-105
          16 Inch TX  >AFRS Basic Mus.Lib.  USA   P-545
```

```
2710   POOR BUTTERFLY (3:23 + 0:03 spoken introduction by Tatum)
       (mx JDB19, serial  B44987)
                  12 Inch 78  >V-Disc (Army)       USA   634
                  10 Inch LP   Palm Club           Fr.   PALM 20
                  12 Inch LP   Black Lion          Eng.  BLP30203
                               Freedom             Fr.   FR.11007
                               Shoestring          USA   SS-105
                               V-Disc              It.   VDL 1008
                  16 Inch TX   AFRS Basic Mus.Lib. USA   P-545

2720   INDIANA (2:33)
       (mx JDB20, serial B44988 & mx JDB20, serial D6-TC-5058)
                  12 Inch 78  >V-Disc (Army)*      USA   634
                  12 Inch LP   Black Lion          Eng.  BLP30203
                               Freedom             Fr.   FR.11007
                  10 Inch LP   Palm Club           Fr.   PALM 18
       *The V-Disc issue of this performance had "Begin the
       Beguine" on the same side.  The latter was performed
       earlier and appears as index #2270.

-----------------------------------------------------------
Hollywood, California                         Between June 15th
                                              & October 1, 1946
             Art Tatum's All-Stars, as they appeared
             in the film "The Fabulous Dorseys."  Ziggy
             Elman, t; Tommy Dorsey, tb; Jimmy Dorsey,
             cl; Charlie Barnet, ts; Art Tatum, p.;
             Ray Bauduc, d.
2750   TURQUOISE* (1:37)

                                              USA   Unissued
       *Piano solo by Art Tatum in background behind dialogue.

2760   ART'S BLUES (2:39)

                  12 Inch LP   Europa Jazz         It.   EJ-1011
                              >Extreme Rarities    USA   ER-1002

-----------------------------------------------------------
New York, New York                            January 20, 1947
             Piano solos.
2770   SMOKE GETS IN YOUR EYES (2:55)
       (mx D7-VB-74)
                  10 Inch 78   His Master's Voice  Eng.  B9711
                                                         (Unissued)
                              >RCA Victor          USA   20-2911
                               RCA Victor          Braz. 82-0534
                   7 Inch 45EP RCA Camden          USA   CAE419
                  12 Inch LP   Pickwick Camden     USA   ACL 7015
                               Pickwick Camden     Eng.  ACL 7015
                               RCA Black & White   Fr.   FXM3 7143
                               RCA Black & White   Fr.   730.561
                               RCA Camden          USA   CAL384
                               RCA Camden          USA   CAL882
                               RCA Camden          USA   CAS882(e)
                               RCA Camden          Eng.  CDS 1050
                               RCA Camden          Fr.   900.020
                               RCA Victor          Jap.  RA-29

2780   AIN'T MISBEHAVIN' (2:40)
       (mx D7-VB-75)
                  10 Inch 78   His Master's Voice  Eng   B9711
                                                         (Unissued)
                              >RCA Victor          USA   20-2911
                               RCA Victor          Braz. 82-0534
                   7 Inch 45EP RCA Camden          USA   CAE419
                  10 Inch LP   RCA Victor          USA   LEJ-11
                  12 Inch LP   RCA Black & White   Fr.   FXM3 7143
                               RCA Black & White   Fr.   730.561
                               RCA Camden          USA   CAL328
                               RCA Camden          Eng.  CDN.118
                               RCA Camden          Fr.   800210
                               RCA Camden          Jap.  CL-5031
                               RCA Victor          Jap.  RA-29
                  12 Inch TX   AFRS Amer.Pop.Mus.  USA   198
```

```
                  16 Inch TX    AFRS Basic Mus.Lib.  USA    P-1077
                                AFRS Remember        USA    952

2790   OUT OF NOWHERE (2:50)
       (mx D7-VB-76)
                  10 Inch 78  >His Master's Voice   Swiss  JK2617
                   7 Inch 45EP RCA Camden           USA    CAE419
                                His Master's Voice   Eng.   7EG 8074
                  12 Inch LP   Pickwick Camden       USA    ACL 7015
                                Pickwick Camden       Eng.   ACL 7015
                                RCA Black & White     Fr.    FMX2 7080
                                RCA Black & White     Fr.    730.561
                                RCA Camden            USA    CAL384
                                RCA Camden            USA    CAL882
                                RCA Camden            USA    CAS882(e)
                                RCA Camden            Eng.   CDS 1050
                                RCA Camden            Fr.    900.020
                                RCA Victor            USA    LJM3001
                                RCA Victor            It.    EDP 1004(6)
                                RCA Victor            Jap.   RA-29

2800   CHEROKEE (3:00)
       (mx D7-VB-77)
                  10 Inch 78  >RCA Victor            USA    20-3088
                                His Master's Voice   Swiss  JK2617
                   7 Inch 45    RCA Victor            USA    27-0147
                   7 Inch 45EP  RCA Camden            USA    CAE419
                                RCA Victor            USA    EPBT3031
                  10 Inch LP   His Master's Voice    Eng.   DLP1022
                                RCA Victor            USA    LPT31
                  12 Inch LP   Pickwick Camden       USA    ACL 7015
                                Pickwick Camden       Eng.   ACL 7015
                                RCA Black & White     Fr.    FXM3 7143
                                RCA Black & White     Fr.    730.561
                                RCA Camden            USA    CAL384
                                RCA Camden            USA    CAL882
                                RCA Camden            USA    CAS882(e)
                                RCA Camden            Eng.   CDS 1050
                                RCA Camden            Fr.    900.020
                                RCA Victor            USA    DMM4-0342-4
                                RCA Victor            Jap.   RA-29
                  16 Inch TX    AFRS Basic Mus.Lib.  USA    P-1077
                                AFRS Jill's All-      USA    226
                                  Time Juke Box
                                AFRS Jill's All-      USA    398
                                  Time Juke Box
```

```
New York, New York                            April 5, 1947
       Radio broadcast.  "Piano Playhouse,"
       WJZ radio.  Piano solos.
2810   SWEET LORRAINE (2:03)
       (mx 56-GS-33A)
                  16 Inch TX  >US Treasury Dept.,   USA    72
                                Guest Star Series

2820   SMOKE GETS IN YOUR EYES (2:37)
       (mx DS-229)
                  16 Inch TX  >US Dept. of State    USA    10
                                VOA Piano Play-
                                house Series
```

```
Los Angeles, California                       c.1948(rel.8/8/48)
       Piano solo, with spoken introduction by Tatum.
2830   YESTERDAYS (2:59)
       (mx 56-GS-33A)
                  16 Inch TX  >US Treasury Dept.,   USA    72
                                Guest Star Series
```

```
Los Angeles, California                       c. 1948
       Piano solos.
       Note: It is believed that these were recorded
         at the home of pianist Buddy Cole.
```

2840 WRAP YOUR TROUBLES IN DREAMS (2:57)

                 12 Inch LP   Jazz Anthology   Fr.   JA5218
                               Jazz Chronicles   USA   JCS 101
                               >Jazzz   USA   JAZZZ 101
                               Philips   Jap. 25RJ-26

2850 SITTIN´ AND ROCKIN´ (2:45)

                 12 Inch LP   Jazz Anthology   Fr.   JA5218
                               Jazz Chronicles   USA   JCS 101
                               >Jazzz   USA   JAZZZ 101
                               Philips   Jap. 25RJ-26

2860 YOU´RE DRIVING ME CRAZY (2:20)

                 12 Inch LP   Jazz Anthology   Fr.   JA5218
                               Jazz Chronicles   USA   JCS 101
                               >Jazzz   USA   JAZZZ 101
                               Philips   Jap. 25RJ-26

2870 TENDERLY (3:00)

                 12 Inch LP   Jazz Anthology   Fr.   JA5218
                               Jazz Chronicles   USA   JCS 101
                               >Jazzz   USA   JAZZZ 101
                               Philips   Jap. 25RJ-26

2880 OVER THE RAINBOW (3:25)

                 12 Inch LP   Jazz Anthology   Fr.   JA5218
                               Jazz Chronicles   USA   JCS 101
                               >Jazzz   USA   JAZZZ 101
                               Philips·   Jap. 25RJ-26

2890 IN A SENTIMENTAL MOOD (3:16)

                 12 Inch LP   Jazz Anthology   Fr.   JA5218
                               Jazz Chronicles   USA   JCS 101
                               >Jazzz   USA   JAZZZ 101
                               Philips   Jap. 25RJ-26

2900 YOU TOOK ADVANTAGE OF ME (2:58)

                 12 Inch LP   Jazz Anthology   Fr.   JA5218
                               Jazz Chronicles   USA   JCS 101
                               >Jazzz   USA   JAZZZ 101
                               Philips   Jap. 25RJ-26

2910 IT´S THE TALK OF THE TOWN (3:25)

                 12 Inch LP   Jazz Anthology   Fr.   JA5218
                               Jazz Chronicles   USA   JCS 101
                               >Jazzz   USA   JAZZZ 101
                               Philips   Jap. 25RJ-26

2920 SHE´S FUNNY THAT WAY (2:52)

                 12 Inch LP   Jazz Anthology   Fr.   JA5218
                               Jazz Chronicles   USA   JCS 101
                               >Jazzz   USA   JAZZZ 101
                               Philips   Jap. 25RJ-26

2930 I´LL NEVER BE THE SAME (3:20)

                 12 Inch LP   Jazz Anthology   Fr.   JA5218
                               Jazz Chronicles   USA   JCS 101
                               >Jazzz   USA   JAZZZ 101
                               Philips   Jap. 25RJ-26

2940 NIGHT AND DAY (3:25)

                 12 Inch LP   Jazz Anthology   Fr.   JA5218
                               Jazz Chronicles   USA   JCS 101
                               >Jazzz   USA   JAZZZ 101

```
------------------------------------------------------------
Los Angeles, California                          April 2, 1949
          Live, at the Shrine Auditorium.
          Piano solos.
2950  HOW HIGH THE MOON (2:28)
      (mx JJ80)
          10 Inch 78    Jazz Selection      Fr.   655
                        Vogue               Eng.  V2241
           7 Inch 45EP  Columbia            Eng.  SEG7561,
                                                  (Unissued)
                        Fontana             Eng.  TFE.17236
                        Philips             It.   429 622 BE
                        Vogue               Eng.  EPV1008
          10 Inch LP    Columbia            USA   CL 2565
                        Columbia            USA   CL 6301
                       >Columbia            USA   GL 101
                        Columbia            Jap.  ZL-1028
                        Philips             It.   BO7902R
                        Vogue               Eng.  L.D.E.081
                        Vogue               Fr.   L.D. 029
          12 Inch LP    CBS                 Holl. 62615
                        CBS Realm Jazz      Eng.  RM52601
                        Columbia            USA   CS9655
                        Harmony             USA   HL7006

2960  HUMORESQUE (3:48)
      (mx JJ81)
          10 Inch 78    Jazz Selection      Fr.   655
                        Vogue               Eng.  V2241
           7 Inch 45    Columbia            USA   75
           7 Inch 45EP  Columbia            USA   4-75-G
                        Columbia            Eng.  SEG7561,
                                                  (Unissued)
                        Fontana             Eng.  TFE.17237
                        Philips             Eng.  BBE12136
                        Philips             It.   429 287 BE
                        Vogue               Astla EPVA1212
                        Vogue               Eng.  EPV1212
          10 Inch LP    Columbia            USA   CL 2565
                        Columbia            USA   CL 6301
                       >Columbia            USA   GL 101
                        Columbia            Jap.  ZL-1028
                        Philips             It.   BO7902R
                        Vogue               Eng.  L.D.E.081
                        Vogue               Fr.   L.D. 029
          12 Inch LP    CBS                 Eng.  88151
                        CBS                 Holl. 62615
                        CBS Realm Jazz      Eng.  RM52601
                        Columbia            USA   CS9655
                        Columbia            USA   BL 33404
                        Fontana             Eur.  467111TE
                        Harmony             USA   HL7006
          16 Inch TX    AFRS Just Jazz      USA   69

2970  TATUM-POLE BOOGIE (2:28)
      (mx JJ82)
          10 Inch 78    Jazz Selection      Fr.   656
           7 Inch 45EP  Columbia            USA   4-74-G
                        Columbia            Eng.  SEG7561,
                                                  (Unissued)
                        Fontana             Eng.  TFE.17236
                        Philips             Eng.  BBE12136
                        Philips             It.   429 287 BE
                        Vogue               Astla EPVA1212
                        Vogue               Eng.  EPV1212
          10 Inch LP    Columbia            USA   CL 2565
                        Columbia            USA   CL 6301
                       >Columbia            USA   GL 101
                        Columbia            Jap.  ZL-1028
                        Philips             It.   BO7902R
                        Vogue               Fr.   L.D. 029
                        Vogue               Eng.  L.D.E.081
          12 Inch LP    CBS                 Holl. 62615
```

```
                              CBS Realm Jazz        Eng.   RM52601
                              Columbia              USA    CS9655
                              Harmony               USA    HL7006

2980  SOMEONE TO WATCH OVER ME (3:08)
      (mx JJ83)
             10 Inch 78    Jazz Selection           Fr.    656
             7 Inch 45EP   Columbia                 Eng.   SEG7561,
                                                           (Unissued)
                           Fontana                  Eng.   TFE.17235
                           Vogue                    Eng.   EPV1008
             10 Inch LP    Columbia                 USA    CL 6301
                          >Columbia                 USA    GL 101
                           Columbia                 Jap.   PMS 55
                           Columbia                 Jap.   ZL-1028
                           Philips                  It.    BO7902R
                           Vogue                    Eng.   L.D.E.081
                           Vogue                    Fr.    L.D. 029
             12 Inch LP    CBS                       Holl.  62615
                           CBS Realm Jazz           Eng.   RM52601
                           Columbia                 USA    CS9655
                           Harmony                  USA    HL7006

2990  YESTERDAYS (3:23)
      (mx JJ84)
             10 Inch 78    Jazz Selection           Fr.    657
                           Jazz Selection           Swed.  4051
             7 Inch 45EP   Fontana                  Eng.   TFE.17237
                           Philips                  Eng.   BBE12136
                           Philips                  It.    429 287 BE
                           Vogue                    Astla  EPVA1212
                           Vogue                    Eng.   EPV1212
             10 Inch LP    Columbia                 USA    CL 2565
                           Columbia                 USA    CL 6301
                           Columbia                 USA    GL 101
                           Columbia                 Jap.   ZL-1028
                           Philips                  It.    BO7902R
                           Vogue                    Eng.   L.D.E.081
                           Vogue                    Fr.    L.D. 029
             12 Inch LP    CBS                       Holl.  62615
                           CBS Realm Jazz           Eng.   RM52601
                           Columbia                 USA    CS9655
                           Fontana                  Eur.   467111TE
                           Harmony                  USA    HL7006
                           Time-Life                USA    P 15515
             16 Inch TX   >AFRS Just Jazz           USA    69

3000  I KNOW THAT YOU KNOW (2:30)
      (mx JJ85)
             10 Inch 78    Jazz Selection           Fr.    657
             7 Inch 45     Columbia                 USA    75
             7 Inch 45EP   Columbia                 USA    4-75-G
                           Fontana                  Eng.   TFE.17236
                           Philips                  Eng.   BBE12136
                           Philips                  It.    429 287 BE
                           Vogue                    Astla  EPVA1212
                           Vogue                    Eng.   EPV1212
             10 Inch LP    Columbia                 USA    CL 2565
                           Columbia                 USA    CL 6301
                           Columbia                 USA    GL 101
                           Columbia                 Jap.   ZL-1028
                           Philips                  It.    BO7902R
                           Vogue                    Eng.   L.D.E.081
                           Vogue                    Fr.    L.D. 029
             12 Inch LP    CBS                       Holl.  62615
                           CBS Realm Jazz           Eng.   RM52601
                           Columbia                 USA    CS9655
                           Harmony                  USA    HL7006
             16 Inch TX   >AFRS Just Jazz           USA    69

3010  WILLOW WEEP FOR ME (3:13)
      (mx JJ86)
             10 Inch 78    Jazz Selection           Fr.    658
                           Jazz Selection           Swed.  4051
             7 Inch 45EP   Fontana                  Eng.   TFE.17237
```

```
                    Vogue          Eng.  EPV1008
     10 Inch LP     Columbia       USA   GL 101
                    Columbia       USA   CL 2565
                    Columbia       USA   CL 6301
                    Columbia       Jap.  ZL-1028
                    Philips        It.   BO7902R
                    Vogue          Eng.  L.D.E.081
                    Vogue          Fr.   L.D. 029
     12 Inch LP     CBS            Holl. 62615
                    CBS Realm Jazz Eng.  RM52601
                    Columbia       USA   CS9655
                    Fontana        Eur.  467111TE
                    Fontana        Eur.  R47121
                    Harmony        USA   HL7006
                    Philips        Eng.  BBL7511
     16 Inch TX   >AFRS Just Jazz  USA   69
```

3020   GERSHWIN MEDLEY (3:53) (Also titled "The Man I Love" and
                               "Tatum Plays Pretty")
       (mx JJ87)
```
     10 Inch 78    Jazz Selection [4]  Fr.   658
      7 Inch 45    Columbia [1]        USA   74
      7 Inch 45EP  Columbia [1]        USA   4-74-G
                   Fontana [1]         Eng.  TFE.17236
                   Vogue [2]           Eng.  EPV1008
     10 Inch LP    Columbia [1]        USA   CL 6301
                   Columbia [1]        USA   GL 101
                   Columbia [1]        Jap.  ZL-1028
                   Vogue [2]           Eng.  L.D.E.081
                   Vogue [3]           Fr.   L.D. 029
     12 Inch LP    CBS [1]             Holl. 62615
                   CBS Realm Jazz [1]  Eng.  RM52601
                   Columbia [1]        USA   CS9655
                   Harmony [1]         USA   HL7006
     16 Inch TX  >AFRS Just Jazz [5]   USA   69
```
[1] Abridged version (2:05), entitled, "The Man
I Love." It is believed that the segments containing
other Gershwin tunes were eliminated to save royalties.
[2] Abridged version (3:01), differently abridged
than [1], entitled, "Tatum Plays Pretty."
[3] Identical to [2], but entitled, "Gershwin Medley."
[4] It is not known which version appears here.
[5] The only issued complete version appears on
this disc.

3030   THE KERRY DANCE (1:58)
```
      7 Inch 45    Columbia       USA   74
      7 Inch 45EP  Columbia       USA   4-74-G
                   Fontana        Eng.  TFE.17237
                   Vogue          Astla EPVA1212
                   Vogue          Eng.  EPV1212
     10 Inch LP    Columbia       USA   CL 6301
                  >Columbia       USA   GL 101
                   Columbia       Jap.  ZL-1028
                   Philips        It.   BO7902R
                   Vogue          Eng.  L.D.E.081
                   Vogue          Fr.   L.D. 029
     12 Inch LP    CBS            Holl. 62615
                   CBS Realm Jazz Eng.  RM52601
                   Columbia       USA   CS9655
                   Fontana        Eur.  467111TE
                   Harmony        USA   HL7006
```

Los Angeles, California   July 13, 1949
       Piano solos.
3040   PROMOTIONAL INTERVIEW by Paul Weston, with gaps for questions
                        to be inserted by local disc jockeys.
                        Part One.
       (mx 4448-1D2)
```
     10 Inch 78   >Capitol        USA   Spec. Promo.
```

3050 PROMOTIONAL INTERVIEW by Paul Weston, with gaps for questions
      to be inserted by local disc jockeys.
      Part Two.
      (mx 5541z)
              10 Inch 78   >Capitol   USA   Spec. Promo.

3060 WILLOW WEEP FOR ME (2:50)
      (mx 5039-1D1, 5039-1D2)
              10 Inch 78   >Capitol   USA   15520
                            Capitol   USA   15782
                            Capitol   USA   Spec. Promo.
              7 Inch 45   Capitol   USA   F15520
              7 Inch 45EP   Capitol   USA   2-216
              10 Inch LP   Capitol   USA   H-216
                            Capitol   Eng.   LC.6524
              12 Inch LP   Capitol   USA   M-11028
                            Capitol   USA   T-216
                            Capitol   Braz. C-13.014
                            Capitol   Fr.   CO62-80800
                            Capitol   Ger.   1C 054-81 999M
                            Capitol   Holl. 5C 052-80800
                            Emigold   Holl. DAG125
                            Smithsonian   USA   P 11894
                            Time-Life   USA   P 15515
                            World Record Club   Eng.   T208
              12 Inch TX   AFRS Amer.Pop.Mus.   USA   149
                            AFRS Amer.Pop.Mus.   USA   194
                            USVA Here's to Vets USA   Series 104,
                                                        Prog.1353

3070 I COVER THE WATERFRONT (2:28)
      (mx 5040-2D1, 5040 2D-1, 5040-2D4)
              10 Inch 78   >Capitol   USA   15518
                            Capitol   USA   Spec. Promo.
              7 Inch 45   Capitol   USA   F15518
              7 Inch 45EP   Capitol   USA   1-216
              10 Inch LP   Capitol   USA   H-216
                            Capitol   Eng.   LC.6524
              12 Inch LP   Capitol   USA   M-11028
                            Capitol   USA   T-216
                            Capitol   Braz. C-13.014
                            Capitol   Fr.   CO62-80800
                            Capitol   Ger.   1C 054-81 999M
                            Capitol   Holl. 5C 052-80800
                            Emigold   Holl. DAG125
                            World Record Club   Eng.   T208

3080 AUNT HAGAR'S BLUES (2:37)
      (mx 5041-1D1)
              10 Inch 78   >Capitol   USA   15520
                            Capitol   USA   15782
                            Capitol   Ger.   C.80154
              7 Inch 45   Capitol   USA   F15520
              7 Inch 45EP   Capitol   USA   2-216
              10 Inch LP   Capitol   USA   H-216
                            Capitol   Eng.   LC.6524
              12 Inch LP   Capitol   USA   M-11028
                            Capitol   USA   T-216
                            Capitol   Braz. C-13.014
                            Capitol   Fr.   CO62-80800
                            Capitol   Holl. 5C 052-80800
                            Emigold   Holl. DAG125
                            Time-Life   USA   P 15516
                            World Record Club   Eng.   T208
              16 Inch TX   AFR&TS, Music   USA   P-S-18
                             Transcription Lib.
                            AFRS 1/4 Century   USA   184
                             of Swing
                            USVA Here's to Vets USA   Program 201

3090 NICE WORK IF YOU CAN GET IT (2:43)
      (mx 5042-1D1, 5042 1D-1)
              10 Inch 78   >Capitol   USA   15519
              7 Inch 45   Capitol   USA   F15519
              7 Inch 45EP   Capitol   USA   2-216

                                    65

```
                10 Inch LP    Capitol              USA   H-216
                              Capitol              Eng.  LC.6524
                12 Inch LP    Capitol              USA   M-11028
                              Capitol              USA   T-216
                              Capitol              Braz. C-13.014
                              Capitol              Fr.   CO62-80800
                              Capitol              Ger.  1C 054-81 999M
                              Capitol              Holl. 5C 052-80800
                              Emigold              Holl. DAG125
                              Time-Life            USA   P 15516
                              World Record Club    Eng.  T208
                12 Inch TX    AFRS Amer.Pop.Mus.   USA   149
                              USVA Here's to Vets  USA   Series 104,
                                                         Prog. 1353
                16 Inch TX    USVA Here's to Vets  USA   Program 201

3100   SOMEONE TO WATCH OVER ME (2:44)
       (mx 5043-D2)
                10 Inch 78   >Capitol              USA   15714
                 7 Inch 45    Capitol              USA   F15714
                 7 Inch 45EP  Capitol              USA   3-269
                10 Inch LP    Capitol              USA   H-269
                              Capitol              Eng.  LC.6638
                12 Inch LP    Capitol              USA   M-11028
                              Capitol              Braz. C-13.014
                              Capitol              Fr.   CO62-80800
                              Capitol              Fr.   T-20640S
                              Capitol              Ger.  1C 054-81 999
                              Capitol              Holl. 5C 052-80800
                              Emigold              Holl. DAG125
                12 Inch TX    USVA Here's to Vets  USA   Series 104,
                                                         Program
                                                         1353
                              USVA Here's to Vets  USA   Series 121,
                                                         Program
                                                         1561
                16 Inch TX    AFRS Basic Mus.Lib.  USA   P-1957

3110   DARDANELLA (2:47)
       (mx 5044)
                 7 Inch 45EP  Capitol              USA   1-216
                10 Inch LP   >Capitol              USA   H-216
                              Capitol              Eng.  LC.6524
                12 Inch LP    Capitol              USA   M-11028
                              Capitol              USA   T-216
                              Capitol              Braz. C-13.014
                              Capitol              Fr.   CO62-80800
                              Capitol              Holl. 5C 052-80800
                              Emigold              Holl. DAG125
                              World Record Club    Eng.  T208
                16 Inch TX    AFRS Bud's Bandwagon USA   319
                              AFR&TS, Music        USA   P-S-18
                               Transcription Lib.
                              USVA Here's to Vets  USA   Program 201

------------------------------------------------------------
Los Angeles, California                     July 25, 1949
          Piano solos.
3120   TIME ON MY HANDS (2:57)
       (mx 5045)
                10 Inch 78   >Capitol              USA   15712
                 7 Inch 45    Capitol              USA   F15712
                 7 Inch 45EP  Capitol              USA   1-269
                10 Inch LP    Capitol              USA   H-269
                              Capitol              Eng.  LC.6638
                12 Inch LP    Capitol              USA   M-11028
                              Capitol              USA   TBO-1970
                              Capitol              Braz. C-13.014
                              Capitol              Fr.   CO62-80800
                              Capitol              Fr.   T-20640S
                              Capitol              Ger.  1C 054-81 999M
                              Capitol              Holl. 5C 052-80800
                              Emigold              Holl. DAG125
                16 Inch TX    AFRS Basic Mus.Lib.  USA   P-1957
```

```
3130   SWEET LORRAINE (2:35)
       (mx 5046-D1)
              10 Inch 78   >Capitol         USA    15713
               7 Inch 45    Capitol          USA    F15713
               7 Inch 45EP  Capitol          USA    2-269
              10 Inch LP    Capitol          USA    H-269
                            Capitol          Eng.   LC.6638
              12 Inch LP    Capitol          USA    M-11028
                            Capitol          Braz.  C-13.014
                            Capitol          Fr.    CO62-80800
                            Capitol          Fr.    T-20640S
                            Capitol          Ger.   1C 054-81 999M
                            Capitol          Holl.  5C 052-80800
                            Emigold          Holl.  DAG125
              12 Inch TX    USVA Here's to Vets USA Series 104,
                                                     Prog. 1353
                            USVA Here's to Vets USA Series 121,
                                                     Prog. 1561
              16 Inch TX    AFRS Basic Mus.Lib. USA P-1957

3140   SOMEBODY LOVES ME (2:36)
       (mx 5047-D1)
              10 Inch 78   >Capitol         USA    15714
               7 Inch 45    Capitol          USA    F15714
               7 Inch 45EP  Capitol          USA    3-269
              10 Inch LP    Capitol          USA    H-269
                            Capitol          Eng.   LC.6638
              12 Inch LP    Capitol          USA    M-11028
                            Capitol          Braz.  C-13.014
                            Capitol          Fr.    CO62-80800
                            Capitol          Fr.    T-20640S
                            Capitol          Ger.   1C 054-81 999M
                            Capitol          Holl.  5C 052-80800
                            Capitol          Jap.   CR-8810
                            Emigold          Holl.  DAG125
              16 Inch TX    AFRS Basic Mus.Lib. USA P-1957

3150   DON'T BLAME ME (2:49)
       (mx 5048-D1)
              10 Inch 78   >Capitol         USA    15713
               7 Inch 45    Capitol          USA    F15713
               7 Inch 45EP  Capitol          USA    2-269
              10 Inch LP    Capitol          USA    H-269
                            Capitol          Eng.   LC.6638
              12 Inch LP    Capitol          USA    M-11028
                            Capitol          Braz.  C-13.014
                            Capitol          Fr.    CO62-80800
                            Capitol          Fr.    T-20640S
                            Capitol          Ger.   1C 054-81 999M
                            Capitol          Holl.  5C 052-80800
                            Emigold          Holl.  DAG125
              12 Inch TX    USVA Here's to Vets USA Series 121,
                                                     Prog. 1561
              16 Inch TX    AFRS Basic Mus.Lib. USA P-1957

----------------------------------------------------------
Los Angeles, California                    September 29, 1949
          Piano solos.
3160   MY HEART STOOD STILL (3:03)
       (mx 5049)
              10 Inch 78   >Capitol         USA    15712
               7 Inch 45    Capitol          USA    F15712
                            Capitol          USA    1-269
              10 Inch LP    Capitol          USA    H-269
                            Capitol          Eng.   LC.6638
              12 Inch LP    Capitol          USA    M-11028
                            Capitol          Braz.  C-13.014
                            Capitol          Fr.    CO62-80800
                            Capitol          Fr.    T-20640S
                            Capitol          Ger.   1C 054-81 999M
                            Capitol          Holl.  5C 052-80800
                            Emigold          Holl.  DAG125
              12 Inch TX    USVA Here's to Vets USA Series 121,
                                                     Prog. 1561
              16 Inch TX    AFRS Basic Mus.Lib. USA P-1957
```

```
3170  YOU TOOK ADVANTAGE OF ME (3:08)
      (mx 5050)
             10 Inch 78  >Capitol                USA   15841
              7 Inch 45   Capitol                USA   F15841
              7 Inch 45EP Capitol                USA   1-323
             10 Inch LP   Capitol                USA   H-323
                          Capitol                Eng.  LC.6559
             12 Inch LP   Capitol                USA   M-11028
                          Capitol                Braz. C-13.014
                          Capitol                Fr.   CO62-80800
                          Capitol                Holl. 5C 052-80800
                          Emigold                Holl. DAG125

3180  I GOTTA RIGHT TO SING THE BLUES (2:53)
      (mx 5051-1D1)
             10 Inch 78  >Capitol                USA   15518
              7 Inch 45   Capitol                USA   F15518
              7 Inch 45EP Capitol                USA   1-216
             10 Inch LP   Capitol                USA   H-216
                          Capitol                Eng.  LC.6524
             12 Inch LP   Capitol                USA   M-11028
                          Capitol                USA   T-216
                          Capitol                Braz. C-13.014
                          Capitol                Fr.   CO62-80800
                          Capitol                Holl. 5C 052-80800
                          Emigold                Holl. DAG125
                          World Record Club      Eng.  T208
             16 Inch TX   AFR&TS, Music          USA   P-S-18
                            Transcription Lib.

3190  HOW HIGH THE MOON (3:00)
      (mx 5052)
                          Capitol                USA   Unissued

3200  MAKIN´ WHOOPEE (2:40)
      (mx 5053)
                          Capitol                USA   Unissued

3210  GOIN´ HOME (3:05)
      (mx 5054)
             10 Inch LP  >Capitol                USA   H-269
                          Capitol                Eng.  LC.6638
             12 Inch LP   Capitol                Fr.   T-20640S
                          Capitol                Ger.  1C 054-81 999M

3220  BLUE SKIES (2:48)
      (mx 5055)
              7 Inch 45EP Capitol                USA   2-216
             10 Inch LP  >Capitol                USA   H-216
                          Capitol                Eng.  LC.6524
             12 Inch LP   Capitol                USA   M-11028
                          Capitol                USA   T-216
                          Capitol                Braz. C-13.014
                          Capitol                Fr.   CO62-80800
                          Capitol                Holl. 5C 052-80800
                          Emigold                Holl. DAG125
                          Time-Life              USA   P 15516
                          World Record Club      Eng.  T208
             16 Inch TX   AFRS 1/4 Century       USA   184
                            of Swing
                          USVA Here´s to Vets    USA   Program 201

3230  IT´S THE TALK OF THE TOWN (3:13)
      (mx 5056)
             10 Inch LP  >Capitol                USA   H-269
                          Capitol                Eng.  LC.6638
             12 Inch LP   Capitol                USA   M-11028
                          Capitol                Braz. C-13.014
                          Capitol                USA   T795
                          Capitol                Fr.   CO62-80800
                          Capitol                Fr.   T-20640S
                          Capitol                Holl. 5C 052-80800
                          Capitol                Jap.  2LP-22
                          Capitol                Jap.  CR-8810
                          Capitol                Span. 1J 060 80.155M
```

```
                        Emigold              Holl. DAG125

3240   DANCING IN THE DARK (2:52)
       (mx 5057-1D1, 5057 1D-1)
            10 Inch 78  >Capitol            USA   15519
                         Capitol            Ger.  C.80154
             7 Inch 45   Capitol            USA   F15519
             7 Inch 45EP Capitol            USA   1-216
            10 Inch LP   Capitol            USA   H-216
                         Capitol            Eng.  LC.6524
            12 Inch LP   Capitol            USA   M-11028
                         Capitol            USA   T-216
                         Capitol            Braz. C-13.014
                         Capitol            Fr.   CO62-80800
                         Capitol            Holl. 5C 052-80800
                         Emigold            Holl. DAG125
                         World Record Club  Eng.  T208

3241   TENDERLY (3:05)
       (mx 5058)
                         Capitol            USA   Unissued

---------------------------------------------------------------
New York, New York                          c. 1950
            Piano solos.
3250   POOR BUTTERFLY (2:30)

            12 Inch LP   Black Lion         Eng.  BLP30166
                         Freedom            Fr.   BLP30166
                         Intercord Black LionGer. 147.000
            16 Inch TX  >US Dept. of State  USA   44
                         VOA Piano Play-
                         house Series

3255   WILLOW WEEP FOR ME (3:00)
       (mx DS-1970)
            16 Inch TX  >US Dept. of State, USA   45
                         VOA Piano Play-
                         house Series

3260   I GOTTA RIGHT TO SING THE BLUES (1:58)
       (mx DS-2320)
            12 Inch LP   Black Lion         Eng.  BLP30166
                         Freedom            Fr.   BLP30166
                         Intercord Black LionGer. 147.000
            16 Inch TX  >US Dept. of State  USA   55
                         VOA Piano Play-
                         house Series

3270   TABOO (2:20)
       (mx DS-2321)
            12 Inch LP   Black Lion         Eng.  BLP30166
                         Freedom            Fr.   BLP30166
                         Intercord Black LionGer. 147.000
            16 Inch TX  >US Dept. of State  USA   56
                         VOA Piano Play-
                         house Series

---------------------------------------------------------------
Beverly Hills, California                   April 16, 1950
            Recorded live, believed to be at the
            home of Ray Heindorf.  Piano solos.
3280   MR. FREDDIE BLUES (3:06)

            12 Inch LP   Ember              Eng.  EMB3326
                         20th Century Fox   USA   TFM3163
                         20th Century Fox   USA   TFS4163
                         20th Century Fox   Fr.   T608
                        >20th Fox           USA   Fox 3033
                         20th Fox           USA   SFX-3033
                         20th Fox           USA   TCF102-2
                         20th Fox           USA   TCF102-2S
                         Time-Life          USA   P 15516
                         Vega               Fr.   30 TCF 6
                         World Record Club  Eng.  T. 279
```

```
3290   MEMORIES OF YOU* (3:41)
                    7 Inch 45EP Ember                   Eng.  EMB4502
                   12 Inch LP   Ember                   Eng.  EMB3326
                                20th Century Fox         USA   TFM3163
                                20th Century Fox         USA   TFS4163
                                20th Century Fox         Fr.   T608
                              >20th Fox                  USA   Fox 3033
                                20th Fox                 USA   SFX-3033
                                20th Fox                 USA   TCF102-2
                                20th Fox                 USA   TCF102-2S
                                Vega                     Fr.   30 TCF 6
                                World Record Club        Eng.  T. 279
          *Note: All issues lack the introduction and a
          few notes at the end.

----------------------------------------------------------
New York, New York                           July, 1950
          Live recording at Cafe Society Downtown.
          Piano solos.
3300   GERSHWIN MEDLEY (3:39)
                   12 Inch LP   Epitaph                USA   E-4006
                              >RI Disc                 Swiss RI-DISC 7

3310   I KNOW THAT YOU KNOW (2:37)

                                                       Unissued

3320   SWEET LORRAINE (2:04)

                                                       Unissued

3330   ROSETTA (2:31)

                                                       Unissued

3340   A GHOST OF A CHANCE (4:03)

                                                       Unissued

3350   HALLELUJAH (5:08)

                                                       Unissued

3360   SOMEONE TO WATCH OVER ME (3:40)

                                                       Unissued

3370   TABOO (3:22)
                   12 Inch LP   Epitaph                USA   E-4006
                              >RI Disc                 Swiss RI-DISC 7

----------------------------------------------------------
New York, New York                           c. 1951
          Live recording at The Embers.  The
          Art Tatum Trio.  Art Tatum, p; Everett
          Barksdale, g; Slam Stewart, b.
3390   TENDERLY (3:50)
       (mx 856)
                   16 Inch TX  >US Dept. of State,    USA   J72
                               VOA Jazz Series

3400   THE MAN I LOVE (4:53)
       (mx 856 & SPE782-3)
                   16 Inch TX   US Dept. of State     USA   J72
                                VOA Jazz Series
                              >US Dept. of State      USA   JC44
                                VOA Jazz Club
                                Series
```

		Decca	Fr.	MU-60515
7 Inch 45		Decca	USA	9-25201
7 Inch 45EP		Brunswick	Ger.	10116EPB
		Decca	USA	91574
10 Inch LP		Decca	USA	DL5086
		Festival	Astla	CFR10 506
12 Inch LP		Ace of Hearts	Eng.	AH133
		Brunswick	Eng.	LAT.8358
		Brunswick	Ger.	LPBM87507
		Cathala	Fr.	BLP 100.005
		Coral	Eng.	CP62
		Coral	Ger.	COP 2686
		Decca	USA	DL8715
		MCA	USA	MCA2-4019
		MCA	Fr.	510082
		MCA	Fr.	MAP 2686
		MCA	It.	MAPD 7028
		MCA	Jap.	MCA-3074
		Swaggie	Astla	S1223

0900 SWEET EMALINA, MY GAL
      (mx DLA1942A)

	Decca	USA	Rejected

0901 SWEET EMALINA, MY GAL
      (mxDLA1942B)

	Decca	USA	Unissued

0910 EMALINE (2:16)
      (mx DLA1943A)

10 Inch 78		>Decca	USA	155
		Decca	USA	25202
7 Inch 45		Decca	USA	9-25202
7 Inch 45EP		Decca	USA	91574
10 Inch LP		Decca	USA	DL5086
		Festival	Astla	CFR10 506
12 Inch LP		Ace of Hearts	Eng.	AH133
		Brunswick	Eng.	LAT.8358
		Brunswick	Ger.	LPBM87507
		Cathala	Fr.	BLP 100.005
		Coral	Eng.	CP62
		Coral	Ger.	COP 2686
		Decca	USA	DL8715
		MCA	USA	MCA2-4019
		MCA	Fr.	510082
		MCA	Fr.	MAP 2686
		MCA	It.	MAPD 7028
		MCA	Jap.	MCA-3074
		Swaggie	Astla	S1223

0920 MOONGLOW (2:57)
      (mx DLA1944A)

10 Inch 78		>Decca	USA	155
12 Inch LP		Cathala	Fr.	BLP 100.005
		MCA	Fr.	510082

0921 MOONGLOW
      (mx DLA1944B)

	Decca	USA	Unissued

0930 LOVE ME (2:38)
      (mx DLA1945A)

10 Inch 78		>Decca	USA	156
12 Inch LP		Ace of Hearts	Eng.	AH133
		Brunswick	Eng.	LAT.8358
		Brunswick	Ger.	LPBM87507
		Cathala	Fr.	BLP 100.005
		Coral	Eng.	CP62
		Coral	Ger.	COP 2686
		Decca	USA	DL8715
		MCA	USA	MCA2-4019
		MCA	Fr.	510082
		MCA	Fr.	MAP 2686
		MCA	It.	MAPD 7028
		MCA	Jap.	MCA-3074

```
3410   BODY AND SOUL (4:59)
       (mx 856)
              12 Inch TX    Gotham*              USA    Unnumbered
                            (Mastered Works of 1951)
              16 Inch TX    >US Dept. of State   USA    J72
                            VOA Jazz Series
              *Contains last two choruses only.

3420   FLYING HOME* (1:10)
       (mx 856)
              16 Inch TX    >US Dept. of State   USA    J72
                            VOA Jazz Series
              *Erroneously titled "A Riff Tune."
-----------------------------------------------------------
Washington, D. C.                          c. 1951 (Release
                                              date 6/21/51)
              Narrated by Willis Conover.
              Piano solos.
3430   MY HEART STOOD STILL (2:25)
       (mx D-73535)
              12 Inch LP    Giants of Jazz       USA    GOJ-1015
              16 Inch TX    >US Treasury Dept.   USA    222
                            Savings Bond Div.,
                            "Guest Star" Series

3440   HOW HIGH THE MOON (2:14)
       (mx D-73535)
              12 Inch LP    Giants of Jazz       USA    GOJ-1015
              16 Inch TX    >US Treasury Dept.   USA    222
                            Savings Bond Div.,
                            "Guest Star" Series
-----------------------------------------------------------
New York, New York                         c. 1951. (Mfg. date
              Live recording at The Embers.    July 25, 1951)
              Piano solos.
3450   COME RAIN OR COME SHINE (3:23)
       (mx 506)
              12 Inch LP    Alamac               USA    QSR 2402
                            Alamac               Fr.    180.040
              16 Inch TX    >US Dept. of State   USA    J35
                            VOA- Jazz Series

3460   BEGIN THE BEGUINE (3:25)
       (mx 506)
              12 Inch LP    Alamac               USA    QSR 2402
                            Alamac               Fr.    180.040
              16 Inch TX    >US Dept. of State   USA    J35
                            VOA- Jazz Series

3470   BODY AND SOUL (4:03)
       (mx 506)
              12 Inch LP    Alamac               USA    QSR 2402
                            Alamac               Fr.    180.040
              16 Inch TX    >US Dept. of State   USA    J35
                            VOA- Jazz Series

3480   I KNOW THAT YOU KNOW (2:15)
       (mx 506)
              12 Inch LP    Alamac               USA    QSR 2402
                            Alamac               Fr.    180.040
              16 Inch TX    >US Dept. of State   USA    J35
                            VOA- Jazz Series

3490   HONEYSUCKLE ROSE (3:05)
       (mx 507)
              12 Inch LP    Alamac               USA    QSR 2402
                            Alamac               Fr.    180.040
              16 Inch TX    >US Dept. of State   USA    J36
                            VOA- Jazz Series
```

```
3500   SITTIN' AND ROCKIN' (2:47)
       (mx 507)
               12 Inch LP    Alamac              USA    QSR 2402
                             Alamac              Fr.    180.040
               16 Inch TX    >US Dept. of State  USA    J36
                             VOA- Jazz Series

3510   MEMORIES OF YOU (4:14)
       (mx 507)
               12 Inch LP    Alamac              USA    QSR 2402
                             Alamac              Fr.    180.040
               16 Inch TX    >US Dept. of State  USA    J36
                             VOA- Jazz Series

3520   THE KERRY DANCE (1:04 + 0:13 false start)
       (mx 507)
               12 Inch LP    Alamac              USA    QSR 2402*
                             Alamac              Fr.    180.040*
               16 Inch TX    >US Dept. of State  USA    J36
                             VOA- Jazz Series
       *These issues do not include the (0:13) false start.

------------------------------------------------------------
New York, New York                          c. 1951
           Live recording at The Embers.
3530   INTERVIEW* (3:11)
       (mx SPE245)
               16 Inch TX    >US Dept. of State  USA    JC24,Part
                                                               One
       *Interview of Tatum by Leonard Feather.
                             VOA Jazz Club
                             Series

3540   TABOO
       (mx SPE246)
               16 Inch TX    >US Dept. of State  USA    JC24,Part
                                                               Two

                             VOA Jazz Club
                             Series

3550   COME RAIN OR COME SHINE
       (mx SPE246)
               16 Inch TX    >US Dept. of State  USA    JC24,Part
                                                               Two

                             VOA Jazz Club
                             Series

3560   HONEYSUCKLE ROSE
       (mx SPE246)
               16 Inch TX    >US Dept. of State  USA    JC24,Part
                                                               Two

                             VOA Jazz Club
                             Series

------------------------------------------------------------
New York, New York                          c. 1951. (Mfg. date
           Live recording at The Embers.        July 18, 1951)
           Piano solos.
3610   DON'T BLAME ME (4:00)
       (mx 359)
               12 Inch LP    Shoestring          USA    SS-105
               16 Inch TX    >US Dept. of State  USA    J16
                             VOA Jazz Series

3620   TABOO (3:30)
       (mx 359)
               16 Inch TX    >US Dept. of State  USA    J16
                             VOA Jazz Series

3630   GERSHWIN MEDLEY (4:20)
       (mx 359)
               12 Inch LP    Shoestring          USA    SS-105
               16 Inch TX    >US Dept. of State  USA    J16
                             VOA Jazz Series
```

```
-----------------------------------------------------------
New York, New York                              c. 1951
          Live recording at Cafe Society Downtown.
          The Art Tatum Trio.  Art Tatum, p;
          Everett Barksdale, g; Slam Stewart, b.
3640  TENDERLY (3:36)
      (mx SPE511)
          16 Inch TX  >US Dept. of State   USA    JC33
                       VOA Jazz Club
                       Series

3650  FLYING HOME* (1:06)
      (mx SPE511)
          16 Inch TX  >US Dept. of State   USA    JC33
                       VOA Jazz Club
                       Series
          *Erroneously titled "Air Mail Special."

3660  THE MAN I LOVE (4:41)
      (mx SPE511)
          16 Inch Tx  >US Dept. of State   USA    JC33
                       VOA Jazz Club
                       Series

-----------------------------------------------------------
New York, New York                          May 10, 1952
          Live recording at Birdland. The
          Art Tatum Trio.  Art Tatum, p; Everett
          Barksdale, g; Slam Stewart, b.
3670  TEA FOR TWO (3:13)

          12 Inch LP  >Alto              USA    AL712
                       Kings of Jazz     It.    KLJ20000
                       Kings of Jazz     It.    KLJ20020

3680  TENDERLY (3:26)

          12 Inch LP  >Alto              USA    AL712
                       Kings of Jazz     It.    KLJ20000
                       Kings of Jazz     It.    KLJ20020

3690  OUT OF NOWHERE (3:33)

          12 Inch LP  >Alto              USA    AL712
                       Kings of Jazz     It.    KLJ20000
                       Kings of Jazz     It.    KLJ20020

3700  BODY AND SOUL (5:55)

          12 Inch LP  >Alto              USA    AL712
                       Kings of Jazz     It.    KLJ20000
                       Kings of Jazz     It.    KLJ20020

-----------------------------------------------------------
New York, New York                      December 20, 1952
          The Art Tatum Trio.  Art Tatum, p;
          Everett Barksdale, g; Slam Stewart, b.
3710  MELODY IN F (3:16)
      (mx 10935)
           7 Inch 45EP Capitol            USA    1-408
          10 Inch LP  >Capitol            USA    H-408
                       Capitol            Astla  CLP 047
                       Capitol            Braz.  H-408
                       Capitol            Eng.   LC.6625
          12 Inch LP   Capitol            Fr.    T-20640S

3720  SEPTEMBER SONG (3:15)
      (mx 10936)
           7 Inch 45EP Capitol            USA    2-408
          10 Inch LP  >Capitol            USA    H-408
                       Capitol            Astla  CLP 047
                       Capitol            Braz.  H-408
                       Capitol            Eng.   LC.6625
          12 Inch LP   Capitol            USA    T-216
                       Capitol            Ger.   1C 054-81 999M

                          73
```

```
                      World Record Club    Eng.   T208

3730  WOULD YOU LIKE TO TAKE A WALK (3:13)
      (mx 10937)
             7 Inch 33    Storia della Musica It.   Vol.X N.8
             7 Inch 45EP Capitol          USA    1-408
            10 Inch LP  >Capitol          USA    H-408
                         Capitol          Astla  CLP 047
                         Capitol          Braz.  H-408
                         Capitol          Eng.   LC.6625
            12 Inch LP   Capitol          USA    2109
                         Capitol          USA    W-2140
                         Capitol          Fr.    T-20640S
                         Capitol          Ger.   K83924
                         Capitol Silver   USA    129
                          Platter Service

3740  TEA FOR TWO (3:03)
      (mx 10938)
             7 Inch 45EP Capitol          USA    2-408
            10 Inch LP  >Capitol          USA    H-408
                         Capitol          Astla  CLP 047
                         Capitol          Braz.  H-408
                         Capitol          Eng.   LC.6625
            12 Inch LP   Capitol          USA    T-216
                         Capitol          Ger.   1C 054-81 999M
                         World Record Club Eng.  T208
            16 Inch TX   AFRS 1/4 Century  USA   76
                          of Swing

3750  OUT OF NOWHERE (2:43)
      (mx 10939)
             7 Inch 45EP Capitol          USA    1-408
            10 Inch LP  >Capitol          USA    H-408
                         Capitol          Astla  CLP 047
                         Capitol          Braz.  H-408
                         Capitol          Eng.   LC.6625
            12 Inch LP   Capitol          USA    T-216
                         Capitol          Ger.   1C 054-81 999M
                         World Record Club Eng.  T208

3760  LOVER (3:07)
      (mx 10940)
             7 Inch 45EP Capitol          USA    1-408
            10 Inch LP  >Capitol          USA    H-408
                         Capitol          Astla  CLP 047
                         Capitol          Braz.  H-408
                         Capitol          Eng.   LC.6625
            12 Inch LP   Capitol          Fr.    T-20640S

3770  JUST ONE OF THOSE THINGS (3:12)
      (mx 10941)
             7 Inch 45EP Capitol          USA    2-408
            10 Inch LP  >Capitol          USA    H-408
                         Capitol          Astla  CLP 047
                         Capitol          Braz.  H-408
                         Capitol          Eng.   LC.6625
            12 Inch LP   Capitol          Fr.    T-20640S

3780  INDIANA (3:23)
      (mx 10942)
             7 Inch 45EP Capitol          USA    2-408
            10 Inch LP  >Capitol          USA    H-408
                         Capitol          Astla  CLP 047
                         Capitol          Braz.  H-408
                         Capitol          Eng.   LC.6625
            12 Inch LP   Capitol          USA    T-216
                         Capitol          Ger.   1C 054-81 999M
                         World Record Club Eng.  T208
            16 Inch TX   AFRS 1/4 Century  USA   76
                          of Swing
```

74

```
          -----------------------------------------------------
New York, New York                          February 16, 1953
          TV broadcast.  The Bandbox Show, with
          Art Ford.  WPIX-TV.  Piano solos.
3790  WHERE OR WHEN (2:59)

          12 Inch LP  >Teppa              USA   76

3800  TABOO (2:50)

          12 Inch LP  >Teppa              USA   76

          -----------------------------------------------------
New York, New York                          February 16, 1953
          Radio broadcast from the Bandbox night club.
          Announcer is Ed Stokes.  The Art Tatum Trio.
          Art Tatum, p; Everett Barksdale, g; Slam
          Stewart, b.
3810  CARAVAN (0:33) [Theme]

                                            Unissued

3820  IF (4:09)

          12 Inch LP  >Session Disc        USA   120

3830  SOFT WINDS (3:13)

          12 Inch LP  >Session Disc        USA   120

3840  MEMORIES OF YOU (5:35)

          12 Inch LP  >Session Disc        USA   120

          -----------------------------------------------------
Los Angeles, California                     December 28, 1953
          Piano solos.
3850  CAN'T WE BE FRIENDS (3:43)
      (mx 1411-1)
          7 Inch 45EP  Barclay         Fr.   GEP12602
                       Clef            USA   EP-263
                       Karusell        Swed. KEP279
          12 Inch LP   Barclay         Fr.   GLP3501
                       >Clef           USA   MG C-612
                       Columbia        Eng.  33CX10024
                       Metro           Ger.  2356 081
                       Norgran         USA   MG N-1036
                       Pablo           USA   2625-703
                       Pablo           Eng.  2310 812
                       Pablo           Eng.  2660 110
                       Pablo           Ger.  2625 703
                       Verve           USA   MG V-8036
                       Verve           USA   MG V-8127
          12 Inch TX   Thesaurus       USA   JATP-6

3860  THIS CAN'T BE LOVE (2:34)
      (mx 1412-1)
          10 Inch 78   Columbia        Eng.  LB 10069
          7 Inch 45EP  Barclay         Fr.   GEP12602
                       Clef            USA   EP-263
                       Karusell        Swed. KEP279
          12 Inch LP   Barclay         Fr.   GLP3501
                       Book-of-the-Month USA 51-400
                       >Clef           USA   MG C-612
                       Metro           Ger.  2356 081
                       Pablo           USA   2310-729
                       Pablo           USA   2625-703
                       Pablo           Can.  2310-729
                       Pablo           Eng.  2310 729
                       Pablo           Eng.  2660 110
                       Pablo           Ger.  2310 729
                       Pablo           Ger.  2625 703
                       Pablo           It.   2310 729A
                       Pablo           Jap.  MTF 1074
                       Verve           USA   MG V-8036
          12 Inch TX   Thesaurus       USA   JATP-6
```

```
3870   ELEGIE (3:37)
       (mx 1413-1)
                7 Inch 45EP Barclay              Fr.    GEP12603
                            Clef                 USA    EP-264
                            Karusell             Swed.  KEP280
               12 Inch LP   Barclay              Fr.    GLP3501
                           >Clef                 USA    MG C-612
                            Metro                Ger.   2356 081
                            Pablo                USA    2310-729
                            Pablo                USA    2625-703
                            Pablo                Can.   2310-729
                            Pablo                Eng.   2310 729
                            Pablo                Eng.   2660 110
                            Pablo                Ger.   2310 729
                            Pablo                Ger.   2625 703
                            Pablo                It.    2310 729A
                            Pablo                Jap.   MTF 1074
                            Verve                USA    MG V-8036
                            Verve                USA    V-8433
                            Verve                USA    V6-8433
                            Verve                Ger.   511 063
               12 Inch TX   Thesaurus            USA    JATP-6

3880   MEMORIES OF YOU (4:57)
       (mx 1414-1)
                7 Inch 45EP Barclay              Fr.    GEP12602
                            Clef                 USA    EP-263
                            Karusell             Swed.  KEP279
               12 Inch LP   Barclay              Fr.    GLP3502
                           >Clef                 USA    MG C-613
                            Columbia             Eng.   33CX10005
                            Metro                Ger.   2356 081
                            Pablo                USA    2310-870
                            Pablo                Can.   2310-870
                            Pablo                USA    2625-703
                            Pablo                Eng.   2310 811
                            Pablo                Eng.   2660 110
                            Pablo                Ger.   2625 703
                            Pablo                Jap.   28MJ 3147
                            Verve                USA    MG V-8037

3890   OVER THE RAINBOW (3:39)
       (mx 1415-1)
                7 Inch 45EP Barclay              Fr.    GEP12603
                            Clef                 USA    EP-264
                            Karusell             Swed.  KEP280
               12 Inch LP   Barclay              Fr.    GLP3502
                            Book-of-the-Month    USA    51-400
                           >Clef                 USA    MG C-613
                            Columbia             Eng.   33CX10005
                            Metro                Ger.   2356 081
                            Pablo                USA    2310-870
                            Pablo                Can.   2310-870
                            Pablo                USA    2625-703
                            Pablo                Eng.   2310 811
                            Pablo                Eng.   2660 110
                            Pablo                Ger.   2625 703
                            Pablo                Jap.   28MJ 3147
                            Verve                USA    MG V-8037

3900   IF YOU HADN'T GONE AWAY (4:04) (Mis-titled "Blues in My
                                       Heart")
       (mx 1416-2)
                7 Inch 45EP Barclay              Fr.    GEP12666
                            Clef                 USA    EP-265
                            Karusell             Swed.  KEP281
               12 Inch LP   Barclay              Fr.    GLP3501
                            Book-of-the-Month    USA    51-400
                           >Clef                 USA    MG C-612
                            Metro                Ger.   2356 081
                            Pablo                USA    2310-862
                            Pablo                USA    2625-703
                            Pablo                Can.   2310-862
                            Pablo                Eng.   2310 809
                            Pablo                Eng.   2660 110
```

```
                    Pablo                Fr.   2310 809
                    Pablo                Ger.  2310 809
                    Pablo                Ger.  2625 703
                    Pablo                Jap.  MTF 1096
                    Verve                USA   MG V-8036
        12 Inch TX  Thesaurus            USA   JATP-6

3910  BODY AND SOUL (5:44)
      (mx 1417-1)
        7 Inch 45EP Barclay              Fr.   GEP12603
                    Clef                 USA   EP-264
                    Karusell             Swed. KEP280
        12 Inch LP  Barclay              Fr.   GLP3502
                   >Clef                 USA   MG C-613
                    Columbia             Eng.  33CX10005
                    Pablo                USA   2310-723
                    Pablo                USA   2625-703
                    Pablo                Braz. 2310 723
                    Pablo                Can.  2310-723
                    Pablo                Eng.  2310 723
                    Pablo                Eng.  2660 110
                    Pablo                Ger.  2310 723
                    Pablo                Ger.  2625 703
                    Pablo                It.   2310 723A
                    Pablo                Jap.  MTF 1073
                    Verve                USA   MG V-8037

3920  THE MAN I LOVE (4:24)
      (mx 1418-2)
        7 Inch 45EP Barclay              Fr.   GEP12666
                    Clef                 USA   EP-265
                    Karusell             Swe.  KEP281
        12 Inch LP  Barclay              Fr.   GLP3502
                   >Clef                 USA   MG C-613
                    Columbia             Eng.  33CX10005
                    Columbia             Eng.  33CX10024
                    Metro                Ger.  2356 081
                    MGM                  USA   E4242
                    MGM                  USA   SE4242
                    Norgran              USA   MG N-1036
                    Pablo                USA   2310-789
                    Pablo                USA   2625-703
                    Pablo                Can.  2310-789
                    Pablo                Eng.  2310 789
                    Pablo                Eng.  2660 110
                    Pablo                Ger.  2310 789
                    Pablo                Ger.  2625 703
                    Pablo                It.   2310 789A
                    Pablo                Jap.  MTF 1076
                    Verve                USA   MG V-8037
                    Verve                USA   MG V-8127
                    VSP Verve            USA   VSP 33
                    VSP Verve            USA   VSPS33
                    VSP Verve            It.   SVSP57.009

3930  MAKIN´ WHOOPEE (2:42)
      (mx 1419-1)
        7 Inch 45EP Barclay              Fr.   GEP12666
                    Clef                 USA   EP-265
                    Karusell             Swed. KEP281
        12 Inch LP  Barclay              Fr.   GLP3502
                   >Clef                 USA   MG C-613
                    Columbia             Eng.  33CX10005
                    Pablo                USA   2310-790
                    Pablo                USA   2625-703
                    Pablo                Can.  2310-790
                    Pablo                Eng.  2310 790
                    Pablo                Eng.  2660 110
                    Pablo                Ger.  2310 790
                    Pablo                Ger.  2625 703
                    Pablo                It.   2310 790A
                    Pablo                Jap.  MTF 1077
                    Verve                USA   MG V-8037
```

```
3940   SEPTEMBER SONG (4:02)
       (mx 1420-1)
              7 Inch 45EP  Clef                USA    EP-C-349
                           Karusell            Swed.  KEP291
             10 Inch LP    Columbia            Eng.   33C 9033
             12 Inch LP    Barclay             Fr.    GLP3524
                          >Clef                USA    MG C-657
                           Pablo               USA    2310-729
                           Pablo               USA    2625-703
                           Pablo               Can.   2310-729
                           Pablo               Eng.   2310 729
                           Pablo               Eng.   2660 110
                           Pablo               Ger.   2310 729
                           Pablo               Ger.   2625 703
                           Pablo               It.    2310 729A
                           Pablo               Jap.   MTF 1074
                           Verve               USA    MG V-8055

3950   BEGIN THE BEGUINE (2:58)
       (mx 1421-1)
             10 Inch 78    Columbia            Eng.   LB 10069
              7 Inch 45EP  Clef                USA    EP-266
                           Karusell            Swed.  KEP282
             12 Inch LP    Barclay             Fr.    GLP3501
                          >Clef                USA    MG C-612
                           Metro               Ger.   2356 081
                           Pablo               USA    2310-730
                           Pablo               USA    2625-703
                           Pablo               Can.   2310-730
                           Pablo               Eng.   2310 730
                           Pablo               Eng.   2660 110
                           Pablo               Ger.   2310 730
                           Pablo               Ger.   2625 703
                           Pablo               It.    2310 730A
                           Pablo               Jap.   MTF 1075
                           Verve               USA    MG V-8036

3960   HUMORESQUE (3:55)
       (mx 1422-1)
              7 Inch 45EP  Clef                USA    EP-266
                           Karusell            Swed.  KEP282
             12 Inch LP    Barclay             Fr.    GLP3501
                          >Clef                USA    MG C-612
                           Metro               Ger.   2356 081
                           Pablo               USA    2310-792
                           Pablo               USA    2625-703
                           Pablo               Can.   2310-792
                           Pablo               Eng.   2310 792
                           Pablo               Eng.   2660 110
                           Pablo               Ger.   2310 792
                           Pablo               Ger.   2625 703
                           Pablo               It.    2310 792A
                           Pablo               Jap.   MTF 1079
                           Verve               USA    MG V-8036

3970   LOUISE (4:57)
       (mx 1423-1)
              7 Inch 45EP  Clef                USA    EP-266
                           Karusell            Swed.  KEP282
             12 Inch LP    Barclay             Fr.    GLP3503
                           Blue Star           Fr.    GLP 3503
                          >Clef                USA    MG C-614
                           Pablo               USA    2310-790
                           Pablo               USA    2625-703
                           Pablo               Can.   2310-790
                           Pablo               Eng.   2310 790
                           Pablo               Eng.   2660 110
                           Pablo               Ger.   2310 790
                           Pablo               Ger.   2625 703
                           Pablo               It.    2310 790A
                           Pablo               Jap.   MTF 1077
                           Verve               USA    MG V-8038
```

3980 LOVE FOR SALE (4:37)
     (mx 1424-1)
          7 Inch 45EP Clef   USA   EP-267
          12 Inch LP   Barclay   Fr.   GLP3503
                       Blue Star   Fr.   GLP 3503
                       >Clef   USA   MG C-614
                       Pablo   USA   2310-723
                       Pablo   USA   2625-703
                       Pablo   Braz. 2310 723
                       Pablo   Can.   2310-723
                       Pablo   Eng.   2310 723
                       Pablo   Eng.   2660 110
                       Pablo   Ger.   2310 723
                       Pablo   Ger.   2625 703
                       Pablo   It.   2310 723A
                       Pablo   Jap.   MTF 1073
                       Verve   USA   MG V-8038

3990 JUDY (3:44)
     (mx 1425-1)
          7 Inch 45EP Clef   USA   EP-267
          12 Inch LP   Barclay   Fr.   GLP3501
                       >Clef   USA   MG C-612
                       Columbia   Eng.   33CX10115
                       Metro   Ger.   2356 081
                       Pablo   USA   2310-870
                       Pablo   Can.   2310-870
                       Pablo   USA   2625-703
                       Pablo   Eng.   2310 811
                       Pablo   Eng.   2660 110
                       Pablo   Ger.   2625 703
                       Pablo   Jap.   28MJ 3147
                       Verve   USA   MG V-8036

4000 I´M COMING VIRGINIA (3:34)
     (mx 1426-1)
          10 Inch 78   Columbia   Eng.   LB 10053
          7 Inch 45EP Clef   USA   EP-267
          12 Inch LP   Barclay   Fr.   GLP3503
                       Blue Star   Fr.   GLP 3503
                       >Clef   USA   MG C-614
                       Pablo   USA   2310-791
                       Pablo   USA   2625-703
                       Pablo   Can.   2310-791
                       Pablo   Eng.   2310 791
                       Pablo   Eng.   2660 110
                       Pablo   Ger.   2310 791
                       Pablo   Ger.   2625 703
                       Pablo   It.   2310 791A
                       Pablo   Jap.   MTF 1078
                       Verve   USA   MG V-8038

4010 WRAP YOUR TROUBLES IS DREAMS (3:38)
     (mx 1427-2)
          10 Inch 78   Columbia   Eng.   LB 10053
          7 Inch 45EP Clef   USA   EP-268
          12 Inch LP   Barclay   Fr.   GLP3503
                       Blue Star   Fr.   GLP 3503
                       >Clef   USA   MG C-614
                       Pablo   USA   2625-703
                       Pablo   Eng.   2310 812
                       Pablo   Eng.   2660 110
                       Pablo   Ger.   2625 703
                       Verve   USA   MG V-8038

4020 DIXIELAND BAND (3:06)
     (mx 1428-1)
          7 Inch 45EP Clef   USA   EP-268
          12 Inch LP   Barclay   Fr.   GLP3501
                       Book-of-the-Month USA   51-400
                       >Clef   USA   MG C-612
                       Columbia   Eng.   33CX10115
                       Metro   Ger.   2356 081
                       Pablo   USA   2310-730

		Pablo	USA	2625-703
		Pablo	Can.	2310-730
		Pablo	Eng.	2310 730
		Pablo	Eng.	2660 110
		Pablo	Ger.	2310 730
		Pablo	Ger.	2625 703
		Pablo	It.	2310 730A
		Pablo	Jap.	MTF 1075
		Verve	USA	MG V-8036
		Verve	USA	V-8433
		Verve	USA	V6-8433
		Verve	Ger.	511 063

4030 EMBRACEABLE YOU (4:35)
(mx 1429-1)

7 Inch 45EP	Clef	USA	EP-269
	Columbia	Eng.	SEB 10003
12 Inch LP	Barclay	Fr.	GLP3503
	Blue Star	Fr.	GLP 3503
	>Clef	USA	MG C-614
	Pablo	USA	2310-835
	Pablo	USA	2625-703
	Pablo	Can.	2310-835
	Pablo	Eng.	2310 808
	Pablo	Eng.	2660 110
	Pablo	Fr.	2310 808
	Pablo	Ger.	2310 808
	Pablo	Ger.	2625 703
	Pablo	Jap.	MTF 1095
	Verve	USA	MG V-8038

4040 COME RAIN OR COME SHINE (5:05)
(mx 1430-1)

7 Inch 45EP	Clef	USA	EP-269
	Columbia	Eng.	SEB 10003
12 Inch LP	Barclay	Fr.	GLP3503
	Blue Star	Fr.	GLP 3503
	>Clef	USA	MG C-614
	Pablo	USA	2310-835
	Pablo	USA	2625-703
	Pablo	Can.	2310-835
	Pablo	Eng.	2310 808
	Pablo	Eng.	2660 110
	Pablo	Fr.	2310 808
	Pablo	Ger.	2310 808
	Pablo	Ger.	2625 703
	Pablo	Jap.	MTF 1095
	Verve	USA	MG V-8038

4050 SITTIN´ AND ROCKIN´ (3:54)
(mx 1431-1)

7 Inch 45EP	Clef	USA	EP-268
12 Inch LP	Barclay	Fr.	GLP3504
	Book-of-the-Month	USA	51-400
	>Clef	USA	MG C-615
	Columbia	Eng.	33CX10053
	Pablo	USA	2310-723
	Pablo	USA	2625-703
	Pablo	Braz.	2310 723
	Pablo	Can.	2310-723
	Pablo	Eng.	2310 723
	Pablo	Eng.	2660 110
	Pablo	Ger.	2310 723
	Pablo	Ger.	2625 703
	Pablo	It.	2310 723A
	Pablo	Jap.	MTF 1073
	Verve	USA	MG V-8039

4060 THERE WILL NEVER BE ANOTHER YOU (5:26)
(mx 1432-1)

7 Inch 45EP	Clef	USA	EP-270
12 Inch LP	Barclay	Fr.	GLP3504
	>Clef	USA	MG C-615
	Columbia	Eng.	33CX10053
	Pablo	USA	2310-729

```
                              Pablo                USA   2625-703
                              Pablo                Can.  2310-729
                              Pablo                Eng.  2310 729
                              Pablo                Eng.  2660 110
                              Pablo                Ger.  2310 729
                              Pablo                Ger.  2625 703
                              Pablo                It.   2310 729A
                              Pablo                Jap.  MTF 1074
                              Verve                USA   MG V-8039

4070  TENDERLY (5:03)
      (mx 1433-1)
          7 Inch 45EP Clef                         USA   EP-270
          12 Inch LP  Barclay                      Fr.   GLP3504
                     >Clef                         USA   MG C-615
                      Columbia                      Eng.  33CX10053
                      Pablo                         USA   2310-730
                      Pablo                         USA   2625-703
                      Pablo                         Can.  2310-730
                      Pablo                         Eng.  2310 730
                      Pablo                         Eng.  2660 110
                      Pablo                         Ger.  2310 730
                      Pablo                         Ger.  2625 703
                      Pablo                         It.   2310 730A
                      Pablo                         Jap.  MTF 1075
                      Verve                         USA   MG V-8039
                      Verve                         USA   V-8433
                      Verve                         USA   V6-8433
                      Verve                         Ger.  511 063

4080  WHAT DOES IT TAKE? (2:50)
      (mx 1434-1)
          7 Inch 45EP Clef                         USA   EP-271
          12 Inch LP  Barclay                      Fr.   GLP3504
                     >Clef                         USA   MG C-615
                      Columbia                      Eng.  33CX10053
                      Pablo                         USA   2310-792
                      Pablo                         USA   2625-703
                      Pablo                         Can.  2310-792
                      Pablo                         Eng.  2310 792
                      Pablo                         Eng.  2660 110
                      Pablo                         Ger.  2310 792
                      Pablo                         Ger.  2625 703
                      Pablo                         It.   2310 792A
                      Pablo                         Jap.  MTF 1079
                      Verve                         USA   MG V-8039

4090  YOU TOOK ADVANTAGE OF ME (3:14)
      (mx 1435-1)
          7 Inch 45EP Clef                         USA   EP-271
          12 Inch LP  Barclay                      Fr.   GLP3504
                      Book-of-the-Month            USA   51-400
                     >Clef                         USA   MG C-615
                      Columbia                      Eng.  33CX10053
                      Pablo                         USA   2310-835
                      Pablo                         USA   2625-703
                      Pablo                         Can.  2310-835
                      Pablo                         Eng.  2310 808
                      Pablo                         Eng.  2660 110
                      Pablo                         Fr.   2310 808
                      Pablo                         Ger.  2310 808
                      Pablo                         Ger.  2625 703
                      Pablo                         Jap.  MTF 1095
                      Verve                         USA   MG V-8039

4100  MIGHTY LAK A ROSE
      (mx 1436-1)
                      Clef                         USA   Unissued

4110  I'VE GOT THE WORLD ON A STRING (3:52)
      (mx 1437-1)
          7 Inch 45EP Clef                         USA   EP-272
          12 Inch LP  Barclay                      Fr.   GLP3504
                     >Clef                         USA   MG C-615
                      Columbia                      Eng.  33CX10053
```

```
                                    Pablo              USA   2310-789
                                    Pablo              USA   2625-703
                                    Pablo              Can.  2310-789
                                    Pablo              Eng.  2310 789
                                    Pablo              Eng.  2660 110
                                    Pablo              Ger.  2310 789
                                    Pablo              Ger.  2625 703
                                    Pablo              It.   2310 789A
                                    Pablo              Jap.  MTF 1076
                                    Verve              USA   MG V-8039

4120  YESTERDAYS (3:26)
      (mx 1438-1)
            7 Inch 45EP  Clef      USA   EP-272
           12 Inch  LP   Barclay   Fr.   GLP3504
                        >Clef      USA   MG C-615
                         Columbia  Eng.  33CX10053
                         Pablo     USA   2310-730
                         Pablo     USA   2625-703
                         Pablo     Can.  2310-730
                         Pablo     Eng.  2310 730
                         Pablo     Eng.  2660 110
                         Pablo     Ger.  2310 730
                         Pablo     Ger.  2625 703
                         Pablo     It.   2310 730A
                         Pablo     Jap.  MTF 1075
                         Verve     USA   MG V-8039

4130  I HADN´T ANYONE ´TILL YOU (3:28)
      (mx 1439-1)
            7 Inch 45EP  Clef              USA   EP-C-349
                         Karusell          Swed. KEP291
           12 Inch  LP   Barclay           Fr.   GLP3524
                         Book-of-the-Month USA   51-400
                        >Clef              USA   MG C-657
                         Pablo             USA   2310-864
                         Pablo             USA   2625-703
                         Pablo             Can.  2310-864
                         Pablo             Eng.  2310 810
                         Pablo             Eng.  2660 110
                         Pablo             Ger.  2625 703
                         Pablo             Jap.  28MJ 3146
                         Verve             USA   MG V-8055

4140  NIGHT AND DAY (3:10)
      (mx 1440-1)
            7 Inch 45EP  Clef      USA   EP-C-349
                         Karusell  Swed. KEP291
           10 Inch  LP   Columbia  Eng.  33C 9033
           12 Inch  LP   Barclay   Fr.   GLP3524
                        >Clef      USA   MG C-657
                         Pablo     USA   2310-791
                         Pablo     USA   2625-703
                         Pablo     Can.  2310-791
                         Pablo     Eng.  2310 791
                         Pablo     Eng.  2660 110
                         Pablo     Ger.  2310 791
                         Pablo     Ger.  2625 703
                         Pablo     It.   2310 791A
                         Pablo     Jap.  MTF 1078
                         Verve     USA   MG V-8055

4150  JITTERBUG WALTZ (3:47)
      (mx 1441-1)
            7 Inch 45EP  Clef              USA   EP-C-350
           10 Inch  LP   Columbia          Eng.  33C 9033
           12 Inch  LP   Barclay           Fr.   GLP3524
                         Book-of-the-Month USA   51-400
                        >Clef              USA   MG C-657
                         Pablo             USA   2310-730
                         Pablo             USA   2625-703
                         Pablo             Can.  2310-730
                         Pablo             Eng.  2310 730
                         Pablo             Eng.  2660 110
                         Pablo             Ger.  2310 730
```

	Pablo	Ger.	2625 703
	Pablo	It.	2310 730A
	Pablo	Jap.	MTF 1075
	Verve	USA	MG V-8055
	Verve	USA	V-8433
	Verve	USA	V6-8433
	Verve	Ger.	511 063

4160 SOMEONE TO WATCH OVER ME (3:47)
(mx 1442-1)

7 Inch 45EP	Clef	USA	EP-C-350
12 Inch LP	Barclay	Fr.	GLP3525
	>Clef	USA	MG C-658
	Pablo	USA	2310-870
	Pablo	Can.	2310-870
	Pablo	USA	2625-703
	Pablo	Eng.	2310 811
	Pablo	Eng.	2660 110
	Pablo	Ger.	2625 703
	Pablo	Jap.	28MJ 3147
	Verve	USA	MG V-8056
	Verve	USA	V-8433
	Verve	USA	V6-8433
	Verve	Ger.	511 063

4170 THE VERY THOUGHT OF YOU (4:25)
(mx 1443-1)

7 Inch 45EP	Clef	USA	EP-C-352
12 Inch LP	Barclay	Fr.	GLP3525
	>Clef	USA	MG C-658
	Pablo	USA	2310-862
	Pablo	USA	2625-703
	Pablo	Can.	2310-862
	Pablo	Eng.	2310 809
	Pablo	Eng.	2660 110
	Pablo	Fr.	2310 809
	Pablo	Ger.	2310 809
	Pablo	Ger.	2625 703
	Pablo	Jap.	MTF 1096
	Verve	USA	MG V-8056

4180 YOU´RE DRIVING ME CRAZY (2:37)
(mx 1444-1)

7 Inch 45EP	Clef	USA	EP-C-351
	Karusell	Swed.	KEP292
10 Inch LP	Columbia	Eng.	33C 9033
12 Inch LP	Barclay	Fr.	GLP3524
	>Clef	USA	MG C-657
	Pablo	USA	2310-790
	Pablo	USA	2625-703
	Pablo	Can.	2310-790
	Pablo	Eng.	2310 790
	Pablo	Eng.	2660 110
	Pablo	Ger.	2310 790
	Pablo	Ger.	2625 703
	Pablo	It.	2310 790A
	Pablo	Jap.	MTF 1077
	Verve	USA	MG V-8055

4190 A GHOST OF A CHANCE (4:09)
(mx 1445-1)

7 Inch 45EP	Clef	USA	EP-C-351
	Karusell	Swed.	KEP292
12 Inch LP	Barclay	Fr.	GLP3525
	>Clef	USA	MG C-658
	Pablo	USA	2310-729
	Pablo	USA	2625-703
	Pablo	Can.	2310-729
	Pablo	Eng.	2310 729
	Pablo	Eng.	2660 110
	Pablo	Ger.	2310 729
	Pablo	Ger.	2625 703
	Pablo	It.	2310 729A
	Pablo	Jap.	MTF 1074
	Verve	USA	MG V-8056

```
-----------------------------------------------------------------
Los Angeles, California                        December 29, 1953
           Piano solos.
4200   STAR DUST (5:00)
       (mx 1446-1)
              7 Inch 45EP  Clef                   USA    EP-C-352
              12 Inch LP   Barclay                Fr.    GLP3525
                          >Clef                   USA    MG C-658
                           Pablo                  USA    2310-789
                           Pablo                  USA    2625-703
                           Pablo                  Can.   2310-789
                           Pablo                  Eng.   2310 789
                           Pablo                  Eng.   2660 110
                           Pablo                  Ger.   2310 789
                           Pablo                  Ger.   2625 703
                           Pablo                  It.    2310 789A
                           Pablo                  Jap.   MTF 1076
                           Verve                  USA    MG V-8056
              12 Inch TX   AFRS Amer.Pop.Mus.     USA    149
                           AFRS Amer.Pop.Mus.     USA    194


4210   I COVER THE WATERFRONT (3:42)
       (mx 1447-1)
              7 Inch 45EP  Clef                   USA    EP-C-351
                           Karusell               Swed.  KEP292
              12 Inch LP   Barclay                Fr.    GLP3526
                          >Clef                   USA    MG C-659
                           Pablo                  USA    2310-790
                           Pablo                  USA    2625-703
                           Pablo                  Can.   2310-790
                           Pablo                  Eng.   2310 790
                           Pablo                  Eng.   2660 110
                           Pablo                  Ger.   2310 790
                           Pablo                  Ger.   2625 703
                           Pablo                  It.    2310 790A
                           Pablo                  Jap.   MTF 1077
                           Verve                  USA    MG V-8057


4220   WHERE OR WHEN (5:12)
       (mx 1448-1)
              7 Inch 45EP  Clef                   USA    EP-C-353
              12 Inch LP   Barclay                Fr.    GLP3525
                          >Clef                   USA    MG C-658
                           Pablo                  USA    2625-703
                           Pablo                  Eng.   2310 812
                           Pablo                  Eng.   2660 110
                           Pablo                  Ger.   2625 703
                           Verve                  USA    MG V-8056


4230   STAY AS SWEET AS YOU ARE (5:06)
       (mx 1449-1)
              7 Inch 45EP  Clef                   USA    EP-C-353
              12 Inch LP   Barclay                Fr.    GLP3525
                           Book-of-the-Month      USA    51-400
                          >Clef                   USA    MG C-658
                           Pablo                  USA    2310-723
                           Pablo                  USA    2625-703
                           Pablo                  Braz.  2310 723
                           Pablo                  Can.   2310-723
                           Pablo                  Eng.   2310 723
                           Pablo                  Eng.   2660 110
                           Pablo                  Ger.   2310 723
                           Pablo                  Ger.   2625 703
                           Pablo                  It.    2310 723A
                           Pablo                  Jap.   MTF 1073
                           Verve                  USA    MG V-8056


4240   FINE AND DANDY (2:59)
       (mx 1450-1)
              7 Inch 45EP  Clef                   USA    EP-C-354
              12 Inch LP   Barclay                Fr.    GLP3526
                           Book-of-the-Month      USA    51-400
                          >Clef                   USA    MG C-659
                           Pablo                  USA    2310-790
                           Pablo                  USA    2625-703
```

```
                           Pablo                      Can.  2310-790
                           Pablo                      Eng.  2310 790
                           Pablo                      Eng.  2660 110
                           Pablo                      Ger.  2310 790
                           Pablo                      Ger.  2625 703
                           Pablo                      It.   2310 790A
                           Pablo                      Jap.  MTF 1077
                           Verve                      USA   MG V-8057

4250   ALL THE THINGS YOU ARE (5:59)
       (mx 1451-1)
            7 Inch 45EP Clef                          USA   EP-C-355
           12 Inch LP    Barclay                      Fr.   GLP3526
                        >Clef                         USA   MG C-659
                         MGM                          USA   E4241
                         MGM                          USA   SE4241
                         Pablo                        USA   2310-730
                         Pablo                        USA   2625-703
                         Pablo                        Can.  2310-730
                         Pablo                        Eng.  2310 730
                         Pablo                        Eng.  2660 110
                         Pablo                        Ger.  2310 730
                         Pablo                        Ger.  2625 703
                         Pablo                        It.   2310 730A
                         Pablo                        Jap.  MTF 1075
                         Verve                        USA   MG V-8057

4260   HAVE YOU MET MISS JONES (4:45)
       (mx 1452-1)
            7 Inch 45EP Clef                          USA   EP-272
           12 Inch LP    Barclay                      Fr.   GLP3505
                         Book-of-the-Month            USA   51-400
                        >Clef                         USA   MG C-618
                         Pablo                        USA   2310-723
                         Pablo                        USA   2625-703
                         Pablo                        Braz. 2310 723
                         Pablo                        Can.  2310-723
                         Pablo                        Eng.  2310 723
                         Pablo                        Eng.  2660 110
                         Pablo                        Ger.  2310 723
                         Pablo                        Ger.  2625 703
                         Pablo                        It.   2310 723A
                         Pablo                        Jap.  MTF 1073
                         Verve                        USA   MG V-8040

4270   IN A SENTIMENTAL MOOD (5:59)
       (mx 1453-1)
            7 Inch 45EP Clef                          USA   EP-273
           12 Inch LP    Barclay                      Fr.   GLP3505
                        >Clef                         USA   MG C-618
                         Pablo                        USA   2310-793
                         Pablo                        USA   ?625-703
                         Pablo                        Can.  2310-793
                         Pablo                        Eng.  2310 793
                         Pablo                        Eng.  2660 110
                         Pablo                        Ger.  2310 793
                         Pablo                        Ger.  2625 703
                         Pablo                        It.   2310 793A
                         Pablo                        Jap.  MTF 1080
                         Verve                        USA   MG V-8040

4280   I'LL SEE YOU AGAIN (4:49)
       (mx 1454-1)
            7 Inch 45EP Clef                          USA   EP-C-354
           12 Inch LP    Barclay                      Fr.   GLP3525
                        >Clef                         USA   MG C-658
                         Pablo                        USA   2310-864
                         Pablo                        USA   2625-703
                         Pablo                        Can.  2310-864
                         Pablo                        Eng.  2310 810
                         Pablo                        Eng.  2660 110
                         Pablo                        Ger.  2625 703
                         Pablo                        Jap.  28MJ 3146
                         Verve                        USA   MG V-8056
```

85

```
4290  I'LL SEE YOU IN MY DREAMS (3:15)
      (mx 1455-1)
            7 Inch 45EP  Clef                    USA    EP-C-354
            12 Inch LP   Barclay                 Fr.    GLP3527
                         Book-of-the-Month       USA    51-400
                        >Clef                    USA    MG C-660
                         Pablo                   USA    2310-729
                         Pablo                   USA    2625-703
                         Pablo                   Can.   2310-729
                         Pablo                   Eng.   2310 729
                         Pablo                   Eng.   2660 110
                         Pablo                   Ger.   2310 729
                         Pablo                   Ger.   2625 703
                         Pablo                   It.    2310 729A
                         Pablo                   Jap.   MTF 1074
                         Verve                   USA    MG V-8058
            12 Inch TX   AFRS Amer.Pop.Mus.      USA    149
                         AFRS Amer.Pop.Mus.      USA    194

4300  ILL WIND (5:16)
      (mx 1456-1)
            7 Inch 45EP  Clef                    USA    EP-C-355
            12 Inch LP   Barclay                 Fr.    GLP3527
                         Book-of-the Month       USA    51-400
                        >Clef                    USA    MG C-660
                         Pablo                   USA    2310-789
                         Pablo                   USA    2625-703
                         Pablo                   Can.   2310-789
                         Pablo                   Eng.   2310 789
                         Pablo                   Eng.   2660 110
                         Pablo                   Ger.   2310 789
                         Pablo                   Ger.   2625 703
                         Pablo                   It.    2310 789A
                         Pablo                   Jap.   MTF 1076
                         Verve                   USA    MG V-8058

4310  ISN'T THIS A LOVELY DAY (3:29)
      (mx 1457-1)
            7 Inch 45EP  Clef                    USA    EP-273
            12 Inch LP   Barclay                 Fr.    GLP3505
                         Book-of-the-Month       USA    51-400
                        >Clef                    USA    MG C-618
                         Pablo                   USA    2310-789
                         Pablo                   USA    2625-703
                         Pablo                   Can.   2310-789
                         Pablo                   Eng.   2310 789
                         Pablo                   Eng.   2660 110
                         Pablo                   Ger.   2310 789
                         Pablo                   Ger.   2625 703
                         Pablo                   It.    2310 789A
                         Pablo                   Jap.   MTF 1076
                         Verve                   USA    MG V-8040

4320  BLUE SKIES (2:56)
      (mx 1458-1)
            7 Inch 45EP  Clef                    USA    EP-C-356
                         Clef                    Astla  EP-C-356
                         Karusell                Swed.  KEP293
            12 Inch LP   Barclay                 Fr.    GLP3527
                        >Clef                    USA    MG C-660
                         Pablo                   USA    2310-793
                         Pablo                   USA    2625-703
                         Pablo                   Can.   2310-793
                         Pablo                   Eng.   2310 793
                         Pablo                   Eng.   2660 110
                         Pablo                   Ger.   2310 793
                         Pablo                   Ger.   2625 703
                         Pablo                   It.    2310 793A
                         Pablo                   Jap.   MTF 1080
                         Verve                   USA    MG V-8058
            12 Inch TX   AFRS Amer.Pop.Mus.      USA    149
                         AFRS Amer.Pop.Mus.      USA    194
```

```
4330   WITHOUT A SONG (5:47)
       (mx 1459-1)
            7 Inch 45EP Clef                   USA    EP-274
           12 Inch LP    Barclay               Fr.    GLP3505
                        >Clef                  USA    MG C-618
                         Pablo                 USA    2310-864
                         Pablo                 USA    2625-703
                         Pablo                 Can.   2310-864
                         Pablo                 Eng.   2310 810
                         Pablo                 Eng.   2660 110
                         Pablo                 Ger.   2625 703
                         Pablo                 Jap.   28MJ 3146
                         Verve                 USA    MG V-8040
           12 Inch TX    AFRS Amer.Pop.Mus.    USA    194

4340   STOMPIN´ AT THE SAVOY (2:57)
       (mx 1460-1)
            7 Inch 45EP Clef                   USA    EP-273
           12 Inch LP    Barclay               Fr.    GLP3505
                        >Clef                  USA    MG C-618
                         Columbia              Eng.   33CX10024
                         Norgran               USA    MG N-1036
                         Pablo                 USA    2310-790
                         Pablo                 USA    2625-703
                         Pablo                 Can.   2310-790
                         Pablo                 Eng.   2310 790
                         Pablo                 Eng.   2660 110
                         Pablo                 Ger.   2310 790
                         Pablo                 Ger.   2625 703
                         Pablo                 It.    2310 790A
                         Pablo                 Jap.   MTF 1077
                         Verve                 USA    MG V-8040
                         Verve                 USA    MG V-8127
                         VSP Verve             USA    VSP 33
                         VSP Verve             USA    VSPS33
                         VSP Verve             It.    SVSP57.009

4350   MY LAST AFFAIR (2:50)
       (mx 1461-1)
            7 Inch 45EP Clef                   USA    EP-274
           12 Inch LP    Barclay               Fr.    GLP3505
                        >Clef                  USA    MG C-618
                         Pablo                 USA    2310-723
                         Pablo                 USA    2625-703
                         Pablo                 Braz.  2310 723
                         Pablo                 Can.   2310-723
                         Pablo                 Eng.   2310 723
                         Pablo                 Eng.   2660 110
                         Pablo                 Ger.   2310 723
                         Pablo                 Ger.   2625 703
                         Pablo                 It.    2310 723A
                         Pablo                 Jap.   MTF 1073
                         Verve                 USA    MG V-8040

4360   I´M IN THE MOOD FOR LOVE (4:22)
       (mx 1462-1)
            7 Inch 45EP Clef                   USA    EP-C-357
           12 Inch LP    Barclay               Fr.    GLP3526
                        >Clef                  USA    MG C-659
                         MGM                   USA    RFM-816
                         Pablo                 USA    2310-835
                         Pablo                 USA    2625-703
                         Pablo                 Can.   2310-835
                         Pablo                 Eng.   2310 808
                         Pablo                 Eng.   2660 110
                         Pablo                 Fr.    2310 808
                         Pablo                 Ger.   2310 808
                         Pablo                 Ger.   2625 703
                         Pablo                 Jap.   MTF 1095
                         Verve                 USA    MG V-8057

4370   TABOO (2:46)
       (mx 1463-1)
            7 Inch 45EP Clef                   USA    EP-274
           12 Inch LP    Barclay               Fr.    GLP3505
```

```
                     Book-of-the-Month   USA   51-400
                    >Clef                USA   MG C-618
                     Pablo               USA   2310-792
                     Pablo               USA   2625-703
                     Pablo               Can.  2310-792
                     Pablo               Eng.  2310 792
                     Pablo               Eng.  2660 110
                     Pablo               Ger.  2310 792
                     Pablo               Ger.  2625 703
                     Pablo               It.   2310 792A
                     Pablo               Jap.  MTF 1079
                     Verve               USA   MG V-8040

4380  WOULD YOU LIKE TO TAKE A WALK (4:13)
      (mx 1464-1)
         7 Inch 45EP Clef                USA   EP-C-350
         12 Inch LP  Barclay             Fr.   GLP3527
                    >Clef                USA   MG C-660
                     Pablo               USA   2310-862
                     Pablo               USA   2625-703
                     Pablo               Can.  2310-862
                     Pablo               Eng.  2310 809
                     Pablo               Eng.  2660 110
                     Pablo               Fr.   2310 809
                     Pablo               Ger.  2310 809
                     Pablo               Ger.  2625 703
                     Pablo               Jap.  MTF 1096
                     Verve               USA   MG V-8058
                     Verve               USA   V-8433
                     Verve               USA   V6-8433
                     Verve               Ger.  511 063

4390  I'VE GOT A CRUSH ON YOU (3:34)
      (mx 1465-1)
         7 Inch 45EP Clef                USA   EP-C-356
                     Clef                Astla EP-C-356
                     Karusell            Swed. KEP293
         12 Inch LP  Barclay             Fr.   GLP3527
                    >Clef                USA   MG C-660
                     Pablo               USA   2310-791
                     Pablo               USA   2625-703
                     Pablo               Can.  2310-791
                     Pablo               Eng.  2310 791
                     Pablo               Eng.  2660 110
                     Pablo               Ger.  2310 791
                     Pablo               Ger.  2625 703
                     Pablo               It.   2310 791A
                     Pablo               Jap.  MTF 1078
                     Verve               USA   MG V-8058

4400  THE JAPANESE SANDMAN (3:01)
      (mx 1466-1)
         7 Inch 45EP Clef                USA   EP-C-357
         12 Inch LP  Barclay             Fr.   GLP3527
                     Book-of-the-Month   USA   51-400
                    >Clef                USA   MG C-660
                     Pablo               USA   2310-792
                     Pablo               USA   2625-703
                     Pablo               Can.  2310-792
                     Pablo               Eng.  2310 792
                     Pablo               Eng.  2660 110
                     Pablo               Ger.  2310 792
                     Pablo               Ger.  2625 703
                     Pablo               It.   2310 792A
                     Pablo               Jap.  MTF 1079
                     Verve               USA   MG V-8058

4410  TOO MARVELOUS FOR WORDS (2:57)
      (mx 1467-1)
         7 Inch 45EP Clef                USA   EP-C-357
         12 Inch LP  Barclay             Fr.   GLP3528
                    >Clef                USA   MG C-661
                     Pablo               USA   2310-835
                     Pablo               USA   2625-703
                     Pablo               Can.  2310-835
```

```
                              Pablo              Eng.   2310 808
                              Pablo              Eng.   2660 110
                              Pablo              Fr.    2310 808
                              Pablo              Ger.   2310 808
                              Pablo              Ger.   2625 703
                              Pablo              Jap.   MTF 1095
                              Time-Life          USA    P 15516
                              Verve              USA    MG V-8059

4420  AUNT HAGAR'S BLUES (4:50)
      (mx 1468-1)
           7 Inch 45EP Clef                     USA    EP-C-358
                       Clef                     Astla  EP-C-358
          12 Inch LP   Barclay                  Fr.    GLP3527
                      >Clef                     USA    MG C-660
                       Pablo                     USA    2310-789
                       Pablo                     USA    2625-703
                       Pablo                     Can.   2310-789
                       Pablo                     Eng.   2310 789
                       Pablo                     Eng.   2660 110
                       Pablo                     Ger.   2310 789
                       Pablo                     Ger.   2625 703
                       Pablo                     It.    2310 789A
                       Pablo                     Jap.   MTF 1076
                       Verve                     USA    MG V-8058

4430  JUST LIKE A BUTTERFLY THAT'S CAUGHT IN THE RAIN (3:48)
      (mx 1469-1)
           7 Inch 45EP Clef                     USA    EP-C-358
                       Clef                     Astla  EP-C-358
          12 Inch LP   Barclay                  Fr.    GLP3528
                      >Clef                     USA    MG C-661
                       Pablo                     USA    2310-870
                       Pablo                     Can.   2310-870
                       Pablo                     USA    2625-703
                       Pablo                     Eng.   2310 811
                       Pablo                     Eng.   2660 110
                       Pablo                     Ger.   2625 703
                       Pablo                     Jap.   28MJ 3147
                       Verve                     USA    MG V-8059

4440  GONE WITH THE WIND (2:57)
      (mx 1470-1)
           7 Inch 45EP Clef                     USA    EP-C-359
          12 Inch LP   Barclay                  Fr.    GLP3528
                       Book-of-the-Month        USA    51-400
                      >Clef                     USA    MG C-661
                       Pablo                     USA    2310-729
                       Pablo                     USA    2625-703
                       Pablo                     Can.   2310-729
                       Pablo                     Eng.   2310 729
                       Pablo                     Eng.   2335 749
                       Pablo                     Eng.   2660 110
                       Pablo                     Ger.   2310 729
                       Pablo                     Ger.   2625 703
                       Pablo                     It.    2310 729A
                       Pablo                     Jap.   MTF 1074
                       Verve                     USA    MG V-8059

4450  DANNY BOY (4:08)
      (mx 1471-1)
           7 Inch 45EP Clef                     USA    EP-C-359
          12 Inch LP   Barclay                  Fr.    GLP3528
                      >Clef                     USA    MG C-661
                       Pablo                     USA    2310-870
                       Pablo                     Can.   2310-870
                       Pablo                     USA    2625-703
                       Pablo                     Eng.   2310 811
                       Pablo                     Eng.   2660 110
                       Pablo                     Ger.   2625 703
                       Pablo                     Jap.   28MJ 3147
                       Verve                     USA    MG V-8059
```

```
4460  THEY CAN´T TAKE THAT AWAY FROM ME (4:45)
      (mx 1472-1)
            7 Inch 45EP Clef                 USA   EP-C-359
           12 Inch LP   Barclay              Fr.   GLP3528
                       >Clef                 USA   MG C-661
                        Pablo                USA   2310-789
                        Pablo                USA   2625-703
                        Pablo                Can.  2310-789
                        Pablo                Eng.  2310 789
                        Pablo                Eng.  2660 110
                        Pablo                Ger.  2310 789
                        Pablo                Ger.  2625 703
                        Pablo                It.   2310 789A
                        Pablo                Jap.  MTF 1076
                        Verve                USA   MG V-8059

4470  TEA FOR TWO (3:29)
      (mx 1473-1)
            7 Inch 45EP Clef                 USA   EP-C-360
           12 Inch LP   Barclay              Fr.   GLP3528
                       >Clef                 USA   MG C-661
                        Pablo                USA   2310-835
                        Pablo                USA   2625-703
                        Pablo                Can.  2310-835
                        Pablo                Eng.  2310 808
                        Pablo                Eng.  2660 110
                        Pablo                Fr.   2310 808
                        Pablo                Ger.  2310 808
                        Pablo                Ger.  2625 703
                        Pablo                Jap.  MTF 1095
                        Verve                USA   MG V-8059

4480  IT´S THE TALK OF THE TOWN (3:40)
      (mx 1474-1)
            7 Inch 45EP Clef                 USA   EP-C-358
                        Clef                 Astla EP-C-358
           12 Inch LP   Barclay              Fr.   GLP3528
                       >Clef                 USA   MG C-661
                        Pablo                USA   2310-793
                        Pablo                USA   2625-703
                        Pablo                Can.  2310-793
                        Pablo                Eng.  2310 793
                        Pablo                Eng.  2660 110
                        Pablo                Ger.  2310 793
                        Pablo                Ger.  2625 703
                        Pablo                It.   2310 793A
                        Pablo                Jap.  MTF 1080
                        Verve                USA   MG V-8059

4490  BLUE LOU (2:40)
      (mx 1475-1)
            7 Inch 45EP Clef                 USA   EP-C-360
           12 Inch LP   Barclay              Fr.   GLP3528
                       >Clef                 USA   MG C-661
                        Pablo                USA   2310-679
                        Pablo                USA   2310-835
                        Pablo                USA   2625-703
                        Pablo                Can.  2310-835
                        Pablo                Eng.  2310 808
                        Pablo                Eng.  2660 110
                        Pablo                Fr.   2310 808
                        Pablo                Ger.  2310 808
                        Pablo                Ger.  2625 703
                        Pablo                Jap.  MTF 1095
                        Verve                USA   MG V-8059

4500  WHEN A WOMAN LOVES A MAN (5:30)
      (mx 1476-1)
            7 Inch 45EP Clef                 USA   EP-C-361
           12 Inch LP   Barclay              Fr.   GLP3526
                       >Clef                 USA   MG C-659
                        Pablo                USA   2625-703
                        Pablo                Eng.  2310 812
                        Pablo                Eng.  2660 110
                        Pablo                Ger.  2625 703
```

```
                        Verve              USA   MG V-8057

4510  WILLOW WEEP FOR ME (4:32)
      (mx 1477-1)
           7 Inch 45EP Clef                USA   EP-C-361
          12 Inch LP    Barclay            Fr.   GLP3526
                        Book-of-the-Month  USA   51-400
                       >Clef               USA   MG C-659
                        Pablo              USA   2310-723
                        Pablo              USA   2625-703
                        Pablo              Braz. 2310 723
                        Pablo              Can.  2310-723
                        Pablo              Eng.  2310 723
                        Pablo              Eng.  2660 110
                        Pablo              Ger.  2310 723
                        Pablo              Ger.  2625 703
                        Pablo              It.   2310 723A
                        Pablo              Jap.  MTF 1073
                        Verve              USA   MG V-8057
                        Verve              USA   V-8433
                        Verve              USA   V6-8433
                        Verve              Ger.  511 063

4520  AIN'T MISBEHAVIN' (2:32)
      (mx 1478-1)
           7 Inch 45EP Clef                USA   EP-C-360
          12 Inch LP    Barclay            Fr.   GLP3526
                        Book-of-the-Month  USA   51-400
                       >Clef               USA   MG C-659
                        Pablo              USA   2310-791
                        Pablo              USA   2625-703
                        Pablo              Can.  2310-791
                        Pablo              Eng.  2310 791
                        Pablo              Eng.  2660 110
                        Pablo              Ger.  2310 791
                        Pablo              Ger.  2625 703
                        Pablo              It.   2310 791A
                        Pablo              Jap.  MTF 1078
                        Verve              USA   MG V-8057

4530  SMOKE GETS IN YOUR EYES (3:51)
      (mx 1479-1)
           7 Inch 45EP Clef                USA   EP-C-362
          10 Inch LP    Columbia           Eng.  33C 9033
          12 Inch LP    Barclay            Fr.   GLP3524
                       >Clef               USA   MG C-657
                        Pablo              USA   2310-792
                        Pablo              USA   2625-703
                        Pablo              Can.  2310-792
                        Pablo              Eng   2310 792
                        Pablo              Eng.  2660 110
                        Pablo              Ger.  2310 792
                        Pablo              Ger.  2625 703
                        Pablo              It.   2310 792A
                        Pablo              Jap.  MTF 1079
                        Verve              USA   MG V-8055

4540  MIGHTY LAK A ROSE (6:06)
      (mx 1480-1)
           7 Inch 45EP Clef                USA   EP-271
          12 Inch LP    Barclay            Fr.   GLP3502
                       >Clef               USA   MG C-613
                        Columbia           Eng.  33CX10005
                        Pablo              USA   2310-792
                        Pablo              USA   2625-703
                        Pablo              Can.  2310-792
                        Pablo              Eng.  2310 792
                        Pablo              Eng.  2660 110
                        Pablo              Ger.  2310 792
                        Pablo              Ger.  2625 703
                        Pablo              It.   2310 792A
                        Pablo              Jap.  MTF 1079
                        Verve              USA   MG V-8037
```

```
                    Piano solos.
4550   STARS FELL ON ALABAMA (5:51)
       (mx 1586-1)
               7 Inch 45EP Clef                  USA   EP-C-363
               10 Inch LP   Columbia             Eng.  33C 9033
               12 Inch LP   Barclay              Fr.   GLP3524
                           >Clef                 USA   MG C-657
                            Pablo                USA   2310-790
                            Pablo                USA   2625-703
                            Pablo                Can.  2310-790
                            Pablo                Eng.  2310 790
                            Pablo                Eng.  2660 110
                            Pablo                Ger.  2310 790
                            Pablo                Ger.  2625 703
                            Pablo                It.   2310 790A
                            Pablo                Jap.  MTF 1077
                            Verve                USA   MG V-8055

4560   BLUE MOON (4:57)
       (mx 1587-1)
               7 Inch 45EP Clef                  USA   EP-C-363
               10 Inch LP   Columbia             Eng.  33C 9033
               12 Inch LP   Barclay              Fr.   GLP3524
                            Book-of-the-Month     USA   51-400
                           >Clef                 USA   MG C-657
                            Pablo                USA   2310-790
                            Pablo                USA   2625-703
                            Pablo                Can.  2310-790
                            Pablo                Eng.  2310 790
                            Pablo                Eng.  2660 110
                            Pablo                Ger.  2310 790
                            Pablo                Ger.  2625 703
                            Pablo                It.   2310 790A
                            Pablo                Jap   MTF 1077
                            Verve                USA   MG V-8055

4570   THERE'S A SMALL HOTEL (5:05)
       (mx 1588-1)
               12 Inch LP  >Clef                 USA   MG C-712
                            Pablo                USA   2310-791
                            Pablo                USA   2625-703
                            Pablo                Can.  2310-791
                            Pablo                Eng.  2310 791
                            Pablo                Eng.  2660 110
                            Pablo                Ger.  2310 791
                            Pablo                Ger.  2625 703
                            Pablo                It.   2310 791A
                            Pablo                Jap.  MTF 1078
                            Verve                USA   MG V-8095

4580   CARAVAN (2:34)
       (mx 1589-1)
               7 Inch 45EP Clef                  USA   EP-C-356
                            Clef                 Astla EP-C-356
                            Karusell             Swed. KEP293
               12 Inch LP   Barclay              Fr.   GLP3528
                           >Clef                 USA   MG C-661
                            Pablo                USA   2625-703
                            Pablo                Eng.  2310 812
                            Pablo                Eng.  2660 110
                            Pablo                Ger.  2625 703
                            Verve                USA   MG V-8059

4590   THE WAY YOU LOOK TONIGHT (6:34)
       (mx 1590-3)
               12 Inch LP  >Clef                 USA   MG C-712
                            Pablo                USA   2310-791
                            Pablo                USA   2625-703
                            Pablo                Can.  2310-791
                            Pablo                Eng.  2310 791
                            Pablo                Eng   2660 110
                            Pablo                Ger.  2310 791
                            Pablo                Ger.  2625 703
```

```
                          Pablo                     It.    2310 791A
                          Pablo                     Jap.   MTF 1078
                          Verve                     USA    MG V-8095

4600  YOU GO TO MY HEAD (4:52)
      (mx 1591-1)
            12 Inch LP   >Clef                      USA    MG C-712
                          Pablo                     USA    2310-793
                          Pablo                     USA    2625-703
                          Pablo                     Can.   2310-793
                          Pablo                     Eng.   2310 793
                          Pablo                     Eng.   2660 110
                          Pablo                     Ger.   2310 793
                          Pablo                     Ger.   2625 703
                          Pablo                     It.    2310 793A
                          Pablo                     Jap.   MTF 1080
                          Verve                     USA    MG V-8095

4610  GONE WITH THE WIND
      (mx 1592-1)
                          Clef                      USA    Unissued

4620  LOVER, COME BACK TO ME! (6:43)
      (mx 1593-1)
            7 Inch 45EP  Clef                       USA    EP -C-362
            12 Inch LP   Barclay                    Fr.    GLP3527
                          Book-of-the-Month         USA    51-400
                         >Clef                      USA    MG C-660
                          Pablo                     USA    2310-729
                          Pablo                     USA    2625-703
                          Pablo                     Can.   2310-729
                          Pablo                     Eng.   2310 729
                          Pablo                     Eng.   2660 110
                          Pablo                     Ger.   2310 729
                          Pablo                     Ger.   2625 703
                          Pablo                     It.    2310 729A
                          Pablo                     Jap.   MTF 1074
                          Verve                     USA    MG V-8058
            12 Inch TX   AFRS Amer.Pop.Mus.         USA    149
                          AFRS Amer.Pop.Mus.         USA    194

4630  SOPHISTICATED LADY (3:32)
      (mx 1594-1)
            12 Inch LP   Book-of-the-Month         USA    51-400
                         >Clef                      USA    MG C-712
                          Pablo                     USA    2310-679
                          Pablo                     USA    2310-835
                          Pablo                     USA    2625-703
                          Pablo                     Can.   2310-835
                          Pablo                     Eng.   2310 808
                          Pablo                     Eng.   2660 110
                          Pablo                     Fr.    2310 808
                          Pablo                     Ger.   2310 808
                          Pablo                     Ger.   2625 703
                          Pablo                     Jap.   MTF 1095
                          Verve                     USA    MG V-8095

4640  DANCING IN THE DARK (4:27)
      (mx 1595-1)
            12 Inch LP   >Clef                      USA    MG C-712
                          Pablo                     USA    2310-792
                          Pablo                     USA    2625-703
                          Pablo                     Can.   2310-792
                          Pablo                     Eng.   2310 792
                          Pablo                     Eng.   2660 110
                          Pablo                     Ger.   2310 792
                          Pablo                     Ger.   2625 703
                          Pablo                     It.    2310 792A
                          Pablo                     Jap.   MTF 1079
                          Verve                     USA    MG V-8095

4650  LOVE ME OR LEAVE ME (3:18)
      (mx 1596-1)
            7 Inch 45EP  Clef                       USA    EP-C-356
                          Clef                       Astla  EP-C-356

                                93
```

	Karusell	Swed.	KEP293
12 Inch LP	Barclay	Fr.	GLP3526
	Book-of-the-Month	USA	51-400
	>Clef	USA	MG C-659
	Pablo	USA	2310-730
	Pablo	USA	2625-703
	Pablo	Can.	2310-730
	Pablo	Eng.	2310 730
	Pablo	Eng.	2660 110
	Pablo	Ger.	2310 730
	Pablo	Ger.	2625 703
	Pablo	It.	2310 730A
	Pablo	Jap.	MTF 1075
	Verve	USA	MG V-8057

4660 CHEROKEE (3:37)
      (mx 1597-1)

12 Inch LP	>Clef	USA	MG C-712
	Pablo	USA	2310-791
	Pablo	USA	2625-703
	Pablo	Can.	2310-791
	Pablo	Eng.	2310 791
	Pablo	Eng.	2660 110
	Pablo	Ger.	2310 791
	Pablo	Ger.	2625 703
	Pablo	It.	2310 791A
	Pablo	Jap.	MTF 1078
	Verve	USA	MG V-8095

4670 THESE FOOLISH THINGS REMIND ME OF YOU (4:49)
      (mx 1598-1)

12 Inch LP	Book-of-the-Month	USA	51-400
	>Clef	USA	MG C-712
	Pablo	USA	2310-793
	Pablo	USA	2625-703
	Pablo	Can.	2310-793
	Pablo	Eng.	2310 793
	Pablo	Eng.	2660 110
	Pablo	Ger.	2310 793
	Pablo	Ger.	2625 703
	Pablo	It.	2310 793A
	Pablo	Jap.	MTF 1080
	Verve	USA	MG V-8095

4680 DEEP PURPLE (4:57)
      (mx 1599-1)

7 Inch 45EP	Verve	Ger.	EPV5131
12 Inch LP	Book of-the-Month	USA	51-400
	Pablo	USA	2310-730
	Pablo	USA	2625-703
	Pablo	Can.	2310-730
	Pablo	Eng.	2310 730
	Pablo	Eng.	2660 110
	Pablo	Ger.	2310 730
	Pablo	Ger.	2625 703
	Pablo	It.	2310 730A
	Pablo	Jap.	MTF 1075
	>Verve	USA	MG V-8323

4690 AFTER YOU´VE GONE (3:59)
      (mx 1600-1)

12 Inch LP	>Clef	USA	MG C-712
	Pablo	USA	2310-862
	Pablo	USA	2625-703
	Pablo	Can.	2310-862
	Pablo	Eng.	2310 809
	Pablo	Eng.	2660 110
	Pablo	Fr.	2310 809
	Pablo	Ger.	2310 809
	Pablo	Ger.	2625 703
	Pablo	Jap.	MTF 1096
	Verve	USA	MG V-8095

```
4700  I DIDN'T KNOW WHAT TIME IT WAS (4:12)
      (mx 1601-1)
                12 Inch LP   Book-of-the-Month   USA    51-400
                             Pablo               USA    2310-835
                             Pablo               USA    2625-703
                             Pablo               Can.   2310-835
                             Pablo               Eng.   2310 808
                             Pablo               Eng.   2660 110
                             Pablo               Fr.    2310 808
                             Pablo               Ger.   2310 808
                             Pablo               Ger.   2625 703
                             Pablo               Jap.   MTF 1095
                            >Verve               USA    MG V-8323

4710  SOMEBODY LOVES ME (3:46)
      (mx 1602-1)
                12 Inch LP   Book-of-the-Month   USA    51-400
                             Pablo               USA    2625-703
                             Pablo               Eng.   2310 812
                             Pablo               Eng.   2660 110
                             Pablo               Ger.   2625 703
                            >Verve               USA    MG V-8323

4720  WHAT'S NEW? (4:30)
      (mx 1603-1)
                12 Inch LP   Pablo               USA    2310-789
                             Pablo               USA    2625-703
                             Pablo               Can.   2310-789
                             Pablo               Eng.   2310 789
                             Pablo               Eng.   2660 110
                             Pablo               Ger.   2310 789
                             Pablo               Ger.   2625 703
                             Pablo               It.    2310 789A
                             Pablo               Jap.   MTF 1076
                            >Verve               USA    MG V-8323

4730  SWEET LORRAINE (4:19)
      (mx 1604-1)
                12 Inch LP   Pablo               USA    2310-793
                             Pablo               USA    2625-703
                             Pablo               Can.   2310-793
                             Pablo               Eng.   2310 793
                             Pablo               Eng.   2660 110
                             Pablo               Ger.   2310 793
                             Pablo               Ger.   2625 703
                             Pablo               It.    2310 793A
                             Pablo               Jap.   MTF 1080
                            >Verve               USA    MG V-8347

4740  CRAZY RHYTHM (2:53)
      (mx 1605-1)
                12 Inch LP   Pablo               USA    2310-730
                             Pablo               USA    2625-703
                             Pablo               Can.   2310-730
                             Pablo               Eng.   2310 730
                             Pablo               Eng.   2660 110
                             Pablo               Ger.   2310 730
                             Pablo               Ger.   2625 703
                             Pablo               It.    2310 730A
                             Pablo               Jap.   MTF 1075
                            >Verve               USA    MG V-8347

4750  ISN'T IT ROMANTIC (4:33)
      (mx 1606-1)
                 7 Inch 45EP His Master's Voice  Eng.   7EG 8604
                12 Inch LP   Pablo               USA    2625-703
                             Pablo               Eng.   2310 812
                             Pablo               Eng.   2660 110
                             Pablo               Ger.   2625 703
                            >Verve               USA    MG V-8347
                             Verve               Eng.   VLP9110
                12 Inch TX   AFRS Jazz Book      USA    12/2
```

4760 YOU´RE BLASE (4:55)
     (mx 1607-1)
              12 Inch LP   Pablo   USA   2310-791
                            Pablo   USA   2625-703
                            Pablo   Can.   2310-791
                            Pablo   Eng.   2310 791
                            Pablo   Eng.   2660 110
                            Pablo   Ger.   2310 791
                            Pablo   Ger.   2625 703
                            Pablo   It.   2310 791A
                            Pablo   Jap.   MTF 1078
                           >Verve   USA   MG V-8323
                            Verve   USA   V-8433
                            Verve   USA   V6-8433
                            Verve   Ger.   511 063

4770 YOU´RE MINE, YOU (4:50)
     (mx 1608-1)
              12 Inch LP   Pablo   USA   2310-864
                            Pablo   USA   2625-703
                            Pablo   Can.   2310-864
                            Pablo   Eng.   2310 810
                            Pablo   Eng.   2660 110
                            Pablo   Ger.   2625 703
                            Pablo   Jap.   28MJ 3146
                           >Verve   USA   MG V-8323

4780 INDIANA (3:02)
     (mx 1609-1)
              12 Inch LP   Book-of-the-Month   USA   51-400
                            Pablo   USA   2310-862
                            Pablo   USA   2625-703
                            Pablo   Can.   2310-862
                            Pablo   Eng.   2310 809
                            Pablo   Eng.   2660 110
                            Pablo   Fr.   2310 809
                            Pablo   Ger.   2310 809
                            Pablo   Ger.   2625 703
                            Pablo   Jap.   MTF 1096
                           >Verve   USA   MG V-8347
                            VSP Verve   USA   VSP 33
                            VSP Verve   USA   VSPS33
                            VSP Verve   It.   SVSP57.009

4790 THAT OLD FEELING (5:10)
     (mx 1610-1)
              12 Inch LP   Book-of-the-Month   USA   51-400
                            Pablo   USA   2310-790
                            Pablo   USA   2625-703
                            Pablo   Can.   2310-790
                            Pablo   Eng.   2310 790
                            Pablo   Eng.   2660 110
                            Pablo   Ger.   2310 790
                            Pablo   Ger.   2625 703
                            Pablo   It.   2310 790A
                            Pablo   Jap.   MTF 1077
                           >Verve   USA   MG V-8323

4800 HEAT WAVE (3:16)
     (mx 1611-1)
              7 Inch 45EP   Verve   Ger.   EPV5131
              12 Inch LP   Pablo   USA   2310-729
                            Pablo   USA   2625-703
                            Pablo   Can.   2310-729
                            Pablo   Eng.   2310 729
                            Pablo   Eng.   2660 110
                            Pablo   Ger.   2310 729
                            Pablo   Ger.   2625 703
                            Pablo   It.   2310 729A
                            Pablo   Jap.   MTF 1074
                           >Verve   USA   MG V-8323

```
4810  SHE'S FUNNY THAT WAY (3:50)
      (mx 1612-1)
            7 Inch 45EP Verve                     Ger.  EPV5131
            12 Inch LP  Book-of-the-Month         USA   51-400
                        Pablo                     USA   2310-793
                        Pablo                     USA   2625-703
                        Pablo                     Can.  2310-793
                        Pablo                     Eng.  2310 793
                        Pablo                     Eng.  2660 110
                        Pablo                     Ger.  2310 793
                        Pablo                     Ger.  2625 703
                        Pablo                     It.   2310 793A
                        Pablo                     Jap.  MTF 1080
                       >Verve                     USA   MG V-8323

------------------------------------------------------------
Hollywood, California                        April 23, 1954

4815  INTERVIEW by Jack Wagner of National Radio & TV Department
          of Capitol Records Distributing Corp.
      (mx 3129)
            12 Inch LP  >Capitol Silver          USA    129
                         Platter Service*
      *Contains three brief statements by Tatum from
      the above interview.

------------------------------------------------------------
Los Angeles, California                      June 25, 1954
          The Art Tatum-Benny Carter-Louis Bellson
          Trio.  Benny Carter, as; Art Tatum, p;
          Louis Bellson, d.
4820  MY BLUE HEAVEN (4:00)
      (mx 1788-1)
            7 Inch 45EP Clef                      USA   EP-320
            12 Inch LP  Book-of-the-Month         USA   51-400
                       >Clef                      USA   MG C-643
                        Clef                      Astla MG C-643
                        Metro                     Eng.  2364013
                        Pablo                     USA   2310-733
                        Pablo                     USA   2625-0706
                        Pablo                     Braz. 2310 733
                        Pablo                     Can.  2310-733
                        Pablo                     Eng.  2310 733
                        Pablo                     Eng.  2625 706
                        Pablo                     Fr.   2310 733
                        Pablo                     Ger.  2310 733
                        Pablo                     Ger.  2625 706
                        Pablo                     It.   2310 733A
                        Pablo                     Jap.  MTF 1063
                        Verve                     USA   MG V-8013

4830  BLUES IN B FLAT (5:40)
      (mx 1789-2)
            7 Inch 45EP Clef                      USA   EP-319
                        Columbia                  Eng.  SEB 10027
            12 Inch LP  >Clef                     USA   MG C-643
                        Clef                      Astla MG C-643
                        Columbia                  Eng.  33CX10141
                        Metro                     Eng.  2364013
                        Pablo                     USA   2310-732
                        Pablo                     USA   2625-0706
                        Pablo                     Braz. 2310 732
                        Pablo                     Can.  2310-732
                        Pablo                     Eng.  2310 732
                        Pablo                     Eng.  2625 706
                        Pablo                     Fr.   2310 732
                        Pablo                     Ger.  2310 732
                        Pablo                     Ger.  2625 706
                        Pablo                     Jap.  MTF 1062
                        Verve                     USA   MG V-8013
                        Verve                     USA   MG V-8230
                        World Record Club         Eng.  F. 526
            12 Inch TX  Amer.Cancer Soc.          USA   Jazz Pano-
                         1957 Cancer Crusade            rama
                                                        Platter*5&6
```

97

*1:07 excerpt.

4840 BLUES IN C (8:00)
      (mx 1790-1)
                12 Inch LP   Metro   Eng.   2364014
                              Pablo   USA   2310-732
                              Pablo   USA   2625-0706
                              Pablo   Braz. 2310 732
                              Pablo   Can.   2310-732
                              Pablo   Eng.   2310 732
                              Pablo   Eng.   2625 706
                              Pablo   Fr.   2310 732
                              Pablo   Ger.   2310 732
                              Pablo   Ger.   2625 706
                              Pablo   Jap.   MTF 1062
                             >Verve   USA   MG V-8227
                              Verve   Astla MG V-8227

4850 A FOGGY DAY (5:25)
      (mx 1791-2)
                12 Inch LP   Amer.Recording Soc. USA   G 424
                              Metro   Eng.   2364014
                              Pablo   USA   2310-732
                              Pablo   USA   2625-0706
                              Pablo   Braz. 2310 732
                              Pablo   Can.   2310-732
                              Pablo   Eng.   2310 732
                              Pablo   Eng.   2625 706
                              Pablo   Fr.   2310 732
                              Pablo   Ger.   2310 732
                              Pablo   Ger.   2625 706
                              Pablo   Jap.   MTF 1062
                             >Verve   USA   MG V-8227
                              Verve   Astla MG V-8227

4860 BLUES IN MY HEART (6:00)
      (mx 1792-1)
                7 Inch 45EP Clef   USA   EP-318
                            Columbia   Eng.   SEB 10062
                12 Inch LP >Clef   USA   MG C-643
                            Clef   Astla MG C-643
                            Metro   Eng.   2364013
                            Pablo   USA   2310-733
                            Pablo   USA   2625-0706
                            Pablo   Braz. 2310 733
                            Pablo   Can.   2310-733
                            Pablo   Eng.   2310 733
                            Pablo   Eng.   2625 706
                            Pablo   Fr.   2310 733
                            Pablo   Ger.   2310 733
                            Pablo   Ger.   2625 706
                            Pablo   It.   2310 733A
                            Pablo   Jap.   MTF 1063
                            Verve   USA   MG V-8013

4870 STREET OF DREAMS (3:50)
      (mx 1793-2)
                7 Inch 45EP Clef   USA   EP-320
                12 Inch LP >Clef   USA   MG C-643
                            Clef   Astla MG C-643
                            Metro   Eng.   2364013
                            Pablo   USA   2310-732
                            Pablo   USA   2625-0706
                            Pablo   Braz. 2310 732
                            Pablo   Can.   2310-732
                            Pablo   Eng.   2310 732
                            Pablo   Eng.   2625 706
                            Pablo   Fr.   2310 732
                            Pablo   Ger.   2310 732
                            Pablo   Ger.   2625 706
                            Pablo   Jap.   MTF 1062
                            Verve   USA   MG V-8013

```
4880    IDAHO (4:15)
        (mx 1794-2)
                  7 Inch 45EP Clef                        USA    EP-320
                 12 Inch LP   >Clef                       USA    MG C-643
                             Clef                         Astla  MG C-643
                             Columbia                     Eng.   33CX10115
                             Metro                        Eng.   2364013
                             Pablo                        USA    2310-733
                             Pablo                        USA    2625-0706
                             Pablo                        Braz.  2310 733
                             Pablo                        Can.   2310-733
                             Pablo                        Eng.   2310 733
                             Pablo                        Eng.   2625 706
                             Pablo                        Fr.    2310 733
                             Pablo                        Ger.   2310 733
                             Pablo                        Ger.   2625 706
                             Pablo                        It.    2310 733A
                             Pablo                        Jap.   MTF 1063
                             Time-Life                    USA    P 15516
                             Verve                        USA    MG V-8013
                 16 Inch TX   AFRS Bud's BandwagonUSA            334

4890    YOU'RE MINE, YOU (5:10)
        (mx 1795-1)
                 12 Inch LP   Metro                       Eng.   2364014
                             Pablo                        USA    2310-733
                             Pablo                        USA    2625-0706
                             Pablo                        Braz.  2310 733
                             Pablo                        Can.   2310-733
                             Pablo                        Eng.   2310 733
                             Pablo                        Eng.   2625 706
                             Pablo                        Fr.    2310 733
                             Pablo                        Ger.   2310 733
                             Pablo                        Ger.   2625 706
                             Pablo                        It.    2310 733A
                             Pablo                        Jap.   MTF 1063
                            >Verve                        USA    MG V-8227
                             Verve                        Astla  MG V-8227

4900    UNDECIDED (4:50)
        (mx 1796-2)
                 12 Inch LP   Metro                       Eng.   2364014
                             Pablo                        USA    2310-732
                             Pablo                        USA    2625-0706
                             Pablo                        Braz.  2310 732
                             Pablo                        Can.   2310-732
                             Pablo                        Eng.   2310 732
                             Pablo                        Eng.   2625 706
                             Pablo                        Fr.    2310 732
                             Pablo                        Ger.   2310 732
                             Pablo                        Ger.   2625 706
                             Pablo                        Jap.   MTF 1062
                            >Verve                        USA    MG V-8227
                             Verve                        Astla  MG V-8227

4910    UNDER A BLANKET OF BLUE (6:10)
        (mx 1797-2)
                 12 Inch LP   Metro                       Eng.   2364014
                             Pablo                        USA    2310-732
                             Pablo                        USA    2625-0706
                             Pablo                        Braz.  2310 732
                             Pablo                        Can.   2310-732
                             Pablo                        Eng.   2310 732
                             Pablo                        Eng.   2625 706
                             Pablo                        Fr.    2310 732
                             Pablo                        Ger.   2310 732
                             Pablo                        Ger.   2625 706
                             Pablo                        Jap.   MTF 1062
                            >Verve                        USA    MG V-8227
                             Verve                        Astla  MG V-8227

4920    MAKIN' WHOOPEE (3:36)
        (mx 1798-1)
                             Verve                        USA    Unissued
```

```
4921   MAKIN' WHOOPEE (6:10)
       (mx 1798-2)
                 12 Inch LP    Book-of-the-Month    USA    51-400
                               Metro                Eng.   2364014
                               Pablo                USA    2310-379
                               Pablo                USA    2310-733
                               Pablo                USA    2625-0706
                               Pablo                Braz.  2310 733
                               Pablo                Can.   2310-733
                               Pablo                Eng.   2310 733
                               Pablo                Eng.   2625 706
                               Pablo                Fr.    2310 733
                               Pablo                Ger.   2310 733
                               Pablo                Ger.   2625 706
                               Pablo                It.    2310 733A
                               Pablo                Jap.   MTF 1063
                              >Verve                USA    MG V-8227
                               Verve                Astla  MG V-8227

4930   OLD FASHIONED LOVE (5:00)
       (mx 1799-1)
                 7 Inch 45EP  Clef                  USA    EP-318
                               Columbia             Eng.   SEB 10062
                 12 Inch LP   >Clef                 USA    MG C-643
                               Clef                 Astla  MG C-643
                               Metro                Eng.   2364013
                               Pablo                USA    2310-733
                               Pablo                USA    2625-0706
                               Pablo                Braz.  2310 733
                               Pablo                Can.   2310-733
                               Pablo                Eng.   2310 733
                               Pablo                Eng.   2625 706
                               Pablo                Fr.    2310 733
                               Pablo                Ger.   2310 733
                               Pablo                Ger.   2625 706
                               Pablo                It.    2310 733A
                               Pablo                Jap.   MTF 1063
                               Verve                USA    MG V-8013

4940   'S WONDERFUL (3:20)
       (mx 1800-2)
                 7 Inch 45EP  Clef                  USA    EP-319
                               Columbia             Eng.   SEB 10027
                 12 Inch LP   >Clef                 USA    MG C-643
                               Clef                 Astla  MG C-643
                               Metro                Eng.   2364013
                               Pablo                USA    2310-732
                               Pablo                USA    2625-0706
                               Pablo                Braz.  2310 732
                               Pablo                Can.   2310-732
                               Pablo                Eng.   2310 732
                               Pablo                Eng.   2625 706
                               Pablo                Fr.    2310 732
                               Pablo                Ger.   2310 732
                               Pablo                Ger.   2625 706
                               Pablo                Jap.   MTF 1062
                               Verve                USA    MG V-8013
                               Verve                USA    DJ V-3
                               Verve                Eng.   VLP9110

4950   HANDS ACROSS THE TABLE (3:40)
       (mx 1801-1)
                 7 Inch 45EP  Clef                  USA    EP-319
                               Columbia             Eng.   SEB 10027
                 12 Inch LP   >Clef                 USA    MG C-643
                               Clef                 Astla  MG C-643
                               Metro                Eng.   2364013
                               Pablo                USA    2310-733
                               Pablo                USA    2625-0706
                               Pablo                Braz.  2310 733
                               Pablo                Can.   2310-733
                               Pablo                Eng.   2310 733
                               Pablo                Eng.   2625 706
                               Pablo                Fr.    2310 733
                               Pablo                Ger.   2310 733
```

```
                       Pablo                    Ger.  2625 706
                       Pablo                    It.   2310 733A
                       Pablo                    Jap.  MTF 1063
                       Verve                    USA   MG V-8013

4960  MOON SONG*

                       Verve                    USA   Unissued
              *Without Benny Carter

------------------------------------------------------------
Los Angeles, California                         January 19,1955
          Piano solos.
4970  I SURRENDER DEAR (3:51)
      (mx 2193-1)
          7 Inch 45EP His Master's Voice  Eng.  7EG 8684
         12 Inch LP   Pablo                USA  2310-862
                      Pablo                USA  2625-703
                      Pablo                Can. 2310-862
                      Pablo                Eng. 2310 809
                      Pablo                Eng. 2660 110
                      Pablo                Fr.  2310 809
                      Pablo                Ger. 2310 809
                      Pablo                Ger. 2625 703
                      Pablo                Jap. MTF 1096
                     >Verve                USA  MG V-8332

4980  HAPPY FEET (2:34)
      (mx 2194-1)
          7 Inch 45EP His Master's Voice  Eng.  7EG 8604
         12 Inch LP   Pablo                USA  2310-870
                      Pablo                Can. 2310-870
                      Pablo                USA  2625-703
                      Pablo                Eng. 2310 811
                      Pablo                Eng. 2660 110
                      Pablo                Ger. 2625 703
                      Pablo                Jap. 28MJ 3147
                     >Verve                USA  MG V-8347

4990  MEAN TO ME (2:54)
      (mx 2195-1)
         12 Inch LP   Book-of-the-Month    USA  51-400
                      Pablo                USA  2310-864
                      Pablo                USA  2625-703
                      Pablo                Can. 2310-864
                      Pablo                Eng. 2310 810
                      Pablo                Eng. 2660 110
                      Pablo                Ger. 2625 703
                      Pablo                Jap. 28MJ 3146
                     >Verve                USA  MG V-8347

5000  BOULEVARD OF BROKEN DREAMS (5:18)
      (mx 2196-1)
         12 Inch LP   Pablo                USA  2310-870
                      Pablo                Can. 2310-870
                      Pablo                USA  2625-703
                      Pablo                Eng. 2310 811
                      Pablo                Eng. 2660 110
                      Pablo                Ger. 2625 703
                      Pablo                Jap. 28MJ 3147
                     >Verve                USA  MG V-8347
                      VSP Verve            USA  VSP 33
                      VSP Verve            USA  VSPS33
                      VSP Verve            It.  SVSP57.009

5010  MOONLIGHT ON THE GANGES (2:13)
      (mx 2197-1)
          7 Inch 45EP His Master's Voice  Eng.  7EG 8604
         12 Inch LP   Amer.Recording Soc.  USA  G-406
                      Pablo                USA  2625-703
                      Pablo                Eng. 2310 812
                      Pablo                Eng. 2660 110
                      Pablo                Ger. 2625 703
                     >Verve                USA  MG V-8347
                      VSP Verve            USA  VSP 33
```

```
                              VSP Verve            USA   VSPS33
                              VSP Verve            It.   SVSP57.009

5020   MOON SONG (4:36)
       (mx 2198-1)
              7 Inch 45EP  His Master´s Voice  Eng.  7EG 8604
              12 Inch LP   Pablo               USA   2310-792
                           Pablo               USA   2625-703
                           Pablo               Can.  2310-792
                           Pablo               Eng.  2310 792
                           Pablo               Eng.  2660 110
                           Pablo               Ger.  2310 792
                           Pablo               Ger.  2625 703
                           Pablo               It.   2310 792A
                           Pablo               Jap.  MTF 1079
                          >Verve               USA   MG V-8347
                           VSP Verve           USA   VSP 33
                           VSP Verve           USA   VSPS33
                           VSP Verve           It.   SVSP57.009

5030   WHEN YOUR LOVER HAS GONE (3:39)
       (mx 2199-1)
              7 Inch 45EP  His Master´s Voice  Eng.  7EG 8684
              12 Inch LP   Amer.Recording Soc. USA   G-406
                           Book-of-the-Month   USA   51-400
                           Pablo               USA   2310-862
                           Pablo               USA   2625-703
                           Pablo               Can.  2310-862
                           Pablo               Eng.  2310 809
                           Pablo               Eng.  2660 110
                           Pablo               Fr.   2310 809
                           Pablo               Ger.  2310 809
                           Pablo               Ger.  2625 703
                           Pablo               Jap.  MTF 1096
                          >Verve               USA   MG V-8332

5040   THE MOON IS LOW (4:11)
       (mx 2200-1)
              12 Inch LP   Book-of-the-Month   USA   51-400
                           Pablo               USA   2310-864
                           Pablo               USA   2625-703
                           Pablo               Can.  2310-864
                           Pablo               Eng.  2310 810
                           Pablo               Eng.  2660 110
                           Pablo               Ger.  2625 703
                           Pablo               Jap.  28MJ 3146
                          >Verve               USA   MG V-8332

5050   IF I HAD YOU (4:10)
       (mx 2201-1)
              7 Inch 45EP  His Master´s Voice  Eng.  7EG 8684
              12 Inch LP   Book-of-the-Month   USA   51-400
                           Pablo               USA   2625-703
                           Pablo               Eng.  2310 812
                           Pablo               Eng.  2660 110
                           Pablo               Ger.  2625 703
                          >Verve               USA   MG V-8332
              12 Inch TX   AFRS Jazz Book      USA   12/2

5060   S´POSIN´ (3:20)
       (mx 2202-1)
              12 Inch LP   Book-of-the-Month   USA   51-400
                           Pablo               USA   2310-864
                           Pablo               USA   2625-703
                           Pablo               Can.  2310-864
                           Pablo               Eng.  2310 810
                           Pablo               Eng.  2660 110
                           Pablo               Ger.  2625 703
                           Pablo               Jap.  28MJ 3146
                          >Verve               USA   MG V-8347

5070   DON´T WORRY ´BOUT ME (4:10)
       (mx 2203-1)
              7 Inch 45EP  Columbia            Eng.  SEB 10116
              12 Inch LP   Book-of-the-Month   USA   51-400
```

```
                           Pablo                USA    2310-790
                           Pablo                USA    2625-703
                           Pablo                Can.   2310-790
                           Pablo                Eng.   2310 790
                           Pablo                Eng.   2660 110
                           Pablo                Ger.   2310 790
                           Pablo                Ger.   2625 703
                           Pablo                It.    2310 790A
                          >Verve                USA    MG V-8332

5080  PRISONER OF LOVE (4:15)
      (mx 2204-1)
           7 Inch 45EP Columbia                 Eng.   SEB 10116
          12 Inch LP   Book-of-the-Month        USA    51-400
                       Pablo                     USA    2310-730
                       Pablo                     USA    2625-703
                       Pablo                     Can.   2310-730
                       Pablo                     Eng.   2310 730
                       Pablo                     Eng.   2660 110
                       Pablo                     Ger.   2310 730
                       Pablo                     Ger.   2625 703
                       Pablo                     It.    2310 730A
                       Pablo                     Jap.   MTF 1075
                      >Verve                     USA    MG V-8332

5090  MOONGLOW (2:52)
      (mx 2205-1)
           7 Inch 45EP Columbia                 Eng.   SEB 10116
          12 Inch LP   Band                      Braz.  BR33.007
                       Book-of-the-Month         USA    51-400
                       Pablo                     USA    2310-723
                       Pablo                     USA    2625-703
                       Pablo                     Braz.  2310 723
                       Pablo                     Can.   2310-723
                       Pablo                     Eng.   2310 723
                       Pablo                     Eng.   2660 110
                       Pablo                     Ger.   2310 723
                       Pablo                     Ger.   2625 703
                       Pablo                     It.    2310 723A
                       Pablo                     Jap.   MTF 1073
                      >Verve                     USA    MG V-8360

5100  I WON'T DANCE (2:55)
      (mx 2206-1)
           7 Inch 45EP Columbia                 Eng.   SEB 10116
          12 Inch LP   Pablo                     USA    2310-793
                       Pablo                     USA    2625-703
                       Pablo                     Can.   2310-793
                       Pablo                     Eng.   2310 793
                       Pablo                     Eng.   2660 110
                       Pablo                     Ger.   2310 793
                       Pablo                     Ger.   2625 703
                       Pablo                     It.    2310 793A
                       Pablo                     Jap.   MTF 1080
                      >Verve                     USA    MG V-8360

5110  I CAN'T GIVE YOU ANYTHING BUT LOVE (3:33)
      (mx 2207-1)
          12 Inch LP   Amer.Recording Soc.       USA    G 424
                       Book-of-the-Month         USA    51-400
                       Pablo                     USA    2310-862
                       Pablo                     USA    2625-703
                       Pablo                     Can.   2310-862
                       Pablo                     Eng.   2310 809
                       Pablo                     Eng.   2660 110
                       Pablo                     Fr.    2310 809
                       Pablo                     Ger.   2310 809
                       Pablo                     Ger.   2625 703
                       Pablo                     Jap.   MTF 1096
                      >Verve                     USA    MG V-8360

5120  LULLABY IN RHYTHM (3:06)
      (mx 2208-1)
          12 Inch LP   Amer.Recording Soc.       USA    G 424
                       Pablo                     USA    2310-870
```

```
                              Pablo              Can.   2310-870
                              Pablo              USA    2625-703
                              Pablo              Eng.   2310 811
                              Pablo              Eng.   2660 110
                              Pablo              Ger.   2625 703
                              Pablo              Jap.   28MJ 3147
                             >Verve              USA    MG V-8360

5130   OUT OF NOWHERE (3:43)
       (mx 2209-1)
              12 Inch LP     Amer.Recording Soc. USA   G 424
                             Book-of-the-Month   USA   51-400
                              Pablo              USA    2310-870
                              Pablo              Can.   2310-870
                              Pablo              USA    2625-703
                              Pablo              Eng.   2310 811
                              Pablo              Eng.   2660 110
                              Pablo              Ger.   2625 703
                              Pablo              Jap.   28MJ 3147
                             >Verve              USA    MG V-8360

5140   I GOTTA RIGHT TO SING THE BLUES (3:50)
       (mx 2210-1)
              12 Inch LP     Amer.Recording Soc. USA   G 424
                             Book-of-the-Month   USA   51-400
                              Pablo              USA    2310-864
                              Pablo              USA    2625-703
                              Pablo              Can.   2310-864
                              Pablo              Eng.   2310 810
                              Pablo              Eng.   2660 110
                              Pablo              Ger.   2625 703
                              Pablo              Jap.   28MJ 3146
                             >Verve              USA    MG V-8360

5150   IT´S ONLY A PAPER MOON (2:35)
       (mx 2211-1)
              12 Inch LP     Amer.Recording Soc. USA   G 424
                             Book-of-the-Month   USA   51-400
                              Pablo              USA    2310-723
                              Pablo              USA    2625-703
                              Pablo              Braz.  2310 723
                              Pablo              Can.   2310-723
                              Pablo              Eng.   2310 723
                              Pablo              Eng.   2660 110
                              Pablo              Ger.   2310 723
                              Pablo              Ger.   2625 703
                              Pablo              It.    2310 723A
                              Pablo              Jap.   MTF 1073
                             >Verve              USA    MG V-8360

5160   EVERYTHING I HAVE IS YOURS (5:31)
       (mx 2212-1)
              12 Inch LP      Pablo              USA    2310-835
                              Pablo              USA    2625-703
                              Pablo              Can.   2310-835
                              Pablo              Eng.   2310 808
                              Pablo              Eng.   2660 110
                              Pablo              Fr.    2310 808
                              Pablo              Ger.   2310 808
                              Pablo              Ger.   2625 703
                              Pablo              Jap.   MTF 1095
                             >Verve              USA    MG V-8332

5170   I ONLY HAVE EYES FOR YOU (2:48)
       (mx 2213-1)
              7 Inch 45EP    His Master´s Voice  Eng.   7EG 8684
              12 Inch LP     Book-of-the-Month   USA    51-400
                              Pablo              USA    2310-864
                              Pablo              USA    2625-703
                              Pablo              Can.   2310-864
                              Pablo              Eng.   2310 810
                              Pablo              Eng.   2660 110
                              Pablo              Ger.   2625 703
                              Pablo              Jap.   28MJ 3146
                             >Verve              USA    MG V-8332

                              104
```

```
5180   ON THE SUNNY SIDE OF THE STREET (3:03)
       (mx 2214-1)
                 12 Inch LP     Amer.Recording Soc. USA   G 401
                                Book-of-the-Month   USA   51-400
                                Pablo               USA   2310-793
                                Pablo               USA   2625-703
                                Pablo               Can.  2310-793
                                Pablo               Eng.  2310 793
                                Pablo               Eng.  2660 110
                                Pablo               Ger.  2310 793
                                Pablo               Ger.  2625 703
                                Pablo               It.   2310 793A
                                Pablo               Jap.  MTF 1080
                                >Verve              USA   MG V-8360

5190   WITH A SONG IN MY HEART
       (mx 2215-1)
                                Verve               USA   Unissued

5200   DO NOTHIN´ TILL YOU HEAR FROM ME (4:55)
       (mx 2216-1)
                 12 Inch LP     Pablo               USA   2310-791
                                Pablo               USA   2625-703
                                Pablo               Can.  2310-791
                                Pablo               Eng.  2310 791
                                Pablo               Eng.  2660 110
                                Pablo               Ger.  2310 791
                                Pablo               Ger.  2625 703
                                Pablo               It.   2310 791A
                                Pablo               Jap.  MTF 1078
                                >Verve              USA   MG V-8360

5210   SO BEATS MY HEART FOR YOU (5:19)
       (mx 2217-1)
                 12 Inch LP     Amer.Recording Soc. USA   G 424
                                Pablo               USA   2310-792
                                Pablo               USA   2625-703
                                Pablo               Can.  2310-792
                                Pablo               Eng.  2310 792
                                Pablo               Eng.  2660 110
                                Pablo               Ger.  2310 792
                                Pablo               Ger.  2625 703
                                Pablo               It.   2310 792A
                                Pablo               Jap.  MTF 1079
                                >Verve              USA   MG V-8360

5220   IF YOU HADN´T GONE AWAY (3:52)
       (mx 2218-1)
                 12 Inch LP     Pablo               USA   2310-864
                                Pablo               USA   2625-703
                                Pablo               Can.  2310-864
                                Pablo               Eng.  2310 810
                                Pablo               Eng.  2660 110
                                Pablo               Ger.  2625 703
                                Pablo               Jap.  28MJ 3146
                                >Verve              USA   MG V-8332

5230   PLEASE BE KIND (5:05)
       (mx 2219-1)
                 12 Inch LP     Pablo               USA   2310-862
                                Pablo               USA   2625-703
                                Pablo               Can.  2310-862
                                Pablo               Eng.  2310 809
                                Pablo               Eng.  2660 110
                                Pablo               Fr.   2310 809
                                Pablo               Ger.  2310 809
                                Pablo               Ger.  2625 703
                                Pablo               Jap.  MTF 1096
                                >Verve              USA   MG V-8332
```

```
Los Angeles, California                         March 23&29, 1955
          The Art Tatum-Roy Eldridge-Alvin Stoller-
          John Simmons Quartet.  Roy Eldridge, t;
          Art Tatum, p; John Simmons, b; Alvin
```

```
                 Stoller, d.
5240   I SURRENDER DEAR (6:52)
       (mx 2302-1)
                 12 Inch LP  Barclay            Fr.   GLP3562
                            >Clef               USA   MG C-679
                             Columbia           Eng.  33CX10042
                             Pablo              USA   2310-734
                             Pablo              USA   2625-0706
                             Pablo              Braz. 2310 734
                             Pablo              Can.  2310-734
                             Pablo              Eng.  2310 734
                             Pablo              Eng.  2625 706
                             Pablo              Fr.   2310 734
                             Pablo              Ger.  2310 734
                             Pablo              Ger.  2625 706
                             Pablo              It.   2310 734A
                             Pablo              Jap.  MTF 1071
                             Verve              USA   MG V-8064
                             Verve              Eng.  VLP9110

5250   THE MOON IS LOW* (4:09)
       (mx 2303-1)
                 7 Inch 45EP Barclay            Fr.   GEP12615
                             Clef               USA   EP-C-373
                             Karusell           Swed. KEP312
                 12 Inch LP  Barclay            Fr.   GLP3562
                            >Clef               USA   MG C-679
                             Columbia           Eng.  33CX10042
                             Pablo              USA   2310-734
                             Pablo              USA   2625-0706
                             Pablo              Braz. 2310 734
                             Pablo              Can.  2310-734
                             Pablo              Eng.  2310 734
                             Pablo              Eng.  2625 706
                             Pablo              Fr.   2310 734
                             Pablo              Ger.  2310 734
                             Pablo              Ger.  2625 706
                             Pablo              It.   2310 734A
                             Pablo              Jap.  MTF 1071
                             Verve              USA   MG V-8064
                 16 Inch TX  AFRS Basic Mus.Lib. USA  P-4927
       *Roy Eldridge, fl instead of t.

5260   YOU TOOK ADVANTAGE OF ME (3:33)
       (mx 2304-1)
                 7 Inch 45EP Barclay            Fr.   GEP12615
                             Clef               USA   EP-C-373
                             Karusell           Swed. KEP312
                 12 Inch LP  Barclay            Fr.   GLP3562
                            >Clef               USA   MG C-679
                             Columbia           Eng.  33CX10042
                             Pablo              USA   2310-734
                             Pablo              USA   2625-0706
                             Pablo              Braz. 2310 734
                             Pablo              Can.  2310-734
                             Pablo              Eng.  2310 734
                             Pablo              Eng.  2625 706
                             Pablo              Fr.   2310 734
                             Pablo              Ger.  2310 734
                             Pablo              Ger.  2625 706
                             Pablo              It.   2310 734A
                             Pablo              Jap.  MTF 1071
                             Verve              USA   MG V-8064
                 16 Inch TX  AFRS Basic Mus.Lib. USA  P-4928

5270   I WON'T DANCE (3:26)
       (mx 2305-5)
                 7 Inch 45EP Barclay            Fr.   GEP12615
                             Clef               USA   EP-C-373
                             Karusell           Swed. KEP312
                 12 Inch LP  Amer.Recording Soc. USA  G 424
                             Barclay            Fr.   GLP3562
                            >Clef               USA   MG C-679
                             Columbia           Eng.  33CX10042
                             Columbia           Eng.  33CX10115
```

	Metro	Ger.	2356 105
	Pablo	USA	2310-734
	Pablo	USA	2625-0706
	Pablo	Braz.	2310 734
	Pablo	Can.	2310-734
	Pablo	Eng.	2310 734
	Pablo	Eng.	2625 706
	Pablo	Fr.	2310 734
	Pablo	Ger.	2310 734
	Pablo	Ger.	2625 706
	Pablo	It.	2310 734A
	Pablo	Jap.	MTF 1071
	Verve	USA	MG V-8064
16 Inch TX	AFRS Basic Mus.Lib.	USA	P-4928

5280 MOON SONG (5:04)
(mx 2306-2)

12 Inch LP	Barclay	Fr.	GLP3562
	>Clef	USA	MG C-679
	Columbia	Eng.	33CX10042
	Pablo	USA	2310-734
	Pablo	USA	2625-0706
	Pablo	Braz.	2310 734
	Pablo	Can.	2310-734
	Pablo	Eng.	2310 734
	Pablo	Eng.	2625 706
	Pablo	Fr.	2310 734
	Pablo	Ger.	2310 734
	Pablo	Ger.	2625 706
	Pablo	It.	2310 734A
	Pablo	Jap.	MTF 1071
	Verve	USA	MG V-8064
16 Inch TX	AFRS Basic Mus.Lib.	USA	P-4927

5290 THIS CAN'T BE LOVE (3:48)
(mx 2307-1)

7 Inch 45EP	Barclay	Fr.	GEP12615
	Clef	USA	EP-C-373
	Karusell	Swed.	KEP312
12 Inch LP	Barclay	Fr.	GLP3562
	>Clef	USA	MG C-679
	Columbia	Eng.	33CX10042
	Metro	Ger.	2356 105
	Pablo	USA	2310-734
	Pablo	USA	2625-0706
	Pablo	Braz.	2310 734
	Pablo	Can.	2310-734
	Pablo	Eng.	2310 734
	Pablo	Eng.	2625 706
	Pablo	Fr.	2310 734
	Pablo	Ger.	2310 734
	Pablo	Ger.	2625 706
	Pablo	It.	2310 734A
	Pablo	Jap.	MTF 1071
	Verve	USA	MG V-8064
	Verve	Eng.	VLP9110
16 Inch TX	AFRS Basic Mus.Lib.	USA	P-4928

5300 IN A SENTIMENTAL MOOD (4:59)
(mx 2308-4)

12 Inch LP	Barclay	Fr.	GLP3562
	>Clef	USA	MG C-679
	Columbia	Eng.	33CX10042
	Pablo	USA	2310-734
	Pablo	USA	2625-0706
	Pablo	Braz.	2310 734
	Pablo	Can.	2310-734
	Pablo	Eng.	2310 734
	Pablo	Eng.	2625 706
	Pablo	Fr.	2310 734
	Pablo	Ger.	2310 734
	Pablo	Ger.	2625 706
	Pablo	It.	2310 734A
	Pablo	Jap.	MTF 1071
	Verve	USA	MG V-8064

```
                16 Inch TX    AFRS Basic Mus.Lib. USA    P-4928

5310  NIGHT AND DAY (6:06)
      (mx 2309-1)
                12 Inch LP    Barclay           Fr.   GLP3562
                             >Clef              USA   MG C-679
                              Columbia          Eng.  33CX10042
                              Pablo             USA   2310-734
                              Pablo             USA   2625-0706
                              Pablo             Braz. 2310 734
                              Pablo             Can.  2310-734
                              Pablo             Eng.  2310 734
                              Pablo             Eng.  2625 706
                              Pablo             Fr.   2310 734
                              Pablo             Ger.  2310 734
                              Pablo             Ger.  2625 706
                              Pablo             It.   2310 734A
                              Pablo             Jap.  MTF 1071
                              Verve             USA   MG V-8064
                16 Inch TX    AFRS Basic Mus.Lib. USA  P-4927
```

```
New York, New York                            June 2, 1955
        TV broadcast, "The Tonight Show," featuring
        Steve Allen, on NBC-TV.  The Art Tatum Trio.
        Art Tatum, p; Everett Barksdale, g; Slam
        Stewart, b.
        The listed LP also contains dialogue between
        Steve Allen and Art Tatum.
5320  TEA FOR TWO (2:47)

                12 Inch LP   >Giants of Jazz    USA   GOJ-1015

5330  SOMEONE TO WATCH OVER ME* (0:27)

                                                Unissued
      *Piano solo by Art Tatum.

5340  SWEET LORRAINE (4:05)

                12 Inch LP   >Giants of Jazz    USA   GOJ-1015

5350  FINE AND DANDY** (1:45)

                12 Inch LP   >Giants of Jazz    USA   GOJ-1015
      **Also includes Steve Allen, p.
```

```
Beverly Hills, California                     July 3, 1955
        Live performances recorded at a private
        party at the home of Ray Heindorf.
        Piano solos.
5360  BEGIN THE BEGUINE (2:55) (Note B)

                12 Inch LP    Ember             Eng.  EMB3314
                              Fontana           It.   9286 307
                              Mercury           Holl. 9286 092
                              Movietone         USA   71021
                              Movietone         USA   S72021
                              RCA Victor        Jap.  MJ-7093
                              20th Century Fox  USA   TFM3162
                              20th Century Fox  USA   TFS4162
                              20th Century Fox  Fr.   468.004
                              20th Century Fox  Fr.   T607
                              20th Century Fox  Fr.   XBLY 921.041
                             >20th Fox          USA   Fox 3029
                              20th Fox          USA   SFX-3029
                              20th Fox          USA   TCF102-2
                              20th Fox          USA   TCF102-2S
                              Top Rank          USA   35/067
                              Vega              Fr.   30 TCF 5
                              World Record Club Eng.  76
                              World Record Club Eng.  TP. 226
```

5370 SOMEONE TO WATCH OVER ME (3:08) (Note C)

	12 Inch LP	Ember	Eng.	EMB3314
		Fontana	It.	9286 307
		Mercury	Holl.	9286 092
		Movietone	USA	71021
		Movietone	USA	S72021
		RCA Victor	Jap.	MJ-7093
		20th Century Fox	USA	TFM3162
		20th Century Fox	USA	TFS4162
		20th Century Fox	Fr.	468.004
		20th Century Fox	Fr.	T607
		20th Century Fox	Fr.	XBLY 921.041
		>20th Fox	USA	Fox 3029
		20th Fox	USA	SFX-3029
		20th Fox	USA	TCF102-2
		20th Fox	USA	TCF102-2S
		Top Rank	USA	35/067
		Vega	Fr.	30 TCF 5
		World Record Club	Eng.	76
		World Record Club	Eng.	TP. 226

5380 BODY AND SOUL (3:28)

	12 Inch LP	Ember	Eng.	EMB3314
		Fontana	It.	9286 307
		Mercury	Holl.	9286 092
		Movietone	USA	71021
		Movietone	USA	S72021
		RCA Victor	Jap.	MJ-7093
		20th Century Fox	USA	TFM3162
		20th Century Fox	USA	TFS4162
		20th Century Fox	Fr.	468.004
		20th Century Fox	Fr.	T607
		20th Century Fox	Fr.	XBLY 921.041
		>20th Fox	USA	Fox 3029
		20th Fox	USA	SFX-3029
		20th Fox	USA	TCF102-2
		20th Fox	USA	TCF102-2S
		Top Rank	USA	35/067
		Vega	Fr.	30 TCF 5
		World Record Club	Eng.	76
		World Record Club	Eng.	TP. 226

5390 WILLOW WEEP FOR ME (3:39) (Note D)

	12 Inch LP	Ember	Eng.	EMB3314
		Fontana	It.	9286 307
		Mercury	Holl.	9286 092
		Movietone	USA	71021
		Movietone	USA	S72021
		RCA Victor	Jap.	MJ-7093
		20th Century Fox	USA	TFM3162
		20th Century Fox	USA	TFS4162
		20th Century Fox	Fr.	468.004
		20th Century Fox	Fr.	T607
		20th Century Fox	Fr.	XBLY 921.041
		>20th Fox	USA	Fox 3029
		20th Fox	USA	SFX-3029
		20th Fox	USA	TCF102-2
		20th Fox	USA	TCF102-2S
		Top Rank	USA	35/067
		Vega	Fr.	30 TCF 5
		World Record Club	Eng.	76
		World Record Club	Eng.	TP. 226

5400 TOO MARVELOUS FOR WORDS (2:21)

	12 Inch LP	Ember	Eng.	EMB3314
		Fontana	It.	9286 307
		Mercury	Holl.	9286 092
		Movietone	USA	71021
		Movietone	USA	S72021
		RCA Victor	Jap.	MJ-7093
		Smithsonian	USA	P 11894

```
                         20th Century Fox    USA    TFM3162
                         20th Century Fox    USA    TFS4162
                         20th Century Fox    Fr.    468.004
                         20th Century Fox    Fr.    T607
                         20th Century Fox    Fr.    XBLY 921.041
                        >20th Fox            USA    Fox 3029
                         20th Fox            USA    SFX-3029
                         20th Fox            USA    TCF102-2
                         20th Fox            USA    TCF102-2S
                         Top Rank            USA    35/067
                         Vega                Fr.    30 TCF 5
                         World Record Club   Eng.   76
                         World Record Club   Eng.   TP. 226

5410   DANNY BOY (3:02)

          12 Inch LP     Ember               Eng.   EMB3314
                         RCA Victor          Jap.   MJ-7093
                         20th Century Fox    USA    TFM3162
                         20th Century Fox    USA    TFS4162
                         20th Century Fox    Fr.    468.004
                         20th Century Fox    Fr.    T607
                         20th Century Fox    Fr.    XBLY 921.041
                        >20th Fox            USA    Fox 3029
                         20th Fox            USA    SFX-3029
                         20th Fox            USA    TCF102-2
                         20th Fox            USA    TCF102-2S
                         Top Rank            USA    35/067
                         Vega                Fr.    30 TCF 5
                         World Record Club   Eng.   76
                         World Record Club   Eng.   TP. 226

5420   TENDERLY (3:57) (Note E)

          12 Inch LP     Ember               Eng.   EMB3314
                         Fontana             It.    9286 307
                         Mercury             Holl.  9286 092
                         Movietone           USA    71021
                         Movietone           USA    S72021
                         RCA Victor          Jap.   MJ-7093
                         20th Century Fox    USA    TFM3162
                         20th Century Fox    USA    TFS4162
                         20th Century Fox    Fr.    468.004
                         20th Century Fox    Fr.    T607
                         20th Century Fox    Fr.    XBLY 921.041
                        >20th Fox            USA    Fox 3029
                         20th Fox            USA    SFX-3029
                         20th Fox            USA    TCF102-2
                         20th Fox            USA    TCF102-2S
                         Top Rank            USA    35/067
                         Vega                Fr.    30 TCF 5
                         World Record Club   Eng.   76
                         World Record Club   Eng.   TP. 226
          12 Inch TX     AFRS Amer.Pop.Mus.  USA    434
                         AFRS Amer.Pop.Mus.  USA    732

5430   YOU TOOK ADVANTAGE OF ME (3:25)

          12 Inch LP     Ember               Eng.   EMB3314
                         Fontana             It.    9286 307
                         Mercury             Holl.  9286 092
                         Movietone           USA    71021
                         Movietone           USA    S72021
                         RCA Victor          Jap.   MJ-7093
                         20th Century Fox    USA    TFM3162
                         20th Century Fox    USA    TFS4162
                         20th Century Fox    Fr.    468.004
                         20th Century Fox    Fr.    T607
                         20th Century Fox    Fr.    XBLY 921.041
                        >20th Fox            USA    Fox 3029
                         20th Fox            USA    SFX-3029
                         20th Fox            USA    TCF102-2
                         20th Fox            USA    TCF102-2S
                         Top Rank            USA    35/067
                         Vega                Fr.    30 TCF 5
```

	World Record Club	Eng.	76
	World Record Club	Eng.	TP. 226
12 Inch TX	AFRS Amer.Pop.Mus.	USA	732

5440 YESTERDAYS (3:05)

12 Inch LP	Ember	Eng.	EMB3314
	Fontana	It.	9286 307
	Mercury	Holl.	9286 092
	Movietone	USA	71021
	Movietone	USA	S72021
	RCA Victor	Jap.	MJ-7093
	20th Century Fox	USA	TFM3162
	20th Century Fox	USA	TFS4162
	20th Century Fox	Fr.	468.004
	20th Century Fox	Fr.	T607
	20th Century Fox	Fr.	XBLY 921.041
	>20th Fox	USA	Fox 3029
	20th Fox	USA	SFX-3029
	20th Fox	USA	TCF102-2
	20th Fox	USA	TCF102-2S
	Top Rank	USA	35/067
	Vega	Fr.	30 TCF 5
	World Record Club	Eng.	76
	World Record Club	Eng.	TP. 226
12 Inch TX	AFRS Amer.Pop.Mus.	USA	732

5450 I´LL NEVER BE THE SAME (2:41) (Note F)

12 Inch LP	Ember	Eng.	EMB3314
	Fontana	It.	9286 307
	Mercury	Holl.	9286 092
	Movietone	USA	71021
	Movietone	USA	S72021
	RCA Victor	Jap.	MJ-7093
	20th Century Fox	USA	TFM3162
	20th Century Fox	USA	TFS4162
	20th Century Fox	Fr.	468.004
	20th Century Fox	Fr.	T607
	20th Century Fox	Fr.	XBLY 921.041
	>20th Fox	USA	Fox 3029
	20th Fox	USA	SFX-3029
	20th Fox	USA	TCF102-2
	20th Fox	USA	TCF102-2S
	Top Rank	USA	35/067
	Vega	Fr.	30 TCF 5
	World Record Club	Eng.	76
	World Record Club	Eng.	TP. 226

5460 WITHOUT A SONG (2:29)

12 Inch LP	Ember	Eng.	EMB3314
	Fontana	It.	9286 307
	Mercury	Holl.	9286 092
	Movietone	USA	71021
	Movietone	USA	S72021
	RCA Victor	Jap.	MJ-7093
	20th Century Fox	USA	TFM3162
	20th Century Fox	USA	TFS4162
	20th Century Fox	Fr.	468.004
	20th Century Fox	Fr.	T607
	20th Century Fox	Fr.	XBLY 921.041
	>20th Fox	USA	Fox 3029
	20th Fox	USA	SFX-3029
	20th Fox	USA	TCF102-2
	20th Fox	USA	TCF102-2S
	Top Rank	USA	35/067
	Vega	Fr.	30 TCF 5
	World Record Club	Eng.	76
	World Record Club	Eng.	TP. 226

5470 LITTLE MAN, YOU´VE HAD A BUSY DAY (4:40) (Note G)

12 Inch LP	Ember	Eng.	EMB3314
	RCA Victor	Jap.	MJ-7093

```
                         20th Century Fox     USA   TFM3162
                         20th Century Fox     USA   TFS4162
                         20th Century Fox     Fr.   468.004
                         20th Century Fox     Fr.   T607
                         20th Century Fox     Fr.   XBLY 921.041
                       >20th Fox              USA   Fox 3029
                         20th Fox             USA   SFX-3029
                         20th Fox             USA   TCF102-2
                         20th Fox             USA   TCF102-2S
                         Top Rank             USA   35/067
                         Vega                 Fr.   30 TCF 5
                         World Record Club    Eng.  76
                         World Record Club    Eng.  TP. 226

5480  MY HEART STOOD STILL (4:21) (Note H)

       12 Inch LP      Ember                 Eng.  EMB3326
                         20th Century Fox     USA   TFM3163
                         20th Century Fox     USA   TFS4163
                         20th Century Fox     Fr.   T608
                       >20th Fox              USA   Fox 3033
                         20th Fox             USA   SFX-3033
                         20th Fox             USA   TCF102-2
                         20th Fox             USA   TCF102-2S
                         Vega                 Fr.   30 TCF 6
                         World Record Club    Eng.  T. 279

5490  JITTERBUG WALTZ (4:03) (Note I)

       12 Inch LP      Ember                 Eng.  EMB3326
                         Smithsonian          USA   R 029*
                         20th Century Fox     USA   TFM3163
                         20th Century Fox     USA   TFS4163
                         20th Century Fox     Fr.   T608
                       >20th Fox              USA   Fox 3033
                         20th Fox             USA   SFX-3033
                         20th Fox             USA   TCF102-2
                         20th Fox             USA   TCF102-2S
                         Vega                 Fr.   30 TCF 6
                         World Record Club    Eng.  T. 279
       *This issue is complete, Note I does not apply.

5500  OVER THE RAINBOW (3:03)

        7 Inch 45EP    Ember                 Eng.  EMB4502
       12 Inch LP      Ember                 Eng.  EMB3326
                         20th Century Fox     USA   TFM3163
                         20th Century Fox     USA   TFS4163
                         20th Century Fox     Fr.   T608
                       >20th Fox              USA   Fox 3033
                         20th Fox             USA   SFX-3033
                         20th Fox             USA   TCF102-2
                         20th Fox             USA   TCF102-2S
                         Vega                 Fr.   30 TCF 6
                         World Record Club    Eng.  T. 279

5510  IN A SENTIMENTAL MOOD (3:09) (Note E)

       12 Inch LP      Ember                 Eng.  EMB3326
                         20th Century Fox     USA   TFM3163
                         20th Century Fox     USA   TFS4163
                         20th Century Fox     Fr.   T608
                       >20th Fox              USA   Fox 3033
                         20th Fox             USA   SFX-3033
                         20th Fox             USA   TCF102-2
                         20th Fox             USA   TCF102-2S
                         Vega                 Fr.   30 TCF 6
                         World Record Club    Eng.  T. 279

5520  THERE WILL NEVER BE ANOTHER YOU (3:33)

       12 Inch LP      Ember                 Eng.  EMB3326
                         20th Century Fox     USA   TFM3163
                         20th Century Fox     USA   TFS4163
                         20th Century Fox     Fr.   T608
```

>20th Fox	USA	Fox 3033
20th Fox	USA	SFX-3033
20th Fox	USA	TCF102-2
20th Fox	USA	TCF102-2S
Vega	Fr.	30 TCF 6
World Record Club	Eng.	T. 279

5530   SEPTEMBER SONG (3:18)

7 Inch 45EP	Ember	Eng.	EMB4502
12 Inch LP	Ember	Eng.	EMB3326
	20th Century Fox	USA	TFM3163
	20th Century Fox	USA	TFS4163
	20th Century Fox	Fr.	T608
	>20th Fox	USA	Fox 3033
	20th Fox	USA	SFX-3033
	20th Fox	USA	TCF102-2
	20th Fox	USA	TCF102-2S
	Vega	Fr.	30 TCF 6
	World Record Club	Eng.	T. 279

5540   WRAP YOUR TROUBLES IN DREAMS (3:11) (Note J)

12 Inch LP	Ember	Eng.	EMB3326
	20th Century Fox	USA	TFM3163
	20th Century Fox	USA	TFS4163
	20th Century Fox	Fr.	T608
	>20th Fox	USA	Fox 3033
	20th Fox	USA	SFX-3033
	20th Fox	USA	TCF102-2
	20th Fox	USA	TCF102-2S
	Vega	Fr.	30 TCF 6
	World Record Club	Eng.	T. 279

5550   I COVER THE WATERFRONT (4:04) (Note K)

12 Inch LP	Ember	Eng.	EMB3326
	Smithsonian	USA	R 029*
	20th Century Fox	USA	TFM3163
	20th Century Fox	USA	TFS4163
	20th Century Fox	Fr.	T608
	>20th Fox	USA	Fox 3033
	20th Fox	USA	SFX-3033
	20th Fox	USA	TCF102-2
	20th Fox	USA	TCF102-2S
	Vega	Fr.	30 TCF 6
	World Record Club	Eng.	T. 279

*This issue is complete, Note K does not apply.

5560   MOON SONG (3:46)

12 Inch LP	Ember	Eng.	EMB3326
	20th Century Fox	USA	TFM3163
	20th Century Fox	USA	TFS4163
	20th Century Fox	Fr.	T608
	>20th Fox	USA	Fox 3033
	20th Fox	USA	SFX-3033
	20th Fox	USA	TCF102-2
	20th Fox	USA	TCF102-2S
	Vega	Fr.	30 TCF 6
	World Record Club	Eng.	T. 279

5570   DON'T BLAME ME (3:24) (Note E)

7 Inch 45EP	Ember	Eng.	EMB4502
12 Inch LP	Ember	Eng.	EMB3326
	20th Century Fox	USA	TFM3163
	20th Century Fox	USA	TFS4163
	20th Century Fox	Fr.	T608
	>20th Fox	USA	Fox 3033
	20th Fox	USA	SFX-3033
	20th Fox	USA	TCF102-2
	20th Fox	USA	TCF102-2S
	Vega	Fr.	30 TCF 6
	World Record Club	Eng.	T. 279

113

5580 LOVE FOR SALE (2:46)

          12 Inch LP >Smithsonian   USA   R 029

5590 JUST LIKE A BUTTERFLY THAT'S CAUGHT IN THE RAIN (2:37)

          12 Inch LP >Smithsonian   USA   R 029

5600 SWEET LORRAINE (3:49)

          12 Inch LP >Smithsonian   USA   R 029
     Note A: Discs lack introduction and a few notes
             at the end.
     Note B: Discs lack a few notes at the start.
     Note C: Discs lack a few notes at the end.
     Note D: Discs lack first two bars of introduction
             and one note at the end.
     Note E: Discs lack the introduction.
     Note F: Discs lack a few notes at the start and one
             at the end.
     Note G: Discs lack the introduction and first chorus.
     Note H: Discs lack the introduction and first full chorus.
     Note I: Original has four choruses. Except for
             Smithsonian R 029, which is complete, all
             discs have first chorus, 24 bars of second
             chorus, then last 8 bars of fourth chorus.
     Note J: Discs lack the introduction and one note at
             the end.
     Note K: Except for Smithsonian R 029, which is complete,
             all discs lack the introduction, the first full
             chorus, and a few notes at the end.

Hollywood, California   July 8, 1955
          TV broadcast, "The Tonight Show," featuring
          Steve Allen, NBC-TV. Piano solos.
          The listed LP also contains dialogue between
          Steve Allen and Art Tatum.
5610 SOMEONE TO WATCH OVER ME (2:54)

          12 Inch LP >Giants of Jazz   USA   GOJ-1015

5620 THIS CAN'T BE LOVE* (1:30)

          12 Inch LP >Giants of Jazz   USA   GOJ-1015
     *Also includes Frank Carroll, b; Bobby Rosengarden, d.

5630 MY HEART STOOD STILL (3:02)

          12 Inch LP >Giants of Jazz   USA   GOJ-1015

Los Angeles, California   August 1, 1955
          The Lionel Hampton, Art Tatum, Buddy
          Rich Trio. Art Tatum, p; Buddy Rich, d;
          Lionel Hampton, vib.
5640 PERDIDO (5:03)
     (mx 2374-2)
          12 Inch LP   Barclay   Fr.   GLP3566
                        >Clef   USA   MG C-709
                         Columbia   Eng. 33CX10045
                         Pablo   USA   2310-720
                         Pablo   USA   2625-0706
                         Pablo   Braz. 2310 720
                         Pablo   Can. 2310-720
                         Pablo   Eng. 2310 720
                         Pablo   Eng. 2625 706
                         Pablo   Fr.   2310 720
                         Pablo   Ger. 2310 720
                         Pablo   Ger. 2625 706
                         Pablo   It.   2310 720A
                         Pablo   Jap. MW 2140
                         Verve   USA   MG V-8093
                         Verve   Braz. 2332 009
                         Verve   Ger. 511114

114

```
                          Verve                    Ger.  2332 009

5650  HALLELUJAH (4:50)
      (mx 2375-2)
            7 Inch 45EP  Karusell              Swed. KEP354
           12 Inch LP    Barclay               Fr.   GLP3566
                         Book-of-the-Month     USA   51-400
                        >Clef                  USA   MG C-709
                         Columbia              Eng.  33CX10045
                         Pablo                 USA   2310-720
                         Pablo                 USA   2625-0706
                         Pablo                 Braz. 2310 720
                         Pablo                 Can.  2310-720
                         Pablo                 Eng.  2310 720
                         Pablo                 Eng.  2625 706
                         Pablo                 Fr.   2310 720
                         Pablo                 Ger.  2310 720
                         Pablo                 Ger.  2625 706
                         Pablo                 It.   2310 720A
                         Pablo                 Jap.  MW 2140
                         Verve                 USA   MG V-8093
                         Verve                 Braz. 2332 009
                         Verve                 Eng.  VLP9124
                         Verve                 Ger.  511114
                         Verve                 Ger.  2332 009

5660  I´LL NEVER BE THE SAME (6:33)
      (mx 2376-2)
           12 Inch LP    Barclay               Fr.   GLP3566
                        >Clef                  USA   MG C-709
                         Columbia              Eng.  33CX10045
                         Pablo                 USA   2310-720
                         Pablo                 USA   2625-0706
                         Pablo                 Braz. 2310 720
                         Pablo                 Can.  2310-720
                         Pablo                 Eng.  2310 720
                         Pablo                 Eng.  2625 706
                         Pablo                 Fr.   2310 720
                         Pablo                 Ger.  2310 720
                         Pablo                 Ger.  2625 706
                         Pablo                 It.   2310 720A
                         Pablo                 Jap.  MW 2140
                         Verve                 USA   MG V-8093
                         Verve                 Ger.  511114

5670  LOVE FOR SALE (9:38)
      (mx 2377-1)
           12 Inch LP   >Pablo                 USA   2310-775
                         Pablo                 Can.  2310-775
                         Pablo                 Eng.  2310 775
                         Pablo                 Ger.  2310 775
                         Pablo                 Jap.  MTF 1114

5680  LOVE FOR SALE (6:15)
      (mx 2377-2)
           12 Inch LP   >Pablo                 USA   2310-775
                         Pablo                 Can.  2310-775
                         Pablo                 Eng.  2310 775
                         Pablo                 Ger.  2310 775
                         Pablo                 Jap.  MTF 1114

5690  BODY AND SOUL (5:21)
      (mx 2378-2)
           12 Inch LP   >Amer.Recording Soc.  USA   G 424
                         Columbia              Eng.  33CX10115
                         Pablo                 USA   2310-775
                         Pablo                 Can.  2310-775
                         Pablo                 Eng.  2310 775
                         Pablo                 Ger.  2310 775
                         Pablo                 Jap.  MTF 1114

5700  PLEASE BE KIND (4:45)
      (mx 2379-1)
           12 Inch LP   >Pablo                 USA   2310-775
                         Pablo                 Can.  2310-775
```

	Pablo	Eng.	2310 775
	Pablo	Ger.	2310 775
	Pablo	Jap.	MTF 1114

5710 WHAT IS THIS THING CALLED LOVE (6:59)
(mx 2380-2)

12 Inch LP	Barclay	Fr.	GLP3566
	Book-of-the-Month	USA	51-400
	>Clef	USA	MG C-709
	Columbia	Eng.	33CX10045
	Pablo	USA	2310-720
	Pablo	USA	2625-0706
	Pablo	Braz.	2310 720
	Pablo	Can.	2310-720
	Pablo	Eng.	2310 720
	Pablo	Eng.	2625 706
	Pablo	Fr.	2310 720
	Pablo	Ger.	2310 720
	Pablo	Ger.	2625 706
	Pablo	It.	2310 720A
	Pablo	Jap.	MW 2140
	Verve	USA	MG V-8093
	Verve	Braz.	2332 010
	Verve	Ger.	511114
	Verve	Ger.	2332 010
16 Inch TX	AFRS 1/4 Century of Swing	USA	236

5720 STARS FELL ON ALABAMA (5:38)
(mx 2381-2)

12 Inch LP	>Pablo	USA	2310-775
	Pablo	Can.	2310-775
	Pablo	Eng.	2310 775
	Pablo	Ger.	2310 775
	Pablo	Jap.	MTF 1114

5730 THIS CAN'T BE LOVE (6:16)
(mx 2382-2)

12 Inch LP	>Pablo	USA	2310-775
	Pablo	Can.	2310-775
	Pablo	Eng.	2310 775
	Pablo	Ger.	2310 775
	Pablo	Jap.	MTF 1114

5740 LOVER MAN (5:58)
(mx 2383-1)

12 Inch LP	>Pablo	USA	2310-775
	Pablo	Can.	2310-775
	Pablo	Eng.	2310 775
	Pablo	Ger.	2310 775
	Pablo	Jap.	MTF 1114

5750 PRISONER OF LOVE (6:07)
(mx 2384-2)

12 Inch LP	>Pablo	USA	2310-775
	Pablo	Can.	2310-775
	Pablo	Eng.	2310 775
	Pablo	Ger.	2310 775
	Pablo	Jap.	MTF 1114

5760 MAKIN' WHOOPEE (7:00)
(mx 2385-1)

12 Inch LP	Barclay	Fr.	GLP3566
	>Clef	USA	MG C-709
	Columbia	Eng.	33CX10045
	Pablo	USA	2310-720
	Pablo	USA	2625-0706
	Pablo	Braz.	2310 720
	Pablo	Can.	2310-720
	Pablo	Eng.	2310 720
	Pablo	Eng.	2625 706
	Pablo	Fr.	2310 720
	Pablo	Ger.	2310 720
	Pablo	Ger.	2625 706

```
                              Pablo              It.   2310 720A
                              Pablo              Jap.  MW 2140
                              Verve              USA   MG V-8093
                              Verve              Eng.  VLP9110
                              Verve              Ger.  511114
            16 Inch TX        AFRS 1/4 Century   USA   242
                                of Swing

5770  MORE THAN YOU KNOW (4:12)
      (mx 2386-1)
            12 Inch LP        Barclay            Fr.   GLP3566
                             >Clef               USA   MG C-709
                              Columbia           Eng.  33CX10045
                              Pablo              USA   2310-720
                              Pablo              USA   2625-0706
                              Pablo              Braz. 2310 720
                              Pablo              Can.  2310-720
                              Pablo              Eng.  2310 720
                              Pablo              Eng.  2625 706
                              Pablo              Fr.   2310 720
                              Pablo              Ger.  2310 720
                              Pablo              Ger.  2625 706
                              Pablo              It.   2310 720A
                              Pablo              Jap.  MW 2140
                              Time-Life          USA   P 15516
                              Verve              USA   MG V-8093
                              Verve              Ger.  511114

5780  HOW HIGH THE MOON (5:03)
      (mx 2387-2)
            12 Inch LP        Barclay            Fr.   GLP3566
                             >Clef               USA   MG C-709
                              Columbia           Eng.  33CX10045
                              Pablo              USA   2310-720
                              Pablo              USA   2625-0706
                              Pablo              Braz. 2310 720
                              Pablo              Can.  2310 -720
                              Pablo              Eng.  2310 720
                              Pablo              Eng.  2625 706
                              Pablo              Fr.   2310 720
                              Pablo              Ger.  2310 720
                              Pablo              Ger.  2625 706
                              Pablo              It.   2310 720A
                              Pablo              Jap.  MW 2140
                              Verve              USA   MG V-8093
                              Verve              Ger.  511114
            16 Inch TX        AFRS 1/4 Century   USA   183
                                of Swing

-----------------------------------------------------------
Los Angeles, California                  September 7, 1955
            Lionel Hampton and His Giants.  Harry
            Edison, t; Art Tatum, p; Buddy
            Rich, d; Lionel Hampton, vib.
5790  PLAID[1] (6:35)
      (mx 2489-2)
            12 Inch LP        Columbia           Eng.  33CX10063
                              Jazz Spectrum      USA   Vol. 7
                             >Norgran            USA   MG N-1080
                              Pablo              USA   2310-731
                              Pablo              USA   2625-0706
                              Pablo              Braz. 2310 731
                              Pablo              Can.  2310-731
                              Pablo              Eng.  2310 731
                              Pablo              Eng.  2625 706
                              Pablo              Fr.   2310 731
                              Pablo              Ger.  2310 731
                              Pablo              Ger.  2625 706
                              Pablo              Jap.  MTF 1072
                              Verve              USA   MG V-8170
                              Verve              Eng.  VLP9110
                              Verve              Fr.   711.068
            12 Inch TX        Thesaurus          USA   JATP-12
      [1]Also includes Red Callender, b; Barney Kessel, g.
```

```
5800    SOMEBODY LOVES ME[2]  (7:09)
        (mx 2490-2)
                12 Inch LP    Columbia              Eng.   33CX10063
                             >Norgran               USA    MG N-1080
                              Pablo                 USA    2310-731
                              Pablo                 USA    2625-0706
                              Pablo                 Braz.  2310 731
                              Pablo                 Can.   2310-731
                              Pablo                 Eng.   2310 731
                              Pablo                 Eng.   2625 706
                              Pablo                 Fr.    2310 731
                              Pablo                 Ger.   2310 731
                              Pablo                 Ger.   2625 706
                              Pablo                 Jap.   MTF 1072
                              Verve                 USA    MG V-8170
                              Verve                 Braz.  2332 010
                              Verve                 Fr.    711.068
                              Verve                 Ger.   2331 010
                12 Inch TX    Thesaurus             USA    JATP-12
        [2]Also includes Barney Kessel, g; John Simmons, b.

5810    DEEP PURPLE[3]  (7:57)
        (mx 2491-5)
                12 Inch LP    Columbia              Eng.   33CX10063
                             >Norgran               USA    MG N-1080
                              Pablo                 USA    2310-731
                              Pablo                 USA    2625-0706
                              Pablo                 Braz.  2310 731
                              Pablo                 Can.   2310-731
                              Pablo                 Eng.   2310 731
                              Pablo                 Eng.   2625 706
                              Pablo                 Fr.    2310 731
                              Pablo                 Ger.   2310 731
                              Pablo                 Ger.   2625 706
                              Pablo                 Jap.   MTF 1072
                              Verve                 USA    MG V-8170
                              Verve                 Fr.    711.068
                12 Inch TX    Thesaurus             USA    JATP-12
        [3]Also includes Barney Kessel, g; John Simmons, b.

5820    WHAT IS THIS THING CALLED LOVE[4]  (7:42)
        (mx 2492-4)
                12 Inch LP    Columbia              Eng.   33CX10115
                             >Verve                 USA    MG V-8215
        [4]Also includes Barney Kessel, g; Red Callender, b.

5830    SEPTEMBER SONG[5]  (7:00)
        (mx 2493-1)
                12 Inch LP    Columbia              Eng.   33CX10063
                             >Norgran               USA    MG N-1080
                              Pablo                 USA    2310-731
                              Pablo                 USA    2625-0706
                              Pablo                 Braz.  2310 731
                              Pablo                 Can.   2310-731
                              Pablo                 Eng.   2310 731
                              Pablo                 Eng.   2625 706
                              Pablo                 Fr.    2310 731
                              Pablo                 Ger.   2310 731
                              Pablo                 Ger.   2625 706
                              Pablo                 Jap.   MTF 1072
                              Verve                 USA    MG V-8170
                              Verve                 Fr.    711.068
        [5]Also includes Red Callender, b.

5831    SEPTEMBER SONG[6]
        (mx 2493-3)
                              Verve                 USA    Unissued
        [6]Also includes Red Callender, b.

5840    VERVE BLUES[7]  (12:43)
        (mx 2494-1)
                12 Inch LP    Columbia              Eng.   33CX10063
                             >Norgran               USA    MG N-1080
                              Pablo                 USA    2310-731
                              Pablo                 USA    2625-0706
```

```
                        Pablo                  Braz. 2310 731
                        Pablo                  Can.  2310-731
                        Pablo                  Eng.  2310 731
                        Pablo                  Eng.  2625 706
                        Pablo                  Fr.   2310 731
                        Pablo                  Ger.  2310 731
                        Pablo                  Ger.  2625 706
                        Pablo                  Jap.  MTF 1072
                        Verve                  USA   MG V-8170
                        Verve                  Fr.   711.068
      [7]Also includes Red Callender, b; Lionel Hampton, vib & v.
```

```
New York, New York                        November 5, 1955
          Radio broadcast, CBS radio, live at Basin
          Street night club.  The Art Tatum Trio.
          Art Tatum, p; Everett Barksdale, g.;
          Slam Stewart, b.
5850  FLYING HOME (0:43)

          12 Inch LP   Jazz Anthology       Fr.    JA5138
                       >RI Disc             Swiss  RI-DISC 8

5860  I COVER THE WATERFRONT (4:17)

          12 Inch LP   Jazz Anthology       Fr.    JA5138
                       >RI Disc             Swiss  RI-DISC 8

5870  SOFT WINDS (3:10)

          12 Inch LP   Jazz Anthology       Fr.    JA5138
                       Europa               It.    EJ-1011
                       >RI Disc             Swiss  RI-DISC 8

5880  TENDERLY (4:42)

          12 Inch LP   Jazz Anthology       Fr.    JA5138
                       >RI Disc             Swiss  RI-DISC 8

5890  TEA FOR TWO (2:58)

          12 Inch LP   Jazz Anthology       Fr.    JA5138
                       >RI Disc             Swiss  RI-DISC 8

5900  WRAP YOUR TROUBLES IN DREAMS (4:59)

          12 Inch LP   Jazz Anthology       Fr.    JA5138
                       >RI Disc             Swiss  RI-DISC 8

5910  BODY AND SOUL (0:57)

          12 Inch LP   Jazz Anthology       Fr.    JA5138
                       >RI Disc             Swiss  RI-DISC 8
```

```
Los Angeles, California                   January 27, 1956
          The Art Tatum Trio.  Art Tatum, p;
          Red Callender, b; Jo Jones, d.
5920  BLUE LOU (3:01)
      (mx 2667-1)
          10 Inch LP   Columbia             Eng.  33C 9039
          12 Inch LP   Amer.Recording Soc.  USA   G 424
                       Barclay              Fr.   GLP3592
                       Pablo                USA   2310-735
                       Pablo                USA   2625 0706
                       Pablo                Braz. 2310 735
                       Pablo                Can.  2310-735
                       Pablo                Eng.  2310 735
                       Pablo                Eng.  2625 706
                       Pablo                Fr.   2310 735
                       Pablo                Ger.  2310 735
                       Pablo                Ger.  2625 706
                       Pablo                It.   2310 735A
                       Pablo                Jap.  MW 2175
                       >Verve               USA   MG V-8118
```

	Verve	Astla	MG V-8118
	Verve	Ger.	511.107
	Verve	Jap.	MV 2021
	Verve	Jap.	MV 2537
	Verve	Jap.	VL-1032
	VSP Verve	It.	SVSP 57.030

5930 IF (3:30)
(mx 2668-1)

12 Inch LP	Barclay	Fr.	GLP3592
	Columbia	Eng.	33CX10115
	Pablo	USA	2310-735
	Pablo	USA	2625-0706
	Pablo	Braz.	2310 735
	Pablo	Can.	2310-735
	Pablo	Eng.	2310 735
	Pablo	Eng.	2625 706
	Pablo	Fr.	2310 735
	Pablo	Ger.	2310 735
	Pablo	Ger.	2625 706
	Pablo	It.	2310 735A
	Pablo	Jap.	MW 2175
	>Verve	USA	MG V-8118
	Verve	Astla	MG V-8118
	Verve	Ger.	511.107
	Verve	Jap.	MV 2021
	Verve	Jap.	MV 2537
	Verve	Jap.	VL-1032
	VSP Verve	It.	SVSP 57.030

5940 SOME OTHER SPRING (4:44)
(mx 2669-1)

12 Inch LP	Barclay	Fr.	GLP3592
	Pablo	USA	2310-735
	Pablo	USA	2625-0706
	Pablo	Braz.	2310 735
	Pablo	Can.	2310-735
	Pablo	Eng.	2310 735
	Pablo	Eng.	2625 706
	Pablo	Fr.	2310 735
	Pablo	Ger.	2310 735
	Pablo	Ger.	2625 706
	Pablo	It.	2310 735A
	Pablo	Jap.	MW 2175
	>Verve	USA	MG V-8118
	Verve	Astla	MG V-8118
	Verve	Ger.	511.107
	Verve	Jap.	MV 2021
	Verve	Jap.	MV 2537
	Verve	Jap.	VL-1032
	VSP Verve	It.	SVSP 57.030

5950 MORE THAN YOU KNOW (3:36)
(mx 2670-1)

10 Inch LP	Columbia	Eng.	33C 9039
12 Inch LP	Barclay	Fr.	GLP3592
	Pablo	USA	2310-735
	Pablo	USA	2625-0706
	Pablo	Braz.	2310 735
	Pablo	Can.	2310-735
	Pablo	Eng.	2310 735
	Pablo	Eng.	2625 706
	Pablo	Fr.	2310 735
	Pablo	Ger.	2310 735
	Pablo	Ger.	2625 706
	Pablo	It.	2310 735A
	Pablo	Jap.	MW 2175
	>Verve	USA	MG V-8118
	Verve	Astla	MG V-8118
	Verve	Ger.	511.107
	Verve	Jap.	MV 2021
	Verve	Jap.	MV 2537
	Verve	Jap.	VL-1032
	VSP Verve	It.	SVSP 57.030

```
5960   JUST ONE OF THOSE THINGS (7:11)
       (mx 2671-1)
           10 Inch LP    Columbia            Eng.   33C 9039
           12 Inch LP    Barclay             Fr.    GLP3592
                         Pablo               USA    2310-735
                         Pablo               USA    2625-0706
                         Pablo               Braz.  2310 735
                         Pablo               Can.   2310-735
                         Pablo               Eng.   2310 735
                         Pablo               Eng.   2625 706
                         Pablo               Fr.    2310 735
                         Pablo               Ger.   2310 735
                         Pablo               Ger.   2625 706
                         Pablo               It.    2310 735A
                         Pablo               Jap.   MW 2175
                        >Verve               USA    MG V-8118
                         Verve               Astla  MG V-8118
                         Verve               Ger.   511.107
                         Verve               Jap.   MV 2021
                         Verve               Jap.   MV 2537
                         Verve               Jap.   VL-1032
                         VSP Verve           It.    SVSP 57.030
           16 Inch TX    AFRS 1/4 Century    USA    183
                          of Swing

5970   I'LL NEVER BE THE SAME (4:53)
       (mx 2672-1)
           10 Inch LP    Columbia            Eng.   33C 9039
           12 Inch LP    Barclay             Fr.    GLP3592
                         Pablo               USA    2310-735
                         Pablo               USA    2625-0706
                         Pablo               Braz.  2310 735
                         Pablo               Can.   2310-735
                         Pablo               Eng.   2310 735
                         Pablo               Eng.   2625 706
                         Pablo               Fr.    2310 735
                         Pablo               Ger.   2310 735
                         Pablo               Ger.   2625 706
                         Pablo               It.    2310 735A
                         Pablo               Jap.   MW 2175
                        >Verve               USA    MG V-8118
                         Verve               Astla  MG V-8118
                         Verve               Ger.   511.107
                         Verve               Jap.   MV 2021
                         Verve               Jap.   MV 2537
                         Verve               Jap.   VL-1032
                         VSP Verve           USA    VSP 13
                         VSP Verve           USA    VSPS-13
                         VSP Verve           It.    SVSP 57.030

5980   LOVE FOR SALE (5:28)
       (mx 2673-2)
           10 Inch LP    Columbia            Eng.   33C 9039
           12 Inch LP    Barclay             Fr.    GLP3592
                         Pablo               USA    2310-735
                         Pablo               USA    2625-0706
                         Pablo               Braz.  2310 735
                         Pablo               Can.   2310-735
                         Pablo               Eng.   2310 735
                         Pablo               Eng.   2625 706
                         Pablo               Fr.    2310 735
                         Pablo               Ger.   2310 735
                         Pablo               Ger.   2625 706
                         Pablo               It.    2310 735A
                         Pablo               Jap.   MW 2175
                        >Verve               USA    MG V-8118
                         Verve               Astla  MG V-8118
                         Verve               Ger.   511.107
                         Verve               Jap.   MV 2021
                         Verve               Jap.   MV 2537
                         Verve               Jap.   VL-1032
                         VSP Verve           It.    SVSP 57.030
```

```
5990   I GUESS I'LL HAVE TO CHANGE MY PLANS (3:37)
       (mx 2674-2)
                  10 Inch LP    Columbia          Eng.   33C 9039
                  12 Inch LP    Barclay           Fr.    GLP3592
                                Pablo             USA    2310-735
                                Pablo             USA    2625-0706
                                Pablo             Braz.  2310 735
                                Pablo             Can.   2310-735
                                Pablo             Eng.   2310 735
                                Pablo             Eng.   2625 706
                                Pablo             Fr.    2310 735
                                Pablo             Ger.   2310 735
                                Pablo             Ger.   2625 706
                                Pablo             It.    2310 735A
                                Pablo             Jap.   MW 2175
                               >Verve             USA    MG V-8118
                                Verve             Astla  MG V-8118
                                Verve             Ger.   511.107
                                Verve             Jap.   MV 2021
                                Verve             Jap.   MV 2537
                                Verve             Jap.   VL-1032
                                VSP Verve         It.    SVSP 57.030

6000   ISN'T IT ROMANTIC (3:57)
       (mx 2675-2)
                  10 Inch LP    Columbia          Eng.   33C 9039
                  12 Inch LP    Barclay           Fr.    GLP3592
                                Pablo             USA    2310-735
                                Pablo             USA    2625-0706
                                Pablo             Braz.  2310 735
                                Pablo             Can.   2310-735
                                Pablo             Eng.   2310 735
                                Pablo             Eng.   2625 706
                                Pablo             Fr.    2310 735
                                Pablo             Ger.   2310 735
                                Pablo             Ger.   2625 706
                                Pablo             It.    2310 735A
                                Pablo             Jap.   MW 2175
                               >Verve             USA    MG V-8118
                                Verve             Astla  MG V-8118
                                Verve             Ger.   511.107
                                Verve             Jap.   MV 2021
                                Verve             Jap.   MV 2537
                                Verve             Jap.   VL-1032
                                VSP Verve         It.    SVSP 57.030

6010   TRIO BLUES (5:06)
       (mx 2676-2)
                  12 Inch LP    Barclay           Fr.    GLP3592
                                Columbia          Eng.   33CX10115
                                Pablo             USA    2310-735
                                Pablo             USA    2625-0706
                                Pablo             Braz.  2310 735
                                Pablo             Can.   2310-735
                                Pablo             Eng.   2310 735
                                Pablo             Eng.   2625 706
                                Pablo             Fr.    2310 735
                                Pablo             Ger.   2310 735
                                Pablo             Ger.   2625 706
                                Pablo             It.    2310 735A
                                Pablo             Jap.   MW 2175
                                Time-Life         USA    P 15516
                               >Verve             USA    MG V-8118
                                Verve             Astla  MG V-8118
                                Verve             USA    MG V-8320
                                Verve             USA    PRS 2-3
                                Verve             Eng.   VLP9110
                                Verve             Ger.   511.107
                                Verve             Jap.   MV 2021
                                Verve             Jap.   MV 2537
                                Verve             Jap.   VL-1032
                                VSP Verve         USA    VSP 13
                                VSP Verve         USA    VSPS-13
                                VSP Verve         It.    SVSP 57.030
                  16 Inch TX    AFRS 1/4 Century  USA    183
```

```
----------------------------------------------------------
Los Angeles, California                     February 6, 1956
        Art Tatum-Buddy De Franco Quartet.
        Buddy De Franco, cl; Art Tatum, p;
        Red Callender, b; Bill Douglass, d.
6020  DEEP NIGHT (5:43)
      (mx 2677-3)
            7 Inch 45EP Columbia              Eng.  SEB 10101
            12 Inch LP  Amer.Recording Soc.   USA   G 412
                        Pablo                 USA   2310-736
                        Pablo                 USA   2625-0706
                        Pablo                 Braz. 2310 736
                        Pablo                 Can.  2310-736
                        Pablo                 Eng.  2310 736
                        Pablo                 Eng.  2625 706
                        Pablo                 Fr.   2310 736
                        Pablo                 Ger.  2310 736
                        Pablo                 Ger.  2625 706
                        Pablo                 It.   2310 736A
                        Pablo                 Jap.  MTF 1064
                       >Verve                 USA   MG V-8229
                        Verve                 Eng.  VLP9110

6030  ONCE IN A WHILE (5:12)
      (mx 2678-3)
            12 Inch LP  Amer.Recording Soc.   USA   G 412
                        Pablo                 USA   2310-736
                        Pablo                 USA   2625-0706
                        Pablo                 Braz. 2310 736
                        Pablo                 Can.  2310-736
                        Pablo                 Eng.  2310 736
                        Pablo                 Eng.  2625 706
                        Pablo                 Fr.   2310 736
                        Pablo                 Ger.  2310 736
                        Pablo                 Ger.  2625 706
                        Pablo                 It.   2310 736A
                        Pablo                 Jap.  MTF 1064
                       >Verve                 USA   MG V-8229

6040  THIS CAN'T BE LOVE (4:34)
      (mx 2679-3)
            12 Inch LP  Amer.Recording Soc.   USA   G 412
                        Columbia              Eng.  33CX10115
                        Pablo                 USA   2310-736
                        Pablo                 USA   2625-0706
                        Pablo                 Braz. 2310 736
                        Pablo                 Can.  2310-736
                        Pablo                 Eng.  2310 736
                        Pablo                 Eng.  2625 706
                        Pablo                 Fr.   2310 736
                        Pablo                 Ger.  2310 736
                        Pablo                 Ger.  2625 706
                        Pablo                 It.   2310 736A
                        Pablo                 Jap.  MTF 1064
                       >Verve                 USA   MG V-8229

6050  MEMORIES OF YOU (7:09)
      (mx 2680-2)
            7 Inch 45EP Columbia              Eng.  SEB 10101
            12 Inch LP  Amer.Recording Soc.   USA   G 412
                        Pablo                 USA   2310-736
                        Pablo                 USA   2625-0706
                        Pablo                 Braz. 2310 736
                        Pablo                 Can.  2310-736
                        Pablo                 Eng.  2310 736
                        Pablo                 Eng.  2625 706
                        Pablo                 Fr.   2310 736
                        Pablo                 Ger.  2310 736
                        Pablo                 Ger.  2625 706
                        Pablo                 It.   2310 736A
                        Pablo                 Jap.  MTF 1064
                       >Verve                 USA   MG V-8229
```

```
6060   YOU'RE MINE, YOU (7:01)
       (mx 2681-1)
             12 Inch LP    Amer.Recording Soc. USA   G 412
                           Pablo               USA   2310-736
                           Pablo               USA   2625-0706
                           Pablo               Braz. 2310 736
                           Pablo               Can.  2310-736
                           Pablo               Eng.  2310 736
                           Pablo               Eng.  2625 706
                           Pablo               Fr.   2310 736
                           Pablo               Ger.  2310 736
                           Pablo               Ger.  2625 706
                           Pablo               It.   2310 736A
                           Pablo               Jap.  MTF 1064
                          >Verve               USA   MG V-8229

6070   A FOGGY DAY (3:21)
       (mx 2682-4)
             10 Inch 78    Columbia            Eng.  LB 10039
              7 Inch 45    Karusell            Swed. AFF1116
              7 Inch 45EP  Clef                USA   89170x45
                           His Master's Voice  Eng.  7EG 8619
             12 Inch LP    Amer.Recording Soc. USA   G 412
                           Pablo               USA   2310-736
                           Pablo               USA   2625-0706
                           Pablo               Braz. 2310 736
                           Pablo               Can.  2310-736
                           Pablo               Eng.  2310 736
                           Pablo               Eng.  2625 706
                           Pablo               Fr.   2310 736
                           Pablo               Ger.  2310 736
                           Pablo               Ger.  2625 706
                           Pablo               It.   2310 736A
                           Pablo               Jap.  MTF 1064
                          >Verve               USA   MG V-8229
                           Verve               Eng.  VLP9110

6080   LOVER MAN (6:40)
       (mx 2683-2)
              7 Inch 45EP  His Master's Voice  Eng.  7EG 8619
             12 Inch LP    Amer.Recording Soc. USA   G 412
                           Pablo               USA   2310-736
                           Pablo               USA   2625-0706
                           Pablo               Braz. 2310 736
                           Pablo               Can.  2310-736
                           Pablo               Eng.  2310 736
                           Pablo               Eng.  2625 706
                           Pablo               Fr.   2310 736
                           Pablo               Ger.  2310 736
                           Pablo               Ger.  2625 706
                           Pablo               It.   2310 736A
                           Pablo               Jap.  MTF 1064
                          >Verve               USA   MG V-8229

6090   MAKIN' WHOOPEE (3:29)
       (mx 2684-4)
             10 Inch 78    Columbia            Eng.  LB 10039
              7 Inch 45    Karusell            Swed. AFF1116
              7 Inch 45EP  Clef                USA   89170x45
                           His Master's Voice  Eng.  7EG 8619
             12 Inch LP    Amer.Recording Soc. USA   G 412
                           Pablo               USA   2310-736
                           Pablo               USA   2625-0706
                           Pablo               Braz. 2310 736
                           Pablo               Can.  2310-736
                           Pablo               Eng.  2310 736
                           Pablo               Eng.  2625 706
                           Pablo               Fr.   2310 736
                           Pablo               Ger.  2310 736
                           Pablo               Ger.  2625 706
                           Pablo               It.   2310 736A
                           Pablo               Jap.  MTF 1064
                          >Verve               USA   MG V-8229
```

```
------------------------------------------------------------
Chicago, Illinois                                March 25, 1956
          Radio broadcast, live at London House.
          NBC "Monitor" program, with Tom Mercein,
          narrator. The Art Tatum Trio. Art
          Tatum, p; Everett Barksdale, g;
          Slam Stewart, b.
6100  SWEET LORRAINE (3:59)

          12 Inch LP  >Giants of Jazz       USA   GOJ-1015

6110  SEPTEMBER SONG (4:48)

          12 Inch LP  >Giants of Jazz       USA   GOJ-1015

------------------------------------------------------------
Hollywood, California                            August 11, 1956
          Live recording at the Hollywood Bowl.
          Piano solos.
6120  BEGIN THE BEGUINE (3:01)

          7 Inch 45EP Columbia              Eng.  SEB 10084
                      Verve                 Ger.  EPV6036
          12 Inch LP  >Verve                USA   MG V-8231-2
                      Verve                 Fr.   2367 396
                      Verve                 Jap.  VL-1007

6130  HUMORESQUE (3:26)

          7 Inch 45EP Barclay              Fr.   74058
                      Columbia              Eng.  SEB 10084
                      Verve                 Ger.  EPV6036
          12 Inch LP  >Verve                USA   MG V-8231-2
                      Verve                 Eng.  VLP9110
                      Verve                 Fr.   2367 396
                      Verve                 Jap.  Vl-1007
                      VSP Verve             USA   VSP 33
                      VSP Verve             USA   VSPS33
                      VSP Verve             It.   SVSP57.009

6140  SOMEONE TO WATCH OVER ME (3:09)

          7 Inch 45EP Columbia              Eng.  SEB 10084
                      Verve                 Ger.  EPV6036
          12 Inch LP  >Verve                USA   MG V-8231-2
                      Verve                 Fr.   2367 396
                      Verve                 Jap.  VL-1007

6150  WILLOW WEEP FOR ME (3:46)

          7 Inch 45EP Barclay              Fr.   74058
                      Columbia              Eng.  SEB 10084
                      Verve                 Ger.  EPV6036
          12 Inch LP  >Verve                USA   MG V-8231-2
                      Verve                 Fr.   2367 396
                      Verve                 Jap.  VL-1007
                      VSP Verve             USA   VSP 33
                      VSP Verve             USA   VSPS33
                      VSP Verve             It.   SVSP57.009

------------------------------------------------------------
Los Angeles, California                          September 11, 1956
          Art Tatum-Ben Webster Quartet. Ben
          Webster, ts; Art Tatum, p; Red
          Callender, b; Bill Douglass, d.
6160  ALL THE THINGS YOU ARE (7:07)
      (mx 2990-1)
          7 Inch 45EP Barclay              Fr.   74058
          12 Inch LP  Amer.Recording Soc.  USA   G 424
                      Columbia              Eng.  33CX10115
                      Pablo                 USA   2310-737
                      Pablo                 USA   2625-0706
                      Pablo                 Braz. 2310 737
                      Pablo                 Can.  2310-737
                      Pablo                 Eng.  2310 737

                               125
```

Pablo	Eng.	2625 706
Pablo	Fr.	2310 737
Pablo	Ger.	2310 737
Pablo	Ger.	2625 706
Pablo	Jap.	MW 2174
Time-Life	USA	P 15516
>Verve	USA	MG V-8220
Verve	Astla	MG V-8220
Verve	Eng.	VLP9090
Verve	Eur.	711.048
Verve	Ger.	511.108
Verve	Jap.	MV 1106
Verve	Jap.	MV 2025
Verve	Jap.	MV 2505
Verve	Jap.	VL-1024

6170 MY ONE AND ONLY LOVE (6:09)
(mx 2991-1)

7 Inch 45EP	Barclay	Fr.	74045
12 Inch LP	Columbia	Eng.	33CX10137
	His Master's Voice	Span.	LCLP 207
	Pablo	USA	2310-737
	Pablo	USA	2625-0706
	Pablo	Braz.	2310 737
	Pablo	Can.	2310-737
	Pablo	Eng.	2310 737
	Pablo	Eng.	2625 706
	Pablo	Fr.	2310 737
	Pablo	Ger.	2310 737
	Pablo	Ger.	2625 706
	Pablo	Jap.	MW 2174
	>Verve	USA	MG V-8220
	Verve	Astla	MG V-8220
	Verve	Eng.	VLP9090
	Verve	Eur.	711.048
	Verve	Ger.	511.108
	Verve	Jap.	MV 1106
	Verve	Jap.	MV 2025
	Verve	Jap.	MV 2505
	Verve	Jap.	VL-1024

6180 MY IDEAL (7:12)
(mx 2992-1)

7 Inch 45EP	Barclay	Fr.	GEP4033
	Barclay	Fr.	74033
12 Inch LP	Columbia	Eng.	33CX10137
	His Master's Voice	Span.	LCLP 207
	Pablo	USA	2310-737
	Pablo	USA	2625-0706
	Pablo	Braz.	2310 737
	Pablo	Can.	2310-737
	Pablo	Eng.	2310 737
	Pablo	Eng.	2625 706
	Pablo	Fr.	2310 737
	Pablo	Ger.	2310 737
	Pablo	Ger.	2625 706
	Pablo	Jap.	MW 2174
	>Verve	USA	MG V-8220
	Verve	Astla	MG V-8220
	Verve	USA	V-8433
	Verve	USA	V6-8433
	Verve	Eng.	VLP9090
	Verve	Eur.	711.048
	Verve	Ger.	511 063
	Verve	Ger.	511.108
	Verve	Jap.	MV 1106
	Verve	Jap.	MV 2025
	Verve	Jap.	MV 2505
	Verve	Jap.	VL-1024

6190 GONE WITH THE WIND (4:44)
(mx 2993-3)

7 Inch 45EP	Barclay	Fr.	74033
12 Inch LP	Columbia	Eng.	33CX10137
	His Master's Voice	Span.	LCLP 207

```
                              Pablo                 USA    2310-737
                              Pablo                 USA    2625-0706
                              Pablo                 Braz.  2310 737
                              Pablo                 Can.   2310-737
                              Pablo                 Eng.   2310 737
                              Pablo                 Eng.   2625 706
                              Pablo                 Fr.    2310 737
                              Pablo                 Ger.   2310 737
                              Pablo                 Ger.   2625 706
                              Pablo                 Jap.   MW 2174
                             >Verve                 USA    MG V-8220
                              Verve                 Astla  MG V-8220
                              Verve                 Eng.   VLP9090
                              Verve                 Eur.   711.048
                              Verve                 Ger.   511.108
                              Verve                 Jap.   MV 1106
                              Verve                 Jap.   MV 2025
                              Verve                 Jap.   MV 2505
                              Verve                 Jap.   VL-1024

6200  HAVE YOU MET MISS JONES (4:46)
      (mx 2994-3)
         7 Inch 45EP  Barclay                       Fr.    74045
        12 Inch LP    Columbia                      Eng.   33CX10137
                      His Master's Voice            Span.  LCLP 207
                      Pablo                         USA    2310-737
                      Pablo                         USA    2625-0706
                      Pablo                         Braz.  2310 737
                      Pablo                         Can.   2310-737
                      Pablo                         Eng.   2310 737
                      Pablo                         Eng.   2625 706
                      Pablo                         Fr.    2310 737
                      Pablo                         Ger.   2310 737
                      Pablo                         Ger.   2625 706
                      Pablo                         Jap.   MW 2174
                     >Verve                         USA    MG V-8220
                      Verve                         Astla  MG V-8220
                      Verve                         Eng.   VLP9090
                      Verve                         Eur.   711.048
                      Verve                         Ger.   511.108
                      Verve                         Jap.   MV 1106
                      Verve                         Jap.   MV 2025
                      Verve                         Jap.   MV 2505
                      Verve                         Jap.   VL-1024

6210  NIGHT AND DAY (5:25)
      (mx 2995-2)
         7 Inch 45EP  Barclay                       Fr.    74030
        12 Inch LP    Columbia                      Eng.   33CX10137
                      His Master's Voice            Span   LCLP 207
                      Pablo                         USA    2310-737
                      Pablo                         USA    2625-0706
                      Pablo                         Braz.  2310 737
                      Pablo                         Can.   2310-737
                      Pablo                         Eng.   2310 737
                      Pablo                         Eng.   2625 706
                      Pablo                         Fr.    2310 737
                      Pablo                         Ger.   2310 737
                      Pablo                         Ger.   2625 706
                      Pablo                         Jap.   MW 2174
                      Time-Life                     USA    P 15516
                     >Verve                         USA    MG V-8220
                      Verve                         Astla  MG V-8220
                      Verve                         Eng.   VLP9090
                      Verve                         Eur.   711.048
                      Verve                         Ger.   511.108
                      Verve                         Jap.   MV 1106
                      Verve                         Jap.   MV 2025
                      Verve                         Jap.   MV 2505
                      Verve                         Jap.   VL-1024

6220  WHERE OR WHEN (6:22)
      (mx 2996-2)
         7 Inch 45EP  Barclay                       Fr.    74030
        12 Inch LP    Columbia                      Eng.   33CX10137
```

```
                    His Master's Voice  Span.  LCLP 207
                    Pablo               USA    2310-737
                    Pablo               USA    2625-0706
                    Pablo               Braz.  2310 737
                    Pablo               Can.   2310-737
                    Pablo               Eng.   2310 737
                    Pablo               Eng.   2625 706
                    Pablo               Fr.    2310 737
                    Pablo               Ger.   2310 737
                    Pablo               Ger.   2625 706
                    Pablo               Jap.   MW 2174
                    Time-Life           USA    P 15516
                   >Verve               USA    MG V 8220
                    Verve               Astla  MG V-8220
                    Verve               Eng.   VLP9090
                    Verve               Eur.   711.048
                    Verve               Ger    511.108
                    Verve               Jap.   MV 1106
                    Verve               Jap.   MV 2025
                    Verve               Jap.   MV 2505
                    Verve               Jap.   VL-1024
```

Washington, D. C.   October 7, 1956
         Radio broadcast from Olivia's Patio
         Lounge. The Art Tatum Trio. Art
         Tatum, p; Everett Barksdale, g;
         Bill Pemberton, b.
6230 FLYING HOME (1:25)

```
           12 Inch LP   Jazz Anthology    Fr.    JA5138
                       >RI Disc           Swiss  RI-DISC 8
```

6240 MOON SONG (5:42)

```
           12 Inch LP   Jazz Anthology    Fr.    JA5138
                       >RI Disc           Swiss  RI-DISC 8
```

6250 JUST ONE OF THOSE THINGS (3:42)

```
           12 Inch LP   Jazz Anthology    Fr.    JA5138
                       >RI Disc           Swiss  RI-DISC 8
```

Pennsauken, New Jersey   October 14, 1956
         Radio broadcast from the Red Hill Inn.
         The Art Tatum Trio. Art Tatum, p;
         Everett Barksdale, g; Bill Pemberton, b.
6260 FLYING HOME (1:32)

```
           12 Inch LP   Jazz Anthology    Fr.    JA5138
                       >RI Disc           Swiss  RI-DISC 8
                        Teppa             USA    76
```

6270 WOULD YOU LIKE TO TAKE A WALK (5:21)

```
           12 Inch LP   Jazz Anthology    Fr.    JA5138
                       >RI Disc           Swiss  RI-DISC 8
                        Teppa             USA    76
```

6280 YOU GO TO MY HEAD (5:07)

```
           12 Inch LP   Jazz Anthology    Fr.    JA5138
                       >RI Disc           Swiss  RI-DISC 8
                        Teppa             USA    76
```

New York, New York   December 31, 1936
          Radio broadcast, "Kraft Phoenix Cheese Program,"
          on NBC radio.
T7000 UNKNOWN TITLE(S)

----
                                            c. 1939
          Acetates transcribed by Peter Maurice Music
          Co., Ltd., London, and published as parts of
          four piano albums entitled, "The Famous Style
          Piano Solo Album," 1939.
T7005 SAPPHIRE (Album 1)
T7006 AMETHYST (Album 2) (Previously recorded by Tatum as,
          "The Shout." See [240], [241], [310].)
T7007 TURQUOISE (Album 3) (Later played by Tatum in the
          film, "The Fabulous Dorseys." See [2750].)
T7008 JADE (Album 4) [Seems related to the tune published by Leeds
          Music Corp. in 1944 as "Gang O´ Nothin´." See [T8062].

New York, New York   c. 1939
          Acetates made for Robbins Music Corporation
          which were transcribed by Morris (Murray)
          Feldman and published as, "Art Tatum Improv-
          isations, No. 1," in 1939. The published
          versions are selected segments only and
          therefore do not have the integrity or
          continuity of the original performances.
T7011 IF I HAD YOU
T7012 STOMPIN´ AT THE SAVOY
T7013 I´M IN THE MOOD FOR LOVE
T7014 WHEN I GROW TOO OLD TO DREAM
T7015 HOW AM I TO KNOW?
T7016 GOODNIGHT SWEETHEART
T7017 I´M COMING VIRGINIA
T7018 THE MOON IS LOW
T7019 SHOULD I?
T7020 DON´T BLAME ME
T7021 BLUE MOON
T7022 JUST YOU, JUST ME
T7023 PAGAN LOVE SONG
T7024 SWEET AND LOVELY

California   May 16, 1940
          Radio broadcast. Piano solo.
T7030 I GOT RHYTHM (2:02)

New York, New York   April 5, 1941
          Radio broadcast. Piano solos.
T7040 ALL THE THINGS YOU ARE (2:25)
T7041 IT HAD TO BE YOU (1:36)

New York, New York   April 6, 1941
          Radio broadcast, on WABC radio.
          Piano solos.
T7070 HUMORESQUE (3:34)
T7071 GEORGIA ON MY MIND (1:41)

New York, New York   July 28, 1941
          Radio broadcast. Alfred Evans, cl;
          Art Tatum, p; Frank Gurasso, g; Harry
          Patent, b; Harry Stiffman, d.
T8000 HUMORESQUE* (3:53)
          *Piano solo.
T8001 GEORGIA ON MY MIND (1:42)

129

```
            ------------------------------------------------
New York, New York                          November 28, 1941
            Radio station WHN carried a "Bundles for
            Britain" program purporting to include a
            live appearance by Art Tatum playing,
            "Elegie." A voice, not Tatum´s, was
            dubbed in and the performance was actually
            a recording. See [0840].

            ------------------------------------------------
New York, New York                           October 7, 1943
            Radio broadcast, on WJZ radio. The Art
            Tatum Trio. Art Tatum, p; Tiny Grimes, g;
            Slam Stewart, b.
T8020   TEA FOR TWO (2:33)
T8021   SWEET LORRAINE (2:15)

            ------------------------------------------------
New York, New York                      c. Sept.-Dec., 1943
            Film short, "Music In America,"
            produced by the March of Time. This
            segment was shot at the Three Deuces
            Night Club. The Art Tatum Trio. Art
            Tatum, p; Tiny Grimes, g; Slam
            Stewart, b.
            Note: The total running time of film
            taken was (3:44), of which the segment
            listed below appeared in the final
            film.
T8030   TINY´S EXERCISE (0:33)

            ------------------------------------------------
New York, New York                                c. 1944
            Acetates made for Leeds Music Corp.,
            transcribed subsequently by Frank
            Paparelli and published by Leeds as,
            "5 Jazz Piano Solos by Art Tatum."
T8060   CARNEGIE HALL BOUNCE (2:45)
T8061   NIGHT SCENE (3:00)
T8062   GANG O´ NOTHIN´ [See T7008.]
T8063   JUMPIN´ FOR SUMPIN´ (2:44)
T8064   LIVE JIVE (2:20)

            ------------------------------------------------
New York, New York                             July 8, 1944
            Radio broadcast, "Atlantic Spotlight
            Program," on NBC radio. The Art Tatum
            Duo. Art Tatum, p; Slam Stewart, b.
            Note: Tiny Grimes was in the studio
            but was unable to perform because he
            had blown a tube in his amplifier.
T8100   SWEET LORRAINE* (2:45)
        *Piano solo.
T8105   I KNOW THAT YOU KNOW (3:39)

            ------------------------------------------------
Buffalo, New York                          November 11, 1944
            Private party at the home of Jim Hedrick.
            Art Tatum, p.
T8110   SCAT[1] (3:42)
        [1]Also includes George Clark, v; Art Tatum p and v.
T8111   HONEYSUCKLE ROSE[2] (1:23)
        [2]Also includes Flo Clark, v.
T8112   NOTHIN´ TO DO BUT LOVE[3] (2:58)
        [3]Art Tatum, p and v.
T8113   I CAN´T BELIEVE THAT YOU´RE IN LOVE WITH ME[4] (2:54)
        [4]Also includes Edna Day, v.
T8114   I´VE FOUND A NEW BABY (1:59)
T8115   ALL THE THINGS YOU ARE (2:44)
T8116   BEGIN THE BEGUINE (3:31)
T8117   SWEET LORRAINE (1:29)
```

```
          ----------------------------------------------------------
New York, New York                          January 6, 1945
               Radio broadcast, "Atlantic Spotlight
               Program," on NBC radio.  Piano solo.
T8130  MORE THAN YOU KNOW (1:22)

          ----------------------------------------------------------
New York, New York                          February 21, 1945
               Radio broadcast, "Schaefer Revue Program,"
               on NBC radio.
T8150  UNKNOWN TITLE(S)

          ----------------------------------------------------------
New York, New York                          March 5, 1945
               Radio broadcast, "Schaefer Revue Program,"
               on NBC radio.  Alan Roth Orchestra; Art
               Tatum, p.
T8170  TEA FOR TWO* (2:35)
       *Piano solo.
T8180  ST. LOUIS BLUES (3:36)

          ----------------------------------------------------------
New York, New York                          April 8, 1945
               Radio broadcast, "Music America Loves
               Best," on NBC radio.  Art Tatum, p; Snags
               Allen, g; Billy Taylor, b.
T8200  UNKNOWN TITLE(S)*
       *Snags Allen believes that "How High the Moon" was played.

          ----------------------------------------------------------
New York, New York                          October 2, 1945
               Radio broadcast, "Johnny Presents Program,"
               the Phillip Morris Hour, on NBC radio.
               Piano solos.
T8220  I KNOW THAT YOU KNOW (0:43)
T8221  TEA FOR TWO* (2:30)
       *Also includes orchestra, chorus, and Barry Wood, v.
T8222  THE MAN I LOVE (2:44)

          ----------------------------------------------------------
New York, New York                          c. 1946
               Acetates made for Robbins Music Corporation
               which were transcribed by Morris (Murray)
               Feldman and published as, "Art Tatum Improv-
               isations, No. 2," in 1946.  The published
               versions are selected segments only and
               therefore do not have the integrity or
               continuity of the original performances.
T8227  LULLABY IN RHYTHM
T8228  CHINA BOY
T8229  DON´T GET AROUND MUCH ANYMORE
T8230  WABASH BLUES
T8231  SUNDAY
T8232  I´LL NEVER BE THE SAME
T8233  JA-DA
T8234  WHAT CAN I SAY AFTER I SAY I´M SORRY
T8235  I GOT IT BAD AND THAT AIN´T GOOD
T8236  THE WANG WANG BLUES
T8237  HOT LIPS
T8238  AT SUNDOWN
T8239  RUNNIN´ WILD

          ----------------------------------------------------------
New York, New York                          April 5, 1946
               Radio broadcast.  Fred Robbins,
               announcer.  Piano solos.
T8240  SWEET LORRAINE (2:20)
T8241  TEA FOR TWO (2:59)
T8242  BODY AND SOUL (3:08)

          ----------------------------------------------------------
Chicago, Illinois                           c. 1946
               Radio broadcast, "Piano Playhouse
               Program," originating from WENR
               radio.  Milton Gross, announcer.
```

```
                   Piano solo.
                   Pianist Earl Wild also appeared
                   on this program.
      T8260   ROSETTA (1:43)


             --------------------------------------------------------
                                                        C. 1946
                   Radio broadcast, "Piano Playhouse
                   Program." Milton Gross, announcer.
                   Piano solos.
      T8280   YESTERDAYS (2:56)
      T8281   HONEYSUCKLE ROSE* (0:35)
             *Also includes Stan Freeman and Cy Walter, p.


             --------------------------------------------------------
      New York, New York                   September 20, 1947
                   Radio broadcast, "Piano Playhouse
                   Program." Piano solos.
      T8300   BEGIN THE BEGUINE
      T8301   BODY AND SOUL


             --------------------------------------------------------
      Chicago, Illinois                    November 16, 1947
                   Radio broadcast.  Piano solos.
      T8320   TEA FOR TWO[1] 3:11)
                   [1]A harp is heard, playing a concluding arpeggio,
                   immediately after Tatum finishes playing.
      T8321   AIN´T MISBEHAVIN´[2] (2:20)
                   [2]An orchestra is heard, playing a very brief concluding
                   sequence, immediately after Tatum finishes playing.


             --------------------------------------------------------
      Toronto, Ontario, Canada             November, 1949
                   Live recordings made privately at a night club.
                   Piano solos.
      T8340   THE VERY THOUGHT OF YOU (6:42+)
      T8341   SOMEBODY LOVES ME (5:19)
      T8342   THE CONTINENTAL (3:02+)
      T8343   I COVER THE WATERFRONT (3:01+)


             --------------------------------------------------------
      Toronto, Ontario, Canada             November, 1949
                   Live recordings made privately at a night club.
                   Piano solos.
      T8360   DON´T BLAME ME (3:13)
      T8361   DARDANELLA (3:51)
      T8362   THE VERY THOUGHT OF YOU (4:34)
      T8363   COME RAIN OR COME SHINE (5:26)
      T8364   SOMEONE TO WATCH OVER ME (4:28)
      T8365   VALSE IN C# MINOR, OPUS 64, #2 [Chopin] (3:49+)


             --------------------------------------------------------
      Toronto, Ontario, Canada             November, 1949
                   Private recordings at Club Normand.
                   Bill Carter, t; Bill Povey, as; Johnny
                   Ord, ts; Art Tatum, p; Ned Ciashine,
                   acc; Murray Lauder, b; Don Hilton, d.
      T8380   IF I HAD YOU (3:55)
      T8381   NIGHT AND DAY (8:58+)
      T8382   FINE AND DANDY (3:56+)
      T8383   FINE AND DANDY (3:05+)
      T8384   FINE AND DANDY (4:10+)


             --------------------------------------------------------
      New York, New York                   c. 1950
                   TV broadcast, "Faye Emerson Show."
                   Piano solo.
      T8400   HUMORESQUE (3:28)


             --------------------------------------------------------
      Chicago, Illinois                    c. 1951
                   Live recording made privately at
                   the Blue Note Club.  The Art Tatum Trio.
                   Art Tatum, p; Everett Barksdale,
                   g; Slam Stewart, b.
```

```
T8420  TENDERLY (4:17)
T8421  INDIANA (3:05)
T8422  WOULD YOU LIKE TO TAKE A WALK (6:11)
T8423  COCKTAILS FOR TWO (3:02)
T8424  BODY AND SOUL (5:27)
T8425  FLYING HOME (Theme)* (0:57)
       *This was preceded by some unidentified doodling.
```

New York, New York   c. 1951
            Radio broadcast, "Piano Playhouse
            Program." Piano solos.
```
T8430  WHERE OR WHEN (2:17)
T8431  BETWEEN THE DEVIL AND THE DEEP BLUE SEA (0:34)
```

New York, New York   c. 1951
            Radio broadcast, "Piano Playhouse
            Program." Piano solos.
```
T8432  I COVER THE WATERFRONT (2:18)
T8433  JUST ONE OF THOSE THINGS (1:06)
```

New York, New York   August 5, 1951
            Radio broadcast, "Quiz Kids Program,"
            on NBC radio. It is not known whether
            Tatum performed or merely appeared
            as a guest on the program.
```
T8440  UNKNOWN TITLE(S)
```

                                      November 24, 1951
            TV broadcast. "Mel Torme Show."
            Piano solos.
```
T8460  TABOO* (0:32)
       *Tatum plays in the background as Mel Torme narrates.
T8461  SOMEONE TO WATCH OVER ME (3:04)
```

New York, New York   c. 1951
            Radio broadcast, on WNEW radio. Al
            (Jazzbo) Collins, announcer. Live
            from the Embers, 161 East 54th Street.
            Piano solos.
```
T8480  WILLOW WEEP FOR ME (3:03)
T8481  BEGIN THE BEGUINE (3:03)
T8482  SITTIN' AND ROCKIN' (2:12)
T8483  HONEYSUCKLE ROSE (2:26)
```

New York, New York   c. 1951
            Radio broadcast, on WNEW radio. Al
            (Jazzbo) Collins, announcer. Live
            from the Embers, 161 East 54th Street.
            The Art Tatum Trio. Art Tatum, p; John
            Collins, g; Slam Stewart, b.
```
T8500  OUT OF NOWHERE (6:05)
T8501  THREE LITTLE WORDS (4:15)
T8502  WHERE OR WHEN (1:35)
```

New York, New York   c. 1951
            Radio broadcast, on WNEW radio. Al
            (Jazzbo) Collins, announcer. Live
            from the Embers, 161 East 54th Street.
            The Art Tatum Trio. Art Tatum, p; John
            Collins, g; Slam Stewart, b.
```
T8520  ALL THE THINGS YOU ARE (2:28+)
T8521  TEA FOR TWO (3:28+)
T8522  YOU GO TO MY HEAD (2:35)
```

New York, New York   c. 1951
            Radio broadcast, on WNEW radio. Al
            (Jazzbo) Collins, announcer. Live

```
                from the Embers, 161 East 54 Street.
                The Art Tatum Trio.  Art Tatum, p; John
                Collins, g; Slam Stewart, b.
T8540   TENDERLY (4:16)
T8541   ON THE SUNNY SIDE OF THE STREET (3:27)
T8542   DARK EYES (2:50)

------------------------------------------------------------
New York, New York                          c. 1951
                Radio broadcast, on WNEW radio. Al
                (Jazzbo) Collins, announcer.  Live
                from the Embers, 161 East 54 Street.
                The Art Tatum Trio.  Art Tatum, p; John
                Collins, g; Slam Stewart, b.
T8550   THESE FOOLISH THINGS REMIND ME OF YOU(4:36)
T8551   CRAZY RHYTHM (2:30)
T8552   WHERE OR WHEN (1:15, incomplete)

------------------------------------------------------------
Los Angeles, California                 November 5, 1951
                Live recordings from Art Tatum's
                home.  Piano solos on his own
                Steinway.
T8560   GOIN' HOME (4:10)
T8561   TENDERLY (2:15)
T8562   SWEET LORRAINE (2:15)
T8563   YOU TOOK ADVANTAGE OF ME (1:10)

------------------------------------------------------------
Los Angeles, California                 November 5, 1951
                Live recordings made privately at
                Jessie's night club.  Piano solos.
T8580   DON'T TAKE YOUR LOVE FROM ME[1] (2:45)
                [1]Also includes Unknown, v.
T8581   I'LL SEE YOU IN MY DREAMS (3:05)
T8582   SOMEONE TO WATCH OVER ME (3:19)
T8583   ART'S BOOGIE (1:13)
T8584   IF YOU HADN'T GONE AWAY[2] (3:24)
                [2]Art Tatum, p and v

------------------------------------------------------------
Montreal, Quebec, Canada                 April 19, 1952
                Radio broadcast, on CBS radio.
                Interview by Ted Miller.
T8600   INTERVIEW (3:20)

------------------------------------------------------------
New York, New York                          c. 1952
                Art Tatum, p; Joe Shulman, b;
                Billy Exiner, d.
T8620   THREE LITTLE WORDS (3:35)
T8621   MEAN TO ME (4:45)
T8622   AIN'T MISBEHAVIN' (3:10)
T8623   OH! LADY BE GOOD (4:50)
T8624   BODY AND SOUL (4:15)

------------------------------------------------------------
New York, New York                          c. 1952
                Live recording by Ed Fuerst,
                made at his apartment.  Art
                Tatum, p; Tal Farlow, g.
T8640   INDIANA (2:50)

------------------------------------------------------------
New York, New York                          c. 1952
                Live recording made privately
                at the Embers by Ed Fuerst.  Art
                Tatum, p; Joe Mooney, org.
T8660   MOONGLOW (2:00)
T8661   THREE LITTLE WORDS (3:00)
T8662   CONFESSIN' (4:20)
T8663   AIN'T MISBEHAVIN' (3:15)
```

```
                   ----------------------------------------------
New York, New York                             February 2, 1953
            Radio broadcast from the Bandbox night club.
            Announcer is Ed Stokes.  The Art Tatum Trio.
            Art Tatum, p; Everett Barksdale, g; Slam
            Stewart, b.
T8680  SWEET LORRAINE (4:15)
T8681  TEA FOR TWO (3:10)
T8682  MOONGLOW (4:16)
T8683  TENDERLY (4:39)

                   ----------------------------------------------
New York, New York                             February 9, 1953
            Radio broadcast from the Bandbox night club.
            Announcer is Ed Stokes.  The Art Tatum Trio.
            Art Tatum, p; Everett Barksdale, g; Slam
            Stewart, b.
T8700  I'VE GOT THE WORLD ON A STRING (4:08)
T8701  SEPTEMBER SONG (3:39)
T8702  BODY AND SOUL (5:16)

                   ----------------------------------------------
New York, New York                             February, 1953
            Live private recordings made in the
            apartment of Joe Springer on West
            72d Street.
            Piano solos.
T8720  THE MOON WAS YELLOW (3:23)
T8721  OVER THE RAINBOW (3:07)
T8722  WITHOUT A SONG (2:19)
T8723  HAVE YOU MET MISS JONES (3:01, including gap)
T8724  SWEET LORRAINE (3:21)
T8725  IF I HAD YOU[1] (4:07)
            [1]Also includes Sylvia Syms, v.
T8726  JUST FRIENDS[2] (3:40 incomplete, including gap)
            [2]Also includes Sylvia Syms, v.
T8727  THERE WILL NEVER BE ANOTHER YOU (4:03)
T8728  SHE'S FUNNY THAT WAY[3] (3:39)
            [3]Also includes Sylvia Syms, v.
T8729  UNKNOWN TITLE [Tatum original] (2:23)

                   ----------------------------------------------
New York, New York                             c. 1953
            Live private recording made at
            the Embers night club.
            Piano solo.
T8740  TABOO (2:47)

                   ----------------------------------------------
Portland, Oregon                           September 21, 1954
            Live private recording made at the
            "Festival of Modern American Jazz"
            at the Civic Auditorium.  The Art
            Tatum Trio.  Art Tatum, p; Everett
            Barksdale, g; Slam Stewart, b.
T8759  SOMEONE TO WATCH OVER ME*  (3:08)
            *Piano solo by Art Tatum.
T8760  FLYING HOME (1:18)
T8761  TENDERLY (5:16)
T8762  TEA FOR TWO (2:58)
T8763  SWEET LORRAINE (4:27)
T8764  BODY AND SOUL (5:17)

                   ----------------------------------------------
Chicago, Illinois                              c. 1954
            Radio broadcast, "Sunday With
            Garroway" #37, Part 4, Side 4.
T8780  INTERVIEW, over records

                   ----------------------------------------------
New York, New York                             December, 1954
            Radio broadcast, on WRCA radio, from
            the Basin Street night club.  The
            Art Tatum Trio.  Art Tatum, p;
            Everett Barksdale, g; Slam Stewart, b.
```

```
T8800    SWEET LORRAINE (4:19)
T8801    MEMORIES OF YOU (5:04)
T8802    AIR MAIL SPECIAL (1:22, incomplete)
```

                                                    Early 1955
             Radio broadcast, Voice of
             America. Interview by
             Willis Conover.
```
T8820    INTERVIEW
```

New York, New York   September, 1955
             TV Broadcast, "The Tonight Show," on NBC-TV.
             The Art Tatum Trio. Art Tatum, p; Everett
             Barksdale, g; Slam Stewart, b.
             This session has not been confirmed.
```
T8840    WOULD YOU LIKE TO TAKE A WALK
T8841    SOFT WINDS
```

                                                    November, 1955
             Radio broadcast, Voice of
             America. Interview by
             Willis Conover.
```
T8860    INTERVIEW
```

New York, New York   c. 1955
             Radio broadcast, taped in New
             York for Radio Sweden. Piano
             solos, with narration by Tatum.
```
T8880    SOMEONE TO WATCH OVER ME (3:01)
T8881    SMOKE GETS IN YOUR EYES (4:24)
T8882    BEGIN THE BEGUINE (2:57)
T8883    I COVER THE WATERFRONT (3:43)
T8884    BODY AND SOUL (2:16)
T8885    I KNOW THAT YOU KNOW (1:02)
```

Chicago, Illinois   March 11, 1956
             Radio broadcast, from London House.
             The Art Tatum Trio. Art Tatum, p;
             Everett Barksdale, g; Slam Stewart, b.
```
T8900    WILLOW WEEP FOR ME (5:19)
T8901    NIGHT AND DAY* (3:51)
```
             *Also includes "voice over" by announcer Tom Mercein.

                                                    Date Unknown
             Radio broadcast, with Raymond
             Paige Orchestra.
```
T8921    THIS CAN'T BE LOVE (1:21, incomplete)
```

New York, New York   Date Unknown
             Radio broadcast, on WOR radio.
             Piano solos.
```
T8940    IF I HAD YOU (3:06)
T8941    ELEGIE (3:31)
```

20th Century Fox   468.004   Fr.   12 Inch LP

```
5360  BEGIN THE BEGUINE
5380  BODY AND SOUL
5410  DANNY BOY
5450  I'LL NEVER BE THE SAME
5470  LITTLE MAN, YOU'VE HAD A BUSY DAY
5370  SOMEONE TO WATCH OVER ME
5420  TENDERLY
5400  TOO MARVELOUS FOR WORDS
5390  WILLOW WEEP FOR ME
5460  WITHOUT A SONG
5440  YESTERDAYS
5430  YOU TOOK ADVANTAGE OF ME
```

20th Century Fox   T607   Fr.   12 Inch LP

```
5360  BEGIN THE BEGUINE
5380  BODY AND SOUL
5410  DANNY BOY
5450  I'LL NEVER BE THE SAME
5470  LITTLE MAN, YOU'VE HAD A BUSY DAY
5370  SOMEONE TO WATCH OVER ME
5420  TENDERLY
5400  TOO MARVELOUS FOR WORDS
5390  WILLOW WEEP FOR ME
5460  WITHOUT A SONG
5440  YESTERDAYS
5430  YOU TOOK ADVANTAGE OF ME
```

20th Century Fox   T608   Fr.   12 Inch LP

```
5570  DON'T BLAME ME
5550  I COVER THE WATERFRONT
5510  IN A SENTIMENTAL MOOD
5490  JITTERBUG WALTZ
3290  MEMORIES OF YOU
5560  MOON SONG
3280  MR. FREDDIE BLUES
5480  MY HEART STOOD STILL
5500  OVER THE RAINBOW
5530  SEPTEMBER SONG
5520  THERE WILL NEVER BE ANOTHER YOU
5540  WRAP YOUR TROUBLES IN DREAMS
```

20th Century Fox   TFM3162   USA   12 Inch LP

```
5360  BEGIN THE BEGUINE
5380  BODY AND SOUL
5410  DANNY BOY
5450  I'LL NEVER BE THE SAME
5470  LITTLE MAN, YOU'VE HAD A BUSY DAY
5370  SOMEONE TO WATCH OVER ME
5420  TENDERLY
5400  TOO MARVELOUS FOR WORDS
5390  WILLOW WEEP FOR ME
5460  WITHOUT A SONG
5440  YESTERDAYS
5430  YOU TOOK ADVANTAGE OF ME
```

20th Century Fox   TFM3163   USA   12 Inch LP

```
5570  DON'T BLAME ME
5550  I COVER THE WATERFRONT
5510  IN A SENTIMENTAL MOOD
5490  JITTERBUG WALTZ
3290  MEMORIES OF YOU
5560  MOON SONG
```

```
        3280  MR. FREDDIE BLUES
        5480  MY HEART STOOD STILL
        5500  OVER THE RAINBOW
        5530  SEPTEMBER SONG
        5520  THERE WILL NEVER BE ANOTHER YOU
        5540  WRAP YOUR TROUBLES IN DREAMS


20th Century Fox                 TFS4162          USA    s 12 Inch LP

        5360  BEGIN THE BEGUINE
        5380  BODY AND SOUL
        5410  DANNY BOY
        5450  I´LL NEVER BE THE SAME
        5470  LITTLE MAN, YOU´VE HAD A BUSY DAY
        5370  SOMEONE TO WATCH OVER ME
        5420  TENDERLY
        5400  TOO MARVELOUS FOR WORDS
        5390  WILLOW WEEP FOR ME
        5460  WITHOUT A SONG
        5440  YESTERDAYS
        5430  YOU TOOK ADVANTAGE OF ME


20th Century Fox                 TFS4163          USA    s 12 Inch LP

        5570  DON´T BLAME ME
        5550  I COVER THE WATERFRONT
        5510  IN A SENTIMENTAL MOOD
        5490  JITTERBUG WALTZ
        3290  MEMORIES OF YOU
        5560  MOON SONG
        3280  MR. FREDDIE BLUES
        5480  MY HEART STOOD STILL
        5500  OVER THE RAINBOW
        5530  SEPTEMBER SONG
        5520  THERE WILL NEVER BE ANOTHER YOU
        5540  WRAP YOUR TROUBLES IN DREAMS


20th Century Fox                 XBLY 921.041     Fr.      12 Inch LP

        5360  BEGIN THE BEGUINE
        5380  BODY AND SOUL
        5410  DANNY BOY
        5450  I´LL NEVER BE THE SAME
        5470  LITTLE MAN, YOU´VE HAD A BUSY DAY
        5370  SOMEONE TO WATCH OVER ME
        5420  TENDERLY
        5400  TOO MARVELOUS FOR WORDS
        5390  WILLOW WEEP FOR ME
        5460  WITHOUT A SONG
        5440  YESTERDAYS
        5430  YOU TOOK ADVANTAGE OF ME


20th Fox                         Fox 3029         USA      12 Inch LP

        5360  BEGIN THE BEGUINE
        5380  BODY AND SOUL
        5410  DANNY BOY
        5450  I´LL NEVER BE THE SAME
        5470  LITTLE MAN, YOU´VE HAD A BUSY DAY
        5370  SOMEONE TO WATCH OVER ME
        5420  TENDERLY
        5400  TOO MARVELOUS FOR WORDS
        5390  WILLOW WEEP FOR ME
        5460  WITHOUT A SONG
        5440  YESTERDAYS
        5430  YOU TOOK ADVANTAGE OF ME
```

```
20th Fox                        Fox 3033        USA    12 Inch LP

     5570  DON'T BLAME ME
     5550  I COVER THE WATERFRONT
     5510  IN A SENTIMENTAL MOOD
     5490  JITTERBUG WALTZ
     3290  MEMORIES OF YOU
     5560  MOON SONG
     3280  MR. FREDDIE BLUES
     5480  MY HEART STOOD STILL
     5500  OVER THE RAINBOW
     5530  SEPTEMBER SONG
     5520  THERE WILL NEVER BE ANOTHER YOU
     5540  WRAP YOUR TROUBLES IN DREAMS


20th Fox                        SFX-3029        USA    s 12 Inch LP

     5360  BEGIN THE BEGUINE
     5380  BODY AND SOUL
     5410  DANNY BOY
     5450  I'LL NEVER BE THE SAME
     5470  LITTLE MAN, YOU'VE HAD A BUSY DAY
     5370  SOMEONE TO WATCH OVER ME
     5420  TENDERLY
     5400  TOO MARVELOUS FOR WORDS
     5390  WILLOW WEEP FOR ME
     5460  WITHOUT A SONG
     5440  YESTERDAYS
     5430  YOU TOOK ADVANTAGE OF ME


20th Fox                        SFX-3033        USA    s 12 Inch LP

     5570  DON'T BLAME ME
     5550  I COVER THE WATERFRONT
     5510  IN A SENTIMENTAL MOOD
     5490  JITTERBUG WALTZ
     3290  MEMORIES OF YOU
     5560  MOON SONG
     3280  MR. FREDDIE BLUES
     5480  MY HEART STOOD STILL
     5500  OVER THE RAINBOW
     5530  SEPTEMBER SONG
     5520  THERE WILL NEVER BE ANOTHER YOU
     5540  WRAP YOUR TROUBLES IN DREAMS


20th Fox                        TCF102-2        USA    12 Inch LP
  [2-record set.]
     5360  BEGIN THE BEGUINE
     5380  BODY AND SOUL
     5410  DANNY BOY
     5570  DON'T BLAME ME
     5550  I COVER THE WATERFRONT
     5450  I'LL NEVER BE THE SAME
     5510  IN A SENTIMENTAL MOOD
     5490  JITTERBUG WALTZ
     5470  LITTLE MAN, YOU'VE HAD A BUSY DAY
     3290  MEMORIES OF YOU
     5560  MOON SONG
     3280  MR. FREDDIE BLUES
     5480  MY HEART STOOD STILL
     5500  OVER THE RAINBOW
     5530  SEPTEMBER SONG
     5370  SOMEONE TO WATCH OVER ME
     5420  TENDERLY
     5520  THERE WILL NEVER BE ANOTHER YOU
     5400  TOO MARVELOUS FOR WORDS
     5390  WILLOW WEEP FOR ME
     5460  WITHOUT A SONG
     5540  WRAP YOUR TROUBLES IN DREAMS
     5440  YESTERDAYS
     5430  YOU TOOK ADVANTAGE OF ME
```

```
20th Fox                           TCF102-2S       USA    s 12 Inch LP
   [2-record set.]
      5360   BEGIN THE BEGUINE
      5380   BODY AND SOUL
      5410   DANNY BOY
      5570   DON´T BLAME ME
      5550   I COVER THE WATERFRONT
      5450   I´LL NEVER BE THE SAME
      5510   IN A SENTIMENTAL MOOD
      5490   JITTERBUG WALTZ
      5470   LITTLE MAN, YOU´VE HAD A BUSY DAY
      3290   MEMORIES OF YOU
      5560   MOON SONG
      3280   MR. FREDDIE BLUES
      5480   MY HEART STOOD STILL
      5500   OVER THE RAINBOW
      5530   SEPTEMBER SONG
      5370   SOMEONE TO WATCH OVER ME
      5420   TENDERLY
      5520   THERE WILL NEVER BE ANOTHER YOU
      5400   TOO MARVELOUS FOR WORDS
      5390   WILLOW WEEP FOR ME
      5460   WITHOUT A SONG
      5540   WRAP YOUR TROUBLES IN DREAMS
      5440   YESTERDAYS
      5430   YOU TOOK ADVANTAGE OF ME


ARA                                4501            USA     10 Inch 78
   [Part of 4-record set A-1.]
      2190   HALLELUJAH
      2230   MEMORIES OF YOU


ARA                                4502            USA     10 Inch 78
   [Part of 4-record set A-1.]
      2220   LOVER
      2200   POOR BUTTERFLY


ARA                                4503            USA     10 Inch 78
   [Part of 4-record set A-1.]
      2240   RUNNIN´ WILD
      2250   YESTERDAYS


ARA                                4504            USA     10 Inch 78
   [Part of 4-record set A-1.]
      2260   KERRY DANCE, THE
      2210   SONG OF THE VAGABONDS


ARA                                A-1             USA
   [4-record set containing 4501,4502,4503,4504.]


Ace of Hearts                      AH.109          Eng.    12 Inch LP

      1430   AFTER YOU´VE GONE
      0960   BEGIN THE BEGUINE
      1410   COCKTAILS FOR TWO
      1450   DEEP PURPLE
      0460   GONE WITH THE WIND
      1490   HONEYSUCKLE ROSE
      1400   I GOT RHYTHM
      1440   MOONGLOW
      0970   ROSETTA
      0950   ST. LOUIS BLUES
      0470   STORMY WEATHER
      0740   TEA FOR TWO
```

```
Ace of Hearts                    AH133           Eng.    12 Inch LP

     0940   COCKTAILS FOR TWO
     0840   ELEGIE
     0910   EMALINE
     0870   GET HAPPY
     0850   HUMORESQUE
     1460   I WOULD DO ANYTHING FOR YOU
     0980   INDIANA
     0930   LOVE ME
     0880   LULLABY OF THE LEAVES
     1440   MOONGLOW
     0860   SWEET LORRAINE
     0890   TIGER RAG


Aircheck                          21            USA     12 Inch LP

     2000   AIN´T MISBEHAVIN´
     0130   CHINATOWN, MY CHINATOWN
     2310   HOW HIGH THE MOON
     1880   HUMORESQUE
     1890   I KNOW THAT YOU KNOW
     0270   LULU´S BACK IN TOWN
     0100   MORNING, NOON, AND NIGHT
     2010   SMOKE GETS IN YOUR EYES
     2690   SONG OF THE VAGABONDS
     0120   STAR DUST
     2300   SWEET LORRAINE
     0001   TIGER RAG
     0110   WHEN DAY IS DONE
     0090   YOUNG AND HEALTHY


Aircheck                          27            USA     12 Inch LP

     1500   BASIN STREET BLUES
     1640   BASIN STREET BLUES
     1510   ESQUIRE BLUES
     1630   ESQUIRE BOUNCE
     1520   HONEYSUCKLE ROSE
     1650   I´LL GET BY
     1660   TEA FOR TWO
     1665   THEME FOR COCA-COLA/CONCLUSION
     1620   THEME FOR COCA-COLA/INTRODUCTIONS


Alamac                          180.040         Fr.     12 Inch LP

     3460   BEGIN THE BEGUINE
     3470   BODY AND SOUL
     3450   COME RAIN OR COME SHINE
     3490   HONEYSUCKLE ROSE
     3480   I KNOW THAT YOU KNOW
            INTROSPECTION (See "Sittin´ and Rockin´")
     3520   KERRY DANCE, THE
     3510   MEMORIES OF YOU
     3500   SITTIN´ AND ROCKIN´ (Incorrectly titled "Introspection")


Alamac                          180.050         Fr.     12 Inch LP

     0760   ALL GOD´S CHILLUN GOT RHYTHM
     2410   CAN´T WE BE FRIENDS
            EMALINE (See "Sweet Emalina")
     0800   FINE AND DANDY
     0820   I GOTTA RIGHT TO SING THE BLUES
     2380   I GUESS I´LL HAVE TO CHANGE MY PLANS
     0830   I´M COMING VIRGINIA
     0810   I´VE GOT THE WORLD ON A STRING
     0780   INDIANA
     2420   LIMEHOUSE BLUES
     0770   SWEET EMALINA, MY GAL (Incorrectly titled "Emaline")
     2390   WHAT IS THIS THING CALLED LOVE
     2360   YOU TOOK ADVANTAGE OF ME

                              141
```

```
Alamac                             QSR 2402        USA      12 Inch LP

     3460  BEGIN THE BEGUINE
     3470  BODY AND SOUL
     3450  COME RAIN OR COME SHINE
     3490  HONEYSUCKLE ROSE
     3480  I KNOW THAT YOU KNOW
           INTROSPECTION (See "Sittin´ and Rockin´")
     3520  KERRY DANCE, THE
     3510  MEMORIES OF YOU
     3500  SITTIN´ AND ROCKIN´ (Incorrectly titled "Introspection")


Alamac                             QSR 2428        USA      12 Inch LP

     0760  ALL GOD´S CHILLUN GOT RHYTHM
     2410  CAN´T WE BE FRIENDS
           EMALINE (See "Sweet Emalina")
     0800  FINE AND DANDY
     0820  I GOTTA RIGHT TO SING THE BLUES
     2380  I GUESS I´LL HAVE TO CHANGE MY PLANS
     0830  I´M COMING VIRGINIA
     0810  I´VE GOT THE WORLD ON A STRING
     0780  INDIANA
     2420  LIMEHOUSE BLUES
     0770  SWEET EMALINA, MY GAL (Incorrectly titled "Emaline")
     2390  WHAT IS THIS THING CALLED LOVE
     2360  YOU TOOK ADVANTAGE OF ME


Albatros                           VPA8474         It.      12 Inch LP

     1070  LAST GOODBYE BLUES


Alto                               AL712           USA      12 Inch LP

     3700  BODY AND SOUL
     3690  OUT OF NOWHERE
     3670  TEA FOR TWO
     3680  TENDERLY


Amer.Cancer Soc. 1957 Cancer
  Crusade - Jazz Panorama          Platter 5 and 6  USA     12 Inch TX
     4830  BLUES IN B FLAT


American Recording Society         G 401           USA      12 Inch LP

     5180  ON THE SUNNY SIDE OF THE STREET


American Recording Society         G-406           USA      12 Inch LP

     5010  MOONLIGHT ON THE GANGES
     5030  WHEN YOUR LOVER HAS GONE


American Recording Society         G 412           USA      12 Inch LP

     6020  DEEP NIGHT
     6070  FOGGY DAY, A
     6080  LOVER MAN
     6090  MAKIN´ WHOOPEE
     6050  MEMORIES OF YOU
     6030  ONCE IN A WHILE
     6040  THIS CAN´T BE LOVE
     6060  YOU´RE MINE, YOU


American Recording Society         G 424           USA      12 Inch LP

     6160  ALL THE THINGS YOU ARE
     5920  BLUE LOU
```

```
5690    BODY AND SOUL
4850    FOGGY DAY, A
5110    I CAN'T GIVE YOU ANYTHING BUT LOVE
5140    I GOTTA RIGHT TO SING THE BLUES
5270    I WON'T DANCE
5150    IT'S ONLY A PAPER MOON
5120    LULLABY IN RHYTHM
5130    OUT OF NOWHERE
5210    SO BEATS MY HEART FOR YOU
```

riston   AR/LP/12023   It.   12 Inch LP

```
0290    AFTER YOU'VE GONE
0760    ALL GOD'S CHILLUN GOT RHYTHM
0280    BOOTS AND SADDLE
0400    DEVIL IN THE MOON
0300    DIXIELAND BAND
0390    I WISH I WERE TWINS
0350    I WOULD DO ANYTHING FOR YOU
0370    IN THE MIDDLE OF A KISS
0780    INDIANA
0340    MONDAY IN MANHATTAN
0380    ROSETTA
0330    STAY AS SWEET AS YOU ARE
0770    SWEET EMALINA, MY GAL
0360    THEME FOR PIANO
```

riston   AR/LP/12059   It.   12 Inch LP

```
1670    BACK O' TOWN BLUES
1640    BASIN STREET BLUES
1610    BLUES
1630    ESQUIRE BOUNCE
1740    FLYING HOME
1560    I LOVE MY MAN
1540    MOP-MOP
1720    MY IDEAL
1730    ROSE ROOM
1660    TEA FOR TWO
```

rmed Forces Radio Service,
America's Popular Music   149   USA   12 Inch TX

```
1430    AFTER YOU'VE GONE
4320    BLUE SKIES
1830    DARK EYES
1490    HONEYSUCKLE ROSE
1400    I GOT RHYTHM
1850    I KNOW THAT YOU KNOW
4290    I'LL SEE YOU IN MY DREAMS
4620    LOVER, COME BACK TO ME!
3090    NICE WORK IF YOU CAN GET IT
1860    ON THE SUNNY SIDE OF THE STREET
0060    ST. LOUIS BLUES
4200    STAR DUST
0470    STORMY WEATHER
3060    WILLOW WEEP FOR ME
```

rmed Forces Radio Service,
America's Popular Music   194   USA   12 Inch TX

```
1430    AFTER YOU'VE GONE
4320    BLUE SKIES
1830    DARK EYES
1850    I KNOW THAT YOU KNOW
4290    I'LL SEE YOU IN MY DREAMS
4620    LOVER, COME BACK TO ME!
1860    ON THE SUNNY SIDE OF THE STREET
0060    ST. LOUIS BLUES
4200    STAR DUST
0470    STORMY WEATHER
```

```
       3060   WILLOW WEEP FOR ME
       4330   WITHOUT A SONG


Armed Forces Radio Service,
  America's Popular Music              198              USA        12 Inch TX

       2780   AIN'T MISBEHAVIN'


Armed Forces Radio Service,
  America's Popular Music              345              USA        12 Inch TX

       1430   AFTER YOU'VE GONE


Armed Forces Radio Service,
  America's Popular Music              434              USA        12 Inch TX

       0460   GONE WITH THE WIND
       1400   I GOT RHYTHM
       5420   TENDERLY


Armed Forces Radio Service,
  America's Popular Music              732              USA        12 Inch TX

       5420   TENDERLY
       5440   YESTERDAYS
       5430   YOU TOOK ADVANTAGE OF ME


Armed Forces Radio Service,
  America's Popular Music              887              USA        12 Inch TX

       1050   WEE BABY BLUES


Armed Forces Radio Service,
  Basic Musical Library              P-68              USA        16 Inch TX

       1380   EXACTLY LIKE YOU


Armed Forces Radio Service,
  Basic Musical Library              P-172             USA        16 Inch TX

       1770   HUMORESQUE
       1780   IT HAD TO BE YOU
       1760   JA-DA


Armed Forces Radio Service,
  Basic Musical Library              P-205             USA        16 Inch TX

       1790   I'VE FOUND A NEW BABY
       1800   OH! LADY BE GOOD
       1810   SOMEBODY LOVES ME


Armed Forces Radio Service,
  Basic Musical Library              P-232             USA        16 Inch TX

       2170   MAN I LOVE, THE


Armed Forces Radio Service,
  Basic Musical Library              P-233             USA        16 Inch TX

       2180   I CAN'T GIVE YOU ANYTHING BUT LOVE
```

```
Armed Forces Radio Service,
  Basic Musical Library            P-545          USA        16 Inch TX

     2270   BEGIN THE BEGUINE
     2700   NIGHT AND DAY
     2710   POOR BUTTERFLY
     2680   WHERE OR WHEN


Armed Forces Radio Service,
  Basic Musical Library            P-774          USA        16 Inch TX

     2260   KERRY DANCE, THE
     2220   LOVER
     2240   RUNNIN' WILD
     2210   SONG OF THE VAGABONDS


Armed Forces Radio Service,
  Basic Musical Library            P-1077         USA        16 Inch TX

     2780   AIN'T MISBEHAVIN'
     2800   CHEROKEE


Armed Forces Radio Service,
  Basic Musical Library            P-1957         USA        16 Inch TX

     3150   DON'T BLAME ME
     3160   MY HEART STOOD STILL
     3140   SOMEBODY LOVES ME
     3100   SOMEONE TO WATCH OVER ME
     3130   SWEET LORRAINE
     3120   TIME ON MY HANDS


Armed Forces Radio Service,
  Basic Musical Library            P-2035         USA        16 Inch TX

     0960   BEGIN THE BEGUINE
     0480   CHLOE
     0460   GONE WITH THE WIND
     0950   ST. LOUIS BLUES
     0470   STORMY WEATHER
     0490   SHEIK OF ARABY, THE


Armed Forces Radio Service,
  Basic Musical Library            P-4927         USA        16 Inch TX
  [The reverse side of this disc is P-4928.]
     5280   MOON SONG
     5310   NIGHT AND DAY
     5250   MOON IS LOW, THE


Armed Forces Radio Service,
  Basic Musical Library            P-4928         USA        16 Inch TX
  [The reverse side of this disc is P-4927.]
     5270   I WON'T DANCE
     5300   IN A SENTIMENTAL MOOD
     5290   THIS CAN'T BE LOVE
     5260   YOU TOOK ADVANTAGE OF ME


Armed Forces Radio Service,
  Bud's Bandwagon                  319            USA        16 Inch TX

     3110   DARDANELLA


Armed Forces Radio Service,
  Bud's Bandwagon                  334            USA        16 Inch TX

     4880   IDAHO
```

Armed Forces Radio Service, Command Performance	141	USA	16 Inch TX

2000 AIN'T MISBEHAVIN'

Armed Forces Radio Service, Downbeat	322	USA	16 Inch TX

0870 GET HAPPY

Armed Forces Radio Service, Downbeat	330	USA	16 Inch TX

1850 I KNOW THAT YOU KNOW

Armed Forces Radio Service, Downbeat	415	USA	16 Inch TX

0870 GET HAPPY

Armed Forces Radio Service, Downbeat	434	USA	16 Inch TX

0860 SWEET LORRAINE

Armed Forces Radio Service, Jazz Book	12/2	USA	12 Inch TX

5050 IF I HAD YOU
4750 ISN'T IT ROMANTIC

Armed Forces Radio Service, Jill's All-Time Juke Box	226	USA	16 Inch TX

2800 CHEROKEE

Armed Forces Radio Service, Jill's All-Time Juke Box	398	USA	16 Inch TX

2800 CHEROKEE

Armed Forces Radio Service, Jubilee	11	USA	16 Inch TX

1270 MELODY IN F

Armed Forces Radio Service, Jubilee	17	USA	16 Inch TX

1280 (Title unknown)

Armed Forces Radio Service, Jubilee	31	USA	16 Inch TX

1290 (Title Unknown)

Armed Forces Radio Service, Jubilee	32	USA	16 Inch TX

1300 AFTER YOU'VE GONE
1310 SWEET LORRAINE

```
rmed Forces Radio Service,
  Jubilee                          67              USA      16 Inch TX

    1530   ESQUIRE BLUES


rmed Forces Radio Service,
  Jubilee                          69              USA      16 Inch TX

    1380   EXACTLY LIKE YOU
    1390   SWEET LORRAINE

rmed Forces Radio Service,
  Jubilee                          97              USA      16 Inch TX

    2010   SMOKE GETS IN YOUR EYES


rmed Forces Radio Service,
  Jubilee                         123              USA      16 Inch TX

    2010   SMOKE GETS IN YOUR EYES


rmed Forces Radio Service,
  Jubilee                         142              USA      16 Inch TX

    2150   DANNY BOY
    2160   HOW HIGH THE MOON

rmed Forces Radio Service,
  Jubilee                         167              USA      16 Inch TX

    2685   LOUISE


rmed Forces Radio Service,
  Jubilee                         168              USA      16 Inch TX

    2690   SONG OF THE VAGABONDS


rmed Forces Radio Service,
  Jubilee 1947 Christmas Show   (Unnumbered)       USA      16 Inch TX

    2250   YESTERDAYS


rmed Forces Radio Service,
  Just Jazz                        69              USA      16 Inch TX

    3020   GERSHWIN MEDLEY
    2960   HUMORESQUE
    3000   I KNOW THAT YOU KNOW
    3010   WILLOW WEEP FOR ME
    2990   YESTERDAYS

rmed Forces Radio Service,
  Mail Call                       132              USA      16 Inch TX

    2180   I CAN'T GIVE YOU ANYTHING BUT LOVE
    1810   SOMEBODY LOVES ME


rmed Forces Radio Service,
  Mildred Bailey Series            13              USA      16 Inch TX

    2020   I CAN'T GIVE YOU ANYTHING BUT LOVE
```

Armed Forces Radio & Television Service,
  Music Transcription Library   P-S-18   USA   16 Inch TX

    3080   AUNT HAGAR'S BLUES
    3110   DARDANELLA
    3180   I GOTTA RIGHT TO SING THE BLUES

Armed Forces Radio Service,
  One Night Stand   186   USA   16 Inch TX

    1610   BLUES
    1690   BUCK JUMPIN'
    1630   ESQUIRE BOUNCE*
    1570   I CAN'T GIVE YOU ANYTHING BUT LOVE
    1600   I GOT RHYTHM
    1620   INTRODUCTION (Does not include "Theme For Coca-Cola."]
    1720   MY IDEAL
    1700   STOMPIN' AT THE SAVOY
      *Has some voice-over and is abbreviated.

Armed Forces Radio Service,
  One Night Stand   187   USA   16 Inch TX

    1630   ESQUIRE BOUNCE*
    1580   I GOTTA RIGHT TO SING THE BLUES
    1560   I LOVE MY MAN
    1540   MOP-MOP
    1730   ROSE ROOM
    1590   SWEET LORRAINE
      *Contains only a small portion used as a theme.

Armed Forces Radio Service,
  One Night Stand   188   USA   16 Inch TX

    1630   ESQUIRE BOUNCE*
    1710   FOR BASS FACES ONLY
    1650   I'LL GET BY
    1660   TEA FOR TWO
    1750   VIBE BLUES (JAMMIN' THE BLUES)
      *Contains only a small portion used as a theme.

Armed Forces Radio Service,
  A Quarter Century of Swing   76   USA   16 Inch TX

    3780   INDIANA
    3740   TEA FOR TWO

Armed Forces Radio Service,
  A Quarter Century of Swing   183   USA   16 Inch TX

    5780   HOW HIGH THE MOON
    5960   JUST ONE OF THOSE THINGS
    6010   TRIO BLUES

Armed Forces Radio Service,
  A Quarter Century of Swing   184   USA   16 Inch TX

    3080   AUNT HAGAR'S BLUES
    3220   BLUE SKIES

Armed Forces Radio Service,
  A Quarter Century of Swing   236   USA   16 Inch TX

    5710   WHAT IS THIS THING CALLED LOVE

```
Armed Forces Radio Service,
  A Quarter Century of Swing       242              USA      16 Inch TX

     5760  MAKIN´ WHOOPEE


Armed Forces Radio Service,
  Purple Heart                     205              USA      16 Inch TX

     0960  BEGIN THE BEGUINE


Armed Forces Radio Service,
  Remember                         782              USA      16 Inch TX

     2200  POOR BUTTERFLY


Armed Forces Radio Service,
  Remember                         952              USA      16 Inch TX

     2780  AIN´T MISBEHAVIN´


Armed Forces Radio Service,
  Remember                         H54-586          USA      16 Inch TX

     1395  I KNOW THAT YOU KNOW


Armed Forces Radio Service,
  Spotlight Bands                  261              USA      16 Inch TX

     1640  BASIN STREET BLUES
     1630  ESQUIRE BOUNCE


Armed Forces Radio Service,
  Swing Years                      135              USA      16 Inch TX

     0870  GET HAPPY


Armed Forces Radio Service,
  Swingtime                        H52-37           USA      16 Inch TX

     2270  BEGIN THE BEGUINE
     2280  CHEROKEE
     2290  DOWN BY THE OLD MILL STREAM


Armed Forces Radio Service,
  Today´s the Day                  36               USA      16 Inch TX

     0880  LULLABY OF THE LEAVES


Armed Forces Radio Service,
  Today´s the Day                  77               USA      16 Inch TX

     1460  I WOULD DO ANYTHING FOR YOU


Armed Forces Radio Service,
  Yank Swing Session               81               USA      16 Inch TX

     1370  SWEET GEORGIA BROWN


Armed Forces Radio Service,
  Yank Swing Session               82               USA      16 Inch TX

     1360  SUGAR FOOT STOMP
```

Armed Forces Radio Service, Yank Swing Session	86	USA	16 Inch TX

    1660   TEA FOR TWO

Armed Forces Radio Service, Yank Swing Session	90	USA	16 Inch TX

    1590   SWEET LORRAINE

Armed Forces Radio Service, Yank Swing Session	91	USA	16 Inch Tx

    1550   DO NOTHIN´ TILL YOU HEAR FROM ME

Armed Forces Radio Service, Yank Swing Session	116,Part 2 Series H-2	USA	16 Inch TX

    1990   HUMORESQUE

Armed Forces Radio Service, Yank Swing Session	121	USA	16 Inch TX

    1560   I LOVE MY MAN

Artia-Parliament [Part of 10-record boxed set.]	WGM(s)-2AB	USA	s	12 Inch LP

    1830   DARK EYES

Artia-Parliament [Part of 5-record boxed set.]	WGM-2A	USA	12 Inch LP

    1830   DARK EYES

Artia-Parliament [Part of 10-record boxed set.]	WGM-2AB	USA	12 Inch LP

    1830   DARK EYES

Asch [3-record set containing 356-1,356-2,356-3.]	356	USA

Asch [Part of 3-record set 356.]	356-1	USA	10 Inch 78

    2030   FINE AND DANDY
    2040   IT HAD TO BE YOU

Asch [Part of 3-record set 356.]	356-2	USA	10 Inch 78

    2050   JA-DA
    2060   WHERE OR WHEN

Asch [Part of 3-record set 356.]	356-3	USA	10 Inch 78

    2080   DANNY BOY
    2070   SWEET AND LOVELY

Asch [2-record set containing either 452-1,452-2 or Stinson 452-1,452-2.]	452	USA

Asch [Part of 2-record set 452.]	452-1	USA	12 Inch 78

    1950   BOOGIE
    1970   IF I HAD YOU

Label		Catalog	Country	Format
Asch [Part of 2-record set 452.]		452-2	USA	12 Inch 78
1980	SOFT WINDS			
1960	TOPSY			
Asch		AA2	USA	12 Inch LP
1960	TOPSY			
Astor		GGS-1389	Astla	12 Inch LP
1550	DO NOTHIN´ TILL YOU HEAR FROM ME			
Atlantic [Part of 2-record set.]		SD2-306	USA	12 Inch LP
1351	ESQUIRE BLUES			
1320	ESQUIRE BOUNCE			
1321	ESQUIRE BOUNCE			
1331	MOP-MOP (Also called Boff-Boff)			
1340	MY IDEAL			
1341	MY IDEAL			
Band		BR33.007	Braz.	12 Inch LP
5090	MOONGLOW			
Barclay		74030	Fr.	7 Inch 45EP
6210	NIGHT AND DAY			
6220	WHERE OR WHEN			
Barclay		74033	Fr.	7 Inch 45EP
6190	GONE WITH THE WIND			
6180	MY IDEAL			
Barclay		74045	Fr.	7 Inch 45EP
6200	HAVE YOU MET MISS JONES			
6170	MY ONE AND ONLY LOVE			
Barclay		74058	Fr.	7 Inch 45EP
6160	ALL THE THINGS YOU ARE			
6130	HUMORESQUE			
6150	WILLOW WEEP FOR ME			
Barclay		GEP4033	Fr.	7 Inch 45EP
6180	MY IDEAL			
Barclay		GEP12602	Fr.	7 Inch 45EP
3850	CAN´T WE BE FRIENDS			
3880	MEMORIES OF YOU			
3860	THIS CAN´T BE LOVE			
Barclay		GEP12603	Fr.	7 Inch 45EP
3910	BODY AND SOUL			
3870	ELEGIE			
3890	OVER THE RAINBOW			

Barclay		GEP12615	Fr.	7 Inch 45E

```
5270  I WON'T DANCE
5250  MOON IS LOW, THE
5290  THIS CAN'T BE LOVE
5260  YOU TOOK ADVANTAGE OF ME
```

Barclay		GEP12666	Fr.	7 Inch 45E

```
      BLUES IN MY HEART (See "If You Hadn't Gone Away")
3900  IF YOU HADN'T GONE AWAY (Incorrectly titled "Blues in
       My Heart")
3930  MAKIN' WHOOPEE
3920  MAN I LOVE, THE
```

Barclay		GLP3501	Fr.	12 Inch LP

```
3950  BEGIN THE BEGUINE
      BLUES IN MY HEART (See "If You Hadn't Gone Away")
3850  CAN'T WE BE FRIENDS
4020  DIXIELAND BAND
3870  ELEGIE
3960  HUMORESQUE
3900  IF YOU HADN'T GONE AWAY (Incorrectly titled "Blues in
       My Heart")
3990  JUDY
3860  THIS CAN'T BE LOVE
```

Barclay		GLP3502	Fr.	12 Inch LP

```
3910  BODY AND SOUL
3930  MAKIN' WHOOPEE
3880  MEMORIES OF YOU
4540  MIGHTY LAK A ROSE
3890  OVER THE RAINBOW
3920  MAN I LOVE, THE
```

Barclay		GLP3503	Fr.	12 Inch LP

```
4040  COME RAIN OR COME SHINE
4030  EMBRACEABLE YOU
4000  I'M COMING VIRGINIA
3970  LOUISE
3980  LOVE FOR SALE
4010  WRAP YOUR TROUBLES IS DREAMS
```

Barclay		GLP3504	Fr.	12 Inch LP

```
4110  I'VE GOT THE WORLD ON A STRING
4050  SITTIN' AND ROCKIN'
4070  TENDERLY
4060  THERE WILL NEVER BE ANOTHER YOU
4080  WHAT DOES IT TAKE?
4120  YESTERDAYS
4090  YOU TOOK ADVANTAGE OF ME
```

Barclay		GLP3505	Fr.	12 Inch LP

```
4260  HAVE YOU MET MISS JONES
4270  IN A SENTIMENTAL MOOD
4310  ISN'T THIS A LOVELY DAY
4350  MY LAST AFFAIR
4340  STOMPIN' AT THE SAVOY
4370  TABOO
4330  WITHOUT A SONG
```

```
Barclay                          GLP3524        Fr.    12 Inch LP

    4560  BLUE MOON
    4130  I HADN'T ANYONE 'TILL YOU
    4150  JITTERBUG WALTZ
    4140  NIGHT AND DAY
    3940  SEPTEMBER SONG
    4530  SMOKE GETS IN YOUR EYES
    4550  STARS FELL ON ALABAMA
    4180  YOU'RE DRIVING ME CRAZY


Barclay                          GLP3525        Fr.    12 Inch LP

    4190  GHOST OF A CHANCE, A
    4280  I'LL SEE YOU AGAIN
    4160  SOMEONE TO WATCH OVER ME
    4200  STAR DUST
    4230  STAY AS SWEET AS YOU ARE
    4170  VERY THOUGHT OF YOU, THE
    4220  WHERE OR WHEN


Barclay                          GLP3526        Fr.    12 Inch LP

    4520  AIN'T MISBEHAVIN'
    4250  ALL THE THINGS YOU ARE
    4240  FINE AND DANDY
    4210  I COVER THE WATERFRONT
    4360  I'M IN THE MOOD FOR LOVE
    4650  LOVE ME OR LEAVE ME
    4500  WHEN A WOMAN LOVES A MAN
    4510  WILLOW WEEP FOR ME


Barclay                          GLP3527        Fr.    12 Inch LP

    4420  AUNT HAGAR'S BLUES
    4320  BLUE SKIES
    4290  I'LL SEE YOU IN MY DREAMS
    4390  I'VE GOT A CRUSH ON YOU
    4300  ILL WIND
    4400  JAPANESE SANDMAN, THE
    4620  LOVER, COME BACK TO ME!
    4380  WOULD YOU LIKE TO TAKE A WALK


Barclay                          GLP3528        Fr.    12 Inch LP

    4490  BLUE LOU
    4580  CARAVAN
    4450  DANNY BOY
    4440  GONE WITH THE WIND
    4480  IT'S THE TALK OF THE TOWN
    4430  JUST LIKE A BUTTERFLY THAT'S CAUGHT IN THE RAIN
    4470  TEA FOR TWO
    4460  THEY CAN'T TAKE THAT AWAY FROM ME
    4410  TOO MARVELOUS FOR WORDS


Barclay                          GLP3562        Fr.    12 Inch LP

    5240  I SURRENDER DEAR
    5270  I WON'T DANCE
    5300  IN A SENTIMENTAL MOOD
    5280  MOON SONG
    5310  NIGHT AND DAY
    5250  MOON IS LOW, THE
    5290  THIS CAN'T BE LOVE
    5260  YOU TOOK ADVANTAGE OF ME
```

```
Barclay                       GLP3566        Fr.      12 Inch LP

   5650   HALLELUJAH
   5780   HOW HIGH THE MOON
   5660   I'LL NEVER BE THE SAME
   5760   MAKIN' WHOOPEE
   5770   MORE THAN YOU KNOW
   5640   PERDIDO
   5710   WHAT IS THIS THING CALLED LOVE


Barclay                       GLP3592        Fr.      12 Inch LP

   5920   BLUE LOU
   5990   I GUESS I'LL HAVE TO CHANGE MY PLANS
   5970   I'LL NEVER BE THE SAME
   5930   IF
   6000   ISN'T IT ROMANTIC
   5960   JUST ONE OF THOSE THINGS
   5980   LOVE FOR SALE
   5950   MORE THAN YOU KNOW
   5940   SOME OTHER SPRING
   6010   TRIO BLUES


Bellaphon                     BLST 6557      Ger.     12 Inch LP

   1840   BODY AND SOUL
   1830   DARK EYES
   1870   FLYING HOME
   1850   I KNOW THAT YOU KNOW
   1860   ON THE SUNNY SIDE OF THE STREET


Black & White                 13             USA      10 Inch 78

   2120   BLUES FOR ART'S SAKE
   2110   SWEET MARIJUANA BROWN


Black & White                 14             USA      10 Inch 78

   2090   CAN'T HELP LOVIN' DAT MAN OF MINE
   2100   PLEASE DON'T TALK ABOUT ME WHEN I'M GONE


Black Lion                    180.059        Fr.      12 Inch LP

   2620   APOLLO BOOGIE
   2650   BETWEEN MIDNIGHT AND DAWN
   2580   FIFTY SECOND STREET BLUES*
   2570   GANG O' NOTES
   2191   HALLELUJAH
   2590   JUST BEFORE DAWN*
   2260   KERRY DANCE, THE
   2230   MEMORIES OF YOU
   2610   MIDNIGHT MELODY, A*
   2200   POOR BUTTERFLY
   2240   RUNNIN' WILD
   2210   SONG OF THE VAGABONDS
          *Not believed to be Tatum.  See Chronological Discography.

Black Lion                    2460-158       Eng.     12 Inch LP

   2620   APOLLO BOOGIE
   2650   BETWEEN MIDNIGHT AND DAWN
   2580   FIFTY SECOND STREET BLUES*
   2570   GANG O' NOTES
   2191   HALLELUJAH
   2590   JUST BEFORE DAWN*
   2260   KERRY DANCE, THE
   2230   MEMORIES OF YOU
   2610   MIDNIGHT MELODY, A*
   2200   POOR BUTTERFLY
   2240   RUNNIN' WILD
```

154

```
        2210    SONG OF THE VAGABONDS
                *Not believed to be Tatum.  See Chronological Discography.

Black Lion                              BL-158          USA      12 Inch LP

        2620    APOLLO BOOGIE
        2650    BETWEEN MIDNIGHT AND DAWN
        2580    FIFTY SECOND STREET BLUES*
        2570    GANG O´ NOTES
        2191    HALLELUJAH
        2590    JUST BEFORE DAWN*
        2260    KERRY DANCE, THE
        2230    MEMORIES OF YOU
        2610    MIDNIGHT MELODY, A*
        2200    POOR BUTTERFLY
        2240    RUNNIN´ WILD
        2210    SONG OF THE VAGABONDS
                *Not believed to be Tatum.  See Chronological Discography.

Black Lion                              BLP30124        It.      12 Inch LP
   [Jacket reads "Jazz Idea."]
        2620    APOLLO BOOGIE
        2650    BETWEEN MIDNIGHT AND DAWN
        2580    FIFTY SECOND STREET BLUES*
        2570    GANG O´ NOTES
        2191    HALLELUJAH
        2590    JUST BEFORE DAWN*
        2260    KERRY DANCE, THE
        2230    MEMORIES OF YOU
        2610    MIDNIGHT MELODY, A*
        2200    POOR BUTTERFLY
        2240    RUNNIN´ WILD
        2210    SONG OF THE VAGABONDS
                *Not believed to be Tatum.  See Chronological Discography.

Black Lion                              BLP30166        Eng.     12 Inch LP

        2000    AIN´T MISBEHAVIN´
        2190    HALLELUJAH
        2191    HALLELUJAH
        1986    I GOT RHYTHM
        3260    I GOTTA RIGHT TO SING THE BLUES
        2260    KERRY DANCE, THE
        2220    LOVER
        2230    MEMORIES OF YOU
        2200    POOR BUTTERFLY
        3250    POOR BUTTERFLY
        1984    ROYAL GARDEN BLUES
        2240    RUNNIN´ WILD
        2210    SONG OF THE VAGABONDS
        3270    TABOO
        1480    TEA FOR TWO
        2250    YESTERDAYS

Black Lion                              BLP30194        Eng.     12 Inch LP

        0550    AIN´T MISBEHAVIN´
        0670    BEGIN THE BEGUINE
        0660    GET HAPPY
        0700    HALLELUJAH
        0530    HAPPY FEET
        0690    HUMORESQUE
        0520    I CAN´T GET STARTED
        0570    IN A SENTIMENTAL MOOD
        0680    IT HAD TO BE YOU
        0710    LULLABY IN RHYTHM
        0500    MAN I LOVE, THE
        0720    OH, YOU CRAZY MOON
        0730    OVER THE RAINBOW
        0540    ROYAL GARDEN BLUES
        0510    RUNNIN´ WILD
        0560    STAR DUST
```

```
Black Lion                        BLP30203        Eng.    12 Inch LP

    2270  BEGIN THE BEGUINE
    2350  BODY AND SOUL
    2320  GERSHWIN MEDLEY
    2354  I'M BEGINNING TO SEE THE LIGHT
    2720  INDIANA
    1470  LIZA
    2340  LOVER
    2355  NINE TWENTY SPECIAL
    2710  POOR BUTTERFLY
    2330  SHE'S FUNNY THAT WAY
    2690  SONG OF THE VAGABONDS
    1590  SWEET LORRAINE
    2680  WHERE OR WHEN


Blue Star                         179             Fr.     10 Inch 78r

    1850  I KNOW THAT YOU KNOW
    1820  MAN I LOVE, THE


Blue Star                         191             Fr.     10 Inch 78r

    1870  FLYING HOME
    1860  ON THE SUNNY SIDE OF THE STREET


Blue Star                         6810            Fr.     10 Inch LP

    1840  BODY AND SOUL
    1830  DARK EYES
    1870  FLYING HOME
    1850  I KNOW THAT YOU KNOW
    1820  MAN I LOVE, THE
    1860  ON THE SUNNY SIDE OF THE STREET


Blue Star                         BLP6810         Fr.     12 Inch LP

    1840  BODY AND SOUL
    1830  DARK EYES
    1870  FLYING HOME
    1850  I KNOW THAT YOU KNOW
    1820  MAN I LOVE, THE
    1860  ON THE SUNNY SIDE OF THE STREET


Blue Star                         GLP 3503        Fr.     12 Inch LP
  [Issued in a Clef jacket.]
    4040  COME RAIN OR COME SHINE
    4030  EMBRACEABLE YOU
    4000  I'M COMING VIRGINIA
    3970  LOUISE
    3980  LOVE FOR SALE
    4010  WRAP YOUR TROUBLES IS DREAMS


Book-of-the-Month Records         51-400          USA     12 Inch LP
  [4-record boxed set.]
    4520  AIN'T MISBEHAVIN'
    4560  BLUE MOON
          BLUES IN MY HEART (See "If You Hadn't Gone Away")
    4680  DEEP PURPLE
    4020  DIXIELAND BAND
    5070  DON'T WORRY 'BOUT ME
    4240  FINE AND DANDY
    4440  GONE WITH THE WIND
    5650  HALLELUJAH
    4260  HAVE YOU MET MISS JONES
    5110  I CAN'T GIVE YOU ANYTHING BUT LOVE
    4700  I DIDN'T KNOW WHAT TIME IT WAS
    5140  I GOTTA RIGHT TO SING THE BLUES
    4130  I HADN'T ANYONE 'TILL YOU
```

156

```
5170   I ONLY HAVE EYES FOR YOU
5050   IF I HAD YOU
3900   IF YOU HADN'T GONE AWAY (Incorrectly titled "Blues in
       My Heart")
4290   I'LL SEE YOU IN MY DREAMS
4300   ILL WIND
4780   INDIANA
4310   ISN'T THIS A LOVELY DAY
5150   IT'S ONLY A PAPER MOON
4400   JAPANESE SANDMAN, THE
4150   JITTERBUG WALTZ
4650   LOVE ME OR LEAVE ME
4620   LOVER, COME BACK TO ME!
4921   MAKIN' WHOOPEE
4990   MEAN TO ME
5090   MOONGLOW
5040   MOON IS LOW, THE
4820   MY BLUE HEAVEN
5180   ON THE SUNNY SIDE OF THE STREET
5130   OUT OF NOWHERE
3890   OVER THE RAINBOW
5080   PRISONER OF LOVE
5060   S'POSIN'
4810   SHE'S FUNNY THAT WAY
4050   SITTIN' AND ROCKIN'
4710   SOMEBODY LOVES ME
4630   SOPHISTICATED LADY
4230   STAY AS SWEET AS YOU ARE
4370   TABOO
4790   THAT OLD FEELING
4670   THESE FOOLISH THINGS REMIND ME OF YOU
3860   THIS CAN'T BE LOVE
5710   WHAT IS THIS THING CALLED LOVE
5030   WHEN YOUR LOVER HAS GONE
4510   WILLOW WEEP FOR ME
4090   YOU TOOK ADVANTAGE OF ME
```

Bravo	BR374	Eng.	7 Inch 45EP

```
1550   DO NOTHIN' TILL YOU HEAR FROM ME
1560   I LOVE MY MAN (Billie's Blues)
```

Brunswick	1348	Eng.	10 Inch 78

```
0020   I'LL NEVER BE THE SAME
0010   STRANGE AS IT SEEMS
```

Brunswick	01442	Eng.	10 Inch 78

```
0040   THIS TIME IT'S LOVE
0030   YOU GAVE ME EVERYTHING BUT LOVE
```

Brunswick	01506	Eng.	10 Inch 78

```
0060   ST. LOUIS BLUES
0070   TIGER RAG
```

Brunswick	01554	Eng.	10 Inch 78

```
0080   SOPHISTICATED LADY
0050   TEA FOR TWO
```

Brunswick	01862	Eng.	10 Inch 78

```
0200   AFTER YOU'VE GONE
0170   EMALINE
```

Brunswick		01877	Eng.	10 Inch 78

0140 MOONGLOW
0240 SHOUT, THE

Brunswick		01978	Eng.	10 Inch 78

0221 I AIN´T GOT NOBODY
0162 WHEN A WOMAN LOVES A MAN

Brunswick		02015	Eng.	10 Inch 78

0150 I WOULD DO ANYTHING FOR YOU
0180 LOVE ME

Brunswick		02051	Eng.	10 Inch 78

0230 ILL WIND
0211 STAR DUST

Brunswick		02417	Eng.	10 Inch 78

0440 WHAT WILL I TELL MY HEART
0430 WITH PLENTY OF MONEY AND YOU

Brunswick		02489	Eng.	10 Inch 78

0251 BEAUTIFUL LOVE
0262 LIZA

Brunswick		02518	Eng.	10 Inch 78

0420 BODY AND SOUL
0450 I´VE GOT MY LOVE TO KEEP ME WARM

Brunswick		02564	Eng.	10 Inch 78

0460 GONE WITH THE WIND
0470 STORMY WEATHER

Brunswick		02591	Eng.	10 Inch 78

0480 CHLOE
0490 SHEIK OF ARABY, THE

Brunswick		02772	Eng.	10 Inch 78

0751 DEEP PURPLE
0740 TEA FOR TWO

Brunswick		03121	Eng.	10 Inch 78

0960 BEGIN THE BEGUINE
0950 ST. LOUIS BLUES

Brunswick		03162	Eng.	10 Inch 78

0840 ELEGIE
0850 HUMORESQUE

Brunswick		0.3162	India	10 Inch 78

0840 ELEGIE
0850 HUMORESQUE

Brunswick		03430	Eng.	10 Inch 78

1080 BATTERY BOUNCE
1131 LUCILLE

Brunswick		0.3430	India	10 Inch 78

1080 BATTERY BOUNCE
1131 LUCILLE

Brunswick		03462	Eng.	10 Inch 78

1160 LONESOME GRAVEYARD BLUES

Brunswick		0.3462	India	10 Inch 78

1160 LONESOME GRAVEYARD BLUES

Brunswick		04318	Eng.	10 Inch 78

0880 LULLABY OF THE LEAVES
0860 SWEET LORRAINE

Brunswick		04319	Eng.	10 Inch 78

0970 ROSETTA
0890 TIGER RAG

Brunswick		6362	USA	10 Inch 78

0020 I´LL NEVER BE THE SAME
0040 THIS TIME IT´S LOVE

Brunswick		6376	USA	10 Inch 78

0010 STRANGE AS IT SEEMS
0030 YOU GAVE ME EVERYTHING BUT LOVE

Brunswick		6543	USA	10 Inch 78

0060 ST. LOUIS BLUES
0070 TIGER RAG
     Note: Others have indicated that this record was also
     issued with 0061 "St. Louis Blues" instead of 0060. This
     has not been confirmed.

Brunswick		6553	USA	10 Inch 78

0080 SOPHISTICATED LADY
0050 TEA FOR TWO
     Note: It is possible that this record was also
     released with "Tea For Two" [0051] instead of
     as shown. See note at [0051] in the Chronological
     Discography.

Brunswick		10116EPB	Ger.	7 Inch 45EP

0870 GET HAPPY
0880 LULLABY OF THE LEAVES

159

```
          0860  SWEET LORRAINE
          0890  TIGER RAG


Brunswick                          80102        USA      10 Inch 78

          1400  I GOT RHYTHM
          1460  I WOULD DO ANYTHING FOR YOU


Brunswick                          80114        USA      10 Inch 78

          1490  HONEYSUCKLE ROSE
          1440  MOONGLOW


Brunswick                          80131        USA      10 Inch 78

          1410  COCKTAILS FOR TWO
          1420  I AIN´T GOT NOBODY


Brunswick                          80141        USA      10 Inch 78

          1430  AFTER YOU´VE GONE
          1450  DEEP PURPLE


Brunswick                          80159        USA      10 Inch 78

          0460  GONE WITH THE WIND
          0470  STORMY WEATHER


Brunswick                          80160        USA      10 Inch 78

          0480  CHLOE
          0490  SHEIK OF ARABY, THE


Brunswick                          80161        USA      10 Inch 78

          0960  BEGIN THE BEGUINE
          0950  ST. LOUIS BLUES


Brunswick                          80162        USA      10 Inch 78

          0970  ROSETTA
          0740  TEA FOR TWO


Brunswick                          82455        Ger.     10 Inch 78

          0460  GONE WITH THE WIND
          0470  STORMY WEATHER


Brunswick                          82455        Nor.     10 Inch 78

          0460  GONE WITH THE WIND
          0470  STORMY WEATHER


Brunswick                          88066        Swiss    10 Inch 78

          1160  LONESOME GRAVEYARD BLUES
          1131  LUCILLE


Brunswick                          233649       Nor.     10 Inch 78

          0940  COCKTAILS FOR TWO
```

```
Brunswick                        9-7006          USA
  [4-record boxed set containing 9-80159,9-80160,9-80161,9-80162.]


Brunswick                        9-80131         USA      7 Inch 45

     1410   COCKTAILS FOR TWO
     1420   I AIN'T GOT NOBODY


Brunswick                        9-80159         USA      7 Inch 45
  [Part of 4-record boxed set 9-7006.]
     0460   GONE WITH THE WIND
     0470   STORMY WEATHER


Brunswick                        9-80160         USA      7 Inch 45
  [Part of 4-record boxed set 9-7006.]
     0480   CHLOE
     0490   SHEIK OF ARABY, THE


Brunswick                        9-80161         USA      7 Inch 45
  [Part of 4-record boxed set 9-7006.]
     0960   BEGIN THE BEGUINE
     0950   ST. LOUIS BLUES


Brunswick                        9-80162         USA      7 Inch 45
  [Part of 4-record boxed set 9-7006.]
     0970   ROSETTA
     0740   TEA FOR TWO


Brunswick                        A-9433          Fr.     10 Inch 78

     0060   ST. LOUIS BLUES
     0070   TIGER RAG


Brunswick                        A-9790          Ger.    10 Inch 78

     0150   I WOULD DO ANYTHING FOR YOU
     0180   LOVE ME


Brunswick                        A-9905          Ger.    10 Inch 78

     0080   SOPHISTICATED LADY
     0050   TEA FOR TWO


Brunswick                        A-81278         Ger.    10 Inch 78

     0420   BODY AND SOUL
     0450   I'VE GOT MY LOVE TO KEEP ME WARM


Brunswick                        A-81298         Ger.    10 Inch 78

     0251   BEAUTIFUL LOVE
     0262   LIZA


Brunswick                        A-81407         Ger.    10 Inch 78

     0460   GONE WITH THE WIND
     0470   STORMY WEATHER


Brunswick                        A-81552         Ger.    10 Inch 78

     0480   CHLOE
     0490   SHEIK OF ARABY, THE
```

Brunswick		A-82196	Ger.	10 Inch 78

| 0751 | DEEP PURPLE |
| 0740 | TEA FOR TWO |

Brunswick		A-82493	Ger.	10 Inch 78

| 0850 | HUMORESQUE |
| 0890 | TIGER RAG |

Brunswick		A-500265	Fr.	10 Inch 78

| 0060 | ST. LOUIS BLUES |
| 0070 | TIGER RAG |

Brunswick		A-500337	Fr.	10 Inch 78

| 0080 | SOPHISTICATED LADY |
| 0050 | TEA FOR TWO |

Brunswick		A-505015	Fr.	10 Inch 78

| 0200 | AFTER YOU´VE GONE |
| 0240 | SHOUT, THE |

Brunswick		BL54004	USA	12 Inch LP

1430	AFTER YOU´VE GONE
0960	BEGIN THE BEGUINE
1410	COCKTAILS FOR TWO
1450	DEEP PURPLE
0460	GONE WITH THE WIND
1490	HONEYSUCKLE ROSE
1400	I GOT RHYTHM
1440	MOONGLOW
0970	ROSETTA
0950	ST. LOUIS BLUES
0470	STORMY WEATHER
0740	TEA FOR TWO

Brunswick		BL58013	USA	10 Inch LP

1430	AFTER YOU´VE GONE
1410	COCKTAILS FOR TWO
1450	DEEP PURPLE
1490	HONEYSUCKLE ROSE
1420	I AIN´T GOT NOBODY
1400	I GOT RHYTHM
1460	I WOULD DO ANYTHING FOR YOU
1440	MOONGLOW

Brunswick		BL58023	USA	10 Inch LP

0960	BEGIN THE BEGUINE
0480	CHLOE
0460	GONE WITH THE WIND
0970	ROSETTA
0950	ST. LOUIS BLUES
0470	STORMY WEATHER
0740	TEA FOR TWO
0490	SHEIK OF ARABY, THE

Brunswick		BL58038	USA	10 Inch LP

1080	BATTERY BOUNCE
1070	LAST GOODBYE BLUES
1060	STOMPIN´ AT THE SAVOY

162

```
       1050  WEE BABY BLUES

runswick                              EB 71020        USA      7 Inch 45EP

       1490  HONEYSUCKLE ROSE
       1400  I GOT RHYTHM
       1460  I WOULD DO ANYTHING FOR YOU
       1440  MOONGLOW

runswick                              EB 71021        USA      7 Inch 45EP

       1430  AFTER YOU´VE GONE
       1410  COCKTAILS FOR TWO
       1450  DEEP PURPLE
       1420  I AIN´T GOT NOBODY

runswick                              LAT.8168        Eng.     12 Inch LP

       1050  WEE BABY BLUES

runswick                              LAT.8358        Eng.     12 Inch LP

       0940  COCKTAILS FOR TWO
       0840  ELEGIE
       0910  EMALINE
       0870  GET HAPPY
       0850  HUMORESQUE
       1460  I WOULD DO ANYTHING FOR YOU
       0980  INDIANA
       0930  LOVE ME
       0880  LULLABY OF THE LEAVES
       1440  MOONGLOW
       0860  SWEET LORRAINE
       0890  TIGER RAG

runswick                              LPBM87015       Ger.     12 Inch LP

       1050  WEE BABY BLUES

runswick                              LPBM87019       Ger.     12 Inch LP

       1070  LAST GOODBYE BLUES

runswick                              LPBM87507       Ger.     12 Inch LP

       0960  BEGIN THE BEGUINE
       0940  COCKTAILS FOR TWO
       0840  ELEGIE
       0910  EMALINE
       0870  GET HAPPY
       0850  HUMORESQUE
       0980  INDIANA
       0930  LOVE ME
       0880  LULLABY OF THE LEAVES
       0970  ROSETTA
       0950  ST. LOUIS BLUES
       0860  SWEET LORRAINE
       0740  TEA FOR TWO
       0890  TIGER RAG

runswick                              LPBM87527       Ger.     12 Inch LP

       1080  BATTERY BOUNCE
       1060  STOMPIN´ AT THE SAVOY
```

```
Bulldog                          BDL 1007        Eng.    12 Inch LP

      1550   DO NOTHIN´ TILL YOU HEAR FROM ME


CBS                              62615           Holl.   12 Inch LP

      2950   HOW HIGH THE MOON
      2960   HUMORESQUE
      3000   I KNOW THAT YOU KNOW
      3030   KERRY DANCE, THE
      3020   MAN I LOVE, THE (Abridged version of "Gershwin Medley")
      2980   SOMEONE TO WATCH OVER ME
      0080   SOPHISTICATED LADY
      2970   TATUM-POLE BOOGIE
      0050   TEA FOR TWO
      0070   TIGER RAG
      3010   WILLOW WEEP FOR ME
      2990   YESTERDAYS


CBS                              64946           Fr.     12 Inch LP
   [Part of 2-record set 67257.]
      0070   TIGER RAG


CBS                              67257           Fr.
   [2-record set containing 64946.]


CBS                              88061           Eng.
   [2-record set containing M 80244.]


CBS                              88151           Eng.    12 Inch LP

      2960   HUMORESQUE


CBS                              M 80244         Eng.    12 Inch LP
   [Part of 2-record set 88061.]
      0070   TIGER RAG


CBS Realm Jazz                   RM52601         Eng.    12 Inch LP

      2950   HOW HIGH THE MOON
      2960   HUMORESQUE
      3000   I KNOW THAT YOU KNOW
      3030   KERRY DANCE, THE
      3020   MAN I LOVE, THE (Abridged version of "Gershwin Medley")
      2980   SOMEONE TO WATCH OVER ME
      0080   SOPHISTICATED LADY
      0060   ST. LOUIS BLUES
      2970   TATUM-POLE BOOGIE
      0050   TEA FOR TWO
      0070   TIGER RAG
      3010   WILLOW WEEP FOR ME
      2990   YESTERDAYS


CID                              CVM42.004       Fr.     12 Inch LP

      1840   BODY AND SOUL
      1830   DARK EYES
      1870   FLYING HOME
      1850   I KNOW THAT YOU KNOW
      1860   ON THE SUNNY SIDE OF THE STREET


Camden                           (See RCA Camden)


Capitol                          1-216           USA     7 Inch 45E
   [Part of 2-record set EBF-216.]
```

```
        3240  DANCING IN THE DARK
        3110  DARDANELLA
        3070  I COVER THE WATERFRONT
        3180  I GOTTA RIGHT TO SING THE BLUES


Capitol                               1-269        USA       7 Inch 45EP
   [Part of 3-record set EBF-269.]
        3160  MY HEART STOOD STILL
        3120  TIME ON MY HANDS


Capitol                               1-323        USA       7 Inch 45EP
   [Part of 2-record set EBF-323.]
        3170  YOU TOOK ADVANTAGE OF ME


Capitol                               1-408        USA       7 Inch 45EP
   [Part of 2-record set EBF-408.]
        3760  LOVER
        3710  MELODY IN F
        3750  OUT OF NOWHERE
        3730  WOULD YOU LIKE TO TAKE A WALK


Capitol                               2-216        USA       7 Inch 45EP
   [Part of 2-record set EBF-216.]
        3080  AUNT HAGAR'S BLUES
        3220  BLUE SKIES
        3090  NICE WORK IF YOU CAN GET IT
        3060  WILLOW WEEP FOR ME


Capitol                               2-269        USA      12 Inch 45EP
   [Part of 3-record set EBF-269.]
        3150  DON'T BLAME ME
        3130  SWEET LORRAINE


Capitol                               2-408        USA       7 Inch 45EP
   [Part of 2-record set EBF-408.]
        3780  INDIANA
        3770  JUST ONE OF THOSE THINGS
        3720  SEPTEMBER SONG
        3740  TEA FOR TWO


Capitol                               3-269        USA      12 Inch 45EP
   [Part of 3-record set EBF-269.]
        3140  SOMEBODY LOVES ME
        3100  SOMEONE TO WATCH OVER ME


Capitol                               2109         USA      12 Inch LP

        3730  WOULD YOU LIKE TO TAKE A WALK


Capitol                               15518        USA      10 Inch 78
   [Part of 3-record set CC-216.]
        3070  I COVER THE WATERFRONT
        3180  I GOTTA RIGHT TO SING THE BLUES


Capitol                               15519        USA      10 Inch 78
   [Part of 3-record set CC-216.]
        3240  DANCING IN THE DARK
        3090  NICE WORK IF YOU CAN GET IT


Capitol                               15520        USA      10 Inch 78
   [Part of 3-record set CC-216.]
        3080  AUNT HAGAR'S BLUES
        3060  WILLOW WEEP FOR ME
```

```
Capitol                              15712          USA     10 Inch 78
   [Part of 3-record set CCN-269.]
   3160  MY HEART STOOD STILL
   3120  TIME ON MY HANDS


Capitol                              15713          USA     10 Inch 78
   [Part of 3-record set CCN-269.]
   3150  DON´T BLAME ME
   3130  SWEET LORRAINE


Capitol                              15714          USA     10 Inch 78
   [Part of 3-record set CCN-269.]
   3140  SOMEBODY LOVES ME
   3100  SOMEONE TO WATCH OVER ME


Capitol                              15782          USA     10 Inch 78

   3080  AUNT HAGAR´S BLUES
   3060  WILLOW WEEP FOR ME


Capitol                              15841          USA     10 Inch 78

   3170  YOU TOOK ADVANTAGE OF ME


Capitol                         1C 054-81 999M   Ger.    12 Inch LP

   3150  DON´T BLAME ME
   3210  GOIN´ HOME
   3070  I COVER THE WATERFRONT
   3780  INDIANA
   3160  MY HEART STOOD STILL
   3090  NICE WORK IF YOU CAN GET IT
   3750  OUT OF NOWHERE
   3720  SEPTEMBER SONG
   3140  SOMEBODY LOVES ME
   3100  SOMEONE TO WATCH OVER ME
   3130  SWEET LORRAINE
   3740  TEA FOR TWO
   3120  TIME ON MY HANDS
   3060  WILLOW WEEP FOR ME


Capitol                         1J 060 80.155M   Span.   12 Inch LP

   3230  IT´S THE TALK OF THE TOWN


Capitol                              2LP-22       Jap.    12 Inch LP

   3230  IT´S THE TALK OF THE TOWN


Capitol                         5C 052-80800     Holl.   12 Inch LP

   3080  AUNT HAGAR´S BLUES
   3220  BLUE SKIES
   3240  DANCING IN THE DARK
   3110  DARDANELLA
   3150  DON´T BLAME ME
   3070  I COVER THE WATERFRONT
   3180  I GOTTA RIGHT TO SING THE BLUES
   3230  IT´S THE TALK OF THE TOWN
   3160  MY HEART STOOD STILL
   3090  NICE WORK IF YOU CAN GET IT
   3140  SOMEBODY LOVES ME
   3100  SOMEONE TO WATCH OVER ME
   3130  SWEET LORRAINE
   3120  TIME ON MY HANDS
   3060  WILLOW WEEP FOR ME
   3170  YOU TOOK ADVANTAGE OF ME
```

```
Capitol                           C-13.014        Braz.    12 Inch LP

   3080   AUNT HAGAR'S BLUES
   3220   BLUE SKIES
   3240   DANCING IN THE DARK
   3110   DARDANELLA
   3150   DON'T BLAME ME
   3070   I COVER THE WATERFRONT
   3180   I GOTTA RIGHT TO SING THE BLUES
   3230   IT'S THE TALK OF THE TOWN
   3160   MY HEART STOOD STILL
   3090   NICE WORK IF YOU CAN GET IT
   3140   SOMEBODY LOVES ME
   3100   SOMEONE TO WATCH OVER ME
   3130   SWEET LORRAINE
   3120   TIME ON MY HANDS
   3060   WILLOW WEEP FOR ME
   3170   YOU TOOK ADVANTAGE OF ME


Capitol                           C.80154         Ger.     10 Inch 78

   3080   AUNT HAGAR'S BLUES
   3240   DANCING IN THE DARK


Capitol                           CC-216          USA
   [Three-record set containing 15518,15519,15520.]


Capitol                           CCF-216         USA
   [Three-record set containing F15518,F15519,F15520.]


Capitol                           CCF-269         USA
   [Three-record boxed set containing F15712,F15713,F15714.]


Capitol                           CCF-323         USA
   [Three-record boxed set containing F15841.]


Capitol                           CCN-269         USA
   [Three-record set containing 15712,15713,15714.]


Capitol                           CLP 047         Astla    10 Inch LP

   3780   INDIANA
   3770   JUST ONE OF THOSE THINGS
   3760   LOVER
   3710   MELODY IN F
   3750   OUT OF NOWHERE
   3720   SEPTEMBER SONG
   3740   TEA FOR TWO
   3730   WOULD YOU LIKE TO TAKE A WALK


Capitol                           CO62-80800      Fr.      12 Inch LP

   3080   AUNT HAGAR'S BLUES
   3220   BLUE SKIES
   3240   DANCING IN THE DARK
   3110   DARDANELLA
   3150   DON'T BLAME ME
   3070   I COVER THE WATERFRONT
   3180   I GOTTA RIGHT TO SING THE BLUES
   3230   IT'S THE TALK OF THE TOWN
   3160   MY HEART STOOD STILL
   3090   NICE WORK IF YOU CAN GET IT
   3140   SOMEBODY LOVES ME
   3100   SOMEONE TO WATCH OVER ME
   3130   SWEET LORRAINE
   3120   TIME ON MY HANDS
   3060   WILLOW WEEP FOR ME
```

```
     3170  YOU TOOK ADVANTAGE OF ME


Capitol                              CR-8810      Jap.     12 Inch LP

     3230  IT'S THE TALK OF THE TOWN
     3140  SOMEBODY LOVES ME


Capitol                              EBF-216      USA
     [Two-record set containing 1-216,2-216.]


Capitol                              EBF-269      USA
     [Three-record boxed set containing 1-269,2-269,3-269.]


Capitol                              EBF-323      USA
     [2-record set containing 1-323.]


Capitol                              EBF-408      USA
     [Two-record set containing 1-408,2-408.]


Capitol                              F15518       USA     7 Inch 45
     [Part of 3-record boxed set CCF-216.]
     3070  I COVER THE WATERFRONT
     3180  I GOTTA RIGHT TO SING THE BLUES


Capitol                              F15519       USA     7 Inch 45
     [Part of 3-record boxed set CCF-216.]
     3240  DANCING IN THE DARK
     3090  NICE WORK IF YOU CAN GET IT


Capitol                              F15520       USA     7 Inch 45
     [Part of 3-record boxed set CCF-216.]
     3080  AUNT HAGAR'S BLUES
     3060  WILLOW WEEP FOR ME


Capitol                              F15712       USA     7 Inch 45
     [Part of 3-record boxed set CCF-269.]
     3160  MY HEART STOOD STILL
     3120  TIME ON MY HANDS


Capitol                              F15713       USA     7 Inch 45
     [Part of 3-record boxed set CCF-269.]
     3150  DON'T BLAME ME
     3130  SWEET LORRAINE


Capitol                              F15714       USA     7 Inch 45
     [Part of 3-record boxed set CCF-269.]
     3140  SOMEBODY LOVES ME
     3100  SOMEONE TO WATCH OVER ME


Capitol                              F15841       USA     7 Inch 45
     [Part of 3-record boxed set CCF-323.]
     3170  YOU TOOK ADVANTAGE OF ME


Capitol                              H-216        USA     10 Inch LP

     3080  AUNT HAGAR'S BLUES
     3220  BLUE SKIES
     3240  DANCING IN THE DARK
     3110  DARDANELLA
     3070  I COVER THE WATERFRONT
     3180  I GOTTA RIGHT TO SING THE BLUES
     3090  NICE WORK IF YOU CAN GET IT
```

```
     3060   WILLOW WEEP FOR ME


Capitol                              H-269          USA     10 Inch LP

     3150   DON'T BLAME ME
     3210   GOIN' HOME
     3230   IT'S THE TALK OF THE TOWN
     3160   MY HEART STOOD STILL
     3140   SOMEBODY LOVES ME
     3100   SOMEONE TO WATCH OVER ME
     3130   SWEET LORRAINE
     3120   TIME ON MY HANDS


Capitol                              H-323          USA     10 Inch LP

     3170   YOU TOOK ADVANTAGE OF ME


Capitol                              H-408          Braz.   10 Inch LP

     3780   INDIANA
     3770   JUST ONE OF THOSE THINGS
     3760   LOVER
     3710   MELODY IN F
     3750   OUT OF NOWHERE
     3720   SEPTEMBER SONG
     3740   TEA FOR TWO
     3730   WOULD YOU LIKE TO TAKE A WALK


Capitol                              H-408          USA     10 Inch LP

     3780   INDIANA
     3770   JUST ONE OF THOSE THINGS
     3760   LOVER
     3710   MELODY IN F
     3750   OUT OF NOWHERE
     3720   SEPTEMBER SONG
     3740   TEA FOR TWO
     3730   WOULD YOU LIKE TO TAKE A WALK


Capitol                              K83924         Ger.    12 Inch LP

     3730   WOULD YOU LIKE TO TAKE A WALK


Capitol                              LC.6524        Eng.    10 Inch LP

     3080   AUNT HAGAR'S BLUES
     3220   BLUE SKIES
     3240   DANCING IN THE DARK
     3110   DARDANELLA
     3070   I COVER THE WATERFRONT
     3180   I GOTTA RIGHT TO SING THE BLUES
     3090   NICE WORK IF YOU CAN GET IT
     3060   WILLOW WEEP FOR ME


Capitol                              LC.6559        Eng.    10 Inch LP

     3170   YOU TOOK ADVANTAGE OF ME


Capitol                              LC.6625        Eng.    10 Inch LP

     3780   INDIANA
     3770   JUST ONE OF THOSE THINGS
     3760   LOVER
     3710   MELODY IN F
     3750   OUT OF NOWHERE
     3720   SEPTEMBER SONG
     3740   TEA FOR TWO
```

3730 WOULD YOU LIKE TO TAKE A WALK

Capitol   LC.6638   Eng.   10 Inch LP

    3150 DON´T BLAME ME
    3210 GOIN´ HOME
    3230 IT´S THE TALK OF THE TOWN
    3160 MY HEART STOOD STILL
    3140 SOMEBODY LOVES ME
    3100 SOMEONE TO WATCH OVER ME
    3130 SWEET LORRAINE
    3120 TIME ON MY HANDS

Capitol   M-11028   USA   12 Inch LP

    3080 AUNT HAGAR´S BLUES
    3220 BLUE SKIES
    3240 DANCING IN THE DARK
    3110 DARDANELLA
    3150 DON´T BLAME ME
    3070 I COVER THE WATERFRONT
    3180 I GOTTA RIGHT TO SING THE BLUES
    3230 IT´S THE TALK OF THE TOWN
    3160 MY HEART STOOD STILL
    3090 NICE WORK IF YOU CAN GET IT
    3140 SOMEBODY LOVES ME
    3100 SOMEONE TO WATCH OVER ME
    3130 SWEET LORRAINE
    3120 TIME ON MY HANDS
    3060 WILLOW WEEP FOR ME
    3170 YOU TOOK ADVANTAGE OF ME

Capitol   Spec. Promo.   USA   10 Inch 78
  [Interview of Art Tatum by Paul Weston with space provided for
  local disc jockey to participate by reading in part of the script.]
    3040 PROMOTIONAL INTERVIEW (Part One)
    3060 WILLOW WEEP FOR ME

Capitol   Spec. Promo.   USA   10 Inch 78
  [Interview of Art Tatum by Paul Weston with space provided for
  local disc jockey to participate by reading in his part of script.]
    3070 I COVER THE WATERFRONT
    3050 PROMOTIONAL INTERVIEW (Part Two)

Capitol   T-20640S   Fr.   12 Inch LP

    3150 DON´T BLAME ME
    3210 GOIN´ HOME
    3230 IT´S THE TALK OF THE TOWN
    3770 JUST ONE OF THOSE THINGS
    3760 LOVER
    3710 MELODY IN F
    3160 MY HEART STOOD STILL
    3140 SOMEBODY LOVES ME
    3100 SOMEONE TO WATCH OVER ME
    3130 SWEET LORRAINE
    3120 TIME ON MY HANDS
    3730 WOULD YOU LIKE TO TAKE A WALK

Capitol   T-216   USA   12 Inch LP

    3080 AUNT HAGAR´S BLUES
    3220 BLUE SKIES
    3240 DANCING IN THE DARK
    3110 DARDANELLA
    3070 I COVER THE WATERFRONT
    3180 I GOTTA RIGHT TO SING THE BLUES
    3780 INDIANA
    3090 NICE WORK IF YOU CAN GET IT

```
          3750  OUT OF NOWHERE
          3720  SEPTEMBER SONG
          3740  TEA FOR TWO
          3060  WILLOW WEEP FOR ME


Capitol                               T795           USA      12 Inch LP

          3230  IT'S THE TALK OF THE TOWN


Capitol                               TBO-1970       USA      12 Inch LP
      [Part of 2-record set with same number.]
          3120  TIME ON MY HANDS


Capitol                               W-2140         USA      12 Inch LP
      [Part of 5-record boxed set WEO-2109.]
          3730  WOULD YOU LIKE TO TAKE A WALK


Capitol                               WEO-2109       USA
      [5-record boxed set containing W-2140.]


Capitol Silver Platter Service        129            USA      12 Inch LP
      [Contains three brief statements by Tatum from interview by
       Jack Wagner, and the selection listed below.]

          3730  WOULD YOU LIKE TO TAKE A WALK
          4815  INTERVIEW SEGMENTS


Caracol                               CAR 426        Fr.      12 Inch LP

          1410  COCKTAILS FOR TWO
          1470  LIZA


Caracol                               CAR.428        Fr.      12 Inch LP

          0550  AIN'T MISBEHAVIN'
          0670  BEGIN THE BEGUINE
          0660  GET HAPPY
          0700  HALLELUJAH
          0530  HAPPY FEET
          0690  HUMORESQUE
          0520  I CAN'T GET STARTED
          0570  IN A SENTIMENTAL MOOD
          0680  IT HAD TO BE YOU
          0710  LULLABY IN RHYTHM
          0500  MAN I LOVE, THE
          0720  OH, YOU CRAZY MOON
          0730  OVER THE RAINBOW
          0540  ROYAL GARDEN BLUES
          0510  RUNNIN' WILD
          0560  STAR DUST


Carrere                               67.061         Fr.
      [Two-record set containing 67.406.]


Carrere                               67.406         Fr.      12 Inch LP
      [Part of 2-record set 67.061.]
          1000  BEAUTIFUL LOVE
          1120  BEGIN THE BEGUINE
          1200  BODY AND SOUL
          1110  FINE AND DANDY
          1090  GEORGIA ON MY MIND
          1180  KNOCKIN' MYSELF OUT
          1010  LAUGHING AT LIFE
          1170  MIGHTY LAK A ROSE
          1250  OH! LADY BE GOOD
          1260  SWEET GEORGIA BROWN
```

```
        1100   SWEET LORRAINE
        1240   THERE'LL BE SOME CHANGES MADE
        1190   TOLEDO BLUES


Cathala                              BLP 100.005    Fr.     12 Inch LP

        0940   COCKTAILS FOR TWO
        0910   EMALINE
        0460   GONE WITH THE WIND
        1490   HONEYSUCKLE ROSE
        0980   INDIANA
        0930   LOVE ME
        0880   LULLABY OF THE LEAVES
        0920   MOONGLOW
        0950   ST. LOUIS BLUES
        0470   STORMY WEATHER
        0740   TEA FOR TWO
        0890   TIGER RAG


Celson                               RA8004         It.     12 Inch 78

        1850   I KNOW THAT YOU KNOW
        1820   MAN I LOVE, THE


Celson                               RA8006         It.     12 Inch 78

        1870   FLYING HOME
        1860   ON THE SUNNY SIDE OF THE STREET


Celson                               RA8008         It.     12 Inch 78

        1840   BODY AND SOUL
        1830   DARK EYES


Clef                                 89170x45       USA     7 Inch 45EP

        6070   FOGGY DAY, A
        6090   MAKIN' WHOOPEE


Clef                                 EP-263         USA     7 Inch 45EP

        3850   CAN'T WE BE FRIENDS
        3880   MEMORIES OF YOU
        3860   THIS CAN'T BE LOVE


Clef                                 EP-264         USA     7 Inch 45EP

        3910   BODY AND SOUL
        3870   ELEGIE
        3890   OVER THE RAINBOW


Clef                                 EP-265         USA     7 Inch 45EP

               BLUES IN MY HEART (See "If You Hadn't Gone Away".)
        3900   IF YOU HADN'T GONE AWAY (Incorrectly titled "Blues in
                 My Heart")
        3930   MAKIN' WHOOPEE
        3920   MAN I LOVE, THE


Clef                                 EP-266         USA     7 Inch 45EP

        3950   BEGIN THE BEGUINE
        3960   HUMORESQUE
        3970   LOUISE
```

Clef		EP-267	USA	7 Inch 45EP

    4000 I'M COMING VIRGINIA
    3990 JUDY
    3980 LOVE FOR SALE

Clef		EP-268	USA	7 Inch 45EP

    4020 DIXIELAND BAND
    4050 SITTIN' AND ROCKIN'
    4010 WRAP YOUR TROUBLES IS DREAMS

Clef		EP-269	USA	7 Inch 45EP

    4040 COME RAIN OR COME SHINE
    4030 EMBRACEABLE YOU

Clef		EP-270	USA	7 Inch 45EP

    4070 TENDERLY
    4060 THERE WILL NEVER BE ANOTHER YOU

Clef		EP-271	USA	7 Inch 45EP

    4540 MIGHTY LAK A ROSE
    4080 WHAT DOES IT TAKE?
    4090 YOU TOOK ADVANTAGE OF ME

Clef		EP-272	USA	7 Inch 45EP

    4260 HAVE YOU MET MISS JONES
    4110 I'VE GOT THE WORLD ON A STRING
    4120 YESTERDAYS

Clef		EP-273	USA	7 Inch 45EP

    4270 IN A SENTIMENTAL MOOD
    4310 ISN'T THIS A LOVELY DAY
    4340 STOMPIN' AT THE SAVOY

Clef		EP-274	USA	7 Inch 45EP

    4350 MY LAST AFFAIR
    4370 TABOO
    4330 WITHOUT A SONG

Clef		EP-318	USA	7 Inch 45EP

    4860 BLUES IN MY HEART
    4930 OLD FASHIONED LOVE

Clef		EP-319	USA	7 Inch 45EP

    4940 'S WONDERFUL
    4830 BLUES IN B FLAT
    4950 HANDS ACROSS THE TABLE

Clef		EP-320	USA	7 Inch 45EP

    4880 IDAHO
    4820 MY BLUE HEAVEN
    4870 STREET OF DREAMS

```
Clef                              EP-C-349        USA      7 Inch 45EP

      4130   I HADN´T ANYONE ´TILL YOU
      4140   NIGHT AND DAY
      3940   SEPTEMBER SONG


Clef                              EP-C-350        USA      7 Inch 45EP

      4150   JITTERBUG WALTZ
      4160   SOMEONE TO WATCH OVER ME
      4380   WOULD YOU LIKE TO TAKE A WALK


Clef                              EP-C-351        USA      7 Inch 45EP

      4190   GHOST OF A CHANCE, A
      4210   I COVER THE WATERFRONT
      4180   YOU´RE DRIVING ME CRAZY


Clef                              EP-C-352        USA      7 Inch 45EP

      4200   STAR DUST
      4170   VERY THOUGHT OF YOU, THE


Clef                              EP-C-353        USA      7 Inch 45EP

      4230   STAY AS SWEET AS YOU ARE
      4220   WHERE OR WHEN


Clef                              EP-C-354        USA      7 Inch 45EP

      4240   FINE AND DANDY
      4280   I´LL SEE YOU AGAIN
      4290   I´LL SEE YOU IN MY DREAMS


Clef                              EP-C-355        USA      7 Inch 45EP

      4250   ALL THE THINGS YOU ARE
      4300   ILL WIND


Clef                              EP-C-356        Astla    7 Inch 45EP

      4320   BLUE SKIES
      4580   CARAVAN
      4390   I´VE GOT A CRUSH ON YOU
      4650   LOVE ME OR LEAVE ME


Clef                              EP-C-356        USA      7 Inch 45EP

      4320   BLUE SKIES
      4580   CARAVAN
      4390   ´I´VE GOT A CRUSH ON YOU
      4650   LOVE ME OR LEAVE ME


Clef                              EP-C-357        USA      7 Inch 45EP

      4360   I´M IN THE MOOD FOR LOVE
      4400   JAPANESE SANDMAN, THE
      4410   TOO MARVELOUS FOR WORDS


Clef                              EP-C-358        Astla    7 Inch 45EP

      4420   AUNT HAGAR´S BLUES
      4480   IT´S THE TALK OF THE TOWN
      4430   JUST LIKE A BUTTERFLY THAT´S CAUGHT IN THE RAIN
```

```
Clef                                    EP-C-358       USA      7 Inch 45EP

   4420   AUNT HAGAR´S BLUES
   4480   IT´S THE TALK OF THE TOWN
   4430   JUST LIKE A BUTTERFLY THAT´S CAUGHT IN THE RAIN


Clef                                    EP-C-359       USA      7 Inch 45EP

   4450   DANNY BOY
   4440   GONE WITH THE WIND
   4460   THEY CAN´T TAKE THAT AWAY FROM ME


Clef                                    EP-C-360       USA      7 Inch 45EP

   4520   AIN´T MISBEHAVIN´
   4490   BLUE LOU
   4470   TEA FOR TWO


Clef                                    EP-C-361       USA      7 Inch 45EP

   4500   WHEN A WOMAN LOVES A MAN
   4510   WILLOW WEEP FOR ME


Clef                                    EP-C-362       USA      7 Inch 45EP

   4620   LOVER, COME BACK TO ME!
   4530   SMOKE GETS IN YOUR EYES


Clef                                    EP-C-363       USA      7 Inch 45EP

   4560   BLUE MOON
   4550   STARS FELL ON ALABAMA


Clef                                    EP-C-373       USA      7 Inch 45EP

   5270   I WON´T DANCE
   5250   MOON IS LOW, THE
   5290   THIS CAN´T BE LOVE
   5260   YOU TOOK ADVANTAGE OF ME


Clef                                    MG C-612       USA      12 Inch LP
  [Issued individually and as part of 5-record boxed set.]
   3950   BEGIN THE BEGUINE
          BLUES IN MY HEART (See "If You Hadn´t Gone Away".)
   3850   CAN´T WE BE FRIENDS
   4020   DIXIELAND BAND
   3870   ELEGIE
   3960   HUMORESQUE
   3900   IF YOU HADN´T GONE AWAY (Incorrectly titled "Blues in
          My Heart")
   3990   JUDY
   3860   THIS CAN´T BE LOVE


Clef                                    MG C-613       USA      12 Inch LP
  [Issued individually and as part of 5-record boxed set.]
   3910   BODY AND SOUL
   3930   MAKIN´ WHOOPEE
   3920   MAN I LOVE, THE
   3880   MEMORIES OF YOU
   4540   MIGHTY LAK A ROSE
   3890   OVER THE RAINBOW


Clef                                    MG C-614       USA      12 Inch LP
  [Issued individually and as part of 5-record boxed set.]
   4040   COME RAIN OR COME SHINE
   4030   EMBRACEABLE YOU

                         175
```

```
            4000   I´M COMING VIRGINIA
            3970   LOUISE
            3980   LOVE FOR SALE
            4010   WRAP YOUR TROUBLES IS DREAMS


Clef                                    MG C-615        USA      12 Inch LP
   [Issued individually and as part of 5-record boxed set.]
            4110   I´VE GOT THE WORLD ON A STRING
            4050   SITTIN´ AND ROCKIN´
            4070   TENDERLY
            4060   THERE WILL NEVER BE ANOTHER YOU
            4080   WHAT DOES IT TAKE?
            4120   YESTERDAYS
            4090   YOU TOOK ADVANTAGE OF ME


Clef                                    MG C-618        USA      12 Inch LP
   [Issued individually and as part of 5-record boxed set.]
            4260   HAVE YOU MET MISS JONES
            4270   IN A SENTIMENTAL MOOD
            4310   ISN´T THIS A LOVELY DAY
            4350   MY LAST AFFAIR
            4340   STOMPIN´ AT THE SAVOY
            4370   TABOO
            4330   WITHOUT A SONG


Clef                                    MG C-643        Astla    12 Inch LP

            4940   ´S WONDERFUL
            4830   BLUES IN B FLAT
            4860   BLUES IN MY HEART
            4950   HANDS ACROSS THE TABLE
            4880   IDAHO
            4820   MY BLUE HEAVEN
            4930   OLD FASHIONED LOVE
            4870   STREET OF DREAMS


Clef                                    MG C-643        USA      12 Inch LP

            4940   ´S WONDERFUL
            4830   BLUES IN B FLAT
            4860   BLUES IN MY HEART
            4950   HANDS ACROSS THE TABLE
            4880   IDAHO
            4820   MY BLUE HEAVEN
            4930   OLD FASHIONED LOVE
            4870   STREET OF DREAMS


Clef                                    MG C-657        USA      12 Inch LP
   [Issued individually and as part of 5-record boxed set MGC-2002-5.]
            4560   BLUE MOON
            4130   I HADN´T ANYONE ´TILL YOU
            4150   JITTERBUG WALTZ
            4140   NIGHT AND DAY
            3940   SEPTEMBER SONG
            4530   SMOKE GETS IN YOUR EYES
            4550   STARS FELL ON ALABAMA
            4180   YOU´RE DRIVING ME CRAZY


Clef                                    MG C-658        USA      12 Inch LP
   [Issued individually and as part of 5-record boxed set MGC-2002-5.]
            4190   GHOST OF A CHANCE, A
            4280   I´LL SEE YOU AGAIN
            4160   SOMEONE TO WATCH OVER ME
            4200   STAR DUST
            4230   STAY AS SWEET AS YOU ARE
            4170   VERY THOUGHT OF YOU, THE
            4220   WHERE OR WHEN
```

```
Clef                              MG C-659        USA     12 Inch LP
  [Issued individually and as part of 5-record boxed set MGC-2002-5.]
     4520   AIN´T MISBEHAVIN´
     4250   ALL THE THINGS YOU ARE
     4240   FINE AND DANDY
     4210   I COVER THE WATERFRONT
     4360   I´M IN THE MOOD FOR LOVE
     4650   LOVE ME OR LEAVE ME
     4500   WHEN A WOMAN LOVES A MAN
     4510   WILLOW WEEP FOR ME


Clef                              MG C-660        USA     12 Inch LP
  [Issued individually and as part of 5-record boxed set MGC-2002-5.]
     4420   AUNT HAGAR´S BLUES
     4320   BLUE SKIES
     4290   I´LL SEE YOU IN MY DREAMS
     4390   I´VE GOT A CRUSH ON YOU
     4300   ILL WIND
     4400   JAPANESE SANDMAN, THE
     4620   LOVER, COME BACK TO ME!
     4380   WOULD YOU LIKE TO TAKE A WALK


Clef                              MG C-661        USA     12 Inch LP
  [Issued individually and as part of 5-record boxed set MGC-2002-5.]
     4490   BLUE LOU
     4580   CARAVAN
     4450   DANNY BOY
     4440   GONE WITH THE WIND
     4480   IT´S THE TALK OF THE TOWN
     4430   JUST LIKE A BUTTERFLY THAT´S CAUGHT IN THE RAIN
     4470   TEA FOR TWO
     4460   THEY CAN´T TAKE THAT AWAY FROM ME
     4410   TOO MARVELOUS FOR WORDS


Clef                              MG C-679        USA     12 Inch LP

     5240   I SURRENDER DEAR
     5270   I WON´T DANCE
     5300   IN A SENTIMENTAL MOOD
     5280   MOON SONG
     5310   NIGHT AND DAY
     5250   MOON IS LOW, THE
     5290   THIS CAN´T BE LOVE
     5260   YOU TOOK ADVANTAGE OF ME


Clef                              MG C-709        USA     12 Inch LP

     5650   HALLELUJAH
     5780   HOW HIGH THE MOON
     5660   I´LL NEVER BE THE SAME
     5760   MAKIN´ WHOOPEE
     5770   MORE THAN YOU KNOW
     5640   PERDIDO
     5710   WHAT IS THIS THING CALLED LOVE


Clef                              MG C-712        USA     12 Inch LP

     4690   AFTER YOU´VE GONE
     4660   CHEROKEE
     4640   DANCING IN THE DARK
     4630   SOPHISTICATED LADY
     4590   WAY YOU LOOK TONIGHT, THE
     4570   THERE´S A SMALL HOTEL
     4670   THESE FOOLISH THINGS REMIND ME OF YOU
     4600   YOU GO TO MY HEAD
```

```
Clef                                    MGC-2002-5       USA
    [Five-record boxed set containing MG C-657,MG C-658,MG C-659,
    MG C-660,MG C-661.]


Columbia                                    74          USA      7 Inch 45

    3030   KERRY DANCE, THE
    3020   MAN I LOVE, THE (Abridged version of "Gershwin Medley")


Columbia                                    75          USA      7 Inch 45

    2960   HUMORESQUE
    3000   I KNOW THAT YOU KNOW


Columbia                                   4-74-G       USA      7 Inch 45E

    3030   KERRY DANCE, THE
    3020   MAN I LOVE, THE (Abridged version of "Gershwin Medley")
    2970   TATUM-POLE BOOGIE


Columbia                                   4-75-G       USA      7 Inch 45E

    2960   HUMORESQUE
    3000   I KNOW THAT YOU KNOW


Columbia                                 33C 9033       Eng.    10 Inch LP

    4560   BLUE MOON
    4150   JITTERBUG WALTZ
    4140   NIGHT AND DAY
    3940   SEPTEMBER SONG
    4530   SMOKE GETS IN YOUR EYES
    4550   STARS FELL ON ALABAMA
    4180   YOU´RE DRIVING ME CRAZY


Columbia                                 33C 9039       Eng.    10 Inch LP

    5920   BLUE LOU
    5990   I GUESS I´LL HAVE TO CHANGE MY PLANS
    5970   I´LL NEVER BE THE SAME
    6000   ISN´T IT ROMANTIC
    5960   JUST ONE OF THOSE THINGS
    5980   LOVE FOR SALE
    5950   MORE THAN YOU KNOW


Columbia                                33CX10005       Eng.    12 Inch LP

    3910   BODY AND SOUL
    3930   MAKIN´ WHOOPEE
    3920   MAN I LOVE, THE
    3880   MEMORIES OF YOU
    4540   MIGHTY LAK A ROSE
    3890   OVER THE RAINBOW


Columbia                                33CX10024       Eng.    12 Inch LP

    3850   CAN´T WE BE FRIENDS
    4340   STOMPIN´ AT THE SAVOY
    3920   MAN I LOVE, THE


Columbia                                33CX10042       Eng.    12 Inch LP

    5240   I SURRENDER DEAR
    5270   I WON´T DANCE
    5300   IN A SENTIMENTAL MOOD
    5280   MOON SONG

                              178
```

```
        5310  NIGHT AND DAY
        5250  MOON IS LOW, THE
        5290  THIS CAN'T BE LOVE
        5260  YOU TOOK ADVANTAGE OF ME


Columbia                          33CX10045      Eng.    12 Inch LP

        5650  HALLELUJAH
        5780  HOW HIGH THE MOON
        5660  I'LL NEVER BE THE SAME
        5760  MAKIN' WHOOPEE
        5770  MORE THAN YOU KNOW
        5640  PERDIDO
        5710  WHAT IS THIS THING CALLED LOVE


Columbia                          33CX10053      Eng.    12 Inch LP

        4110  I'VE GOT THE WORLD ON A STRING
        4050  SITTIN' AND ROCKIN'
        4070  TENDERLY
        4060  THERE WILL NEVER BE ANOTHER YOU
        4080  WHAT DOES IT TAKE?
        4120  YESTERDAYS
        4090  YOU TOOK ADVANTAGE OF ME


Columbia                          33CX10063      Eng.    12 Inch LP

        5810  DEEP PURPLE
        5790  PLAID
        5830  SEPTEMBER SONG
        5800  SOMEBODY LOVES ME
        5840  VERVE BLUES


Columbia                          33CX10115      Eng.    12 Inch LP

        6160  ALL THE THINGS YOU ARE
        5690  BODY AND SOUL
        4020  DIXIELAND BAND
        5270  I WON'T DANCE
        4880  IDAHO
        5930  IF
        3990  JUDY
        6040  THIS CAN'T BE LOVE
        6010  TRIO BLUES
        5820  WHAT IS THIS THING CALLED LOVE


Columbia                          33CX10137      Eng.    12 Inch LP

        6190  GONE WITH THE WIND
        6200  HAVE YOU MET MISS JONES
        6180  MY IDEAL
        6170  MY ONE AND ONLY LOVE
        6210  NIGHT AND DAY
        6220  WHERE OR WHEN


Columbia                          33CX10141      Eng.    12 Inch LP

        4830  BLUES IN B FLAT


Columbia                          33SX1506       Eng.    12 Inch LP

        0080  SOPHISTICATED LADY
        0050  TEA FOR TWO
```

```
Columbia                            33SX1557        Eng.    12 Inch LP

     1840   BODY AND SOUL
     1830   DARK EYES
     1870   FLYING HOME
     1850   I KNOW THAT YOU KNOW
     1860   ON THE SUNNY SIDE OF THE STREET


Columbia                            BL 33404        USA     12 Inch LP
   [Part of 2-record set PG 33402.]
     2960   HUMORESQUE


Columbia                            CL 2565         USA     10 Inch LP

     2950   HOW HIGH THE MOON
     2960   HUMORESQUE
     3000   I KNOW THAT YOU KNOW
     2970   TATUM-POLE BOOGIE
     3010   WILLOW WEEP FOR ME
     2990   YESTERDAYS


Columbia                            CL 6301         USA     10 Inch LP

     2950   HOW HIGH THE MOON
     2960   HUMORESQUE
     3000   I KNOW THAT YOU KNOW
     3030   KERRY DANCE, THE
     3020   MAN I LOVE, THE (Abridged version of "Gershwin Medley")
     2980   SOMEONE TO WATCH OVER ME
     2970   TATUM-POLE BOOGIE
     3010   WILLOW WEEP FOR ME
     2990   YESTERDAYS


Columbia                            CS9655          USA     12 Inch LP

     2950   HOW HIGH THE MOON
     2960   HUMORESQUE
     3000   I KNOW THAT YOU KNOW
     3030   KERRY DANCE, THE
     3020   MAN I LOVE, THE (Abridged version of "Gershwin Medley")
     2980   SOMEONE TO WATCH OVER ME
     0080   SOPHISTICATED LADY
     0060   ST. LOUIS BLUES
     2970   TATUM-POLE BOOGIE
     0050   TEA FOR TWO
     0070   TIGER RAG
     3010   WILLOW WEEP FOR ME
     2990   YESTERDAYS


Columbia                            DO-1227         Astla   10 Inch 78

     0060   ST. LOUIS BLUES
     0070   TIGER RAG


Columbia                            EM-72           Jap.    7 Inch 45E.

     0080   SOPHISTICATED LADY
     0060   ST. LOUIS BLUES
     0050   TEA FOR TWO
     0070   TIGER RAG


Columbia                            GL 101          USA     10 Inch LP

     2950   HOW HIGH THE MOON
     2960   HUMORESQUE
     3000   I KNOW THAT YOU KNOW
     3030   KERRY DANCE, THE
     3020   MAN I LOVE, THE (Abridged version of "Gershwin Medley")
```

```
      2980   SOMEONE TO WATCH OVER ME
      2970   TATUM-POLE BOOGIE
      3010   WILLOW WEEP FOR ME
      2990   YESTERDAYS


Columbia                          KG32355       USA      12 Inch LP
   [Some record jackets call this PG32355; record number is KG32355.]
      0070   TIGER RAG


Columbia                          LB 10039      Eng.     10 Inch 78

      6070   FOGGY DAY, A
      6090   MAKIN´ WHOOPEE


Columbia                          LB 10053      Eng.     10 Inch 78

      4000   I´M COMING VIRGINIA
      4010   WRAP YOUR TROUBLES IS DREAMS


Columbia                          LB 10069      Eng.     10 Inch 78

      3950   BEGIN THE BEGUINE
      3860   THIS CAN´T BE LOVE


Columbia                          PG32355  (See KG32355)

Columbia                          PG33402       USA
   [2-record set containing BL 33404.]


Columbia                          PMS 53-54-55  Jap.
   [3-record boxed set containing PMS 55.]


Columbia                          PMS 55        Jap.    12 Inch LP
   [Part of 3-record boxed set PMS 53-54-55.]
      2980   SOMEONE TO WATCH OVER ME


Columbia                          SEB 10003     Eng.     7 Inch 45E

      4040   COME RAIN OR COME SHINE
      4030   EMBRACEABLE YOU


Columbia                          SEB 10027     Eng.     7 Inch 45E

      4940   ´S WONDERFUL
      4830   BLUES IN B FLAT
      4950   HANDS ACROSS THE TABLE


Columbia                          SEB 10062     Eng.     7 Inch 45E

      4860   BLUES IN MY HEART
      4930   OLD FASHIONED LOVE


Columbia                          SEB 10084     Eng.     7 Inch 45E

      6120   BEGIN THE BEGUINE
      6130   HUMORESQUE
      6140   SOMEONE TO WATCH OVER ME
      6150   WILLOW WEEP FOR ME


Columbia                          SEB 10101     Eng.     7 Inch 45E

      6020   DEEP NIGHT
      6050   MEMORIES OF YOU
```
181

Columbia	SEB 10116	Eng.	7 Inch 45EP

```
5070  DON'T WORRY 'BOUT ME
5100  I WON'T DANCE
5090  MOONGLOW
5080  PRISONER OF LOVE
```

Columbia	SEG7540	Eng.	7 Inch 45EP

```
0080  SOPHISTICATED LADY
0060  ST. LOUIS BLUES
0050  TEA FOR TWO
0070  TIGER RAG
```

Columbia	ZL-1028	Jap.	10 Inch LP

```
2950  HOW HIGH THE MOON
2960  HUMORESQUE
3000  I KNOW THAT YOU KNOW
3030  KERRY DANCE, THE
3020  MAN I LOVE, THE (Abridged version of "Gershwin Medley")
2980  SOMEONE TO WATCH OVER ME
2970  TATUM-POLE BOOGIE
3010  WILLOW WEEP FOR ME
2990  YESTERDAYS
```

Columbia House	P3S5932	USA	12 Inch LP

```
[Part of 3-record set.]
0070  TIGER RAG
```

Columbia Special Products	JLN 24028	USA	12 Inch LP

```
[Part of 4-record boxed set JSN 6042.]
0080  SOPHISTICATED LADY
0050  TEA FOR TWO
```

Columbia Special Products	JSN 6042		

```
[4-record boxed set containing JLN 24028.]
```

Comet	T-1	USA	12 Inch 78

```
1830  DARK EYES
1820  MAN I LOVE, THE
```

Comet	T-2	USA	12 Inch 78

```
1840  BODY AND SOUL
1850  I KNOW THAT YOU KNOW
```

Comet	T-3	USA	12 Inch 78

```
1870  FLYING HOME
1860  ON THE SUNNY SIDE OF THE STREET
```

Commodore	547	USA	10 Inch 78

```
1351  ESQUIRE BLUES
1320  ESQUIRE BOUNCE
```

Commodore	548	USA	10 Inch 78

```
1331  MOP-MOP
1340  MY IDEAL
```

Commodore	7540	USA	10 Inch 78

```
        1351   ESQUIRE BLUES
        1320   ESQUIRE BOUNCE


Commodore                        7541          USA      10 Inch 78

        1331   MOP-MOP
        1340   MY IDEAL


Commodore                        45-7540       USA      7 Inch 45

        1351   ESQUIRE BLUES
        1320   ESQUIRE BOUNCE


Commodore                        45-7541       USA      7 Inch 45

        1331   MOP-MOP
        1340   MY IDEAL


Commodore                        FL20 025      USA      10 Inch LP

        1351   ESQUIRE BLUES
        1320   ESQUIRE BOUNCE
        1331   MOP-MOP (Also called Boff-Boff)
        1340   MY IDEAL


Commodore                        GXC-3146      Jap.     12 Inch LP

        1351   ESQUIRE BLUES
        1320   ESQUIRE BOUNCE
        1331   MOP-MOP (Also called Boff-Boff)
        1340   MY IDEAL


Commodore                        GXC-3147      Jap.     12 Inch LP

        1341   MY IDEAL


Commodore                        XFL14936      USA      12 Inch LP

        1350   ESQUIRE BLUES
        1351   ESQUIRE BLUES
        1320   ESQUIRE BOUNCE
        1321   ESQUIRE BOUNCE
        1330   MOP-MOP (Also called Boff-Boff)
        1331   MOP-MOP (Also called Boff-Boff)
        1340   MY IDEAL
        1341   MY IDEAL


Coral                            (See also "Vogue Coral" & "MCA Coral"


Coral                            CJE 100       USA
   [5-record boxed set containing CRL57223.]


Coral                            COP 2686      Ger.     12 Inch LP

        0940   COCKTAILS FOR TWO
        0840   ELEGIE
        0910   EMALINE
        0870   GET HAPPY
        0850   HUMORESQUE
        1460   I WOULD DO ANYTHING FOR YOU
        0980   INDIANA
        0930   LOVE ME
        0880   LULLABY OF THE LEAVES
        1440   MOONGLOW
        0860   SWEET LORRAINE

                            183
```

        0890   TIGER RAG

Coral   COPS 3443   Ger.   12 Inch LP

        1430   AFTER YOU´VE GONE
        0960   BEGIN THE BEGUINE
        0940   COCKTAILS FOR TWO
        1450   DEEP PURPLE
        0460   GONE WITH THE WIND
        1490   HONEYSUCKLE ROSE
        1400   I GOT RHYTHM
        1440   MOONGLOW
        0970   ROSETTA
        0950   ST. LOUIS BLUES
        0470   STORMY WEATHER
        0740   TEA FOR TWO

Coral   CP62   Eng.   12 Inch LP
     [Some record jackets have EMI CRLM 1044; record number is CP62.]
        0940   COCKTAILS FOR TWO
        0840   ELEGIE
        0910   EMALINE
        0870   GET HAPPY
        0850   HUMORESQUE
        1460   I WOULD DO ANYTHING FOR YOU
        0980   INDIANA
        0930   LOVE ME
        0880   LULLABY OF THE LEAVES
        1440   MOONGLOW
        0860   SWEET LORRAINE
        0890   TIGER RAG

Coral   CRL57223   Eng.   12 Inch LP
     [Part of 5-record boxed set CJE 100.]
        0950   ST. LOUIS BLUES

Coral   CVM.40006   Fr.   10 Inch LP

        0960   BEGIN THE BEGUINE
        0480   CHLOE
        0460   GONE WITH THE WIND
        0970   ROSETTA
        0490   SHEIK OF ARABY, THE
        0950   ST. LOUIS BLUES
        0470   STORMY WEATHER
        0740   TEA FOR TWO

Coral   CVM.40007   Fr.   10 Inch LP

        1430   AFTER YOU´VE GONE
        1410   COCKTAILS FOR TWO
        1450   DEEP PURPLE
        1490   HONEYSUCKLE ROSE
        1420   I AIN´T GOT NOBODY
        1400   I GOT RHYTHM
        1460   I WOULD DO ANYTHING FOR YOU
        1440   MOONGLOW

Coral   EPC 94 020   Ger.   7 Inch 45E

        0960   BEGIN THE BEGUINE
        1400   I GOT RHYTHM
        1440   MOONGLOW
        0950   ST. LOUIS BLUES

Coral   EPC 94 122   Ger.   7 Inch 45EP

```
0460   GONE WITH THE WIND
0970   ROSETTA
0470   STORMY WEATHER
0740   TEA FOR TWO
```

Coral   LPCM-2009   Jap.   12 Inch LP

```
1430   AFTER YOU'VE GONE
0960   BEGIN THE BEGUINE
1410   COCKTAILS FOR TWO
1450   DEEP PURPLE
0460   GONE WITH THE WIND
1490   HONEYSUCKLE ROSE
1400   I GOT RHYTHM
1440   MOONGLOW
0970   ROSETTA
0950   ST. LOUIS BLUES
0470   STORMY WEATHER
0740   TEA FOR TWO
```

Core   100C   USA   12 Inch LP
  [Part of 2-record set C100.]
```
1830   DARK EYES
```

Core   C100   USA
  [2-record set containing 100C.]

Crystal   12.501   Fr.   12 Inch LP
  [Jacket reads, "Comet Sessions."]
```
1840   BODY AND SOUL
1830   DARK EYES
1870   FLYING HOME
1850   I KNOW THAT YOU KNOW
1820   MAN I LOVE, THE
1860   ON THE SUNNY SIDE OF THE STREET
```

DJM   DJD 28002   Eng.   12 Inch LP
  [2-record set.]
```
0760   ALL GOD'S CHILLUN GOT RHYTHM
2430   AMONG MY SOUVENIRS
2410   CAN'T WE BE FRIENDS
2400   CRAZY RHYTHM
0790   DAY IN - DAY OUT
0800   FINE AND DANDY
2180   I CAN'T GIVE YOU ANYTHING BUT LOVE
0820   I GOTTA RIGHT TO SING THE BLUES
2540   I GOTTA RIGHT TO SING THE BLUES
2380   I GUESS I'LL HAVE TO CHANGE MY PLANS
0830   I'M COMING VIRGINIA
2440   I'M GONNA SIT RIGHT DOWN AND WRITE MYSELF A LETTER
0810   I'VE GOT THE WORLD ON A STRING
2480   IF I COULD BE WITH YOU
0780   INDIANA
2420   LIMEHOUSE BLUES
2170   MAN I LOVE, THE
2500   MEAN TO ME
2550   ON THE SUNNY SIDE OF THE STREET
2460   SOMEBODY LOVES ME
2450   STAY AS SWEET AS YOU ARE
0770   SWEET EMALINA, MY GAL
2490   TEA FOR TWO
2530   THREE LITTLE WORDS
2390   WHAT IS THIS THING CALLED LOVE
2470   WHY WAS I BORN
2360   YOU TOOK ADVANTAGE OF ME*
       *Note: The record contains two tracks of this tune which
       are identical; they are incorrectly identified as different
       versions.
```

185

```
DJM                                    DJLMD.8002    Eng.    12 Inch LP
  [2-record set.]
       0760   ALL GOD´S CHILLUN GOT RHYTHM
       2430   AMONG MY SOUVENIRS
       2410   CAN´T WE BE FRIENDS
       2400   CRAZY RHYTHM
       0790   DAY IN - DAY OUT
       0800   FINE AND DANDY
       2180   I CAN´T GIVE YOU ANYTHING BUT LOVE
       0820   I GOTTA RIGHT TO SING THE BLUES
       2540   I GOTTA RIGHT TO SING THE BLUES
       2380   I GUESS I´LL HAVE TO CHANGE MY PLANS
       0830   I´M COMING VIRGINIA
       2440   I´M GONNA SIT RIGHT DOWN AND WRITE MYSELF A LETTER
       0810   I´VE GOT THE WORLD ON A STRING
       2480   IF I COULD BE WITH YOU
       0780   INDIANA
       2420   LIMEHOUSE BLUES
       2170   MAN I LOVE, THE
       2500   MEAN TO ME
       2550   ON THE SUNNY SIDE OF THE STREET
       2460   SOMEBODY LOVES ME
       2450   STAY AS SWEET AS YOU ARE
       0770   SWEET EMALINA, MY GAL
       2490   TEA FOR TWO
       2530   THREE LITTLE WORDS
       2390   WHAT IS THIS THING CALLED LOVE
       2470   WHY WAS I BORN
       2360   YOU TOOK ADVANTAGE OF ME*
       *Note: The record contains two tracks of this tune which
        are identical; they are incorrectly identified as different
        versions.


DJM                                    DJM 22047     Eng.    12 Inch LP

       1550   DO NOTHIN´ TILL YOU HEAR FROM ME


Dan                                    VC-5006       Jap.    12 Inch LP

       1670   BACK O´ TOWN BLUES
       1640   BASIN STREET BLUES


Dan                                    VC-5010       Jap.    12 Inch LP

       2320   SHE´S FUNNY THAT WAY


Dan                                    VC-5011       Jap.    12 Inch LP

       1630   ESQUIRE BOUNCE
       1740   FLYING HOME (Listed as "Flyin´ On a V-Disc")
       1540   MOP-MOP
       1720   MY IDEAL


Dan                                    VC-5014       Jap.    12 Inch LP

       1550   DO NOTHIN´ TILL YOU HEAR FROM ME
       1560   I LOVE MY MAN
       1650   I´LL GET BY


Dan                                    VC-5029       Jap.    12 Inch LP

       1640   BASIN STREET BLUES
       1610   BLUES
       1550   DO NOTHIN´ TILL YOU HEAR FROM ME
       1530   ESQUIRE BLUES
```

```
1630  ESQUIRE BOUNCE
1570  I CAN'T GIVE YOU ANYTHING BUT LOVE
1600  I GOT RHYTHM
1580  I GOTTA RIGHT TO SING THE BLUES
1560  I LOVE MY MAN
1650  I'LL GET BY
1540  MOP-MOP
1590  SWEET LORRAINE
1620  THEME FOR COCA-COLA/INTRODUCTIONS(Spotlight Band Theme)
```

Dan   VC-5030   Jap.   12 Inch LP

```
1670  BACK O' TOWN BLUES
1690  BUCK JUMPIN'
1740  FLYING HOME
1710  FOR BASS FACES ONLY
1680  MUSKRAT RAMBLE
1720  MY IDEAL
1730  ROSE ROOM
1700  STOMPIN' AT THE SAVOY
1660  TEA FOR TWO
1665  THEME FOR COCA-COLA/CONCLUSION(Spotlight Band Theme)
1750  VIBE BLUES (Listed as "Jammin' the Blues")
```

Decca   126   USA
  [3-record set containing 18049,18050,18051.]

Decca   155   USA   10 Inch 78
  [Issued as shown here and also as in the next listing below.]
  0170 EMALINE
  0140 MOONGLOW

Decca   155   USA   10 Inch 78
  [Issued as shown here and also as in the preceding listing above.]
  0910 EMALINE
  0920 MOONGLOW

Decca   156   USA   10 Inch 78
  [Issued as shown here and also as in the next listing below.]
  0190 COCKTAILS FOR TWO
  0180 LOVE ME

Decca   156   USA   10 Inch 78
  [Issued as shown here and also as in the preceding listing above.]
  0940 COCKTAILS FOR TWO
  0930 LOVE ME

Decca   306   USA   10 Inch 78
  [Issued as shown here and also as in the next listing below.]
  0251 BEAUTIFUL LOVE
  0211 STAR DUST

Decca   306   USA   10 Inch 78
  [Issued as shown here and also as in the preceding listing above.]
  0252 BEAUTIFUL LOVE
  0211 STAR DUST

Decca   468   USA   10 Inch 78

  0201 AFTER YOU'VE GONE
  0240 SHOUT, THE
```
```

Decca   741   Can.   10 Inch 78

    0221 I AIN'T GOT NOBODY
    0160 WHEN A WOMAN LOVES A MAN

Decca   741   USA   10 Inch 78
  [Issued as shown here and also as in the next listing below.]
    0221 I AIN'T GOT NOBODY
    0160 WHEN A WOMAN LOVES A MAN

Decca   741   USA   10 Inch 78
  [Issued as shown here and also as in the preceding listing above.]
    0221 I AIN'T GOT NOBODY
    0162 WHEN A WOMAN LOVES A MAN

Decca   1197   USA   10 Inch 78

    0420 BODY AND SOUL
    0440 WHAT WILL I TELL MY HEART

Decca   1198   USA   10 Inch 78

    0450 I'VE GOT MY LOVE TO KEEP ME WARM
    0430 WITH PLENTY OF MONEY AND YOU

Decca   1373   Can.   10 Inch 78

    0152 I WOULD DO ANYTHING FOR YOU
    0262 LIZA

Decca   1373   USA   10 Inch 78
  [Issued as shown here and also as in the next listing below.]
    0152 I WOULD DO ANYTHING FOR YOU
    0260 LIZA

Decca   1373   USA   10 Inch 78
  [Issued as shown here and also as in the preceding listing above.]
    0152 I WOULD DO ANYTHING FOR YOU
    0262 LIZA

Decca   1603   USA   10 Inch 78

    0460 GONE WITH THE WIND
    0470 STORMY WEATHER
Decca   2052   Can.   10 Inch 78

    0481 CHLOE
    0490 SHEIK OF ARABY, THE

Decca   2052   USA   10 Inch 78

    0480 CHLOE
    0490 SHEIK OF ARABY, THE

Decca   2456   Can.   10 Inch 78

    0750 DEEP PURPLE
    0740 TEA FOR TWO

Decca   2456   USA   10 Inch 78
  [Issued as shown here and also as in the next listing below.]
    0750 DEEP PURPLE
    0740 TEA FOR TWO

188

Decca   2456   USA   10 Inch 78
     [Issued as shown here and also as in the preceding listing above.]
     0751   DEEP PURPLE
     0740   TEA FOR TWO

Decca   8502   USA   10 Inch 78

     0960   BEGIN THE BEGUINE
     0970   ROSETTA

Decca   8526   USA   10 Inch 78

     1080   BATTERY BOUNCE
     1050   WEE BABY BLUES

Decca   8536   USA   10 Inch 78

     1070   LAST GOODBYE BLUES
     1060   STOMPIN´ AT THE SAVOY

Decca   8550   USA   10 Inch 78

     0980   INDIANA
     0950   ST. LOUIS BLUES

Decca   8563   USA   10 Inch 78
     [Issued as shown here and also as in the next listing below.]
     1150   CORRINE, CORRINA
     1160   LONESOME GRAVEYARD BLUES

Decca   8563   USA   10 Inch 78
     [Issued as shown here and also as in the preceding listing above.]
     1150   CORRINE, CORRINA
     1161   LONESOME GRAVEYARD BLUES

Decca   8577   USA   10 Inch 78
     [Issued as shown here and also as in the next listing below.]
     1130   LUCILLE
     1140   ROCK ME MAMA

Decca   8577   USA   10 Inch 78
     [Issued as shown here and also as in the preceding listing above.]
     1131   LUCILLE
     1140   ROCK ME MAMA

Decca   18049   USA   10 Inch 78
     [Part of 3-record set 126]
     0840   ELEGIE
     0850   HUMORESQUE

Decca   18050   USA   10 Inch 78
     [Part of 3-record set 126]
     0870   GET HAPPY
     0860   SWEET LORRAINE

Decca   18051   Can.   10 Inch 78

     0880   LULLABY OF THE LEAVES
     0890   TIGER RAG

```
Decca                             18051         USA      10 Inch 78
   [Part of 3-record set 126]
      0880  LULLABY OF THE LEAVES
      0890  TIGER RAG


Decca                             25199         USA      10 Inch 78
   [Part of 4-record set A-585.]
      0840  ELEGIE
      0850  HUMORESQUE


Decca                             25200         USA      10 Inch 78
   [Part of 4-record set A-585.]
      0870  GET HAPPY
      0860  SWEET LORRAINE


Decca                             25201         USA      10 Inch 78
   [Part of 4-record set A-585.]
      0880  LULLABY OF THE LEAVES
      0890  TIGER RAG


Decca                             25202         USA      10 Inch 78
   [Part of 4-record set A-585.]
      0940  COCKTAILS FOR TWO
      0910  EMALINE


Decca                             29924         USA      10 Inch 78

      1150  CORRINE, CORRINA


Decca                             48062         USA      10 Inch 78

      1150  CORRINE, CORRINA
      1050  WEE BABY BLUES


Decca                             60.060        Belg.    10 Inch 78

      0870  GET HAPPY
      0860  SWEET LORRAINE


Decca                             60.516        Belg.    10 Inch 78

      0751  DEEP PURPLE
      0740  TEA FOR TWO


Decca                             91573         USA       7 Inch 45E
   [Part of 2-record set ED 713.]
      0840  ELEGIE
      0870  GET HAPPY
      0850  HUMORESQUE
      0860  SWEET LORRAINE


Decca                             91574         USA       7 Inch 45E
   [Part of 2-record set ED 713.]
      0940  COCKTAILS FOR TWO
      0910  EMALINE
      0880  LULLABY OF THE LEAVES
      0890  TIGER RAG


Decca                             9-304         USA
   [4-record boxed set containing 9-25199,9-25200,9-25201,9-25202.]


Decca                             9-25199       USA       7 Inch 45
   [Part of 4-record boxed set 9-304.]
```

```
          0840   ELEGIE
          0850   HUMORESQUE


Decca                                 9-25200        USA       7 Inch 45
     [Part of 4-record boxed set 9-304.]
          0870   GET HAPPY
          0860   SWEET LORRAINE


Decca                                 9-25201        USA       7 Inch 45
     [Part of 4-record boxed set 9-304.]
          0880   LULLABY OF THE LEAVES
          0890   TIGER RAG


Decca                                 9-25202        USA       7 Inch 45
     [Part of 4-record boxed set 9-304.]
          0940   COCKTAILS FOR TWO
          0910   EMALINE


Decca                                 A-585          USA
     [4-record set containing 25199,25200,25201,25202.]


Decca                                 BM 01203       Eng.      10 Inch 78

          0230   ILL WIND
          0211   STAR DUST


Decca                                 BM 01204       Eng.      10 Inch 78

          0200   AFTER YOU'VE GONE
          0170   EMALINE


Decca                                 BM 01232       Eng.      10 Inch 78

          0460   GONE WITH THE WIND
          0470   STORMY WEATHER


Decca                                 BM 02518       Eng.      10 Inch 78

          0420   BODY AND SOUL
          0450   I'VE GOT MY LOVE TO KEEP ME WARM


Decca                                 BM 02591       Eng.      10 Inch 78

          0480   CHLOE
          0490   SHEIK OF ARABY, THE


Decca                                 BM 03121       Eng.      10 Inch 78

          0960   BEGIN THE BEGUINE
          0950   ST. LOUIS BLUES


Decca                                 BM 03462       Eng.      10 Inch 78

          1160   LONESOME GRAVEYARD BLUES


Decca                                 DL5086         USA       10 Inch LP

          0940   COCKTAILS FOR TWO
          0840   ELEGIE
          0910   EMALINE
          0870   GET HAPPY
          0850   HUMORESQUE
          0880   LULLABY OF THE LEAVES
```

191

```
          0860   SWEET LORRAINE
          0890   TIGER RAG


Decca                                   DL8385        USA      12 Inch LP

          1050   WEE BABY BLUES


Decca                                   DL8400        USA      12 Inch LP

          1050   WEE BABY BLUES


Decca                                   DL8715        USA      12 Inch LP

          0940   COCKTAILS FOR TWO
          0840   ELEGIE
          0910   EMALINE
          0870   GET HAPPY
          0850   HUMORESQUE
          1460   I WOULD DO ANYTHING FOR YOU
          0980   INDIANA
          0930   LOVE ME
          0880   LULLABY OF THE LEAVES
          1440   MOONGLOW
          0860   SWEET LORRAINE
          0890   TIGER RAG


Decca                                   DL78385       USA      12 Inch LP

          1050   WEE BABY BLUES


Decca                                   DXF140        USA      12 Inch LP

          1050   WEE BABY BLUES


Decca                                   DXSF140       USA
     [4-record set containing DL78385.]


Decca                                   ED 713        USA
     [2-record set containing 91573, 91574.]


Decca                                   F 8059        Eng.     10 Inch 78

          1080   BATTERY BOUNCE
          1050   WEE BABY BLUES


Decca                                   F 8069        Eng.     10 Inch 78

          0460   GONE WITH THE WIND
          0470   STORMY WEATHER


Decca                                   JDL 6025      Jap.     12 Inch LP

          1050   WEE BABY BLUES


Decca                                   M.30777       Eng.     10 Inch 78

          0190   COCKTAILS FOR TWO
          0170   EMALINE


Decca                                   M.39029       Eng.     10 Inch 78

          0440   WHAT WILL I TELL MY HEART
          0430   WITH PLENTY OF MONEY AND YOU
```

```
Decca                            MU-60515      Fr.     10 Inch 78

    0970   ROSETTA
    0890   TIGER RAG


Decca                            MU-60516      Fr.     10 Inch 78
    [Issued as shown here and also as in the next listing below.]
    0750   DEEP PURPLE
    0740   TEA FOR TWO


Decca                            MU-60516      Fr.     10 Inch 78
    [Issued as shown here and also as in the preceding listing above.]
    0751   DEEP PURPLE
    0740   TEA FOR TWO


Decca                            MU-60517      Fr.     10 Inch 78

    0480   CHLOE
    0490   SHEIK OF ARABY, THE


Decca                            MU-60524      Fr.     10 Inch 78

    0980   INDIANA


Decca                            PD 12005      Ger.    12 Inch LP

    1610   BLUES
    1740   FLYING HOME
    2180   I CAN'T GIVE YOU ANYTHING BUT LOVE
    1540   MOP-MOP
    1720   MY IDEAL


Decca                            PD 12006      Ger.    12 Inch LP

    1550   DO NOTHIN' TILL YOU HEAR FROM ME
    1560   I LOVE MY MAN
    1650   I'LL GET BY


Decca                            PD-12008      Ger.    12 Inch LP

    1670   BACK O' TOWN BLUES
    1640   BASIN STREET BLUES
    1580   I GOTTA RIGHT TO SING THE BLUES


Decca                            Y5165         Astla   10 Inch 78

    0420   BODY AND SOUL
    0440   WHAT WILL I TELL MY HEART


Decca                            Y5168         Astla   10 Inch 78

    0450   I'VE GOT MY LOVE TO KEEP ME WARM
    0430   WITH PLENTY OF MONEY AND YOU


Decca                            Y5206         Astla   10 Inch 78

    0460   GONE WITH THE WIND
    0470   STORMY WEATHER


Decca                            Y5562         Astla   10 Inch 78

    0880   LULLABY OF THE LEAVES
    0890   TIGER RAG
```

```
Decca                              Y5892        Astla   10 Inch 78

    1080   BATTERY BOUNCE
    1050   WEE BABY BLUES


Decca                              Y6088        Astla   10 Inch 78

    0870   GET HAPPY
    0860   SWEET LORRAINE


Dial                               1036         USA     10 Inch 78EP

    1850   I KNOW THAT YOU KNOW
    1820   MAN I LOVE, THE


Dial                               1046         USA     10 Inch 78EP

    1840   BODY AND SOUL
    1870   FLYING HOME


Dial                               LP206        USA     10 Inch LP

    1840   BODY AND SOUL
    1830   DARK EYES
    1870   FLYING HOME
    1850   I KNOW THAT YOU KNOW
    1820   MAN I LOVE, THE
    1860   ON THE SUNNY SIDE OF THE STREET


Dick James Music          (See "DJM")


Discomania                         101          Jap.    12 Inch LP

    1640   BASIN STREET BLUES
    1740   FLYING HOME
    1540   MOP-MOP


Discophon                          (S) 4174     Span. s 12 Inch LP

    0790   DAY IN - DAY OUT
    0800   FINE AND DANDY
    0820   I GOTTA RIGHT TO SING THE BLUES
    0830   I'M COMING VIRGINIA
    0810   I'VE GOT THE WORLD ON A STRING


EMI                                CRLM 1044    Eng.
  [See Coral CP62]


Elec                               KV-401       Jap.    12 Inch LP
  [3-record set.]
    1670   BACK O' TOWN BLUES
    1640   BASIN STREET BLUES
    1610   BLUES
    1690   BUCK JUMPIN'
    1550   DO NOTHIN' TILL YOU HEAR FROM ME
    1530   ESQUIRE BLUES
    1630   ESQUIRE BOUNCE
    1740   FLYING HOME
    1710   FOR BASS FACES ONLY
    1570   I CAN'T GIVE YOU ANYTHING BUT LOVE
    1600   I GOT RHYTHM
    1580   I GOTTA RIGHT TO SING THE BLUES
    1650   I'LL GET BY
    1560   I LOVE MY MAN (Billie's Blues)
    1750   JAMMIN' THE VIBES (Vibe Blues)
    1540   MOP-MOP
```

194

```
1680  MUSKRAT RAMBLE
1720  MY IDEAL
1730  ROSE ROOM
1700  STOMPIN´ AT THE SAVOY
1590  SWEET LORRAINE
1660  TEA FOR TWO
1665  THEME FOR COCA-COLA/CONCLUSION
1620  THEME FOR COCA-COLA/INTRODUCTIONS(Spotlight Band Theme)
```

Ember   CJS848   Eng.   12 Inch LP

```
2430  AMONG MY SOUVENIRS
2410  CAN´T WE BE FRIENDS
0790  DAY IN - DAY OUT
0800  FINE AND DANDY
2180  I CAN´T GIVE YOU ANYTHING BUT LOVE
2540  I GOTTA RIGHT TO SING THE BLUES
0780  INDIANA
2420  LIMEHOUSE BLUES
2550  ON THE SUNNY SIDE OF THE STREET
0770  SWEET EMALINA, MY GAL
2490  TEA FOR TWO
```

Ember   EMB3314   Eng.   12 Inch LP

```
5360  BEGIN THE BEGUINE
5380  BODY AND SOUL
5410  DANNY BOY
5450  I´LL NEVER BE THE SAME
5470  LITTLE MAN, YOU´VE HAD A BUSY DAY
5370  SOMEONE TO WATCH OVER ME
5420  TENDERLY
5400  TOO MARVELOUS FOR WORDS
5390  WILLOW WEEP FOR ME
5460  WITHOUT A SONG
5440  YESTERDAYS
5430  YOU TOOK ADVANTAGE OF ME
```

Ember   EMB3326   Eng.   12 Inch LP

```
5570  DON´T BLAME ME
5550  I COVER THE WATERFRONT
5510  IN A SENTIMENTAL MOOD
5490  JITTERBUG WALTZ
3290  MEMORIES OF YOU
5560  MOON SONG
3280  MR. FREDDIE BLUES
5480  MY HEART STOOD STILL
5500  OVER THE RAINBOW
5530  SEPTEMBER SONG
5520  THERE WILL NEVER BE ANOTHER YOU
5540  WRAP YOUR TROUBLES IN DREAMS
```

Ember   EMB4502   Eng.   7 Inch 45EP

```
5570  DON´T BLAME ME
3290  MEMORIES OF YOU
5500  OVER THE RAINBOW
5530  SEPTEMBER SONG
```

Emigold   DAG125   Holl.   12 Inch LP

```
3080  AUNT HAGAR´S BLUES
3220  BLUE SKIES
3240  DANCING IN THE DARK
3110  DARDANELLA
3150  DON´T BLAME ME
3070  I COVER THE WATERFRONT
3180  I GOTTA RIGHT TO SING THE BLUES
3230  IT´S THE TALK OF THE TOWN
```

3160	MY HEART STOOD STILL			
3090	NICE WORK IF YOU CAN GET IT			
3140	SOMEBODY LOVES ME			
3100	SOMEONE TO WATCH OVER ME			
3130	SWEET LORRAINE			
3120	TIME ON MY HANDS			
3060	WILLOW WEEP FOR ME			
3170	YOU TOOK ADVANTAGE OF ME			

Epic   LA-16000   USA   12 Inch LP

        0080   SOPHISTICATED LADY

Epic   LN3295   USA   12 Inch LP

        0080   SOPHISTICATED LADY
        0050   TEA FOR TWO
        0070   TIGER RAG

Epic   LN 24028   USA   12 Inch LP
  [Part of 4-record boxed set SN 6042.]
        0080   SOPHISTICATED LADY
        0050   TEA FOR TWO

Epic   SN 6042   USA
  [4-record boxed set containing LN 24028.]

Epitaph   E-4006   USA   12 Inch LP

        0130   CHINATOWN, MY CHINATOWN
        2540   I GOTTA RIGHT TO SING THE BLUES
        2480   IF I COULD BE WITH YOU
        2510   IT'S ONLY A PAPER MOON
        2520   JUST A GIGOLO
        3300   MAN I LOVE, THE (Gershwin Medley)
        2500   MEAN TO ME
        0100   MORNING, NOON, AND NIGHT
        2460   SOMEBODY LOVES ME
        0120   STAR DUST
        3370   TABOO
        2490   TEA FOR TWO
        2530   THREE LITTLE WORDS
        0110   WHEN DAY IS DONE
        2470   WHY WAS I BORN
        0090   YOUNG AND HEALTHY

Esquire   10-156   Eng.   10 Inch 78E

        1850   I KNOW THAT YOU KNOW
        1820   MAN I LOVE, THE

Esquire Jazz Book,   (Unnumbered)   USA   8 Inch 78

        0950   ST. LOUIS BLUES

Europa Jazz   EJ-1011   It.   12 Inch LP

        2760   ART'S BLUES
        2354   I'M BEGINNING TO SEE THE LIGHT
        5870   SOFT WINDS
        1590   SWEET LORRAINE

Everest   FS-265   USA   12 Inch LP

        1550   DO NOTHIN' TILL YOU HEAR FROM ME

```
Explosive                           528012        Fr.      12 Inch LP

     1830   DARK EYES
     1870   FLYING HOME
     1850   I KNOW THAT YOU KNOW
     1820   MAN I LOVE, THE
     1860   ON THE SUNNY SIDE OF THE STREET


Extreme Rarities                    ER-1002       USA      12 Inch LP
   [Record jacket has LP 1002 instead.]
     2760   ART'S BLUES


Extreme Rarities                    LP 1002       USA
   [See ER-1002.]


FDC                              (See "For Discriminate Collector")


Festival                            100.100       Fr.      12 Inch LP
   [Part of 2-record set ALBUM 144.]
     1550   DO NOTHIN' TILL YOU HEAR FROM ME


Festival                            100.101       Fr.      12 Inch LP
   [Part of 2-record set ALBUM 144.]
     1560   I LOVE MY MAN
     1650   I'LL GET BY


Festival                            100.350       Fr.      12 Inch LP
   [Part of 2-record set ALBUM 269.]
     1640   BASIN STREET BLUES
     1610   BLUES
     1550   DO NOTHIN' TILL YOU HEAR FROM ME
     1530   ESQUIRE BLUES (Incorrectly titled "Esquire Bounce")
     1570   I CAN'T GIVE YOU ANYTHING BUT LOVE
     1600   I GOT RHYTHM
     1580   I GOTTA RIGHT TO SING THE BLUES
     1560   I LOVE MY MAN (Billie's Blues)
     1650   I'LL GET BY
     1540   MOP-MOP
     1590   SWEET LORRAINE


Festival                            100.351       Fr.      12 Inch LP
   [Part of 2-record set ALBUM 269.]
     1670   BACK O' TOWN BLUES
     1690   BUCK JUMPIN'
     1740   FLYING HOME (Titled "Flying On")
     1710   FOR BASS FACES ONLY
     1680   MUSKRAT RAMBLE
     1720   MY IDEAL
     1730   ROSE ROOM
     1700   STOMPIN' AT THE SAVOY
     1660   TEA FOR TWO


Festival                            ALBUM 144     Fr.
   [2-record set containing 100.100,100.101.]


Festival                            ALBUM 269     Fr.
   [2-record set containing 100.350,100.351.]


Festival                            CFR10 506     Astla    10 Inch LP

     0940   COCKTAILS FOR TWO
     0840   ELEGIE
     0910   EMALINE
     0870   GET HAPPY
     0850   HUMORESQUE
```

```
          0880   LULLABY OF THE LEAVES
          0860   SWEET LORRAINE
          0890   TIGER RAG


Festival                        CFR10 648      Astla    10 Inch LP

          0960   BEGIN THE BEGUINE
          1410   COCKTAILS FOR TWO
          0460   GONE WITH THE WIND
          1490   HONEYSUCKLE ROSE
          1400   I GOT RHYTHM
          1440   MOONGLOW
          0950   ST. LOUIS BLUES
          0740   TEA FOR TWO


Festival                        XP 45 658      Astla    7 Inch 45E

          1430   AFTER YOU´VE GONE
          1450   DEEP PURPLE
          0970   ROSETTA
          0470   STORMY WEATHER


Folkways                        FJ2293         USA      10 Inch LP

          1900   BOOGIE (Rehearsal excerpt titled "Long, Long Ago")
          1910   BOOGIE (Rehearsal excerpt titled "Variations On a Theme
                    By Flotow")
          1920   IF I HAD YOU (Rehearsal excerpt)
          1921   IF I HAD YOU (Rehearsal excerpt)
          1930   JAPANESE SANDMAN, THE (Warm Up With Sandman)
                 LONG, LONG AGO (See "Boogie," [1900])
          1940   SOFT WINDS (Rehearsal excerpt titled "Thou Swell")
          1941   SOFT WINDS (Rehearsal excerpt titled "Thou Swell")
          1942   SOFT WINDS (Rehearsal excerpt titled "Thou Swell")
                 VARIATIONS ON A THEME BY FLOTOW (See "Boogie," [1910])


Folkways                        FJ2852         USA      12 Inch LP

          2080   DANNY BOY
          2031   FINE AND DANDY
          2040   IT HAD TO BE YOU
          2050   JA-DA
          2060   WHERE OR WHEN


Folkways                        FJ2893         USA      12 Inch LP

          1900   BOOGIE (Rehearsal excerpt titled "Long, Long Ago")
          1910   BOOGIE (Rehearsal excerpt titled "Variations On a Theme
                    By Flotow")
          1920   IF I HAD YOU (Rehearsal excerpt)
          1921   IF I HAD YOU (Rehearsal excerpt)
          1930   JAPANESE SANDMAN, THE (Warm Up With Sandman)
                 LONG, LONG AGO (See "Boogie," [1900])
          1940   SOFT WINDS (Rehearsal excerpt titled "Thou Swell")
          1941   SOFT WINDS (Rehearsal excerpt titled "Thou Swell")
          1942   SOFT WINDS (Rehearsal excerpt titled "Thou Swell")
                 VARIATIONS ON A THEME BY FLOTOW (See "Boogie," [1910])


Folkways                        FJ12293        USA      12 Inch LP

          1900   BOOGIE (Rehearsal excerpt titled "Long, Long Ago")
          1910   BOOGIE (Rehearsal excerpt titled "Variations On a Theme
                    By Flotow")
          1920   IF I HAD YOU (Rehearsal excerpt)
          1921   IF I HAD YOU (Rehearsal excerpt)
          1930   JAPANESE SANDMAN, THE (Warm Up With Sandman)
                 LONG, LONG AGO (See "Boogie," [1900])
          1940   SOFT WINDS (Rehearsal excerpt titled "Thou Swell")
          1941   SOFT WINDS (Rehearsal excerpt titled "Thou Swell")
```

```
     1942  SOFT WINDS (Rehearsal excerpt titled "Thou Swell")
           VARIATIONS ON A THEME BY FLOTOW (See "Boogie," [1910])


Folkways                          FP 33          USA      10 Inch LP

     1900  BOOGIE (Rehearsal excerpt titled "Long, Long Ago")
     1910  BOOGIE (Rehearsal excerpt titled "Variations On a Theme
                   By Flotow")
     1920  IF I HAD YOU (Rehearsal excerpt)
     1921  IF I HAD YOU (Rehearsal excerpt)
     1930  JAPANESE SANDMAN, THE (Warm Up With Sandman)
           LONG, LONG AGO (See "Boogie," [1900])
     1940  SOFT WINDS (Rehearsal excerpt titled "Thou Swell")
     1941  SOFT WINDS (Rehearsal excerpt titled "Thou Swell")
     1942  SOFT WINDS (Rehearsal excerpt titled "Thou Swell")
           VARIATIONS ON A THEME BY FLOTOW (See "Boogie," [1910])


Fonit                             8001           It.      12 Inch LP

     1840  BODY AND SOUL
     1830  DARK EYES
     1870  FLYING HOME
     1850  I KNOW THAT YOU KNOW
     1860  ON THE SUNNY SIDE OF THE STREET


Fontana                           467111TE       Eur.     12 Inch LP

     2960  HUMORESQUE
     3030  KERRY DANCE, THE
     3010  WILLOW WEEP FOR ME
     2990  YESTERDAYS


Fontana                           883 904JCY     Holl.    12 Inch LP

     2620  APOLLO BOOGIE
     2650  BETWEEN MIDNIGHT AND DAWN
     2600  CRYSTAL CLEAR
     2580  FIFTY SECOND STREET BLUES*
     2570  GANG O´ NOTES
     2590  JUST BEFORE DAWN*
     2610  MIDNIGHT MELODY, A*
     2660  PLAYING IN RIDDLES*
     2640  THIS AND THAT*
     2630  TOO SHARP FOR THIS FLAT*
           *Not believed to be Tatum.  See Chronological Discography.


Fontana                           9286 307       It.      12 Inch LP

     5360  BEGIN THE BEGUINE
     5380  BODY AND SOUL
     5450  I´LL NEVER BE THE SAME
     5370  SOMEONE TO WATCH OVER ME
     5420  TENDERLY
     5400  TOO MARVELOUS FOR WORDS
     5390  WILLOW WEEP FOR ME
     5460  WITHOUT A SONG
     5440  YESTERDAYS
     5430  YOU TOOK ADVANTAGE OF ME


Fontana                           FJL.904        Eng.     12 Inch LP

     2620  APOLLO BOOGIE
     2650  BETWEEN MIDNIGHT AND DAWN
     2600  CRYSTAL CLEAR
     2580  FIFTY SECOND STREET BLUES*
     2570  GANG O´ NOTES
     2590  JUST BEFORE DAWN*
     2610  MIDNIGHT MELODY, A*
     2660  PLAYING IN RIDDLES*
```

```
        2640   THIS AND THAT*
        2630   TOO SHARP FOR THIS FLAT*
               *Not believed to be Tatum.  See Chronological Discography.


Fontana                              LPU8001        It.    12 Inch LP

        1830   DARK EYES
        1870   FLYING HOME
        1850   I KNOW THAT YOU KNOW
        1820   MAN I LOVE, THE


Fontana                              R47121         Eur.   12 Inch LP

        3010   WILLOW WEEP FOR ME


Fontana                              TFE.17235      Eng.   7 Inch 45EP

        2980   SOMEONE TO WATCH OVER ME
        0080   SOPHISTICATED LADY
        0050   TEA FOR TWO
        0070   TIGER RAG


Fontana                              TFE.17236      Eng.   7 Inch 45EP

        3020   GERSHWIN MEDLEY
        2950   HOW HIGH THE MOON
        3000   I KNOW THAT YOU KNOW
        2970   TATUM-POLE BOOGIE


Fontana                              TFE.17237      Eng.   7 Inch 45EP

        2960   HUMORESQUE
        3030   KERRY DANCE, THE
        3010   WILLOW WEEP FOR ME
        2990   YESTERDAYS


Fontana                              TL5273         Eng.   12 Inch LP

        1351   ESQUIRE BLUES
        1320   ESQUIRE BOUNCE
        1331   MOP-MOP (Also called Boff-Boff)
        1340   MY IDEAL


Fontana                              TL5294         Eng.   12 Inch LP

        1351   ESQUIRE BLUES


For Discriminate Collector           FDC1001        It.    12 Inch LP
     [This was later reissued in Denmark with the same number.]
        1670   BACK O´ TOWN BLUES
        1640   BASIN STREET BLUES
        1610   BLUES
        1630   ESQUIRE BOUNCE
        1740   FLYING HOME
        1560   I LOVE MY MAN
        1540   MOP-MOP
        1720   MY IDEAL
        1730   ROSE ROOM
        1660   TEA FOR TWO


For Discriminate Collector           FDC1007        It.    12 Inch LP

        1690   BUCK JUMPIN´
        1550   DO NOTHIN´ TILL YOU HEAR FROM ME
        1530   ESQUIRE BLUES
        1570   I CAN´T GIVE YOU ANYTHING BUT LOVE
```

```
       1600  I GOT RHYTHM
       1580  I GOTTA RIGHT TO SING THE BLUES
       1650  I'LL GET BY
       1620  THEME FOR COCA-COLA/INTRODUCTIONS


For Discriminate Collector        FDC1008/1009    It.
  [2-record set containing FDC1009.]


For Discriminate Collector        FDC1009         It.   12 Inch LP
  [Part of 2-record set containing FDC1008/1009.]
       2180  I CAN'T GIVE YOU ANYTHING BUT LOVE
       2170  MAN I LOVE, THE


For Discriminate Collector        FDC1010         It.   12 Inch LP

       1710  FOR BASS FACES ONLY
       1680  MUSKRAT RAMBLE
       1700  STOMPIN' AT THE SAVOY
       1590  SWEET LORRAINE
       1750  VIBE DUET (Vibe Blues)


Forum                             F-9056          USA   12 Inch LP

       1870  FLYING HOME


Freedom                           BLP30.124       Fr.   12 Inch LP

       2620  APOLLO BOOGIE
       2650  BETWEEN MIDNIGHT AND DAWN
       2580  FIFTY SECOND STREET BLUES*
       2570  GANG O' NOTES
       2191  HALLELUJAH
       2590  JUST BEFORE DAWN*
       2260  KERRY DANCE, THE (Incorrectly titled "Henry Dance")
       2230  MEMORIES OF YOU
       2610  MIDNIGHT MELODY, A*
       2200  POOR BUTTERFLY
       2240  RUNNIN' WILD
       2210  SONG OF THE VAGABONDS
             *Not believed to be Tatum.  See Chronological Discography.


Freedom                           BLP30166        Fr.   12 Inch LP

       2000  AIN'T MISBEHAVIN'
       2190  HALLELUJAH
       2191  HALLELUJAH
       1986  I GOT RHYTHM
       3260  I GOTTA RIGHT TO SING THE BLUES
       2260  KERRY DANCE, THE
       2220  LOVER
       2230  MEMORIES OF YOU
       2200  POOR BUTTERFLY
       3250  POOR BUTTERFLY
       1984  ROYAL GARDEN BLUES
       2240  RUNNIN' WILD
       2210  SONG OF THE VAGABONDS
       3270  TABOO
       1480  TEA FOR TWO
       2250  YESTERDAYS


Freedom                           FR.11007        Fr.   12 Inch LP

       2270  BEGIN THE BEGUINE
       2350  BODY AND SOUL
       2320  GERSHWIN MEDLEY
       2354  I'M BEGINNING TO SEE THE LIGHT
       2720  INDIANA
       1470  LIZA
```

```
            2340  LOVER
            2355  NINE TWENTY SPECIAL
            2710  POOR BUTTERFLY
            2330  SHE'S FUNNY THAT WAY
            2690  SONG OF THE VAGABONDS
            1590  SWEET LORRAINE
            2680  WHERE OR WHEN
```

GNP Crescendo   GNP9025*   USA   12 Inch LP

```
            2370  BODY AND SOUL
            2540  I GOTTA RIGHT TO SING THE BLUES
            2380  I GUESS I'LL HAVE TO CHANGE MY PLANS
            2480  IF I COULD BE WITH YOU
            2510  IT'S ONLY A PAPER MOON
            2520  JUST A GIGOLO
            2500  MEAN TO ME
            2550  ON THE SUNNY SIDE OF THE STREET
            2460  SOMEBODY LOVES ME
            2530  THREE LITTLE WORDS
            2470  WHY WAS I BORN
            2360  YOU TOOK ADVANTAGE OF ME
                  *Applause has been dubbed onto these performances.
```

GNP Crescendo   GNP9026*   USA   12 Inch LP

```
            0760  ALL GOD'S CHILLUN GOT RHYTHM
            2430  AMONG MY SOUVENIRS
            2410  CAN'T WE BE FRIENDS
            2400  CRAZY RHYTHM
            0800  FINE AND DANDY
            0820  I GOTTA RIGHT TO SING THE BLUES
            0830  I'M COMING VIRGINIA
            2440  I'M GONNA SIT RIGHT DOWN AND WRITE MYSELF A LETTER
            0810  I'VE GOT THE WORLD ON A STRING
            2420  LIMEHOUSE BLUES
            2450  STAY AS SWEET AS YOU ARE
            2390  WHAT IS THIS THING CALLED LOVE
                  *Applause has been dubbed onto these performances.
```

GNP Crescendo   LAX-3088*   Jap.   12 Inch LP

```
            2370  BODY AND SOUL
            2540  I GOTTA RIGHT TO SING THE BLUES
            2380  I GUESS I'LL HAVE TO CHANGE MY PLANS
            2480  IF I COULD BE WITH YOU
            2510  IT'S ONLY A PAPER MOON
            2520  JUST A GIGOLO
            2500  MEAN TO ME
            2550  ON THE SUNNY SIDE OF THE STREET
            2460  SOMEBODY LOVES ME
            2530  THREE LITTLE WORDS
            2470  WHY WAS I BORN
            2360  YOU TOOK ADVANTAGE OF ME
                  *Applause has been dubbed onto these performances.
```

GNP Crescendo   LAX-3089*   Jap.   12 Inch LP

```
            0760  ALL GOD'S CHILLUN GOT RHYTHM
            2430  AMONG MY SOUVENIRS
            2410  CAN'T WE BE FRIENDS
            2400  CRAZY RHYTHM
            0800  FINE AND DANDY
            0820  I GOTTA RIGHT TO SING THE BLUES
            0830  I'M COMING VIRGINIA
            2440  I'M GONNA SIT RIGHT DOWN AND WRITE MYSELF A LETTER
            0810  I'VE GOT THE WORLD ON A STRING
            2420  LIMEHOUSE BLUES
            2450  STAY AS SWEET AS YOU ARE
            2390  WHAT IS THIS THING CALLED LOVE
                  *Applause has been dubbed onto these performances.
```

```
Gazell                          2033              Swed.    10 Inch 78

    1986   I GOT RHYTHM
    1984   ROYAL GARDEN BLUES


Giants of Jazz                  GOJ-1015          USA      12 Inch LP

    5350   FINE AND DANDY
    3440   HOW HIGH THE MOON
    3430   MY HEART STOOD STILL
    5630   MY HEART STOOD STILL
    6110   SEPTEMBER SONG
    5610   SOMEONE TO WATCH OVER ME
    5340   SWEET LORRAINE
    6100   SWEET LORRAINE
    5320   TEA FOR TWO
    5620   THIS CAN'T BE LOVE


Giants of Jazz                  GOJ-1018          USA      12 Inch LP

    2270   BEGIN THE BEGUINE
    2280   CHEROKEE


Golden Tone                     C-4068            USA      12 Inch LP

    2090   CAN'T HELP LOVIN' DAT MAN OF MINE


Gotham,
    Mastered Works of 1951      (Unnumbered)      USA      12 Inch TX

    3410   BODY AND SOUL (Last 2 choruses only)


Guest Star                      G1403             USA      12 Inch LP

    1830   DARK EYES
    1860   ON THE SUNNY SIDE OF THE STREET


Guest Star                      GS1403            USA    s 12 Inch LP

    1830   DARK EYES
    1860   ON THE SUNNY SIDE OF THE STREET


Guild                           (See Rem Hollywood)


Guilde du Jazz                  J701              Fr.       7 Inch 33EP

    1870   FLYING HOME
    1850   I KNOW THAT YOU KNOW
    1820   MAN I LOVE, THE
    1860   ON THE SUNNY SIDE OF THE STREET


Hall of Fame                    JG-607            USA      12 Inch LP

    1830   DARK EYES
    1870   FLYING HOME
    1850   I KNOW THAT YOU KNOW
    1820   MAN I LOVE, THE
    1860   ON THE SUNNY SIDE OF THE STREET


Harlem Hit Parade               HHP5011           USA      12 Inch LP

    2100   PLEASE DON'T TALK ABOUT ME WHEN I'M GONE
```

```
Harmony                          HL7006*         USA    12 Inch LP

   3020   GERSHWIN MEDLEY (Titled "The Man I Love")
   2950   HOW HIGH THE MOON
   2960   HUMORESQUE
   3000   I KNOW THAT YOU KNOW
   3030   KERRY DANCE, THE
   2980   SOMEONE TO WATCH OVER ME
   2970   TATUM-POLE BOOGIE
   3010   WILLOW WEEP FOR ME
   2990   YESTERDAYS
          *Cover photo shows the hands of a white pianist!


His Master's Voice               7EG 8074        Eng.    7 Inch 45EP

   2790   OUT OF NOWHERE


His Master's Voice               7EG 8604        Eng.    7 Inch 45EP

   4980   HAPPY FEET
   4750   ISN'T IT ROMANTIC
   5020   MOON SONG
   5010   MOONLIGHT ON THE GANGES


His Master's Voice               7EG 8619        Eng.    7 Inch 45EP

   6070   FOGGY DAY, A
   6080   LOVER MAN
   6090   MAKIN' WHOOPEE


His Master's Voice               7EG 8684        Eng.    7 Inch 45EP

   5170   I ONLY HAVE EYES FOR YOU
   4970   I SURRENDER DEAR
   5050   IF I HAD YOU
   5030   WHEN YOUR LOVER HAS GONE


His Master's Voice               DLP1022         Eng.   10 Inch LP

   2800   CHEROKEE


His Master's Voice               JK2617          Swiss  10 Inch 78

   2800   CHEROKEE
   2790   OUT OF NOWHERE


His Master's Voice               LCLP 207        Span.  12 Inch LP

   6190   GONE WITH THE WIND
   6200   HAVE YOU MET MISS JONES
   6180   MY IDEAL
   6170   MY ONE AND ONLY LOVE
   6210   NIGHT AND DAY
   6220   WHERE OR WHEN


Intercord Black Lion             147.000*        Ger.   12 Inch LP

   2000   AIN'T MISBEHAVIN'
   2190   HALLELUJAH
   2191   HALLELUJAH
   1986   I GOT RHYTHM
   3260   I GOTTA RIGHT TO SING THE BLUES
   2260   KERRY DANCE, THE
   2220   LOVER
   2230   MEMORIES OF YOU
   2200   POOR BUTTERFLY
   3250   POOR BUTTERFLY
```

```
       1984   ROYAL GARDEN BLUES
       2240   RUNNIN' WILD
       2210   SONG OF THE VAGABONDS
       3270   TABOO
       1480   TEA FOR TWO
       2250   YESTERDAYS
              *Number on jacket only is INT.147.000.


Intercord Black Lion            28 440-6 U      Ger.     12 Inch LP

       2620   APOLLO BOOGIE
       2650   BETWEEN MIDNIGHT AND DAWN
       2580   FIFTY SECOND STREET BLUES*
       2570   GANG O' NOTES
       2191   HALLELUJAH
       2590   JUST BEFORE DAWN*
       2260   KERRY DANCE, THE
       2230   MEMORIES OF YOU
       2610   MIDNIGHT MELODY, A*
       2200   POOR BUTTERFLY
       2240   RUNNIN' WILD
       2210   SONG OF THE VAGABONDS
              *Not believed to be Tatum.  See Chronological Discography.


Intercord                       INT.147.000  (See 147.000)


Intercord Xanadu                INT.197.105     Ger.     12 Inch LP

       1020   ALL THE THINGS YOU ARE


Jazz Anthology                  JA5102          Fr.      12 Inch LP

       1670   BACK O' TOWN BLUES
       1640   BASIN STREET BLUES
       1740   FLYING ON (Flying Home)
       1540   MOP-MOP
       1730   ROSE ROOM


Jazz Anthology                  JA5111          Fr.      12 Inch LP

       1000   BEAUTIFUL LOVE
       1120   BEGIN THE BEGUINE
       1200   BODY AND SOUL
       1110   FINE AND DANDY
       1090   GEORGIA ON MY MIND
       1010   LAUGHING AT LIFE
       1170   MIGHTY LAK A ROSE
       1250   OH! LADY BE GOOD
       1260   SWEET GEORGIA BROWN
       1100   SWEET LORRAINE
       1240   THERE'LL BE SOME CHANGES MADE


Jazz Anthology                  JA5138          Fr.      12 Inch LP

       5910   BODY AND SOUL
       5850   FLYING HOME
       6230   FLYING HOME
       6260   FLYING HOME
       5860   I COVER THE WATERFRONT
       6250   JUST ONE OF THOSE THINGS
       6240   MOON SONG
       5870   SOFT WINDS
       5890   TEA FOR TWO
       5880   TENDERLY
       6270   WOULD YOU LIKE TO TAKE A WALK
       5900   WRAP YOUR TROUBLES IN DREAMS
       6280   YOU GO TO MY HEAD
```

```
Jazz Anthology                    JA5146        Fr.     12 Inch LP

    1550   DO NOTHIN' TILL YOU HEAR FROM ME
    1530   ESQUIRE BLUES
    1710   FOR BASS FACES ONLY
    1570   I CAN'T GIVE YOU ANYTHING BUT LOVE
    1600   I GOT RHYTHM
    1650   I'LL GET BY
    1680   MUSKRAT RAMBLE
    1700   STOMPIN' AT THE SAVOY
    1590   SWEET LORRAINE
    1620   THEME FOR COCA-COLA/INTRODUCTIONS
    1750   VIBES DUET (Vibe Blues)


Jazz Anthology                    JA5177        Fr.     12 Inch LP

    0630   BODY AND SOUL
    0640   CAN'T WE BE FRIENDS
    0790   DAY IN - DAY OUT
    0620   ELEGIE
    0800   FINE AND DANDY
    0820   I GOTTA RIGHT TO SING THE BLUES
    0590   I'LL GET BY
    0600   I'LL NEVER BE THE SAME
    0830   I'M COMING VIRGINIA
    0810   I'VE GOT THE WORLD ON A STRING
    0610   JUDY
    0650   MAKE BELIEVE
    0580   SWEET LORRAINE


Jazz Anthology                    JA5208        Fr.     12 Inch LP

    1840   BODY AND SOUL
    1950   BOOGIE
    1830   DARK EYES
    1870   FLYING HOME
    1850   I KNOW THAT YOU KNOW
    1970   IF I HAD YOU
    1820   MAN I LOVE, THE
    1860   ON THE SUNNY SIDE OF THE STREET
    1980   SOFT WINDS
    1960   TOPSY


Jazz Anthology                    JA5218        Fr.     12 Inch LP

    2930   I'LL NEVER BE THE SAME
    2890   IN A SENTIMENTAL MOOD
    2910   IT'S THE TALK OF THE TOWN
    2940   NIGHT AND DAY
    2880   OVER THE RAINBOW
    2920   SHE'S FUNNY THAT WAY
    2850   SITTIN' AND ROCKIN'
    2870   TENDERLY
    2840   WRAP YOUR TROUBLES IN DREAMS
    2900   YOU TOOK ADVANTAGE OF ME
    2860   YOU'RE DRIVING ME CRAZY


Jazz Archives                     JA-40         USA     12 Inch LP

    0410   BOOTS AND SADDLE


Jazz Chronicles                   JCS 101       USA     12 Inch LP

    2930   I'LL NEVER BE THE SAME
    2890   IN A SENTIMENTAL MOOD
    2910   IT'S THE TALK OF THE TOWN
    2940   NIGHT AND DAY
    2880   OVER THE RAINBOW
    2920   SHE'S FUNNY THAT WAY
    2850   SITTIN' AND ROCKIN'
```

```
2870   TENDERLY
2840   WRAP YOUR TROUBLES IN DREAMS
2900   YOU TOOK ADVANTAGE OF ME
2860   YOU'RE DRIVING ME CRAZY
```

Jazz Man   JAZ-5024   USA   12 Inch LP

```
2620   APOLLO BOOGIE
2650   BETWEEN MIDNIGHT AND DAWN
2580   FIFTY SECOND STREET BLUES*
2570   GANG O' NOTES
2191   HALLELUJAH
2590   JUST BEFORE DAWN*
2260   KERRY DANCE, THE
2230   MEMORIES OF YOU
2610   MIDNIGHT MELODY, A*
2200   POOR BUTTERFLY
2240   RUNNIN' WILD
2210   SONG OF THE VAGABONDS
       *Not believed to be Tatum.  See Chronological Discography.
```

Jazz Panorama   JPLP15   Swed.   12 Inch LP

```
0290   AFTER YOU'VE GONE
0760   ALL GOD'S CHILLUN GOT RHYTHM
0280   BOOTS AND SADDLE
0400   DEVIL IN THE MOON
0300   DIXIELAND BAND
0390   I WISH I WERE TWINS
0350   I WOULD DO ANYTHING FOR YOU
0370   IN THE MIDDLE OF A KISS
0780   INDIANA
0340   MONDAY IN MANHATTAN
0380   ROSETTA
0330   STAY AS SWEET AS YOU ARE
0770   SWEET EMALINA, MY GAL
0310   SHOUT, THE
0360   THEME FOR PIANO
0320   TIGER RAG
```

Jazz Panorama   LP15   Swed.   12 Inch LP

```
0290   AFTER YOU'VE GONE
0760   ALL GOD'S CHILLUN GOT RHYTHM
0280   BOOTS AND SADDLE
0400   DEVIL IN THE MOON
0300   DIXIELAND BAND
0390   I WISH I WERE TWINS
0350   I WOULD DO ANYTHING FOR YOU
0370   IN THE MIDDLE OF A KISS
0780   INDIANA
0340   MONDAY IN MANHATTAN
0380   ROSETTA
0330   STAY AS SWEET AS YOU ARE
0770   SWEET EMALINA, MY GAL
0310   SHOUT, THE
0360   THEME FOR PIANO
0320   TIGER RAG
```

Jazz Piano   JP5005   Dan.   12 Inch LP

```
2430   AMONG MY SOUVENIRS
0630   BODY AND SOUL
0640   CAN'T WE BE FRIENDS
2400   CRAZY RHYTHM (Incorrectly titled "Chrzy Rhythm".)
0620   ELEGIE
2380   I GUESS I'LL HAVE TO CHANGE MY PLANS
0590   I'LL GET BY
0600   I'LL NEVER BE THE SAME
0610   JUDY
2420   LIMEHOUSE BLUES
0650   MAKE BELIEVE
```

```
          0580   SWEET LORRAINE
          2390   WHAT IS THIS THING CALLED LOVE
          2360   YOU TOOK ADVANTAGE OF ME


Jazz Selection                        655           Fr.      10 Inch 78

          2950   HOW HIGH THE MOON
          2960   HUMORESQUE


Jazz Selection                        656           Fr.      10 Inch 78

          2980   SOMEONE TO WATCH OVER ME
          2970   TATUM-POLE BOOGIE


Jazz Selection                        657           Fr.      10 Inch 78

          3000   I KNOW THAT YOU KNOW
          2990   YESTERDAYS


Jazz Selection                        658           Fr.      10 Inch 78

          3020   GERSHWIN MEDLEY
          3010   WILLOW WEEP FOR ME


Jazz Selection                        4051          Swed.    10 Inch 78

          3010   WILLOW WEEP FOR ME
          2990   YESTERDAYS


Jazz Series 4000FC                 JAZ4005*          It.      12 Inch LP

          2370   BODY AND SOUL
          2540   I GOTTA RIGHT TO SING THE BLUES
          2380   I GUESS I´LL HAVE TO CHANGE MY PLANS
          2480   IF I COULD BE WITH YOU
          2510   IT´S ONLY A PAPER MOON
          2520   JUST A GIGOLO
          2500   MEAN TO ME
          2550   ON THE SUNNY SIDE OF THE STREET
          2460   SOMEBODY LOVES ME
          2530   THREE LITTLE WORDS
          2470   WHY WAS I BORN
          2360   YOU TOOK ADVANTAGE OF ME
                 *Applause has been dubbed onto these performances.


Jazz Series 4000FC                 JAZ4006*          It.      12 Inch LP

          0760   ALL GOD´S CHILLUN GOT RHYTHM
          2430   AMONG MY SOUVENIRS
          2410   CAN´T WE BE FRIENDS
          2400   CRAZY RHYTHM
          0800   FINE AND DANDY
          0820   I GOTTA RIGHT TO SING THE BLUES
          0830   I´M COMING VIRGINIA
          2440   I´M GONNA SIT RIGHT DOWN AND WRITE MYSELF A LETTER
          0810   I´VE GOT THE WORLD ON A STRING
          2420   LIMEHOUSE BLUES
          2450   STAY AS SWEET AS YOU ARE
          2390   WHAT IS THIS THING CALLED LOVE
                 *Applause has been dubbed onto these performances.


Jazz Society                          67.406        Fr.      12 Inch LP

          1000   BEAUTIFUL LOVE
          1120   BEGIN THE BEGUINE
          1200   BODY AND SOUL
          1110   FINE AND DANDY
```

```
      1090   GEORGIA ON MY MIND
      1180   KNOCKIN' MYSELF OUT
      1010   LAUGHING AT LIFE
      1170   MIGHTY LAK A ROSE
      1250   OH! LADY BE GOOD
      1260   SWEET GEORGIA BROWN
      1100   SWEET LORRAINE
      1240   THERE'LL BE SOME CHANGES MADE
      1190   TOLEDO BLUES


Jazz Society                        AA522           Swed.   12 Inch LP
   [Part of 2-record set AA522/523.]
      1640   BASIN STREET BLUES
      1610   BLUES
      1550   DO NOTHIN' TILL YOU HEAR FROM ME
      1530   ESQUIRE BLUES
      1600   I GOT RHYTHM
      1580   I GOTTA RIGHT TO SING THE BLUES
      1560   I LOVE MY MAN
      1650   I'LL GET BY
      1540   MOP-MOP
      1590   SWEET LORRAINE
      1660   TEA FOR TWO


Jazz Society                        AA523           Swed.   12 Inch LP
   [Part of 2-record set AA522/523.]
      1670   BACK O' TOWN BLUES
      1690   BUCK JUMPIN'
      1740   FLYING HOME
      1710   FOR BASS FACES ONLY
      1720   MY IDEAL
      1700   STOMPIN' AT THE SAVOY
      1750   VIBE BLUES (Jammin' the Vibes)


Jazz Society                        AA522/523       Swed.
   [2-record set containing AA522, AA523.]


Jazz Spectrum                       Vol. 7          USA     12 Inch LP

      5790   PLAID


Jazztone                            J-1203          USA     12 Inch LP

      1830   DARK EYES
      1870   FLYING HOME
      1850   I KNOW THAT YOU KNOW
      1820   MAN I LOVE, THE
      1860   ON THE SUNNY SIDE OF THE STREET


Jazztone                            J-1221          USA     12 Inch LP

      1351   ESQUIRE BLUES
      1320   ESQUIRE BOUNCE
      1331   MOP-MOP


Jazztone                            J1280           USA     12 Inch LP

      1830   DARK EYES
      1870   FLYING HOME
      1850   I KNOW THAT YOU KNOW
      1820   MAN I LOVE, THE
      1860   ON THE SUNNY SIDE OF THE STREET


Jazztone                            J-SPEC-100      USA     10 Inch LP

      1830   DARK EYES
```

```
Jazztone                          J-SPEC-101      USA     10 Inch LP

    1830   DARK EYES


Jazz Trip                         (See Trip)


Jazzz                             JAZZZ 101       USA     12 Inch LP

    2930   I'LL NEVER BE THE SAME
    2890   IN A SENTIMENTAL MOOD
    2910   IT'S THE TALK OF THE TOWN
    2940   NIGHT AND DAY
    2880   OVER THE RAINBOW
    2920   SHE'S FUNNY THAT WAY
    2850   SITTIN' AND ROCKIN'
    2870   TENDERLY
    2840   WRAP YOUR TROUBLES IN DREAMS
    2900   YOU TOOK ADVANTAGE OF ME
    2860   YOU'RE DRIVING ME CRAZY


Joker                             SM 3117         It.     12 Inch LP

    2430   AMONG MY SOUVENIRS
    2370   BODY AND SOUL
    2410   CAN'T WE BE FRIENDS
    2400   CRAZY RHYTHM
    2380   I GUESS I'LL HAVE TO CHANGE MY PLANS
    2440   I'M GONNA SIT RIGHT DOWN AND WRITE MYSELF A LETTER
    2420   LIMEHOUSE BLUES
    2450   STAY AS SWEET AS YOU ARE
    1360   SUGAR FOOT STOMP
    1370   SWEET GEORGIA BROWN
    2390   WHAT IS THIS THING CALLED LOVE
    2360   YOU TOOK ADVANTAGE OF ME


Joker                             SM 3119         It.     12 Inch LP

    1410   COCKTAILS FOR TWO
    1470   LIZA


Joker                             SM 3131         It.     12 Inch LP

    1550   DO NOTHIN' TILL YOU HEAR FROM ME
    1560   I LOVE MY MAN
    1650   I'LL GET BY


Joker                             SM 3132         It.     12 Inch LP

    1610   BLUES
    1740   FLYING HOME
    2180   I CAN'T GIVE YOU ANYTHING BUT LOVE
    1540   MOP-MOP
    1720   MY IDEAL


Joker                             SM 3133         It.     12 Inch LP

    1670   BACK O' TOWN BLUES
    1640   BASIN STREET BLUES
    1580   I GOTTA RIGHT TO SING THE BLUES


Joker                             SM 3428         It.     12 Inch LP

    1640   BASIN STREET BLUES
    1610   BLUES
    1740   FLYING HOME
    1560   I LOVE MY MAN


                          210
```

```
Joyce                           LP-5005        USA      12 Inch LP

     2010   SMOKE GETS IN YOUR EYES


Karusell                        AFF1116        Swed.    7 Inch 45

     6070   FOGGY DAY, A
     6090   MAKIN´ WHOOPEE


Karusell                        KEP279         Swed.    7 Inch 45EP

     3850   CAN´T WE BE FRIENDS
     3880   MEMORIES OF YOU
     3860   THIS CAN´T BE LOVE


Karusell                        KEP280         Swed.    7 Inch 45EF

     3910   BODY AND SOUL
     3870   ELEGIE
     3890   OVER THE RAINBOW


Karusell                        KEP281         Swed.    7 Inch 45EF

            BLUES IN MY HEART (See "If You Hadn´t Gone Away")
     3900   IF YOU HADN´T GONE AWAY (Incorrectly titled "Blues in
              My Heart")
     3930   MAKIN´ WHOOPEE
     3920   MAN I LOVE, THE


Karusell                        KEP282         Swed.    7 Inch 45EF

     3950   BEGIN THE BEGUINE
     3960   HUMORESQUE
     3970   LOUISE


Karusell                        KEP291         Swed.    7 Inch 45EF

     4130   I HADN´T ANYONE ´TILL YOU
     4140   NIGHT AND DAY
     3940   SEPTEMBER SONG


Karusell                        KEP292         Swed.    7 Inch 45EF

     4190   GHOST OF A CHANCE, A
     4210   I COVER THE WATERFRONT
     4180   YOU´RE DRIVING ME CRAZY


Karusell                        KEP293         Swed.    7 Inch 45EF

     4320   BLUE SKIES
     4580   CARAVAN
     4390   I´VE GOT A CRUSH ON YOU
     4650   LOVE ME OR LEAVE ME


Karusell                        KEP312         Swed.    7 Inch 45EF

     5270   I WON´T DANCE
     5250   MOON IS LOW, THE
     5290   THIS CAN´T BE LOVE
     5260   YOU TOOK ADVANTAGE OF ME


Karusell                        KEP354         Swed.    7 Inch 45EP

     5650   HALLELUJAH
```

Kaydee   KAYDEE-2 (See KD-2)

Kaydee   KD-2*   USA   12 Inch LP

    2150   DANNY BOY
    2160   HOW HIGH THE MOON
            *Jacket only shows KAYDEE-2 instead.

Keystone Broadcasting System   KBS402   USA   16 Inch TX

    0530   HAPPY FEET
    0520   I CAN'T GET STARTED
    0510   RUNNIN' WILD
    0500   MAN I LOVE, THE

Keystone Broadcasting System   KBS414   USA   16 Inch TX

    0630   BODY AND SOUL
    0640   CAN'T WE BE FRIENDS
    0620   ELEGIE
    0650   MAKE BELIEVE

Keystone Broadcasting System   KBS452   USA   16 Inch TX

    0550   AIN'T MISBEHAVIN'
    0570   IN A SENTIMENTAL MOOD
    0540   ROYAL GARDEN BLUES
    0560   STAR DUST

Keystone Broadcasting System   KBS472   USA   16 Inch TX

    0590   I'LL GET BY
    0600   I'LL NEVER BE THE SAME
    0610   JUDY
    0580   SWEET LORRAINE

Kings of Jazz   KLJ20.002   It.   12 Inch LP

    1550   DO NOTHIN' TILL YOU HEAR FROM ME
    1560   I LOVE MY MAN
    1650   I'LL GET BY

Kings of Jazz   KLJ20000   It.   12 Inch LP

    3700   BODY AND SOUL
    3690   OUT OF NOWHERE
    3670   TEA FOR TWO
    3680   TENDERLY

Kings of Jazz   KLJ20020   It.   12 Inch LP

    3700   BODY AND SOUL
    3690   OUT OF NOWHERE
    3670   TEA FOR TWO
    3680   TENDERLY

Koala   K.O. 14278   USA   12 Inch LP

    0760   ALL GOD'S CHILLUN GOT RHYTHM
    2400   CRAZY RHYTHM
    0790   DAY IN - DAY OUT
    0800   FINE AND DANDY
    2380   I GUESS I'LL HAVE TO CHANGE MY PLANS
    0780   INDIANA
    0770   SWEET EMALINA, MY GAL
    2390   WHAT IS THIS THING CALLED LOVE

```
        2360   YOU TOOK ADVANTAGE OF ME*
               *Note: The record contains two tracks of this tune which
               are identical; they are incorrectly identified as different
               versions.


Konsa                              8400          USA      12 Inch LP

        2110   SWEET MARIJUANA BROWN


London                             6.24056       Ger.     12 Inch LP

        1350   ESQUIRE BLUES
        1351   ESQUIRE BLUES
        1320   ESQUIRE BOUNCE
        1321   ESQUIRE BOUNCE
        1330   MOP-MOP (Also called Boff-Boff)
        1331   MOP-MOP (Also called Boff-Boff)
        1340   MY IDEAL
        1341   MY IDEAL


London                             180006        Fr.      12 Inch LP

        1351   ESQUIRE BLUES
        1320   ESQUIRE BOUNCE
        1331   MOP-MOP (Also called Boff-Boff)
        1340   MY IDEAL


London                             HMC5006       Eng.     12 Inch LP

        1351   ESQUIRE BLUES
        1320   ESQUIRE BOUNCE
        1331   MOP-MOP
        1340   MY IDEAL


London                             SLC 450       Jap.     12 Inch LP

        1351   ESQUIRE BLUES
        1320   ESQUIRE BOUNCE
        1331   MOP-MOP (Also called Boff-Boff)
        1340   MY IDEAL


London                             SLC 512       Jap.     12 Inch LP

        1350   ESQUIRE BLUES
        1341   MY IDEAL


Longines                           LWS262        USA      12 Inch LP

        0840   ELEGIE


MCA                                510.080       Fr.      12 Inch LP

        1070   LAST GOODBYE BLUES
        1140   ROCK ME MAMA


MCA                                510.081       Fr.      12 Inch LP

        0201   AFTER YOU'VE GONE
        0251   BEAUTIFUL LOVE
        0480   CHLOE
        0170   EMALINE
        0460   GONE WITH THE WIND
        0221   I AIN'T GOT NOBODY
        0152   I WOULD DO ANYTHING FOR YOU
        0230   ILL WIND
```

```
         0260  LIZA
         0262  LIZA
         0140  MOONGLOW
         0211  STAR DUST
         0470  STORMY WEATHER
         0490  SHEIK OF ARABY, THE
         0240  SHOUT, THE
         0162  WHEN A WOMAN LOVES A MAN


MCA                                    510082      Fr.      12 Inch LP

         0960  BEGIN THE BEGUINE
         0940  COCKTAILS FOR TWO
         0751  DEEP PURPLE (Liner notes erroneously list this as [0750].)
         0840  ELEGIE
         0910  EMALINE
         0870  GET HAPPY
         0850  HUMORESQUE
         0980  INDIANA
         0930  LOVE ME TONIGHT (Love Me)
         0880  LULLABY OF THE LEAVES
         0920  MOONGLOW
         0970  ROSETTA
         0950  ST. LOUIS BLUES
         0860  SWEET LORRAINE
         0740  TEA FOR TWO
         0890  TIGER RAG


MCA                                    510 105     Fr.      12 Inch LP

         1430  AFTER YOU'VE GONE
         1080  BATTERY BOUNCE
         1410  COCKTAILS FOR TWO
         1150  CORRINE, CORRINA
         1450  DEEP PURPLE
         1490  HONEYSUCKLE ROSE
         1420  I AIN'T GOT NOBODY
         1400  I GOT RHYTHM
         1460  I WOULD DO ANYTHING FOR YOU
         1070  LAST GOODBYE BLUES
         1160  LONESOME GRAVEYARD BLUES
         1131  LUCILLE
         1440  MOONGLOW
         1140  ROCK ME MAMA
         1060  STOMPIN' AT THE SAVOY
         1050  WEE BABY BLUES


MCA                                    510 123     Fr.      12 Inch LP
    [Jacket says "M.C.A.510.123".]
         0421  BODY AND SOUL
         0450  I'VE GOT MY LOVE TO KEEP ME WARM
         0440  WHAT WILL I TELL MY HEART
         0431  WITH PLENTY OF MONEY AND YOU


MCA                                    MAP 2686    Fr.      12 Inch LP

         0940  COCKTAILS FOR TWO
         0840  ELEGIE
         0910  EMALINE
         0870  GET HAPPY
         0850  HUMORESQUE
         1460  I WOULD DO ANYTHING FOR YOU
         0980  INDIANA
         0930  LOVE ME
         0880  LULLABY OF THE LEAVES
         1440  MOONGLOW
         0860  SWEET LORRAINE
         0890  TIGER RAG
```

```
MCA                              MAPD 7028          It.      12 Inch LP
   [2-record set.]
       1430   AFTER YOU'VE GONE
       1080   BATTERY BOUNCE
       0960   BEGIN THE BEGUINE
       1410   COCKTAILS FOR TWO
       1150   CORRINE, CORRINA
       1450   DEEP PURPLE
       0840   ELEGIE
       0910   EMALINE
       0870   GET HAPPY
       0460   GONE WITH THE WIND
       1490   HONEYSUCKLE ROSE
       0850   HUMORESQUE
       1400   I GOT RHYTHM
       1460   I WOULD DO ANYTHING FOR YOU
       0980   INDIANA
       1070   LAST GOODBYE BLUES
       1160   LONESOME GRAVEYARD BLUES
       0930   LOVE ME
       1131   LUCILLE
       0880   LULLABY OF THE LEAVES
       1440   MOONGLOW
       1140   ROCK ME MAMA
       0970   ROSETTA
       0950   ST. LOUIS BLUES
       1060   STOMPIN' AT THE SAVOY
       0470   STORMY WEATHER
       0860   SWEET LORRAINE
       0740   TEA FOR TWO
       0890   TIGER RAG
       1050   WEE BABY BLUES


MCA                              MCA-1325           USA      12 Inch LP

       1070   LAST GOODBYE BLUES
       1140   ROCK ME MAMA


MCA                              MCA-3001/2/3/4/5 Jap.      12 Inch LP
   [5-record boxed set containing MCA-3004.]


MCA                              MCA-3004           Jap.     12 Inch LP
   [Part of 5-record boxed set MCA-3001/2/3/4/5.]
       1080   BATTERY BOUNCE


MCA                              MCA-3073           Jap.     12 Inch LP
   [Part of 3-record boxed set MCA-3073-75.]
       0201   AFTER YOU'VE GONE
       0251   BEAUTIFUL LOVE
       0190   COCKTAILS FOR TWO
       0170   EMALINE
       0221   I AIN'T GOT NOBODY
       0152   I WOULD DO ANYTHING FOR YOU
       0260   LIZA
       0180   LOVE ME
       0140   MOONGLOW
       0211   STAR DUST
       0240   SHOUT, THE
              WHEN A WOMAN LOVES A MAN (Incorrect listing, see Note)
   Note: Although listed on the label and in the liner notes, this
     title does not appear on the disc; instead there is a piano solo
     of "Narcissus" by an unknown pianist, clearly not Tatum.


MCA                              MCA-3074           Jap.     12 Inch LP
   [Part of 3-record boxed set MCA-3073-75.]
       0480   CHLOE
       0940   COCKTAILS FOR TWO
       0840   ELEGIE
       0910   EMALINE
       0870   GET HAPPY

                              215
```

```
          0460   GONE WITH THE WIND
          0850   HUMORESQUE
          0930   LOVE ME
          0880   LULLABY OF THE LEAVES
          0490   SHEIK OF ARABY, THE
          0470   STORMY WEATHER
          0860   SWEET LORRAINE
          0740   TEA FOR TWO
          0890   TIGER RAG


MCA                                    MCA-3075          Jap.      12 Inch LP
     [Part of 3-record boxed set MCA-3073-75.]
          1430   AFTER YOU'VE GONE
          0960   BEGIN THE BEGUINE
          1410   COCKTAILS FOR TWO
          1450   DEEP PURPLE
          1490   HONEYSUCKLE ROSE
          1420   I AIN'T GOT NOBODY
          1400   I GOT RHYTHM
          1460   I WOULD DO ANYTHING FOR YOU
          0980   INDIANA
          1440   MOONGLOW
          0970   ROSETTA
          0950   ST. LOUIS BLUES


MCA                                    MCA-3073-75     Jap.
     [3-record boxed set containing MCA-3073,MCA-3074,MCA-3075.]


MCA                                    MCA-3107          Jap.      12 Inch LP

          1080   BATTERY BOUNCE
          0421   BODY AND SOUL
          1150   CORRINE, CORRINA
          0450   I'VE GOT MY LOVE TO KEEP ME WARM
          1070   LAST GOODBYE BLUES
          1160   LONESOME GRAVEYARD BLUES
          1131   LUCILLE
          1140   ROCK ME MAMA
          1060   STOMPIN' AT THE SAVOY
          1050   WEE BABY BLUES
          0440   WHAT WILL I TELL MY HEART
          0431   WITH PLENTY OF MONEY AND YOU


MCA                                    MCA-3519          Jap.      12 Inch LP
     [Part of 2-record set MCA-3519-20.]

          1070   LAST GOODBYE BLUES


MCA                                    MCA-3519-20       Jap.
     [2-record set containing MCA-3519.]


MCA                                    MCA-3524          Jap.      12 Inch LP

          1150   CORRINE, CORRINA
          1140   ROCK ME MAMA
          1050   WEE BABY BLUES


MCA                                    MCA2-4019         USA       12 Inch LP
     [2-record set.]
          1430   AFTER YOU'VE GONE
          1080   BATTERY BOUNCE
          0960   BEGIN THE BEGUINE
          1410   COCKTAILS FOR TWO
          1150   CORRINE, CORRINA
          1450   DEEP PURPLE
          0840   ELEGIE
          0910   EMALINE
          0870   GET HAPPY
```

```
      0460  GONE WITH THE WIND
      1490  HONEYSUCKLE ROSE
      0850  HUMORESQUE
      1400  I GOT RHYTHM
      1460  I WOULD DO ANYTHING FOR YOU
      0980  INDIANA
      1070  LAST GOODBYE BLUES
      1160  LONESOME GRAVEYARD BLUES
      0930  LOVE ME
      1131  LUCILLE
      0880  LULLABY OF THE LEAVES
      1440  MOONGLOW
      1140  ROCK ME MAMA
      0970  ROSETTA
      0950  ST. LOUIS BLUES
      1060  STOMPIN´ AT THE SAVOY
      0470  STORMY WEATHER
      0860  SWEET LORRAINE
      0740  TEA FOR TWO
      0890  TIGER RAG
      1050  WEE BABY BLUES
```

```
MCA                              MCA2-4062      USA      12 Inch LP
   [Part of 2-record set.]
      1050  WEE BABY BLUES


MCA                              MCA2-4112      USA      12 Inch LP
   [Part of 2-record set.]
      0251  BEAUTIFUL LOVE
      0420  BODY AND SOUL
      0480  CHLOE
      0221  I AIN´T GOT NOBODY
      0450  I´VE GOT MY LOVE TO KEEP ME WARM
      0230  ILL WIND
      0260  LIZA
      0211  STAR DUST
      0490  SHEIK OF ARABY, THE
      0240  SHOUT, THE
      0440  WHAT WILL I TELL MY HEART
      0160  WHEN A WOMAN LOVES A MAN
      0431  WITH PLENTY OF MONEY AND YOU


MCA Coral                        82040-4        Ger.     12 Inch LP
   [Part of 4-record boxed set.]
      1150  CORRINE, CORRINA


MGM                              E4241          USA      12 Inch LP

      4250  ALL THE THINGS YOU ARE


MGM                              E4242          USA      12 Inch LP

      3920  MAN I LOVE, THE


MGM                              RFM-816        USA      12 Inch LP

      4360  I´M IN THE MOOD FOR LOVE


MGM                              SE4241         USA    s 12 Inch LP

      4250  ALL THE THINGS YOU ARE


MGM                              SE4242         USA    s 12 Inch LP

      3920  MAN I LOVE, THE
```

Mainstream	56002	USA	12 Inch LP

    1340 MY IDEAL

Mainstream	56008	USA	12 Inch LP

    1331 MOP-MOP

Mainstream	56009	USA	12 Inch LP

    1351 ESQUIRE BLUES

Mainstream	56017	USA	12 Inch LP

    1320 ESQUIRE BOUNCE

Mainstream	56037	USA	12 Inch LP

    1351 ESQUIRE BLUES
    1320 ESQUIRE BOUNCE
    1331 MOP-MOP
    1340 MY IDEAL

Mainstream	PS-1240	Jap.	12 Inch LP

    1331 MOP-MOP

Mainstream	PS-1291	Jap.	12 Inch LP

    1340 MY IDEAL

Mainstream	S/6002	USA	s 12 Inch LP

    1340 MY IDEAL

Mainstream	S/6008	USA	s 12 Inch LP

    1331 MOP-MOP

Mainstream	S/6009	USA	s 12 Inch LP

    1351 ESQUIRE BLUES

Mainstream	S/6017	USA	s 12 Inch LP

    1320 ESQUIRE BOUNCE

Mainstream	S/6037	USA	s 12 Inch LP

    1351 ESQUIRE BLUES
    1320 ESQUIRE BOUNCE
    1331 MOP-MOP
    1340 MY IDEAL

Mainstream	SL 1210	Jap.	12 Inch LP

    1351 ESQUIRE BLUES
    1320 ESQUIRE BOUNCE
    1331 MOP-MOP
    1340 MY IDEAL

```
Mecolico*                          1/8              Eng.    10 Inch LP

    2430  AMONG MY SOUVENIRS
    2370  BODY AND SOUL
    2410  CAN'T WE BE FRIENDS
    2400  CRAZY RHYTHM
    2380  I GUESS I'LL HAVE TO CHANGE MY PLANS
    2440  I'M GONNA SIT RIGHT DOWN AND WRITE MYSELF A LETTER
    2420  LIMEHOUSE BLUES
    2450  STAY AS SWEET AS YOU ARE
    1360  SUGAR FOOT STOMP
    1370  SWEET GEORGIA BROWN
    2390  WHAT IS THIS THING CALLED LOVE
    2360  YOU TOOK ADVANTAGE OF ME
          *This was actually a limited private release on a disc
          which had a plain white label.  Some of these labels
          bore the trade name of the label supplier, "Mecolico."


Melodisc                          1157             Eng.    10 Inch 78

    2030  FINE AND DANDY
    2050  JA-DA


Melodisc                          EPM7-108         Eng.     7 Inch 45EP

    2030  FINE AND DANDY
    1970  IF I HAD YOU
    1980  SOFT WINDS
    2070  SWEET AND LOVELY


Melojazz                          7003             Fr.     12 Inch 78

    1950  BOOGIE
    1970  IF I HAD YOU


Melojazz                          7004             Fr.     12 Inch 78

    1980  SOFT WINDS
    1960  TOPSY


Melojazz                          7011             Fr.     10 Inch 78

    2040  IT HAD TO BE YOU
    2060  WHERE OR WHEN


Melojazz                          7012             Fr.     10 Inch 78

    2030  FINE AND DANDY
    2050  JA-DA


Melojazz                          7013             Fr.     10 Inch 78

    2080  DANNY BOY
    2070  SWEET AND LOVELY


Mercury                           9286 092         Holl.   12 Inch LP

    5360  BEGIN THE BEGUINE
    5380  BODY AND SOUL
    5450  I'LL NEVER BE THE SAME
    5370  SOMEONE TO WATCH OVER ME
    5420  TENDERLY
    5400  TOO MARVELOUS FOR WORDS
    5390  WILLOW WEEP FOR ME
    5460  WITHOUT A SONG
    5440  YESTERDAYS
    5430  YOU TOOK ADVANTAGE OF ME
```

```
Mercury                        BT-5049        Jap.    12 Inch LP

    0760   ALL GOD'S CHILLUN GOT RHYTHM
    2410   CAN'T WE BE FRIENDS
    2400   CRAZY RHYTHM
    0790   DAY IN - DAY OUT
           EMALINE, MY GAL (See "Sweet Emalina")
    0800   FINE AND DANDY
    0820   I GOTTA RIGHT TO SING THE BLUES
    2380   I GUESS I'LL HAVE TO CHANGE MY PLANS
    0830   I'M COMING VIRGINIA
    0810   I'VE GOT THE WORLD ON A STRING
    0780   INDIANA
    2420   LIMEHOUSE BLUES
    0770   SWEET EMALINA, MY GAL
    2390   WHAT IS THIS THING CALLED LOVE
    2360   YOU TOOK ADVANTAGE OF ME*
           *Note: The record contains two tracks of this tune which
            are identical; they are incorrectly identified as different
            versions.


Mercury                        BT-5050        Jap.    12 Inch LP

    2430   AMONG MY SOUVENIRS
    2180   I CAN'T GIVE YOU ANYTHING BUT LOVE
    2540   I GOTTA RIGHT TO SING THE BLUES
    2440   I'M GONNA SIT RIGHT DOWN AND WRITE MYSELF A LETTER
    2480   IF I COULD BE WITH YOU
    2170   MAN I LOVE, THE
    2500   MEAN TO ME
    2550   ON THE SUNNY SIDE OF THE STREET
    2460   SOMEBODY LOVES ME
    2450   STAY AS SWEET AS YOU ARE
    2490   TEA FOR TWO
    2530   THREE LITTLE WORDS
    2470   WHY WAS I BORN


Meritt                         4              USA     12 Inch LP

    0481   CHLOE


Metro                          2356 081       Ger.    12 Inch LP

    3950   BEGIN THE BEGUINE
           BLUES IN MY HEART (See "If You Hadn't Gone Away")
    3850   CAN'T WE BE FRIENDS
    4020   DIXIELAND BAND
    3870   ELEGIE
    3960   HUMORESQUE
    3900   IF YOU HADN'T GONE AWAY (Incorrectly titled "Blues in
            My Heart")
    3990   JUDY
    3920   MAN I LOVE, THE
    3880   MEMORIES OF YOU
    3890   OVER THE RAINBOW
    3860   THIS CAN'T BE LOVE


Metro                          2356 105       Ger.    12 Inch LP

    5270   I WON'T DANCE
    5290   THIS CAN'T BE LOVE


Metro                          2364013        Eng.    12 Inch LP
    [Part of 2-record set 2682 024.]
    4830   BLUES IN B FLAT
    4860   BLUES IN MY HEART
    4950   HANDS ACROSS THE TABLE
    4880   IDAHO
    4820   MY BLUE HEAVEN
    4930   OLD FASHIONED LOVE
```

```
       4940   'S WONDERFUL
       4870   STREET OF DREAMS


Metro                              2364014         Eng.    12 Inch LP
   [Part of 2-record set 2682 024.]
       4840   BLUES IN C
       4850   FOGGY DAY, A
       4921   MAKIN' WHOOPEE
       4900   UNDECIDED
       4910   UNDER A BLANKET OF BLUE
       4890   YOU'RE MINE, YOU


Metro                              2682 024        Eng.
   [2-record set containing 2364013,2364014.]


Metro Hollywood                    23001           USA     10 Inch 78

       2260   KERRY DANCE, THE
       2250   YESTERDAYS


Metro Hollywood                    23002           USA     10 Inch 78

       2230   MEMORIES OF YOU
       2240   RUNNIN' WILD


Metro Hollywood                    23003           USA     10 Inch 78

       2220   LOVER
       2210   SONG OF THE VAGABONDS


Metro Hollywood                    23004           USA     10 Inch 78

       2191   HALLELUJAH
       2200   POOR BUTTERFLY


Metronome                          B515            Swed.   10 Inch 78EP

       1850   I KNOW THAT YOU KNOW
       1820   MAN I LOVE, THE


Mode                               MDINT.9168      Fr.     12 Inch LP
   [Jacket reads MDR 9 168.]
       1840   BODY AND SOUL
       1830   DARK EYES
       1870   FLYING HOME
       1850   I KNOW THAT YOU KNOW
       1860   ON THE SUNNY SIDE OF THE STREET


Mode                               MDINT9201       Fr.     12 Inch LP

       1830   DARK EYES


Mode                               MDR9161         Fr.     12 Inch LP

       1870   FLYING HOME


Mode                               CLVLXR401       Fr.     12 Inch LP

       1850   I KNOW THAT YOU KNOW
```

```
Movietone                         71021            USA      12 Inch LP

    5360  BEGIN THE BEGUINE
    5380  BODY AND SOUL
    5450  I'LL NEVER BE THE SAME
    5370  SOMEONE TO WATCH OVER ME
    5420  TENDERLY
    5400  TOO MARVELOUS FOR WORDS
    5390  WILLOW WEEP FOR ME
    5460  WITHOUT A SONG
    5440  YESTERDAYS
    5430  YOU TOOK ADVANTAGE OF ME


Movietone                         S72021           USA    s 12 Inch LP

    5360  BEGIN THE BEGUINE
    5380  BODY AND SOUL
    5450  I'LL NEVER BE THE SAME
    5370  SOMEONE TO WATCH OVER ME
    5420  TENDERLY
    5400  TOO MARVELOUS FOR WORDS
    5390  WILLOW WEEP FOR ME
    5460  WITHOUT A SONG
    5440  YESTERDAYS
    5430  YOU TOOK ADVANTAGE OF ME


Music Parade                      LEL 14           It.      12 Inch LP

    1830  DARK EYES
    1870  FLYING HOME
    1850  I KNOW THAT YOU KNOW
    1820  MAN I LOVE, THE
    1860  ON THE SUNNY SIDE OF THE STREET


Musidisc                          (See "Jazz Anthology")

Musidisc                          30 CV 1522       Fr.      12 Inch LP
   [Part of 4-record set CCV 2521.]
    1850  I KNOW THAT YOU KNOW


Musidisc                          CCV 2521         Fr.
   [4-record set containing 30 CV 1522.]


Neiman Marcus                     DMM4-0342        USA
   [4-record boxed set containing RCA DMM4-0342-4.]


Norgran                           MG N-1036        USA      12 Inch LP

    3850  CAN'T WE BE FRIENDS
    3920  MAN I LOVE, THE
    4340  STOMPIN' AT THE SAVOY


Norgran                           MG N-1080        USA      12 Inch LP

    5810  DEEP PURPLE
    5790  PLAID
    5830  SEPTEMBER SONG
    5800  SOMEBODY LOVES ME
    5840  VERVE BLUES


ORL                               8166             It.      12 Inch LP

    1050  WEE BABY BLUES
```

```
Odeon                              284030        Arg.   10 Inch 78

    0221  I AIN'T GOT NOBODY
    0162  WHEN A WOMAN LOVES A MAN


Odeon                              284255        Arg.   10 Inch 78

    0450  I'VE GOT MY LOVE TO KEEP ME WARM
    0430  WITH PLENTY OF MONEY AND YOU


Odeon                              284289        Arg.   10 Inch 78

    0420  BODY AND SOUL
    0440  WHAT WILL I TELL MY HEART


Odeon                              284465        Arg.   10 Inch 78

    0410  BOOTS AND SADDLE
    0152  I WOULD DO ANYTHING FOR YOU


Odeon                              284832        Arg.   10 Inch 78

    1050  BLUES DEL BEBE (Wee Baby Blues)
    1070  BLUES DEL ULTIMO ADIOS (Last Goodbye Blues)


Odeon                              286291        Arg.   10 Inch 78

    0740  TE PARA DOS (Tea For Two)
    0950  ST. LOUIS BLUES


Odeon                              286310        Arg.   10 Inch 78

    0751  DEEP PURPLE
    0221  I AIN'T GOT NOBODY


Odeon                              286320        Arg.   10 Inch 78

    0970  ROSETTA


Odeon                              286341        Arg.   10 Inch 78

    0980  INDIANA


Odeon                              288.050       Braz.  10 Inch 78

    0750  DEEP PURPLE
    0740  TEA FOR TWO


Odeon                              288.099       Braz.  10 Inch 78

    0950  ST. LOUIS BLUES
    0470  STORMY WEATHER


Office of War Information,         51            USA    16 Inch TX
  Music of Jazz Bands

    1860  ON THE SUNNY SIDE OF THE STREET


Olympic                            OL-7120 (E)   USA    12 Inch LP

    2430  AMONG MY SOUVENIRS
    2410  CAN'T WE BE FRIENDS
    0790  DAY IN - DAY OUT
```

```
          EMALINE, MY GAL (See "Sweet Emalina")
0800      FINE AND DANDY
2180      I CAN'T GIVE YOU ANYTHING BUT LOVE
2540      I GOTTA RIGHT TO SING THE BLUES
0780      INDIANA
2420      LIMEHOUSE BLUES
2550      ON THE SUNNY SIDE OF THE STREET
0770      SWEET EMALINA, MY GAL
2490      TEA FOR TWO
```

Omniamusic Napoleon   OLP-19002   It.   12 Inch LP

```
1550      DO NOTHIN' TILL YOU HEAR FROM ME
1560      I LOVE MY MAN
1650      I'LL GET BY
```

Onyx   MP2349   Jap.   12 Inch LP

```
1000      BEAUTIFUL LOVE
1120      BEGIN THE BEGUINE
1200      BODY AND SOUL
1110      FINE AND DANDY
1090      GEORGIA ON MY MIND
1180      KNOCKIN' MYSELF OUT
1010      LAUGHING AT LIFE
1170      MIGHTY LAK A ROSE
1250      OH! LADY BE GOOD
1260      SWEET GEORGIA BROWN
1100      SWEET LORRAINE
1240      THERE'LL BE SOME CHANGES MADE
1190      TOLEDO BLUES
```

Onyx   ORI 205   USA   12 Inch LP

```
1000      BEAUTIFUL LOVE
1120      BEGIN THE BEGUINE
1200      BODY AND SOUL
1110      FINE AND DANDY
1090      GEORGIA ON MY MIND
1180      KNOCKIN' MYSELF OUT
1010      LAUGHING AT LIFE
1170      MIGHTY LAK A ROSE
1250      OH! LADY BE GOOD
1260      SWEET GEORGIA BROWN
1100      SWEET LORRAINE
1240      THERE'LL BE SOME CHANGES MADE
1190      TOLEDO BLUES
```

Oscar Disco   OS 050   It.   12 Inch LP

```
0290      AFTER YOU'VE GONE
0760      ALL GOD'S CHILLUN GOT RHYTHM
0280      BOOTS AND SADDLE
0400      DEVIL IN THE MOON
0300      DIXIELAND BAND
          EMALINE, MY GAL (See "Sweet Emalina")
0390      I WISH I WERE TWINS
0350      I WOULD DO ANYTHING FOR YOU
0370      IN THE MIDDLE OF A KISS
0780      INDIANA
0340      MONDAY IN MANHATTAN
0380      ROSETTA
0770      SWEET EMALINA, MY GAL
0330      STAY AS SWEET AS YOU ARE
0360      THEME FOR PIANO
```

Overseas   ULS-1559R   Jap.   12 Inch LP

```
2120      BLUES FOR ART'S SAKE
2090      CAN'T HELP LOVIN' DAT MAN OF MINE
```

```
      2100   PLEASE DON'T TALK ABOUT ME WHEN I'M GONE
      2110   SWEET MARIJUANA BROWN


Ozone                              3              USA      12 Inch LP

      1550   DO NOTHIN' TILL YOU HEAR FROM ME
      1560   I LOVE MY MAN (Billie's Blues)
      1650   I'LL GET BY


Pablo                          2310-379          USA    s 12 Inch LP

      4921   MAKIN' WHOOPEE


Pablo                          2310-679          USA    s 12 Inch LP

      4490   BLUE LOU
      4630   SOPHISTICATED LADY


Pablo                          2310 720          Braz.  s 12 Inch LP

      5650   HALLELUJAH
      5780   HOW HIGH THE MOON
      5660   I'LL NEVER BE THE SAME
      5760   MAKIN' WHOOPEE
      5770   MORE THAN YOU KNOW
      5640   PERDIDO
      5710   WHAT IS THIS THING CALLED LOVE


Pablo                          2310-720          Can.   s 12 Inch LP

      5650   HALLELUJAH
      5780   HOW HIGH THE MOON
      5660   I'LL NEVER BE THE SAME
      5760   MAKIN' WHOOPEE
      5770   MORE THAN YOU KNOW
      5640   PERDIDO
      5710   WHAT IS THIS THING CALLED LOVE


Pablo                          2310 720          Eng.   s 12 Inch LP

      5650   HALLELUJAH
      5780   HOW HIGH THE MOON
      5660   I'LL NEVER BE THE SAME
      5760   MAKIN' WHOOPEE
      5770   MORE THAN YOU KNOW
      5640   PERDIDO
      5710   WHAT IS THIS THING CALLED LOVE


Pablo                          2310 720          Fr.    s 12 Inch LP

      5650   HALLELUJAH
      5780   HOW HIGH THE MOON
      5660   I'LL NEVER BE THE SAME
      5760   MAKIN' WHOOPEE
      5770   MORE THAN YOU KNOW
      5640   PERDIDO
      5710   WHAT IS THIS THING CALLED LOVE


Pablo                          2310 720          Ger.   s 12 Inch LP

      5650   HALLELUJAH
      5780   HOW HIGH THE MOON
      5660   I'LL NEVER BE THE SAME
      5760   MAKIN' WHOOPEE
      5770   MORE THAN YOU KNOW
      5640   PERDIDO
      5710   WHAT IS THIS THING CALLED LOVE
```

```
Pablo                              2310 720A        It.   s 12 Inch LP

    5650  HALLELUJAH
    5780  HOW HIGH THE MOON
    5660  I´LL NEVER BE THE SAME
    5760  MAKIN´ WHOOPEE
    5770  MORE THAN YOU KNOW
    5640  PERDIDO
    5710  WHAT IS THIS THING CALLED LOVE


Pablo                              2310-720         USA   s 12 Inch LP

    5650  HALLELUJAH
    5780  HOW HIGH THE MOON
    5660  I´LL NEVER BE THE SAME
    5760  MAKIN´ WHOOPEE
    5770  MORE THAN YOU KNOW
    5640  PERDIDO
    5710  WHAT IS THIS THING CALLED LOVE


Pablo                              2310 723         Braz. s 12 Inch LP

    3910  BODY AND SOUL
    4260  HAVE YOU MET MISS JONES
    5150  IT´S ONLY A PAPER MOON
    3980  LOVE FOR SALE
    5090  MOONGLOW
    4350  MY LAST AFFAIR
    4050  SITTIN´ AND ROCKIN´
    4230  STAY AS SWEET AS YOU ARE
    4510  WILLOW WEEP FOR ME


Pablo                              2310-723         Can.  s 12 Inch LP

    3910  BODY AND SOUL
    4260  HAVE YOU MET MISS JONES
    5150  IT´S ONLY A PAPER MOON
    3980  LOVE FOR SALE
    5090  MOONGLOW
    4350  MY LAST AFFAIR
    4050  SITTIN´ AND ROCKIN´
    4230  STAY AS SWEET AS YOU ARE
    4510  WILLOW WEEP FOR ME


Pablo                              2310 723         Eng.  s 12 Inch LP

    3910  BODY AND SOUL
    4260  HAVE YOU MET MISS JONES
    5150  IT´S ONLY A PAPER MOON
    3980  LOVE FOR SALE
    5090  MOONGLOW
    4350  MY LAST AFFAIR
    4050  SITTIN´ AND ROCKIN´
    4230  STAY AS SWEET AS YOU ARE
    4510  WILLOW WEEP FOR ME


Pablo                              2310 723         Ger.  s 12 Inch LP

    3910  BODY AND SOUL
    4260  HAVE YOU MET MISS JONES
    5150  IT´S ONLY A PAPER MOON
    3980  LOVE FOR SALE
    5090  MOONGLOW
    4350  MY LAST AFFAIR
    4050  SITTIN´ AND ROCKIN´
    4230  STAY AS SWEET AS YOU ARE
    4510  WILLOW WEEP FOR ME
```

```
Pablo                          2310 723A       It.   s 12 Inch LP

     3910  BODY AND SOUL
     4260  HAVE YOU MET MISS JONES
     5150  IT'S ONLY A PAPER MOON
     3980  LOVE FOR SALE
     5090  MOONGLOW
     4350  MY LAST AFFAIR
     4050  SITTIN' AND ROCKIN'
     4230  STAY AS SWEET AS YOU ARE
     4510  WILLOW WEEP FOR ME


Pablo                          2310-723        USA   s 12 Inch LP

     3910  BODY AND SOUL
     4260  HAVE YOU MET MISS JONES
     5150  IT'S ONLY A PAPER MOON
     3980  LOVE FOR SALE
     5090  MOONGLOW
     4350  MY LAST AFFAIR
     4050  SITTIN' AND ROCKIN'
     4230  STAY AS SWEET AS YOU ARE
     4510  WILLOW WEEP FOR ME


Pablo                          2310 729        Can.  s 12 Inch LP

     3870  ELEGIE
     4190  GHOST OF A CHANCE, A
     4440  GONE WITH THE WIND
     4800  HEAT WAVE
     4290  I'LL SEE YOU IN MY DREAMS
     4620  LOVER, COME BACK TO ME!
     3940  SEPTEMBER SONG
     4060  THERE WILL NEVER BE ANOTHER YOU
     3860  THIS CAN'T BE LOVE


Pablo                          2310 729        Eng.  s 12 Inch LP

     3870  ELEGIE
     4190  GHOST OF A CHANCE, A
     4440  GONE WITH THE WIND
     4800  HEAT WAVE
     4290  I'LL SEE YOU IN MY DREAMS
     4620  LOVER, COME BACK TO ME!
     3940  SEPTEMBER SONG
     4060  THERE WILL NEVER BE ANOTHER YOU
     3860  THIS CAN'T BE LOVE


Pablo                          2310 729        Ger.  s 12 Inch LP

     3870  ELEGIE
     4190  GHOST OF A CHANCE, A
     4440  GONE WITH THE WIND
     4800  HEAT WAVE
     4290  I'LL SEE YOU IN MY DREAMS
     4620  LOVER, COME BACK TO ME!
     3940  SEPTEMBER SONG
     4060  THERE WILL NEVER BE ANOTHER YOU
     3860  THIS CAN'T BE LOVE


Pablo                          2310 729A       It.   s 12 Inch LP

     3870  ELEGIE
     4190  GHOST OF A CHANCE, A
     4440  GONE WITH THE WIND
     4800  HEAT WAVE
     4290  I'LL SEE YOU IN MY DREAMS
     4620  LOVER, COME BACK TO ME!
     3940  SEPTEMBER SONG
     4060  THERE WILL NEVER BE ANOTHER YOU
```

3860   THIS CAN´T BE LOVE

Pablo   2310-729   USA   s 12 Inch LP

    3870   ELEGIE
    4190   GHOST OF A CHANCE, A
    4440   GONE WITH THE WIND
    4800   HEAT WAVE
    4290   I´LL SEE YOU IN MY DREAMS
    4620   LOVER, COME BACK TO ME!
    3940   SEPTEMBER SONG
    4060   THERE WILL NEVER BE ANOTHER YOU
    3860   THIS CAN´T BE LOVE

Pablo   2310-730   Can. s 12 Inch LP

    4250   ALL THE THINGS YOU ARE
    3950   BEGIN THE BEGUINE
    4740   CRAZY RHYTHM
    4680   DEEP PURPLE
    4020   DIXIELAND BAND
    4150   JITTERBUG WALTZ
    4650   LOVE ME OR LEAVE ME
    5080   PRISONER OF LOVE
    4070   TENDERLY
    4120   YESTERDAYS

Pablo   2310 730   Eng. s 12 Inch LP

    4250   ALL THE THINGS YOU ARE
    3950   BEGIN THE BEGUINE
    4740   CRAZY RHYTHM
    4680   DEEP PURPLE
    4020   DIXIELAND BAND
    4150   JITTERBUG WALTZ
    4650   LOVE ME OR LEAVE ME
    5080   PRISONER OF LOVE
    4070   TENDERLY
    4120   YESTERDAYS

Pablo   2310 730   Ger. s 12 Inch LP

    4250   ALL THE THINGS YOU ARE
    3950   BEGIN THE BEGUINE
    4740   CRAZY RHYTHM
    4680   DEEP PURPLE
    4020   DIXIELAND BAND
    4150   JITTERBUG WALTZ
    4650   LOVE ME OR LEAVE ME
    5080   PRISONER OF LOVE
    4070   TENDERLY
    4120   YESTERDAYS

Pablo   2310 730A   It.   s 12 Inch LP

    4250   ALL THE THINGS YOU ARE
    3950   BEGIN THE BEGUINE
    4740   CRAZY RHYTHM
    4680   DEEP PURPLE
    4020   DIXIELAND BAND
    4150   JITTERBUG WALTZ
    4650   LOVE ME OR LEAVE ME
    5080   PRISONER OF LOVE
    4070   TENDERLY
    4120   YESTERDAYS

```
Pablo                              2310-730      USA    s 12 Inch LP

     4250  ALL THE THINGS YOU ARE
     3950  BEGIN THE BEGUINE
     4740  CRAZY RHYTHM
     4680  DEEP PURPLE
     4020  DIXIELAND BAND
     4150  JITTERBUG WALTZ
     4650  LOVE ME OR LEAVE ME
     5080  PRISONER OF LOVE
     4070  TENDERLY
     4120  YESTERDAYS


Pablo                              2310 731      Braz.  s 12 Inch LP

     5810  DEEP PURPLE
     5790  PLAID
     5830  SEPTEMBER SONG
     5800  SOMEBODY LOVES ME
     5840  VERVE BLUES


Pablo                              2310-731      Can.   s 12 Inch LP

     5810  DEEP PURPLE
     5790  PLAID
     5830  SEPTEMBER SONG
     5800  SOMEBODY LOVES ME
     5840  VERVE BLUES


Pablo                              2310 731      Eng.   s 12 Inch LP

     5810  DEEP PURPLE
     5790  PLAID
     5830  SEPTEMBER SONG
     5800  SOMEBODY LOVES ME
     5840  VERVE BLUES


Pablo                              2310 731      Fr.    s 12 Inch LP

     5810  DEEP PURPLE
     5790  PLAID
     5830  SEPTEMBER SONG
     5800  SOMEBODY LOVES ME
     5840  VERVE BLUES


Pablo                              2310 731      Ger.   s 12 Inch LP

     5810  DEEP PURPLE
     5790  PLAID
     5830  SEPTEMBER SONG
     5800  SOMEBODY LOVES ME
     5840  VERVE BLUES


Pablo                              2310-731      USA    s 12 Inch LP

     5810  DEEP PURPLE
     5790  PLAID
     5830  SEPTEMBER SONG
     5800  SOMEBODY LOVES ME
     5840  VERVE BLUES


Pablo                              2310 732      Braz.  s 12 Inch LP

     4940  ´S WONDERFUL
     4830  BLUES IN B FLAT
     4840  BLUES IN C
     4850  FOGGY DAY, A
     4870  STREET OF DREAMS
```

```
        4900   UNDECIDED
        4910   UNDER A BLANKET OF BLUE


Pablo                                  2310-732        Can.  s 12 Inch LP

        4940   'S WONDERFUL
        4830   BLUES IN B FLAT
        4840   BLUES IN C
        4850   FOGGY DAY, A
        4870   STREET OF DREAMS
        4900   UNDECIDED
        4910   UNDER A BLANKET OF BLUE


Pablo                                  2310 732        Eng.  s 12 Inch LP

        4940   'S WONDERFUL
        4830   BLUES IN B FLAT
        4840   BLUES IN C
        4850   FOGGY DAY, A
        4870   STREET OF DREAMS
        4900   UNDECIDED
        4910   UNDER A BLANKET OF BLUE


Pablo                                  2310 732        Fr.   s 12 Inch LP

        4940   'S WONDERFUL
        4830   BLUES IN B FLAT
        4840   BLUES IN C
        4850   FOGGY DAY, A
        4870   STREET OF DREAMS
        4900   UNDECIDED
        4910   UNDER A BLANKET OF BLUE


Pablo                                  2310 732        Ger.  s 12 Inch LP

        4940   'S WONDERFUL
        4830   BLUES IN B FLAT
        4840   BLUES IN C
        4850   FOGGY DAY, A
        4870   STREET OF DREAMS
        4900   UNDECIDED
        4910   UNDER A BLANKET OF BLUE


Pablo                                  2310-732        USA   s 12 Inch LP

        4940   'S WONDERFUL
        4830   BLUES IN B FLAT
        4840   BLUES IN C
        4850   FOGGY DAY, A
        4870   STREET OF DREAMS
        4900   UNDECIDED
        4910   UNDER A BLANKET OF BLUE


Pablo                                  2310 733        Braz. s 12 Inch LP

        4860   BLUES IN MY HEART
        4950   HANDS ACROSS THE TABLE
        4880   IDAHO
        4921   MAKIN' WHOOPEE
        4820   MY BLUE HEAVEN
        4930   OLD FASHIONED LOVE
        4890   YOU'RE MINE, YOU


Pablo                                  2310-733        Can.  s 12 Inch LP

        4860   BLUES IN MY HEART
        4950   HANDS ACROSS THE TABLE
        4880   IDAHO
```

```
       4921  MAKIN' WHOOPEE
       4820  MY BLUE HEAVEN
       4930  OLD FASHIONED LOVE
       4890  YOU'RE MINE, YOU


Pablo                            2310 733        Eng.  s 12 Inch LP

       4860  BLUES IN MY HEART
       4950  HANDS ACROSS THE TABLE
       4880  IDAHO
       4921  MAKIN' WHOOPEE
       4820  MY BLUE HEAVEN
       4930  OLD FASHIONED LOVE
       4890  YOU'RE MINE, YOU


Pablo                            2310 733        Fr.   s 12 Inch LP

       4860  BLUES IN MY HEART
       4950  HANDS ACROSS THE TABLE
       4880  IDAHO
       4921  MAKIN' WHOOPEE
       4820  MY BLUE HEAVEN
       4930  OLD FASHIONED LOVE
       4890  YOU'RE MINE, YOU


Pablo                            2310 733        Ger.  s 12 Inch LP

       4860  BLUES IN MY HEART
       4950  HANDS ACROSS THE TABLE
       4880  IDAHO
       4921  MAKIN' WHOOPEE
       4820  MY BLUE HEAVEN
       4930  OLD FASHIONED LOVE
       4890  YOU'RE MINE, YOU


Pablo                            2310 733A       It.   s 12 Inch LP

       4860  BLUES IN MY HEART
       4950  HANDS ACROSS THE TABLE
       4880  IDAHO
       4921  MAKIN' WHOOPEE
       4820  MY BLUE HEAVEN
       4930  OLD FASHIONED LOVE
       4890  YOU'RE MINE, YOU


Pablo                            2310-733        USA   s 12 Inch LP

       4860  BLUES IN MY HEART
       4950  HANDS ACROSS THE TABLE
       4880  IDAHO
       4921  MAKIN' WHOOPEE
       4820  MY BLUE HEAVEN
       4930  OLD FASHIONED LOVE
       4890  YOU'RE MINE, YOU


Pablo                            2310 734        Braz. s 12 Inch LP

       5240  I SURRENDER DEAR
       5270  I WON'T DANCE
       5300  IN A SENTIMENTAL MOOD
       5280  MOON SONG
       5310  NIGHT AND DAY
       5250  MOON IS LOW, THE
       5290  THIS CAN'T BE LOVE
       5260  YOU TOOK ADVANTAGE OF ME
```

```
Pablo                         2310-734        Can.  s 12 Inch LP

    5240  I SURRENDER DEAR
    5270  I WON'T DANCE
    5300  IN A SENTIMENTAL MOOD
    5280  MOON SONG
    5310  NIGHT AND DAY
    5250  MOON IS LOW, THE
    5290  THIS CAN'T BE LOVE
    5260  YOU TOOK ADVANTAGE OF ME


Pablo                         2310 734        Eng.  s 12 Inch LP

    5240  I SURRENDER DEAR
    5270  I WON'T DANCE
    5300  IN A SENTIMENTAL MOOD
    5280  MOON SONG
    5310  NIGHT AND DAY
    5250  MOON IS LOW, THE
    5290  THIS CAN'T BE LOVE
    5260  YOU TOOK ADVANTAGE OF ME


Pablo                         2310 734        Fr.   s 12 Inch LP

    5240  I SURRENDER DEAR
    5270  I WON'T DANCE
    5300  IN A SENTIMENTAL MOOD
    5280  MOON SONG
    5310  NIGHT AND DAY
    5250  MOON IS LOW, THE
    5290  THIS CAN'T BE LOVE
    5260  YOU TOOK ADVANTAGE OF ME


Pablo                         2310 734        Ger.  s 12 Inch LP

    5240  I SURRENDER DEAR
    5270  I WON'T DANCE
    5300  IN A SENTIMENTAL MOOD
    5280  MOON SONG
    5310  NIGHT AND DAY
    5250  MOON IS LOW, THE
    5290  THIS CAN'T BE LOVE
    5260  YOU TOOK ADVANTAGE OF ME


Pablo                         2310 734A       It.   s 12 Inch LP

    5240  I SURRENDER DEAR
    5270  I WON'T DANCE
    5300  IN A SENTIMENTAL MOOD
    5280  MOON SONG
    5310  NIGHT AND DAY
    5250  MOON IS LOW, THE
    5290  THIS CAN'T BE LOVE
    5260  YOU TOOK ADVANTAGE OF ME


Pablo                         2310-734        USA   s 12 Inch LP

    5240  I SURRENDER DEAR
    5270  I WON'T DANCE
    5300  IN A SENTIMENTAL MOOD
    5280  MOON SONG
    5310  NIGHT AND DAY
    5250  MOON IS LOW, THE
    5290  THIS CAN'T BE LOVE
    5260  YOU TOOK ADVANTAGE OF ME
```

Pablo   2310 735   Braz. s 12 Inch LP

    5920   BLUE LOU
    5990   I GUESS I´LL HAVE TO CHANGE MY PLANS
    5970   I´LL NEVER BE THE SAME
    5930   IF
    6000   ISN´T IT ROMANTIC
    5960   JUST ONE OF THOSE THINGS
    5980   LOVE FOR SALE
    5950   MORE THAN YOU KNOW
    5940   SOME OTHER SPRING
    6010   TRIO BLUES

Pablo   2310-735   Can. s 12 Inch LP

    5920   BLUE LOU
    5990   I GUESS I´LL HAVE TO CHANGE MY PLANS
    5970   I´LL NEVER BE THE SAME
    5930   IF
    6000   ISN´T IT ROMANTIC
    5960   JUST ONE OF THOSE THINGS
    5980   LOVE FOR SALE
    5950   MORE THAN YOU KNOW
    5940   SOME OTHER SPRING
    6010   TRIO BLUES

Pablo   2310 735   Eng. s 12 Inch LP

    5920   BLUE LOU
    5990   I GUESS I´LL HAVE TO CHANGE MY PLANS
    5970   I´LL NEVER BE THE SAME
    5930   IF
    6000   ISN´T IT ROMANTIC
    5960   JUST ONE OF THOSE THINGS
    5980   LOVE FOR SALE
    5950   MORE THAN YOU KNOW
    5940   SOME OTHER SPRING
    6010   TRIO BLUES

Pablo   2310 735   Fr.   s 12 Inch LP

    5920   BLUE LOU
    5990   I GUESS I´LL HAVE TO CHANGE MY PLANS
    5970   I´LL NEVER BE THE SAME
    5930   IF
    6000   ISN´T IT ROMANTIC
    5960   JUST ONE OF THOSE THINGS
    5980   LOVE FOR SALE
    5950   MORE THAN YOU KNOW
    5940   SOME OTHER SPRING
    6010   TRIO BLUES

Pablo   2310 735   Ger. s 12 Inch LP

    5920   BLUE LOU
    5990   I GUESS I´LL HAVE TO CHANGE MY PLANS
    5970   I´LL NEVER BE THE SAME
    5930   IF
    6000   ISN´T IT ROMANTIC
    5960   JUST ONE OF THOSE THINGS
    5980   LOVE FOR SALE
    5950   MORE THAN YOU KNOW
    5940   SOME OTHER SPRING
    6010   TRIO BLUES

Pablo   2310 735A   It.   s 12 Inch LP

    5920   BLUE LOU
    5990   I GUESS I´LL HAVE TO CHANGE MY PLANS
    5970   I´LL NEVER BE THE SAME

```
        5930   IF
        6000   ISN'T IT ROMANTIC
        5960   JUST ONE OF THOSE THINGS
        5980   LOVE FOR SALE
        5950   MORE THAN YOU KNOW
        5940   SOME OTHER SPRING
        6010   TRIO BLUES
```

Pablo   2310-735   USA   s 12 Inch LP

```
        5920   BLUE LOU
        5990   I GUESS I'LL HAVE TO CHANGE MY PLANS
        5970   I'LL NEVER BE THE SAME
        5930   IF
        6000   ISN'T IT ROMANTIC
        5960   JUST ONE OF THOSE THINGS
        5980   LOVE FOR SALE
        5950   MORE THAN YOU KNOW
        5940   SOME OTHER SPRING
        6010   TRIO BLUES
```

Pablo   2310 736   Braz. s 12 Inch LP

```
        6020   DEEP NIGHT
        6070   FOGGY DAY, A
        6080   LOVER MAN
        6090   MAKIN' WHOOPEE
        6050   MEMORIES OF YOU
        6030   ONCE IN A WHILE
        6040   THIS CAN'T BE LOVE
        6060   YOU'RE MINE, YOU
```

Pablo   2310-736   Can. s 12 Inch LP

```
        6020   DEEP NIGHT
        6070   FOGGY DAY, A
        6080   LOVER MAN
        6090   MAKIN' WHOOPEE
        6050   MEMORIES OF YOU
        6030   ONCE IN A WHILE
        6040   THIS CAN'T BE LOVE
        6060   YOU'RE MINE, YOU
```

Pablo   2310 736   Eng. s 12 Inch LP

```
        6020   DEEP NIGHT
        6070   FOGGY DAY, A
        6080   LOVER MAN
        6090   MAKIN' WHOOPEE
        6050   MEMORIES OF YOU
        6030   ONCE IN A WHILE
        6040   THIS CAN'T BE LOVE
        6060   YOU'RE MINE, YOU
```

Pablo   2310 736   Fr.   s 12 Inch LP

```
        6020   DEEP NIGHT
        6070   FOGGY DAY, A
        6080   LOVER MAN
        6090   MAKIN' WHOOPEE
        6050   MEMORIES OF YOU
        6030   ONCE IN A WHILE
        6040   THIS CAN'T BE LOVE
        6060   YOU'RE MINE, YOU
```

Pablo   2310 736   Ger. s 12 Inch LP

```
        6020   DEEP NIGHT
        6070   FOGGY DAY, A
```

```
       6080   LOVER MAN
       6090   MAKIN' WHOOPEE
       6050   MEMORIES OF YOU
       6030   ONCE IN A WHILE
       6040   THIS CAN'T BE LOVE
       6060   YOU'RE MINE, YOU


Pablo                              2310 736A      It.   s 12 Inch LP

       6020   DEEP NIGHT
       6070   FOGGY DAY, A
       6080   LOVER MAN
       6090   MAKIN' WHOOPEE
       6050   MEMORIES OF YOU
       6030   ONCE IN A WHILE
       6040   THIS CAN'T BE LOVE
       6060   YOU'RE MINE, YOU


Pablo                              2310-736       USA   s 12 Inch LP

       6020   DEEP NIGHT
       6070   FOGGY DAY, A
       6080   LOVER MAN
       6090   MAKIN' WHOOPEE
       6050   MEMORIES OF YOU
       6030   ONCE IN A WHILE
       6040   THIS CAN'T BE LOVE
       6060   YOU'RE MINE, YOU


Pablo                              2310 737       Braz. s 12 Inch LP

       6160   ALL THE THINGS YOU ARE
       6190   GONE WITH THE WIND
       6200   HAVE YOU MET MISS JONES
       6180   MY IDEAL
       6170   MY ONE AND ONLY LOVE
       6210   NIGHT AND DAY
       6220   WHERE OR WHEN


Pablo                              2310-737       Can.  s 12 Inch LP

       6160   ALL THE THINGS YOU ARE
       6190   GONE WITH THE WIND
       6200   HAVE YOU MET MISS JONES
       6180   MY IDEAL
       6170   MY ONE AND ONLY LOVE
       6210   NIGHT AND DAY
       6220   WHERE OR WHEN


Pablo                              2310 737       Eng.  s 12 Inch LP

       6160   ALL THE THINGS YOU ARE
       6190   GONE WITH THE WIND
       6200   HAVE YOU MET MISS JONES
       6180   MY IDEAL
       6170   MY ONE AND ONLY LOVE
       6210   NIGHT AND DAY
       6220   WHERE OR WHEN


Pablo                              2310 737       Fr.   s 12 Inch LP

       6160   ALL THE THINGS YOU ARE
       6190   GONE WITH THE WIND
       6200   HAVE YOU MET MISS JONES
       6180   MY IDEAL
       6170   MY ONE AND ONLY LOVE
       6210   NIGHT AND DAY
       6220   WHERE OR WHEN
```

```
Pablo                           2310 737        Ger.  s 12 Inch LP

     6160   ALL THE THINGS YOU ARE
     6190   GONE WITH THE WIND
     6200   HAVE YOU MET MISS JONES
     6180   MY IDEAL
     6170   MY ONE AND ONLY LOVE
     6210   NIGHT AND DAY
     6220   WHERE OR WHEN


Pablo                           2310-737        USA   s 12 Inch LP

     6160   ALL THE THINGS YOU ARE
     6190   GONE WITH THE WIND
     6200   HAVE YOU MET MISS JONES
     6180   MY IDEAL
     6170   MY ONE AND ONLY LOVE
     6210   NIGHT AND DAY
     6220   WHERE OR WHEN


Pablo                           2310-775        Can.  s 12 Inch LP

     5690   BODY AND SOUL
     5670   LOVE FOR SALE
     5680   LOVE FOR SALE
     5740   LOVER MAN
     5700   PLEASE BE KIND
     5750   PRISONER OF LOVE
     5720   STARS FELL ON ALABAMA
     5730   THIS CAN'T BE LOVE


Pablo                           2310 775        Eng.  s 12 Inch LP

     5690   BODY AND SOUL
     5670   LOVE FOR SALE
     5680   LOVE FOR SALE
     5740   LOVER MAN
     5700   PLEASE BE KIND
     5750   PRISONER OF LOVE
     5720   STARS FELL ON ALABAMA
     5730   THIS CAN'T BE LOVE


Pablo                           2310 775        Ger.  s 12 Inch LP

     5690   BODY AND SOUL
     5670   LOVE FOR SALE
     5680   LOVE FOR SALE
     5740   LOVER MAN
     5700   PLEASE BE KIND
     5750   PRISONER OF LOVE
     5720   STARS FELL ON ALABAMA
     5730   THIS CAN'T BE LOVE


Pablo                           2310-775        USA   s 12 Inch LP

     5690   BODY AND SOUL
     5670   LOVE FOR SALE
     5680   LOVE FOR SALE
     5740   LOVER MAN
     5700   PLEASE BE KIND
     5750   PRISONER OF LOVE
     5720   STARS FELL ON ALABAMA
     5730   THIS CAN'T BE LOVE


Pablo                           2310-789        Can.  s 12 Inch LP

     4420   AUNT HAGAR'S BLUES
     4110   I'VE GOT THE WORLD ON A STRING
     4300   ILL WIND
```

```
       4310   ISN'T THIS A LOVELY DAY
       4200   STAR DUST
       3920   MAN I LOVE, THE
       4460   THEY CAN'T TAKE THAT AWAY FROM ME
       4720   WHAT'S NEW?


Pablo                               2310 789        Eng.  s 12 Inch LP

       4420   AUNT HAGAR'S BLUES
       4110   I'VE GOT THE WORLD ON A STRING
       4300   ILL WIND
       4310   ISN'T THIS A LOVELY DAY
       4200   STAR DUST
       3920   MAN I LOVE, THE
       4460   THEY CAN'T TAKE THAT AWAY FROM ME
       4720   WHAT'S NEW?


Pablo                               2310 789        Ger.  s 12 Inch LP

       4420   AUNT HAGAR'S BLUES
       4110   I'VE GOT THE WORLD ON A STRING
       4300   ILL WIND
       4310   ISN'T THIS A LOVELY DAY
       4200   STAR DUST
       3920   MAN I LOVE, THE
       4460   THEY CAN'T TAKE THAT AWAY FROM ME
       4720   WHAT'S NEW?


Pablo                               2310 789A       It.   s 12 Inch LP

       4420   AUNT HAGAR'S BLUES
       4110   I'VE GOT THE WORLD ON A STRING
       4300   ILL WIND
       4310   ISN'T THIS A LOVELY DAY
       4200   STAR DUST
       3920   MAN I LOVE, THE
       4460   THEY CAN'T TAKE THAT AWAY FROM ME
       4720   WHAT'S NEW?


Pablo                               2310-789        USA   s 12 Inch LP

       4420   AUNT HAGAR'S BLUES
       4110   I'VE GOT THE WORLD ON A STRING
       4300   ILL WIND
       4310   ISN'T THIS A LOVELY DAY
       4200   STAR DUST
       3920   MAN I LOVE, THE
       4460   THEY CAN'T TAKE THAT AWAY FROM ME
       4720   WHAT'S NEW?


Pablo                               2310-790        Can.  s 12 Inch LP

       4560   BLUE MOON
       5070   DON'T WORRY 'BOUT ME
       4240   FINE AND DANDY
       4210   I COVER THE WATERFRONT
       3970   LOUISE
       3930   MAKIN' WHOOPEE
       4550   STARS FELL ON ALABAMA
       4340   STOMPIN' AT THE SAVOY
       4790   THAT OLD FEELING
       4180   YOU'RE DRIVING ME CRAZY


Pablo                               2310 790        Eng.  s 12 Inch LP

       4560   BLUE MOON
       5070   DON'T WORRY 'BOUT ME
       4240   FINE AND DANDY
       4210   I COVER THE WATERFRONT
```

```
       3970  LOUISE
       3930  MAKIN' WHOOPEE
       4550  STARS FELL ON ALABAMA
       4340  STOMPIN' AT THE SAVOY
       4790  THAT OLD FEELING
       4180  YOU'RE DRIVING ME CRAZY


Pablo                                 2310 790        Ger.  s 12 Inch LP

       4560  BLUE MOON
       5070  DON'T WORRY 'BOUT ME
       4240  FINE AND DANDY
       4210  I COVER THE WATERFRONT
       3970  LOUISE
       3930  MAKIN' WHOOPEE
       4550  STARS FELL ON ALABAMA
       4340  STOMPIN' AT THE SAVOY
       4790  THAT OLD FEELING
       4180  YOU'RE DRIVING ME CRAZY


Pablo                                 2310 790A       It.   s 12 Inch LP

       4560  BLUE MOON
       5070  DON'T WORRY 'BOUT ME
       4240  FINE AND DANDY
       4210  I COVER THE WATERFRONT
       3970  LOUISE
       3930  MAKIN' WHOOPEE
       4550  STARS FELL ON ALABAMA
       4340  STOMPIN' AT THE SAVOY
       4790  THAT OLD FEELING
       4180  YOU'RE DRIVING ME CRAZY


Pablo                                 2310-790        USA   s 12 Inch LP

       4560  BLUE MOON
       5070  DON'T WORRY 'BOUT ME
       4240  FINE AND DANDY
       4210  I COVER THE WATERFRONT
       3970  LOUISE
       3930  MAKIN' WHOOPEE
       4550  STARS FELL ON ALABAMA
       4340  STOMPIN' AT THE SAVOY
       4790  THAT OLD FEELING
       4180  YOU'RE DRIVING ME CRAZY


Pablo                                 2310-791        Can.  s 12 Inch LP

       4520  AIN'T MISBEHAVIN'
       4660  CHEROKEE
       5200  DO NOTHIN' TILL YOU HEAR FROM ME
       4000  I'M COMING VIRGINIA
       4390  I'VE GOT A CRUSH ON YOU
       4140  NIGHT AND DAY
       4570  THERE'S A SMALL HOTEL
       4590  WAY YOU LOOK TONIGHT, THE
       4760  YOU'RE BLASE


Pablo                                 2310 791        Eng.  s 12 Inch LP

       4520  AIN'T MISBEHAVIN'
       4660  CHEROKEE
       5200  DO NOTHIN' TILL YOU HEAR FROM ME
       4000  I'M COMING VIRGINIA
       4390  I'VE GOT A CRUSH ON YOU
       4140  NIGHT AND DAY
       4570  THERE'S A SMALL HOTEL
       4590  WAY YOU LOOK TONIGHT, THE
       4760  YOU'RE BLASE
```

```
Pablo                          2310 791          Ger.  s 12 Inch LP

     4520   AIN'T MISBEHAVIN'
     4660   CHEROKEE
     5200   DO NOTHIN' TILL YOU HEAR FROM ME
     4000   I'M COMING VIRGINIA
     4390   I'VE GOT A CRUSH ON YOU
     4140   NIGHT AND DAY
     4570   THERE'S A SMALL HOTEL
     4590   WAY YOU LOOK TONIGHT, THE
     4760   YOU'RE BLASE


Pablo                          2310 791A         It.   s 12 Inch LP

     4520   AIN'T MISBEHAVIN'
     4660   CHEROKEE
     5200   DO NOTHIN' TILL YOU HEAR FROM ME
     4000   I'M COMING VIRGINIA
     4390   I'VE GOT A CRUSH ON YOU
     4140   NIGHT AND DAY
     4570   THERE'S A SMALL HOTEL
     4590   WAY YOU LOOK TONIGHT, THE
     4760   YOU'RE BLASE


Pablo                          2310-791          USA   s 12 Inch LP

     4520   AIN'T MISBEHAVIN'
     4660   CHEROKEE
     5200   DO NOTHIN' TILL YOU HEAR FROM ME
     4000   I'M COMING VIRGINIA
     4390   I'VE GOT A CRUSH ON YOU
     4140   NIGHT AND DAY
     4570   THERE'S A SMALL HOTEL
     4590   WAY YOU LOOK TONIGHT, THE
     4760   YOU'RE BLASE


Pablo                          2310-792          Can.  s 12 Inch LP

     4640   DANCING IN THE DARK
     3960   HUMORESQUE
     4400   JAPANESE SANDMAN, THE
     4540   MIGHTY LAK A ROSE
     5020   MOON SONG
     4530   SMOKE GETS IN YOUR EYES
     5210   SO BEATS MY HEART FOR YOU
     4370   TABOO
     4080   WHAT DOES IT TAKE?


Pablo                          2310 792          Eng.  s 12 Inch LP

     4640   DANCING IN THE DARK
     3960   HUMORESQUE
     4400   JAPANESE SANDMAN, THE
     4540   MIGHTY LAK A ROSE
     5020   MOON SONG
     4530   SMOKE GETS IN YOUR EYES
     5210   SO BEATS MY HEART FOR YOU
     4370   TABOO
     4080   WHAT DOES IT TAKE?


Pablo                          2310 792          Ger.  s 12 Inch LP

     4640   DANCING IN THE DARK
     3960   HUMORESQUE
     4400   JAPANESE SANDMAN, THE
     4540   MIGHTY LAK A ROSE
     5020   MOON SONG
     4530   SMOKE GETS IN YOUR EYES
     5210   SO BEATS MY HEART FOR YOU
     4370   TABOO
```

        4080   WHAT DOES IT TAKE?

Pablo   2310 792A   It.   s 12 Inch LP

        4640   DANCING IN THE DARK
        3960   HUMORESQUE
        4400   JAPANESE SANDMAN, THE
        4540   MIGHTY LAK A ROSE
        5020   MOON SONG
        4530   SMOKE GETS IN YOUR EYES
        5210   SO BEATS MY HEART FOR YOU
        4370   TABOO
        4080   WHAT DOES IT TAKE?

Pablo   2310-792   USA   s 12 Inch LP

        4640   DANCING IN THE DARK
        3960   HUMORESQUE
        4400   JAPANESE SANDMAN, THE
        4540   MIGHTY LAK A ROSE
        5020   MOON SONG
        4530   SMOKE GETS IN YOUR EYES
        5210   SO BEATS MY HEART FOR YOU
        4370   TABOO
        4080   WHAT DOES IT TAKE?

Pablo   2310-793   Can.   s 12 Inch LP

        4320   BLUE SKIES
        5100   I WON´T DANCE
        4270   IN A SENTIMENTAL MOOD
        4480   IT´S THE TALK OF THE TOWN
        5180   ON THE SUNNY SIDE OF THE STREET
        4810   SHE´S FUNNY THAT WAY
        4730   SWEET LORRAINE
        4670   THESE FOOLISH THINGS REMIND ME OF YOU
        4600   YOU GO TO MY HEAD

Pablo   2310 793   Eng.   s 12 Inch LP

        4320   BLUE SKIES
        5100   I WON´T DANCE
        4270   IN A SENTIMENTAL MOOD
        4480   IT´S THE TALK OF THE TOWN
        5180   ON THE SUNNY SIDE OF THE STREET
        4810   SHE´S FUNNY THAT WAY
        4730   SWEET LORRAINE
        4670   THESE FOOLISH THINGS REMIND ME OF YOU
        4600   YOU GO TO MY HEAD

Pablo   2310 793   Ger.   s 12 Inch LP

        4320   BLUE SKIES
        5100   I WON´T DANCE
        4270   IN A SENTIMENTAL MOOD
        4480   IT´S THE TALK OF THE TOWN
        5180   ON THE SUNNY SIDE OF THE STREET
        4810   SHE´S FUNNY THAT WAY
        4730   SWEET LORRAINE
        4670   THESE FOOLISH THINGS REMIND ME OF YOU
        4600   YOU GO TO MY HEAD

Pablo   2310 793A   It.   s 12 Inch LP

        4320   BLUE SKIES
        5100   I WON´T DANCE
        4270   IN A SENTIMENTAL MOOD
        4480   IT´S THE TALK OF THE TOWN
        5180   ON THE SUNNY SIDE OF THE STREET

```
     4810  SHE'S FUNNY THAT WAY
     4730  SWEET LORRAINE
     4670  THESE FOOLISH THINGS REMIND ME OF YOU
     4600  YOU GO TO MY HEAD

Pablo                           2310-793        USA   s 12 Inch LP

     4320  BLUE SKIES
     5100  I WON'T DANCE
     4270  IN A SENTIMENTAL MOOD
     4480  IT'S THE TALK OF THE TOWN
     5180  ON THE SUNNY SIDE OF THE STREET
     4810  SHE'S FUNNY THAT WAY
     4730  SWEET LORRAINE
     4670  THESE FOOLISH THINGS REMIND ME OF YOU
     4600  YOU GO TO MY HEAD

Pablo                           2310 808        Eng.  s 12 Inch LP

     4490  BLUE LOU
     4040  COME RAIN OR COME SHINE
     4030  EMBRACEABLE YOU
     5160  EVERYTHING I HAVE IS YOURS
     4700  I DIDN'T KNOW WHAT TIME IT WAS
     4360  I'M IN THE MOOD FOR LOVE
     4630  SOPHISTICATED LADY
     4470  TEA FOR TWO
     4410  TOO MARVELOUS FOR WORDS
     4090  YOU TOOK ADVANTAGE OF ME

Pablo                           2310 808        Fr.   s 12 Inch LP

     4490  BLUE LOU
     4040  COME RAIN OR COME SHINE
     4030  EMBRACEABLE YOU
     5160  EVERYTHING I HAVE IS YOURS
     4700  I DIDN'T KNOW WHAT TIME IT WAS
     4360  I'M IN THE MOOD FOR LOVE
     4630  SOPHISTICATED LADY
     4470  TEA FOR TWO
     4410  TOO MARVELOUS FOR WORDS
     4090  YOU TOOK ADVANTAGE OF ME

Pablo                           2310 808        Ger.  s 12 Inch LP

     4490  BLUE LOU
     4040  COME RAIN OR COME SHINE
     4030  EMBRACEABLE YOU
     5160  EVERYTHING I HAVE IS YOURS
     4700  I DIDN'T KNOW WHAT TIME IT WAS
     4360  I'M IN THE MOOD FOR LOVE
     4630  SOPHISTICATED LADY
     4470  TEA FOR TWO
     4410  TOO MARVELOUS FOR WORDS
     4090  YOU TOOK ADVANTAGE OF ME

Pablo                           2310 809        Eng.  s 12 Inch LP

     4690  AFTER YOU'VE GONE
           BLUES IN MY HEART (See "If You Hadn't Gone Away")
     5110  I CAN'T GIVE YOU ANYTHING BUT LOVE
     4970  I SURRENDER DEAR
     3900  IF YOU HADN'T GONE AWAY (Incorrectly titled "Blues in
             My Heart")
     4780  INDIANA
     5230  PLEASE BE KIND
     4170  VERY THOUGHT OF YOU, THE
     5030  WHEN YOUR LOVER HAS GONE
     4380  WOULD YOU LIKE TO TAKE A WALK
```

```
Pablo                      2310 809        Fr.   s 12 Inch LP

    4690   AFTER YOU'VE GONE
           BLUES IN MY HEART (See "If You Hadn't Gone Away")
    5110   I CAN'T GIVE YOU ANYTHING BUT LOVE
    4970   I SURRENDER DEAR
    3900   IF YOU HADN'T GONE AWAY (Incorrectly titled "Blues in
           My Heart")
    4780   INDIANA
    5230   PLEASE BE KIND
    4170   VERY THOUGHT OF YOU, THE
    5030   WHEN YOUR LOVER HAS GONE
    4380   WOULD YOU LIKE TO TAKE A WALK


Pablo                      2310 809        Ger.  s 12 Inch LP

    4690   AFTER YOU'VE GONE
           BLUES IN MY HEART (See "If You Hadn't Gone Away")
    5110   I CAN'T GIVE YOU ANYTHING BUT LOVE
    4970   I SURRENDER DEAR
    3900   IF YOU HADN'T GONE AWAY (Incorrectly titled "Blues in
           My Heart")
    4780   INDIANA
    5230   PLEASE BE KIND
    4170   VERY THOUGHT OF YOU, THE
    5030   WHEN YOUR LOVER HAS GONE
    4380   WOULD YOU LIKE TO TAKE A WALK


Pablo                      2310 810        Eng.  s 12 Inch LP

    5140   I GOTTA RIGHT TO SING THE BLUES
    4130   I HADN'T ANYONE 'TILL YOU
    5170   I ONLY HAVE EYES FOR YOU
    4280   I'LL SEE YOU AGAIN
    5220   IF YOU HADN'T GONE AWAY
    4990   MEAN TO ME
    5040   MOON IS LOW, THE
    5060   S'POSIN'
    4330   WITHOUT A SONG
    4770   YOU'RE MINE, YOU


Pablo                      2310 811        Eng.  s 12 Inch LP

    5000   BOULEVARD OF BROKEN DREAMS
    4450   DANNY BOY
    4980   HAPPY FEET
    3990   JUDY
    4430   JUST LIKE A BUTTERFLY THAT'S CAUGHT IN THE RAIN
    5120   LULLABY IN RHYTHM
    3880   MEMORIES OF YOU
    5130   OUT OF NOWHERE
    3890   OVER THE RAINBOW
    4160   SOMEONE TO WATCH OVER ME


Pablo                      2310 812        Eng.  s 12 Inch LP

    3850   CAN'T WE BE FRIENDS
    4580   CARAVAN
    5050   IF I HAD YOU
    4750   ISN'T IT ROMANTIC
    5010   MOONLIGHT ON THE GANGES
    4710   SOMEBODY LOVES ME
    4500   WHEN A WOMAN LOVES A MAN
    4220   WHERE OR WHEN
    4010   WRAP YOUR TROUBLES IS DREAMS


Pablo                      2310-835        Can.  s 12 Inch LP

    4490   BLUE LOU
    4040   COME RAIN OR COME SHINE
```

```
          4030   EMBRACEABLE YOU
          5160   EVERYTHING I HAVE IS YOURS
          4700   I DIDN'T KNOW WHAT TIME IT WAS
          4360   I'M IN THE MOOD FOR LOVE
          4630   SOPHISTICATED LADY
          4470   TEA FOR TWO
          4410   TOO MARVELOUS FOR WORDS
          4090   YOU TOOK ADVANTAGE OF ME

Pablo                           2310-835      USA   s 12 Inch LP

          4490   BLUE LOU
          4040   COME RAIN OR COME SHINE
          4030   EMBRACEABLE YOU
          5160   EVERYTHING I HAVE IS YOURS
          4700   I DIDN'T KNOW WHAT TIME IT WAS
          4360   I'M IN THE MOOD FOR LOVE
          4630   SOPHISTICATED LADY
          4470   TEA FOR TWO
          4410   TOO MARVELOUS FOR WORDS
          4090   YOU TOOK ADVANTAGE OF ME

Pablo                           2310-862      Can.  s 12 Inch LP

          4690   AFTER YOU'VE GONE
                 BLUES IN MY HEART (See "If You Hadn't Gone Away")
          5110   I CAN'T GIVE YOU ANYTHING BUT LOVE
          4970   I SURRENDER DEAR
          3900   IF YOU HADN'T GONE AWAY (Incorrectly titled "Blues in
                 My Heart")
          4780   INDIANA
          5230   PLEASE BE KIND
          4170   VERY THOUGHT OF YOU, THE
          5030   WHEN YOUR LOVER HAS GONE
          4380   WOULD YOU LIKE TO TAKE A WALK

Pablo                           2310-862      USA   s 12 Inch LP

          4690   AFTER YOU'VE GONE
                 BLUES IN MY HEART (See "If You Hadn't Gone Away")
          5110   I CAN'T GIVE YOU ANYTHING BUT LOVE
          4970   I SURRENDER DEAR
          3900   IF YOU HADN'T GONE AWAY (Incorrectly titled "Blues in
                 My Heart")
          4780   INDIANA
          5230   PLEASE BE KIND
          4170   VERY THOUGHT OF YOU, THE
          5030   WHEN YOUR LOVER HAS GONE
          4380   WOULD YOU LIKE TO TAKE A WALK

Pablo                           2310-864      Can.  s 12 Inch LP

          5140   I GOTTA RIGHT TO SING THE BLUES
          4130   I HADN'T ANYONE 'TILL YOU
          5170   I ONLY HAVE EYES FOR YOU
          4280   I'LL SEE YOU AGAIN
          5220   IF YOU HADN'T GONE AWAY
          4990   MEAN TO ME
          5040   MOON IS LOW, THE
          5060   S'POSIN'
          4330   WITHOUT A SONG
          4770   YOU'RE MINE, YOU

Pablo                           2310-864      USA   s 12 Inch LP

          5140   I GOTTA RIGHT TO SING THE BLUES
          4130   I HADN'T ANYONE 'TILL YOU
          5170   I ONLY HAVE EYES FOR YOU
          4280   I'LL SEE YOU AGAIN
          5220   IF YOU HADN'T GONE AWAY
```

```
          4990  MEAN TO ME
          5040  MOON IS LOW, THE
          5060  S'POSIN'
          4330  WITHOUT A SONG
          4770  YOU'RE MINE, YOU


Pablo                              2310-870      Can.  s 12 Inch LP

          5000  BOULEVARD OF BROKEN DREAMS
          4450  DANNY BOY
          4980  HAPPY FEET
          3990  JUDY
          4430  JUST LIKE A BUTTERFLY THAT'S CAUGHT IN THE RAIN
          5120  LULLABY IN RHYTHM
          3880  MEMORIES OF YOU
          5130  OUT OF NOWHERE
          3890  OVER THE RAINBOW
          4160  SOMEONE TO WATCH OVER ME


Pablo                              2310-870      USA   s 12 Inch LP

          5000  BOULEVARD OF BROKEN DREAMS
          4450  DANNY BOY
          4980  HAPPY FEET
          3990  JUDY
          4430  JUST LIKE A BUTTERFLY THAT'S CAUGHT IN THE RAIN
          5120  LULLABY IN RHYTHM
          3880  MEMORIES OF YOU
          5130  OUT OF NOWHERE
          3890  OVER THE RAINBOW
          4160  SOMEONE TO WATCH OVER ME


Pablo            [Part of 2-record set 2625 713.]   2335 749   Eng.  s 12 Inch LP
          4440  GONE WITH THE WIND


Pablo                              2625 703      Ger.  s 12 Inch LP
     [13-record boxed set.]
          4690  AFTER YOU'VE GONE
          4520  AIN'T MISBEHAVIN'
          4250  ALL THE THINGS YOU ARE
                ANYTHING BUT LOVE (See "I Can't Give You Anything But Love")
          4420  AUNT HAGAR'S BLUES
          3950  BEGIN THE BEGUINE
          4490  BLUE LOU
          4560  BLUE MOON
          4320  BLUE SKIES
                BLUES IN MY HEART (See "If You Hadn't Gone Away")
          3910  BODY AND SOUL
          5000  BOULEVARD OF BROKEN DREAMS
          3850  CAN'T WE BE FRIENDS
          4580  CARAVAN
          4660  CHEROKEE
          4040  COME RAIN OR COME SHINE
          4740  CRAZY RHYTHM
          4640  DANCING IN THE DARK
          4450  DANNY BOY
          4680  DEEP PURPLE
          4020  DIXIELAND BAND
          5200  DO NOTHIN' TILL YOU HEAR FROM ME
          5070  DON'T WORRY 'BOUT ME
          3870  ELEGIE
          4030  EMBRACEABLE YOU
          5160  EVERYTHING I HAVE IS YOURS
          4240  FINE AND DANDY
          4190  GHOST OF A CHANCE, A
          4440  GONE WITH THE WIND
          4980  HAPPY FEET
          4260  HAVE YOU MET MISS JONES
          4800  HEAT WAVE
          3960  HUMORESQUE
```

```
5110  I CAN´T GIVE YOU ANYTHING BUT LOVE [Incorrectly titled
         "Anything But Love."]
4210  I COVER THE WATERFRONT
4700  I DIDN´T KNOW WHAT TIME IT WAS
5140  I GOTTA RIGHT TO SING THE BLUES
4130  I HADN´T ANYONE ´TILL YOU
5170  I ONLY HAVE EYES FOR YOU
4970  I SURRENDER DEAR
5100  I WON´T DANCE
4280  I´LL SEE YOU AGAIN
4290  I´LL SEE YOU IN MY DREAMS
4000  I´M COMING VIRGINIA
4360  I´M IN THE MOOD FOR LOVE
4390  I´VE GOT A CRUSH ON YOU
4110  I´VE GOT THE WORLD ON A STRING
5050  IF I HAD YOU
3900  IF YOU HADN´T GONE AWAY (Incorrectly titled "Blues in
         My Heart")
5220  IF YOU HADN´T GONE AWAY
4300  ILL WIND
4270  IN A SENTIMENTAL MOOD
4780  INDIANA
4750  ISN´T IT ROMANTIC
4310  ISN´T THIS A LOVELY DAY
5150  IT´S ONLY A PAPER MOON
4480  IT´S THE TALK OF THE TOWN
4400  JAPANESE SANDMAN, THE
4150  JITTERBUG WALTZ
3990  JUDY
4430  JUST LIKE A BUTTERFLY THAT´S CAUGHT IN THE RAIN
3970  LOUISE
3980  LOVE FOR SALE
4650  LOVE ME OR LEAVE ME
4620  LOVER, COME BACK TO ME!
5120  LULLABY IN RHYTHM
3930  MAKIN´ WHOOPEE
3920  MAN I LOVE, THE
4990  MEAN TO ME
3880  MEMORIES OF YOU
4540  MIGHTY LAK A ROSE
5040  MOON IS LOW, THE
5020  MOON SONG
5090  MOONGLOW
5010  MOONLIGHT ON THE GANGES
4350  MY LAST AFFAIR
4140  NIGHT AND DAY
5180  ON THE SUNNY SIDE OF THE STREET
5130  OUT OF NOWHERE
3890  OVER THE RAINBOW
5230  PLEASE BE KIND
5080  PRISONER OF LOVE
5060  S´POSIN´
3940  SEPTEMBER SONG
4810  SHE´S FUNNY THAT WAY
4050  SITTIN´ AND ROCKIN´
4530  SMOKE GETS IN YOUR EYES
5210  SO BEATS MY HEART FOR YOU
4710  SOMEBODY LOVES ME
4160  SOMEONE TO WATCH OVER ME
4630  SOPHISTICATED LADY
4200  STAR DUST
4550  STARS FELL ON ALABAMA
4230  STAY AS SWEET AS YOU ARE
4340  STOMPIN´ AT THE SAVOY
4730  SWEET LORRAINE
4370  TABOO
4470  TEA FOR TWO
4070  TENDERLY
4790  THAT OLD FEELING
4060  THERE WILL NEVER BE ANOTHER YOU
4570  THERE´S A SMALL HOTEL
4670  THESE FOOLISH THINGS REMIND ME OF YOU
4460  THEY CAN´T TAKE THAT AWAY FROM ME
3860  THIS CAN´T BE LOVE
4410  TOO MARVELOUS FOR WORDS
```

```
      4170  VERY THOUGHT OF YOU, THE
      4590  WAY YOU LOOK TONIGHT, THE
      4080  WHAT DOES IT TAKE?
      4720  WHAT'S NEW?
      4500  WHEN A WOMAN LOVES A MAN
      5030  WHEN YOUR LOVER HAS GONE
      4220  WHERE OR WHEN
      4510  WILLOW WEEP FOR ME
      4330  WITHOUT A SONG
      4380  WOULD YOU LIKE TO TAKE A WALK
      4010  WRAP YOUR TROUBLES IS DREAMS
      4120  YESTERDAYS
      4600  YOU GO TO MY HEAD
      4090  YOU TOOK ADVANTAGE OF ME
      4760  YOU'RE BLASE
      4180  YOU'RE DRIVING ME CRAZY
      4770  YOU'RE MINE, YOU
```

Pablo   2625-703   USA   s 12 Inch LP
   [13-record boxed set.]

```
      4690  AFTER YOU'VE GONE
      4520  AIN'T MISBEHAVIN'
      4250  ALL THE THINGS YOU ARE
            ANYTHING BUT LOVE (See "I Can't Give You Anything But Love.")
      4420  AUNT HAGAR'S BLUES
      3950  BEGIN THE BEGUINE
      4490  BLUE LOU
      4560  BLUE MOON
      4320  BLUE SKIES
            BLUES IN MY HEART (See "If You Hadn't Gone Away")
      3910  BODY AND SOUL
      5000  BOULEVARD OF BROKEN DREAMS
      3850  CAN'T WE BE FRIENDS
      4580  CARAVAN
      4660  CHEROKEE
      4040  COME RAIN OR COME SHINE
      4740  CRAZY RHYTHM
      4640  DANCING IN THE DARK
      4450  DANNY BOY
      4680  DEEP PURPLE
      4020  DIXIELAND BAND
      5200  DO NOTHIN' TILL YOU HEAR FROM ME
      5070  DON'T WORRY 'BOUT ME
      3870  ELEGIE
      4030  EMBRACEABLE YOU
      5160  EVERYTHING I HAVE IS YOURS
      4240  FINE AND DANDY
      4190  GHOST OF A CHANCE, A
      4440  GONE WITH THE WIND
      4980  HAPPY FEET
      4260  HAVE YOU MET MISS JONES
      4800  HEAT WAVE
      3960  HUMORESQUE
      5110  I CAN'T GIVE YOU ANYTHING BUT LOVE [Incorrectly titled
               "Anything But Love."]
      4210  I COVER THE WATERFRONT
      4700  I DIDN'T KNOW WHAT TIME IT WAS
      5140  I GOTTA RIGHT TO SING THE BLUES
      4130  I HADN'T ANYONE 'TILL YOU
      5170  I ONLY HAVE EYES FOR YOU
      4970  I SURRENDER DEAR
      5100  I WON'T DANCE
      4280  I'LL SEE YOU AGAIN
      4290  I'LL SEE YOU IN MY DREAMS
      4000  I'M COMING VIRGINIA
      4360  I'M IN THE MOOD FOR LOVE
      4390  I'VE GOT A CRUSH ON YOU
      4110  I'VE GOT THE WORLD ON A STRING
      5050  IF I HAD YOU
      3900  IF YOU HADN'T GONE AWAY (Incorrectly titled "Blues in
               My Heart")
      5220  IF YOU HADN'T GONE AWAY
      4300  ILL WIND
      4270  IN A SENTIMENTAL MOOD
```

```
4780   INDIANA
4750   ISN'T IT ROMANTIC
4310   ISN'T THIS A LOVELY DAY
5150   IT'S ONLY A PAPER MOON
4480   IT'S THE TALK OF THE TOWN
4400   JAPANESE SANDMAN, THE
4150   JITTERBUG WALTZ
3990   JUDY
4430   JUST LIKE A BUTTERFLY THAT'S CAUGHT IN THE RAIN
3970   LOUISE
3980   LOVE FOR SALE
4650   LOVE ME OR LEAVE ME
4620   LOVER, COME BACK TO ME!
5120   LULLABY IN RHYTHM
3930   MAKIN' WHOOPEE
3920   MAN I LOVE, THE
4990   MEAN TO ME
3880   MEMORIES OF YOU
4540   MIGHTY LAK A ROSE
5040   MOON IS LOW, THE
5020   MOON SONG
5090   MOONGLOW
5010   MOONLIGHT ON THE GANGES
4350   MY LAST AFFAIR
4140   NIGHT AND DAY
5180   ON THE SUNNY SIDE OF THE STREET
5130   OUT OF NOWHERE
3890   OVER THE RAINBOW
5230   PLEASE BE KIND
5080   PRISONER OF LOVE
5060   S'POSIN'
3940   SEPTEMBER SONG
4810   SHE'S FUNNY THAT WAY
4050   SITTIN' AND ROCKIN'
4530   SMOKE GETS IN YOUR EYES
5210   SO BEATS MY HEART FOR YOU
4710   SOMEBODY LOVES ME
4160   SOMEONE TO WATCH OVER ME
4630   SOPHISTICATED LADY
4200   STAR DUST
4550   STARS FELL ON ALABAMA
4230   STAY AS SWEET AS YOU ARE
4340   STOMPIN' AT THE SAVOY
4730   SWEET LORRAINE
4370   TABOO
4470   TEA FOR TWO
4070   TENDERLY
4790   THAT OLD FEELING
4060   THERE WILL NEVER BE ANOTHER YOU
4570   THERE'S A SMALL HOTEL
4670   THESE FOOLISH THINGS REMIND ME OF YOU
4460   THEY CAN'T TAKE THAT AWAY FROM ME
3860   THIS CAN'T BE LOVE
4410   TOO MARVELOUS FOR WORDS
4170   VERY THOUGHT OF YOU, THE
4590   WAY YOU LOOK TONIGHT, THE
4080   WHAT DOES IT TAKE?
4720   WHAT'S NEW?
4500   WHEN A WOMAN LOVES A MAN
5030   WHEN YOUR LOVER HAS GONE
4220   WHERE OR WHEN
4510   WILLOW WEEP FOR ME
4330   WITHOUT A SONG
4380   WOULD YOU LIKE TO TAKE A WALK
4010   WRAP YOUR TROUBLES IS DREAMS
4120   YESTERDAYS
4600   YOU GO TO MY HEAD
4090   YOU TOOK ADVANTAGE OF ME
4760   YOU'RE BLASE
4180   YOU'RE DRIVING ME CRAZY
4770   YOU'RE MINE, YOU
```

```
Pablo                           2625 706        Eng.  s 12 Inch LP
  [8-record boxed set.]
    4940   'S WONDERFUL
    6160   ALL THE THINGS YOU ARE
    5920   BLUE LOU
    4830   BLUES IN B FLAT
    4840   BLUES IN C
    4860   BLUES IN MY HEART
    6020   DEEP NIGHT
    5810   DEEP PURPLE
    4850   FOGGY DAY, A
    6070   FOGGY DAY, A
    6190   GONE WITH THE WIND
    5650   HALLELUJAH
    4950   HANDS ACROSS THE TABLE
    6200   HAVE YOU MET MISS JONES
    5780   HOW HIGH THE MOON
    5990   I GUESS I'LL HAVE TO CHANGE MY PLANS
    5240   I SURRENDER DEAR
    5270   I WON'T DANCE
    5660   I'LL NEVER BE THE SAME
    5970   I'LL NEVER BE THE SAME
    4880   IDAHO
    5930   IF
    5300   IN A SENTIMENTAL MOOD
    6000   ISN'T IT ROMANTIC
    5960   JUST ONE OF THOSE THINGS
    5980   LOVE FOR SALE
    6080   LOVER MAN
    4921   MAKIN' WHOOPEE
    5760   MAKIN' WHOOPEE
    6090   MAKIN' WHOOPEE
    6050   MEMORIES OF YOU
    5250   MOON IS LOW, THE
    5280   MOON SONG
    5770   MORE THAN YOU KNOW
    5950   MORE THAN YOU KNOW
    4820   MY BLUE HEAVEN
    6180   MY IDEAL
    6170   MY ONE AND ONLY LOVE
    5310   NIGHT AND DAY
    6210   NIGHT AND DAY
    4930   OLD FASHIONED LOVE
    6030   ONCE IN A WHILE
    5640   PERDIDO
    5790   PLAID
    5830   SEPTEMBER SONG
    5940   SOME OTHER SPRING
    5800   SOMEBODY LOVES ME
    4870   STREET OF DREAMS
    5290   THIS CAN'T BE LOVE
    6040   THIS CAN'T BE LOVE
    6010   TRIO BLUES
    4900   UNDECIDED
    4910   UNDER A BLANKET OF BLUE
    5840   VERVE BLUES
    5710   WHAT IS THIS THING CALLED LOVE
    6220   WHERE OR WHEN
    5260   YOU TOOK ADVANTAGE OF ME
    4890   YOU'RE MINE, YOU
    6060   YOU'RE MINE, YOU


Pablo                           2625 706        Ger.  s 12 Inch LP
  [8-record boxed set.]
    4940   'S WONDERFUL
    6160   ALL THE THINGS YOU ARE
    5920   BLUE LOU
    4830   BLUES IN B FLAT
    4840   BLUES IN C
    4860   BLUES IN MY HEART
    6020   DEEP NIGHT
    5810   DEEP PURPLE
    4850   FOGGY DAY, A
    6070   FOGGY DAY, A
```

```
6190  GONE WITH THE WIND
5650  HALLELUJAH
4950  HANDS ACROSS THE TABLE
6200  HAVE YOU MET MISS JONES
5780  HOW HIGH THE MOON
5990  I GUESS I'LL HAVE TO CHANGE MY PLANS
5240  I SURRENDER DEAR
5270  I WON'T DANCE
5660  I'LL NEVER BE THE SAME
5970  I'LL NEVER BE THE SAME
4880  IDAHO
5930  IF
5300  IN A SENTIMENTAL MOOD
6000  ISN'T IT ROMANTIC
5960  JUST ONE OF THOSE THINGS
5980  LOVE FOR SALE
6080  LOVER MAN
4921  MAKIN' WHOOPEE
5760  MAKIN' WHOOPEE
6090  MAKIN' WHOOPEE
6050  MEMORIES OF YOU
5250  MOON IS LOW, THE
5280  MOON SONG
5770  MORE THAN YOU KNOW
5950  MORE THAN YOU KNOW
4820  MY BLUE HEAVEN
6180  MY IDEAL
6170  MY ONE AND ONLY LOVE
5310  NIGHT AND DAY
6210  NIGHT AND DAY
4930  OLD FASHIONED LOVE
6030  ONCE IN A WHILE
5640  PERDIDO
5790  PLAID
5830  SEPTEMBER SONG
5940  SOME OTHER SPRING
5800  SOMEBODY LOVES ME
4870  STREET OF DREAMS
5290  THIS CAN'T BE LOVE
6040  THIS CAN'T BE LOVE
6010  TRIO BLUES
4900  UNDECIDED
4910  UNDER A BLANKET OF BLUE
5840  VERVE BLUES
5710  WHAT IS THIS THING CALLED LOVE
6220  WHERE OR WHEN
5260  YOU TOOK ADVANTAGE OF ME
4890  YOU'RE MINE, YOU
6060  YOU'RE MINE, YOU
```

Pablo   2625-0706   USA   s 12 Inch LP

[8-record boxed set.]

```
4940  'S WONDERFUL
6160  ALL THE THINGS YOU ARE
5920  BLUE LOU
4830  BLUES IN B FLAT
4840  BLUES IN C
4860  BLUES IN MY HEART
6020  DEEP NIGHT
5810  DEEP PURPLE
4850  FOGGY DAY, A
6070  FOGGY DAY, A
6190  GONE WITH THE WIND
5650  HALLELUJAH
4950  HANDS ACROSS THE TABLE
6200  HAVE YOU MET MISS JONES
5780  HOW HIGH THE MOON
5990  I GUESS I'LL HAVE TO CHANGE MY PLANS
5240  I SURRENDER DEAR
5270  I WON'T DANCE
5660  I'LL NEVER BE THE SAME
5970  I'LL NEVER BE THE SAME
4880  IDAHO
5930  IF
```

```
5300    IN A SENTIMENTAL MOOD
6000    ISN´T IT ROMANTIC
5960    JUST ONE OF THOSE THINGS
5980    LOVE FOR SALE
6080    LOVER MAN
4921    MAKIN´ WHOOPEE
5760    MAKIN´ WHOOPEE
6090    MAKIN´ WHOOPEE
6050    MEMORIES OF YOU
5250    MOON IS LOW, THE
5280    MOON SONG
5770    MORE THAN YOU KNOW
5950    MORE THAN YOU KNOW
4820    MY BLUE HEAVEN
6180    MY IDEAL
6170    MY ONE AND ONLY LOVE
5310    NIGHT AND DAY
6210    NIGHT AND DAY
4930    OLD FASHIONED LOVE
6030    ONCE IN A WHILE
5640    PERDIDO
5790    PLAID
5830    SEPTEMBER SONG
5940    SOME OTHER SPRING
5800    SOMEBODY LOVES ME
4870    STREET OF DREAMS
5290    THIS CAN´T BE LOVE
6040    THIS CAN´T BE LOVE
6010    TRIO BLUES
4900    UNDECIDED
4910    UNDER A BLANKET OF BLUE
5840    VERVE BLUES
5710    WHAT IS THIS THING CALLED LOVE
6220    WHERE OR WHEN
5260    YOU TOOK ADVANTAGE OF ME
4890    YOU´RE MINE, YOU
6060    YOU´RE MINE, YOU
```

Pablo   2625 713   Eng.
  [2-record set containing 2335 749.]

Pablo   2660 110   Eng. s 12 Inch LP
  [13-record boxed set.]
```
    4690    AFTER YOU´VE GONE
    4520    AIN´T MISBEHAVIN´
    4250    ALL THE THINGS YOU ARE
            ANYTHING BUT LOVE (See "I Can´t Give You Anything But Love"]
    4420    AUNT HAGAR´S BLUES
    3950    BEGIN THE BEGUINE
    4490    BLUE LOU
    4560    BLUE MOON
    4320    BLUE SKIES
            BLUES IN MY HEART (See "If You Hadn´t Gone Away")
    3910    BODY AND SOUL
    5000    BOULEVARD OF BROKEN DREAMS
    3850    CAN´T WE BE FRIENDS
    4580    CARAVAN
    4660    CHEROKEE
    4040    COME RAIN OR COME SHINE
    4740    CRAZY RHYTHM
    4640    DANCING IN THE DARK
    4450    DANNY BOY
    4680    DEEP PURPLE
    4020    DIXIELAND BAND
    5200    DO NOTHIN´ TILL YOU HEAR FROM ME
    5070    DON´T WORRY ´BOUT ME
    3870    ELEGIE
    4030    EMBRACEABLE YOU
    5160    EVERYTHING I HAVE IS YOURS
    4240    FINE AND DANDY
    4190    GHOST OF A CHANCE, A
    4440    GONE WITH THE WIND
    4980    HAPPY FEET
```

```
4260   HAVE YOU MET MISS JONES
4800   HEAT WAVE
3960   HUMORESQUE
5110   I CAN'T GIVE YOU ANYTHING BUT LOVE [Incorrectly titled
          "Anything But Love."]
4210   I COVER THE WATERFRONT
4700   I DIDN'T KNOW WHAT TIME IT WAS
5140   I GOTTA RIGHT TO SING THE BLUES
4130   I HADN'T ANYONE 'TILL YOU
5170   I ONLY HAVE EYES FOR YOU
4970   I SURRENDER DEAR
5100   I WON'T DANCE
4280   I'LL SEE YOU AGAIN
4290   I'LL SEE YOU IN MY DREAMS
4000   I'M COMING VIRGINIA
4360   I'M IN THE MOOD FOR LOVE
4390   I'VE GOT A CRUSH ON YOU
4110   I'VE GOT THE WORLD ON A STRING
5050   IF I HAD YOU
3900   IF YOU HADN'T GONE AWAY (Incorrectly titled "Blues in
          My Heart")
5220   IF YOU HADN'T GONE AWAY
4300   ILL WIND
4270   IN A SENTIMENTAL MOOD
4780   INDIANA
4750   ISN'T IT ROMANTIC
4310   ISN'T THIS A LOVELY DAY
5150   IT'S ONLY A PAPER MOON
4480   IT'S THE TALK OF THE TOWN
4400   JAPANESE SANDMAN, THE
4150   JITTERBUG WALTZ
3990   JUDY
4430   JUST LIKE A BUTTERFLY THAT'S CAUGHT IN THE RAIN
3970   LOUISE
3980   LOVE FOR SALE
4650   LOVE ME OR LEAVE ME
4620   LOVER, COME BACK TO ME!
5120   LULLABY IN RHYTHM
3930   MAKIN' WHOOPEE
3920   MAN I LOVE, THE
4990   MEAN TO ME
3880   MEMORIES OF YOU
4540   MIGHTY LAK A ROSE
5040   MOON IS LOW, THE
5020   MOON SONG
5090   MOONGLOW
5010   MOONLIGHT ON THE GANGES
4350   MY LAST AFFAIR
4140   NIGHT AND DAY
5180   ON THE SUNNY SIDE OF THE STREET
5130   OUT OF NOWHERE
3890   OVER THE RAINBOW
5230   PLEASE BE KIND
5080   PRISONER OF LOVE
5060   S'POSIN'
3940   SEPTEMBER SONG
4810   SHE'S FUNNY THAT WAY
4050   SITTIN' AND ROCKIN'
4530   SMOKE GETS IN YOUR EYES
5210   SO BEATS MY HEART FOR YOU
4710   SOMEBODY LOVES ME
4160   SOMEONE TO WATCH OVER ME
4630   SOPHISTICATED LADY
4200   STAR DUST
4550   STARS FELL ON ALABAMA
4230   STAY AS SWEET AS YOU ARE
4340   STOMPIN' AT THE SAVOY
4730   SWEET LORRAINE
4370   TABOO
4470   TEA FOR TWO
4070   TENDERLY
4790   THAT OLD FEELING
4060   THERE WILL NEVER BE ANOTHER YOU
4570   THERE'S A SMALL HOTEL
4670   THESE FOOLISH THINGS REMIND ME OF YOU
```

```
4460  THEY CAN'T TAKE THAT AWAY FROM ME
3860  THIS CAN'T BE LOVE
4410  TOO MARVELOUS FOR WORDS
4170  VERY THOUGHT OF YOU, THE
4590  WAY YOU LOOK TONIGHT, THE
4080  WHAT DOES IT TAKE?
4720  WHAT'S NEW?
4500  WHEN A WOMAN LOVES A MAN
5030  WHEN YOUR LOVER HAS GONE
4220  WHERE OR WHEN
4510  WILLOW WEEP FOR ME
4330  WITHOUT A SONG
4380  WOULD YOU LIKE TO TAKE A WALK
4010  WRAP YOUR TROUBLES IS DREAMS
4120  YESTERDAYS
4600  YOU GO TO MY HEAD
4090  YOU TOOK ADVANTAGE OF ME
4760  YOU'RE BLASE
4180  YOU'RE DRIVING ME CRAZY
4770  YOU'RE MINE, YOU
```

Pablo   28MJ 3146   Jap. s 12 Inch LP

```
5140  I GOTTA RIGHT TO SING THE BLUES
4130  I HADN'T ANYONE 'TILL YOU
5170  I ONLY HAVE EYES FOR YOU
4280  I'LL SEE YOU AGAIN
5220  IF YOU HADN'T GONE AWAY
4990  MEAN TO ME
5040  MOON IS LOW, THE
5060  S'POSIN'
4330  WITHOUT A SONG
4770  YOU'RE MINE, YOU
```

Pablo   28MJ 3147   Jap. s 12 Inch LP

```
5000  BOULEVARD OF BROKEN DREAMS
4450  DANNY BOY
4980  HAPPY FEET
3990  JUDY
4430  JUST LIKE A BUTTERFLY THAT'S CAUGHT IN THE RAIN
5120  LULLABY IN RHYTHM
3880  MEMORIES OF YOU
5130  OUT OF NOWHERE
3890  OVER THE RAINBOW
4160  SOMEONE TO WATCH OVER ME
```

Pablo   MTF 1062   Jap. s 12 Inch LP

```
4940  'S WONDERFUL
4830  BLUES IN B FLAT
4840  BLUES IN C
4850  FOGGY DAY, A
4870  STREET OF DREAMS
4900  UNDECIDED
4910  UNDER A BLANKET OF BLUE
```

Pablo   MTF 1063   Jap. s 12 Inch LP

```
4860  BLUES IN MY HEART
4950  HANDS ACROSS THE TABLE
4880  IDAHO
4921  MAKIN' WHOOPEE
4820  MY BLUE HEAVEN
4930  OLD FASHIONED LOVE
4890  YOU'RE MINE, YOU
```

```
Pablo                          MTF 1064        Jap.  s 12 Inch LP

    6020   DEEP NIGHT
    6070   FOGGY DAY, A
    6080   LOVER MAN
    6090   MAKIN´ WHOOPEE
    6050   MEMORIES OF YOU
    6030   ONCE IN A WHILE
    6040   THIS CAN´T BE LOVE
    6060   YOU´RE MINE, YOU


Pablo                          MTF 1071        Jap.  s 12 Inch LP

    5240   I SURRENDER DEAR
    5270   I WON´T DANCE
    5300   IN A SENTIMENTAL MOOD
    5280   MOON SONG
    5310   NIGHT AND DAY
    5250   MOON IS LOW, THE
    5290   THIS CAN´T BE LOVE
    5260   YOU TOOK ADVANTAGE OF ME


Pablo                          MTF 1072        Jap.  s 12 Inch LP

    5810   DEEP PURPLE
    5790   PLAID
    5830   SEPTEMBER SONG
    5800   SOMEBODY LOVES ME
    5840   VERVE BLUES


Pablo                          MTF 1073        Jap.  s 12 Inch LP

    3910   BODY AND SOUL
    4260   HAVE YOU MET MISS JONES
    5150   IT´S ONLY A PAPER MOON
    3980   LOVE FOR SALE
    5090   MOONGLOW
    4350   MY LAST AFFAIR
    4050   SITTIN´ AND ROCKIN´
    4230   STAY AS SWEET AS YOU ARE
    4510   WILLOW WEEP FOR ME


Pablo                          MTF 1074        Jap.  s 12 Inch LP

    3870   ELEGIE
    4190   GHOST OF A CHANCE, A
    4440   GONE WITH THE WIND
    4800   HEAT WAVE
    4290   I´LL SEE YOU IN MY DREAMS
    4620   LOVER, COME BACK TO ME!
    3940   SEPTEMBER SONG
    4060   THERE WILL NEVER BE ANOTHER YOU
    3860   THIS CAN´T BE LOVE


Pablo                          MTF 1075        Jap.  s 12 Inch LP

    4250   ALL THE THINGS YOU ARE
    3950   BEGIN THE BEGUINE
    4740   CRAZY RHYTHM
    4680   DEEP PURPLE
    4020   DIXIELAND BAND
    4150   JITTERBUG WALTZ
    4650   LOVE ME OR LEAVE ME
    5080   PRISONER OF LOVE
    4070   TENDERLY
    4120   YESTERDAYS
```

Pablo   MTF 1076   Jap. s 12 Inch LP

     4420 AUNT HAGAR'S BLUES
     4110 I'VE GOT THE WORLD ON A STRING
     4300 ILL WIND
     4310 ISN'T THIS A LOVELY DAY
     3920 MAN I LOVE, THE
     4200 STAR DUST
     4460 THEY CAN'T TAKE THAT AWAY FROM ME
     4720 WHAT'S NEW?

Pablo   MTF 1077   Jap. s 12 Inch LP

     4560 BLUE MOON
     4240 FINE AND DANDY
     4210 I COVER THE WATERFRONT
     3970 LOUISE
     3930 MAKIN' WHOOPEE
     4550 STARS FELL ON ALABAMA
     4340 STOMPIN' AT THE SAVOY
     4790 THAT OLD FEELING
     4180 YOU'RE DRIVING ME CRAZY

Pablo   MTF 1078   Jap. s 12 Inch LP

     4520 AIN'T MISBEHAVIN'
     4660 CHEROKEE
     5200 DO NOTHIN' TILL YOU HEAR FROM ME
     4000 I'M COMING VIRGINIA
     4390 I'VE GOT A CRUSH ON YOU
     4140 NIGHT AND DAY
     4570 THERE'S A SMALL HOTEL
     4590 WAY YOU LOOK TONIGHT, THE
     4760 YOU'RE BLASE

Pablo   MTF 1079   Jap. s 12 Inch LP

     4640 DANCING IN THE DARK
     3960 HUMORESQUE
     4400 JAPANESE SANDMAN, THE
     4540 MIGHTY LAK A ROSE
     5020 MOON SONG
     4530 SMOKE GETS IN YOUR EYES
     5210 SO BEATS MY HEART FOR YOU
     4370 TABOO
     4080 WHAT DOES IT TAKE?

Pablo   MTF 1080   Jap. s 12 Inch LP

     4320 BLUE SKIES
     5100 I WON'T DANCE
     4270 IN A SENTIMENTAL MOOD
     4480 IT'S THE TALK OF THE TOWN
     5180 ON THE SUNNY SIDE OF THE STREET
     4810 SHE'S FUNNY THAT WAY
     4730 SWEET LORRAINE
     4670 THESE FOOLISH THINGS REMIND ME OF YOU
     4600 YOU GO TO MY HEAD

Pablo   MTF 1095   Jap. s 12 Inch LP

     4490 BLUE LOU
     4040 COME RAIN OR COME SHINE
     4030 EMBRACEABLE YOU
     5160 EVERYTHING I HAVE IS YOURS
     4700 I DIDN'T KNOW WHAT TIME IT WAS
     4360 I'M IN THE MOOD FOR LOVE
     4630 SOPHISTICATED LADY
     4470 TEA FOR TWO
     4410 TOO MARVELOUS FOR WORDS

4090 YOU TOOK ADVANTAGE OF ME

Pablo   MTF 1096   Jap. s 12 Inch LP

    4690 AFTER YOU´VE GONE
          BLUES IN MY HEART (See "If You Hadn´t Gone Away")
    5110 I CAN´T GIVE YOU ANYTHING BUT LOVE
    4970 I SURRENDER DEAR
    3900 IF YOU HADN´T GONE AWAY (Incorrectly titled "Blues in
           My Heart")
    4780 INDIANA
    5230 PLEASE BE KIND
    4170 VERY THOUGHT OF YOU, THE
    5030 WHEN YOUR LOVER HAS GONE
    4380 WOULD YOU LIKE TO TAKE A WALK

Pablo   MTF 1114   Jap. s 12 Inch LP

    5690 BODY AND SOUL
    5670 LOVE FOR SALE
    5680 LOVE FOR SALE
    5740 LOVER MAN
    5700 PLEASE BE KIND
    5750 PRISONER OF LOVE
    5720 STARS FELL ON ALABAMA
    5730 THIS CAN´T BE LOVE

Pablo   MW 2140   Jap. s 12 Inch LP

    5650 HALLELUJAH
    5780 HOW HIGH THE MOON
    5660 I LL NEVER BE THE SAME
    5760 MAKIN´ WHOOPEE
    5770 MORE THAN YOU KNOW
    5640 PERDIDO
    5710 WHAT IS THIS THING CALLED LOVE

Pablo   MW 2174   Jap. s 12 Inch LP

    6160 ALL THE THINGS YOU ARE
    6190 GONE WITH THE WIND
    6200 HAVE YOU MET MISS JONES
    6180 MY IDEAL
    6170 MY ONE AND ONLY LOVE
    6210 NIGHT AND DAY
    6220 WHERE OR WHEN

Pablo   MW 2175   Jap. s 12 Inch LP

    5920 BLUE LOU
    5990 I GUESS I´LL HAVE TO CHANGE MY PLANS
    5970 I´LL NEVER BE THE SAME
    5930 IF
    6000 ISN´T IT ROMANTIC
    5960 JUST ONE OF THOSE THINGS
    5980 LOVE FOR SALE
    5950 MORE THAN YOU KNOW
    5940 SOME OTHER SPRING
    6010 TRIO BLUES

Palm 30   P.30:07   Eng.   12 Inch LP

    1550 DO NOTHIN´ TILL YOU HEAR FROM ME
    1530 ESQUIRE BLUES
    1570 I CAN´T GIVE YOU ANYTHING BUT LOVE
    1600 I GOT RHYTHM
    1580 I GOTTA RIGHT TO SING THE BLUES
    1560 I LOVE MY MAN (Billie´s Blues)
    1540 MOP MOP

1590   SWEET LORRAINE

Palm 30   P.30:13   Eng.   12 Inch LP

    1670   BACK O´ TOWN BLUES
    1640   BASIN STREET BLUES
    1610   BLUES
    1690   BUCK JUMPIN´
    1630   ESQUIRE BOUNCE (Jacket reads "Esquire Blues")
    1710   FOR BASS FACES ONLY
    1650   I´LL GET BY
    1680   MUSKRAT RAMBLE
    1700   STOMPIN´ AT THE SAVOY
    1660   TEA FOR TWO

Palm 30   P.30:14   Eng.   12 Inch LP

    1740   FLYING HOME
    1720   MY IDEAL
    1730   ROSE ROOM
    1750   VIBE BLUES (JAMMIN´ THE BLUES)

Palm 30   P.30:16   Eng.   12 Inch LP

    2180   I CAN´T GIVE YOU ANYTHING BUT LOVE
    2170   MAN I LOVE, THE

Palm Club   PALM 01   Fr.   10 Inch LP

    1640   BASIN STREET BLUES
    1690   BUCK JUMPIN´
    1740   FLYING HOME
    1650   I´LL GET BY
    1540   MOP-MOP
    1720   MY IDEAL
    1730   ROSE ROOM

Palm Club   #2*   Fr.   10 Inch LP

    1670   BACK O´ TOWN BLUES
    1610   BLUES
    1550   DO NOTHIN´ TILL YOU HEAR FROM ME
    1530   ESQUIRE BLUES
    1630   ESQUIRE BOUNCE
    1560   I LOVE MY MAN
    1660   TEA FOR TWO
            *Label bears this number in ink; there is no printed number.

Palm Club   PALM 14   Fr.   10 Inch LP

    1710   FOR BASS FACES ONLY
    1570   I CAN´T GIVE YOU ANYTHING BUT LOVE
    1600   I GOT RHYTHM
    1580   I GOTTA RIGHT TO SING THE BLUES
    1680   MUSKRAT RAMBLE
    1700   STOMPIN´ AT THE SAVOY
    1750   VIBE BLUES (JAMMIN´ THE BLUES)

Palm Club   PALM 18   Fr.   10 Inch LP

    2270   BEGIN THE BEGUINE
    2320   GERSHWIN MEDLEY
    2720   INDIANA
    2340   LOVER
    2330   SHE´S FUNNY THAT WAY
    2690   SONG OF THE VAGABONDS
    2680   WHERE OR WHEN

```
Palm Club                         PALM 20         Fr.    10 Inch LP

    2355  NINE TWENTY SPECIAL
    2350  BODY AND SOUL
    2354  I'M BEGINNING TO SEE THE LIGHT
    2710  POOR BUTTERFLY


Parlophone                        F1425           Eng.   10 Inch 78

    0040  THIS TIME IT'S LOVE
    0030  YOU GAVE ME EVERYTHING BUT LOVE


Philips                           429 287 BE      It.    7 Inch 45EP

    2960  HUMORESQUE
    3000  I KNOW THAT YOU KNOW
    2970  TATUM-POLE BOOGIE
    2990  YESTERDAYS


Philips                           429 622 BE      It     7 Inch 45EP

    2950  HOW HIGH THE MOON


Philips                           25RJ-26         Jap    12 Inch LP

    2930  I'LL NEVER BE THE SAME
    2890  IN A SENTIMENTAL MOOD
    2910  IT'S THE TALK OF THE TOWN
    2940  NIGHT AND DAY
    2880  OVER THE RAINBOW
    2920  SHE S FUNNY THAT WAY
    2850  SITTIN  AND ROCKIN'
    2870  TENDERLY
    2840  WRAP YOUR TROUBLES IN DREAMS
    2900  YOU TOOK ADVANTAGE OF ME
    2860  YOU'RE DRIVING ME CRAZY


Philips                           BBE12136        Eng.   7 Inch 45EP

    2960  HUMORESQUE
    3000  I KNOW THAT YOU KNOW
    2970  TATUM POLE BOOGIE
    2990  YESTERDAYS


Philips                           BBL7511         Eng    12 Inch LP

    0080  SOPHISTICATED LADY
    3010  WILLOW WEEP FOR ME


Philips                           BO7902R         It.    10 Inch LP

    2950  HOW HIGH THE MOON
    2960  HUMORESQUE
    3000  I KNOW THAT YOU KNOW
    3030  KERRY DANCE   THE
    2980  SOMEONE TO WATCH OVER ME
    2970  TATUM-POLE BOOGIE
    3010  WILLOW WEEP FOR ME
    2990  YESTERDAYS


Phoenix 10                        PHX-312         USA    12 Inch LP
  [Jacket erroneously lists performance as from Boston in 1951.]
    1550  DO NOTHIN  TILL YOU HEAR FROM ME
```

```
Phoenix 10                        PHX313        USA      12 Inch LP

    2430   AMONG MY SOUVENIRS
    0800   FINE AND DANDY
    0820   I GOTTA RIGHT TO SING THE BLUES
    2420   LIMEHOUSE BLUES
    2170   MAN I LOVE, THE
    2500   MEAN TO ME
    2450   STAY AS SWEET AS YOU ARE
    0770   SWEET EMALINA, MY GAL
    2470   WHY WAS I BORN


Pick                              308.0013      Braz.    12 Inch LP

    2430   AMONG MY SOUVENIRS
    2370   BODY AND SOUL
    2410   CAN'T WE BE FRIENDS
    2400   CRAZY RHYTHM
    0800   FINE AND DANDY
    2380   I GUESS I'LL HAVE TO CHANGE MY PLANS
    2480   IF I COULD BE WITH YOU
    2510   IT'S ONLY A PAPER MOON
    2420   LIMEHOUSE BLUES
    2500   MEAN TO ME
    2450   STAY AS SWEET AS YOU ARE
    2360   YOU TOOK ADVANTAGE OF ME


Pickwick                          SPC 3335      USA      12 Inch LP

    1550   DO NOTHIN' TILL YOU HEAR FROM ME


Pickwick Camden                   ACL 7015      Eng.     12 Inch LP

    2800   CHEROKEE
    2790   OUT OF NOWHERE
    2770   SMOKE GETS IN YOUR EYES


Pickwick Camden                   ACL 7015      USA      12 Inch LP

    2800   CHEROKEE
    2790   OUT OF NOWHERE
    2770   SMOKE GETS IN YOUR EYES


Polydor                           2310 325      Ger.     12 Inch LP

    1000   BEAUTIFUL LOVE
    1120   BEGIN THE BEGUINE
    1200   BODY AND SOUL
    1110   FINE AND DANDY
    1090   GEORGIA ON MY MIND
    1180   KNOCKIN' MYSELF OUT
    1010   LAUGHING AT LIFE
    1170   MIGHTY LAK A ROSE
    1250   OH! LADY BE GOOD
    1260   SWEET GEORGIA BROWN
    1100   SWEET LORRAINE
    1240   THERE'LL BE SOME CHANGES MADE
    1190   TOLEDO BLUES


Polydor                           2344 043      Eng.     12 Inch LP

    1000   BEAUTIFUL LOVE
    1120   BEGIN THE BEGUINE
    1200   BODY AND SOUL
    1110   FINE AND DANDY
    1090   GEORGIA ON MY MIND
    1180   KNOCKIN' MYSELF OUT
    1010   LAUGHING AT LIFE
    1170   MIGHTY LAK A ROSE
```

```
      1250   OH! LADY BE GOOD
      1260   SWEET GEORGIA BROWN
      1100   SWEET LORRAINE
      1240   THERE'LL BE SOME CHANGES MADE
      1190   TOLEDO BLUES


Polydor                              580.019        Fr.     10 Inch 78

      2040   IT HAD TO BE YOU
      2060   WHERE OR WHEN


Polydor                              623274         Eng.    12 Inch LP
   [See Sonet SLPS1937.]
      0790   DAY IN - DAY OUT
      0800   FINE AND DANDY
      0820   I GOTTA RIGHT TO SING THE BLUES
      0830   I'M COMING VIRGINIA
      0810   I'VE GOT THE WORLD ON A STRING


Pop Jazz                             WGM 2A         USA     12 Inch LP
   [Part of 5-record boxed set.]
      1830   DARK EYES


Prestige                             P-24052        USA     12 Inch LP
   [Part of 2-record set.]
      2100   PLEASE DON'T TALK ABOUT ME WHEN I'M GONE


Queen Disc                           Q-020          It.     12 Inch LP

      1986   I GOT RHYTHM
      1984   ROYAL GARDEN BLUES


RCA Black & White                    730.561        Fr.     12 Inch LP

      2780   AIN'T MISBEHAVIN'
      2800   CHEROKEE
      2790   OUT OF NOWHERE
      2770   SMOKE GETS IN YOUR EYES


RCA Black & White                    FMX2 7080      Fr.     12 Inch LP
   [Part of 2-record set.]
      2790   OUT OF NOWHERE


RCA Black & White                    FXM3 7143      Fr.     12 Inch LP
   [Part of 3-record boxed set.]
      2780   AIN'T MISBEHAVIN'
      2800   CHEROKEE
      2770   SMOKE GETS IN YOUR EYES


RCA Camden                           800210         Fr.     12 Inch LP

      2780   AIN'T MISBEHAVIN'


RCA Camden                           900.020        Fr.     12 Inch LP

      2800   CHEROKEE
      2790   OUT OF NOWHERE
      2770   SMOKE GETS IN YOUR EYES


RCA Camden                           CAE419         USA     7 Inch 45EP

      2780   AIN'T MISBEHAVIN'
      2800   CHEROKEE
      2790   OUT OF NOWHERE
```

```
        2770   SMOKE GETS IN YOUR EYES


RCA Camden                          CAL328            USA      12 Inch LP
   [Issued with two different cover designs.]
        2780   AIN'T MISBEHAVIN'


RCA Camden                          CAL384            USA      12 Inch LP

        2800   CHEROKEE
        2790   OUT OF NOWHERE
        2770   SMOKE GETS IN YOUR EYES


RCA Camden                          CAL882            USA      12 Inch LP

        2800   CHEROKEE
        2790   OUT OF NOWHERE
        2770   SMOKE GETS IN YOUR EYES


RCA Camden                          CAS882(e)         USA    s 12 Inch LP

        2800   CHEROKEE
        2790   OUT OF NOWHERE
        2770   SMOKE GETS IN YOUR EYES


RCA Camden                          CDN.118           Eng.     12 Inch LP

        2780   AIN'T MISBEHAVIN'


RCA Camden                          CDS 1050          Eng.   s 12 Inch LP

        2800   CHEROKEE
        2790   OUT OF NOWHERE
        2770   SMOKE GETS IN YOUR EYES


RCA Camden                          CL-5030-31        Jap.
   [2-record set containing CL-5031.]


RCA Camden                          CL-5031           Jap.     12 Inch LP

        2780   AIN'T MISBEHAVIN'


RCA Victor                          20-2911           USA      10 Inch 78

        2780   AIN'T MISBEHAVIN'
        2770   SMOKE GETS IN YOUR EYES


RCA Victor                          20-3088           USA      10 Inch 78

        2800   CHEROKEE


RCA Victor                          27-0147           USA       7 Inch 45
   [Part of 4-record boxed set WPT 40.]
        2800   CHEROKEE


RCA Victor                          82-0534           Braz.    10 Inch 78

        2780   AIN'T MISBEHAVIN'
        2770   SMOKE GETS IN YOUR EYES
```

```
RCA Victor                        DMM4-0342-4      USA      12 Inch LP

    2800  CHEROKEE


RCA Victor                        EDP 1004(6)      It.      12 Inch LP
  [Part of 10-record boxed set EDP 1004 (10).]
    2790  OUT OF NOWHERE


RCA Victor                        EDP 1004(10)     It.
  [10-record boxed set containing EDP 1004(6).]


RCA Victor                        EPBT3031         USA      7 Inch 45EP
  [Part of 2-record set.]
    2800  CHEROKEE


RCA Victor                        LEJ-11           USA      10 Inch LP
  [Part of 12-record series.]
    2780  AIN'T MISBEHAVIN


RCA Victor                        LJM3001          USA      12 Inch LP

    2790  OUT OF NOWHERE


RCA Victor                        LPT31            USA      10 Inch LP

    2800  CHEROKEE


RCA Victor                        MJ-7093          Jap.     12 Inch LP

    5360  BEGIN THE BEGUINE
    5380  BODY AND SOUL
    5410  DANNY BOY
    5450  I'LL NEVER BE THE SAME
    5470  LITTLE MAN, YOU'VE HAD A BUSY DAY
    5370  SOMEONE TO WATCH OVER ME
    5420  TENDERLY
    5400  TOO MARVELOUS FOR WORDS
    5390  WILLOW WEEP FOR ME
    5460  WITHOUT A SONG
    5440  YESTERDAYS
    5430  YOU TOOK ADVANTAGE OF ME


RCA Victor                        RA 28-29         Jap.     12 Inch LP
  [2-record boxed set containing RA 29.]


RCA Victor                        RA-29            Jap.     12 Inch LP
  [Part of 2-record boxed set RA 28-29.]
    2780  AIN'T MISBEHAVIN'
    2800  CHEROKEE
    2790  OUT OF NOWHERE
    2770  SMOKE GETS IN YOUR EYES


RCA Victor                        WPT 40           USA
  [4-record boxed set containing 27-0147.]


RI Disc                           RI-DISC 7        Swiss    12 Inch LP

    0130  CHINATOWN, MY CHINATOWN
    3300  GERSHWIN MEDLEY
    2540  I GOTTA RIGHT TO SING THE BLUES
    2480  IF I COULD BE WITH YOU
    2510  IT'S ONLY A PAPER MOON
    2520  JUST A GIGOLO
    2500  MEAN TO ME

                        261
```

```
        0100   MORNING, NOON, AND NIGHT
        2550   ON THE SUNNY SIDE OF THE STREET
        2460   SOMEBODY LOVES ME
        0120   STAR DUST
        3370   TABOO
        2490   TEA FOR TWO
        2530   THREE LITTLE WORDS
        0110   WHEN DAY IS DONE
        2470   WHY WAS I BORN
        0090   YOUNG AND HEALTHY


RI Disc                        RI-DISC 8        Swiss    12 Inch LP

        5910   BODY AND SOUL
        5850   FLYING HOME
        6230   FLYING HOME
        6260   FLYING HOME
        5860   I COVER THE WATERFRONT
        6250   JUST ONE OF THOSE THINGS
        6240   MOON SONG
        5870   SOFT WINDS
        5890   TEA FOR TWO
        5880   TENDERLY
        6270   WOULD YOU LIKE TO TAKE A WALK
        5900   WRAP YOUR TROUBLES IN DREAMS
        6280   YOU GO TO MY HEAD


Radiola                        2MR-5051         USA
   (2-record set containing Release #50,Release #51)

Radiola                        Release #50      USA      12 Inch LP
   (Part of 2-record set 2MR-5051.)
        1640   BASIN STREET BLUES
        1610   BLUES
        1550   DO NOTHIN´ TILL YOU HEAR FROM ME
        1530   ESQUIRE BLUES
        1630   ESQUIRE BOUNCE
        1570   I CAN´T GIVE YOU ANYTHING BUT LOVE
        1600   I GOT RHYTHM
        1580   I GOTTA RIGHT TO SING THE BLUES
        1560   I LOVE MY MAN*
        1650   I´LL GET BY
        1540   MOP-MOP
        1590   SWEET LORRAINE
        1620   THEME FOR COCA-COLA/INTRODUCTIONS
               *This title does is not listed on the jacket nor the label.


Radiola                        Release #51      USA      12 Inch LP
   (Part of 2-record set 2MR-5051.)
        1670   BACK O´ TOWN BLUES
        1690   BUCK JUMPIN´
        1740   FLYING HOME
        1710   FOR BASS FACES ONLY
        1680   MUSKRAT RAMBLE
        1720   MY IDEAL
        1730   ROSE ROOM
        1700   STOMPIN´ AT THE SAVOY
        1660   TEA FOR TWO
        1665   THEME FOR COCA-COLA/CONCLUSION
        1750   VIBE BLUES (JAMMIN´ THE BLUES)


Recollections at 30            22               USA      16 Inch TX

        0270   LULU´S BACK IN TOWN


Redwood                        R.W.J.1001       Can.     12 Inch LP
   [Part of 5-record boxed set.]
        1540   MOP-MOP
```

```
Rem Hollywood*                          LP-3            USA     10 Inch LP

   2191  HALLELUJAH
   2260  KERRY DANCE, THE
   2220  LOVER
   2230  MEMORIES OF YOU
   2200  POOR BUTTERFLY
   2240  RUNNIN´ WILD
   2210  SONG OF THE VAGABONDS
   2250  YESTERDAYS
         *Jacket bears the number "2"; LP-3 is on the disc.
          This LP exists also in a jacket which reads "Guild 3"
          instead of "Rem Hollywood" but the disc shows latter label.


Rex Hollywood                           23001           USA     10 Inch 78

   2260  KERRY DANCE, THE
   2250  YESTERDAYS


Rex Hollywood                           23002           USA     10 Inch 78

   2230  MEMORIES OF YOU
   2240  RUNNIN´ WILD


Rex Hollywood                           23003           USA     10 Inch 78

   2220  LOVER
   2210  SONG OF THE VAGABONDS


Rex Hollywood                           23004           USA     10 Inch 78

   2191  HALLELUJAH
   2200  POOR BUTTERFLY


Roost                         (See Royal Roost, also Roulette)


Roulette                                CLVLXR.600A     Fr.     12 Inch LP

   1870  FLYING HOME


Roulette                                RE-110          USA     12 Inch LP

   1840  BODY AND SOUL
   1830  DARK EYES
   1870  FLYING HOME
   1850  I KNOW THAT YOU KNOW
   1860  ON THE SUNNY SIDE OF THE STREET


Roulette                                YW-7503-RO      Jap.    12 Inch LP
   [Jacket says "Roost"]
   1840  BODY AND SOUL
   1830  DARK EYES
   1870  FLYING HOME
   1850  I KNOW THAT YOU KNOW
   1860  ON THE SUNNY SIDE OF THE STREET


Royal Roost                             YY-7002-RO      Jap.    12 Inch LP

   1840  BODY AND SOUL
   1830  DARK EYES
   1870  FLYING HOME
   1850  I KNOW THAT YOU KNOW
   1860  ON THE SUNNY SIDE OF THE STREET
```

```
Royal Roost                      LP-2256        USA      12 Inch LP

    1840  BODY AND SOUL
    1830  DARK EYES
    1850  I KNOW THAT YOU KNOW


Royal Roost                      OJ-1           USA      12 Inch LP

    1870  FLYING HOME


Royal Roost                      RLP 2213       USA      12 Inch LP

    1840  BODY AND SOUL
    1830  DARK EYES
    1870  FLYING HOME
    1850  I KNOW THAT YOU KNOW
    1860  ON THE SUNNY SIDE OF THE STREET


Royal Roost                      YW-7803-RO     Jap.     12 Inch LP

    1840  BODY AND SOUL
    1830  DARK EYES
    1870  FLYING HOME
    1850  I KNOW THAT YOU KNOW
    1860  ON THE SUNNY SIDE OF THE STREET


S R International                 30 180 4        Ger.
[3-record boxed set containing 30 181 2,30 182 0,30 183 8.
 The cover erroneously lists date as 1945; it should be 1944.]


S R International                 30 181 2        Ger.     12 Inch LP
[Part of 3-record boxed set 30 180 4.]
    1670  BACK O´ TOWN BLUES
    1640  BASIN STREET BLUES
    1690  BUCK JUMPIN´
    1630  ESQUIRE BOUNCE
    1710  FOR BASS FACES ONLY
    1650  I´LL GET BY
    1680  MUSKRAT RAMBLE
    1700  STOMPIN´ AT THE SAVOY
    1660  TEA FOR TWO


S R International                 30 182 0        Ger.     12 Inch LP
[Part of 3-record boxed set 30 180 4.]
    1550  DO NOTHIN´ TILL YOU HEAR FROM ME
    1530  ESQUIRE BLUES
    1570  I CAN´T GIVE YOU ANYTHING BUT LOVE
    1580  I GOTTA RIGHT TO SING THE BLUES
    1560  I LOVE MY MAN (Billie´s Blues)
    1540  MOP-MOP
    1590  SWEET LORRAINE


S R International                 30 183 8        Ger.     12 Inch LP
[Part of 3-record boxed set 30 180 4.]
    1610  BLUES (THREE MINUTES OF BLUES)
    1740  FLYING HOME
    1600  I GOT RHYTHM
    1720  MY IDEAL
    1730  ROSE ROOM
    1750  VIBE BLUES (JAMMIN´ THE BLUES)


Saga                              6915           Eng.     12 Inch LP

    0290  AFTER YOU´VE GONE
    0760  ALL GOD´S CHILLUN GOT RHYTHM
    0280  BOOTS AND SADDLE
    0400  DEVIL IN THE MOON
```

```
0300   DIXIELAND BAND
0390   I WISH I WERE TWINS
0350   I WOULD DO ANYTHING FOR YOU
0370   IN THE MIDDLE OF A KISS
0780   INDIANA
0340   MONDAY IN MANHATTAN
0380   ROSETTA
0330   STAY AS SWEET AS YOU ARE
0770   SWEET EMALINA, MY GAL
0360   THEME FOR PIANO
```

Saga	6918	Eng.	12 Inch LP

```
1550   DO NOTHIN´ TILL YOU HEAR FROM ME
1560   I LOVE MY MAN
```

Saga	6922	Eng.	12 Inch LP

```
1610   BLUES
1550   DO NOTHIN´ TILL YOU HEAR FROM ME
1530   ESQUIRE BLUES
1570   I CAN´T GIVE YOU ANYTHING BUT LOVE
1600   I GOT RHYTHM
1580   I GOTTA RIGHT TO SING THE BLUES
1560   I LOVE MY MAN (Billie´s Blues)
1540   MOP-MOP
```

Saga	6923	Eng.	12 Inch LP

```
1670   BACK O´ TOWN BLUES
1640   BASIN STREET BLUES
1690   BUCK JUMPIN´
1630   ESQUIRE BOUNCE
1740   FLYING HOME
1650   I´LL GET BY
1720   MY IDEAL
1730   ROSE ROOM
1660   TEA FOR TWO
```

Saga	6925	Eng.	12 Inch LP

```
2180   I CAN´T GIVE YOU ANYTHING BUT LOVE
2170   MAN I LOVE, THE
```

Saga	ERO-8014	Eng.	12 Inch LP

```
1550   DO NOTHIN´ TILL YOU HEAR FROM ME
1560   I LOVE MY MAN (Billie´s Blues)
```

Session Disc	120	USA	12 Inch LP

```
3820   IF
3840   MEMORIES OF YOU
3830   SOFT WINDS
```

Shoestring	SS-105	USA	12 Inch LP

```
2270   BEGIN THE BEGUINE
3610   DON´T BLAME ME
1380   EXACTLY LIKE YOU
3630   GERSHWIN MEDLEY [Entitled "The Man I Love"]
1770   HUMORESQUE
1790   I´VE FOUND A NEW BABY
1780   IT HAD TO BE YOU
1760   JA-DA
2700   NIGHT AND DAY
1800   OH! LADY BE GOOD
2710   POOR BUTTERFLY
```

265

```
      1810   SOMEBODY LOVES ME
      2680   WHERE OR WHEN


Smithsonian                          P 11894         USA      12 Inch LP
  [Part of 6-record boxed set P6 11891.]
      5400   TOO MARVELOUS FOR WORDS
      3060   WILLOW WEEP FOR ME


Smithsonian                          P6 11891        USA
  [6-record boxed set containing P 11894.]


Smithsonian                          R 029           USA      12 Inch LP

      0790   DAY IN - DAY OUT
      1815   EXACTLY LIKE YOU
      2190   HALLELUJAH
      2191   HALLELUJAH
      5550   I COVER THE WATERFRONT
      0680   IT HAD TO BE YOU
      5490   JITTERBUG WALTZ
      5590   JUST LIKE A BUTTERFLY THAT'S CAUGHT IN THE RAIN
      5580   LOVE FOR SALE
      2230   MEMORIES OF YOU
      0720   OH, YOU CRAZY MOON
      0730   OVER THE RAINBOW
      5600   SWEET LORRAINE
      2250   YESTERDAYS


Sonet                                SLP1001         Dan.     12 Inch LP

      1351   ESQUIRE BLUES
      1320   ESQUIRE BOUNCE
      1331   MOP-MOP (Also called Boff-Boff)
      1340   MY IDEAL


Sonet                                SLPS1937        Dan.     12 Inch LP
  [Jacket says Polydor 623274.]
      0790   DAY IN - DAY OUT
      0800   FINE AND DANDY
      0820   I GOTTA RIGHT TO SING THE BLUES
      0830   I'M COMING VIRGINIA
      0810   I'VE GOT THE WORLD ON A STRING


Sonet                                SXP 2005        Dan.      7 Inch 45EP

      1351   ESQUIRE BLUES
      1320   ESQUIRE BOUNCE
      1331   MOP-MOP
      1340   MY IDEAL


Special Editions                     5015-S          USA      10 Inch 78

      0080   SOPHISTICATED LADY
      0050   TEA FOR TWO


Standard                             A675            USA      16 Inch TX

      0290   AFTER YOU'VE GONE
      0280   BOOTS AND SADDLE
      0300   DIXIELAND BAND
      0350   I WOULD DO ANYTHING FOR YOU
      0340   MONDAY IN MANHATTAN
      0310   SHOUT, THE
      0330   STAY AS SWEET AS YOU ARE
      0360   THEME FOR PIANO
      0320   TIGER RAG
```

Standard   A684   USA   16 Inch TX

```
0400   DEVIL IN THE MOON
0390   I WISH I WERE TWINS
0370   IN THE MIDDLE OF A KISS
0380   ROSETTA
```

Standard   Q104   USA   16 Inch TX

```
0290   AFTER YOU'VE GONE
0280   BOOTS AND SADDLE
0300   DIXIELAND BAND
0350   I WOULD DO ANYTHING FOR YOU
0340   MONDAY IN MANHATTAN
0310   SHOUT  THE
0330   STAY AS SWEET AS YOU ARE
0360   THEME FOR PIANO
0320   TIGER RAG
```

Standard   Q105   USA   16 Inch TX

```
0400   DEVIL IN THE MOON
0390   I WISH I WERE TWINS
0370   IN THE MIDDLE OF A KISS
0380   ROSETTA
```

Standard   Q126   USA   16 Inch TX

```
0550   AIN'T MISBEHAVIN'
0530   HAPPY FEET
0520   I CAN'T GET STARTED
0570   IN A SENTIMENTAL MOOD
0500   MAN I LOVE, THE
0540   ROYAL GARDEN BLUES
0510   RUNNIN' WILD
0560   STAR DUST
```

Standard   Q129   USA   16 Inch TX

```
0630   BODY AND SOUL
0640   CAN'T WE BE FRIENDS
0620   ELEGIE
0590   I'LL GET BY
0600   I'LL NEVER BE THE SAME
0610   JUDY
0650   MAKE BELIEVE
0580   SWEET LORRAINE
```

Standard   Q135   USA   16 Inch TX

```
0670   BEGIN THE BEGUINE
0660   GET HAPPY
0700   HALLELUJAH
0690   HUMORESQUE
0680   IT HAD TO BE YOU
0710   LULLABY IN RHYTHM
0720   OH, YOU CRAZY MOON
0730   OVER THE RAINBOW
```

Standard   Q140   USA   16 Inch TX

```
0760   ALL GOD'S CHILLUN GOT RHYTHM
0790   DAY IN - DAY OUT
0800   FINE AND DANDY
0820   I GOTTA RIGHT TO SING THE BLUES
0830   I'M COMING VIRGINIA
0810   I'VE GOT THE WORLD ON A STRING
0780   INDIANA
0770   SWEET EMALINA, MY GAL
```

```
Standard                          Q183              USA      16 Inch TX

     0760   ALL GOD´S CHILLUN GOT RHYTHM
     0790   DAY IN - DAY OUT
     0800   FINE AND DANDY
     0820   I GOTTA RIGHT TO SING THE BLUES
     0830   I´M COMING VIRGINIA
     0810   I´VE GOT THE WORLD ON A STRING
     0780   INDIANA
     0770   SWEET EMALINA, MY GAL


Standard                          Q190              USA      16 Inch TX

     2430   AMONG MY SOUVENIRS
     2370   BODY AND SOUL
     2410   CAN´T WE BE FRIENDS
     2400   CRAZY RHYTHM
     2380   I GUESS I´LL HAVE TO CHANGE MY PLANS
     2440   I´M GONNA SIT RIGHT DOWN AND WRITE MYSELF A LETTER
     2420   LIMEHOUSE BLUES
     2450   STAY AS SWEET AS YOU ARE
     2390   WHAT IS THIS THING CALLED LOVE
     2360   YOU TOOK ADVANTAGE OF ME


Standard                          Q191              USA      16 Inch TX

     2540   I GOTTA RIGHT TO SING THE BLUES
     2480   IF I COULD BE WITH YOU
     2510   IT´S ONLY A PAPER MOON
     2520   JUST A GIGOLO
     2500   MEAN TO ME
     2550   ON THE SUNNY SIDE OF THE STREET
     2460   SOMEBODY LOVES ME
     2490   TEA FOR TWO
     2530   THREE LITTLE WORDS
     2470   WHY WAS I BORN


Stash                             ST-100            USA      12 Inch LP

     2110   SWEET MARIJUANA BROWN


Stash                             ST120             USA      12 Inch LP

     2110   SWEET MARIJUANA BROWN


Stinson                           356-3             USA      10 Inch 78
     [356-1 and 356-2 probably also exist, same as Asch issues.]
     2080   DANNY BOY
     2070   SWEET AND LOVELY


Stinson                           452-1             USA      12 Inch 78
     [Part of 2-record set Asch 452.]
     1950   BOOGIE
     1970   IF I HAD YOU


Stinson                           452-2             USA      12 Inch 78
     [Part of 2-record set Asch 452.]
     1980   SOFT WINDS
     1960   TOPSY


Stinson                           SLP-40            USA      10 Inch LP

     1950   BOOGIE
     2080   DANNY BOY
     2030   FINE AND DANDY
     1970   IF I HAD YOU
     2040   IT HAD TO BE YOU
```

```
2050   JA-DA
1980   SOFT WINDS
2070   SWEET AND LOVELY
1960   TOPSY
2060   WHERE OR WHEN


Stinson                          SLP 40          USA      12 Inch LP
1950   BOOGIE
2080   DANNY BOY
2030   FINE AND DANDY
1970   IF I HAD YOU
2040   IT HAD TO BE YOU
2050   JA-DA
1980   SOFT WINDS
2070   SWEET AND LOVELY
1960   TOPSY
2060   WHERE OR WHEN


Storia della Musica Jazz         046             It.      7 Inch 33

1840   BODY AND SOUL
1850   I KNOW THAT YOU KNOW


Storia della Musica              Vol. X N. 8    It.      7 Inch 33
   [Part of 13-book set with companion record volumes. Volume X
   of records consists of 13 records.]
3730   WOULD YOU LIKE TO TAKE A WALK


Storyville                       SLP 807         Dan.     12 Inch LP

2120   BLUES FOR ART'S SAKE
2090   CAN'T HELP LOVIN' DAT MAN OF MINE
2100   PLEASE DON'T TALK ABOUT ME WHEN I'M GONE
2110   SWEET MARIJUANA BROWN


Storyville                       SLP 829         Dan.     12 Inch LP

0790   DAY IN - DAY OUT
0800   FINE AND DANDY
0820   I GOTTA RIGHT TO SING THE BLUES
0830   I'M COMING VIRGINIA
0810   I'VE GOT THE WORLD ON A STRING


Storyville                       ULS-1550        Jap.     12 Inch LP

0790   DAY IN - DAY OUT
0800   FINE AND DANDY
0820   I GOTTA RIGHT TO SING THE BLUES
0830   I'M COMING VIRGINIA
0810   I'VE GOT THE WORLD ON A STRING


Sunbeam                          SB-219          USA      1? Inch LP
   (Part of 2-record set.)
2180   I CAN'T GIVE YOU ANYTHING BUT LOVE
2170   MAN I LOVE, THE


Swaggie                          S1223           Astla    12 Inch LP

0960   BEGIN THE BEGUINE
0940   COCKTAILS FOR TWO
0840   ELEGIE
0910   EMALINE
0870   GET HAPPY
0460   GONE WITH THE WIND
0850   HUMORESQUE
0980   INDIANA
0930   LOVE ME
```

```
        0880   LULLABY OF THE LEAVES
        0970   ROSETTA
        0950   ST. LOUIS BLUES
        0470   STORMY WEATHER
        0860   SWEET LORRAINE
        0740   TEA FOR TWO
        0890   TIGER RAG


Swingfan                        LP 1018        Ger.     12 Inch LP

        0420   BODY AND SOUL
        0450   I´VE GOT MY LOVE TO KEEP ME WARM
        1070   LAST GOODBYE BLUES
        0440   WHAT WILL I TELL MY HEART
        0430   WITH PLENTY OF MONEY AND YOU


Swing House                     SWH 27         Eng.     12 Inch LP

        1550   DO NOTHIN´ TILL YOU HEAR FROM ME
        1560   I LOVE MY MAN (Billie´s Blues)


Teppa                           76             USA      12 Inch LP

               BLUES ON DOWN (See "Taboo")
        6260   FLYING HOME (Incorrectly titled "Flying on the Piano")
               FLYING ON THE PIANO (See "Flying Home")
        3800   TABOO (Incorrectly titled "Blues on Down")
        3790   WHERE OR WHEN
        6270   WOULD YOU LIKE TO TAKE A WALK
        6280   YOU GO TO MY HEAD


Thesaurus                       JATP-6         USA      12 Inch TX

               BLUES IN MY HEART (See "If You Hadn´t Gone Away")
        3850   CAN´T WE BE FRIENDS
        3870   ELEGIE
        3900   IF YOU HADN´T GONE AWAY (Incorrectly titled "Blues in
               My Heart")
        3860   THIS CAN´T BE LOVE


Thesaurus                       JATP-12        USA      12 Inch TX

        5810   DEEP PURPLE
        5790   PLAID
        5800   SOMEBODY LOVES ME


Time-Life                       P 15514        USA      12 Inch LP
   [Part of 3-record boxed set STL-J24.]
        1080   BATTERY BOUNCE
        0420   BODY AND SOUL
        1150   CORRINE, CORRINA
        0840   ELEGIE
        0870   GET HAPPY
        0460   GONE WITH THE WIND
        1070   LAST GOODBYE BLUES
        0970   ROSETTA
        1060   STOMPIN´ AT THE SAVOY
        0470   STORMY WEATHER
        0860   SWEET LORRAINE
        0050   TEA FOR TWO
        0001   TIGER RAG
        0070   TIGER RAG
        1190   TOLEDO BLUES
        1050   WEE BABY BLUES
```

```
Time-Life                         P 15515        USA      12 Inch LP
   [Part of 3-record boxed set STL-J24.]
      2120  BLUES FOR ART'S SAKE
      1840  BODY AND SOUL
      1950  BOOGIE
      1351  ESQUIRE BLUES
      1320  ESQUIRE BOUNCE
      1870  FLYING HOME
      1420  I AIN'T GOT NOBODY
      1400  I GOT RHYTHM
      1340  MY IDEAL
      1250  OH! LADY BE GOOD
      1260  SWEET GEORGIA BROWN
      3060  WILLOW WEEP FOR ME
      2990  YESTERDAYS


Time-Life                         P 15516        USA      12 Inch LP
   [Part of 3-record boxed set STL-J24.]
      6160  ALL THE THINGS YOU ARE
      3080  AUNT HAGAR'S BLUES
      3220  BLUE SKIES
      4880  IDAHO
      5770  MORE THAN YOU KNOW
      3280  MR. FREDDIE BLUES
      3090  NICE WORK IF YOU CAN GET IT
      6210  NIGHT AND DAY
      4410  TOO MARVELOUS FOR WORDS
      6010  TRIO BLUES
      6220  WHERE OR WHEN


Time-Life                         STL-J24        USA
   [3-record boxed set containing P 15514,P 15515,P 15516.]


Top Rank                          35/067         USA      12 Inch LP

      5360  BEGIN THE BEGUINE
      5380  BODY AND SOUL
      5410  DANNY BOY
      5450  I'LL NEVER BE THE SAME
      5470  LITTLE MAN, YOU'VE HAD A BUSY DAY
      5370  SOMEONE TO WATCH OVER ME
      5420  TENDERLY
      5400  TOO MARVELOUS FOR WORDS
      5390  WILLOW WEEP FOR ME
      5460  WITHOUT A SONG
      5440  YESTERDAYS
      5430  YOU TOOK ADVANTAGE OF ME


Tops                              L1508          USA      12 Inch LP

      2120  BLUES FOR ART'S SAKE
      2090  CAN'T HELP LOVIN' DAT MAN OF MINE
      2100  PLEASE DON'T TALK ABOUT ME WHEN I'M GONE


Totem                             1037           USA      12 Inch LP

      1985  ALL OF ME
      1983  FINE AND MELLOW
      1986  I GOT RHYTHM (Not listed on label.)
      1984  ROYAL GARDEN BLUES (Not listed on label.)


Trip                              JT-IX-(2)      USA      12 Inch LP
   [2-record set.]
      0760  ALL GOD'S CHILLUN GOT RHYTHM
      2430  AMONG MY SOUVENIRS
      2410  CAN'T WE BE FRIENDS
      2400  CRAZY RHYTHM
      0790  DAY IN - DAY OUT
      0800  FINE AND DANDY
```

```
2180  I CAN'T GIVE YOU ANYTHING BUT LOVE
0820  I GOTTA RIGHT TO SING THE BLUES
2540  I GOTTA RIGHT TO SING THE BLUES
2380  I GUESS I'LL HAVE TO CHANGE MY PLANS
2480  IF I COULD BE WITH YOU
0830  I'M COMING VIRGINIA
2440  I'M GONNA SIT RIGHT DOWN AND WRITE MYSELF A LETTER
0780  INDIANA
0810  I'VE GOT THE WORLD ON A STRING
2420  LIMEHOUSE BLUES
2170  MAN I LOVE, THE
2500  MEAN TO ME
2550  ON THE SUNNY SIDE OF THE STREET
2460  SOMEBODY LOVES ME
2450  STAY AS SWEET AS YOU ARE
0770  SWEET EMALINA, MY GAL
2490  TEA FOR TWO
2530  THREE LITTLE WORDS
2390  WHAT IS THIS THING CALLED LOVE
2470  WHY WAS I BORN
2360  YOU TOOK ADVANTAGE OF ME*
      *Note: The record contains two tracks of this tune which
      are identical; they are incorrectly identified as different
      versions.
```

Trip   TLP-5024   USA   12 Inch LP

```
1550  DO NOTHIN' TILL YOU HEAR FROM ME
```

Trip   TLX-5813   USA   12 Inch LP
[2-record set.]
```
0760  ALL GOD'S CHILLUN GOT RHYTHM
2430  AMONG MY SOUVENIRS
2410  CAN'T WE BE FRIENDS
2400  CRAZY RHYTHM
0790  DAY IN - DAY OUT
0800  FINE AND DANDY
2180  I CAN'T GIVE YOU ANYTHING BUT LOVE
0820  I GOTTA RIGHT TO SING THE BLUES
2540  I GOTTA RIGHT TO SING THE BLUES
2380  I GUESS I'LL HAVE TO CHANGE MY PLANS
2480  IF I COULD BE WITH YOU
0830  I'M COMING VIRGINIA
2440  I'M GONNA SIT RIGHT DOWN AND WRITE MYSELF A LETTER
0780  INDIANA
0810  I'VE GOT THE WORLD ON A STRING
2420  LIMEHOUSE BLUES
2170  MAN I LOVE, THE
2500  MEAN TO ME
2550  ON THE SUNNY SIDE OF THE STREET
2460  SOMEBODY LOVES ME
2450  STAY AS SWEET AS YOU ARE
0770  SWEET EMALINA, MY GAL
2490  TEA FOR TWO
2530  THREE LITTLE WORDS
2390  WHAT IS THIS THING CALLED LOVE
2470  WHY WAS I BORN
2360  YOU TOOK ADVANTAGE OF ME*
      *Note: The record contains two tracks of this tune which
      are identical; they are incorrectly identified as different
      versions.
```

Tulip   TLP 104   Can.   12 Inch LP

```
1840  BODY AND SOUL
1950  BOOGIE
1830  DARK EYES
1870  FLYING HOME
1850  I KNOW THAT YOU KNOW
1970  IF I HAD YOU
1820  MAN I LOVE, THE
1860  ON THE SUNNY SIDE OF THE STREET
```

```
      1980  SOFT WINDS
      1960  TOPSY


Tulip                              TLP 105         Can.     12 Inch LP

      1320  ESQUIRE BOUNCE


US Dept. of State Voice of America,
  American Jazz Series            AJ32            USA      16 Inch TX

      1690  BUCK JUMPIN´
      1630  ESQUIRE BOUNCE
      1650  I´LL GET BY
      1730  ROSE ROOM


US Dept. of State Voice of America,
  Jazz Club Series               JC24, Part One   USA      16 Inch TX
  [The reverse side of this disc has JC23, Part One.]
      3530  INTERVIEW


US Dept. of State Voice of America,
  Jazz Club Series               JC24, Part Two   USA      16 Inch TX
  [The reverse side of this disc has JC23, Part Two.]
      3550  COME RAIN OR COME SHINE
      3560  HONEYSUCKLE ROSE
      3540  TABOO


US Dept. of State Voice of America,
  Jazz Club Series               JC33            USA      16 Inch TX

            AIR MAIL SPECIAL (See "Flying Home")
      3650  FLYING HOME (Incorrectly titled "Air Mail Special")
      3660  MAN I LOVE, THE
      3640  TENDERLY


US Dept. of State Voice of America,
  Jazz Club Series               JC44            USA      16 Inch TX

      3400  MAN I LOVE, THE


US Dept. of State Voice of America,
  Jazz Series                    J16             USA      16 Inch TX

      3610  DON´T BLAME ME
      3630  GERSHWIN MEDLEY [Entitled "The Man I Love"]
      3620  TABOO


US Dept. of State Voice of America,
  Jazz Series                    J35             USA      16 Inch TX

      3460  BEGIN THE BEGUINE
      3470  BODY AND SOUL
      3450  COME RAIN OR COME SHINE
      3480  I KNOW THAT YOU KNOW


US Dept. of State Voice of America,
  Jazz Series                    J36             USA      16 Inch TX

      3490  HONEYSUCKLE ROSE
      3520  KERRY DANCE, THE
      3510  MEMORIES OF YOU
      3500  SITTIN´ AND ROCKIN´
```

```
US Dept. of State Voice of America,
   Jazz Series                      J72            USA      16 Inch TX

      3410   BODY AND SOUL
      3420   FLYING HOME (Incorrectly titled "A Riff Tune")
      3400   MAN I LOVE, THE
             RIFF TUNE, A (See "Flying Home [3420])
      3390   TENDERLY


US Dept. of State Voice of America,
   Piano Playhouse Series           10             USA      16 Inch TX

      2820   SMOKE GETS IN YOUR EYES


US Dept. of State Voice of America,
   Piano Playhouse Series           44             USA      16 Inch TX

      3250   POOR BUTTERFLY


US Dept. of State Voice of America,
   Piano Playhouse Series           45             USA      16 Inch TX

      3255   WILLOW WEEP FOR ME


US Dept. of State Voice of America,
   Piano Playhouse Series           55             USA      16 Inch TX

      3260   I GOTTA RIGHT TO SING THE BLUES


US Dept. of State Voice of America,
   Piano Playhouse Series           56             USA      16 Inch TX

      3270   TABOO


US Treasury Dept. Savings Bond Division,
   Guest Star Series                72             USA      16 Inch TX

      2810   SWEET LORRAINE
      2830   YESTERDAYS


US Treasury Dept. Savings Bond Division,
   Guest Star Series                222            USA      16 Inch TX

      3440   HOW HIGH THE MOON
      3430   MY HEART STOOD STILL


US Veterans Administration,
   Here's to Vets              Program 201         USA      16 Inch TX

      3080   AUNT HAGAR'S BLUES
      3220   BLUE SKIES
      3110   DARDANELLA
      3090   NICE WORK IF YOU CAN GET IT


US Veterans Administration,
   Here's to Vets, Series 104  Program 1353        USA      12 Inch TX

      3090   NICE WORK IF YOU CAN GET IT
      3100   SOMEONE TO WATCH OVER ME
      3130   SWEET LORRAINE
      3060   WILLOW WEEP FOR ME
```

```
US Veterans Administration,
  Here's to Vets, Series 121       Program 1561    USA    12 Inch TX

      3150   DON'T BLAME ME
      3160   MY HEART STOOD STILL
      3100   SOMEONE TO WATCH OVER ME
      3130   SWEET LORRAINE


Up Front                             5028/2         USA    12 Inch LP
   (2-record set.)
      1670   BACK O' TOWN BLUES
      1640   BASIN STREET BLUES
      1610   BLUES
      1690   BUCK JUMPIN'
      1550   DO NOTHIN' TILL YOU HEAR FROM ME
      1530   ESQUIRE BLUES
      1630   ESQUIRE BOUNCE
      1740   FLYING HOME
      1710   FOR BASS FACES ONLY
      1570   I CAN'T GIVE YOU ANYTHING BUT LOVE
      1600   I GOT RHYTHM
      1580   I GOTTA RIGHT TO SING THE BLUES
      1560   I LOVE MY MAN (Billie's Blues)
      1650   I'LL GET BY
      1540   MOP-MOP
      1680   MUSKRAT RAMBLE
      1720   MY IDEAL
      1730   ROSE ROOM
      1700   STOMPIN' AT THE SAVOY
      1590   SWEET LORRAINE
      1660   TEA FOR TWO
      1750   VIBE BLUES (JAMMIN' THE BLUES)


Up Front                             UPF 156        USA    12 Inch LP

      2430   AMONG MY SOUVENIRS
      0800   FINE AND DANDY
      2540   I GOTTA RIGHT TO SING THE BLUES
      2420   LIMEHOUSE BLUES
      2170   MAN I LOVE, THE
      2500   MEAN TO ME
      2450   STAY AS SWEET AS YOU ARE
      0770   SWEET EMALINA, MY GAL
      2470   WHY WAS I BORN


V-Disc                               VDL 1006       It.    12 Inch LP

      1410   COCKTAILS FOR TWO
      1470   LIZA


V-Disc                               VDL 1008       It.    12 Inch LP

      2710   POOR BUTTERFLY
      2690   SONG OF THE VAGABONDS
      2680   WHERE OR WHEN


V-Disc (Army)                        152            USA    12 Inch 78

      1540   MOP-MOP
      1730   ROSE ROOM


V-Disc (Army)                        163            USA    12 Inch 78

      1610   BLUES
      1630   ESQUIRE BOUNCE
      1660   TEA FOR TWO
```

```
V-Disc (Army)                      234            USA      12 Inch 78
     1640  BASIN STREET BLUES

V-Disc (Army)                      248            USA      12 Inch 78
     1560  I LOVE MY MAN (Billie's Blues)

V-Disc (Army)                      366            USA      12 Inch 78
     1670  BACK O' TOWN BLUES

V-Disc (Army)                      456            USA      12 Inch 78
     1410  COCKTAILS FOR TWO
     1470  LIZA

V-Disc (Army)                      604            USA      12 Inch 78
     2320  GERSHWIN MEDLEY
     2330  SHE'S FUNNY THAT WAY

V-Disc (Army)                      620            USA      12 Inch 78
     2350  BODY AND SOUL
     2340  LOVER

V-Disc (Army)                      634            USA      12 Inch 78
     2270  BEGIN THE BEGUINE
     2720  INDIANA
     2710  POOR BUTTERFLY

V-Disc (Army)                      644            USA      12 Inch 78
     2690  SONG OF THE VAGABONDS
     2680  WHERE OR WHEN

V-Disc (Army)                      663            USA      12 Inch 78
     2355  NINE TWENTY SPECIAL
     2354  I'M BEGINNING TO SEE THE LIGHT

V-Disc (Army)                      665            USA      12 Inch 78
     1720  MY IDEAL

V-Disc (Army)                      672            USA      12 Inch 78
     1550  DO NOTHIN' TILL YOU HEAR FROM ME
     1650  I'LL GET BY

V-Disc (Army)                      674            USA      12 Inch 78
     1740  FLYING HOME (Flyin' On a V-Disc, Parts 1 & 2)

V-Disc (Navy)                       14            USA      12 Inch 78
     1640  BASIN STREET BLUES
```

```
V-Disc (Navy)                    28          USA    12 Inch 78

   1560  I LOVE MY MAN (Billie's Blues)


V-Disc (Navy)                   135          USA    12 Inch 78

   1540  MOP-MOP


V-Disc (Navy)                   148          USA    12 Inch 78

   1670  BACK O' TOWN BLUES


V-Disc (Navy)                   236          USA    12 Inch 78

   1410  COCKTAILS FOR TWO
   1470  LIZA


VSP Verve                   SVSP 57.030      It.  s 12 Inch LP

   5920  BLUE LOU
   5990  I GUESS I'LL HAVE TO CHANGE MY PLANS
   5970  I'LL NEVER BE THE SAME
   5930  IF
   6000  ISN'T IT ROMANTIC
   5960  JUST ONE OF THOSE THINGS
   5980  LOVE FOR SALE
   5950  MORE THAN YOU KNOW
   5940  SOME OTHER SPRING
   6010  TRIO BLUES


VSP Verve                   SVSP57.009       It.  s 12 Inch LP

   5000  BOULEVARD OF BROKEN DREAMS
   6130  HUMORESQUE
   4780  INDIANA
   5020  MOON SONG
   5010  MOONLIGHT ON THE GANGES
   4340  STOMPIN' AT THE SAVOY
   3920  MAN I LOVE, THE
   6150  WILLOW WEEP FOR ME


VSP Verve                   VSP 13           USA    12 Inch LP

   5970  I'LL NEVER BE THE SAME
   6010  TRIO BLUES


VSP Verve                   VSP 33           USA    12 Inch LP

   5000  BOULEVARD OF BROKEN DREAMS
   6130  HUMORESQUE
   4780  INDIANA
   5020  MOON SONG
   5010  MOONLIGHT ON THE GANGES
   4340  STOMPIN' AT THE SAVOY
   3920  MAN I LOVE, THE
   6150  WILLOW WEEP FOR ME


VSP Verve                   VSPS-13          USA  s 12 Inch LP

   5970  I'LL NEVER BE THE SAME
   6010  TRIO BLUES


VSP Verve                   VSPS33           USA  s 12 Inch LP

   5000  BOULEVARD OF BROKEN DREAMS
   6130  HUMORESQUE
```

```
4780  INDIANA
5020  MOON SONG
5010  MOONLIGHT ON THE GANGES
4340  STOMPIN' AT THE SAVOY
3920  MAN I LOVE, THE
6150  WILLOW WEEP FOR ME
```

Varese International   VS 81021   USA   12 Inch LP

```
0550  AIN'T MISBEHAVIN'
0630  BODY AND SOUL
0640  CAN'T WE BE FRIENDS
0620  ELEGIE
0530  HAPPY FEET
0520  I CAN'T GET STARTED
0590  I'LL GET BY
0600  I'LL NEVER BE THE SAME
0570  IN A SENTIMENTAL MOOD
0610  JUDY
0650  MAKE BELIEVE
0500  MAN I LOVE, THE
0540  ROYAL GARDEN BLUES
0510  RUNNIN' WILD
0560  STAR DUST
0580  SWEET LORRAINE
```

Vega   30 TCF 5   Fr.   12 Inch LP

```
5360  BEGIN THE BEGUINE
5380  BODY AND SOUL
5410  DANNY BOY
5450  I'LL NEVER BE THE SAME
5470  LITTLE MAN, YOU'VE HAD A BUSY DAY
5370  SOMEONE TO WATCH OVER ME
5420  TENDERLY
5400  TOO MARVELOUS FOR WORDS
5390  WILLOW WEEP FOR ME
5460  WITHOUT A SONG
5440  YESTERDAYS
5430  YOU TOOK ADVANTAGE OF ME
```

Vega   30 TCF 6   Fr.   12 Inch LP

```
5570  DON'T BLAME ME
5550  I COVER THE WATERFRONT
5510  IN A SENTIMENTAL MOOD
5490  JITTERBUG WALTZ
3290  MEMORIES OF YOU
5560  MOON SONG
3280  MR. FREDDIE BLUES
5480  MY HEART STOOD STILL
5500  OVER THE RAINBOW
5530  SEPTEMBER SONG
5520  THERE WILL NEVER BE ANOTHER YOU
5540  WRAP YOUR TROUBLES IN DREAMS
```

Verve   511 063   Ger.   12 Inch LP

```
4020  DIXIELAND BAND
3870  ELEGIE
4150  JITTERBUG WALTZ
6180  MY IDEAL
4160  SOMEONE TO WATCH OVER ME
4070  TENDERLY
4510  WILLOW WEEP FOR ME
4380  WOULD YOU LIKE TO TAKE A WALK
4760  YOU'RE BLASE
```

Verve   511.107   Ger.   12 Inch LP

```
        5920  BLUE LOU
        5990  I GUESS I'LL HAVE TO CHANGE MY PLANS
        5970  I'LL NEVER BE THE SAME
        5930  IF
        6000  ISN'T IT ROMANTIC
        5960  JUST ONE OF THOSE THINGS
        5980  LOVE FOR SALE
        5950  MORE THAN YOU KNOW
        5940  SOME OTHER SPRING
        6010  TRIO BLUES


Verve                              511.108        Ger.    12 Inch LP

        6160  ALL THE THINGS YOU ARE
        6190  GONE WITH THE WIND
        6200  HAVE YOU MET MISS JONES
        6180  MY IDEAL
        6170  MY ONE AND ONLY LOVE
        6210  NIGHT AND DAY
        6220  WHERE OR WHEN


Verve                              511114         Ger.    12 Inch LP

        5650  HALLELUJAH
        5780  HOW HIGH THE MOON
        5660  I'LL NEVER BE THE SAME
        5760  MAKIN' WHOOPEE
        5770  MORE THAN YOU KNOW
        5640  PERDIDO
        5710  WHAT IS THIS THING CALLED LOVE


Verve                              711.048        Eur.    12 Inch LP

        6160  ALL THE THINGS YOU ARE
        6190  GONE WITH THE WIND
        6200  HAVE YOU MET MISS JONES
        6180  MY IDEAL
        6170  MY ONE AND ONLY LOVE
        6210  NIGHT AND DAY
        6220  WHERE OR WHEN


Verve                              711.068        Fr.     12 Inch LP

        5810  DEEP PURPLE
        5790  PLAID
        5830  SEPTEMBER SONG
        5800  SOMEBODY LOVES ME
        5840  VERVE BLUES


Verve                              2332 009       Braz.   12 Inch LP
     [Part of 2-record set 2332 009/010.]
        5650  HALLELUJAH
        5640  PERDIDO


Verve                              2332 009       Ger.    12 Inch LP
     [Part of 2-record set 2632 005.]
        5650  HALLELUJAH
        5640  PERDIDO


Verve                              2332 010       Braz.   12 Inch LP
     [Part of 2-record set 2332 009/010.]
        5800  SOMEBODY LOVES ME
        5710  WHAT IS THIS THING CALLED LOVE


Verve                              2332 010       Ger.    12 Inch LP
     [Part of 2-record set 2632 005.]
        5800  SOMEBODY LOVES ME
        5710  WHAT IS THIS THING CALLED LOVE
```

```
Verve                          2332 009/010      Braz.
  [2-record set containing 2332 009,2332 010.]


Verve                          2367 396          Fr.       12 Inch LP
  [Part of 2-record set 2610 058.]
     6120  BEGIN THE BEGUINE
     6130  HUMORESQUE
     6140  SOMEONE TO WATCH OVER ME
     6150  WILLOW WEEP FOR ME


Verve                          2610 058
  [2-record set containing 2367 396.]


Verve                          2632 005          Ger.      12 Inch LP
  [2-record set containing 2332 009,2332 010.]


Verve                          DJ V-3            USA       12 Inch LP

     4940  'S WONDERFUL


Verve                          EPV5131           Ger.      7 Inch 45E

     4680  DEEP PURPLE
     4800  HEAT WAVE
     4810  SHE'S FUNNY THAT WAY


Verve                          EPV6036           Ger.      7 Inch 45E

     6120  BEGIN THE BEGUINE
     6130  HUMORESQUE
     6140  SOMEONE TO WATCH OVER ME
     6150  WILLOW WEEP FOR ME


Verve                          MG V-8013         USA       12 Inch LP

     4940  'S WONDERFUL
     4830  BLUES IN B FLAT
     4860  BLUES IN MY HEART
     4950  HANDS ACROSS THE TABLE
     4880  IDAHO
     4820  MY BLUE HEAVEN
     4930  OLD FASHIONED LOVE
     4870  STREET OF DREAMS


Verve                          MG V-8036         USA       12 Inch LP

     3950  BEGIN THE BEGUINE
           BLUES IN MY HEART (See "If You Hadn't Gone Away")
     3850  CAN'T WE BE FRIENDS
     4020  DIXIELAND BAND
     3870  ELEGIE
     3960  HUMORESQUE
     3900  IF YOU HADN'T GONE AWAY (Incorrectly titled "Blues in
           My Heart")
     3990  JUDY
     3860  THIS CAN'T BE LOVE


Verve                          MG V-8037         USA       12 Inch LP

     3910  BODY AND SOUL
     3930  MAKIN' WHOOPEE
     3920  MAN I LOVE, THE
     3880  MEMORIES OF YOU
     4540  MIGHTY LAK A ROSE
```

3890 OVER THE RAINBOW

Verve   MG V-8038   USA   12 Inch LP

    4040 COME RAIN OR COME SHINE
    4030 EMBRACEABLE YOU
    4000 I'M COMING VIRGINIA
    3970 LOUISE
    3980 LOVE FOR SALE
    4010 WRAP YOUR TROUBLES IS DREAMS

Verve   MG V-8039   USA   12 Inch LP

    4110 I'VE GOT THE WORLD ON A STRING
    4050 SITTIN' AND ROCKIN'
    4070 TENDERLY
    4060 THERE WILL NEVER BE ANOTHER YOU
    4080 WHAT DOES IT TAKE?
    4120 YESTERDAYS
    4090 YOU TOOK ADVANTAGE OF ME

Verve   MG V-8040   USA   12 Inch LP

    4260 HAVE YOU MET MISS JONES
    4270 IN A SENTIMENTAL MOOD
    4310 ISN'T THIS A LOVELY DAY
    4350 MY LAST AFFAIR
    4340 STOMPIN' AT THE SAVOY
    4370 TABOO
    4330 WITHOUT A SONG

Verve   MG V-8055   USA   12 Inch LP

    4560 BLUE MOON
    4130 I HADN'T ANYONE 'TILL YOU
    4150 JITTERBUG WALTZ
    4140 NIGHT AND DAY
    3940 SEPTEMBER SONG
    4530 SMOKE GETS IN YOUR EYES
    4550 STARS FELL ON ALABAMA
    4180 YOU'RE DRIVING ME CRAZY

Verve   MG V-8056   USA   12 Inch LP

    4190 GHOST OF A CHANCE, A
    4280 I'LL SEE YOU AGAIN
    4160 SOMEONE TO WATCH OVER ME
    4200 STAR DUST
    4230 STAY AS SWEET AS YOU ARE
    4170 VERY THOUGHT OF YOU, THE
    4220 WHERE OR WHEN

Verve   MG V-8057   USA   12 Inch LP

    4520 AIN'T MISBEHAVIN'
    4250 ALL THE THINGS YOU ARE
    4240 FINE AND DANDY
    4210 I COVER THE WATERFRONT
    4360 I'M IN THE MOOD FOR LOVE
    4650 LOVE ME OR LEAVE ME
    4500 WHEN A WOMAN LOVES A MAN
    4510 WILLOW WEEP FOR ME

Verve   MG V-8058   USA   12 Inch LP

    4420 AUNT HAGAR'S BLUES
    4320 BLUE SKIES
    4290 I'LL SEE YOU IN MY DREAMS

```
      4390  I'VE GOT A CRUSH ON YOU
      4300  ILL WIND
      4400  JAPANESE SANDMAN, THE
      4620  LOVER, COME BACK TO ME!
      4380  WOULD YOU LIKE TO TAKE A WALK


Verve                          MG V-8059      USA      12 Inch LP

      4490  BLUE LOU
      4580  CARAVAN
      4450  DANNY BOY
      4440  GONE WITH THE WIND
      4480  IT'S THE TALK OF THE TOWN
      4430  JUST LIKE A BUTTERFLY THAT'S CAUGHT IN THE RAIN
      4470  TEA FOR TWO
      4460  THEY CAN'T TAKE THAT AWAY FROM ME
      4410  TOO MARVELOUS FOR WORDS


Verve                          MG V-8064      USA      12 Inch LP

      5240  I SURRENDER DEAR
      5270  I WON'T DANCE
      5300  IN A SENTIMENTAL MOOD
      5280  MOON SONG
      5310  NIGHT AND DAY
      5250  MOON IS LOW, THE
      5290  THIS CAN'T BE LOVE
      5260  YOU TOOK ADVANTAGE OF ME


Verve                          MG V-8093      USA      12 Inch LP

      5650  HALLELUJAH
      5780  HOW HIGH THE MOON
      5660  I'LL NEVER BE THE SAME
      5760  MAKIN' WHOOPEE
      5770  MORE THAN YOU KNOW
      5640  PERDIDO
      5710  WHAT IS THIS THING CALLED LOVE


Verve                          MG V-8095      USA      12 Inch LP

      4690  AFTER YOU'VE GONE
      4660  CHEROKEE
      4640  DANCING IN THE DARK
      4630  SOPHISTICATED LADY
      4570  THERE'S A SMALL HOTEL
      4670  THESE FOOLISH THINGS REMIND ME OF YOU
      4590  WAY YOU LOOK TONIGHT, THE
      4600  YOU GO TO MY HEAD


Verve                          MG V-8118      Astla    12 Inch LP

      5920  BLUE LOU
      5990  I GUESS I'LL HAVE TO CHANGE MY PLANS
      5970  I'LL NEVER BE THE SAME
      5930  IF
      6000  ISN'T IT ROMANTIC
      5960  JUST ONE OF THOSE THINGS
      5980  LOVE FOR SALE
      5950  MORE THAN YOU KNOW
      5940  SOME OTHER SPRING
      6010  TRIO BLUES


Verve                          MG V-8118      USA      12 Inch LP

      5920  BLUE LOU
      5990  I GUESS I'LL HAVE TO CHANGE MY PLANS
      5970  I'LL NEVER BE THE SAME
      5930  IF
```

```
6000   ISN´T IT ROMANTIC
5960   JUST ONE OF THOSE THINGS
5980   LOVE FOR SALE
5950   MORE THAN YOU KNOW
5940   SOME OTHER SPRING
6010   TRIO BLUES
```

Verve   MG V-8127   USA   12 Inch LP

```
3850   CAN´T WE BE FRIENDS
3920   MAN I LOVE, THE
4340   STOMPIN´ AT THE SAVOY
```

Verve   MG V-8170   USA   12 Inch LP

```
5810   DEEP PURPLE
5790   PLAID
5830   SEPTEMBER SONG
5800   SOMEBODY LOVES ME
5840   VERVE BLUES
```

Verve   MG V-8215   USA   12 Inch LP

```
5820   WHAT IS THIS THING CALLED LOVE
```

Verve   MG V-8220   Astla   12 Inch LP

```
6160   ALL THE THINGS YOU ARE
6190   GONE WITH THE WIND
6200   HAVE YOU MET MISS JONES
6180   MY IDEAL
6170   MY ONE AND ONLY LOVE
6210   NIGHT AND DAY
6220   WHERE OR WHEN
```

Verve   MG V-8220   USA   12 Inch LP

```
6160   ALL THE THINGS YOU ARE
6190   GONE WITH THE WIND
6200   HAVE YOU MET MISS JONES
6180   MY IDEAL
6170   MY ONE AND ONLY LOVE
6210   NIGHT AND DAY
6220   WHERE OR WHEN
```

Verve   MG V-8227   Astla   12 Inch LP

```
4840   BLUES IN C
4850   FOGGY DAY, A
4921   MAKIN´ WHOOPEE
4900   UNDECIDED
4910   UNDER A BLANKET OF BLUE
4890   YOU´RE MINE, YOU
```

Verve   MG V-8227   USA   12 Inch LP

```
4840   BLUES IN C
4850   FOGGY DAY, A
4921   MAKIN´ WHOOPEE
4900   UNDECIDED
4910   UNDER A BLANKET OF BLUE
4890   YOU´RE MINE, YOU
```

Verve   MG V-8229   USA   12 Inch LP

```
6020   DEEP NIGHT
6070   FOGGY DAY, A
```

```
          6080    LOVER MAN
          6090    MAKIN' WHOOPEE
          6050    MEMORIES OF YOU
          6030    ONCE IN A WHILE
          6040    THIS CAN'T BE LOVE
          6060    YOU'RE MINE, YOU


Verve                              MG V-8230      USA      12 Inch LP

          4830    BLUES IN B FLAT


Verve                              MG V-8231-2    USA      12 Inch LP
     [Part of 2-record set.]
          6120    BEGIN THE BEGUINE
          6130    HUMORESQUE
          6140    SOMEONE TO WATCH OVER ME
          6150    WILLOW WEEP FOR ME


Verve                              MG V-8320      USA      12 Inch LP

          6010    TRIO BLUES


Verve                              MG V-8323      USA      12 Inch LP

          4680    DEEP PURPLE
          4800    HEAT WAVE
          4700    I DIDN'T KNOW WHAT TIME IT WAS
          4810    SHE'S FUNNY THAT WAY
          4710    SOMEBODY LOVES ME
          4790    THAT OLD FEELING
          4720    WHAT'S NEW?
          4760    YOU'RE BLASE
          4770    YOU'RE MINE, YOU


Verve                              MG V-8332      USA      12 Inch LP

          5070    DON'T WORRY 'BOUT ME
          5160    EVERYTHING I HAVE IS YOURS
          5170    I ONLY HAVE EYES FOR YOU
          4970    I SURRENDER DEAR
          5050    IF I HAD YOU
          5220    IF YOU HADN'T GONE AWAY
          5230    PLEASE BE KIND
          5080    PRISONER OF LOVE
          5040    MOON IS LOW, THE
          5030    WHEN YOUR LOVER HAS GONE


Verve                              MG V-8347      USA      12 Inch LP

          5000    BOULEVARD OF BROKEN DREAMS
          4740    CRAZY RHYTHM
          4980    HAPPY FEET
          4780    INDIANA
          4750    ISN'T IT ROMANTIC
          4990    MEAN TO ME
          5020    MOON SONG
          5010    MOONLIGHT ON THE GANGES
          5060    S'POSIN'
          4730    SWEET LORRAINE


Verve                              MG V-8360      USA      12 Inch LP

          5200    DO NOTHIN' TILL YOU HEAR FROM ME
          5110    I CAN'T GIVE YOU ANYTHING BUT LOVE
          5140    I GOTTA RIGHT TO SING THE BLUES
          5100    I WON'T DANCE
          5150    IT'S ONLY A PAPER MOON
          5120    LULLABY IN RHYTHM
```

```
        5090    MOONGLOW
        5180    ON THE SUNNY SIDE OF THE STREET
        5130    OUT OF NOWHERE
        5210    SO BEATS MY HEART FOR YOU
```

Verve   MV 1106   Jap.   12 Inch LP

```
        6160    ALL THE THINGS YOU ARE
        6190    GONE WITH THE WIND
        6200    HAVE YOU MET MISS JONES
        6180    MY IDEAL
        6170    MY ONE AND ONLY LOVE
        6210    NIGHT AND DAY
        6220    WHERE OR WHEN
```

Verve   MV 2021   Jap.   12 Inch LP

```
        5920    BLUE LOU
        5990    I GUESS I'LL HAVE TO CHANGE MY PLANS
        5970    I'LL NEVER BE THE SAME
        5930    IF
        6000    ISN'T IT ROMANTIC
        5960    JUST ONE OF THOSE THINGS
        5980    LOVE FOR SALE
        5950    MORE THAN YOU KNOW
        5940    SOME OTHER SPRING
        6010    TRIO BLUES
```

Verve   MV 2025   Jap.   12 Inch LP

```
        6160    ALL THE THINGS YOU ARE
        6190    GONE WITH THE WIND
        6200    HAVE YOU MET MISS JONES
        6180    MY IDEAL
        6170    MY ONE AND ONLY LOVE
        6210    NIGHT AND DAY
        6220    WHERE OR WHEN
```

Verve   MV 2505   Jap.   12 Inch LP

```
        6160    ALL THE THINGS YOU ARE
        6190    GONE WITH THE WIND
        6200    HAVE YOU MET MISS JONES
        6180    MY IDEAL
        6170    MY ONE AND ONLY LOVE
        6210    NIGHT AND DAY
        6220    WHERE OR WHEN
```

Verve   MV 2537   Jap.   12 Inch LP

```
        5920    BLUE LOU
        5990    I GUESS I'LL HAVE TO CHANGE MY PLANS
        5970    I'LL NEVER BE THE SAME
        5930    IF
        6000    ISN'T IT ROMANTIC
        5960    JUST ONE OF THOSE THINGS
        5980    LOVE FOR SALE
        5950    MORE THAN YOU KNOW
        5940    SOME OTHER SPRING
        6010    TRIO BLUES
```

Verve   PRS 2-3   USA   12 Inch LP
     [Part of 3-record boxed set.]
        6010   TRIO BLUES

```
Verve                          V-8433        USA    12 Inch LP

    4020  DIXIELAND BAND
    3870  ELEGIE
    4150  JITTERBUG WALTZ
    6180  MY IDEAL
    4160  SOMEONE TO WATCH OVER ME
    4070  TENDERLY
    4510  WILLOW WEEP FOR ME
    4380  WOULD YOU LIKE TO TAKE A WALK
    4760  YOU´RE BLASE


Verve                          V6-8433       USA  s 12 Inch LP

    4020  DIXIELAND BAND
    3870  ELEGIE
    4150  JITTERBUG WALTZ
    6180  MY IDEAL
    4160  SOMEONE TO WATCH OVER ME
    4070  TENDERLY
    4510  WILLOW WEEP FOR ME
    4380  WOULD YOU LIKE TO TAKE A WALK
    4760  YOU´RE BLASE


Verve                          VL-1007       Jap.   12 Inch LP

    6120  BEGIN THE BEGUINE
    6130  HUMORESQUE
    6140  SOMEONE TO WATCH OVER ME
    6150  WILLOW WEEP FOR ME


Verve                          VL-1024       Jap.   12 Inch LP

    6160  ALL THE THINGS YOU ARE
    6190  GONE WITH THE WIND
    6200  HAVE YOU MET MISS JONES
    6180  MY IDEAL
    6170  MY ONE AND ONLY LOVE
    6210  NIGHT AND DAY
    6220  WHERE OR WHEN


Verve                          VL-1032       Jap.   12  Inch LP

    5920  BLUE LOU
    5990  I GUESS I´LL HAVE TO CHANGE MY PLANS
    5970  I´LL NEVER BE THE SAME
    5930  IF
    6000  ISN´T IT ROMANTIC
    5960  JUST ONE OF THOSE THINGS
    5980  LOVE FOR SALE
    5950  MORE THAN YOU KNOW
    5940  SOME OTHER SPRING
    6010  TRIO BLUES


Verve                          VLP9090       Eng.   12 Inch LP

    6160  ALL THE THINGS YOU ARE
    6190  GONE WITH THE WIND
    6200  HAVE YOU MET MISS JONES
    6180  MY IDEAL
    6170  MY ONE AND ONLY LOVE
    6210  NIGHT AND DAY
    6220  WHERE OR WHEN


Verve                          VLP9110       Eng.   12 Inch LP

    4940  ´S WONDERFUL
    6020  DEEP NIGHT
    6070  FOGGY DAY, A
```

```
6130   HUMORESQUE
5240   I SURRENDER DEAR
4750   ISN'T IT ROMANTIC
5760   MAKIN' WHOOPEE
5790   PLAID
5290   THIS CAN'T BE LOVE
6010   TRIO BLUES
```

Verve   VLP9124   Eng.   12 Inch LP

```
5650   HALLELUJAH
```

Vogue   416039   Fr.   12 Inch LP
[Part of 2-record set VG304 416039.]
```
2520   JUST A GIGOLO
```

Vogue   DP.31   Fr.
[2-record set containing DP.31A,DP.31B.]

Vogue   DP.31A   Fr.   s 12 Inch LP

```
2370   BODY AND SOUL
2540   I GOTTA RIGHT TO SING THE BLUES
2380   I GUESS I'LL HAVE TO CHANGE MY PLANS
2480   IF I COULD BE WITH YOU
2510   IT'S ONLY A PAPER MOON
2520   JUST A GIGOLO
2500   MEAN TO ME
2550   ON THE SUNNY SIDE OF THE STREET
2460   SOMEBODY LOVES ME
2530   THREE LITTLE WORDS
2470   WHY WAS I BORN
2360   YOU TOOK ADVANTAGE OF ME
```
       *Applause has been dubbed onto these performances.

Vogue   DP.31B   Fr.   s 12 Inch LP

```
0760   ALL GOD'S CHILLUN GOT RHYTHM
2430   AMONG MY SOUVENIRS
2410   CAN'T WE BE FRIENDS
2400   CRAZY RHYTHM
0800   FINE AND DANDY
0820   I GOTTA RIGHT TO SING THE BLUES
0830   I'M COMING VIRGINIA
2440   I'M GONNA SIT RIGHT DOWN AND WRITE MYSELF A LETTER
0810   I'VE GOT THE WORLD ON A STRING
2420   LIMEHOUSE BLUES
2450   STAY AS SWEET AS YOU ARE
2390   WHAT IS THIS THING CALLED LOVE
```
       *Applause has been dubbed onto these performances.

Vogue   DP.64   Fr.
[2-record set containing DP.64B.]

Vogue   DP.64B   Fr.   12 Inch LP

```
1850   I KNOW THAT YOU KNOW
```

Vogue   EPV1008   Eng.   7 Inch 45EP

```
3020   GERSHWIN MEDLEY (Titled "Tatum Plays Pretty")
2950   HOW HIGH THE MOON
2980   SOMEONE TO WATCH OVER ME
3010   WILLOW WEEP FOR ME
```

287

```
Vogue                          EPV1212        Eng.    7 Inch 45E

    2960  HUMORESQUE
    3000  I KNOW THAT YOU KNOW
    3030  KERRY DANCE, THE
    2970  TATUM-POLE BOOGIE
    2990  YESTERDAYS


Vogue                          EPVA1212       Astla   7 Inch 45E

    2960  HUMORESQUE
    3000  I KNOW THAT YOU KNOW
    3030  KERRY DANCE, THE
    2970  TATUM-POLE BOOGIE
    2990  YESTERDAYS


Vogue                          INT40014       Fr.    12 Inch LP

    1340  MY IDEAL


Vogue                          INT40015       Fr.    12 Inch LP

    1331  MOP-MOP (Also called Boff-Boff)


Vogue                          INT40020       Fr.    12 Inch LP

    1351  ESQUIRE BLUES
    1320  ESQUIRE BOUNCE
    1331  MOP-MOP (Also called Boff-Boff)
    1340  MY IDEAL


Vogue                          INT40025       Fr.    12 Inch LP

    1320  ESQUIRE BOUNCE


Vogue                          INT40028       Fr.    12 Inch LP

    1351  ESQUIRE BLUES


Vogue                          L.D. 029       Fr.    10 Inch LP

    3020  GERSHWIN MEDLEY
    2950  HOW HIGH THE MOON
    2960  HUMORESQUE
    3000  I KNOW THAT YOU KNOW
    3030  KERRY DANCE, THE
    2980  SOMEONE TO WATCH OVER ME
    2970  TATUM-POLE BOOGIE (Titled "Boogie Woogie")
    3010  WILLOW WEEP FOR ME
    2990  YESTERDAYS


Vogue                          LAE.12209      Eng.   12 Inch LP

    1840  BODY AND SOUL
    1830  DARK EYES
    1870  FLYING HOME
    1850  I KNOW THAT YOU KNOW
    1860  ON THE SUNNY SIDE OF THE STREET


Vogue                          L.D.E.081      Eng.   10 Inch LP

    3020  GERSHWIN MEDLEY (Titled "Tatum Plays Pretty")
    2950  HOW HIGH THE MOON
    2960  HUMORESQUE
    3000  I KNOW THAT YOU KNOW
    3030  KERRY DANCE, THE
```

```
          2980  SOMEONE TO WATCH OVER ME
          2970  TATUM-POLE BOOGIE (Titled "Boogie Woogie")
          3010  WILLOW WEEP FOR ME
          2990  YESTERDAYS


Vogue                           LDM.30206         Fr.      12 Inch LP
     [Jacket shows number as 530206.]
          1550  DO NOTHIN' TILL YOU HEAR FROM ME


Vogue                           V2241             Eng.     10 Inch 78

          2950  HOW HIGH THE MOON
          2960  HUMORESQUE


Vogue                           VG304 416039      Fr.
     [2-record set containing 416039.]


Vogue                           VJD 511-1         Eng.  s 12 Inch LP

          2370  BODY AND SOUL
          2540  I GOTTA RIGHT TO SING THE BLUES
          2380  I GUESS I'LL HAVE TO CHANGE MY PLANS
          2480  IF I COULD BE WITH YOU
          2510  IT'S ONLY A PAPER MOON
          2520  JUST A GIGOLO
          2500  MEAN TO ME
          2550  ON THE SUNNY SIDE OF THE STREET
          2460  SOMEBODY LOVES ME
          2530  THREE LITTLE WORDS
          2470  WHY WAS I BORN
          2360  YOU TOOK ADVANTAGE OF ME
                *Applause has been dubbed onto these performances.


Vogue                           VJD 511-2         Eng.  s 12 Inch LP

          0760  ALL GOD'S CHILLUN GOT RHYTHM
          2430  AMONG MY SOUVENIRS
          2410  CAN'T WE BE FRIENDS
          2400  CRAZY RHYTHM
          0800  FINE AND DANDY
          0820  I GOTTA RIGHT TO SING THE BLUES
          0830  I'M COMING VIRGINIA
          2440  I'M GONNA SIT RIGHT DOWN AND WRITE MYSELF A LETTER
          0810  I'VE GOT THE WORLD ON A STRING
          2420  LIMEHOUSE BLUES
          2450  STAY AS SWEET AS YOU ARE
          2390  WHAT IS THIS THING CALLED LOVE
                *Applause has been dubbed onto these performances.


Vogue                           VJD 511/1/2       Eng.
     [2-record set containing VJD 511-1,VJD 511-2.]


Vogue                           VK 30             Belg. s 12 Inch LP
          2430  AMONG MY SOUVENIRS
          2370  BODY AND SOUL
          2410  CAN'T WE BE FRIENDS
          2400  CRAZY RHYTHM
          0800  FINE AND DANDY
          2440  I'M GONNA SIT RIGHT DOWN AND WRITE MYSELF A LETTER
          0810  I'VE GOT THE WORLD ON A STRING
          2510  IT'S ONLY A PAPER MOON
          2500  MEAN TO ME
          2550  ON THE SUNNY SIDE OF THE STREET
          2460  SOMEBODY LOVES ME
          2390  WHAT IS THIS THING CALLED LOVE
                *Applause has been dubbed onto these performances.


                               289
```

```
Vogue Coral                    ECV18032        Fr.      7 Inch 45E

     1080   BATTERY BOUNCE
     1070   LAST GOODBYE BLUES
     1060   STOMPIN´ AT THE SAVOY
     1050   WEE BABY BLUES


Vogue Coral                    LRA.10011       Eng.    10 Inch LP

     1430   AFTER YOU´VE GONE
     1410   COCKTAILS FOR TWO
     1450   DEEP PURPLE
     1490   HONEYSUCKLE ROSE
     1420   I AIN´T GOT NOBODY
     1400   I GOT RHYTHM
     1460   I WOULD DO ANYTHING FOR YOU
     1440   MOONGLOW


Vogue Coral                    LVA.9047        Eng.    12 Inch LP

     1430   AFTER YOU´VE GONE
     0960   BEGIN THE BEGUINE
     1410   COCKTAILS FOR TWO
     1450   DEEP PURPLE
     0460   GONE WITH THE WIND
     1490   HONEYSUCKLE ROSE
     1400   I GOT RHYTHM
     1440   MOONGLOW
     0970   ROSETTA
     0950   ST. LOUIS BLUES
     0470   STORMY WEATHER
     0740   TEA FOR TWO


White Label                    (See "Mecolico")


Windmill                       WMD 248         Eng.    12 Inch LP

     1610   BLUES
     1740   FLYING HOME
     1540   MOP-MOP
     1720   MY IDEAL


World Jam Session              JS 31           USA     16 Inch TX

     1450   DEEP PURPLE
     1490   HONEYSUCKLE ROSE
     1460   I WOULD DO ANYTHING FOR YOU
     1470   LIZA
     1480   TEA FOR TWO


World Jam Session              JS32            USA     16 Inch TX

     1430   AFTER YOU´VE GONE
     1410   COCKTAILS FOR TWO
     1420   I AIN´T GOT NOBODY
     1400   I GOT RHYTHM
     1440   MOONGLOW


World Program Service          345             USA     16 Inch TX

     1430   AFTER YOU´VE GONE
     1490   HONEYSUCKLE ROSE
     1440   MOONGLOW
```

```
World Program Service          367          USA      16 Inch TX

     1400  I GOT RHYTHM
     1470  LIZA
     1480  TEA FOR TWO


World Program Service          393          USA      16 Inch TX

     1410  COCKTAILS FOR TWO
     1420  I AIN'T GOT NOBODY
     1460  I WOULD DO ANYTHING FOR YOU


World Program Service       WM1276/1280     USA      16 Inch TX
     [The side of the disc which contains the Tatum listings is numbered
     as shown; the other side is number WM1271/1275.  Each title is
     individually numbered.]
     1410  COCKTAILS FOR TWO
     1490  HONEYSUCKLE ROSE
     1420  I AIN'T GOT NOBODY
     1440  MOONGLOW


World Record Club              76           Eng.     12 Inch LP

     5360  BEGIN THE BEGUINE
     5380  BODY AND SOUL
     5410  DANNY BOY
     5450  I'LL NEVER BE THE SAME
     5470  LITTLE MAN, YOU'VE HAD A BUSY DAY
     5370  SOMEONE TO WATCH OVER ME
     5420  TENDERLY
     5400  TOO MARVELOUS FOR WORDS
     5390  WILLOW WEEP FOR ME
     5460  WITHOUT A SONG
     5440  YESTERDAYS
     5430  YOU TOOK ADVANTAGE OF ME


World Record Club            F. 526         Eng.     12 Inch LP

     4830  BLUES IN B FLAT


World Record Club            T208           Eng.     12 Inch LP

     3080  AUNT HAGAR'S BLUES
     3220  BLUE SKIES
     3240  DANCING IN THE DARK
     3110  DARDANELLA
     3070  I COVER THE WATERFRONT
     3180  I GOTTA RIGHT TO SING THE BLUES
     3780  INDIANA
     3090  NICE WORK IF YOU CAN GET IT
     3750  OUT OF NOWHERE
     3720  SEPTEMBER SONG
     3740  TEA FOR TWO
     3060  WILLOW WEEP FOR ME


World Record Club            T. 279         Eng.     12 Inch LP

     5570  DON'T BLAME ME
     5550  I COVER THE WATERFRONT
     5510  IN A SENTIMENTAL MOOD
     5490  JITTERBUG WALTZ
     3290  MEMORIES OF YOU
     5560  MOON SONG
     3280  MR. FREDDIE BLUES
     5480  MY HEART STOOD STILL
     5500  OVER THE RAINBOW
     5530  SEPTEMBER SONG
     5520  THERE WILL NEVER BE ANOTHER YOU
     5540  WRAP YOUR TROUBLES IN DREAMS
```

291

```
World Record Club              TP. 226        Eng.     12 Inch LP
        5360   BEGIN THE BEGUINE
        5380   BODY AND SOUL
        5410   DANNY BOY
        5450   I'LL NEVER BE THE SAME
        5470   LITTLE MAN, YOU'VE HAD A BUSY DAY
        5370   SOMEONE TO WATCH OVER ME
        5420   TENDERLY
        5400   TOO MARVELOUS FOR WORDS
        5390   WILLOW WEEP FOR ME
        5460   WITHOUT A SONG
        5440   YESTERDAYS
        5430   YOU TOOK ADVANTAGE OF ME


Xanadu                         112           USA      12 Inch LP
        1020   ALL THE THINGS YOU ARE


Xanadu                         VG405-JX.6610  Fr.     12 Inch LP
        1020   ALL THE THINGS YOU ARE


Xtra                           XTRA 1007      Eng.    12 Inch LP
        2080   DANNY BOY
        2031   FINE AND DANDY
               GONE WITH WHAT WIND (See "Topsy" [1960])
        1970   IF I HAD YOU
        2040   IT HAD TO BE YOU
        2050   JA-DA
        1980   SOFT WINDS
        2070   SWEET AND LOVELY
        1960   TOPSY (Incorrectly titled "Gone With What Wind")
        1961   TOPSY
        2060   WHERE OR WHEN
```

```
0200  AFTER YOU'VE GONE (3:06)  [Turner Layton/Henry Creamer]
0201  AFTER YOU'VE GONE (2:28)
0202  AFTER YOU'VE GONE
0290  AFTER YOU'VE GONE (2:25)
1300  AFTER YOU'VE GONE
1430  AFTER YOU'VE GONE (2:25)
4690  AFTER YOU'VE GONE (3:59)
0550  AIN'T MISBEHAVIN' (2:35)  [Fats Waller-Harry Brooks/Andy Razaf]
2000  AIN'T MISBEHAVIN' (4:28)
2780  AIN'T MISBEHAVIN' (2:40)
4520  AIN'T MISBEHAVIN' (2:32)
T8321 AIN'T MISBEHAVIN' (2:20)
T8622 AIN'T MISBEHAVIN' (3:10)
T8663 AIN'T MISBEHAVIN' (3:15)
T8802 AIR MAIL SPECIAL (1:22) [Charlie Christian-Benny Goodman-
      Jimmy Mundy]
0760  ALL GOD'S CHILLUN GOT RHYTHM (1:55) [Bronislaw Kaper-Walter
      Jurmann/Gus Kahn]
1985  ALL OF ME (1:43) [Seymour Simons-Gerald Marks]
1020  ALL THE THINGS YOU ARE (3:46) [Jerome Kern/Oscar Hammerstein II]
4250  ALL THE THINGS YOU ARE (5:59)
6160  ALL THE THINGS YOU ARE (7:07)
T7040 ALL THE THINGS YOU ARE (2:25)
T8115 ALL THE THINGS YOU ARE (2:44)
T8520 ALL THE THINGS YOU ARE (2:28+)
      AMETHYST (Published as "Amethyst", but this is the same tune
      recorded by Tatum as "The Shout".  See 240,241,310.)
T7006 AMETHYST [Art Tatum]
2430  AMONG MY SOUVENIRS (2:45) [Horatio Nicholls/Edgar Leslie]
      ANYTHING BUT LOVE (See "I Can't Give You Anything But Love"[5910])
2620  APOLLO BOOGIE (2:25) [Art Tatum]
2760  ART'S BLUES (2:39)
T8583 ART'S BOOGIE (1:13) [Art Tatum]
T8238 AT SUNDOWN [Walter Donaldson]
3080  AUNT HAGAR'S BLUES (2:37) [W. C. Handy/J. Tim Brymn]
4420  AUNT HAGAR'S BLUES (4:50)
1670  BACK O' TOWN BLUES (3:27) [Louis Armstrong-Luis Russell]
1500  BASIN STREET BLUES (3:37) [Spencer Williams]
1640  BASIN STREET BLUES (3:57)
1080  BATTERY BOUNCE (2:28) [Art Tatum]
0250  BEAUTIFUL LOVE [Victor Young-Wayne King-Egbert Van Alstyne/
      Haven Gillespie]
0251  BEAUTIFUL LOVE (2:51)
0252  BEAUTIFUL LOVE (3:18)
1000  BEAUTIFUL LOVE (3:41)
0670  BEGIN THE BEGUINE (2:45) [Cole Porter]
0960  BEGIN THE BEGUINE (2:37)
0961  BEGIN THE BEGUINE
1120  BEGIN THE BEGUINE (3:52)
2270  BEGIN THE BEGUINE (3:14)
3460  BEGIN THE BEGUINE (3:25)
3950  BEGIN THE BEGUINE (2:58)
5360  BEGIN THE BEGUINE (2:55)
6120  BEGIN THE BEGUINE (3:01)
T8116 BEGIN THE BEGUINE (3:31)
T8300 BEGIN THE BEGUINE
T8481 BEGIN THE BEGUINE (3:03)
T8882 BEGIN THE BEGUINE (2:57)
2650  BETWEEN MIDNIGHT AND DAWN (2:47) [Art Tatum]
T8431 BETWEEN THE DEVIL AND THE DEEP BLUE SEA (0:34) [Harold Arlen/
      Ted Koehler]
      BILLIE'S BLUES (See "I Love My Man")
4490  BLUE LOU (2:40) [Edgar Sampson-Irving Mills]
5920  BLUE LOU (3:01)
4560  BLUE MOON (4:57) [Richard Rodgers/Lorenz Hart]
T7021 BLUE MOON
3220  BLUE SKIES (2:48) [Irving Berlin]
4320  BLUE SKIES (2:56)
1610  BLUES (2:47)
2120  BLUES FOR ART'S SAKE (2:47) [Barney Bigard-Art Tatum]
4830  BLUES IN B FLAT (5:40) [Louis Bellson-Benny Carter]
4840  BLUES IN C (8:00) [Louis Bellson-Benny Carter-Art Tatum]
```

```
        BLUES IN MY HEART (Incorrectly titled- See "If You Hadn't
          Gone Away" [3900])
4860    BLUES IN MY HEART (6:00) [Benny Carter-Irving Mills]
        BLUES ON DOWN (Incorrectly titled- See "Taboo" [3800])
2670    BLUES ON THE ROCKS (3:04) [Art Tatum]
0420    BODY AND SOUL (3:06) [Johnny Green/Edward Heyman-Robert
          Sour-Frank Eyton]
0421    BODY AND SOUL (3:07)
0630    BODY AND SOUL (2:30)
1040    BODY AND SOUL (7:49+)
1200    BODY AND SOUL (3:32)
1840    BODY AND SOUL (4:30)
2350    BODY AND SOUL (3:07
2370    BODY AND SOUL (2:50)
3410    BODY AND SOUL (4:59)
3470    BODY AND SOUL (4:03)
3700    BODY AND SOUL (5:55)
3910    BODY AND SOUL (5:44)
5280    BODY AND SOUL (3:28)
5690    BODY AND SOUL (5:21)
5910    BODY AND SOUL (0:57)
T8242   BODY AND SOUL (3:08)
T8301   BODY AND SOUL
T8424   BODY AND SOUL (5:27)
T8624   BODY AND SOUL (4:15)
T8702   BODY AND SOUL (5:16)
T8764   BODY AND SOUL (5:17)
T8884   BODY AND SOUL (2:16)
        BOFF-BOFF (See "Mop-Mop")
1950    BOOGIE (3:45) [Art Tatum]
1900    BOOGIE (3:38) (Rehearsal excerpt titled "Long, Long Ago")
1910    BOOGIE (1:51) (Rehearsal excerpt titled "Variations On a
          Theme By Flotow")
0280    BOOTS AND SADDLE (2:15) [Walter G. Samuels-Leonard Whitcup-
          Teddy Powell]
0410    BOOTS AND SADDLE (3:07)
5000    BOULEVARD OF BROKEN DREAMS (5:18) [Harry Warren/Al Dubin]
1690    BUCK JUMPIN' (2:42) [Al Casey]
2090    CAN'T HELP LOVIN' DAT MAN OF MINE (3:08) [Jerome Kern/Oscar
          Hammerstein II]
0640    CAN'T WE BE FRIENDS (2:20) [Kay Swift/James Warburg]
2410    CAN'T WE BE FRIENDS (2:30)
3850    CAN'T WE BE FRIENDS (3:43)
3810    CARAVAN (0:33) [Duke Ellington-Juan Tizol/Irving Mills]
4580    CARAVAN (2:34)
T8060   CARNEGIE HALL BOUNCE (2:45) [Art Tatum]
2280    CHEROKEE (5:37) [Ray Noble]
2800    CHEROKEE (3:00)
4660    CHEROKEE (3:37)
T8228   CHINA BOY [Dick Winfree-Phil Boutelje]
0130    CHINATOWN, MY CHINATOWN (1:34) [Jean Schwartz/William Jerome]
0480    CHLOE (3:21) [Charles N. Daniels/Gus Kahn]
0481    CHLOE (3:02)
        CHRZY RHYTHM (Incorrectly titled- See "Crazy Rhythm" [2400])
0190    COCKTAILS FOR TWO (2:46) [Arthur Johnston-Sam Coslow]
0940    COCKTAILS FOR TWO (2:48)
1410    COCKTAILS FOR TWO (2:37)
T8423   COCKTAILS FOR TWO (3:02)
3450    COME RAIN OR COME SHINE (3:23) [Harold Arlen/Johnny Mercer]
3550    COME RAIN OR COME SHINE
4040    COME RAIN OR COME SHINE (5:05)
T8363   COME RAIN OR COME SHINE (5:26)
T8662   CONFESSIN' (4:20) [Doc Daugherty-Ellis Reynolds/Al Neiburg]
T8342   CONTINENTAL, THE (3:02+) [Con Conrad/Herb Magidson]
1150    CORINNE, CORINNA (2:28) [J. Mayo Williams-Bo Chatman]
2400    CRAZY RHYTHM (2:15) [Roger Wolfe Kahn-Joseph Meyer/
          Irving Caesar]
4740    CRAZY RHYTHM (2:53)
T8551   CRAZY RHYTHM (2:30)
2600    CRYSTAL CLEAR (2:57) [Art Tatum]
3240    DANCING IN THE DARK (2:52) [Arthur Schwartz/Howard Dietz]
4640    DANCING IN THE DARK (4:27)
2080    DANNY BOY (2:45) [Irish Air adapted by Fred E. Weatherly]
2150    DANNY BOY (2:32)
4450    DANNY BOY (4:08)
```

```
5410  DANNY BOY (3:02)
3110  DARDANELLA (2:47) [Felix Bernard-Johnny S. Black/Fred Fisher]
T8361 DARDANELLA (3:51)
1830  DARK EYES (4:40) [A. Salama]
T8542 DARK EYES (2:50)
0790  DAY IN - DAY OUT (3:30) [Rube Bloom/Johnny Mercer]
6020  DEEP NIGHT (5:43) [Charlie Henderson/Rudy Vallee]
0750  DEEP PURPLE (3:12) [Peter De Rose/Mitchell Parish]
0751  DEEP PURPLE (3:15)
1450  DEEP PURPLE (3:03)
4680  DEEP PURPLE (4:57)
5810  DEEP PURPLE (7:57)
0400  DEVIL IN THE MOON (3:16) [Alex Hill-Mannie Kurtz-Irving Mills]
      DIPPERMOUTH BLUES (See "Sugar Foot Stomp")
0300  DIXIELAND BAND (2:30) [Bernard Hanighen/Johnny Mercer]
4020  DIXIELAND BAND (3:06)
1550  DO NOTHIN' TILL YOU HEAR FROM ME (3:28) [Duke Ellington/
      Bob Russell]
5200  DO NOTHIN' TILL YOU HEAR FROM ME (4:55)
3150  DON'T BLAME ME (2:49) [Jimmy McHugh/Dorothy Fields]
3610  DON'T BLAME ME (4:00)
5570  DON'T BLAME ME (3:24)
T7020 DON'T BLAME ME
T8360 DON'T BLAME ME (3:13)
T8229 DON'T GET AROUND MUCH ANYMORE [Duke Ellington/Bob Russell]
T8580 DON'T TAKE YOUR LOVE FROM ME (2:45) [Henry Nemo]
5070  DON'T WORRY 'BOUT ME (4:10) [Rube Bloom/Ted Koehler]
2290  DOWN BY THE OLD MILL STREAM (3:39) [Tell Taylor]
0620  ELEGIE (2:25) [Jules Massenet]
0840  ELEGIE (3:10)
0841  ELEGIE
3870  ELEGIE (3:37)
T8941 ELEGIE (3:31)
0170  EMALINE (2:34) [Frank Perkins/Mitchell Parish]
0910  EMALINE (2:16)
1220  EMBRACEABLE YOU (3:51) [George Gershwin/Ira Gershwin]
4030  EMBRACEABLE YOU (4:35)
1350  ESQUIRE BLUES (3:15) [Leonard Feather]
1351  ESQUIRE BLUES (3:16)
1510  ESQUIRE BLUES (2:17)
1530  ESQUIRE BLUES (5:10)
1320  ESQUIRE BOUNCE (3:12) [Leonard Feather]
1321  ESQUIRE BOUNCE (3:10)
1630  ESQUIRE BOUNCE (1:50)
5160  EVERYTHING I HAVE IS YOURS (5:31) [Burton Lane/Harold Adamson]
1380  EXACTLY LIKE YOU (3:22) [Jimmy McHugh/Dorothy Fields]
1815  EXACTLY LIKE YOU (4:56)
2580  FIFTY SECOND STREET BLUES (3:44) [Art Tatum]
0800  FINE AND DANDY (1:50) [Kay Swift/Paul James]
1110  FINE AND DANDY (4:03)
2030  FINE AND DANDY (2:45)
2031  FINE AND DANDY (2:42)
4240  FINE AND DANDY (2:59)
5350  FINE AND DANDY (1:45)
T8382 FINE AND DANDY (3:56+)
T8383 FINE AND DANDY (3:05+)
T8384 FINE AND DANDY (4:10+)
1983  FINE AND MELLOW (3:38) [Billie Holiday]
1740  FLYING HOME (8:27) [Benny Goodman-Lionel Hampton-Sid Robin]
1870  FLYING HOME (4:20)
3420  FLYING HOME (1:10) (Incorrectly titled "A Riff Tune")
3650  FLYING HOME (1:06) (Incorrectly titled "Air Mail Special")
5850  FLYING HOME (0:43)
6230  FLYING HOME (1:25)
6260  FLYING HOME (1:32)
T8425 FLYING HOME (0:57)
T8760 FLYING HOME
      FLYIN' ON A V-DISC (See "Flying Home" [1740])
      FLYING ON THE PIANO (See "Flying Home" [6260])
4850  FOGGY DAY, A (5:25) [George Gershwin/Ira Gershwin]
6070  FOGGY DAY, A (3:21)
1710  FOR BASS FACES ONLY (4:59) [Oscar Pettiford]
2570  GANG O' NOTES (2:42) [Art Tatum]
      GANG O' NOTHIN' (Seems related to "Jade." See [T7008].)
T8062 GANG O' NOTHIN' [Art Tatum]
```

295

```
1090   GEORGIA ON MY MIND (2:15) [Hoagy Carmichael/Stuart Gorrell]
T7071  GEORGIA ON MY MIND (1:41)
T8001  GEORGIA ON MY MIND (1:42)
       GERSHWIN MEDLEY [This medley includes "The Man I Love",
       "Summertime", "I Got Plenty O' Nuttin' ", "It Ain't
       Necessarily So", and "The Man I Love" again.]
2320   GERSHWIN MEDLEY (4:16) [George Gershwin/Ira Gershwin]
3020   GERSHWIN MEDLEY (3:53) (Abridged versions are variously
       entitled "The Man I Love" or "Tatum Plays Pretty")
3300   GERSHWIN MEDLEY (3:39)
3630   GERSHWIN MEDLEY (4:20)
       GERSHWIN MEDLEY (See also "Man I Love, The)
0660   GET HAPPY (1:55) [Harold Arlen/Ted Koehler]
0870   GET HAPPY (2:40)
3340   GHOST OF A CHANCE, A  (4:03) [Victor Young/Ned Washington-
       Bing Crosby]
4190   GHOST OF A CHANCE, A  (4:09)
3210   GOIN' HOME (3:05) [Antonin Dvorak]
T8560  GOIN' HOME (4:10)
0460   GONE WITH THE WIND (2:48) [Allie Wrubel/Herb Magidson]
0461   GONE WITH THE WIND
4440   GONE WITH THE WIND (2:57)
4610   GONE WITH THE WIND
6190   GONE WITH THE WIND (4:44)
T7016  GOODNIGHT SWEETHEART [Ray Noble-James Campbell-Reg Connelly]
0700   HALLELUJAH (2:05) [Vincent Youmans/Leo Robin-Clifford Grey]
2190   HALLELUJAH (3:07)
2191   HALLELUJAH (2:40)
3350   HALLELUJAH (5:08)
5650   HALLELUJAH (4:50)
4950   HANDS ACROSS THE TABLE (3:40) [Jean Deletre/Mitchell Parish]
0530   HAPPY FEET (1:45) [Milton Ager/Jack Yellen]
4980   HAPPY FEET (2:34)
4260   HAVE YOU MET MISS JONES (4:45) [Richard Rodgers/Lorenz Hart]
6200   HAVE YOU MET MISS JONES (4:46)
T8723  HAVE YOU MET MISS JONES (3:01)
4800   HEAT WAVE (3:16) [Irving Berlin]
       HENRY DANCE (Incorrectly titled- See "Kerry Dance" [2260])
1488   HONEYSUCKLE ROSE (0:20) [Fats Waller/Andy Razaf]
1489   HONEYSUCKLE ROSE (2:24)
1490   HONEYSUCKLE ROSE (2:19)
1520   HONEYSUCKLE ROSE (1:59)
3490   HONEYSUCKLE ROSE (3:05)
3560   HONEYSUCKLE ROSE
T8111  HONEYSUCKLE ROSE (1:23)
T8281  HONEYSUCKLE ROSE (0:35)
T8483  HONEYSUCKLE ROSE (2:26)
T8237  HOT LIPS [Henry Busse-Henry Lange-Lou Davis]
T7015  HOW AM I TO KNOW? [Jack King/Dorothy Parker]
2160   HOW HIGH THE MOON (1:59) [Morgan Lewis/Nancy Hamilton]
2310   HOW HIGH THE MOON (2:12)
2950   HOW HIGH THE MOON (2:28)
3190   HOW HIGH THE MOON
3440   HOW HIGH THE MOON (2:14)
5780   HOW HIGH THE MOON (5:03)
0690   HUMORESQUE (2:20) [Antonin Dvorak]
0850   HUMORESQUE
1770   HUMORESQUE (4:13)
1880   HUMORESQUE (1:54)
1990   HUMORESQUE (3:33)
2960   HUMORESQUE (3:48)
3960   HUMORESQUE (3:55)
6130   HUMORESQUE (3:26)
T7070  HUMORESQUE (3:34)
T8000  HUMORESQUE (3:53)
T8400  HUMORESQUE (3:28)
0220   I AIN'T GOT NOBODY [Spencer Williams-Dave Peyton/Roger Graham]
0221   I AIN'T GOT NOBODY (3:21)
0222   I AIN'T GOT NOBODY
1420   I AIN'T GOT NOBODY (2:33)
T8113  I CAN'T BELIEVE THAT YOU'RE IN LOVE WITH ME (2:54) [Clarence
       Gaskill-Jimmy McHugh]
0520   I CAN'T GET STARTED (3:00) [Vernon Duke/Ira Gershwin]
1570   I CAN'T GIVE YOU ANYTHING BUT LOVE (3:15) [Jimmy McHugh/
       Dorothy Fields]
```

```
2020   I CAN'T GIVE YOU ANYTHING BUT LOVE (3:06)
2180   I CAN'T GIVE YOU ANYTHING BUT LOVE (2:20)
5110   I CAN'T GIVE YOU ANYTHING BUT LOVE (3:33) (Sometimes incorrectly
       titled "Anything But Love")
3070   I COVER THE WATERFRONT (2:28) [Johnny Green/Edward Heyman]
4210   I COVER THE WATERFRONT (3:42)
5550   I COVER THE WATERFRONT (4:04)
5860   I COVER THE WATERFRONT (4:17)
T8343  I COVER THE WATERFRONT (3:01+)
T8432  I COVER THE WATERFRONT (2:18)
T8883  I COVER THE WATERFRONT (3:43)
4700   I DIDN'T KNOW WHAT TIME IT WAS (4:12) [Richard Rodgers/Lorenz
       Hart]
T8235  I GOT IT BAD AND THAT AIN'T GOOD [Duke Ellington/Paul
       Francis Webster]
       I GOT PLENTY O' NUTTIN' [George Gershwin/Ira Gershwin]
       (See "Gershwin Medley")
1400   I GOT RHYTHM (2:15) [George Gershwin/Ira Gershwin]
1600   I GOT RHYTHM (8:15)
1986   I GOT RHYTHM (2:30)
T7030  I GOT RHYTHM (2:02)
0820   I GOTTA RIGHT TO SING THE BLUES (2:10) [Harold Arlen/Ted
       Koehler]
1580   I GOTTA RIGHT TO SING THE BLUES (3:39)
2540   I GOTTA RIGHT TO SING THE BLUES (2:32)
3180   I GOTTA RIGHT TO SING THE BLUES (2:53)
3260   I GOTTA RIGHT TO SING THE BLUES (1:58)
5140   I GOTTA RIGHT TO SING THE BLUES (3:50)
2380   I GUESS I'LL HAVE TO CHANGE MY PLANS (2:20) [Arthur Schwartz/
       Howard Dietz]
5990   I GUESS I'LL HAVE TO CHANGE MY PLANS (3:37)
4130   I HADN'T ANYONE 'TILL YOU (3:28) [Ray Noble]
1395   I KNOW THAT YOU KNOW (2:37) [Vincent Youmans/Anne Caldwell]
1850   I KNOW THAT YOU KNOW (4:15)
1890   I KNOW THAT YOU KNOW (3:28)
3000   I KNOW THAT YOU KNOW (2:30)
3310   I KNOW THAT YOU KNOW (2:37)
3480   I KNOW THAT YOU KNOW (2:15)
T8105  I KNOW THAT YOU KNOW (3:39)
T8220  I KNOW THAT YOU KNOW (0:43)
T8885  I KNOW THAT YOU KNOW (1:02)
1560   I LOVE MY MAN (Billie's Blues) (4:04) [Billie Holiday]
5170   I ONLY HAVE EYES FOR YOU (2:48) [Harry Warren/Al Dubin]
1230   I SURRENDER DEAR (4:27) [Harry Barris/Gordon Clifford]
4970   I SURRENDER DEAR (3:51)
5240   I SURRENDER DEAR (6:52)
0390   I WISH I WERE TWINS (2:09) [Joseph Meyer/Frank Loesser-
       Eddie DeLange]
5100   I WON'T DANCE (2:55) [Jerome Kern/Otto Harbach-Oscar
       Hammerstein II]
5270   I WON'T DANCE (3:26)
0150   I WOULD DO ANYTHING FOR YOU (2:36) [Alex Hill-Bob Williams-
       Claude Hopkins]
0151   I WOULD DO ANYTHING FOR YOU
0152   I WOULD DO ANYTHING FOR YOU (2:36)
0153   I WOULD DO ANYTHING FOR YOU
0350   I WOULD DO ANYTHING FOR YOU (2:10)
1460   I WOULD DO ANYTHING FOR YOU (2:29)
4880   IDAHO (4:15) [Jesse Stone]
3820   IF (4:09) [Tolchard Evans/Robert Hargreaves-Stanley J. Damerell]
5930   IF (3:30)
2480   IF I COULD BE WITH YOU (2:41) [Henry Creamer-James P. Johnson]
1920   IF I HAD YOU (Fragments totalling 3:25) [Ted Shapiro-Jimmy
       Campbell-Reg Connelly]
1921   IF I HAD YOU (1:48)
1970   IF I HAD YOU (3:24)
5050   IF I HAD YOU (4:10)
T7011  IF I HAD YOU
T8380  IF I HAD YOU (3:55)
T8725  IF I HAD YOU (4:07)
T8940  IF I HAD YOU (3:06)
3900   IF YOU HADN'T GONE AWAY (4:04) (Incorrectly titled
       "Blues in My Heart") [Lew Brown-Billy Rose-Ray Henderson]
5220   IF YOU HADN'T GONE AWAY (3:52)
T8584  IF YOU HADN'T GONE AWAY (3:24)
```

```
0590  I'LL GET BY (2:25) [Fred E. Ahlert/Roy Turk]
1650  I'LL GET BY (1:25)
0020  I'LL NEVER BE THE SAME (3:09) [Matty Malneck-Frank Signorelli/
      Gus Kahn]
0021  I'LL NEVER BE THE SAME (3:17)
0600  I'LL NEVER BE THE SAME (2:35)
2930  I'LL NEVER BE THE SAME (3:20)
5450  I'LL NEVER BE THE SAME (2:41)
5660  I'LL NEVER BE THE SAME (6:33)
5970  I'LL NEVER BE THE SAME (4:53)
T8232 I'LL NEVER BE THE SAME
4280  I'LL SEE YOU AGAIN (4:49) [Noel Coward]
4290  I'LL SEE YOU IN MY DREAMS (3:15) [Isham Jones/Gus Kahn]
T8581 I'LL SEE YOU IN MY DREAMS (3:05)
0230  ILL WIND (2:55) [Harold Arlen/Ted Koehler]
4300  ILL WIND (5:16)
2354  I'M BEGINNING TO SEE THE LIGHT (3:06) [Harry James-Duke
      Ellington-Johnny Hodges-Don George]
0830  I'M COMING VIRGINIA (2:35) [Donald Heywood/Will Marion Cook]
4000  I'M COMING VIRGINIA (3:34)
T7017 I'M COMING VIRGINIA
2420  I'M GONNA SIT RIGHT DOWN AND WRITE MYSELF A LETTER (2:40) [Fred
      E. Ahlert/Joe Young]
4360  I'M IN THE MOOD FOR LOVE (4:22) [Jimmy McHugh/Dorothy Fields]
T7013 I'M IN THE MOOD FOR LOVE
0570  IN A SENTIMENTAL MOOD (2:22) [Duke Ellington]
2890  IN A SENTIMENTAL MOOD (3:16)
4270  IN A SENTIMENTAL MOOD (5:59)
5300  IN A SENTIMENTAL MOOD (4:59)
5510  IN A SENTIMENTAL MOOD (3:09)
0370  IN THE MIDDLE OF A KISS (2:31) [Sam Coslow]
0780  INDIANA (2:05) [James F. Hanley/Ballard MacDonald]
0980  INDIANA (2:45)
0981  INDIANA
2720  INDIANA (2:33)
3780  INDIANA (3:23)
4780  INDIANA (3:02)
T8421 INDIANA (3:05)
T8640 INDIANA (2:50)
3040  INTERVIEW (PROMOTIONAL) by Paul Weston
3050  INTERVIEW (PROMOTIONAL) by Paul Weston
3530  INTERVIEW (3:11)
4815  INTERVIEW
T8600 INTERVIEW (3:20)
T8780 INTERVIEW
T8820 INTERVIEW
T8860 INTERVIEW
      INTROSPECTION (Incorrectly titled- See "Sittin' and
      Rockin'" [3500])
4750  ISN'T IT ROMANTIC (4:33) [Richard Rodgers/Lorenz Hart]
6000  ISN'T IT ROMANTIC (3:57)
4310  ISN'T THIS A LOVELY DAY (3:29) [Irving Berlin]
      IT AIN'T NECESSARILY SO [George Gershwin/Ira Gershwin]
      (See "Gershwin Medley")
0680  IT HAD TO BE YOU (2:30) [Isham Jones/Gus Kahn]
1780  IT HAD TO BE YOU (3:53)
2040  IT HAD TO BE YOU (2:33)
T7041 IT HAD TO BE YOU (1:36)
2510  IT'S ONLY A PAPER MOON (2:41) [Harold Arlen/Billy Rose-
      E. Y. Harburg]
5150  IT'S ONLY A PAPER MOON (2:35)
2910  IT'S THE TALK OF THE TOWN (3:25) [Marty Symes-Al J. Neiburg]
3230  IT'S THE TALK OF THE TOWN (3:13)
4480  IT'S THE TALK OF THE TOWN (3:40)
1790  I'VE FOUND A NEW BABY (3:36) [Jack Palmer-Spencer Williams]
T8114 I'VE FOUND A NEW BABY (1:59)
4390  I'VE GOT A CRUSH ON YOU (3:34) [George Gershwin/Ira Gershwin]
0450  I'VE GOT MY LOVE TO KEEP ME WARM (3:02) [Irving Berlin]
0451  I'VE GOT MY LOVE TO KEEP ME WARM
0810  I'VE GOT THE WORLD ON A STRING (2:25) [Harold Arlen/Ted Koehler]
4110  I'VE GOT THE WORLD ON A STRING (3:52)
T8700 I'VE GOT THE WORLD ON A STRING (4:08)
1760  JA-DA (3:28) [Bob Carleton]
2050  JA-DA (2:27)
T8233 JA-DA
```

```
         JADE (Seems related to "Gang O' Nothin'." See T8062.)
T7008    JADE [Art Tatum]
1930     JAPANESE SANDMAN, THE (1:35) [Richard A. Whiting/Raymond B. Egan]
4400     JAPANESE SANDMAN, THE (3:01)
4150     JITTERBUG WALTZ (3:47) [Fats Waller]
5490     JITTERBUG WALTZ (4:03)
0610     JUDY (2:20) [Hoagy Carmichael-Sammy Lerner]
3990     JUDY (3:44)
T8063    JUMPIN' FOR SUMPIN' (2:44) [Art Tatum]
2520     JUST A GIGOLO (2:19) [Leonello Casucci/Irving Caesar]
2590     JUST BEFORE DAWN (3:27) [Art Tatum]
T8726    JUST FRIENDS (3:40+) [John Klenner/Sam M. Lewis]
4430     JUST LIKE A BUTTERFLY THAT'S CAUGHT IN THE RAIN (3:48) [Mort
            Dixon-Harry Woods]
5590     JUST LIKE A BUTTERFLY THAT'S CAUGHT IN THE RAIN (2:37)
3770     JUST ONE OF THOSE THINGS (3:12) [Cole Porter]
5960     JUST ONE OF THOSE THINGS (7:11)
6250     JUST ONE OF THOSE THINGS (3:42)
T8433    JUST ONE OF THOSE THINGS (1:06)
T7022    JUST YOU, JUST ME [Jesse Greer/Raymond Klages]
2260     KERRY DANCE, THE (2:32) [James L. Molloy]
3030     KERRY DANCE, THE (1:58)
3520     KERRY DANCE, THE (1:04)
1180     KNOCKIN' MYSELF OUT (4:03) [Lil Green]
1070     LAST GOODBYE BLUES (3:10) [Pete Johnson-Joe Turner]
1010     LAUGHING AT LIFE (3:03) [Cornell & Bob Todd/Nick & Charles
            Kenny]
2410     LIMEHOUSE BLUES (2:15) [Philip Braham/Douglas Furber]
5470     LITTLE MAN, YOU'VE HAD A BUSY DAY (4:40) [Mabel Wayne/
            Maurice Sigler-Al Hoffman]
T8064    LIVE JIVE (2:20) [Art Tatum]
0260     LIZA (2:41) [George Gershwin/Ira Gershwin-Gus Kahn]
0261     LIZA
0262     LIZA (3:03)
1470     LIZA (1:54)
1160     LONESOME GRAVEYARD BLUES (3:05) [Jones-Williams]
1161     LONESOME GRAVEYARD BLUES (3:09)
         LONG, LONG AGO (See "Boogie," [1900])
2685     LOUISE (3:02) [Richard A. Whiting/Leo Robin]
3970     LOUISE (4:57)
3980     LOVE FOR SALE (4:37) [Cole Porter]
5580     LOVE FOR SALE (2:46)
5670     LOVE FOR SALE (9:38)
5680     LOVE FOR SALE (6:15)
5980     LOVE FOR SALE (5:28)
0180     LOVE ME (2:53) [Victor Young/Ned Washington]
0930     LOVE ME (2:38)
4650     LOVE ME OR LEAVE ME (3:18) [Walter Donaldson/Gus Kahn]
2220     LOVER (2:58) [Richard Rodgers/Lorenz Hart]
2340     LOVER (3:50)
3760     LOVER (3:07)
4620     LOVER, COME BACK TO ME! (6:43) [Sigmund Romberg/Oscar
            Hammerstein II]
5740     LOVER MAN (5:58) [Jimmy Davis-Ram Ramirez-Jimmy Sherman]
6080     LOVER MAN (6:40)
1130     LUCILLE (3:03) [Luther Williams]
1131     LUCILLE (3:25)
0710     LULLABY IN RHYTHM (2:00) [Benny Goodman-Edgar Sampson-
            Clarence Profit/Walter Hirsch]
5120     LULLABY IN RHYTHM (3:06)
T8227    LULLABY IN RHYTHM
0880     LULLABY OF THE LEAVES (3:01) [Bernice Petkere/Joe Young]
0270     LULU'S BACK IN TOWN (2:44) [Harry Warren/Al Dubin]
0650     MAKE BELIEVE (2:10) [Jerome Kern/Oscar Hammerstein II]
3200     MAKIN' WHOOPEE (2:40) [Walter Donaldson/Gus Kahn]
3930     MAKIN' WHOOPEE (2:42)
4920     MAKIN' WHOOPEE (3:36)
4921     MAKIN' WHOOPEE (6:10)
5760     MAKIN' WHOOPEE (7:00)
6090     MAKIN' WHOOPEE (3:29)
0500     MAN I LOVE, THE (2:45) [George Gershwin/Ira Gershwin]
1820     MAN I LOVE, THE (4:10)
2170     MAN I LOVE, THE (2:27)
3400     MAN I LOVE, THE (4:53)
3660     MAN I LOVE, THE (4:41)
```

```
3920  MAN I LOVE, THE (4:24)
T8222 MAN I LOVE, THE (2:44)
      MAN I LOVE, THE (See also "Gershwin Medley" )
2500  MEAN TO ME (2:32) [Fred E. Ahlert/Roy Turk]
4990  MEAN TO ME (2:54)
T8621 MEAN TO ME (4:45)
1270  MELODY IN F (5:08) [Anton Rubinstein]
3710  MELODY IN F (3:16)
2230  MEMORIES OF YOU (3:08) [Eubie Blake/Andy Razaf]
3290  MEMORIES OF YOU (3:41)
3510  MEMORIES OF YOU (4:14)
3840  MEMORIES OF YOU (5:35)
3880  MEMORIES OF YOU (4:57)
6050  MEMORIES OF YOU (7:09)
T8801 MEMORIES OF YOU (5:04)
2610  MIDNIGHT MELODY, A (4:02) [Art Tatum]
1170  MIGHTY LAK A ROSE (3:36) [Ethelbert Nevin/Frank L. Stanton]
4100  MIGHTY LAK A ROSE
4540  MIGHTY LAK A ROSE (6:06)
3280  MR. FREDDIE BLUES (3:06) [J. H. "Freddie" Shayne]
0340  MONDAY IN MANHATTAN (2:15) [Richard Himber/Richard
         Himber-Elliott Grennard]
5040  MOON IS LOW, THE (4:11) [Nacio Herb Brown/Arthur Freed]
5250  MOON IS LOW, THE (4:09)
T7018 MOON IS LOW, THE
4960  MOON SONG [Arthur Johnston/Sam Coslow]
5020  MOON SONG (4:36)
5280  MOON SONG (5:04)
5560  MOON SONG (3:46)
6240  MOON SONG (5:42)
T8720 MOON WAS YELLOW, THE (3:23) [Fred E. Ahlert/Edgar Leslie]
0140  MOONGLOW (2:35) [Will Hudson-Eddie DeLange-Irving Mills]
0141  MOONGLOW
0920  MOONGLOW (2:57)
0921  MOONGLOW
1440  MOONGLOW (2:33)
5090  MOONGLOW (2:52)
T8660 MOONGLOW (2:00)
T8682 MOONGLOW (4:16)
5010  MOONLIGHT ON THE GANGES (2:13) [Sherman Meyers/Chester Wallace]
1330  MOP-MOP (Also called Boff-Boff) (3:00) [Coleman Hawkins]
1331  MOP-MOP (Also called Boff-Boff) (3:08)
1540  MOP-MOP (4:38)
5770  MORE THAN YOU KNOW (4:12) [Vincent Youmans/Billy Rose-
         Edward Eliscu]
5950  MORE THAN YOU KNOW (3:36)
T8130 MORE THAN YOU KNOW (1:22)
0100  MORNING, NOON, AND NIGHT (3:19) [Louis Alter/Arthur Swanstrom]
1680  MUSKRAT RAMBLE (2:09) [Kid Ory/Ray Gilbert]
4820  MY BLUE HEAVEN (4:00) [Walter Donaldson/George Whiting]
3160  MY HEART STOOD STILL (3:03) [Richard Rodgers/Lorenz Hart]
3430  MY HEART STOOD STILL (2:25)
5480  MY HEART STOOD STILL (4:21)
5630  MY HEART STOOD STILL (3:02)
1340  MY IDEAL (3:07) [Richard A. Whiting-Newell Chase/Leo Robin]
1341  MY IDEAL (3:07)
1720  MY IDEAL (3:06)
6180  MY IDEAL (7:12)
4350  MY LAST AFFAIR (2:50) [Haven Johnson]
6170  MY ONE AND ONLY LOVE (6:09) [Guy Wood/Robert Mellin]
3090  NICE WORK IF YOU CAN GET IT (2:43) [George Gershwin/Ira
         Gershwin]
2700  NIGHT AND DAY (1:26) [Cole Porter]
2940  NIGHT AND DAY (3:25)
4140  NIGHT AND DAY (3:10)
5310  NIGHT AND DAY (6:06)
6210  NIGHT AND DAY (5:25)
T8381 NIGHT AND DAY (8:58+)
T8901 NIGHT AND DAY (3:51)
T8061 NIGHT SCENE (3:00) [Art Tatum]
2355  NINE TWENTY SPECIAL (2:26) [Earl Warren/Bill Engvick]
T8112 NOTHIN' TO DO BUT LOVE (2:58) [Buddy Fields-Gerald Marks]
1030  OH! LADY BE GOOD (3:47) [George Gershwin/Ira Gershwin]
1250  OH! LADY BE GOOD (4:30)
1800  OH! LADY BE GOOD (3:26)
```

```
T8623  OH! LADY BE GOOD (4:50)
0720   OH, YOU CRAZY MOON (2:25) [James Van Heusen/Johnny Burke]
4930   OLD FASHIONED LOVE (5:00) [James P. Johnson/Cecil Mack]
1860   ON THE SUNNY SIDE OF THE STREET (4:26) [Jimmy McHugh/
         Dorothy Fields]
2550   ON THE SUNNY SIDE OF THE STREET (2:25)
5180   ON THE SUNNY SIDE OF THE STREET (3:03)
T8541  ON THE SUNNY SIDE OF THE STREET (3:27)
6030   ONCE IN A WHILE (5:12) [Michael Edwards/Bud Green]
2790   OUT OF NOWHERE (2:50) [Johnny Green/Edward Heyman]
3690   OUT OF NOWHERE (3:33)
3750   OUT OF NOWHERE (2:43)
5130   OUT OF NOWHERE (3:43)
T8500  OUT OF NOWHERE (6:05)
0730   OVER THE RAINBOW (3:50) [Harold Arlen/E. Y. Harburg]
2880   OVER THE RAINBOW (3:25)
3890   OVER THE RAINBOW (3:39)
5500   OVER THE RAINBOW (3:03)
T8721  OVER THE RAINBOW (3:07)
T7023  PAGAN LOVE SONG [Nacio Herb Brown/Arthur Freed]
5640   PERDIDO (5:03) [Juan Tizol/Harry Lenk-Ervin Drake]
5790   PLAID (6:35) [Harry Edison-Art Tatum-Lionel Hampton]
2660   PLAYING IN RIDDLES (4:02) [Art Tatum]
5230   PLEASE BE KIND (5:05) [Sammy Cahn-Saul Chaplin]
5700   PLEASE BE KIND (4:45)
2100   PLEASE DON'T TALK ABOUT ME WHEN I'M GONE (2:51) [Sam H. Stept/
         Sidney Clare]
2200   POOR BUTTERFLY (3:10) [Raymond Hubbell/John Golden]
2710   POOR BUTTERFLY (3:23)
3250   POOR BUTTERFLY (2:30)
5080   PRISONER OF LOVE (4:15) [Russ Columbo-Clarence Gaskill/
         Leo Robin]
5750   PRISONER OF LOVE (6:07)
       RIFF TUNE, A (See "Flying Home" [3420])
1140   ROCK ME MAMA (2:57) [M. Jones]
1730   ROSE ROOM (5:33) [Art Hickman/Harry Williams]
0380   ROSETTA (2:11) [Earl Hines-Henri Woode]
0970   ROSETTA (2:45)
0971   ROSETTA
3330   ROSETTA (2:31)
T8260  ROSETTA (1:43)
0540   ROYAL GARDEN BLUES (2:25) [Clarence Williams-Spencer Williams]
1984   ROYAL GARDEN BLUES (2:46)
0510   RUNNIN' WILD (2:25) [A. Harrington Gibbs/Joe Grey-Leo Wood]
2240   RUNNIN' WILD (2:55)
T8239  RUNNIN' WILD
4940   'S WONDERFUL (3:20) [George Gershwin/Ira Gershwin]
T7005  SAPPHIRE [Art Tatum]
T8110  SCAT (3:42)
3720   SEPTEMBER SONG (3:15) [Kurt Weill/Maxwell Anderson]
3940   SEPTEMBER SONG (4:02)
5530   SEPTEMBER SONG (3:18)
5830   SEPTEMBER SONG (7:00)
5831   SEPTEMBER SONG
6110   SEPTEMBER SONG (4:48)
T8701  SEPTEMBER SONG (3:39)
0490   SHEIK OF ARABY, THE (2:40) [Ted Snyder/Harry B. Smith-
         Francis Wheeler]
2330   SHE'S FUNNY THAT WAY (3:35) [Neil Moret/Richard A. Whiting]
2920   SHE'S FUNNY THAT WAY (2:52)
4810   SHE'S FUNNY THAT WAY (3:50)
T8728  SHE'S FUNNY THAT WAY (3:39)
T7019  SHOULD I? [Nacio Herb Brown/Arthur Freed]
0240   SHOUT, THE (2:42) [Art Tatum]
0241   SHOUT, THE
0310   SHOUT, THE (1:35)
2850   SITTIN' AND ROCKIN' (2:45) [Billy Strayhorn-Duke Ellington/
         Lee Gaines]
3500   SITTIN' AND ROCKIN' (2:47)
4050   SITTIN' AND ROCKIN' (3:54)
T8482  SITTIN' AND ROCKIN' (2:12)
2010   SMOKE GETS IN YOUR EYES (3:08) [Jerome Kern/Otto Harbach]
2770   SMOKE GETS IN YOUR EYES (2:55)
2820   SMOKE GETS IN YOUR EYES (2:37)
4530   SMOKE GETS IN YOUR EYES (3:51)
```

```
T8881 SMOKE GETS IN YOUR EYES (4:24)
5210  SO BEATS MY HEART FOR YOU (5:19) [Pat Ballard-Charles
      Henderson-Tom Waring]
1940  SOFT WINDS (Incorrectly entitled "Thou Swell") (4:08) [Benny
      Goodman/Fred Royal]
1941  SOFT WINDS (Incorrectly entitled "Thou Swell") (4:16)
1942  SOFT WINDS (Incorrectly entitled "Thou Swell") (4:00)
1980  SOFT WINDS (3:51)
3830  SOFT WINDS (3:13)
5870  SOFT WINDS (3:10)
T8841 SOFT WINDS
5940  SOME OTHER SPRING (4:44) [Irene Kitchings/Arthur Herzog, Jr.]
1810  SOMEBODY LOVES ME (4:40) [George Gershwin/B. G. DeSylva-
      Ballard MacDonald]
2460  SOMEBODY LOVES ME (2:17)
3140  SOMEBODY LOVES ME (2:36)
4710  SOMEBODY LOVES ME (3:46)
5800  SOMEBODY LOVES ME (7:09)
T8341 SOMEBODY LOVES ME (5:19)
2980  SOMEONE TO WATCH OVER ME (3:08) [George Gershwin/Ira Gershwin]
3100  SOMEONE TO WATCH OVER ME (2:44)
3360  SOMEONE TO WATCH OVER ME (3:40)
4160  SOMEONE TO WATCH OVER ME (3:47)
5330  SOMEONE TO WATCH OVER ME (0:27)
5370  SOMEONE TO WATCH OVER ME (3:08)
5610  SOMEONE TO WATCH OVER ME (2:54)
6140  SOMEONE TO WATCH OVER ME (3:09)
T8364 SOMEONE TO WATCH OVER ME (4:28)
T8461 SOMEONE TO WATCH OVER ME (3:04)
T8582 SOMEONE TO WATCH OVER ME (3:19)
T8759 SOMEONE TO WATCH OVER ME (3:08)
T8880 SOMEONE TO WATCH OVER ME (3:01)
2210  SONG OF THE VAGABONDS (3:00) [Rudolf Friml/Brian Hooker]
2690  SONG OF THE VAGABONDS (2:14)
0080  SOPHISTICATED LADY (3:14) [Duke Ellington/Mitchell Parish-
      Irving Mills]
4630  SOPHISTICATED LADY (3:32)
5060  S'POSIN' (3:20) [Paul Denniker/Andy Razaf]
0060  ST. LOUIS BLUES (2:30) [W. C. Handy]
0061  ST. LOUIS BLUES
0950  ST. LOUIS BLUES (2:26)
0951  ST. LOUIS BLUES
T8180 ST. LOUIS BLUES (3:36)
0120  STAR DUST (2:57) [Hoagy Carmichael/Mitchell Parish]
0210  STAR DUST
0211  STAR DUST (3:17)
0212  STAR DUST
0560  STAR DUST (2:30)
1210  STAR DUST (3:46)
4200  STAR DUST (5:00)
4550  STARS FELL ON ALABAMA (5:51) [Frank Perkins/Mitchell Parish]
5720  STARS FELL ON ALABAMA (5:38)
0330  STAY AS SWEET AS YOU ARE (2:30) [Harry Revel/Mack Gordon]
2450  STAY AS SWEET AS YOU ARE (2:40)
4230  STAY AS SWEET AS YOU ARE (5:06)
1060  STOMPIN' AT THE SAVOY (3:12) [Edgar Sampson-Benny Goodman-
      Chick Webb]
1700  STOMPIN' AT THE SAVOY (3:09)
4340  STOMPIN' AT THE SAVOY (2:57)
T7012 STOMPIN' AT THE SAVOY
0470  STORMY WEATHER (3:07) [Harold Arlen/Ted Koehler]
0471  STORMY WEATHER
1816  STORMY WEATHER (4:48)
0010  STRANGE AS IT SEEMS (3:06) [Fats Waller/Andy Razaf]
0011  STRANGE AS IT SEEMS (3:08)
4870  STREET OF DREAMS (3:50) [Victor Young-Sam Lewis]
1360  SUGAR FOOT STOMP (2:07) [Joe "King" Oliver/Walter Melrose]
      SUMMERTIME [George Gershwin/Ira Gershwin] (See "Gershwin
      Medley")
T8231 SUNDAY [Fred Coots/Clifford Grey]
2070  SWEET AND LOVELY (2:51) [Gus Arnheim-Harry Tobias-Jules Lemare
T7024 SWEET AND LOVELY
0770  SWEET EMALINA, MY GAL (2:00) [Turner Layton/Hnery Creamer]
0900  SWEET EMALINA, MY GAL
0901  SWEET EMALINA, MY GAL

                                  302
```

```
1260  SWEET GEORGIA BROWN (7:19) [Ben Bernie-Maceo Pinkard-
      Kenneth Casey]
1370  SWEET GEORGIA BROWN (3:10)
0580  SWEET LORRAINE (2:35) [Cliff Burwell/Mitchell Parish]
0860  SWEET LORRAINE (2:57)
1100  SWEET LORRAINE (3:01)
1310  SWEET LORRAINE
1390  SWEET LORRAINE (3:17)
1590  SWEET LORRAINE (3:20)
1817  SWEET LORRAINE (4:12)
2300  SWEET LORRAINE (2:06)
2810  SWEET LORRAINE (2:03)
3130  SWEET LORRAINE (2:35)
3320  SWEET LORRAINE (2:04)
4730  SWEET LORRAINE (4:19)
5340  SWEET LORRAINE (4:05)
5600  SWEET LORRAINE (3:49)
6100  SWEET LORRAINE (3:59)
T8021 SWEET LORRAINE (2:15)
T8100 SWEET LORRAINE (2:45)
T8117 SWEET LORRAINE (1:29)
T8240 SWEET LORRAINE (2:20)
T8562 SWEET LORRAINE (2:15)
T8680 SWEET LORRAINE (4:15)
T8724 SWEET LORRAINE (3:21)
T8763 SWEET LORRAINE (4:27)
T8800 SWEET LORRAINE (4:19)
2110  SWEET MARIJUANA BROWN (2:51) [Leonard Feather]
3270  TABOO (2:20) [Margarita Lecuona/Al Stillman]
3370  TABOO (3:22)
3540  TABOO
3620  TABOO (3:30)
3800  TABOO (2:50)
4370  TABOO (2:46)
T8460 TABOO (0:32)
T8740 TABOO (2:47)
      TATUM PLAYS PRETTY (Incorrectly titled- See "Gershwin
      Medley" [3020])
2970  TATUM POLE BOOGIE (2:28) [Art Tatum]
0050  TEA FOR TWO (3:11) [Vincent Youmans/Irving Caesar]
0051  TEA FOR TWO
0740  TEA FOR TWO (2:32)
0741  TEA FOR TWO
1475  TEA FOR TWO (0:03)
1480  TEA FOR TWO (2:05)
1660  TEA FOR TWO (3:28)
2490  TEA FOR TWO (2:29)
3670  TEA FOR TWO (3:13)
3740  TEA FOR TWO (3:03)
4470  TEA FOR TWO (3:29)
5320  TEA FOR TWO (2:47)
5890  TEA FOR TWO (2:58)
T8020 TEA FOR TWO (2:33)
T8170 TEA FOR TWO (2:35)
T8221 TEA FOR TWO (2:30)
T8241 TEA FOR TWO (2:59)
T8320 TEA FOR TWO (3:11)
T8521 TEA FOR TWO (3:28+)
T8681 TEA FOR TWO (3:10)
T8762 TEA FOR TWO (2:58)
2870  TENDERLY (3:00) [Walter Gross/Jack Lawrence]
3241  TENDERLY (3:05)
3390  TENDERLY (3:50)
3640  TENDERLY (3:36)
3680  TENDERLY (3:26)
4070  TENDERLY (5:03)
5420  TENDERLY (3:57)
5880  TENDERLY (4:42)
T8420 TENDERLY (4:17)
T8540 TENDERLY (4:16)
T8561 TENDERLY (2:15)
T8683 TENDERLY (4:39)
T8761 TENDERLY (5:16)
4790  THAT OLD FEELING (5:10) [Lew Brown-Sammy Fain]
1665  THEME FOR COCA-COLA/CONCLUSION (0:37) [Leonard Joy]
1620  THEME FOR COCA-COLA/INTRODUCTIONS (1:31)
```

```
0360    THEME FOR PIANO (0:60)
4060    THERE WILL NEVER BE ANOTHER YOU (5:26) [Harry Warren/Mack Gordon]
5520    THERE WILL NEVER BE ANOTHER YOU (3:33)
T8727   THERE WILL NEVER BE ANOTHER YOU (4:03)
1240    THERE'LL BE SOME CHANGES MADE (3:29) [W. Benton Overstreet/
          Billy Higgins]
4570    THERE'S A SMALL HOTEL (5:05) [Richard Rodgers/Lorenz Hart]
4670    THESE FOOLISH THINGS (4:49) [Jack Strachey-Harry Link/
          Eric Maschwitz]
T8550   THESE FOOLISH THINGS (4:36)
4460    THEY CAN'T TAKE THAT AWAY FROM ME (4:45) [George Gershwin-
          Ira Gershwin]
2640    THIS AND THAT (3:32) [Art Tatum]
3860    THIS CAN'T BE LOVE (2:34) [George Gershwin/Ira Gershwin]
5290    THIS CAN'T BE LOVE (3:48)
5620    THIS CAN'T BE LOVE (1:30)
5730    THIS CAN'T BE LOVE (6:16)
6040    THIS CAN'T BE LOVE (4:34)
T8921   THIS CAN'T BE LOVE (1:21+)
0040    THIS TIME IT'S LOVE (3:09) [J. Fred Coots/Sam M. Lewis]
        THOU SWELL (Incorrectly titled- See "Soft Winds"
          [1940/1941/1942])
2530    THREE LITTLE WORDS (2:16) [Harry Ruby/Bert Kalmar]
T8501   THREE LITTLE WORDS (4:15)
T8620   THREE LITTLE WORDS (3:35)
T8661   THREE LITTLE WORDS (3:00)
0001    TIGER RAG (1:58) [D. J. LaRocca/Harry DeCosta]
0070    TIGER RAG (2:17)
0320    TIGER RAG (2:10)
0890    TIGER RAG (2:09)
3120    TIME ON MY HANDS (2:57) [Vincent Youmans/Harry Adamson-
          Mack Gordon]
T8030   TINY'S EXERCISE (0:33) [Tiny Grimes]
1190    TOLEDO BLUES (4:08) [Art Tatum]
4410    TOO MARVELOUS FOR WORDS (2:57) [Richard A. Whiting/Johnny Mercer]
5400    TOO MARVELOUS FOR WORDS (2:21)
2630    TOO SHARP FOR THIS FLAT (3:36) [Art Tatum]
1960    TOPSY (4:07) [Folk tune]
1961    TOPSY (4:14)
6010    TRIO BLUES (5:06) [Art Tatum]
2750    TURQUOISE (1:37) [Art Tatum]
T7007   TURQUOISE
4900    UNDECIDED (4:50) [Charlie Shavers/Sid Robin]
4910    UNDER A BLANKET OF BLUE (6:10) [Jerry Livingston/Marty Symes-
          Al J. Neiburg]
1280    UNKNOWN TITLE
1290    UNKNOWN TITLE
T7000   UNKNOWN TITLE
T8150   UNKNOWN TITLE
T8200   UNKNOWN TITLE
T8440   UNKNOWN TITLE
T8729   UNKNOWN TITLE (2:23)
T8365   VALSE IN C# MINOR, OPUS 64, #2 (3:49+) [Frederic Chopin]
        VARIATIONS ON A THEME BY FLOTOW (See "Boogie" [1910])
5840    VERVE BLUES (12:43) [Harry Edison-Lionel Hampton-Art Tatum]
4170    VERY THOUGHT OF YOU, THE (4:25) [Ray Noble]
T8340   VERY THOUGHT OF YOU, THE (6:42+)
T8362   VERY THOUGHT OF YOU, THE (4:34)
1750    VIBE BLUES (JAMMIN' THE BLUES) (4:13) [Lionel Hampton-Red Norvo]
        VIBES DUET (See "Vibe Blues" [1750])
T8230   WABASH BLUES [Fred Meinken/Dave Ringle]
T8236   WANG WANG BLUES, THE [Gus Mueller-Buster Johnson-Henry Busse/
          Leo Wood]
        WARM UP WITH SANDMAN (Incorrectly titled- See "Japanese
          Sandman" [1930])
4590    WAY YOU LOOK TONIGHT, THE (6:34) [Jerome Kern/Dorothy Fields]
1050    WEE BABY BLUES (2:50) [Pete Johnson-Joe Turner]
T8234   WHAT CAN I SAY AFTER I SAY I'M SORRY [Walter Donaldson/Abe
          Lyman]
4080    WHAT DOES IT TAKE? (2:50) [James Van Heusen/Johnny Burke]
2390    WHAT IS THIS THING CALLED LOVE (2:35) [Cole Porter]
5710    WHAT IS THIS THING CALLED LOVE (6:59)
5820    WHAT IS THIS THING CALLED LOVE (7:42)
0440    WHAT WILL I TELL MY HEART (3:06) [Peter Tinturin-Jack Lawrence]
0441    WHAT WILL I TELL MY HEART
```

```
4720   WHAT'S NEW? (4:30) [Bob Haggart/Johnny Burke]
0160   WHEN A WOMAN LOVES A MAN (3:04) [Bernard Hanighen-Gordon
       Jenkins/Johnny Mercer]
0161   WHEN A WOMAN LOVES A MAN
0162   WHEN A WOMAN LOVES A MAN (2:38)
4500   WHEN A WOMAN LOVES A MAN (5:30)
0110   WHEN DAY IS DONE (2:51) [Robert Katscher/B. G. De Sylva]
T7014  WHEN I GROW TOO OLD TO DREAM [Sigmund Romberg/Oscar
       Hammerstein II]
5030   WHEN YOUR LOVER HAS GONE (3:39) [E. A. Swan]
2060   WHERE OR WHEN (2:40) [Richard Rodgers/Lorenz Hart]
2680   WHERE OR WHEN (3:53)
3790   WHERE OR WHEN (2:59)
4220   WHERE OR WHEN (5:12)
6220   WHERE OR WHEN (6:22)
T8430  WHERE OR WHEN (2:17)
T8502  WHERE OR WHEN (1:35)
T8552  WHERE OR WHEN (1:15, incomplete)
2470   WHY WAS I BORN (2:36) [Jerome Kern/Oscar Hammerstein II]
3010   WILLOW WEEP FOR ME (3:13) [Ann Ronell]
3060   WILLOW WEEP FOR ME (2:50)
3255   WILLOW WEEP FOR ME (3:00)
4510   WILLOW WEEP FOR ME (4:32)
5390   WILLOW WEEP FOR ME (3:39)
6150   WILLOW WEEP FOR ME (3:46)
T8480  WILLOW WEEP FOR ME (3:03)
T8900  WILLOW WEEP FOR ME (5:19)
5190   WITH A SONG IN MY HEART [Richard Rodgers/Lorenz Hart]
0430   WITH PLENTY OF MONEY AND YOU (2:40) [Harry Warren/Al Dubin]
0431   WITH PLENTY OF MONEY AND YOU (2:41)
4330   WITHOUT A SONG (5:47) [Vincent Youmans/Billy Rose-Edward Eliscu]
5460   WITHOUT A SONG (2:29)
T8722  WITHOUT A SONG (2:19)
3730   WOULD YOU LIKE TO TAKE A WALK (3:13) [Harry Warren/Mort Dixon-
       Billy Rose]
4380   WOULD YOU LIKE TO TAKE A WALK (4:13)
6270   WOULD YOU LIKE TO TAKE A WALK (5:21)
T8422  WOULD YOU LIKE TO TAKE A WALK (6:11)
T8840  WOULD YOU LIKE TO TAKE A WALK
2840   WRAP YOUR TROUBLES IN DREAMS (2:57) [Harry Barris/Ted Koehler-
       Billy Moll]
4010   WRAP YOUR TROUBLES IS DREAMS (3:38)
5540   WRAP YOUR TROUBLES IN DREAMS (3:11)
5900   WRAP YOUR TROUBLES IN DREAMS (4:59)
2250   YESTERDAYS (3:07) [Jerome Kern/Otto Harbach]
2830   YESTERDAYS (2:59)
2990   YESTERDAYS (3:23)
4120   YESTERDAYS (3:26)
5440   YESTERDAYS (3:05)
T8280  YESTERDAYS (2:56)
0030   YOU GAVE ME EVERYTHING BUT LOVE (3:12) [Monte Wilhite/Sammy
       Gallop]
0031   YOU GAVE ME EVERYTHING BUT LOVE
4600   YOU GO TO MY HEAD (4:52) [J. Fred Coots/Haven Gillespie]
6280   YOU GO TO MY HEAD (5:07)
T8522  YOU GO TO MY HEAD (2:35)
2360   YOU TOOK ADVANTAGE OF ME (2:10) [Richard Rodgers/Lorenz Hart]
2900   YOU TOOK ADVANTAGE OF ME (2:58)
3170   YOU TOOK ADVANTAGE OF ME (3:08)
4090   YOU TOOK ADVANTAGE OF ME (3:14)
5260   YOU TOOK ADVANTAGE OF ME (3:33)
5430   YOU TOOK ADVANTAGE OF ME (3:25)
T8563  YOU TOOK ADVANTAGE OF ME (1:10)
4760   YOU'RE BLASE (4:55) [Ord Hamilton/Bruce Sievier]
2860   YOU'RE DRIVING ME CRAZY (2:20) [Walter Donaldson]
4180   YOU'RE DRIVING ME CRAZY (2:37)
4770   YOU'RE MINE, YOU (4:50) [Johnny Green/Edward Heyman]
4890   YOU'RE MINE, YOU (5:10)
6060   YOU'RE MINE, YOU (7:01)
0090   YOUNG AND HEALTHY (1:30) [Harry Warren/Al Dubin]
```

Art Tatum plays piano on all performances unless
otherwise noted.

AFRS ORCHESTRA   Orchestra

   2280/2290

ALLEN, SNAGS   Guitar

   T8200

ALLEN, STEVE   Piano

   5350

ARMSTRONG, LOUIS   Trumpet, (Trumpet & Vocal)*

   1500*/1510/1520/1570*/1580/1600/1620/1640*/1670*/1680

BAILEY, JOE   Bass

   0420/0421/0430/0431/0440/0441/0450/0451

BARKSDALE, EVERETT   Guitar

   3390/3400/3410/3420/3640/3650/3660/3670/3680/3690/3700/3710
   3720/3730/3740/3750/3760/3770/3780/3810/3820/3830/3840/5320
   5340/5350/5850/5360/5870/5880/5890/5900/5910/6100/6110/6230
   6240/6250/6260/6270/6280/T8420/T8421/T8422/T8423/T8424/T8425
   T8680/T8681/T8682/T8683/T8700/T8701/T8702/T8760/T8761/T8762
   T8763/T8764/T8765/T8800/T8801/T8802/T8840/T8841/T8900/T8901

BARNET, CHARLIE   Tenor Saxophone

   2760

BAUDUC, RAY   Drums

   2760

BELLSON, LOUIS   Drums

   4820/4830/4840/4850/4860/4870/4880/4890/4900/4910/4920/4921
   4930/4940/4950/4960

BIGARD, LEON (BARNEY)   Clarinet

   1530/1540/1550/1560/1570/1600/1610/1620/16501660/1665/1680
   1700/1730/1740/2090/2100/2110/2120

BRADLEY, OSCAR   Drums

   0420/0421/0430/0431/0440/0441/0450/0451

CALLENDER, GEORGE (RED)   Bass

   5790/5820/5830/5831/5840/5920/5930/5940/5950/5960/5970/5980
   5990/6000/6010/6020/6030/6040/6050/6060/6070/6080/6090/6160
   6170/6180/6190/6200/6210/6220

CANDREVA, PHIL   Trumpet

   2280/2290

CARROLL, FRANK   Bass

   5620

CARTER, BENNY   Alto Saxophone

   4820/4830/4840/4850/4860/4870/4880/4890/4900/4910/4920/4921
   4930/4940/4950

CARTER, BILL   Trumpet

    T8380/T8381/T8382/T8383/T8384

CARTER, FRANCIS   Trumpet

    0010/0011/0020/0021/0030/0031/0040

CASEY, AL   Guitar

    1320/1321/1330/1331/1340/1341/1350/1351/1500/1510/1520/1530
    1540/1550/1560/1570/1580/1600/1610/1620/1630/1640/1650/1660
    1665/1670/1680/1690/1700/1710/1720/1730/1740/1750/1983/1984
    1985/1986

CATLETT, SID   Drums

    1320/1321/1330/1331/1340/1341/1350/1351/1500/1510/1520/1530
    1540/1550/1560/1570/1580/1590/1600/1610/1620/1630/1640/1650
    1660/1665/1670/1680/1690/1700/1710/1720/1730/1740/1750

CHAMBER MUSIC SOCIETY OF LOWER BASIN ST.   Orchestra

    1360

CIASHINE, NED   Accordion

    T8380/T8381/T8382/T8383/T8384

CLARK, FLO   Vocal

    T8111

CLARK, GEORGE   Vocal

    T8110

COLLINS, JOHN   Guitar

    1050/1060/1070/1080/T8500/T8501/T8502/T8520/T8521/T8522
    T8540/T8541/T8542/T8550/T8551/T8552

CONIFF, RAY   Trombone

    2280/2290

DAY, EDNA   Vocal

    T8113

DeFRANCO, BONIFACE (BUDDY)   Clarinet

    6020/6030/6040/6050/6060/6070/6080/6090

DeNAUT, JUD   Bass

    2280/2290

DICKENSON, VIC   Trombone

    1983/1984/1985/1986

DORSEY, JIMMY   Alto Saxophone

    0010(?)/0011(?)/0020(?)/0021(?)/2760

DORSEY, TOMMY   Trombone

    2760

DOUGHERTY, EDDIE   Drums

    1050/1060/1070/1080

DOUGLASS, BILL   Drums
    6020/6030/6040/6050/6060/6070/6080/6090/6160/6170/6180/6190
    6200/6210/6220

EDISON, HARRY (SWEETS)   Trumpet
    5790/5800/5810/5820/5830/5831/5840

ELMAN, HARRY [FINKELMAN] (ZIGGY)   Trumpet
    2760

ELDRIDGE, ROY   Trumpet, Flugelhorn*
    1530/1540/1550/1560/1600/1610/1620/1630/1650/1660/1665/1700
    1710/1740/1750/1983/1984/1985/1986/5240/5250*/5260/5270
    5280/5290/5300/5310

EVANS, ALFRED   Clarinet
    T8001

EXINER, BILLY   Drums
    T8620/T8621/T8622/T8623/T8624

FARLOW, TAL   Guitar
    T8640

FIELDS, HERBIE   Tenor Saxophone
    1030/1040

FREEMAN, STAN   Piano
    T8281

GOODIN, CALVIN   Guitar
    1760/1790/1800/1810

GOODRICH, BOB   Trumpet
    2280/2290

GRIMES, LLOYD (TINY)   Guitar
    1270/1280/1290/1300/1310/1370/1380/1390/1395/1400/1410/1420
    1430/1440/1450/1460/1470/1475/1480/1488/1489/1490/1815/1816
    1817/1820/1830/1840/1850/1860/1870/1890/1900/1910/1920/1921
    1930/1940/1941/1942/1950/1960/1961/1970/1980/T8020/T8021
    T8030

GURASSO, FRANK   Guitar
    T8001

HALL, ADELAIDE   Vocal
    0010/0011/0020/0021/0030/0031/0040

HALL, EDMOND   Clarinet
    1050/1060/1070/1080/1320/1321/1330/1331/1340/1341/1350/1351
    1983/1984/1985/1986

HAMPTON, LIONEL   Vibes, (Vibes and Drums)*,
                                            (Vibes and Vocal)**
    1620/1660/1665/1740*/1750/5640/5650/5660/5670/5680/5690/5700
    5710/5720/5730/5740/5750/5760/5770/5780/5790/5800/5810/5820
    5830/5831/5840**

HARRIS, REUBEN   Whiskbrooms

   1110

HAWKINS, COLEMAN (HAWK)   Tenor Saxophone

   1320/1321/1330/1331/1340/1341/1350/1351/1500/1510/1520/1530
   1560/1560/1570/1600/1620/1630/1640/1650/1665/1680/1700/1710
   1720/1740/1983/1984/1985/1986

HERFURT, ARTHUR (SKEETS)   Alto Saxophone

   2280/2290

HILTON, DON   Drums

   T8380/T8381/T8382/T8383/T8384

HOLIDAY, BILLIE   Vocal

   1550/1560/1650/1983/1985

JENKINS, LES   Trombone

   2280/2290

JONES, JONATHAN (JO)   Drums

   5920/5930/5940/5950/5960/5970/5980/5990/6000/6010

KELLY, GUY   Trumpet

   0410

KESSEL, BARNEY   Guitar

   5790/5800/5810/5820

LaFRENIER, GENE   Trumpet

   2280/2290

LAGUERE, PAYTON   Alto Saxophone

   2280/2290

LAUDER, MURRAY   Bass

   T8380/T8381/T8382/T8383/T8384

LEVEY, STAN   Drums

   2090/2100/2110/2120

LORD, JIMMY   (See 0001)

MARTIN, JACK   Vocal

   2290

McDONOUGH, DICK   Guitar

   0010(?)/0011(?)/0020(?)/0021(?)

McEACHERN, MURRAY   Trombone, Clarinet*,
                                    Alto Saxophone**,
                                    Alto Saxophone & Trombone***

   1000/1010***/1020**/1030/1040/2280*/2290

McREYNOLDS, BOB   Trombone

   2280/2290

MEL-TONES, THE   Vocal Group
    2290
MOONEY, JOE   Organ
    T8660/T8661/T8662/T8663
MOORE, OSCAR   Guitar
    1130/1131/1140/1150/1160/1161
MORTON, HENRY (BENNY)   Trombone
    1983/1984/1985/1986
NEWTON, FRANK   Trumpet
    1250/1260
NORDQUIST, CLINTON   Bass
    1760/1790/1800/1810
NORVO, KENNETH (RED)   Vibes
    1600/1620/1665/1750
ORD, JOHNNY   Tenor Saxophone
    T8380/T8381/T8382/T8383/T8384
PAIGE, RAYMOND   Orchestra
    T8921
PALMIERI, REMO   Guitar
    2020
PATENT, HARRY   Bass
    T8001
PAUL, EBENEZER   Bass
    1250/1260
PAUL, LES   Guitar
    1760/1790/1800/1810/2280/2290
PEMBERTON, BILL   Bass
    6230/6240/6250/6260/6270/6280
PERKINS, BILL   Guitar
    0420/0421/0430/0431/0440/0441/0450/0451
PETTIFORD, OSCAR   Bass
    1320/1321/1330/1331/1340/1341/1350/1351/1500/1510/1520/1530
    1540/1550/1560/1570/1580/1590/1600/1610/1620/1630/1640/1650
    1660/1665/1670/1680/1690/1700/1710/1720/1730/1740/1750
PORTER, YANK   Drums
    1130/1131/1140/1150/1160/1161
POTTER, OLLIE   Vocal

1240

POVEY, BILL   Alto Saxophone

T8380/T8381/T8382/T8383/T8384

POWELL, GORDON (SPECS)   Drums

2020

RAGLIN, JUNIOR   Bass

2180

REESE, LLOYD   Trumpet

0420/0421/0430/0431/0440/0441/0450/0451

RICH, BERNARD (BUDDY)   Drums

5640/5650/5660/5670/5680/5690/5700/5710/5720/5730/5740/5750
5760/5770/5780/5790/5800/5810/5820/5830/5831/5840

ROBINSON, ANNA (Also known as ANN)   Vocal

1210

ROSENGARDEN, BOBBY   Drums

5620

ROTH, ALAN   Orchestra

T8180

ROYAL, MARSHALL   Clarinet

0420/0421/0430/0431/0440/0441/0450/0451

RUSSIN, IRVING (BABE)   Tenor Saxophone

2280/2290

SHAVERS, CHARLIE   Trumpet, (Vocal only)*

1230*/1983/1984/1985/1986

SHULMAN, JOE   Bass

T8620/T8621/T8622/T8623/T8624

SIMMONS, JOHN   Bass

5240/5250/5260/5270/5280/5290/5300/5310/5800/5810

STEWART, LEROY (SLAM)   Bass

1270/1280/1290/1300/1310/1370/1380/1390/1395/1400/1410/1420
1430/1440/1450/1460/1470/1475/1480/1488/1489/1490/1815/1816
1817/1820/1830/1840/1850/1860/1870/1890/1900/1910/1920/1921
1930/1940/1941/1942/1950/1960/1961/1970/1980/1983/1984/1985
1986/3390/3400/3410/3420/3640/3650/3660/3670/3680/3690/3700
3710/3720/3730/3740/3750/3760/3770/3780/3810/3820/3830/3840
5320/5340/5350/5850/5860/5870/5880/5890/5900/5910/6100/6110
T8020/T8021/T8030/T8100/T8105/T8420/T8421/T8422/T8423/T8424
T8425/T8500/T8501/T8502/T8520/T8521/T8522/T8540/T8541/T8542
T8550/T8551/T8552/T8680/T8681/T8682/T8683/T8700/T8701/T8702
T8760/T8761/T8762/T8763/T8764/T8765/T8800/T8801/T8802/T8840
T8841/T8900/T8901

STEWART, MARTHA   Vocal

2290

STIFFMAN, HARRY   Drums

 T8001

STOLLER, ALVIN   Drums

 5240/5250/5260/5270/5280/5290/5300/5310

SYMS, SYLVIA   Vocal

 T8725/T8726/T8728

TATUM, ART   Piano and Celeste
            Piano and Vocal*

 0440/0441/T8110*/T8112*/T8584*

TAYLOR, BILLY   Bass

 1050/1060/1070/1080/1130/1131/1140/1150/1160/1161
 2090/2100/2110/2120/T8200

TEAGARDEN, CHARLIE   Trumpet

 0010/0011/0020/0021

TEAGARDEN, WELDON (JACK) Trombone, (Trombone & Vocal)*

 1500*/1510/1520/1530/1540/1550/1560/1570/1580*/1600/1610/1620
 1640*/1650/1665/1680/1700/1750

THOMAS, JOE   Tenor Saxophone, (Tenor Sax
             & Vocal)*

 2090/2100/2110*/2120

THOMAS, JOE   Trumpet

 1050/1060/1070/1080/1130/1131/1140/1150/1160/1161/2090/2100
 2110/2120

TORME, MEL   Vocal

 2290

TRAPPIER, ARTHUR (TRAPS) Drums

 1983/1984/1985/1986

TURNER, JOE   Vocal

 1050/1070/1130/1131/1140/1150/1160/1161

UNKNOWN PERFORMER(S)   Bass

 0410/1030/1040/2160/2300/2310

UNKNOWN PERFORMER(S)   Clarinet

 0410

UNKNOWN PERFORMER(S)   Drums

 0410/2280/2290

UNKNOWN PERFORMERS   Orchestra

 T8221

UNKNOWN PERFORMER(S)   Trumpet

 1030

UNKNOWN PERFORMER(S)   Vocal
    0410/T8580
WALTER, CY   Piano
    T8281
WEBSTER, BEN   Tenor Saxophone
    1983/1984/1985/1986/6160/6170/6180/6190/6200/6210/6220
WHITE, ETHEL   Vocal
    1220
WILLIAMS, CHOCOLATE   Bass, (Bass and Vocal)*
    1170/1180*/1190/1210/1220/1230/1240
WILLIAMS, CHARLES (COOTIE)   Trumpet
    1320/1321/1330/1331/1340/1341/1350/1351
WOOD, BARRY   Vocal
    T8221

THE IMITATUMS ON DISC

Over the years a number of records have been released on which other pianists have consciously attempted to copy Art Tatum. Some have sought to duplicate previously issued Tatum performances note-for-note, while others have tried to emulate Tatum's style and technique in their approach to a piece. Listed below are those records which indicate in the liner notes that one or more titles were deliberately played as Art Tatum might have done so, or as an attempt to replicate a specific Tatum performance. These do not appear to have been made in an attempt to "challenge" Tatum, but rather out of respect and admiration. Not included are recordings made as a tribute to Tatum by many pianists including Earl Hines, Chick Corea, Bernard Peiffer, and Barry Harris, among others. Also excluded are illustrative recordings by any of the numerous pianists heavily influenced by him. Such a discussion is beyond the scope of this discography and will appear in a subsequent book now in preparation. The efforts known to the authors are described below, with the artists listed in alphabetical order. All discs are 12 Inch LP's unless otherwise noted.

BOLLING, CLAUDE
Who's Who In Jazz   WWLP 21018   "With The Help of My Friends"

Bolling emulates the varying styles of a number of jazz pianists including Oscar Peterson, Count Basie, Scott Joplin, George Shearing, Dave Brubeck, Thelonius Monk, Duke Ellington, Fats Waller, Ramsey Lewis, Jelly Roll Morton, and Erroll Garner. The Tatum track is "With Art and Fun," and it is interesting.

FARRELL, JOHN
Halcyon SHAL 11   "Presenting John Farrell, the Amazing Auto-Roll
Piano Soloist"

Farrell utilizes a special technique to create player piano rolls from written transcriptions. This disc is a recording from such piano rolls; Farrell does not actually play the pieces. The Tatum titles are:
Carnegie Hall Bounce— This is a Tatum original which appeared
in print in a Leeds folio entitled "5 Jazz Piano Solos by
Art Tatum," transcribed by Frank Paparelli. Leeds Music
Corporation, New York, 1946.
Art Tatum Medley— Consisting of Sunday [1], Wang Wang
Blues [2], Ja-Da [1], What Can I Say After I Say I'm Sorry
[1], Stompin' At the Savoy [3]
[1] Originally in print as part of "Art Tatum
Improvisations, No. 1," Robbins Music Corporation, New
York, 1939. Also reprinted in [4] and [5] below.
[2] Originally as in [1]; reprinted in [4] below.
[3] Originally in print as part of "Art Tatum
Improvisations , No. 2," Robbins Music Corporation,
New York, 1946. Also reprinted in [4] and [5] below.
[4] "Art Tatum," EMI, London, 1980.
[5] "The Genius of Art Tatum", The Big 3 Music
Corporation, New York, 1980.
With the exception of "Carnegie Hall Bounce" all the written transcriptions for the above were done by Morris (Murray) Feldman, who was affiliated with Teddy Wilson's School of Music in the late thirties. He used selected segments from longer Tatum performances, and therefore these transcriptions do not have the integrity and continuity of a normal Tatum performance. Further, the whereabouts of the original acetates are unknown and therefore it is not possible to assess the validity of the written transcriptions.

HUG, ARMAND
Dulai 804 "Armand Hug Plays Jazz Piano Greats, Vol. 1"

Hug attempts the style of a number of pianists, including Jelly Roll Morton, Scott, Joplin, Zez Confrey, Pinetop Smith, James P. Johnson, and Duke Ellington, among others, and also plays in his own style. The Tatum track is "Time On My Hands," and it is a superficial, out-of-context performance which bears no resemblance to Tatum's playing.

314

HYMAN, DICK
  Chiaroscuro CR-198 "Themes & Variations on ´A Child Is Born´"

      On this record, Hyman plays "A Child is Born," in the
manner of 12 different pianists, including Tatum. Tatum never
recorded this piece and therefore the effort is original and is
probably the most successful attempt at capturing the Tatum style.
Hyman also does Scott Joplin, Jelly Roll Morton, James P. Johnson,
Earl Hines, Fats Waller, Teddy Wilson, Erroll Garner, George
Shearing, Bill Evans, and Cecil Taylor as well as his own style.

MEHEGAN, JOHN
  Perspective 1 (10 Inch LP)

      Mehegan plays "Sweet Lorraine," in the Tatum style, but does
not try to duplicate any of Tatum´s recordings of the piece. He is
moderately successful.

PETERSON, OSCAR
  Prestige 7595 "Oscar Peterson Soul-O!"
  Someone to Watch Over Me/Perdido/Body and Soul/Who Can I
  Turn To?/Bye, Bye, Blackbird/I Should Care/Lulu´s Back In
  Town/Little Girl Blue/Take the A Train

      In his liner notes, Ralph Berton writes: "...this is the first
time I ever heard him [Peterson] set out - I cannot conceive it as
being done other than consciously - to do homage to that deceased
genius [Tatum] in a deliberate and profoundly beautiful imitation
of all the main elements of his style."

SMITH, PAUL
  Outstanding 004 "Paul Smith, The Art Tatum Touch"
  Yesterdays/Baubles, Bangles & Beads/Humoresque/Blue Skies/Over
  the Rainbow/Nice Work If You Can Get It/Poor Butterfly/
  Tangerine/I Only Have Eyes For You/You and The Night and The
  Music
  Outstanding 007 "Paul Smith, The Art Tatum Touch, Vol. 2"
  I Get a Kick Out of You/My Shining Hour/I Cover the
  Waterfront/Deep Purple/Someone to Watch Over Me/Sweet
  Lorraine/Fly Me to The Moon/Surrey With the Fringe On
  Top/Let´s Fall In Love/Tea For Two

      Both of these discs seem to be aimed at using Tatum´s name for
the commercial purpose of luring the prospective record buyer.
While Smith is a very competent pianist, he does not fulfill the
promise of "The Tatum Touch," used as the title of both these LP´s.

STEIN, LOU
  Chiaroscuro CR-149 "Lou Stein, Tribute to Tatum"
  (The cover of this album has a painting of Tatum by Ron
  Warwell.)

      Elegie[0840]/Indiana[0980]/Begin the Beguine[0960]/Stormy
      Weather[0470]/Deep Purple[0751]/Aunt Hagar´s Blues[3080]/
      Humoresque[0850]/Lullaby of the Leaves[0880]/The Man I
      Love [0500]/Get Happy[0870]/Sweet Lorraine[0860]/Chloe[0480]

      Stein attempts to play these titles, all previously recorded
by Tatum, note for note. He valiantly tries to overcome the twin
handicaps of small hand size and the demands of the material but
one wonders why the recording was made at all, since most of the
original Tatum performances, better in every way, are still
available.

WILLIAMS, ROGER
  Kapp KL-1354 "The Solid Gold Steinway"
  Elegie [0840]

      On one track of this disc Williams does a decent job with
a note-for-note effort to duplicate Tatum´s famous recording. The
other tracks are not intended to, and do not, relate to Tatum.

FILMS

Unfortunately there are only two known instances of
Art Tatum appearances on film. These are listed below:

MARCH OF TIME, Vol. X, Issue 5. Released December, 1943. Total
running time is 16 minutes. A short which is a chapter in a
series entitled "Music In America." The Tatum segment was filmed
during an appearance of the Art Tatum Trio at the Three Deuces
night club in New York City. The trio performs "Tiny's
Exercise," [T8030], and the total playing time of this segment of
the film is 33 seconds. The segment was repeated as part of a
telecast originally shown on ITV Television in England on April
9, 1977, and subsequently reshown on public television stations
in the United States. The show was entitled "All You Need Is
Love - The Story of Popular Music."

The noted jazz film collector David Chertok has obtained the
"out-takes" from this appearance, and the total running time of
film taken is (3:44).

THE FABULOUS DORSEYS, directed by Alfred Green. 1947. Total
running time is 16 minutes. Tatum appears briefly as a pianist
in a night club, and his playing is mostly obscured by dialogue.
He plays part of a Tatum original, "Turquoise," [2750]. This is
followed by a scene in which Tatum is joined by a group of
musicians in a performance of "Art's Blues," [2760].

PUBLISHED MUSIC

ROYAL GARDEN BLUES [0540]
Downbeat Magazine, January 1939. Transcribed by Sharon Pease.
Reprinted in the first Downbeat Book, "About the Piano."
This contains two excerpts from Tatum´s solo performance.

IF I HAD YOU/STOMPIN´ AT THE SAVOY/I´M IN THE MOOD FOR LOVE/WHEN I
GROW TOO OLD TO DREAM/HOW AM I TO KNOW?/JUST YOU, JUST ME*/GOODNIGHT
SWEETHEART/I´M COMING VIRGINIA/THE MOON IS LOW/SHOULD I/DON´T BLAME
ME/BLUE MOON/PAGAN LOVE SONG*/SWEET AND LOVELY*
Art Tatum Improvisations. Edited by Morris Feldman. Robbins Music
Corporation. New York. 1939.
   *The first edition of this book, which had a lime-green cover,
   contained all 14 selections. The second edition, a darker green,
   omitted "Just You, Just Me," and later editions omitted this as
   well as "Pagan Love Song" and "Sweet and Lovely." There were at
   least four editions and the last, which was issued after book
   "No. 2" appeared, called itself "No. 1."

SAPPHIRE
The Famous Style Piano Solo Album, Album 1. The Peter Maurice Music
Co., Ltd. London. 1939.

AMETHYST (This is basically the same composition as "The Shout,"
   see [0240].)
The Famous Style Piano Solo Album, Album 2. The Peter Maurice Music
Co., Ltd. London. 1939.

TURQUOISE
The Famous Style Piano Solo Album, Album 3. The Peter Maurice Music
Co., Ltd. London. 1939.

JADE (Seems related to "Gang O´ Nothin´," see [T8062].)
The Famous Style Piano Solo Album, Album 4. The Peter Maurice Music
Co., Ltd. London. 1939.

SWANEE RIVER
29 Modern Piano Interpretations of "Swanee River." Robbins Music
Corporation. New York. 1939.

WEE BABY BLUES [1050]
Downbeat Magazine, July 1944, transcribed by Sharon Pease. Reprinted
in "Styles of 88ers." This is a transcription of part of the piece.

CARNEGIE HALL BOUNCE [T8060]/GANG O´ NOTHIN´*/JUMPIN´ FOR SUMPIN´
[T8062]/LIVE JIVE [T8063]/NIGHT SCENE [T8061]
5 Jazz Piano Solos by Art Tatum, transcribed by Frank Paparelli.
Leeds Music Corporation. New York. 1944. The introduction to
"Carnegie Hall Bounce" is similar to that used by Tatum in many
recorded versions of "Begin the Beguine."
   *Seems related to "Jade," see [T7008].

WEE BABY BLUES [1050]/NIGHT SCENE [T8061]
4 To the Bar Jazz Piano Method, by Frank Paparelli. Leeds Music
Corporation. New York. 1946.

LULLABY IN RHYTHM/CHINA BOY/DON´T GET AROUND MUCH ANYMORE/WABASH
BLUES/SUNDAY/I´LL NEVER BE THE SAME*/JA-DA/WHAT CAN I SAY AFTER I SAY
I´M SORRY/I GOT IT BAD AND THAT AIN´T GOOD/THE WANG WANG BLUES/HOT
LIPS/AT SUNDOWN*/RUNNIN´ WILD*
Art Tatum Improvisations, No. 2. Edited by Morris Feldman. Robbins
Music Corporation. New York. 1946.
   *The second edition did not include these selections.

BLUES IN Bb [4830]
Norman Granz´ Jazz At the Philharmonic Piano Solos, transcribed by
Frank Metis. JATAP Publishing Co., Inc. New York. 1957. Reprinted
in The Book of Jazz - From Then Till Now, by Leonard Feather. Horizon
Press. New York. 1957. This is a transcription of part of the piece.

317

AUNT HAGAR'S BLUES [3080]
Jazz Improvisation, Volume Two, written and transcribed by John
Mehegan. Watson-Guptill Publications, Inc. New York. 1962.

TATUM-POLE BOOGIE [2970]
The Major Jazz Piano Styles, by Eli H. Newberger.
Scholar-Of-the-House Essay, Yale University. New Haven. 1963.
This is a transcription of the last chorus only.

BLUES IN Bb [4830]
Contemporary Keyboard Magazine, December 1976. Cupertino, California.
Article by Leonard Feather containing an abbreviated version of the
Frank Metis transcription published in 1957. The notation is very
slightly different.

CARNEGIE HALL BOUNCE [T8060]/GANG O' NOTHIN' [T8062]*
Jazz, Blues, Boogie & Swing For Piano - The Jazz Of An Era, edited by
Ronny S. Schiff. Belwin-Mills Publishing Corp. Melville, New York.
1977.
    *Seems related to "Jade," see [T7008].

The Improvisational Techniques of Art Tatum, Vol. 2, Parts I and
II. Case Western Reserve University PhD Thesis. Cleveland,
Ohio. 1978. Lead sheets and graphic analyses of 244 Tatum
performances taken from the recordings.

AMETHYST/AT SUNDOWN/BLUE MOON/CHINA BOY/DON'T GET AROUND MUCH ANYMORE/
HOT LIPS/I GOT IT BAD AND THAT AIN'T GOOD/I'M COMING VIRGINIA/I'M IN
THE MOOD FOR LOVE/JA-DA/JADE*/LULLABY IN RHYTHM/RUNNIN' WILD/SAPPHIRE/
SHOULD I/STOMPIN' AT THE SAVOY/SUNDAY/TURQUOISE/WABASH BLUES/THE WANG
WANG BLUES/WHAT CAN I SAY AFTER I SAY I'M SORRY
The Music Makers - Art Tatum - Piano Solos, edited by Cecil Bolton.
EMI Music Publishing Ltd. London. 1980.
    *Seems related to "Gang O' Nothin'," see [T8062].

HOT LIPS/I'M COMING VIRGINIA/I'M IN THE MOOD FOR LOVE/CHINA BOY/
SHOULD I/THE MOON IS LOW/WABASH BLUES/IF I HAD YOU/BLUE MOON/LULLABY
IN RHYTHM/STOMPIN' AT THE SAVOY/WHAT CAN I SAY AFTER I SAY I'M SORRY/
DON'T GET AROUND MUCH ANYMORE/SUNDAY/GOODNIGHT SWEETHEART/JA-DA/I GOT
IT BAD AND THAT AIN'T GOOD/AT SUNDOWN/DON'T BLAME ME/RUNNIN' WILD/HOW
AM I TO KNOW?/I'LL NEVER BE THE SAME/WHEN I GROW TOO OLD TO DREAM
The Genius of Art Tatum - Piano Solos. The Big 3 Music Corporation.
New York. 1981.

OVER THE RAINBOW [5500]
Contemporary Keyboard Magazine, October 1981 issue. Cupertino,
California. Transcribed by Jim Aiken. Transcription of the second
chorus only.

AIN'T MISBEHAVIN' [0550]/FINE AND DANDY [1110]/MOONGLOW [5090]/I
SURRENDER DEAR [4970]/SWEET LORRAINE [0860]/SWEET LORRAINE [3130]
Jazz Masters - Art Tatum, selected and edited by Jed Distler. Volume
85/Music for Millions Series. Consolidated Music Publishers. New
York. 1981. The first five titles were transcribed by Jed Distler,
the last by Felicity A. Howlett.

DEEP PURPLE [0750]
Le Jazzophone, quarterly magazine of Centre d'Instruction Musical.
Article by Aaron Bridgers, transcription by J. Lawrence Cook. Paris,
France. First Quarter, 1982.

As far as is known, Art Tatum never directly cut any piano rolls. However, there are piano rolls, listed below, which were made by others either as copies of Tatum recordings or as mechanical reproductions from piano scores.

The following Jazzmaster piano rolls were made by John T. Farrell using a proprietary method of cutting piano rolls from a piano score without actually playing the piece. See the section entitled ,"The Imitatums," for details about an issued LP made from these piano rolls.

Jazzmaster   1   Eng.
    [From the Peter Maurice publication. See "Published Music."]
    T7006 AMETHYST

Jazzmaster   11   Eng.
    [This piano roll is entitled "A Tatum Potpourri." Pieces are from
    the Robbins publication. See "Published Music."]
    T8046 JA-DA
    T7012 STOMPIN' AT THE SAVOY
    T8044 SUNDAY
    T8049 WANG WANG BLUES, THE
    T8047 WHAT CAN I SAY AFTER I SAY I'M SORRY

The following Q.R.S. piano rolls were played by J. Lawrence Cook, a prolific transcriber and piano roll performer.

Q.R.S.   4973   USA
    [Transcribed by J. Lawrence Cook from the record.]
    0870   GET HAPPY

Q.R.S.   7960   USA
    [Transcribed by J. Lawrence Cook from the record.]
    0860   SWEET LORRAINE

Q.R.S.   9530   USA
    [The first chorus was taken from the first Robbins publication.
    (See "Published Music.") It is not known whether the remainder
    of the piece was taken from the unpublished portion of the
    original Tatum performance, or was added by J. Lawrence Cook
    to fill out the piano roll.]
    T7012 STOMPIN' AT THE SAVOY

Q.R.S.   9735   USA
    [Transcribed by J. Lawrence Cook from the record.]
    1870   FLYING HOME

Appendix I - Guide To Abbreviations

RECORD TYPES:

78	78 rpm recording
78LP	78 rpm longer playing recording
45	45 rpm recording
EP	Extended play recording, usually 45 rpm
LP	Long playing (microgroove) recording, usually 33 rpm
TX	Electrical transcription, usually 33 rpm

ORIGINS:

Arg.	Argentina
Astla	Australia
Belg.	Belgium
Braz.	Brazil
Can.	Canada
Dan.	Denmark
Eng.	England
Eur.	Europe
Fr.	France
Ger.	Germany
Holl.	Holland
India	India
It.	Italy
Jap.	Japan
Nor.	Norway
Span.	Spain
Swed.	Sweden
Swiss	Switzerland
USA	Unites States of America

INSTRUMENTS:

as	alto saxophone
acc	accordion
b	acoustic string bass
cel	celeste
cl	clarinet
d	drums
fl	flugelhorn
g	guitar
orch	orchestra
org	organ
p	piano
t	trumpet
tb	trombone
ts	tenor saxophone
v	vocal
vg	vocal group
vib	vibraphone or vibes
wh	whiskbrooms
x	xylophone

Appendix II - Matrix Cross Reference List

Matrix No.	Index No.
1-1	2030
1-2	2031
2-1	2040
2-62822A	0460
2-62823A	0470
3-1	2050
4-1	2060
5-1	2070
6-1	2080
56-GS-33A	2810
56-GS-33A	2830
359	3610
359	3620
359	3630
506	3450
506	3460
506	3470
506	3480
507	3490
507	3500
507	3510
507	3520
856	3390
856	3400
856	3410
856	3420
1251-1	1950
1256-1	1970
1411-1	3850
1412-1	3860
1413-1	3870
1414-1	3880
1415-1	3890
1416-2	3900
1417-1	3910
1418-2	3920
1419-1	3930
1420-1	3940
1421-1	3950
1422-1	3960
1423-1	3970
1424-1	3980
1425-1	3990
1426-1	4000
1427-2	4010
1428-1	4020
1429-1	4030
1430-1	4040
1431-1	4050
1432-1	4060
1433-1	4070
1434-1	4080
1435-1	4090
1436-1	4100
1437-1	4110
1438-1	4120
1439-1	4130
1440-1	4140
1441-1	4150
1442-1	4160
1443-1	4170
1444-1	4180
1445-1	4190
1446-1	4200
1447-1	4210
1448-1	4220
1449-1	4230
1450-1	4240
1451-1	4250
1452-1	4260
1453-1	4270
1454-1	4280

Appendix II - Matrix Cross Reference List

1455-1	4290
1456-1	4300
1457-1	4310
1458-1	4320
1459-1	4330
1460-1	4340
1461-1	4350
1462-1	4360
1463-1	4370
1464-1	4380
1465-1	4390
1466-1	4400
1467-1	4410
1468-1	4420
1469-1	4430
1470-1	4440
1471-1	4450
1472-1	4460
1473-1	4470
1474-1	4480
1475-1	4490
1476-1	4500
1477-1	4510
1478-1	4520
1479-1	4530
1480-1	4540
1586-1	4550
1587-1	4560
1588-1	4570
1589-1	4580
1590-3	4590
1591-1	4600
1592-1	4610
1593-1	4620
1594-1	4630
1595-1	4640
1596-1	4650
1597-1	4660
1598-1	4670
1599-1	4680
1600-1	4690
1601-1	4700
1602-1	4710
1603-1	4720
1604-1	4730
1605-1	4740
1606-1	4750
1607-1	4760
1608-1	4770
1609-1	4780
1610-1	4790
1611-1	4800
1612-1	4810
1788-1	4820
1789-2	4830
1790-1	4840
1791-2	4850
1792-1	4860
1793-2	4870
1794-2	4880
1795-1	4890
1796-2	4900
1797-2	4910
1798-1	4920
1798-2	4921
1799-1	4930
1800-2	4940
1801-1	4950
2193-1	4970
2194-1	4980
2195-1	4990
2196-1	5000
2197-1	5010
2198-1	5020

Appendix II - Matrix Cross Reference List

2199-1	5030
2200-1	5040
2201-1	5050
2202-1	5060
2203-1	5070
2204-1	5080
2205-1	5090
2206-1	5100
2207-1	5110
2208-1	5120
2209-1	5130
2210-1	5140
2211-1	5150
2212-1	5160
2213-1	5170
2214-1	5180
2215-1	5190
2216-1	5200
2217-1	5210
2218-1	5220
2219-1	5230
2302-1	5240
2303-1	5250
2304-1	5260
2305-5	5270
2306-2	5280
2307-1	5290
2308-4	5300
2309-1	5310
2374-2	5640
2375-2	5650
2376-2	5660
2377-1	5670
2377-2	5680
2378-2	5690
2379-1	5700
2380-2	5710
2381-2	5720
2382-2	5730
2383-1	5740
2384-2	5750
2385-1	5760
2386-1	5770
2387-2	5780
2489-2	5790
2490-2	5800
2491-5	5810
2492-4	5820
2493-1	5830
2493-3	5831
2494-1	5840
2667-1	5920
2668-1	5930
2669-1	5940
2670-1	5950
2671-1	5960
2672-1	5970
2673-2	5980
2674-2	5990
2675-2	6000
2676-2	6010
2677-3	6020
2678-3	6030
2679-3	6040
2680-2	6050
2681-1	6060
2682-4	6070
2683-2	6080
2684-4	6090
2990-1	6160
2991-1	6170
2992-1	6180
2993-3	6190
2994-3	6200

Appendix II - Matrix Cross Reference List

2995-2	6210
2996-2	6220
3129	4815
4448-1D2	3040
5039-1D1	3060
5039-1D2	3060
5040 2D-1	3070
5040-2D1	3070
5040-2D4	3070
5041-1D1	3080
5042 1D-1	3090
5042-1D1	3090
5043-D2	3100
5044	3110
5045	3120
5046-D1	3130
5047-D1	3140
5048-D1	3150
5049	3160
5050	3170
5051-1D1	3180
5052	3190
5053	3200
5054	3210
5055	3220
5056	3230
5057-1D1	3240
5057 1D-1	3240
5541z	3050
8427A	0210
10935	3710
10936	3720
10937	3730
10938	3740
10939	3750
10940	3760
10941	3770
10942	3780
12551	1960
12571	1980
025348-1	0500
025348-1	0510
025348-1	0520
025348-1	0530
025349-1	0540
025349-1	0550
025349-1	0560
025349-1	0570
025350-1	0580
025350-1	0590
025350-1	0600
025350-1	0610
025351-2	0620
025351-2	0630
025351-2	0640
025351-2	0650
38387A	0140
38387B	0141
38388A	0150
38388B	0151
38388C	0152
38388D	0153
38389A	0160
38389C	0161
38389D	0162
38390A	0170
38391	0180
38391A	0180
38392	0190
38392A	0190
38426A	0200
38426C	0201
38426D	0202
38427A	0210

38427C	0211
38427D	0212
38428A	0220
38428C	0221
38428D	0222
38429A	0230
38430A	0240
38430B	0241
38431A	0250
38431C	0251
38431D	0252
38432A	0260
38432C	0261
38432D	0262
042276-1	0660
042276-1	0670
042276-1	0680
042276-1	0690
042277-1	0700
042277-1	0710
042277-1	0720
042277-1	0730
042377-1	0760
042377-1	0770
042377-1	0780
042377-1	0790
042378-1	0800
042378-1	0810
042378-1	0820
042378-1	0830
62822A	0460
62822B	0461
62823A	0470
62823B	0471
62824A	0480
62824B	0481
62825A	0490
68605-D	1050
68605A	1050
68605AA	1050
68606A	1060
68606AA	1060
68607A	1070
68607AA	1070
68608-D	1080
68608A	1080
68608AA	1080
69356A	1130
69356AA	1130
69356B	1131
69356BB	1131
69357A	1140
69357AA	1140
69358A	1150
69358AA	1150
69359A	1160
69359AA	1160
69359B	1161
90541-A	0410
A4691-1	1320
A4691-2	1321
A4692-1	1330
A4692-2	1331
A4693-1	1340
A4693-2	1341
A4694-1	1350
A4694-2	1351
ARA-1040-1-A	2190
ARA-1040-1-B	2190
ARA-1040-1C	2190
ARA-1041-1-A	2200
ARA-1041-1-B	2200
ARA-1042-1	2210
ARA-1042-1-A	2210

Appendix II - Matrix Cross Reference List

ARA-1042-1-B	2210
ARA-1043-1-A	2220
ARA-1043-1-B	2220
ARA-1044-A	2230
ARA-1044-B	2230
ARA-1044A	2230
ARA-1045-1-A	2240
ARA-1045-1-B	2240
ARA-1046-1	2250
ARA-1046-1-A	2250
ARA-1046-1B	2250
ARA-1046-1-B	2250
ARA-1047-1A	2260
ARA-1047-1-A	2260
ARA-1047-1-B	2260
B12148A	0010
B12148B	0011
B12149A	0020
B12149B	0021
B12166A	0030
B12166B	0031
B12167A	0040
B13162A	0050
B13162B	0051
B13163A	0060
B13163B	0061
B13164A	0070
B13165A	0080
BW63	2090
BW64	2100
BW65	2110
BW66	2120
C-90541	0410
D-73535	3430
D-73535	3440
D7-VB-74	2770
D7-VB-75	2780
D7-VB-76	2790
D7-VB-77	2800
DLA724A	0420
DLA724B	0421
DLA725A	0430
DLA725B	0431
DLA726A	0440
DLA726B	0441
DLA727A	0450
DLA727B	0451
DLA1759A	0740
DLA1759B	0741
DLA1760A	0750
DLA1760B	0751
DLA1936-AT1	0840
DLA1936A	0840
DLA1936B	0841
DLA1937-AT1	0850
DLA1937A	0850
DLA1938A	0860
DLA1939A	0870
DLA1940A	0880
DLA1941A	0890
DLA1942A	0900
DLA1942B	0901
DLA1943A	0910
DLA1944A	0920
DLA1944B	0921
DLA1945A	0930
DLA1946A	0940
DLA2068A	0950
DLA2068B	0951
DLA2069A	0960
DLA2069B	0961
DLA2070A	0970
DLA2070B	0971
DLA2071A	0980

Appendix II - Matrix Cross Reference List

DLA2071B	0981
DS-229	2820
DS-1970	3255
DS-2320	3260
DS-2321	3270
HD5-MM-6636-1	2010
JDB18B, serial D6-TC-5056	2680
JDB19, serial B44987	2710
JDB20, serial B44988	2270
JDB20, serial B44988	2720
JDB20, serial D6-TC-5058	2270
JDB20, serial D6-TC-5058	2720
JDB34B, serial D6-TC-5067	2680
JDB34B, serial D6-TC-5067	2690
JDB72, serial B45222	2354
JDB72, serial B45222	2355
JDB91, serial B45464	1720
JDB100, serial B45590	1550
JDB100, serial B45590	1650
JDB102, serial B45592	1740
JDB103, serial B45593	1740
JJ80	2950
JJ81	2960
JJ82	2970
JJ83	2980
JJ84	2990
JJ85	3000
JJ86	3010
JJ87	3020
MA1251	1950
MA1256	1970
MS-96544-1	0280
MS-96544-1	0290
MS-96544-1	0300
MS-96544-1	0310
MS-96545-1	0320
MS-96545-1	0330
MS-96545-1	0340
MS-96545-1	0350
MS-96545-1	0360
MS-96546-1	0370
MS-96546-1	0380
MS-96546-1	0390
MS-96546-1	0400
METRO 1040	2191
MM4607	2685
ND3-MM-7196-1	2360
ND3-MM-7196-1	2370
ND3-MM-7196-1	2380
ND3-MM-7196-1	2390
ND3-MM-7196-1	2400
ND3-MM-7197-1	2410
ND3-MM-7197-1	2420
ND3-MM-7197-1	2430
ND3-MM-7197-1	2440
ND3-MM-7197-1	2450
ND3-MM-7198-1	2460
ND3-MM-7198-1	2470
ND3-MM-7198-1	2480
ND3-MM-7198-1	2490
ND3-MM-7198-1	2500
ND3-MM-7199-1	2510
ND3-MM-7199-1	2520
ND3-MM-7199-1	2530
ND3-MM-7199-1	2540
ND3-MM-7199-1	2550
PS502	1984
PS503	1986
RG 200	0270
SPE245	3530
SPE246	3540
SPE246	3550
SPE246	3560
SPE511	3640

```
SPE511                          3650
SPE511                          3660
SPE782-3                        3400
SSL-286                         1760
SSL-286                         1770
SSL-286                         1780
SSL-373                         1790
SSL-373                         1800
SSL-373                         1810
SSL-1087                        2700
T-1-A-1                         1820
T-1-A-3                         1820
T-1-A-3 #2                      1820
T-1-A-3 #3                      1820
T-1-B-1                         1830
T-1-B-3                         1830
T-1-B-3 #3                      1830
T-1B-1                          1830
T-2-A-4                         1840
T-2-B-3                         1850
T-2A4-RE                        1840
T-3-A-3                         1860
T-3-B-3                         1870
T2B3-RE                         1850
T3A3-RE                         1860
T3B3-RE                         1870
TO 1192                         0001
VP-467, serial D4-TC-30         1540
VP-468, serial D4-TC-31         1590
VP-469, serial D4-TC-34         1610
VP-469, serial D4-TC-34         1630
VP-470, serial D4-TC-33         1730
VP-472, serial D4-TC-35         1660
VP-665, serial D4-TC-165        1640
VP-670, serial D4-TC-170        1560
VP-1025, serial D4-TC-511       1670
VP1234, serial B42325           1410
VP1234, serial B42325           1470
VP1692, serial B44382           2320
VP1709, serial B44530           2330
VP1710, serial B44441           2340
VP1711, serial B44523           2350
WN1360                          1400
WN1361                          1410
WN1362                          1420
WN1363                          1430
WN1364                          1440
WN1365                          1450
WN1366                          1460
WN1367                          1470
WN1368                          1480
WN1369                          1490
XYZ68608-T1                     1080
XYZ69356                        1131
XYZ69356-T1                     1131
XYZ69359-T1                     1160
```

Borromeo, Filippo. Slam Stewart Discography, in Discographical Forum, #23, 1971. Part Three.

Brigaud, Dominic. Art Tatum - Essai Pour Une Discographie Des Enregistrements Hors Commerce. Paris, France. November, 1979. Privately distributed.

Bruyninckx, Walter. Sixty Years of Recorded Jazz. Mechelen, Belgium. c. 1977; uses loose leaf pages, updated periodically.

Delaunay, Charles. New Hot Discography. Criterion Books. New York. 1981.

Heider, Wally. Transcography; a discography of jazz and "pop" music issued on 16" transcriptions. 1934 through June 1956. Privately distributed.

Howard, Joseph A. The Improvisational Techniques of Art Tatum. Department of Music, Case Western University. Cleveland, Ohio. Doctoral thesis, May 31, 1978.

Jepsen, Jorgen Grunnet. Jazz Records 1942-1962. Vol. 7, S-Te. Karl Emil Knudsen. Holte, Denmark. 1964.

Jepsen, Jorgen Grunnet, et. al. Jazz Records 1962-1980. Draft version.

Jepsen, Jorgen Grunnet. Discographie d´Art Tatum, in Les Cahiers du Jazz, #5. Copenhagen, Denmark. c. 1962.

Jepsen, Jorgen Grunnet. A Discography of Art Tatum/Bud Powell. Debut Records. Copenhagen, Denmark. 1961.

Lange, Horst H. Die deutsche Jazz Discographie; eine geschichte der Jazz auf Schallplatten von 1902 bis 1955. Bote und G. Bock. Berlin. 1955.

McCarthy, Albert and Max Harrison, Alun Morgan, and Paul Oliver. Jazz On Record, 1917-67. Hanover Books. London, England. 1968.

Millar, Jack. Born To Sing, A Discography of Billie Holiday. Jazzmedia ApS. Copenhagen, Denmark. 1979.

Ramsey, Frederic Jr. A Guide To Longplay Records. Long Player Publications. New York, New York. 1954.

Rust, Brian. Jazz Records, A-Z, 1897-1942. Storyville Publications. Chigwell, England. 1971. Also 2nd Edition. Arlington House. New Rochelle, New York. 1978.

Schleman, Hilton R. Rhythm On Record. The Melody Maker. London, England. 1936.

Sears, Richard S. V-Discs - A History and Discography. Greenwood Press. Westport, Connecticut. 1980.

Selchow, Manfred and Karsten Lohmann. Edmond Hall - A Discography. Uhle & Kleimann. Lubbecke, West Germany. 1981.

Spencer, Ray. Art Tatum, An Appreciation. In Jazz Journal, August, September, and October 1966, Vol. 19, Nos. 8, 9, and 10. London, England.

Westerberg, Hans. Boy From New Orleans - Louis >>Satchmo>> Armstrong. Jazzmedia ApS. Copenhagen, Denmark. 1981.

Appendix IV - Quick Dating Guide

| | FIST INDEX NUMBER OF THE YEAR IN: | |
Year	Chronological Discography	Unissued Sessions
1932	0001	
1933	0050	
1934	0090	
1935	0270	
1936		T7000
1937	0420	
1938	0500	
1939	0660	T7005
1940	0840	T7030
1941	1050	T7040
1942		
1943	1270	T8020
1944	1390	T8060
1945	2090	T8130
1946	2680	T8227
1947	2770	T8300
1948	2830	
1949	2950	T8340
1950	3250	T8400
1951	3390	T8420
1952	3670	T8600
1953	3790	T8680
1954	4550	T8759
1955	4970	T8820
1956	5920	T8900
Unknown		T8921

330